The Professional Handbook of Architectural Detailing

JOHN WILEY & SONS

New York
Chichester
Brisbane
Toronto
Singapore

THE PROFESSIONAL HANDBOOK OF ARCHITECTURAL DETAILING

SECOND EDITION

Osamu A. Wakita

Los Angeles Harbor College

Richard M. Linde

A.I.A., Architect

Jacket Photo: © Judith Turner, 1976.
House VI, Frank Residence, Peter Eisenman, architect.

Library of Congress Cataloging in Publication Data:

Wakita, Osamu A.
  The professional handbook of architectural detailing.

  1. Architectural drawing — Detailing.   I. Linde, Richard M.
II. Title.
NA2718.W35   1987   720′.28′4   86-26780
ISBN 0-471-84813-1

Printed in the United States of America

10 9 8 7 6 5 4 3 2 1

This book is dedicated to the students of architecture and to our families

PREFACE

Detailing is important to the architect because it is a means of controlling the total building process. To produce excellent architecture as opposed to ''minimum construction,'' an architect must rely heavily on details. Architects involved in quality work find there is never enough information on a set of drawings, nor enough details drawn.

The purpose of this book is to present the attitudes, skills, and fundamental concepts of architectural drafting and detailing to persons who will benefit from this knowledge in their professional endeavors as well as to provide a reference book for the practitioner.

This book deals primarily with wood and masonry construction. Thus the discussion of most drafting techniques is initially approached with these materials in mind. Other materials are discussed only as they relate to wood and masonry construction. Because there are certain regional differences in construction and variations in codes, we present the basic processes that are common to all good construction. If there are unique differences imposed by a local agency, these, of course, should be considered when designing the detail.

Initially, the presentation of the book is devoted to the intersection of the wall plane and the earth, which is the horizontal base plane. Then the wall plane and its various treatments are discussed, followed by an examination of the intersection of the wall plane to the roof plane, how it is attached, waterproofing problems, and so on. Also included are chapters dealing with office practice production techniques that utilize computers, scissor drafting, pin registration, and appliqué copier processes.

A chapter illustrating the evolution of various architectural details and how they are influenced by code restriction, design, materials, and structural conditions is included.

Finally, related information is given about wood construction, such as window and door construction, stairs as they apply to wood frame, cabinet details, fireplace studies, beam connections, retaining walls, balcony flashing, glass roof details, insulation and flashing conditions, and special construction problems.

However slowly it is adopted, it appears that the metric system will be the way of the future in this country. Hence, there is a chapter dealing with metric measurements. Related drafting information about welding, lumber sizing, and reinforcing is also presented in great detail.

We attempt to cover not only the "whys" and "hows" of the methods by which things are connected but to show actual finished drawn details as well as photographs of a detail in the construction phase. The book examines, in great depth, each area of detailing so that it functions as a real reference. In many instances, the standards established by the American Institute of Architects have been included as a means of national standardization.

Although this book is not meant to be read sequentially, chapter by chapter, but rather in order of the need, we suggest that the conceptual chapters be read first. The chapters, Background to Detailing and Introduction to Principles of Detailing, and those on wood, masonry, and metals are the basis for all subsequent chapters and are fundamental to the detailing process.

Osamu A. Wakita
Richard M. Linde

Acknowledgments   The authors express their sincere thanks to the following people who have helped in the preparation and development of the first and second editions of this book:

In the first edition, Louis Toledo, who was responsible for the drafting of the finished details, two sets of working drawings, and all freehand lettering; Marolyn Young for the translation of preliminary sketches into pictorial drawings; Nancy T. Wakita for typing the initial proposal, correspondence, and permissions; Cynthia and Mark Wakita for aiding in pagination, checking figure numbers, sorting, and reproduction of artwork; Lynne Hallock for her assistance in specialized typing and permissions; Marilyn Gilbert for researching and the development of the information contained in the appendix and teacher's manual; Georgia, Darin, and Jan Linde for typing and criticism of chapter contents; Marilyn Gene Smith for typing, proofreading, trouble shooting, correspondence, and the development of the teacher's manual; and Alan Lesure, our original editor, who guided us through our first book with John Wiley & Sons, Inc.

In the second edition, Andrea C. Kho for her help in the development of the computer and metric chapters, photographic expertise, and the drafting and development of many details and pictorial drawings; Marilyn Gene Smith for her continued typing and correspondence; Gregory Haddon for the drafting and lettering of the newly developed details and correction of existing details; Louis Toledo for continued help in lettering; Huey Lim for her help in preliminary engineering, checking and coordinating the new figures and index; Brian Cravens for drafting the newly developed pictorial drawings; Sally Ann Bailey for the manuscript editing; and Judy Joseph, editor of this edition.

We thank the following reviewers, whose thoughtful comments helped shape this new edition: Roger Kness, Southeast Community College, Milford, Nebraska; Jack H. Paules, West Virginia University, Morgantown, West Virginia; and Thomas D. Peterson, Des Moines Area Community College, Ankeny, Iowa.

O.A.W.
R.M.L.

CONTENTS

The Professional Handbook of Architectural Detailing

1
BACKGROUND TO DETAILING

Preview This chapter conveys to draftspersons and students the importance of the drawings, details, and information required to complete a set of construction documents. These documents are also referred to as working drawings, and they are the final drawings used to build a structure. In this chapter we explain their basic parts.

Besides realizing that construction documents are the prime communicative tool in which to convey all the information required to build a specific structure, the architectural draftsperson will:

1. Learn about the basic services to be considered prior to the erection of a specific building.
2. Understand the principal categories required for a set of construction documents.
3. Learn the necessity for having consultants on specific projects.
4. Review the basic information that each phase of a set of construction documents must relate to the contractors and subcontractors prior to the erection of a structure.
5. Recognize the divisions of specifications that may apply to most structures.
6. Realize the importance of the interrelationship of drawings and how these may be programmed.

Prior to the erection of a building, many people spend much time and effort in preparing the drawings or construction documents and obtaining the information required to build a structure. The principal designer, coordinator, and administrator of this task is the architect. An architect's basic services may consist of research, site development, architectural presentation drawings and models, determination of economic feasibility, seeking acceptance of design by governing agencies, formulation of construction documents and specifications, and supervision of the construction.

Construction Documents

Construction documents — the architect's main concern — dictate the design and construction techniques for a specific structure.

Architectural drawings and details, structural, mechanical, and electrical drawings, landscape design drawings and specifications comprise these documents. They are the means by which the architect, engineers, and consultants communicate their design methods and findings to the general contractor and the various trades that are involved in the construction of a specific structure.

Architectural drawings generally consist of the following:

Plot plan	Cross sections
Foundation plan	Related details
Floor plan	Specifications
Exterior elevations	Interior elevations

Structural drawings are devoted to framing layouts, column and beam sizes and their locations, and the makeup of walls required to stiffen the structure laterally. Also included are details that communicate required structural connections between various members.

The complexity of mechanical drawings depends mainly on the type of structure being built. For residential design, duct sizes and layouts for heating or air-conditioning systems may be incorporated. When necessary, plumbing line sizes and their location are shown, such as waste, vent, drain, and supply lines.

Electrical drawings consist of internal and external lighting design and power supply. Plan layouts show the location and types of switches and lighting fixtures to be used, as well as specialty items, such as door chimes, exhaust fans, and electrical heaters. An electrical legend is incorporated in these drawings that defines what the various electrical symbols represent.

Specifications are an integral part of the construction documents since they define the responsibilities of the general contractor and the various trades that are responsible for their phase of the construction. Also included in this document are the manufacturers' names and their specific equipment that has been designated for the structure. When there is a conflict between the information on a detail and the specifications, the specification will govern.

Landscape design and its related details may not always be incorporated into a set of construction documents. Generally, inclusion depends on the programming of a project and the magnitude of the landscape design. When landscape drawings are incorporated into construction documents, they will include the finish grading necessary to achieve the design of the landscaping, locations and types of paved surfaces, and details of light structures, such as fences, benches, and drains. The location of all ground cover and plant specimens is shown on these drawings along with a plant list indicating the type and size of specific specimens.

Architectural Drawings

Since this textbook is primarily devoted to architectural detailing, the substance of architectural drawings is more clearly defined and illustrated. First, we discuss the plot plan and its primary function, then, most important, the site with its lot line dimensions and bearings and the dimensional relationship of the exterior walls of the building to the property lines. Figure 1.1 illustrates plot plan for a residence, which we use to describe other information pertinent for the construction of this building.

Grading for this site is depicted by the natural and finished contour lines. Contour lines are given a numerical value that indicates the rise and fall occurring on this site. Note that the distance between contours varies and does not always follow any set pattern.

The drawing that shows the property lines, bearings, contours, utilities, and other information that relates to this site is called a topographical survey and is furnished to the architect before any design studies have begun. Existing contours are those that are depicted graphically with a broken line. Finished contours are those that indicate the physical change of the site to facilitate the structure, and they are shown as a solid line. With this information grading contractors can see what amount of grading is required and thus assess costs and perform their phase of construction. Note on Figure 1.1 the definitions of these lines and their numerical values. Floor elevations, driveways, walks, and patios are shown and given a

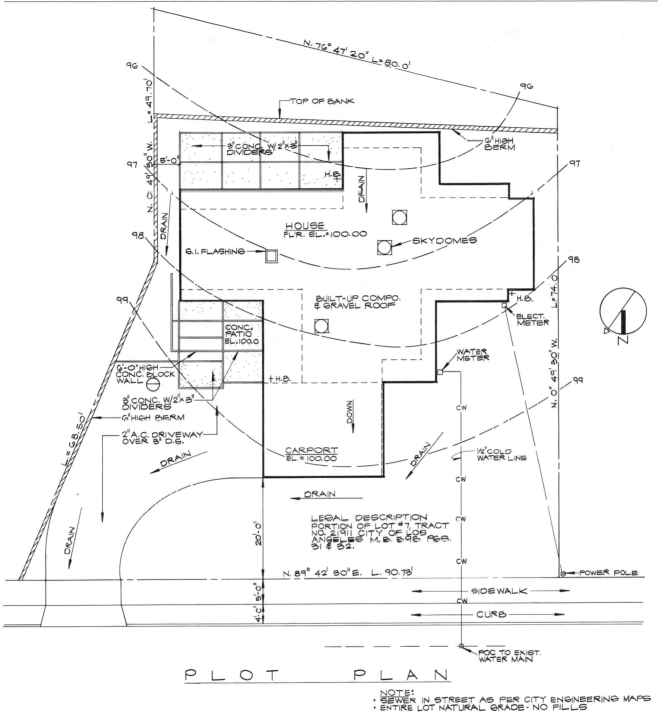

Figure 1.1 Plot plan.

designated numerical value that is directly related to the numerical values of the contours.

In many cases the roof plan may be incorporated with the plot plan. It shows the roof design, slope or pitch of the roof, roof overhangs, gutters, downspouts, and other information that might be relevant to a specific roof design.

Information and location of sanitary and site drainage devices are also shown in Figure 1.1; these devices are incorporated in the plumbing contractor's costs and duties.

In cases where concrete footings and masonry walls are required, but are not a part of the structure, their detail symbols are shown on the plot plan, with

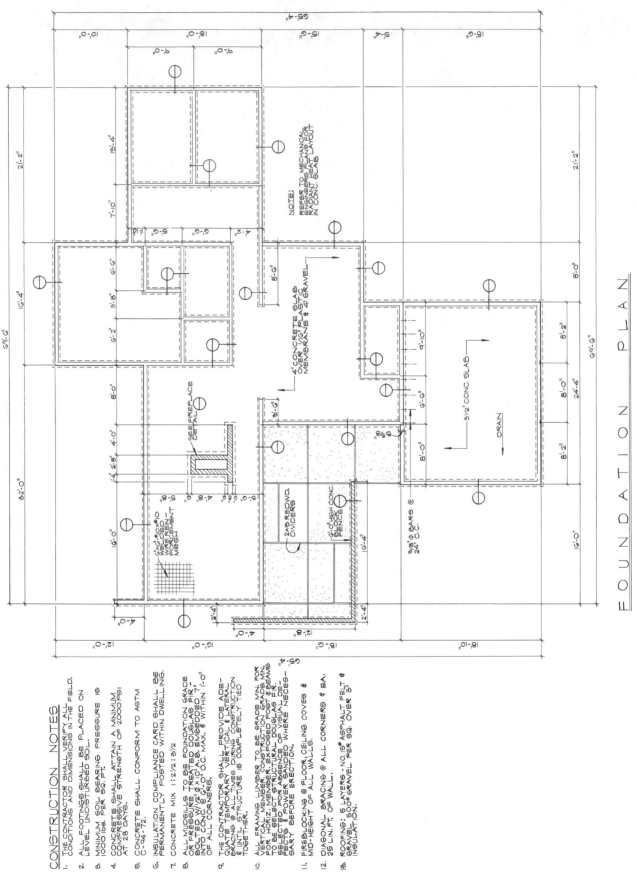

FOUNDATION PLAN

CONSTRUCTION NOTES

1. THE CONTRACTOR SHALL VERIFY ALL CONDITIONS AND DIMENSIONS IN THE FIELD.

2. ALL FOOTINGS SHALL BE PLACED ON LEVEL UNDISTURBED SOIL.

3. MINIMUM SOIL BEARING PRESSURE IS 1000 lbs. PER SQ. FT.

4. CONCRETE SHALL ATTAIN A MINIMUM COMPRESSIVE STRENGTH OF 2000 PSI AT 28 DAYS.

5. CONCRETE SHALL CONFORM TO ASTM C-94-72.

6. INSULATION COMPLIANCE CARD SHALL BE PERMANENTLY POSTED WITHIN DWELLING.

7. CONCRETE MIX 1:2 1/2:3 1/2

8. ALL MUDSILLS TO BE FOUNDATION GRADE OR PRESSURE TREATED DOUGLAS FIR. BOLTED W/ 1/2"Ø x 10" A.B. EMBEDDED 7" INTO CONC. @ 6'-0" O.C. MAX. & WITHIN 1'-0" OF ALL CORNERS.

9. THE CONTRACTOR SHALL PROVIDE ADE-QUATE TEMPORARY VERTICAL & LATERAL BRACING @ ALL TIMES DURING CONSTRUCTION & UNTIL STRUCTURE IS COMPLETELY TIED TOGETHER.

10. ALL FRAMING LUMBER TO BE GRADE MIN. FOR VERTICAL MEMBER, CONSTRUCTION GRADE MIN. FOR HORIZ. MEMBER, EXPOSED POST & BEAMS TO BE SELECT STRUCTURAL DOUGLAS FIR. SELECTED FOR ABSENCE OF VISUAL DE-FECTS & POWER SANDED WHERE NECES-SARY BEFORE ERECTION.

11. FIREBLOCKING @ FLOOR, CEILING COVES & MID-HEIGHT OF ALL WALLS.

12. DIAGONAL BRACING @ ALL CORNERS & EA. 25 LIN. FT. OF WALL.

13. ROOFING: 5 LAYERS - NO. 15 ASPHALT FELT & GRAVEL. 500# GRAVEL PER SQ. OVER 3" INSULATION.

Figure 1.2 Foundation plan.

reference to a detail sheet. Note detail ⊖ in Figure 1.1.

Foundation Plan

The foundation plan is a dimensional drawing reflecting the site and configuration of the floor plan. It shows the dimensional location of concrete footings, concrete piers, wood girders, floor joist sizes and spacing, and other information related to the substructure. Figure 1.2 illustrates a foundation plan incorporating the use of a concrete slab for the residence and a concrete slab for the garage. Note that all exterior and interior footings and supporting members are dimensioned. This is required because they are in direct relationship with the structure above and their numerical values should coincide with one another. Next in order of importance are the detail symbols shown in Figure 1.2. These symbols are referenced to the foundation details that describe to the builder how that particular section is to be built. In general, the accuracy and information on the foundation plan are most important since the plan is the basis for all that will transpire after this phase.

Floor Plan

The floor plan probably contains more information and references than does any other sheet in a set of construction documents. In Figure 1.3 the draftsperson or student should observe the following:

▶ The dimensioning of all exterior and interior walls.
▶ The designations of all rooms, storage areas, location of equipment and appliances and other specialty items.
▶ The location of doors and windows and their hinged or sliding positions. Note the door and window symbols. These are made in reference to a door and window schedule that indicates the dimensions and material of these units.
▶ The location and designation of all plumbing fixtures and their related symbol. This symbol is referenced to a plumbing schedule that indicates the size, type, and manufacturer of a specific fixture.
▶ Kitchen, bathroom, and other cabinets are shown and dimensioned when necessary. Note that there is a symbol at each cabinet. This is referenced to the cabinet elevation sheet, which shows that specific cabinet in its entirety.
▶ Note the cross-sectional reference symbols showing where the framing sections were taken. These and other pertinent detail symbols may be referred to on the floor plan.

The preceding information is most commonly found on the floor plan; however, it must be emphasized that the amount of information supplied depends on the complexity of the structure.

Exterior Elevations

Exterior elevations are drawn to show the exterior design of the structure. These drawings depict all sides of the building, the exterior wall materials, exterior window and door designs, and other related architectural designs.

As shown in Figure 1.4, there are detail symbols for all sections of the window and door frames; these symbols refer to the window and door details. Structural cross-sectional lines and their symbols are given to indicate the exact position of framing sections.

The natural and finish grade lines are shown and directly below them a broken line that indicates the bottom of the concrete footing. In many cases, the footings are stepped so as to maintain the minimum depth required below the natural grade.

Roof overhangs, plate heights, and chimney heights above roof planes should all be clearly dimensioned. All exterior attached elements such as planters, decks, and balustrades should be shown on the exterior elevations and keyed with detail symbols.

Structural Cross Sections

The student should provide as many cross sections as required to show clearly the complexities that may occur in various areas of a structure. Numerous sections not only afford clarity to the builder, but they also point out conditions that the student may not realize exist. The cross-sectional reference lines and symbols are shown on the floor plan and exterior elevations. As shown in Figure 1.5, the sections provide information on the following: plate heights (top of subfloor to top of wall), roof pitch, roofing material, roof sheathing, rafter, beam and joist sizes, partition walls, subflooring, supporting floor joist, concrete slab, and related foundation members.

In most cases, enlarged structural framing details are shown, and they are symbolized and keyed to the cross sections. For example, these details may show bolted framing connections, eave detail, roof to wall flashing conditions, and other enlarged details required for clarity of design and construction technique. Note where these conditions may occur in Figure 1.5.

Interior Elevations

Interior elevations are drawn to depict cabinet design such as door and drawer placement, heights of counters, shelves, and other specific cabinetry items required for a project. Elevations of fireplaces, ward-

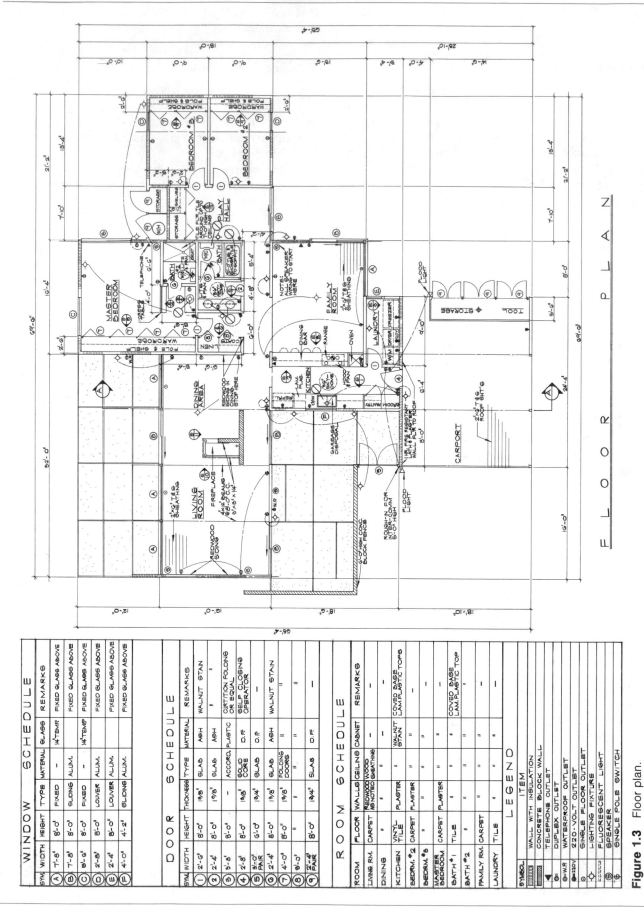

Figure 1.3 Floor plan.

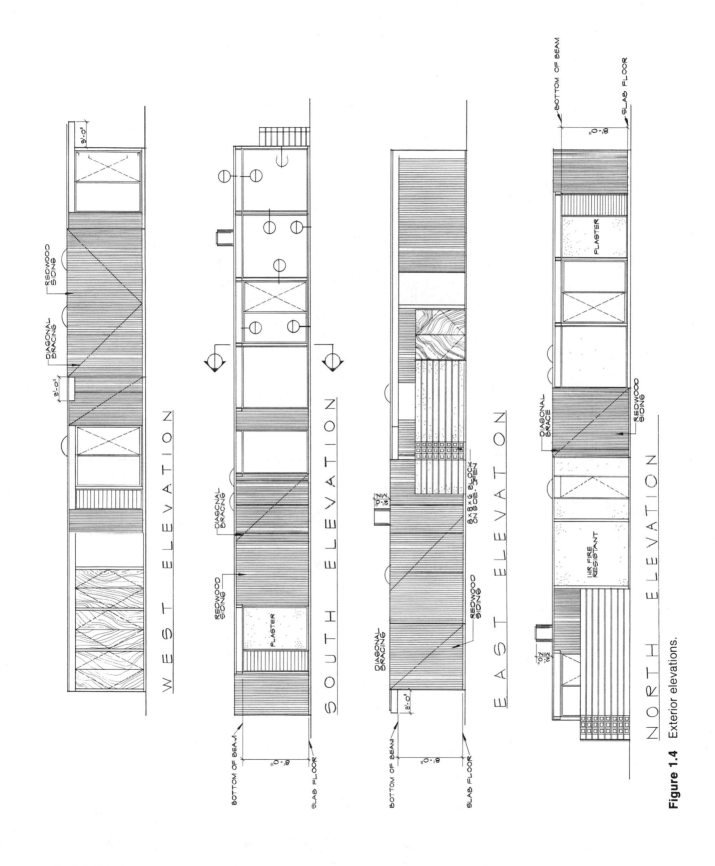

Figure 1.4 Exterior elevations.

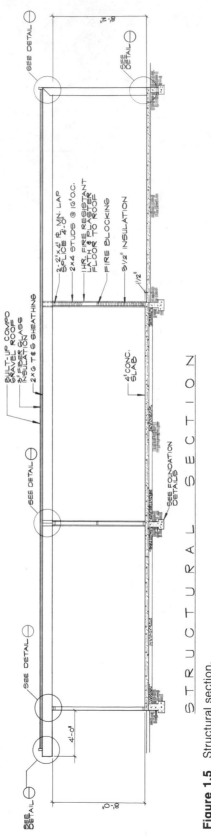

Figure 1.5 Structural section.

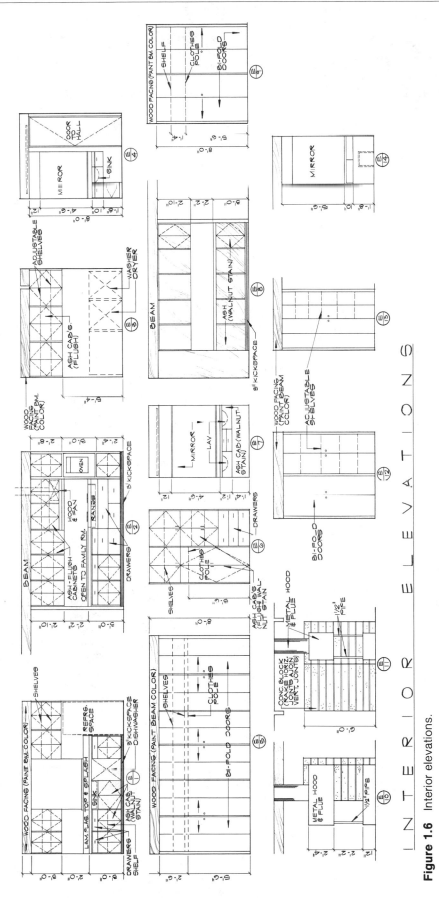

Figure 1.6 Interior elevations.

SPECIFICATIONS

INDEX

CONDITIONS OF THE CONTRACT

GENERAL CONDITIONS (A.I.A. FORM A-201)
SUPPLEMENTARY GENERAL CONDITIONS

DIVISION 1 — GENERAL REQUIREMENTS

1A SPECIAL CONDITIONS
1B ALTERNATES
1C ALLOWANCES
1D UNIT PRICES

DIVISION 2 — SITE WORK

2A DEMOLITION
2B SITE CLEARING
2C EXCAVATION, BACKFILLING, and GRADING
2D SITE DRAINAGE, UTILITIES
2E PAVING
2F LANDSCAPING
2G METAL FENCING
2H IRRIGATION SYSTEM
2I SHORING
2J CAISSONS
2K PILING

DIVISION 3 — CONCRETE

3A FORMWORK
3B REINFORCING STEEL
3C CONCRETE (CAST-IN-PLACE)
3D PRECAST CONCRETE
3E PRESTRESSED CONCRETE
3F INSULATING CONCRETE

DIVISION 4 — MASONRY

4A BLOCK MASONRY
4B BRICK MASONRY
4C STONE MASONRY

DIVISION 5 — METALS

5A STRUCTURAL STEEL
5B METAL DECKING
5C MISCELLANEOUS METALS
5D ARCHITECTURAL METALS
5E PREFINISHED METAL

DIVISION 6 — CARPENTRY

6A ROUGH CARPENTRY
6B FINISH CARPENTRY
6C GLUE-LAMINATED WORK
6D CABINET WORK

DIVISION 7 — MOISTURE PROTECTION

7A MEMBRANE WATERPROOFING
7B BUILTUP ROOFING
7C SHEET METAL
7D CALKING and SEALANTS
7E INSULATION
7F METAL ROOFING
7G ELASTOMERIC COATING
7H BUTYL MEMBRANE
7I LIQUID DAMPPROOFING
7J METALLIC WATERPROOFING
7K TILE ROOFING
7L SHINGLE ROOFING

DIVISION 8 — DOORS, WINDOWS, and GLASS

8A WOOD DOORS
8B METAL FRAMES
8C METAL DOORS
8D ENTRANCE DOORS and FRAMING
8E METAL WINDOWS
8F WOOD WINDOWS
8G GLASS, GLAZING
8H FINISH HARDWARE
8I SPECIAL DOORS
8J CURTAIN WALL

DIVISION 9 — FINISHES

9A LATH and PLASTER
9B VENEER PLASTER
9C DRYWALL
9D TILE WORK
9E RESILIENT FLOORING
9F ACOUSTICAL TILE
9G PAINTING and FINISHING
9H WALL COVERING
9I WOOD FLOORING
9J TERRAZZO
9K SEAMLESS FLOORING
9L SEAMLESS WALL COATING

DIVISION 10 — SPECIALTIES

10A MISCELLANEOUS SPECIALTIES
10B TOILET ROOM ACCESSORIES
10C TOILET PARTITIONS
10D METAL TRACKS and TRIM
10E METAL LOCKERS
10F METAL SHELVING
10G FLAGPOLES
10H MOVABLE PARTITIONS
10I SUN CONTROL
10J LETTERING and NUMBERING

DIVISION 11 — EQUIPMENT

11A LABORATORY FURNITURE
11B LABORATORY/HOSPITAL EQUIPMENT
11C FOOD SERVICE EQUIPMENT
11D PARKING and GARAGE EQUIPMENT
11E SCHOOL and GYMNASIUM EQUIPMENT
11F LIBRARY EQUIPMENT
11G WINDOW WASHING EQUIPMENT
11H STORE EQUIPMENT
11I PLAYGROUND EQUIPMENT
11J BANK EQUIPMENT
11K AUDIO-VISUAL EQUIPMENT

DIVISION 12 — FURNISHINGS

12A SEATING
12B BLINDS and SHADES
12C CABINETS and FIXTURES
12D CARPETING
12E MATS and MATTING

Figure 1.7 Specifications index.

SPECIFICATIONS

INDEX

DIVISION 13—SPECIAL CONSTRUCTION

13A WALK-IN COLD STORAGE
13B ISOLATED ROOMS
13C RADIATION PROTECTION
13D INCINERATORS
13E INFINITE ACCESS FLOORS
13F SWIMMING POOL
13G PREFABRICATED STRUCTURE
13H WOOD TANKS and PIPING
13I SAUNAS

DIVISION 14—CONVEYING EQUIPMENT

14A ELECTRIC ELEVATORS
14B HYDRAULIC ELEVATORS
14C ESCALATORS
14D CONVEYORS
14E DUMBWAITERS
14F LOAD LIFTS
14G PNEUMATIC TUBE SYSTEM

DIVISION 15—MECHANICAL

15A MECHANICAL—GENERAL REQUIREMENTS
15B PLUMBING
15C FIRE EXTINGUISHING SYSTEM
15D STANDPIPE and FIREHOSE SYSTEMS
15E HEATING, VENTILATING, and AIR CONDITIONING
15F HVAC BALANCING
15G RADIANT HEATING

DIVISION 16—ELECTRICAL

16A ELECTRICAL—GENERAL REQUIREMENTS
16B BASIC MATERIALS and METHODS
16C SERVICE SYSTEM
16D DISTRIBUTION SYSTEM
16E LIGHTING FIXTURES
16F COMMUNICATION SYSTEMS
16G ELECTRIC HEATING
16H LIGHTNING PROTECTION SYSTEM
16I FIRE PROTECTION SYSTEM

SECTION 4A

BLOCK MASONRY

GENERAL CONDITIONS, SUPPLEMENTARY GENERAL CONDITIONS, and DIVISION 1 of these Specifications apply to this Section.

SCOPE: Supply and install all Block Masonry Work as shown on the Drawings and as specified herein.

GUARANTEE: As per GENERAL CONDITIONS.

MEASUREMENTS: Verify all dimensions shown on Drawings by taking field measurements; proper fit and attachments of all block masonry is required.

COORDINATION: Coordinate with all other Trades whose Work relates to block masonry installation for placing of all required blocking, subframing, backing, furring, and so on to ensure proper locations.

TESTS AND INSPECTIONS:

A. *General:* The Architect shall require tests and inspections when they are necessary to verify the quality and strength of block materials, mortar, grout, and workmanship. Laboratory tests of materials, mortar, and grout will be made in accordance with current ASTM standard procedures.

B. *Testing Laboratory:* The Architect shall select the Testing Laboratory and the Owner shall pay for all work required by the Testing Laboratory.

C. *Samples and Specimens:* If required, the Contractor shall furnish and deliver to the Testing Laboratory, without charge, identified samples of blocks, mortar, and grout required for tests. Test specimens shall be prepared and cured under the direction of the Architect. One set of at least two test prisms each of mortar and grout shall be made each day for the first three working days at the beginning of block Work.

CERTIFICATION: Contractor shall furnish a certificate in triplicate to the Architect, stating that all concrete blocks have been properly and thoroughly cured at the plant before shipment and that they conform to all the requirements of this specification. Each certificate shall be signed by the block manufacturer and shall contain the name of the Contractor, the project location, and the quantity and date or dates of shipment or delivery to which the certificate applies.

DELIVERY AND STORAGE: Materials shall be delivered and stored in dry, protected areas and kept free of stain or other damage. Damaged material will be replaced at no cost to the Owner.

REINFORCING STEEL: Reinforcing steel for grouted block masonry under this section shall be furnished and installed in accordance with the requirements of Section 3B, REINFORCING STEEL.

CLEAN-UP: As per SUPPLEMENTARY GENERAL CONDITIONS.

CONSTRUCTION (GENERAL):

A. *General:* Walls shall be straight, plumb, and true, with all courses true to line and level, built to dimensions shown. Cells shall be filled solid with grout as indicated. Blocks shall be laid up with waterproof Type S mortar. Units will be cleaned before placing. A masonry saw will be used for cutting.

Figure 1.7 *(Continued)*

B. *Alignment of Vertical Cells:* Masonry shall be built to preserve the unobstructed vertical continuity of the cells. The vertical alignment shall be sufficient to maintain a clear, unobstructed vertical opening not less than 3 inches in all directions. Units to be laid will be clean and dry.

C. *Cleanouts:* Cleanout openings shall be provided at the bottoms of all cells to be filled at each lift or pour of grout, when such lift or pour of grout is in excess of 4 feet in height. Cleanouts shall be sealed after inspection and before grouting.

D. *Reinforcement:* Vertical reinforcing shall be placed prior to laying the wall and shall be held in place by standard reinforcing supports. Horizontal bars shall be tied to vertical bars as the block Work progresses and shall be embedded in grout. Placing of horizontal reinforcing in joints or mortar will not be permitted.

E. *Grouting:*

1. *Grout Mix:* Grout shall be laboratory designed in accordance with ASTM C94 for manufacturer designed mixes. The use of an admixture for the purpose of reducing water content will be permitted, subject to approval by the Architect of the admixture, and provided the strength of grout is not impaired.

2. *Construction:* Grout shall be placed by means of an approved grout pump capable of handling at least 12 cubic yards per hour of the specified ⅜ inch maximum aggregate mix or by other accepted method if first approved by the Architect.

F. *Anchorage Items:* Bolts, straps, hangers, inserts, and other anchorage devices required to support framing and other attachments shall be built in unless otherwise indicated and shall be installed as block Work progresses.

CURING: Attention shall be given to the proper curing of the mortar joints as well as the grout concrete pour. The block Work shall be kept damp but not saturated for at least 4 days to prevent too rapid drying during hot or drying weather and drying winds.

PROTECTION: Block surfaces shall be covered with waterproof paper, plastic sheet, or canvas when necessary to protect them from rain or from hot, dry weather. Surfaces not being worked on shall be protected.

CLEANING: All exposed block shall be cleaned thoroughly, working rom the top downward, with fiber brushes. Mortar and mortar stains shall be removed, using cleaning compound and rinsed thoroughly with water. All finished surfaces of finished Work shall be unmarked and unmarred.

SECTION 4B

BRICK MASONRY

GENERAL CONDITIONS, SUPPLEMENTARY GENERAL CONDITIONS and DIVISION 1 of these Specifications apply to this Section.

SCOPE: Brick Masonry Work shall be supplied and installed as shown on the Drawings and as specified herein.

SAMPLES AND SAMPLE PANEL:

A. As per SUPPLEMENTARY GENERAL CONDITIONS, submit two samples of each type of brick specified.

B. Before proceeding with the Work, a sample brick panel 5 feet × 5 feet shall be erected with tooling, mortar, color, and workmanship to be approved by the Architect. This sample shall be the standard for the balance of the Work.

GUARANTEE: As per GENERAL CONDITIONS.

MEASUREMENTS: Verify all dimensions shown on Drawings by taking field measurements; proper fit and attachments of all brick masonry is required.

COORDINATION: Coordinate with all other Trades whose Work relates to brick masonry installation for placing of all required blocking, subframing, backing, furring, and so on to ensure proper locations.

TESTS AND INSPECTIONS:

A. *General:* The Architect may require tests and inspections as necessary to verify the quality and strength of brick materials, mortar, grout, and workmanship. Laboratory tests of materials, mortar, and grout will be made in accordance with current ASTM standard procedures.

B. *Testing Laboratory:* The Architect will select the Testing Laboratory, and the Owner will pay for all work required by the Testing Laboratory.

C. *Samples and Specimens:* If required, the Contractor shall furnish and deliver to the Testing Laboratory, without charge, identified samples of bricks, mortar, and grout required for tests. Test specimens shall be prepared and cured under the direction of the Architect. One set of at least two test prisms each of mortar and grout shall be made each day for the first three working days at the beginning of brick Work.

Figure 1.7 *(Continued)*

DELIVERY AND STORAGE: Bricks will be stored in manufacturer's original packing, until ready for use. Loaded pallets of delivered bricks will not be stacked. Bricks will be stored in protected location off the ground.

ERECTION:

A. Bricks will be clean and wet before placing. Units will be cut with saw, free from broken or spalled corners and edges. Minimum length of cut: $\frac{1}{2}$ of unit. Full mortar coverage of vertical and horizontal face of joints will be provided. Contractor will step back any unfinished Work for joining with continued work. No warped, spalled, cracked, or broken bricks will be used.

B. *Tolerances:*

Vertical: Within $\frac{1}{8}$ inch in 5 feet.

Horizontal: Within $\frac{1}{4}$ inch for length of wall.

C. On completion of Work, defective joints in exposed brick Work will be raked out, filled with mortar, and retooled.

D. Contractor will grout solidly behind any door jambs or other built-in items.

PROTECTION: All unfinished Work, will be covered at night against the elements with plastic sheet, building paper, heavy canvas, or other material approved by the Architect.

CLEANING: All brick Work will be cleaned thoroughly from top downward using fiber brushes. Mortar stains will be removed with cleaning compound, rinsing thoroughly with water. All finished brick surfaces shall be unmarred.

CLEAN-UP: As per SUPPLEMENTARY GENERAL CONDITIONS.

SECTION 4C

STONE MASONRY

GENERAL CONDITIONS, SUPPLEMENTARY GENERAL CONDITIONS, and DIVISION 1 of these Specifications apply to this Section.

SCOPE: Supply and install all Stone Masonry Work as shown on the Drawings and as specified herein.

SAMPLES: As per SUPPLEMENTARY GENERAL CONDITIONS, submit two 8-inch $\times$ 10-inch samples of all stone specified herein, showing the finish of the materials for approval of the Architect, plus as many samples as the Contractor may require.

SHOP DRAWINGS: As per SUPPLEMENTARY GENERAL CONDITIONS, submit Shop Drawings showing layout and details of construction, adhesion, anchorage, jointing, and setting.

GUARANTEE: As per GENERAL CONDITIONS.

COORDINATION: Coordinate stone Work with other Trades whose Work relates to this Section in any manner for placing of all required backing, blocking, and so on to ensure proper locations.

INSPECTION: Examine all subsurfaces to receive stone Work. Report in writing to the General Contractor, with a copy to the Architect, any undesirable conditions that may prove detrimental to the Work. Failure to observe this injunction will constitute a waiver to any subsequent claims to the contrary and will make this Contractor responsible for any corrections the Architect may require and this Contractor will be required to make such corrections at his own expense. Commencement of Work will be construed as acceptance of all subsurfaces.

SETTING:

A. Contractor shall cut stone to accommodate Work of other Trades.

B. All stone shall be brushed free of dust and other foreign matter and thoroughly washed with clean water before setting. All units shall be spotted, bedded, and joined as indicated on the Drawings. All Work shall be accurately set true to line, level, and plumb. All joints shall be to the widths and configurations as required herein.

C. Stone shall be laid to true vertical face, in sizes selected to minimize joints. All interstices and crevices shall be filled solid with stone chips and mortar. Keep exposed faces of all stone clean of mortar. Stones for any corners or openings shall be carefully selected for squared faces.

D. Generally, stone Work shall be done by competent stone masons and to appearance as approved by the Architect.

GROUTING AND POINTING: Contractor shall fill all joints with mortar, then rake out joints and beds to a depth consistent with thickness of units, taking every precaution to prevent stones from bearing on the edges. After face-joints and beds have been brushed clean of loose material, contractor shall grout to within $\frac{1}{2}$ inch of the exposed surface of the units unless otherwise shown. All joints shall be pointed neatly with specified pointing mortars. Contractor shall press and work pointing material into

Figure 1.7 *(Continued)*

the raked out area to insure solid packing throughout the entire joint. Contractor shall strike joints neatly to profiles required herein.

CLEANING: After completion of stone Work, and after possibility of stain from other operations has passed, the Work shall be carefully cleaned, removing all dirt, mortar, stains, or other defacements. No wire brushes or acid solution shall be used.

PROTECTION: All unfinished Work shall be covered over at night against the elements with plastic sheet, building paper heavy canvas, or other material satisfactory to the Architect.

CLEAN-UP: As per SUPPLEMENTARY GENERAL CONDITIONS.

RELATIONSHIP OF CONSTRUCTION DOCUMENT DRAWINGS

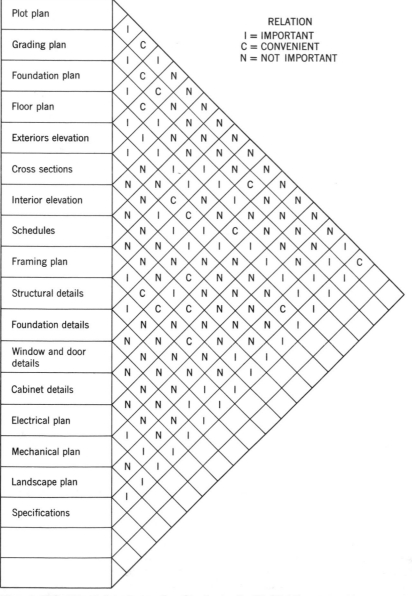

RELATION

I = IMPORTANT
C = CONVENIENT
N = NOT IMPORTANT

Figure 1.8 Matrix chart.

robes, and wall designs are shown with related dimensioning and keyed detail symbols. Again, the draftsperson should provide as many elevations and their related information as necessary for clarity of design and construction. Figure 1.6 illustrates examples of interior elevations for a specific project that incorporate the client's prerequisites.

Specifications

The part of a set of construction documents that defines the general conditions, the responsibilities of all the trades involved, and the specific equipment and methods to be used is called the specifications. This document is in typewritten form with the "general conditions for the construction of the building" defining the execution, correlation, intent, and interpretation of the construction documents.

Generally, specifications are indexed into 16 divisions. Divisions are deleted or added depending on the needs for a specific project. An example of a specifications index with its respective divisions and subtitles is illustrated in Figure 1.7. Division 4—Masonry—has been selected as a example to show what information and technical data are necessary so that the mason and suppliers understand their responsibilities. Refer to Sections 4A, 4B, and 4C (called sheets) in Figure 1.7.

This should precede specification form 5.

Interrelationship of Drawings

As previously discussed, many phases and complexities constitute a set of construction documents. The clarity of these documents depends not only on graphic or drafting skills, but also on the interrelationship of the drawings to each other. Examples include the correlation of dimensioning between the foundation plan and floor plan, or the referencing of detail symbols to related drawings—such as window detail symbols to exterior elevations.

Many architectural offices incorporate the use of a matrix chart to show the relationship or design elements required for a specific project. A similar matrix chart may be used by the architect as a visual aid for various phases of the construction documents and for demonstrating the importance of their relationships. Figure 1.8 illustrates an example of a matrix chart for the relationships of drawings and details within a set of construction documents.

Regional Differences

The contents of different sets of construction documents will be similar. Therefore, it is important to be consistent in the use of symbols, abbreviations, and other graphic representations within a set. To ensure this consistency, it is recommended that the designations follow the format shown in the *Architectural Graphic Standards*. It is also recommended that the organization and code numbering for specifications follow the format established by the Construction Specification Institute. This standardization for all regions will provide uniformity in referencing.

Summary

This chapter gives the architectural draftsperson an understanding of the elements necessary to compose a set of construction documents as well as the input that is required from various professionals. This discussion emphasizes the need for clarity and organization essential for construction documents if they are to convey to builders the design and assembly techniques desired by architects and their consultants.

2
APPROACH TO DETAILING

Preview   This chapter will help draftspersons to develop a comprehensive approach to detailing that will allow them to attack any detail. This involves the philosophy of detailing rather than the stating of facts and imparting of knowledge; it not only answers why details are drawn but how to approach them. To this end, the chapter is divided into 12 basic approaches. Each one is dealt with as an individual topic within the chapter, yet they are very often interrelated and detailing involves more than one of these approaches. This chapter is devoted to the awareness of the forces producing the necessity for details, such as aesthetics, human needs, structural problems, and concern for the environment.

After reading this chapter, the architectural draftsperson will:

1. Be able to locate potential trouble spots in a structure and develop a logical method of approach.
2. Discover the items that necessitate details.
3. Approach nontypical detail logically and systematically.
4. Discriminate details that deal with structure from aesthetics, from the environment, and so on.
5. Be able to detail within certain confined limitations, such as building codes, manufacturing limits, and the ability of the workers out in the field.
6. Build an appreciation of the need for a comprehensive set of details.
7. Comprehend the total scope of detailing as an integral part of the preparation of a full-service contract.

Need for Details

Details are absolutely necessary for architects if architects are to have complete control over every aspect of any structure. There are as many opinions and procedures for doing things in architecture as there are artisans in the field. Therefore, the only way the workers can know exactly what the designer or engineer had in mind is to have these procedures described minutely by details. And because working drawings, specifications, and even the details constitute a legal document, if a conflict of opinion occurs, architects would be lost without a detail explaining their intent. The detail then becomes an architect's evidence of intent in a court of law.

Selection of Proper Details

Chapter 1 discussed the various types of contract documents that are developed, the interrelationship of these drawings, and the typical details derived from them. But why are they so necessary? How does one decide which ones to select? How does the draftsperson know what information to put on a detail? This chapter will answer many of these questions concerning detailing.

Often, the selection of detail is dictated by some type of governmental or financial agency or is even required by the local building department. The selection of details in such instances is a simple matter of checking with the agency to find out precisely what is expected in the form of a contract document. This will vary from region to region, from locale to locale, and even from agency to agency. Hospitals have requirements different from those of schools; public buildings have requirements different from those for residences, and so on.

A detail may be selected to convey an especially difficult idea or concept, such as specifying erection procedure to a contractor. The architect may desire a particular sequence of construction to ensure that the work will go smoothly. The detail may also be selected because it is needed by the contractor to guarantee a certain quality of work. Listed in the sections that follow are various major considerations for selecting a detail and the approach that should be used in drafting it.

Structural Considerations

The overall structural system used is usually described by such drawings as the foundation plan, roof framing plan, the cross section, and so on. How each of these component parts comes together is de-

scribed by the detail. Chapter 9 (Footing Details), Chapter 10 (Exterior Walls), and Chapter 11 (Roof to Wall) show excellent examples of this type of detail.

Special structural conditions do occur quite often. An example is a two-story office building built using the normal 2 × 4 stud construction except in one location where the second story projects beyond the first floor. This condition necessitates the need for a beam connection detail. (Chapter 20 describes such a condition.) Whether it is a special case, such as the beam condition, or showing how the various parts come together, the detailer must determine what information is the most important. The thought process should start with the following.

1. A description of its various parts.
2. A description of the sizes and material of each of the parts.
3. The maximum and minimum dimensions required by codes, engineering, or by various agencies.
4. Correct designation for the materials used.
5. Special treatment or unique features for any piece.

Examples of these principles are found in Figure 2.1. Most of these principles explain themselves with the possible exception of condition 3. Code and good practice, for example, require that a bolt be spaced a certain distance away from the end as well as the edge of the wood (see Chapter 20, "Drilling holes in column or beam"). The structural engineer may have calculated the need for greater strength due to wind

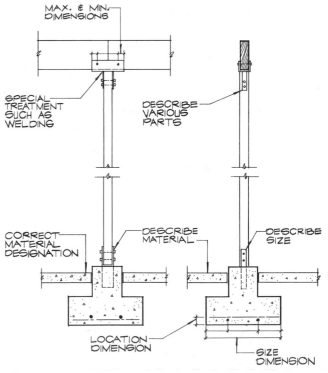

Figure 2.1 Identifying unique or special features.

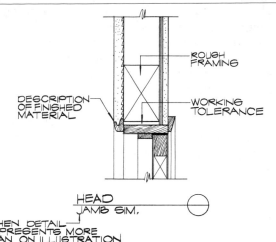

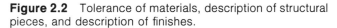

Figure 2.2 Tolerance of materials, description of structural pieces, and description of finishes.

problems. If the detail had not been drawn, the contractor might not have constructed this connection correctly.

Often, the normal structural system such as studs 16″ o.c. (on center) is interrupted. This happens with doors and windows (see Chapters 12 and 13 for specific descriptions), and the approach here is slightly different. The architect must be aware of the tolerance used by the trades involved. First, the rough carpenters are working to $\frac{1}{2}$″ tolerances. If their detail does not reflect this, the window may not fit when delivered at a later time in the construction sequence. The following items are to be considered when drafting this type of detail.

1. The working tolerance of the material and trades involved.
2. The description of structural pieces around the object.
3. The description of finish material around the framing.

A sample of these principles is shown in Figure 2.2 (above). If a detail such as this is used in more than one location, only a general statement is made about those parts that vary. For example, instead of saying 4 × 6 header above the door, the note should read 4 × header. This will force the carpenter to look at the roof framing plan for the exact size of that piece for a specific location.

Aesthetic Considerations

Details are often drawn to describe something other than a structural connection. They are very often used to illustrate an aesthetic feature of the structure or to maintain a degree of expertise. As illustrated in Chapters 12 and 13, there are several methods for finishing lath and plaster around an opening on the inside of a structure — wood or metal trim can be used to hide the ending of the plaster. If a detail is not drawn, you are allowing contractors to use their judgment on how to deal with it. Although this judgment may be sound, it may also be influenced by the cost involved or the speed with which the project can be executed. To detail is to ensure the procedure and method to be used. Figure 2.3 shows a desired method of attaching a trim to a post — a classic illustration of this principle. The architect may want to use a reveal between the post and the trim for aesthetic reasons and because it is almost impossible to get a piece of trim to line up perfectly with a post without expending a great deal of time and effort. Unless this is detailed, there is no guarantee where the trim will be placed, if at all.

Environmental Considerations

Here we are dealing with such factors as sun, its heat and light, wind, rain, noise, hurricane, snow, and so on. By detailing with an awareness of these environmental factors, we can trace water from a rainfall around a window and be sure that it does not enter the structure itself or the building interior. Moisture may enter an area by its normal gravitational flow or by its capillary action. See Figure 2.4. In fact, by drawing a detail we can locate many potential problem locations in a structure that plans and elevations do not reveal.

Due to the resurgent interest in energy conservation, many states are now requiring sectional drawings and details at the roof, the wall, and at the floor showing what has been done to avoid heat loss or

Figure 2.3 Loss of reveal on final assembly when not detailed.

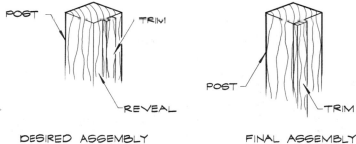

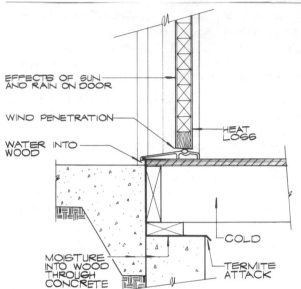

Figure 2.4 Environmental considerations.

describing how the structure has been insulated from the heat or cold. The detail or section is now required to show all materials used in the structure and to indicate their "R" value, which is a numerical value given to each material to show its resistive capability to heat loss. See Figure 2.5. In many instances there have been changes in required window sizes. Initially, only minimums were established, based on the square footage of the rooms. Now many building departments have maximums as well. If these maximums are exceeded, calculations must be submitted to the local building official confirming that the heat loss–heat gain is not excessive. As the nature of architecture changes, the need for more specific drawings and details will increase.

Human Needs

Many details are drawn to show how the needs of the human body can be fulfilled. The concern for people, including the handicapped, has produced the need

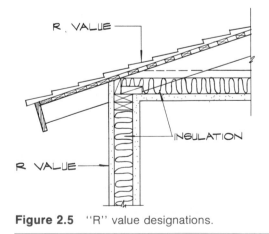

Figure 2.5 "R" value designations.

for selective detailing, which should be based on the ease with which the human body performs. A simple handrail becomes a significant feature when looked at from the standpoint of the young, the handicapped, or the aged because of the human forces exerted upon it. While the average person takes such features for granted, the draftsperson must consider minimum and maximum heights, the forces put upon them, the structural framing necessary to accept them, the materials they are made of, and even the decorative feature each might have. See Figure 2.6.

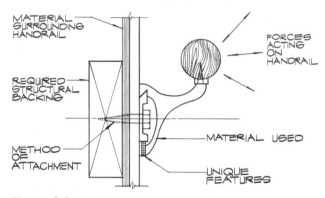

Figure 2.6 Analysis of human needs.

Relationship Between Building Elements

Any time there is a change in a horizontal or vertical plane, this becomes a potential problem for a designer if its problems are not explored with a detail. The draftsperson should explore any intersection of floor to wall, wall to roof, or change of level for a detail. There is always some type of special connection, potential of water penetration, or movement of the structure at this point. Exploration by detail will significantly reduce cracks in the plaster, expose unanticipated structural problems that will halt work in the field, or highlight any of the previously mentioned problems of structure, environment, aesthetics, or functional problems for the human body. Chapters 9, 10, and 11 describe minutely the different ways of dealing with these intersections by using a variety of different materials.

Material Limitation

One of the more often overlooked areas of detailing by students is that of knowing the limitations of the materials with which they are dealing. Concrete, wood, and plaster are the best examples. It is possible to form concrete into a very sharp angle as shown in Figure 2.7, but not practical because it will break. For walks and concrete slabs, the detailer should

POOR SHAPE FOR CONCRETE

BETTER SHAPE

Figure 2.7 Considering material limitations.

never taper the thickness of concrete to form a wedge shape.

One of the poor qualities of wood is that it warps. Therefore, it is very difficult to take two extremely long pieces of wood and put them side by side and expect them, without nails or bolts, to maintain parallelism. Another example of wood warping is a cabinet door made of plywood wider than 16"; here warpage could be great. It is for this and for aesthetic reasons that architects, designers, and draftspersons use what is called a reveal when joining one piece of wood with another piece of wood or straight edge such as an aluminum window casing. See Figure 2.3.

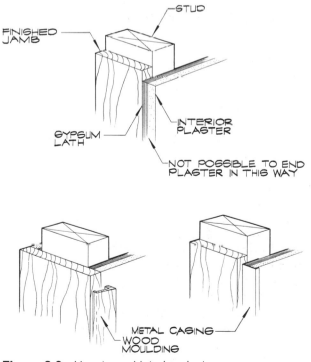

Figure 2.8 How to end interior plaster.

Stucco and interior plaster is another material often misunderstood by the beginning detailer. Beginning detailers often forget that plaster is put on wet and requires an ending. This ending serves two purposes: it gives a definite termination for the plaster, and it allows the plasterer to maintain a consistent thickness. See Figure 2.8. Chapters 12 and 13 demonstrate various ways of ending plaster.

Plaster is also a very brittle material and care must be taken when rounding corners. A metal protective piece called a corner bead is often employed in such cases. See Figure 2.9. A similar device is utilized on outside corners when stucco is used.

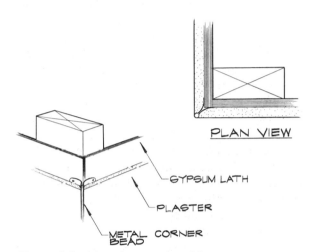

PLAN VIEW

Figure 2.9 Use of corner bead for corners.

Material Change

Whenever there is a change from one material to another, a potential location for a detail exists. A concrete foundation to a wood floor (Chapter 9), steel stairs to a wood frame (Chapter 16), or a brick fireplace to a wood frame (Chapter 18) are good examples of transitions from one material to another that could be trouble spots if not detailed.

Building Codes and Safety

Safety is a main concern of building codes and local building officials. It should also be a primary concern of the designer and detailer. Elevators, playground equipment, industrial workstations, the rise and run of stairs, and so on, should be detailed. When health and safety are concerned, local building codes often require the detail.

An illustration of building codes and safety problems might be best described by the example of a typical door in a hospital. The jamb (the side portion

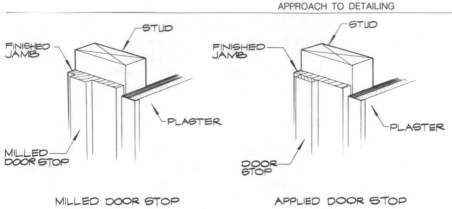

MILLED DOOR STOP   APPLIED DOOR STOP

Figure 2.10 Comparison between milled door stop and applied door stop.

of the door) in many states must be milled (cut out) out of one piece of wood for fire and smoke protection. See Figure 2.10. A contractor unaware of this may use a plant-on doorstop. If the building inspector caught this oversight after the construction, the plaster, jamb, and doorstop would have to be removed and replaced. Detailing might not have stopped this oversight, but it would absolve the architectural firm of the responsibility since it *was detailed.*

Another example of a code dictating a detail is that of requiring venting in a roof or roof overhang. The code requires the vent, but the detail actually positions it. The location may have an effect on structure or on the aesthetic, visual appearance of the building and should be considered.

A final example of a code requirement might be an anchor bolt (which holds the first piece of the foundation), where the local building department may establish a minimum standard in terms of size, length, spacing, how far the bolt must be embedded into concrete, and even how far from the corners of the building a bolt must be. In many cases codes are very specific.

Building Sequence

Unlike mechanical detailing, where you start with a piece of metal and develop the desired shape by cutting, milling, and drilling the material away, the architectural process is one of adding on. Once drafters understand the specific sequence of construction, the details they draft become logical and allow for a smooth progression of construction. For example, cabinet depth is measured from the front face of the cabinet to the interior plaster rather than from the rough framing to the front face of the cabinet door. The reason is simple. If the cabinet is shop-made, it is installed after the rough framing is done and the inte-

rior plaster applied. It would be impossible to verify the distance from the rough framing to the front face of the cabinet. Cabinet doors are installed after the cabinet itself is installed. Because the door is a moving object as opposed to a stationary object, it should not be dimensioned.

Another common error in detailing involves dimensioning to inaccessible locations. A dimension may be inaccessible because of the building sequence or location of the item being detailed. Structural aspects of a building should not be dimensioned from the finished item to be installed at a latter date. Dimensioning a location of a beam from an air-conditioning duct to be installed later is a good example of what an architect must *not* do.

Limits of Manufacturing

Each manufacturer sets individual tolerances — the maximum and minimum size to which an item might be made. In space travel, the tolerance may be a thousandth of an inch for the various parts of a space craft, but on a building the tolerances are less rigid. Most tolerances are determined by the tools used in the field, the characteristic of the material being used, or the accumulation of the errors as an object is being assembled. In cabinetmaking, where the tolerance is very small, variation may develop from one cabinet to another because each piece on one cabinet may have been cut to the absolute minimum while another may have been cut to the absolute maximum.

Draftspersons should not attempt to dimension items over which they have no control. For example, when detailing an aluminum sliding door, it would be foolish if drafters tried to detail the working parts of the door. Their function is to show how the total aluminum door fits into the wall, not to dimension its component parts.

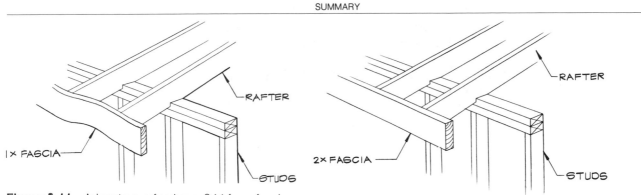

Figure 2.11 Advantages of a change of fascia for a facade.

Craftsmanship

Details are also used to maintain a degree of craftsmanship. A fascia on the end of a roof overhang illustrates this point in Figure 2.11. If a 1 × 8 fascia were used, the rafters would not have to be cut as carefully, because if any rafter were longer or shorter, the 1 × 8 would bend to a certain extend as shown. This only accents poor construction, and the wavy line of the fascia detracts from the structure. A 2 × 8 fascia used in its place cannot bend as easily and forces the workers in the field to be more precise initially. As attempts to maintain expertise increase, along with an awareness on the part of architectural draftspersons of what produces good craftsmanship, detailers will produce better details and subsequently better constructed buildings.

Selection of Proper Scale

The selection of the scale at which the detail is to be drawn is as important as the detail itself. Certain standards have been set up by the architectural industry, yet clarity should dictate the scale architectural draftspersons select. The proper scale should satisfy all the conditions of the detail and translate the intent of the designer so the worker in the field is aided rather than hindered.

The scale should also be drawn large enough so that the architectural draftsperson can discover that assemblies are impossible. All too often we assume a particular situation will work until we draft a large de-

tail and find otherwise. Had the detail not been drawn, the impossible situation may have to be solved in the field — which wastes time and increases costs.

As one can readily see, detailing is a necessary part of a set of contract documents and can be a learning process as well. Talk to any architect or detailer about what he or she has learned or discovered in the process of drawing details and you will be surprised. Many unsolved problems are unearthed at the detailing stage of development.

Details also preserve and produce continuity of the character of the building by maintaining uniformity of approach throughout the structure. As one architect put it: "Details help to maintain a certain rhythm to the building."

Standardization

Before the architectural draftsperson begins any detail, he or she should look at the appendix and become familiar with the standard conventions used.

There are various ways of designating materials in section. Three suggested methods are displayed in Figures A-1 through A-4. Standard material designations are followed by a list of standard abbreviations used nationally and symbols that are used for abbreviations.

Figure A-5 shows the various graphics symbols used by the majority of the offices surveyed by the Committee on Office Practice, American Institute of Architects (national).

Summary

This chapter has given architectural draftspersons enough background so that they might do more than just copy previously drawn details. It is necessary to look beyond the detail itself to the reason for its inception and the underlying causes that produced the need for certain information. This is part of the process of developing an attitude that will help architectural draftspersons in all phases of architecture, not just detailing.

Detailing reduced to its most simple terms becomes a problem-solving adventure using aesthetics, the environment, human needs, and structural considerations as a basis for all thought processes.

INTRODUCTION TO PRINCIPLES OF DETAILING

3

Preview Chapter 3 introduces detailing by describing what a detail is and what makes it necessary to draw a detail; in other words, the intent of the detail is established.

Through 25 rules, this chapter also introduces the do's and don'ts of detailing. These rules cover everything from acceptable drafting procedures to how to note a detail, from dimensioning to sizing of lumber, and are based on acceptable procedures used in industry.

There is a section devoted to scale (ratio of drawing to actual size) as they apply to details. Because employers are always emphasizing the need for good lettering, there is a large section describing the practice of lettering. The final two sections provide an introduction to building codes and use of break-lines.

After reading this chapter, the architectural draftsperson will:

1. Understand the importance of detailing as a means of communication.
2. Develop a method of approach to drafting a set of details.
3. Realize which procedures are acceptable in the industry and which are not.
4. Learn to note and dimension details.
5. Be able to select proper material designation for the specific detail.
6. Learn to reference details to other drawings.
7. Be able to select the proper scale for the detail.
8. Be able to improve lettering skills by emphasizing particular, important aspects of letters and spacing.
9. Begin to understand the role building codes have in architecture and especially detailing.
10. Understand the proper use of the break-line.

What Is a Detail?

A detail is a drawing that minutely describes a particular assembly of a building. It is a refinement of the general drawings such as the floor plans, elevations, plot plans, and so on. While the major working drawings deal predominantly with general information, details deal with specifics. For example, while the general location and size of the kitchen cabinets may be indicated on a floor plan, it is the cabinet detail that describes the mortar under the ceramic tile, the type of joints used, whether the drawer uses metal hardware on the inside, how the edges of the plywood are treated, and so forth.

Since most details do not affect the health and safety of individuals, they are not generally required by the local department of building and safety. However, the use of detail is the *only way* an architect or designer can have complete control over the appearance of the building and mastery over the final resultant assembly.

Intent of Details

The primary purpose of details is to illustrate, on a larger scale, the method of assembly. Details are usually drawn in section, thereby exposing much of the interior members covered up in other drawings. See Figure 3.1. The very nature of details affords the draftsperson the opportunity to give critical dimensions, describe materials, and indicate maximum and minimum dimensions.

Vocabulary of Architectural Lines

A list of the various types of lines used in architectural detailing is shown in Figure 3.2. The lines are very similar to those used in mechanical drafting, although the application is a bit different.

Rules of Detailing

Listed here are some of the fundamental rules that guarantee good details. The majority of these rules apply to all details and as such should be explicitly followed.

Rule 1 Draw as it is built. Unlike mechanical drawing where a piece of metal is cut, slotted, or drilled, architecture is a process of building from the inside out and adding as you go along. For example, in drawing a section through a wall, you draw the studs (wood inside of a wall) including insulation if needed first, then add the gypsum lath

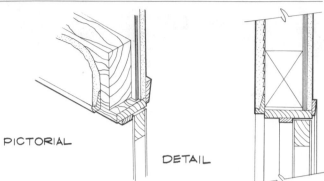

Figure 3.1 Pictorial drawing of a door; drafted detail drawing of a door.

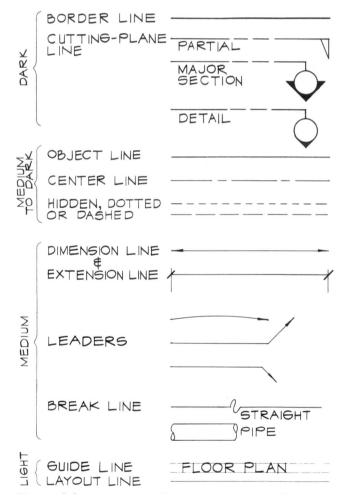

Figure 3.2 Vocabulary of architectural lines. (Reprinted, by permission, from *The Professional Practice of Architectural Working Drawings,* Copyright © 1984 by John Wiley & Sons, Inc.)

(commonly called plaster board), and finally add the plaster.

Rule 2 Follow a definite sequence based on an exact priority: object first, dimensions next, then notes, profiling, and referencing. See Figure 3.3.

Rule 3 Try not to interrupt or cross dimension lines — failure to follow this rule may end in confusion. See Figure 3.4.

Rule 4 Learn how to note drawings. The size of the object usually comes first, then the name of the piece, spacing third, and finally any other pertinent information. For example,

SIZE   NAME

½" X 10" LONG ANCHOR BOLT EMBEDDED 7" INTO CONC., 6'-0" O.C., 12" FROM CORNERS

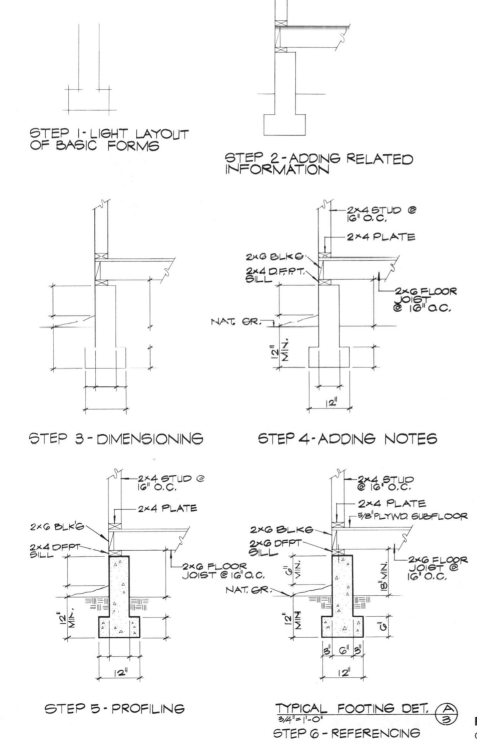

STEP 1 - LIGHT LAYOUT OF BASIC FORMS

STEP 2 - ADDING RELATED INFORMATION

STEP 3 - DIMENSIONING

STEP 4 - ADDING NOTES

STEP 5 - PROFILING

TYPICAL FOOTING DET. Ⓐ/③
3/4" = 1'-0"

STEP 6 - REFERENCING

Figure 3.3 Drafting sequence of a detail.

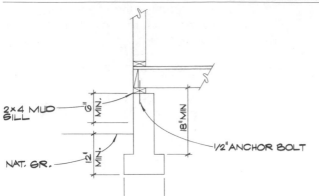

Figure 3.4 How *not* to cross dimension lines.

Rule 5 The inside of the building is always drawn to the right and the outside to the left. See Figure 3.1.

Rule 6 Always draw a surfaced size, which is the actual (net size) lumber size, not what it is said to be (nominal size). For example, don't draw a (nominal size) 2×4 as 2 inches by 4 inches but rather $1\frac{1}{2} \times 3\frac{1}{2}$ in lumber size (see Chapter 6). In fact, *some* architectural offices differentiate between net sizes and nominal sizes by the use of inch marks. An example of this would be not using inch marks when noting (nominal) sizes as 2×4 or 6×8 and using inch marks for exact (net size) measurements such as $\frac{3}{4}''$ plywood or $18''$ minimum.

Rule 7 The leaders from notes should be placed so as not to disturb the integrity of the drawing. Straight lines and curved lines are usually the best, as in Figure 3.5, and are most often used in the profession. Snake-like lines may also be used, but they are not easy to draw consistently. Freehand arcs should not be used for leaders. Using a french curve is recommended for the beginning draftsperson.

Rule 8 Leaders for notes on the right side of a detail should come from the beginning of the

note. Leaders for notes on the left side of a detail should proceed from the end of the note. An exception occurs when the space between the notes is such that there is little question as to what leader belongs to what note. For an example of this situation see Figure 3.6. The 2×4 D.F.P.T. (Douglas fir pressure treated) sill note and that of reinforcing bars in Figure 3.7 are shown incorrectly. The leaders drawn for 2×6 and the anchor bolt notes are correct.

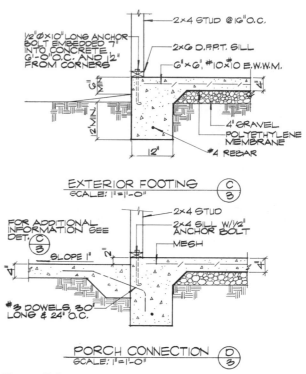

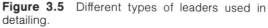

Figure 3.6 How to share notes.

Rule 9 Unless required by the owner of the structure or the designer, brand names should be avoided. For example, the word laminated plastic should be used instead of Formica. Brand names are usually desig-

Figure 3.5 Different types of leaders used in detailing.

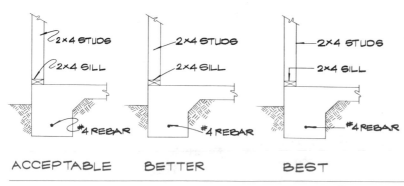

nated in a set of written descriptions called specifications. Also, complete names, not assumed names, should be given. An example of this would be using the word "tile"—there are many types of tiles, and the description is incomplete without specifying the type (e.g., ceramic tile).

Rule 10 Each detail should have its own set of notes. One note should not be shared with another detail. It is very tempting for a beginner to run leaders from one note to more than one detail to some lettering. The principle is: "Each detail should be able to stand on its own."

Rule 11 Rule 10 indicated that each detail should have its own set of notes; however, it is perfectly acceptable to refer one detail to another. If, for example, the first detail of a set of, say, 10 details described the exterior footing and the second described how a porch comes into contact with that exterior footing, the porch detail need only describe the connection definitively and assume that the rest of the information can be gotten by the contractor from the first exterior footing. A note on the second detail that reads "see ⊖ for additional information" is sufficient here. See Figure 3.7. Also note on the sample how the first detail has a complete note referring to the anchor bolt while the detail pertaining to the porch connection does not.

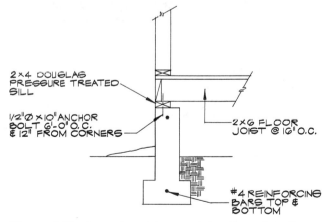

Figure 3.7 Correct and incorrect location of leaders on notes.

Rule 12 Slang or field expressions should be avoided on details. Remember that this is a legal document and there is no room for expressions, such as mud for concrete.

Rule 13 Do not abbreviate unless you know the abbreviation is a standard in the field of architecture. Such terms as A.C. can be abbre-

viations for alternating current as well as asphaltic concrete; F.G. can be mistaken for fuel gas or finish grade. See the Appendix for abbreviations accepted by the American Institute of Architects.

Rule 14 Dimensions and notes, written vertically because of the lack of space, should read from the right. See Figure 3.8.

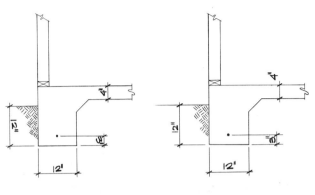

INCORRECT   CORRECT

Figure 3.8 Location and orientation of dimensions.

Rule 15 There are eight different types of dimension notations used.

1. When a dimension line has nothing added to it but the dimension, it should be assumed that workers will hold to that dimension as best they can within the tolerance of the material with which they are working. A rough carpenter, for example, can stay within $\frac{1}{2}$ inch of the dimension requested.

2. If a dimension has the term Maximum next to it or below it, the worker cannot exceed this measurement.

3. If the term Minimum is used, the measurement could and may be larger but not smaller than that indicated.

4. The term Hold means exactly what it indicates. Hold that dimension at all cost. Other dimensions may change, but the Hold dimension cannot. It might be important for a piece of equipment to fit, or necessary for the flow of a piece of merchandise through an industrial building, or may have been required for safety reasons.

5. The notation ± after a dimension means the space dimensioned or the piece of equipment dimensioned may vary somewhat. For example, $3'\text{-}0'' \pm \frac{1}{8}''$ means the $3'\text{-}0$ is not less than $2'\text{-}11\frac{7}{8}''$ or greater than $3'\text{-}\frac{1}{8}''$.

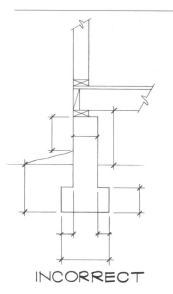
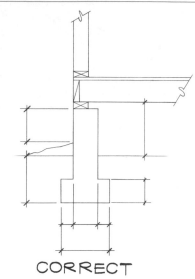

INCORRECT CORRECT

Figure 3.9 How to group dimensions.

6. The term Approximately is seldom used, but it is necessary when the precise dimension is not known. It should be avoided because it is too ambiguous and thus has no place in architecture.

7. The notation Not to Scale under a dimension can be accompanied by a wavy line under it, for example, 3'-0". The term Not to Scale can be abbreviated NTS or N.T.S. This means that the written dimension is correct but the drawing is not. This procedure is employed when there is not enough time to redraw the detail but a change is necessary.

8. When the dimensioning fluctuates, the term Varies is used. For example, on a sloping lot, a concrete wall may be level at the top, but the base may fluctuate. The dimension line from the base to the top of the wall may simply indicate Varies with no exact dimension on it.

Rule 16 Group or align dimensions when possible to facilitate reading. Do not scatter dimensions all over the detail. Attempt to incorporate some logic and organization. See Figure 3.9.

Rule 17 Fractions are not often used in architecture, but when they are, they should be measurable fractions such as $\frac{3}{4}$, $\frac{5}{8}$, $\frac{1}{2}$, $\frac{1}{4}$. Unconventional fractions such as $\frac{7}{9}$, $\frac{3}{7}$, and $\frac{1}{3}$ cannot be measured with the measuring devices now employed. When the metric system is finally adopted by architecture, the problem will be avoided.

Rule 18 Use extension lines freely. If the dimension is more clearly stated by the use of extension lines, they should be used. Dimension lines should touch the object only if there is no other way to dimension an object. See Figure 3.10.

Rule 19 Some offices use a simple way to differentiate among wood members that are continuous, those that are blocking (not continuous), and those that are finished. See Figure 3.11.

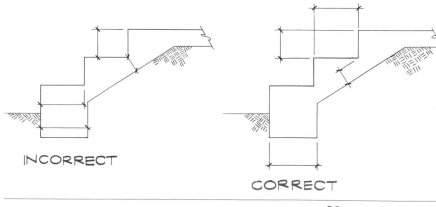

INCORRECT CORRECT

Figure 3.10 Proper use of extension lines.

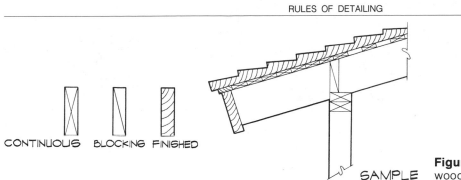

CONTINUOUS BLOCKING FINISHED

SAMPLE

Figure 3.11 Differentiating between wood members.

Rule 20 Use the correct designation for the various types of materials. Concrete in elevation is designated by a series of dots, while the same material in section is shown with dots and triangular forms. See the chart on ''Materials in Section'' in the Appendix.

Rule 21 Scale must also be considered. Plywood, for example, drawn in $3'' = 1'-0''$ would look different from that drawn at $\frac{3}{4}' = 1'-0''$ scale. See Figure 3.12.

Rule 22 Profile the most important part of the detail. Profiling is the process of darkening or outlining the most important features of the

PLYWOOD @ 3'' SCALE

PLYWOOD @ 1½'' SCALE

Figure 3.12 Selecting the *correct* scale.

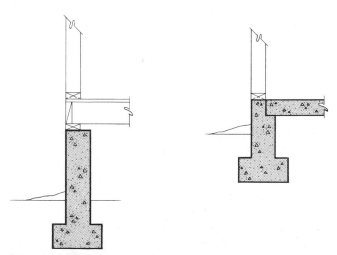

Figure 3.13 Shading (*pouché*) the detail.

detail. If the detail is a footing, the concrete portion should be profiled. See Figure 3.13.

Rule 23 Besides profiling, another method of accenting a particular part of a detail is to *pouché*. This term refers to the process of shading in the area that one desires to emphasize. It is usually done on the reverse side of the vellum and can be shaded, much like coloring with a crayon, with graphite or colored pencil. One should be careful not to use a wax-based material, such as crayon, prismacolor pencil, pastels, or to use such colors as red, yellow, or orange. These colors stop light when reproducing the detail for copies and turn the emphasized area black. Blue seems to be the best color. The right-side illustration on Figure 3.13 has been pouchéd.

Rule 24 The correct use of reference bubbles is imperative because they cross index the detail to the drawing from which it came.

There are various arrangements used. Some architects prefer to put them in front of the title, while others place them after. Whatever position, if the detail is drawn on the same sheet that it is taken from (e.g., footing detail and foundation plan on the same sheet), only one letter or number need occur in the reference bubble. See Figure 3.14.

When the detail is on a completely different sheet from its source, the bubble must be split in two—never vertically as shown incorrectly on Figure 3.15. Figure 3.15 also shows the correct method of splitting the reference bubble horizontally, so that the detail number or letters can go on the top and the sheet number on the bottom.

Rule 25 There is no replacement for legible lettering and clean crisp lines. Unlike mechanical drawing, the object lines may cross slightly to show confidence and mastery over the material to be drawn but *never* so as to be mistaken for sloppiness.

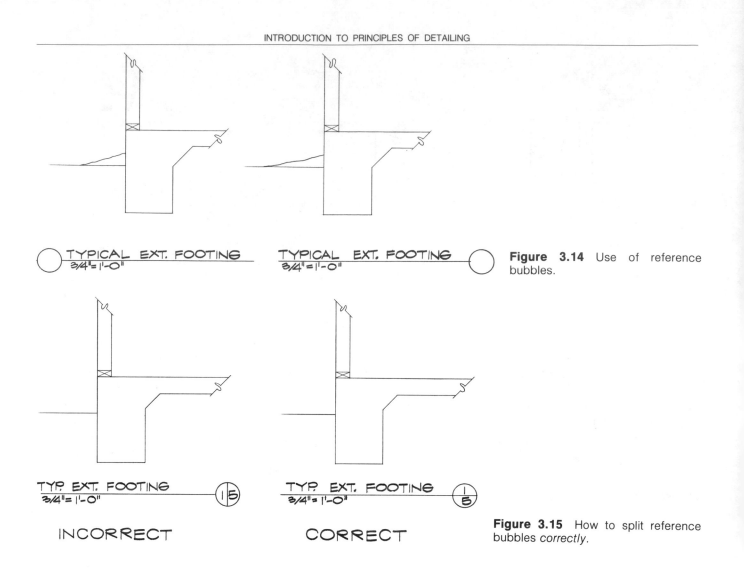

Figure 3.14 Use of reference bubbles.

Figure 3.15 How to split reference bubbles *correctly*.

Scale

Most plans, elevations, and sections are drawn at a very small scale. Details are usually drawn at a larger scale, such as the following.

$\frac{3}{4}'' = 1'\text{-}0''$
$1'' = 1'\text{-}0''$
$1\frac{1}{2}'' = 1'\text{-}0''$
$3'' = 1'\text{-}0''$ (quarter size)
$6'' = 1'\text{-}0''$ (half size)
Full size

The following are suggested typical scales for use in detailing.

Footings	$\frac{3}{4}'' = 1'\text{-}0''$
	$1'' = 1'\text{-}0''$
Intersections of roof to wall	$1\frac{1}{2}'' = 1'\text{-}0''$
	$3'' = 1'\text{-}0''$
Window and door details	$3'' = 1'\text{-}0''$
Cabinet details	$3'' = 1'\text{-}0''$
Others	$\frac{3}{4}'' = 1'\text{-}0''$
	(to full size, depending on clarity needed)

A detail may occasionally be freehand, usually because of the need for speed. The drawing should be designated *Scale: none.*

Lettering

In architectural drafting, as in mechanical drafting, hand-lettering working drawings may not always be a reality. A variety of different types of mechanical devices have been coming on the market in recent years and large engineering and aircraft firms have been experimenting with their effectiveness.

However, the architectural industry is and may always be a small crafts industry. Architectural firms usually contain three to six employees and consequently cannot afford the expense of computerized drafting and lettering machines. For this reason it is important that each draftsperson be proficient in lettering. In fact, good lettering and good line quality help to obtain the first job for the recent graduate.

Architectural lettering differs somewhat from the Gothic letters developed by C. W. Reinhardt about 50 years ago that are now called mechanical lettering. Architectural lettering has evolved from a series of influences. Speed was one of these influences. Mechanically formed letters seem to lack speed in their development—yet we must not interpret speed as sloppiness.

Another influence was style. The architecturally drafted plan was in essence an idea or concept on paper, a creative endeavor. So the lines took on a definite characteristic, as did the lettering.

Finally, stylizing lettering serves to identify the draftsperson in many firms. Many individuals have certain lettering peculiarities and lines alone will not identify them. However, most firms attempt to create a uniform style of lettering for all draftspersons.

Stylizing must not be interpreted as an attempt to overdecorate. Students often think that they can almost create new alphabets and justify this by calling it stylization.

Stylization does not mean more curlicues on letters or the destruction of readability. Here are a few simple rules to follow.

1. Learn to letter with vertical strokes first. Sloping letters may be easier to master, but most architectural offices prefer vertical lettering. It is easier to go from vertical to sloping letters than the reverse. See Figure 3.16.

ANCHOR BOLT   *ANCHOR BOLT*

VERTICAL LETTERS   SLOPING LETTERS

Figure 3.16 Comparison between vertical and sloping lettering.

2. Master mechanical lettering before attempting architectural lettering or any type of stylization. A student who cannot letter well mechanically has less chance to develop good architectural letters. See Figure 3.17.

MECHANICAL   ARCHITECTURAL
M W   /\\ \\/ /\\/\\ ← (Poor)

Figure 3.17 Overworking architectural letters.

3. A student should practice words, phrases, and numbers—not just individual letters. Copy a phrase used in any part of this text.

4. The shape of a letter should not be changed. The proportion of the letter may be slightly altered, but the letter's original image should never be destroyed. While the example in Figure 3.17 is often used for speed, it can be misconstrued for an ''I'' and a ''V'' rather than a ''W'' as intended.

5. Proportion change is shown in Figure 3.18.

MECHANICAL   ARCHITECTURAL
STUD   STUD STUD

Figure 3.18 Changing proportion to produce architectural effect.

6. Certain strokes can be emphasized so that one letter is not mistaken for another. This also forces the draftsperson to be more definitive in the formation of individual strokes. The strokes an architect emphasizes should be those most important to that letter; for example, a ''B'' differs from an ''R'' by certain strokes and an ''L'' from an ''I'' by the bottom stroke. The beginning or end of these strokes can be emphasized by bearing down on the pencil at the point to insure a good reprint of that portion of the stroke. See Figure 3.19.

B L I T R K

Figure 3.19 Emphasis on certain strokes

EXAMPLE

7. Many draftspersons have picked up the bad habit of mixing upper- and lowercase letters. This is not to be copied or regarded as good lettering.

8. Some draftspersons also have developed a style of leaving space within the letter that is not there. This too is to be discouraged. See Figure 3.20.

B O Q D P

Figure 3.20 Leaving space within the letter.

EXAMPLE

9. Consistency produces good lettering. If vertical lines are used, they must all be parallel. A slight variation produces poor lettering. Even round letters such as ''O'' have a center through which imaginary vertical strokes will go. See Figure 3.21.

PLYWOOD   PLYWOOD
(Poor)   (Good)

Figure 3.21 Producing consistency.

EXAMPLE

10. Second only to the letter itself is spacing. Good spacing protects good letter formation. Poor spacing destroys even the best lettering. See Figure 3.22.

P LY WO OD (Poor)

Figure 3.22 Importance of good spacing.

EXAMPLE

11. Always use guidelines and use them to the fullest. See Figure 3.23.

(Poor)   (Good)

Figure 3.23 Full use of guidelines.

Using Guidelines*

While a purist might frown on the practice, a guideline or straightedge can be used in lettering to speed up the learning process. Horizontal lines are easier for a beginner than are vertical lines, and shapes appear better formed when all of the vertical strokes are perfectly perpendicular and parallel to each other. Curved and round strokes are done without the aid of an instrument.

After drawing the guidelines, place a T-square or parallel about 2 or 3 inches below the lines. Locate the triangle to the left of the area to be lettered with the vertical portion of the triangle on the right side. See Figure 3.24. "Eyeball" the spacing of the letters. Position your pencil as if you are ready to make the

Figure 3.24 Pencil placement for vertical lettering. (Reprinted, by permission, from *The Professional Practice of Architectural Working Drawings,* Copyright © 1984 by John Wiley & Sons, Inc.)

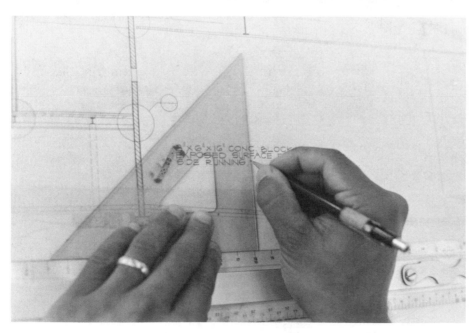

Figure 3.25 Placing the triangle against the pencil. (Reprinted, by permission, from *The Professional Practice of Architectural Working Drawings,* Copyright © 1984 by John Wiley & Sons, Inc.)

* Reprinted, by permission, from *The Professional Practice of Architectural Working Drawings,* copyright © 1984 by John Wiley & Sons, Inc.

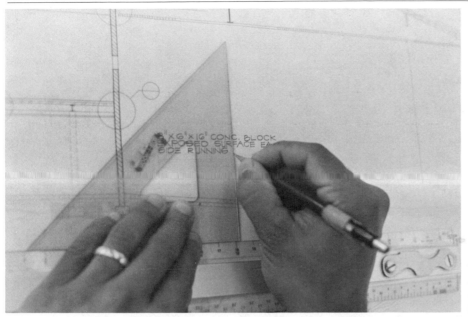

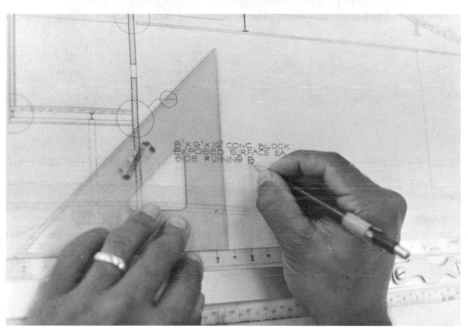

vertical line without the triangle. Before you make the vertical stroke, slide the triangle over against the pencil and make the stroke. See Figures 3.25 and 3.26. Draw nonvertical lines freehand. See Figure 3.27.

Using a straightedge helps build up skills. Eventually you should discontinue its use as practice improves your lettering skills.

Building Codes

An architect should be aware of the existence of building codes. These codes deal primarily with health and safety and not the aesthetics of a building. They are concerned with the stability of a structure and the safety of its occupants.

There is a national code, most states have uniform building codes, and there are local codes. Architectural building codes can be likened to automobile speed regulations. The federal government can institute a law governing the speed of automobiles. A state can adopt these or make them more stringent, but the state cannot make them more lenient.

The local county or city also can adapt the state requirements for automobile safety and, within jurisdiction, make them more stringent. A local agency can legislate to have drivers go slower in its community even if the road is a state highway. However, they cannot allow people to go faster.

Let us say that a state building code calls for a minimum dimension between the finished floor of a structure and the ceiling to be 7'-6". The local code can establish the minimum as 8'-0" but not 7'-0." Do realize that minimum code standards are just what the term indicates: minimum. They may not necessarily be the most desired solution—the best solution is very seldom the minimum.

When developing a set of working drawings, *always* check to see what agency (city, county, or state) dictates the manner in which you build.

Use of Break-Line

The break-line has two functions. If a single break-line is used, it designates that the item in question does continue but was stopped at that point for convenience. Figure 3.28 shows how the stud at the top has

been culminated in a breakline as has the concrete to the right. Both continue, but without purpose since the detail deals primarily with the footing.

A pair of break-lines next to each other indicates that a portion of the drawing has been removed. See Figure 3.29. The object may have been removed for several reasons. Its presence would have made the drawing too large for the drawing area allowed, the removal did not significantly affect the detail, or it was possible to draw the detail larger by eliminating a section of it, thus making the detail clearer. If the dimension of the wall varies, the double break-line is often employed.

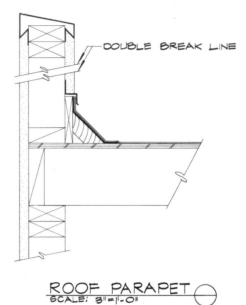

Figure 3.29   Use of double break-line.

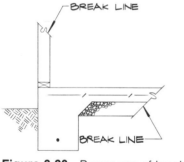

Figure 3.28   Proper use of break-line.

Regional Differences

Regional differences usually involve one of the following items:

Wind—hurricanes, cyclones
Rain and humidity
Soil differences
Frost lines, extreme temperatures, and snow loads
Termites
Seismic pressure
Availability of material
Construction differences

Each subsequent chapter will express these differences as they apply to a specific detailing procedure or according to the impact they create.

It should be noted here that while the attempt of this chapter is to produce a uniform approach to detailing, practices and procedures *do* vary from region to region and even from office to office. If, however, the method of approach is sound and the reasons for a particular procedure are known by the architectural draftsperson, a readjustment to a slightly different practice becomes easy.

Building Codes

Each subsequent chapter will also deal with the code differences that exist nationally from one region to another. No attempt is made here to discuss or explore the variety of differences in code requirements that might exist.

Summary

There is a very precise and systematic method of approaching details. There are also certain standards that the architectural industry tries to maintain for purposes of uniformity. These rules were developed to convey information to the people out in the field.

Selection of scale is a critical part of detailing. Certain standard scales are used by the industry, but the individual detail should, for clarity, dictate the appropriate scale to be used.

Architectural drafting depends on lines, symbols, and words to describe a particular effect, procedure, or method of assembly. It is, therefore, necessary for draftspersons constantly to improve their lettering.

As draftspersons develop these good habits of detailing, they must always be aware of the implications building codes have on them. These codes are usually stated in the form of maximums and minimums, not necessarily good architectural construction practices.

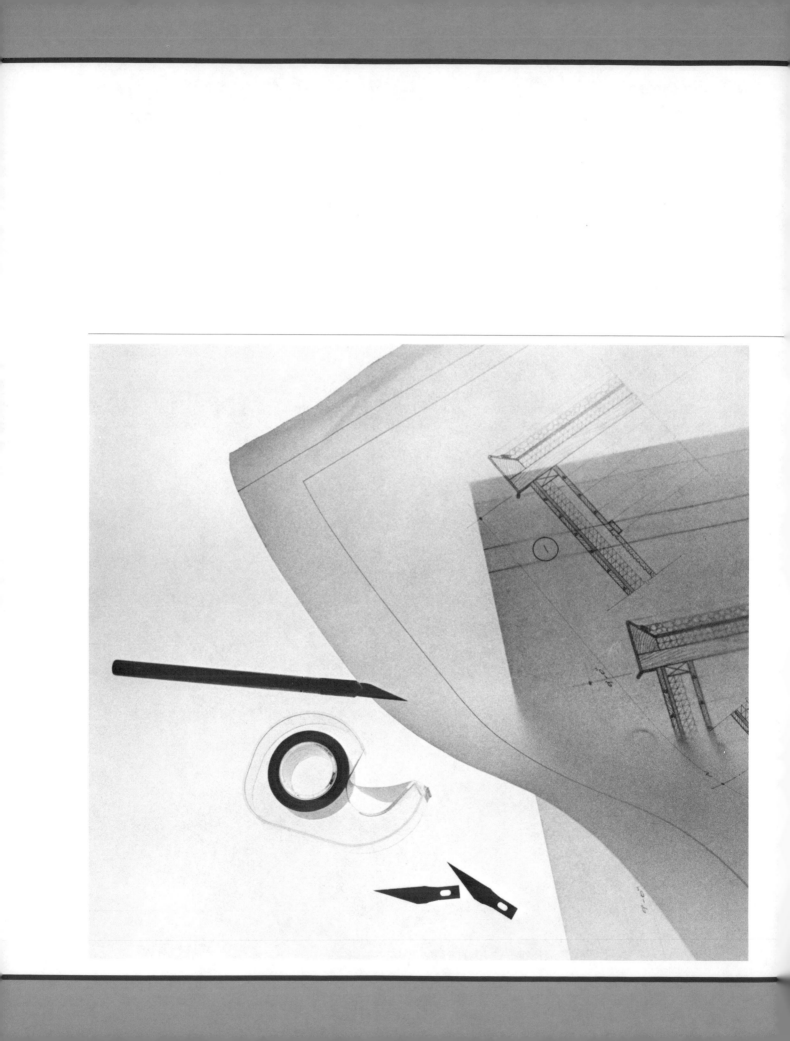

4

APPLIQUÉ FILM, SCISSOR DRAFTING, AND SPLICING

Preview   Chapter 4 introduces architecture office practices of appliqué film drafting, scissor drafting, and splicing. It explains how each of these procedures is used to change an architectural detail. When to use each and the advantages of each are discussed. Emphasis is placed on achieving a professional-looking final detail or drawing.

   After reading this chapter, the architectural draftsperson will:

1.   Understand why office practice calls for frequent use of appliqué-drafting and scissor-drafting techniques.
2.   Be able to draft using diazo and plain-paper copiers as an aid.
3.   Know how to scissor draft.
4.   Have a better understanding of how splicing can speed up the production process.
5.   Be able to use the skills discussed in this chapter to advance his or her own abilities and production.

Appliqué Film Drafting

An appliqué film, or adhesive-type, drafting product has an adhesive on its reverse side that allows one sheet to be applied to another. This is accomplished by using appliqué film, which is a transparent or translucent mylar with an adhesive backing and a carrier. (See Figure 4.1.) The carrier is a sheet on the underside of the adhesive to prevent the adhesive from sticking to any surface while it is being handled or is going through the diazo process, plain-paper copier, or printing machine.

Figure 4.1 Appliqué film and its carrier.

The carrier is often coated with a wax substance that prevents the adhesive from sticking to the carrier. Unfortunately, many plain-paper copiers use a heat process that can melt the wax and possibly jam the copier. Also, for a copier that is sensitive to a specific thickness of paper, the adhesive sheet with its carrier may exceed the capability of the machine and jam it. Be cautious when using an adhesive that has a very slippery surface, such as mylar or a plastic type. The gears of the plain-paper copier may slip as the machine feeds the adhesive sheet. For this reason, some adhesive and carrier combinations have a slightly rough surface on the feeding edge to allow the rubber rollers that feed the copies to grab each sheet individually.

Appliqué film drafting can be done with a diazo machine, plain-paper copier, or printing machine.

The Diazo Process

The diazo process is the same as that used in making diazo prints. The only difference is that the emulsion (light-sensitive chemical) found on regular diazo paper is now placed on an adhesive film.

Here is the step-by-step procedure for appliqué film drafting using the diazo machine.

Step 1   Select the area of the total sheet onto which the appliqué film is to be attached. Draft a heavy border around this area. (See Figure 4.2.)

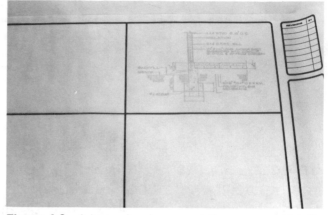

Figure 4.2 A heavy border around the area on which the appliqué is to be attached.

Step 2   Select the detail to be used. Many architectural offices now use standard predrafted details that contain areas to be completed later for a specific job. Figure 4.3 shows predrafted detail of a pair of footings.

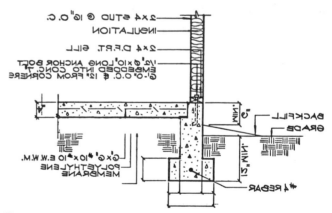

Figure 4.3 A predrafted detail.

Step 3   Make a reverse adhesive film of the details. Note that the detail in Figure 4.3 appears to have been drafted backward. Actually, the footings were drafted normally but were reversed by photography or with a plain-paper copier. Using the plain-paper copier, first make a transparent copy of the detail; then the transparent copy is placed in the copier in reverse to set a reverse detail. This reverse detail can be filed for future use or printed directly onto an adhesive film in reverse.

Step 4 Remove the carrier and position the detail in place. Positioning the adhesive should be done to ensure that the detail area will stay inside the drafted border. Figures 4.4, 4.5, and 4.6 demonstrate a very successful technique of using the adhesive film's carrier as an aid to facilitate positioning. This technique also eliminates the air bubbles often encountered by the beginner.

Step 5 Place a sheet of vellum over the detail, and burnish down the appliqué to ensure a good bond between the original and the appliqué film. Work the burnisher from the center outward or from one edge to the opposite edge. (See Figure 4.7.) Figure 4.8 shows the predrafted detail attached to the appliqué that was used in this procedure.

Figure 4.4 Select the detail and remove the carrier.

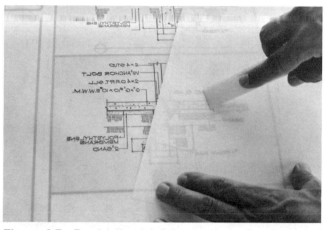

Figure 4.7 Burnish the detail down using vellum to protect the appliqué.

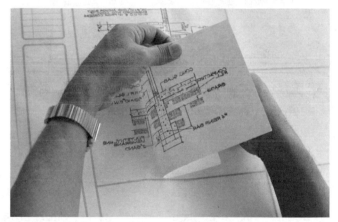

Figure 4.5 Position the artwork using the carrier.

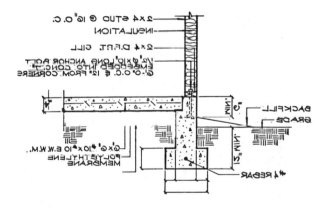

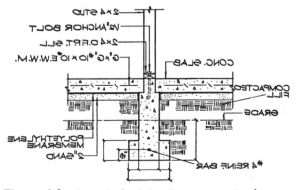

Figure 4.8 A predrafted detail on an appliqué.

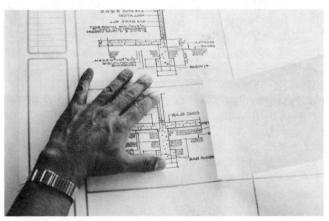

Figure 4.6 Apply the appliqué by pulling the carrier away.

Step 6 Turn the sheet (original) over to its correct side and complete the detail by drafting missing information, dimensions, and a title. The title must include reference bubbles and can also use adhesive film. (See Figure 4.9.)

Step 7 The final step is to check the detail for errors and/or omissions. Note on Figure 4.10, the completed detail on the lower half of the example and the in-progress detail above it.

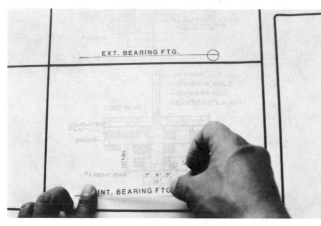

Figure 4.9 Add information, dimensions, title, and reference bubbles to the detail.

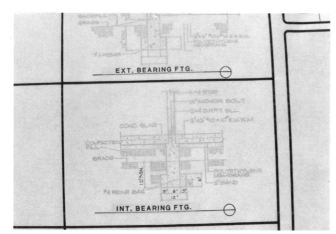

Figure 4.10 Check the finished product.

Ghosting

When appliqué films are mounted on the original, the copy—usually a diazo print—tends to "ghost." This gray ghosting takes place because the original ends up with two thicknesses through which light must penetrate to make a diazo copy. Thus if dark borders are drafted on the original, as shown in Figure 4.11, the ghosting looks more like a planned event and the final copy will look more professional. (See Figure 4.12.)

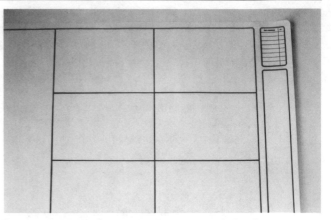

Figure 4.11 Draw border lines around detail area to reduce the appearance of ghosting.

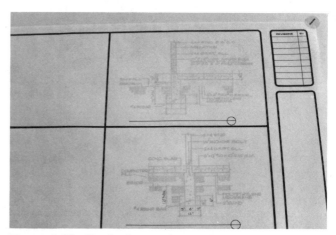

Figure 4.12 Border lines reduce "ghosting."

Offset Printing and Plain-Paper Copiers

In addition to the appliqués made by the diazo process, architectural offices use appliqués made by offset printing. A print shop can produce the appliqués from a good-quality original.

To make an offset printing system cost effective, the adhesives must be made in large quantities. Therefore, anything that is repetitive and typically used by many drafters would be appropriate. For example, the offset process is suitable for use in offices in which there is standardization of room titles and names of specific drawings such as floor plans, building sections, and north elevations. Figure 4.13 shows a sheet of appliqué paper with repetitive titles.

For smaller repetitive projects, plain-paper copiers can be used. Quality is rather good on the new copiers. The advantage with both the plain-paper copier and the offset process is that the original can be pro-

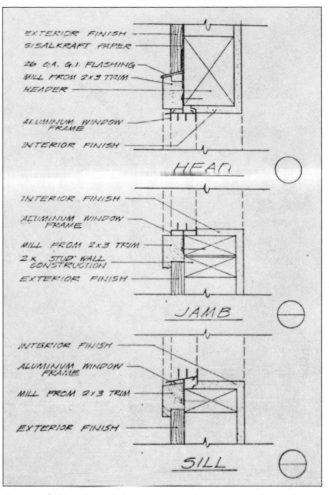

Figure 4.13 Appliqué paper with repetitive titles.

duced on almost anything with a white background — typed material, rub-on letters, drafted material, or chart-type illustrations. Thus a set of general notes or a schedule need not be hand lettered but could be added to a drawing by using an adhesive. The information can be drafted or typed directly on the adhesive. The time-saving possibilities are endless.

The step-by-step procedure and corresponding figures for using appliqués with a diazo process apply to offset printing and plain-paper copiers (see Figures 4.2 to 4.13 and corresponding text).

Scissor Drafting

Adding or subtracting information from a working drawing or detail can be accomplished by scissor drafting. The detail can be drafted or can be taken from printed matter such as a manufacturer's catalog, pamphlet, or brochure. The main purpose of scissor drafting is to reduce drafting time by having clerical aides or those with little experience produce details. Scissor drafting can also eliminate errors as well as the need for rechecking previously drafted portions of the detail. The result will still be a professional-looking detail.

Using a Predrafted Detail

The procedure for scissor drafting with a predrafted detail is as follows:

Step 1 Take a predrafted detail and, using a plain-paper copier, make a duplicate on bond paper. If the scale of the architectural detail is critical, be sure to use a copier that does not reduce or enlarge during the copying process, that is, a copier that makes a one-to-one copy. (See Figure 4.14.)

Step 2 Since you are not working with the original, you are free to cut this copy. Using a sharp

Figure 4.14 An existing detail to be used in the scissor-drafting procedure.

X-Acto–type knife, cut out the unwanted portions of the detail. If the information to be eliminated is minor, use a white liquid correction product. Be sure to use a type made to be applied to copies. (See Figures 4.15 and 4.16.)

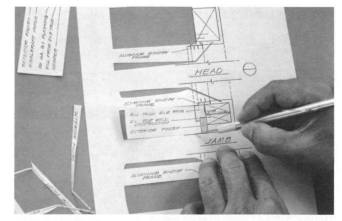

Figure 4.15 Cut out unwanted information from the copy of the detail.

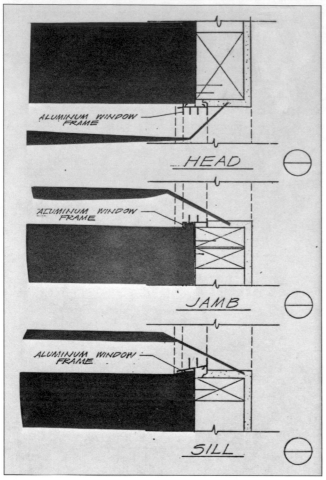

Figure 4.16 The detail with unwanted information removed.

Step 3 Using a plain-paper copier, duplicate the cut copy. Instead of printing it on a sheet of bond paper, print it on vellum. (See Figure 4.17.)

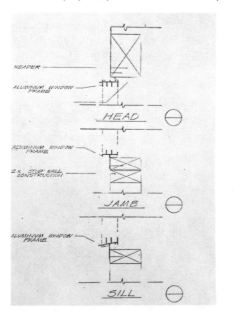

Figure 4.17 Using a plain-paper copier, make a copy of the cut detail on vellum.

Step 4 Now add new information on the vellum detail as discussed for the diazo process. (See Figure 4.18.)

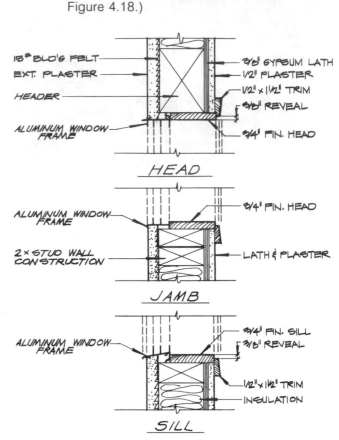

Figure 4.18 Making changes on the detail on vellum.

Step 5 The finished architectural detail can be grouped together with other details or placed onto a large working drawing by using the splicing procedure, discussed shortly.

Using Manufacturers' Catalogs

The scissor-drafting procedure for using information from a manufacturer's catalog is similar to that just described for scissor drafting with a predrafted detail.

Step 1 From a manufacturer's catalog or brochure, select the appropriate detail, which includes all the criteria that satisfies a specific job condition. These may be
   a. Thermo glazing (double glazing).
   b. Waterproofing.
   c. Correct material for the specific region of the country.
   d. Correct style of object for a specific design.
(See Figure 4.19.)

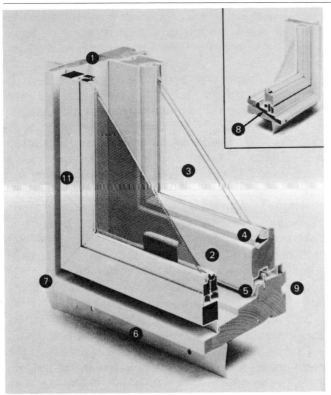

Figure 4.19 Select the appropriate window from a manufacturer's catalog. Reprinted, by permission, from Anderson Corporation, Bayport, Minn.

Step 2 Locate the proper drafted portion in the catalog that corresponds to the detail you selected. This is the detail you will be using. (See Figure 4.20.)

Step 3 On a plain-paper copier, make a copy of the selected detail and cut it out. (See Figure 4.21.)

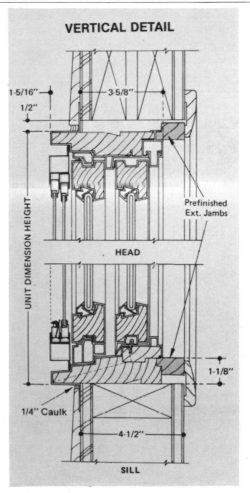

Figure 4.20 Locate the proper detail. Reprinted, by permission, from Anderson Corporation, Bayport, Minn.

Step 4 Cut out any unwanted drawings, notes, and so on. Tape the portion of the detail you want to a piece of plain white paper. (See Figure 4.22.)

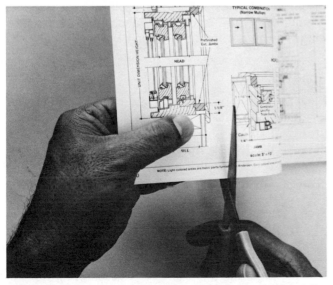

Figure 4.21 Copy the page in the catalog and cut out the detail.

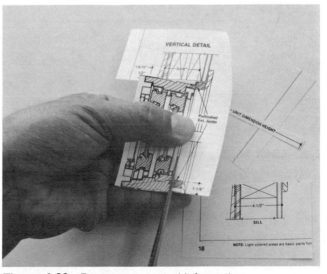

Figure 4.22 Remove unwanted information.

Step 5 Using a plain-paper copier with vellum loaded in the paper carrier, make a vellum duplicate of the detail. (See Figure 4.23.)

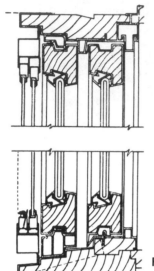

Figure 4.23 Vellum copy of desired portion of the detail.

Step 6 Add any desired information to the vellum copy as discussed for the diazo process. (See Figure 4.24.)

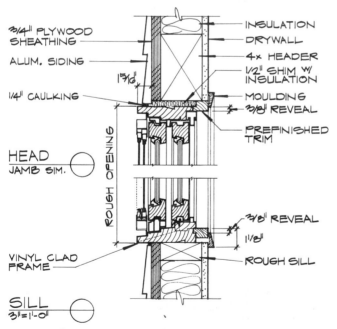

3/4" PLYWOOD SHEATHING

ALUM. SIDING

1/4" CAULKING

INSULATION

DRYWALL

4× HEADER

1/2" SHIM W/ INSULATION

MOULDING

3/8" REVEAL

PREFINISHED TRIM

ROUGH OPENING

1⁵⁄₁₆

HEAD
JAMB SIM.

3/8" REVEAL

1 1/8"

VINYL CLAD FRAME

ROUGH SILL

SILL
3"=1'-0"

Figure 4.24 Add desired information.

Splicing Vellum

Splicing is a method of cutting a piece out of a large sheet of vellum and inserting another piece in its place. The need for splicing rather than taping a small sheet of vellum on top of a large sheet of vellum is dictated by the way in which the vellum is to be duplicated.

In architecture, the majority of the prints are made using the diazo process we described earlier. Remember that the diazo process uses a transparent or translucent paper, usually vellum, as the carrier of information. This sheet can be compared to a negative in photography. It is placed on top of a paper, called diazo paper, which has a light-sensitive coating. As light penetrates the vellum to the diazo paper below, an image is formed by the lines on the vellum because they stop the light from reaching paper and therefore appear dark. If the vellum to be printed has another sheet of vellum taped onto it, the light must penetrate three layers of paper in the taped area, producing a ghost image. Thus, on the final print, the taped area will appear dark, with the tape itself being even darker, and the rest of the sheet will be a normal color (refer back to Figures 4.11 and 4.12).

To maintain a single layer of vellum on top of the diazo paper, the small piece of vellum is spliced into the larger sheet. The taped area will still leave a slight ghosting effect on the diazo print. To minimize this effect, a good-quality tape, such as page mending tape, should be used.

As the original vellum sheet and the diazo paper go through the diazo machine, both sheets rotate around a glass cylinder that exposes them to the light. In addition, the diazo paper rotates around a perforated stainless steel cylinder. The holes act as vents to allow the ammonia vapor to develop the paper.

If a small piece of vellum is taped onto a large piece of vellum instead of being spliced in, the rotation of the taped vellum around the cylinder can cause the vellum to wrinkle. Not only does this prevent good contact with the diazo paper and result in a fuzzy image, it can also ruin the original vellum.

Good Splicing

A few simple steps to ensure a good splice of vellum are as follows:

Step 1 Using a plain-paper copier, make a copy of the detail on a small sheet of vellum. Position it onto the large sheet of vellum in the location to be spliced. (See Figure 4.25.) Tape it down with masking tape or removable tape.

Step 2 Using a sharp mat knife or X-acto knife, cut through *both sheets* of vellum. *Do not* cut along the edge of the top sheet of vellum, but rather slightly inside as if you were making a picture frame. The vellum may move if you try to cut too close to the edge. (See Figures 4.26 and 4.27.)

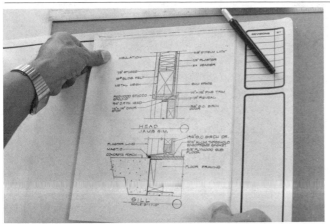

Figure 4.25 Make a vellum copy of the detail on a plain-paper copier and position it onto the large sheet of vellum.

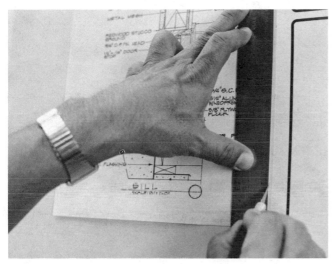

Figure 4.26 Cut slightly inside the edge of the vellum.

Figure 4.27 Cut through both sheets of vellum.

Step 3 Remove the unwanted parts, the picture frame shape, and the portion of the original that was cut out. (See Figure 4.28.)

Step 4 Position the detail in place and temporarily tape it with masking tape on the front side of the sheet. (See Figures 4.29 and 4.30.)

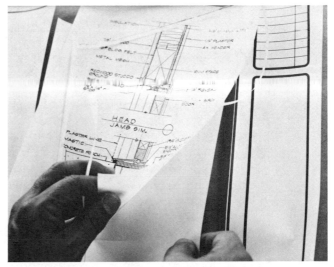

Figure 4.28 Remove the unwanted portions.

Figure 4.29 Position the detail in the opening.

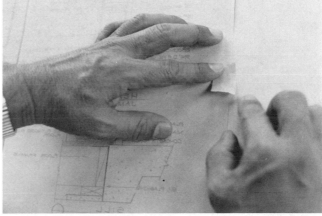

Figure 4.30 Temporarily tape the detail on the front side with masking tape.

Step 5 Turn the sheet over and carefully tape the new detail into place on the back. Allow the pieces of tapes to overlap at the corners, but do not press down hard. (See Figures 4.31 and 4.32.)

Step 6 Cutting the tape is the most difficult task in splicing because you must cut through the two layers of tape but not through the vellum. Cut a miter at the corners. (See Figure 4.33.) A very sharp blade works best, since the weight of the knife plus minimal hand pressure lets you control your cut.

Step 7 Use the knife to remove the unwanted layers of tape. First, lift the top tape by placing the knife blade under the first layer of tape separating the two layers (Figure 4.34). Hold the raised portion with your fingers, and remove the unwanted portion with the knife (Figure 4.35). Repeat the procedure for the tape in the other corners. When the unwanted tape has been removed, replace the mitered tape corners (much like a picture frame corner).

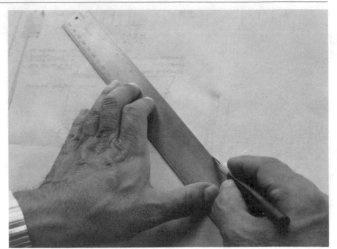

Figure 4.33 Cut a miter at the corners. Be careful to cut through two layers of tape but not through the vellum.

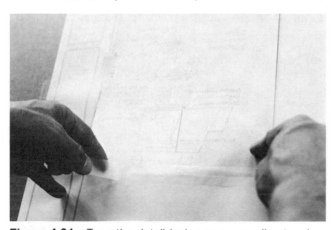

Figure 4.31 Tape the detail (using page mending tape) on the reverse side.

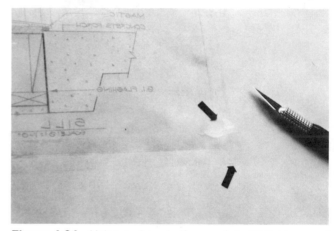

Figure 4.34 Using a sharp knife, carefully lift the layers of tape.

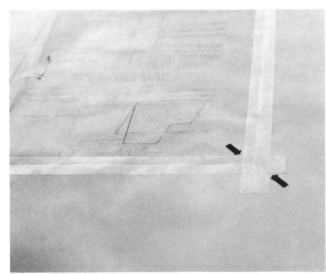

Figure 4.32 Overlap tape at the corners.

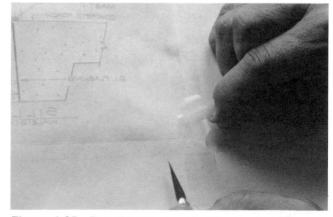

Figure 4.35 Remove the unwanted layers of tape.

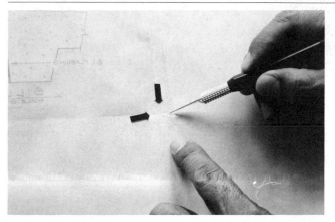

Figure 4.36 After the multiple layers of tape have been removed, carefully replace the mitered tape corners.

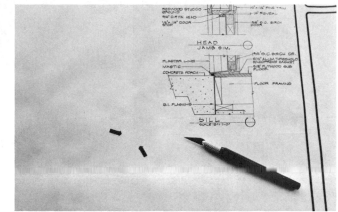

Figure 4.37 Check the detail from the front side.

This is shown in Figure 4.36.

Step 8 As we discussed earlier, once a detail has been taped in place, it should be burnished. To burnish the taped portions, place a sheet of paper on top and press along the taped seams with a burnishing tool.

Step 9 Check the final product from the front side of the vellum. (See Figure 4.37.)

Summary

A thorough understanding of this chapter is essential for architectural draftspersons who want to increase their production time. Shortcuts such as scissor drafting and adhesive drafting are not new to the architectural profession. It is the quality of the adhesives and the advent of and the availability of the plain-paper copier that have popularized the methods again and with excellent results.

The required understanding of the subject matter is accomplished when the draftsperson can assess the task and select any combination of scissor, adhesive, plain-paper copier, or diazo process to achieve a desired solution to the task.

We call these shortcuts, but in reality they are standard practice in the architectural offices today.

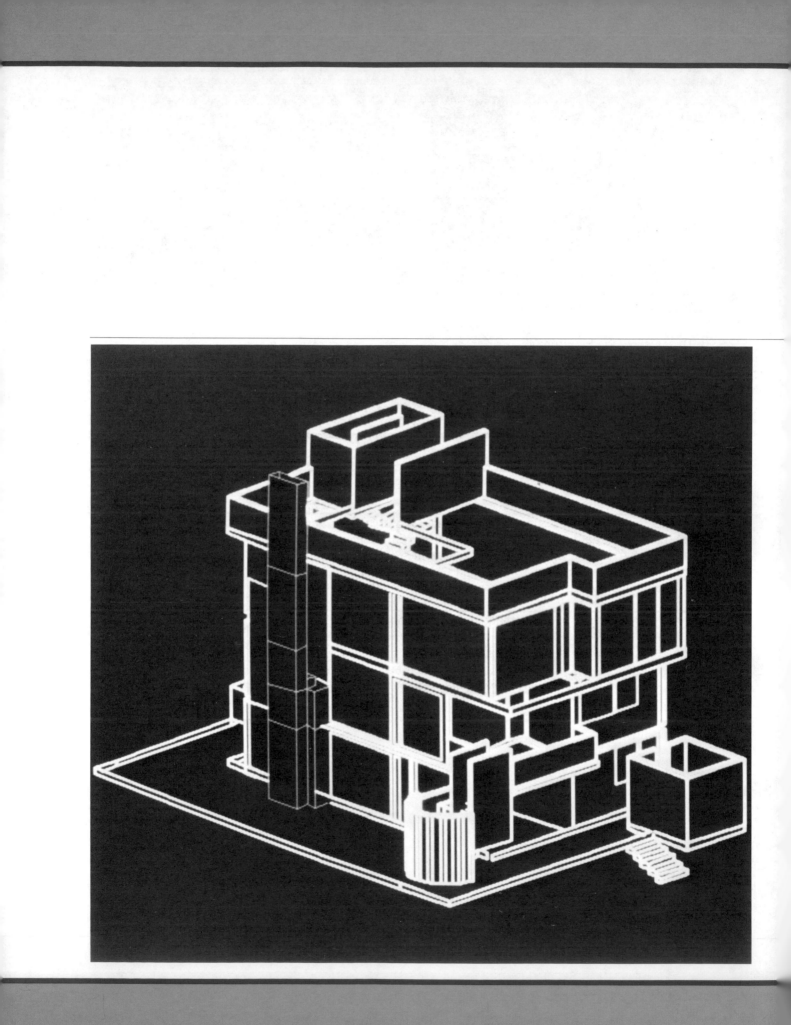

5

COMPUTER-AIDED DRAFTING

Preview   Chapter 5 introduces the topic of computer-aided drafting (or design) (CAD). It gives you a good understanding of the nature of CAD, teaches you about its implications for drafters, and allows you to discover the relationship of communication skills learned in conventional detailing to CAD. You will also learn about the advantages and disadvantages of CAD, changes in the job market for drafters, and the future of CAD in architecture.

   After reading this chapter, the architectural draftsperson will:

1. Understand what computer-aided drafting is, and how it works.
2. Realize that conventional drafting skills are needed to become a computer-aided drafter.
3. Learn how technical information is communicated to the computer.
4. Appreciate the impact of CAD on the architectural detailing process.
5. Learn the advantages and disadvantages of the computer to the architectural office and the drafting industry.
6. Discover the job market for drafters who have a knowledge of CAD and learn about the future of CAD.

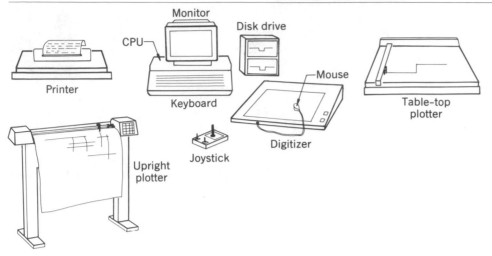

Figure 5.1A Typical computer workstation.

Although the full impact of computers has not yet been completely recognized, architects and designers are exploring the medium and are learning that computer-aided drafting could be a more significant innovation than the parallel bars and drafting machines introduced a few years earlier.

The Workstation

To set up an office, or workstation, for computer-aided drafting, you need a computer and other equipment, called *computer hardware,* which is shown in Figure 5.1A and is described here:

- The *computer* contains the *central processing unit (CPU),* or brain of the system. The CPU takes information that the user enters, processes it, and produces a finished drawing. It accepts data and stores, recalls, corrects, and calculates information.
- The *monitor* is a *screen,* like a television screen, that displays instructions given to the computer and shows the drawing being created in its various stages.
- Information is entered into a computer by typing it on a *keyboard* that is similar to a typewriter keyboard.
- Information is stored on a disk that is similar to a phonograph record. (See Figure 5.1B.) The counterpart of a turntable on a CAD system is a disk drive. One disk is used to run the CAD program, and another is used to store information.
- A letter-quality *printer* produces typewriterlike output. It can print such items as general notes, titles, special call outs, and title block information.
- A *plotter* is the instrument that actually performs the drawing. The two main types are a flat table-

Figure 5.1B Disk.

top model, on which the pen moves on a stationary sheet of paper, and an upright model, on which the paper moves on a cylindrical roller and the pen moves on a bar above the drawing. In the latter, the paper rolls back and forth on the cylinder while the pen (or pens if there are several pen colors or thicknesses used) moves perpendicular to the motion of the paper.
- A *digitizer* is an electronic drawing pad that functions like a small drafting board. Its surface is usually plastic. The underside of the plastic surface is a matrix of hundreds of pieces of electronically sensitive material that responds to stimulus provided by a drawing instrument.
- The drawing instrument can be a device called a *mouse* or a photosensitive device called a *light pen* or *stylus.* By using these instruments on the digitizer as you would a pencil on paper, the beginning and end points of a line can be defined and the drafting of the line can be recorded in the computer.

- The *cursor* is a small light on the monitor that tells you your position. When you use a keyboard, the cursor can be moved horizontally or vertically. If the computer is set up in a drawing mode, the cursor can be moved anywhere on the screen using a joystick, thumb wheel, or track ball similar to those found on video games. If a digitizer is used, the cursor can be moved by moving the attached light pen or the mouse.

Some cursors are shaped like a cross (+), but more sophisticated ones resemble a drafting pencil or paintbrush when using color. When you wish to erase, you press the letter "E" on the keyboard and the pencil cursor flips over, erasing lines as if it were an eraser on a pencil.

CAD Software

When we were describing the computer hardware that comprise the CAD workstation, we referred to information that the user puts into the computer. There are actually several kinds of information. First, you need the instructions that tell the computer how the CAD system works. These instructions, which are on a disk, are called the *program*; they are the *software* part of the workstation. The other information is the specific things you tell the program to do, such as how long a line to draw.

Learning the CAD Program

You can learn a CAD program in a variety of ways. One is via self-teaching, using the instruction manual for the specific CAD program. This method consumes a large amount of time spent in trial and error before you master each specific procedure and learn to solve problems and, thus, is not recommended.

A more successful approach using self-teaching is based on the *tutorial* program that will show you step by step how to run a particular CAD program. As a result, you learn while you are actually performing the various tasks. This teaching method is based on a series of tasks and questions, such as "Did you understand the last procedure?" If you answer "No," the program will review the procedure. If you answer "Yes," the computer will send you on to the next task.

There are several types of places you can go to learn the CAD system. Computer firms and private training facilities conduct seminars and classes on a short-term basis; these can be costly. Alternatively, public and private schools give classes in the use of CAD systems that range from short extension courses at local universities and colleges to formal CAD degree programs that may last as long as two years. Finally, large firms that use CAD will often have training programs for new employees.

What CAD Can Do

A CAD system can make drafters' jobs easier and their use of time more efficient. In general, a computer can assist with tasks that are repetitive and can provide easy access to information and materials that are used over and over again.

Store and Retrieve Information

Information is stored in a *memory bank* that permits easy retrieval. Frequently used material can be stored in a section of the memory called the *library*. In fact, with CAD, drafters use lists of filed information in much the same way people use card catalogs in a library or look at hard copy (paper copy) of previously drawn details or written information. Figure 5.2 on the following page shows a library of details that have been retrieved and printed.

Alter Drawings and Details

The CAD system allows a drafter to retrieve a detail from the memory bank, display it on the monitor, and make changes for a specific job. The detail can be displayed on a grid background (Figure 5.3) or a dot-matrix background (Figure 5.4), each of which helps the CAD drafter to orient the detail. CAD drawings

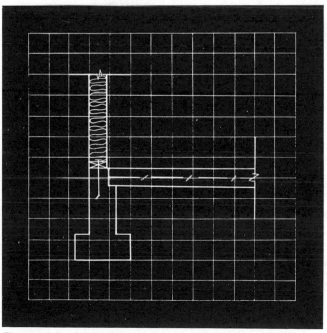

Figure 5.3 Grid background.

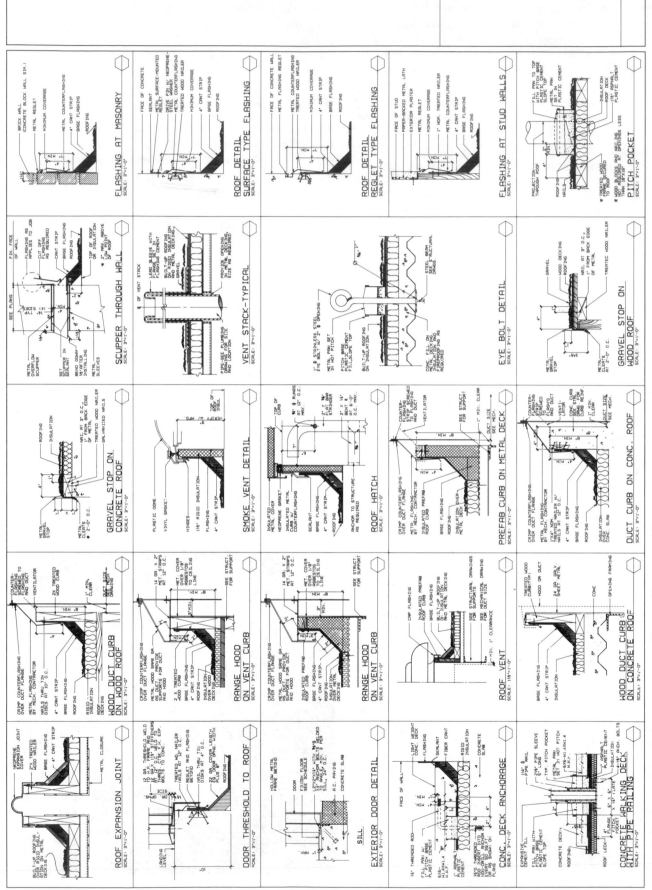

Figure 5.2 A set of details from a computer library. (Courtesy of Peter H. Martin, ARCAD, Los Angeles, California.)

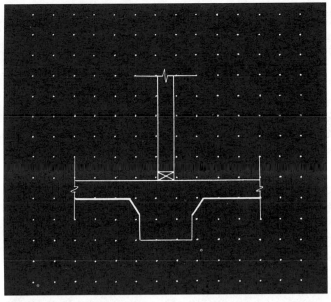

Figure 5.4 Dot matrix.

Figure 5.5 (a) Original detail. (Courtesy of Chester Smith Associates, Architects, Torrance, California.) (b) Windowing (closeup look) in on orginal detail. (c) Extending the concrete pad deeper into the earth. (d) Erasing the unwanted information. (e) Revised detail.

can be fully drafted details that are to be corrected, altered, or changed or partially drafted details that contain a basic foundation upon which a detail can be finished. For example, a footing that goes 12 inches below the grade can be elongated to 18 inches for a specific soil condition, or a 24 inch square pad of concrete under a column can be increased to 32 inches to accommodate a greater weight on the column. Figure 5.5 shows a detail with specific information and dimensions using CAD.

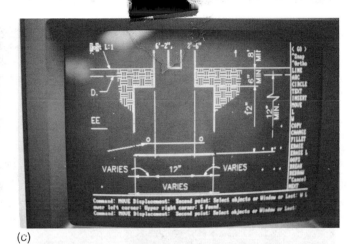

(c)

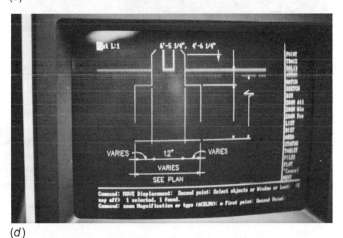

(d)

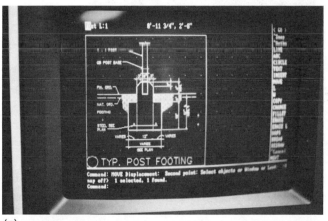

(a)

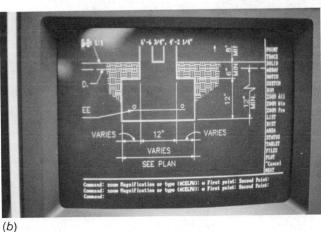

(b)

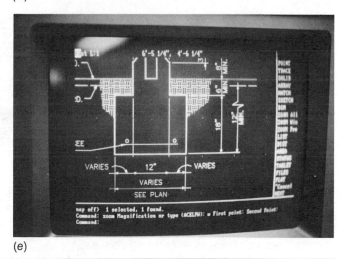

(e)

Create Original Drawings

The CAD system enables drafters to make complete drawings from scratch. These drawings can be a simple detail with material designations, dimensions, and notes or the most complicated building section. Figure 5.6 illustrates the evolution of a computer-drawn detail.

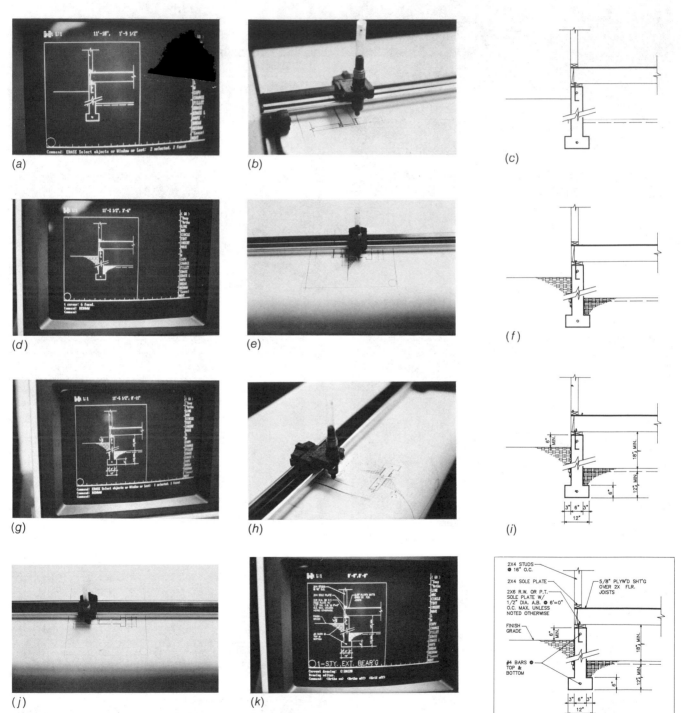

Figure 5.6 Evolution of a computer-drawn detail. (Courtesy of Chester Smith Associates, Architects, Torrance, California.) *(a)*, *(b)*, *(c)*, Step I: Initial phase of detail development. *(d)*, *(e)*, *(f)* Step II: Material designation phase. *(g)*, *(h)*, *(i)* Step III: Dimensioning phase. *(j)*, *(k)*, *(l)* Step IV: Noting, leaders, title, and referencing phase.

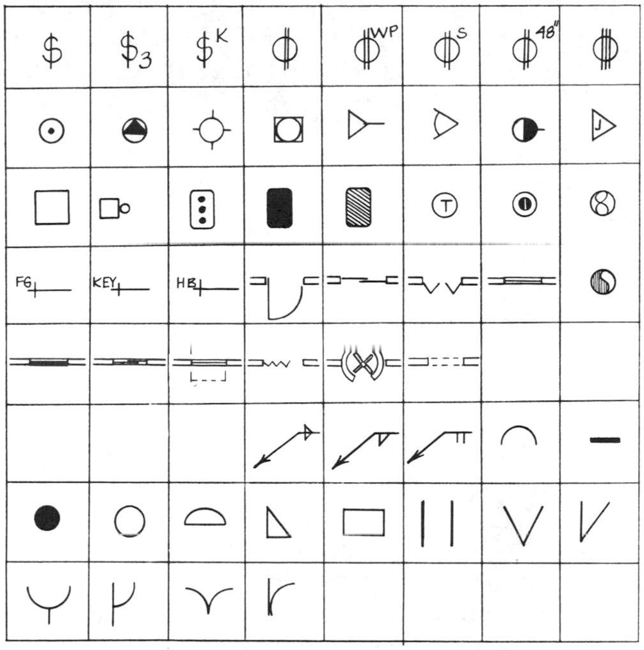

Figure 5.7 A set of symbols from a computer library.

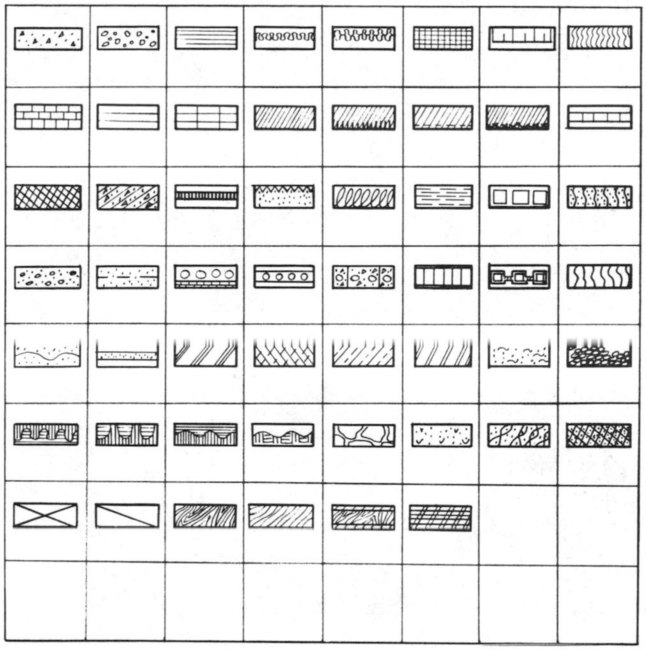

Figure 5.8 A set of material designations from a computer library.

Share Information

The CAD system allows the drafter to create a library of the most commonly used symbols, notes, pictorial descriptions, material designations, and other drafting conventions. One advantage of the library is that other drafters can display, retrieve, and use the information stored there. Another advantage is that symbols, material designations, and so on need to be drawn only once and can be used repeatedly thereafter. In some CAD programs these libraries are already written and stored on a disk. In that case, new symbols can be added to conform to individual office requirements. (See Figures 5.7 and 5.8.)

Figure 5.6 is organized in such a manner that the reader can follow this evolution as it would be seen on the Monitor, as it is being plotted on the upright plotter and the finished detail at different stages. While it is not normal to plot each stage of the evolution, Figure 5.6 does so to enable you to appreciate its development.

Step I shows the initial stages of the development of a footing detail.

Step II shows the addition of the material designation for earth.

Step III illustrates the dimensioning stage of the development of the detail.

Step IV is the noting phase of the computer drafting. This final stage also includes leaders, titles, and a reference symbol. Drafting quality can be improved by taking the information housed on a disk and having a drafting service (such as a blueprint firm) reproduce it on a high-fidelity, high-resolution printer.

Using the CAD Library

The material in a CAD library can be interphased with the program that's doing the drafting. For example, typical material designations such as soil (earth), concrete in section, wood, and masonry can be made to show up on the monitor along side the detail being drawn. As each symbol is needed, it is picked up on the digitizer using the mouse or light pen and transferred onto the detail. (See Figure 5.9.) The library thus becomes a major part of the draftsperson's drawing vocabulary and is easily accessible upon demand.

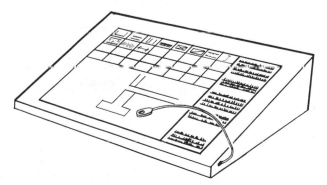

Figure 5.9 Digitizer with a symbol library and menu.

Looking at a Menu

The contents in a computer library is called a *menu;* it is a listing of various things that can be performed by the computer. (See Figure 5.10.)

Figure 5.10 Listing a drafting menu.

A *master menu* lists the specific menus in the library. For example a master menu might include the following:

Master Menu

1. Drafting
2. Plotting
3. Saving drawings
4. Loading drawings

If you select drafting from the master menu, you will then see the drafting menu:

Drafting Menu

1. Construct
2. Draw
3. Dimension
4. Change and edit
5. Symbols

Each of these drafting functions will have its own menu for the specific tasks to be performed; for example,

Construction Menu	Dimension Menu
(1) Line	(1) Horizontal
(2) Circles	(2) Vertical
(3) Geometric solids	(3) Angular
(4) Parallel lines	(4) Curve or arc
(5) Angular lines	(5) Notes
(6) Tangent lines	(6) Arrows
(7) Tangent circles	(7) Leaders

Each of these drafting functions will have its own menu (instructions) for the specific tasks to be per-

formed. Most drafting functions have very elaborate menus. Because of this, the three examples shown have been greatly simplified so you can get a general idea of what they look like.

Symbols Menu

(1) Electrical
(2) Plumbing
(3) Doors
(4) Windows
(5) Material in elevation
(6) Material in section

Necessary Skills and Knowledge

The CAD programs on the market now are known as being "user friendly." This means that once you learn the program, as we discussed earlier, it is easy to operate. You do not need to know a great deal about computers or computer languages.

Although the ability to type can be helpful, such as for typing notes on the computer-drafted detail, it is not absolutely necessary. Because of the nature of how details are created, typing skills are used minimally. Only a few keys are used to activate the computer, and identification stickers may be placed on the most frequently used keys for convenience. Also, a library of typically used notes can be used. Or a drafter can draw the necessary detail, make a hardcopy print, and hand letter the necessary notes on the hard copy for a clerical person to type, thus saving the drafter's skill for additional details. In a small office, however, the ability to type and draft on the computer makes the drafter that much more valuable.

The Drafting Process with CAD

The actual drafting process using the CAD system is a direct function of the specific CAD program. Each available program has its own specialities. One program will enable you to create the appearance of a hand-lettered alphabet for a less mechanical lettering effect. Another will let you draft two parallel lines with one command, which would be helpful when drafting a floor plan. Still another program will let you assemble parts of drawings into a whole.

When you use CAD, you can carry out any task that can be performed by conventional drafting methods. You can draw horizontal and vertical lines, parallel lines, angular lines, circles and arcs, and geometric objects; you can construct and erase lines; and you can create special lines such as hidden lines, object lines, and cutting plane lines. The CAD drafter can also select scale and letter details with the proper note and size of lettering. (See Figure 5.11.)

The CAD system performs many tasks that cannot be carried out with conventional drafting. The computer can rotate a drawing and produce a mirror image, and it can rapidly repeat with great accuracy any shape regardless of its complexity. The computer can also zoom in for a closer look at any portion of the detail. This enables a detail to be drafted with greater accuracy and greater detail. Above all, the computer can save the drawing by storing it, can change it easily, and can retrieve it almost immediately.

Typical CAD Procedures

A typical procedure for drafting an architectural detail is as follows:

Step 1 Load the computer with the proper CAD software and select the proper scale. To do this, you must understand the available scales, how each will look on the screen,

and even more important, how each will look when drawn by the plotter.

Step 2 Choose what you wish to do from the menu of available functions, such as draw a line, construct a circle, or draft a rectangle.

To draw a rectangle choose a rectangular drafting mode. You can use a grid background on the screen, such as those in Figures 5.3 and 5.4, to help you. With a grid, you have only to indicate the coordinates of the rectangle to the computer, and it will draw it. Or you can use the mouse on the digitizer and indicate the start and end points of the individual lines of the detail, which translates into the width and depth of the footing. (See Figure 5.9.)

If you want to draw a circle, the CAD program may require that you use the keyboard to indicate the radius and the mouse and digitizer to locate the center of the circle. The computer can thus draft a perfect circle to your specifications and location. This proce-

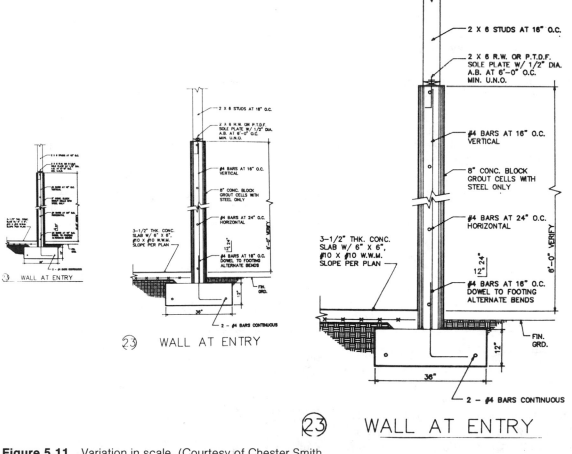

Figure 5.11 Variation in scale. (Courtesy of Chester Smith Associates, Architects, Torrance, California.)

Step 3   dure is followed for an arc, an angle, or any geometrical shape.

Step 3   After you have your drawing on the screen, you can add symbols. Figure 5.9 shows a display format in which a hard (paper) copy of the menu is placed on the right hand side of the digitizer pad and a symbol library along the top. The remaining space on the digitizer pad is for the drawing. When you need a specific symbol, place the mouse on that particular symbol. Pushing the button on the mouse triggers it to pick up the symbol. You then move the mouse to the part of the drawing pad on the digitizer where the symbol is needed. The exact location for the placement of the symbol is monitored on the computer screen, where the cursor simulates the movement of the mouse. This method is very useful for drafting arrowheads, material designations, doors, and the like quickly, without having to plot each specific line. A similar method is used when the menu and library appear directly on the screen. (See Figure 5.10.)

CAD-Drafted Details

Figure 5.12 shows a partly drafted eave detail onto which the CAD drafter can put required information or make changes. Figure 5.13A shows a part of a CAD program that allows the CAD drafter to enter specific information, such as the size of tread and riser of a stair. Figure 5.13B shows the same approach used for a footing detail. In this example the parts of the footing are previously drafted to form a menu and the architectural draftsperson need only enter the height of the stem wall, width of the wall, width of footing, and the depth of the footing. The computer assembles, notes, dimensions, and drafts the material designation.

Figures 5.14 and 5.15 show two additional details drafted in this fashion.

Advantages of CAD

CAD provides a great degree of accuracy and maintains a high level of quality. Because the computer is not subject to fatigue, the drawing has consistent line work. Another advantage is the speed of the computer. Many architectural offices that use CAD claim great increases in production, accompanied by reduced costs of producing construction documents. This, in turn, can create savings for clients.

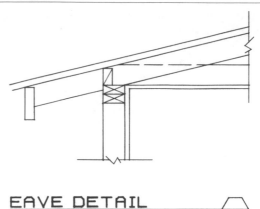

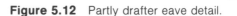

EAVE DETAIL

Figure 5.12   Partly drafter eave detail.

Being arithmetically oriented, computers can easily do preliminary estimates and check drawings against local code ordinances to be sure that certain special requirements (e.g., related to the handicapped) or fire regulations have been met.

Once a drawing has been made on the monitor, it is ready to be drawn by the plotter. The drafter doesn't

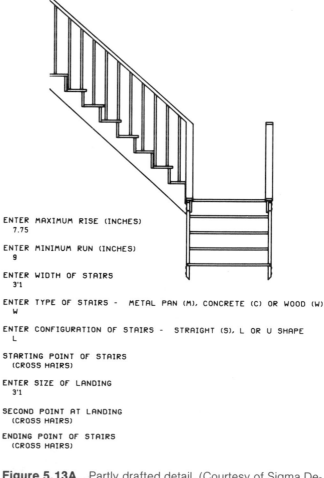

ENTER MAXIMUM RISE (INCHES)
7.75

ENTER MINIMUM RUN (INCHES)
9

ENTER WIDTH OF STAIRS
3'1

ENTER TYPE OF STAIRS - METAL PAN (M), CONCRETE (C) OR WOOD (W)
W

ENTER CONFIGURATION OF STAIRS - STRAIGHT (S), L OR U SHAPE
L

STARTING POINT OF STAIRS
(CROSS HAIRS)

ENTER SIZE OF LANDING
3'1

SECOND POINT AT LANDING
(CROSS HAIRS)

ENDING POINT OF STAIRS
(CROSS HAIRS)

Figure 5.13A   Partly drafted detail. (Courtesy of Sigma Design, Inc., Englewood, Colo.)

MENU KEYS

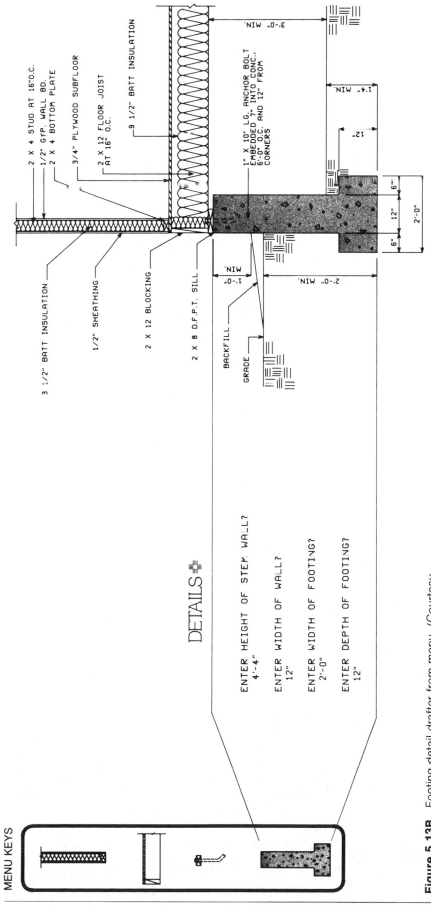

DETAILS

ENTER HEIGHT OF STEM WALL?
4'-4"

ENTER WIDTH OF WALL?
12"

ENTER WIDTH OF FOOTING?
2'-0"

ENTER DEPTH OF FOOTING?
12"

3 1/2" BATT INSULATION

1/2" SHEATHING

2 X 12 BLOCKING

2 X 8 D.F.P.T. SILL

BACKFILL

GRADE

2 X 4 STUD AT 16"O.C.
1/2" GYP. WALL BD.
2 X 4 BOTTOM PLATE

3/4" PLYWOOD SUBFLOOR

2 X 12 FLOOR JOIST
AT 16" O.C.

9 1/2" BATT INSULATION

1" X 10' LG. ANCHOR BOLT
EMBEDDED 7" INTO CONC.,
6'-0" O.C. AND 12" FROM
CORNERS

3'-0" MIN.

1'-4" MIN.

12"

6"

12"

2'-0"

6"

1'-0" MIN.

2'-0" MIN.

Figure 5.13B Footing detail drafter from menu. (Courtesy of Sigma Design, Inc., Englewood, Colo.)

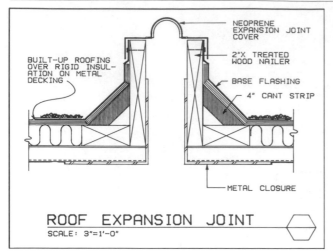

Figure 5.14 CAD-drafted detail of expansion joint. (Courtesy of Peter H. Martin, ARCAD., Los Angeles, California.)

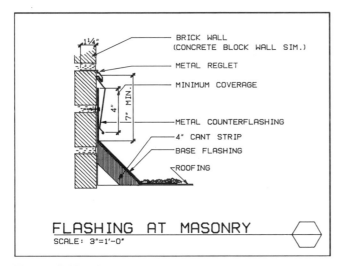

Figure 5.15 CAD-drafted detail of flashing. (Courtesy of Peter H. Martin, ARCAD. Los Angeles, California.)

have to be in attendance when the plotter is drawing, thus making him or her available for other tasks.

CAD adds a new dimension to construction documents in that many originals can be produced. They can easily be modified and new, high-quality originals can be drawn quickly.

Some CAD systems have techniques for adding color to renderings. Architects can therefore use color on construction documents. For example, steel mainframe structures with wood as a secondary building material can be drafted in several colors. In fact, the whole drafting vocabulary might be simplified because of the inclusion of color: revisions, addendums, and changes can all be done in different colors.

One of the biggest design aids of CAD is that of simulation. Structures can be tested against the impact of earthquakes, wind loads, and other natural forces. The computer can simulate and predict the outcome of the construction process, which will in turn change the complexion of a specific detail or configuration of a structure.

Disadvantages of CAD

One disadvantage with CAD is the time it takes to familiarize a staff with the system and to convert office procedures so that CAD becomes a viable means of production. It takes time for drafters to gain speed with CAD, and this training time may become a burden to offices. It also takes time to develop an extensive library to make the investment pay off.

Computers and their programs are constantly being updated and changed so rapidly that within just a few years, a CAD system may be outdated. Consequently, many small offices have to adopt a wait-and-see attitude.

Maintenance and upkeep are other disadvantages. A specialist has to repair and maintain the equipment. And since computers are relatively new on the market, there are only limited guarantees as to how long they will keep working.

Eye fatigue is a very common complaint of CAD users. The computer drafter must look closely into a video screen, often for hours at a time. Little is known about eye care in regard to eye fatigue, but it could cause physical as well as psychological problems. The computer industry has tried to eliminate eye fatigue by producing monitors with low-contrast green, amber, or multicolored screens.

CAD and the Job Market

Initially, architectural firms hired computer specialists who had no experience in architecture. These specialists quickly failed. Architecture speaks a language of symbols, lines, and conventions that the computer specialists did not know. The industry thus discovered that trained drafters had better success with the CAD system than did the computer specialists. A drafter is already familiar with the conventional approach to drafting details; the CAD system is just an adaptation of that method of communicative skills and knowledge, using a new tool. The method of drawing with CAD can be taught very quickly, and then it's only a matter of time before the drafter becomes proficient.

Being Replaced by CAD

A common myth is that computers and CAD will put drafters out of work. If all you can do is trace material or if you have only developed your line quality and lettering skills, you might be displaced by a computer. But if you are a fully trained drafter, the CAD system can be your most important tool, and like any tool it depends on knowledge to operate it. If production time is reduced because it takes less time to draft, an architectural office can take on more work at a savings to the client and thus build up its clientele. Just as teaching machines did not replace teachers, CAD will *not* replace the drafter. In fact, CAD-capable drafters can command 10 to 50 percent higher salary than can those without CAD experience.

The Future of CAD

According to experts, the concept of CAD will not change drastically in the future. But changes are being made in the cost, speed, and memory capacity of CAD.

Cost

In the past few years, the cost of a CAD system for an average architectural office has gone from hundreds of thousands of dollars to tens of thousands of dollars. When drafting services are added that use time sharing, (a system where one set of hardware is shared by many including its expenses), CAD will be WITHIN THE REACH of the most modest office.

Speed

Dual OR parallel systems have now been developed. They are in reality two computers in one. The first one contains to accept commands and instructions while the other orders and performs the task. Thus, the need for the CAD draftsperson to wait for the system to perform its task before adding more information will be a thing of the past. With parallel systems, the computer will not only anticipate and work ahead of the CAD drafter but will allow more than one task at a time to be done, such as flipping from one project to another or from one detail to another as the drafter physically does with a reference table and many sets of plans.

Memory Capacity

The inexpensive computers now used to run CAD programs are limited by their relatively low memory capability. For this reason, two or more disks are used to retrieve information, get instruction, perform particular tasks, and so on. Memory will be greatly expanded in the next few years to allow computers that do not use auxiliary disks to contain instructions for CAD procedures as well as built-in libraries. At the same time, enough space will be left in the computer's own memory to perform, record, and save the most complicated drawings. Presently, only large, expensive computers have this capability.

Summary

This chapter has explained computer-aided drafting and the state of the technology that has infiltrated the drafting profession. After reading it, drafters understand the need to train for the future.

In much the same way, as robotics has affected the manufacturing industry by changing its complexion, speed, and accuracy, CAD can be seen as changing the architectural industry. It still needs people, however, to be the decision makers who program the tasks.

CAD is not a fad or a trend to be taken lightly nor is it a new way to communicate; rather, it's a new tool to continue the communication of the language called architecture — or more accurately *architectonics:* the science of architecture.

6
LUMBER

Preview   Chapter 6 introduces the subject of lumber by explaining the types of wood and their application in the construction industry. This chapter is divided into six sections. The first deals with lumber sizes, accompanied by definitions of nominal and surfaced dimensions. The second describes wood species with explanations about their characteristics and suitability. The third explains lumber grading classifications, grading stamps, manufacturing, and natural defects. The fourth deals with preservative treatment of wood with illustrations of applicable conditions. The fifth discusses and illustrates the fabrication of glued laminated lumber and the flexibility of these members. The final section deals with the manufacturing of plywood panels with explanations of the types used in construction today.

   After reading this chapter, the architectural draftsperson will:

1. Understand nominal and surfaced size lumber.
2. Be familiar with various species and their application in building construction.
3. Have a knowledge of graded lumber and be able to interpret a grading stamp.
4. Be familiar with various wood preservative treatments and their application in construction.
5. Understand glued laminated timbers and the flexibility of these members.
6. Have a knowledge of the fabrication process of plywood panels and the types used in building construction.

Table 6.1

Softwood	Hardwood
Cedars	Birch
Douglas fir	Beech
Firs	Cherry
Hemlock	Hickory
Cypress	Mahogany
Larch	Chestnut
Pines	Oak
Redwood	Maple
Spruce	Teak
	Walnut

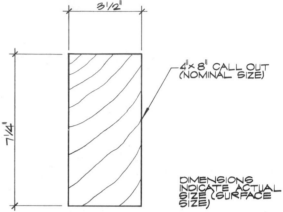

Figure 6.1 Surface size 2″ × 4″.

Figure 6.2 Surface size 4″ × 8″.

Wood is one of civilization's oldest and most widely used construction materials. Its structural capabilities as well as its aesthetic value make it extremely popular.

The terms wood, lumber, and timber are often used interchangeably. However, the term wood usually means the unprocessed fibrous material of a tree. Lumber is wood that has been sawed and milled to size, and timber refers to lumber in large sizes.

Wood is classified into two categories: softwood and hardwood. The terms "hardwood" and "softwood" do not apply to the hardness or softness of the wood but rather to the characteristics of native trees. Trees that are classified hardwood have broad leaves, and most shed these leaves at the end of each growing season. Trees classified softwood are evergreen except for cypress and some exotic species. Examples of some common softwoods and hardwoods used in construction are listed in Table 6.1.

Size

Standard lumber sizes are defined as nominal size and surfaced size. The nominal size is the dimensional size of the rough lumber; the surfaced size is the actual size after the rough lumber has been planed and finished. The dimensional difference between the nominal and surfaced size varies according to the size of the lumber.

When designating the sizes of wood members in a specific detail, the nominal size is used. For example, the call out for wood studs may be 2″ × 4″ while the actual or surfaced size is $1\frac{1}{2}″ × 3\frac{1}{2}″$.

It is important to note that the designer should use the scale of the actual or surfaced dimensions in architectural details rather than the nominal or call-out size. Figures 6.1 and 6.2 illustrate graphically examples of wood members with call-out and actual size dimensions that would be incorporated when detailing wood assemblies.

A further example of a comparison of nominal and surface sizes is illustrated in Table 6.2.

Occasionally, lumber sizes and finishes are changed. It is therefore important that the architectural draftsperson review and be aware of the current lumber sizes before beginning wood detailing.

When reviewing lumber size tables, abbreviated descriptions of how a specific piece of lumber is dressed are shown. Explanations of these abbreviations are given in Table 6.3.

Species

The term "species" refers to the type of tree from which the lumber originated. Each species has its own characteristics and properties that are related to its uses. Species are grouped into various categories concerning their suitability for a specific job. The selection of a species may depend on any of the following: wood color, grain, durability, or other special characteristics.

Types of tree species vary according to the region of the country. Therefore, architectural draftspersons should be familiar with the species and their qualities in their specific regions.

One example of wood species' usability is the appearance and high stress capabilities of Douglas fir

Table 6.2

Nominal Size in inches		Surfaced Size for Design in inches		Nominal Size in inches		Surfaced Size for Design in inches	
b	h	b	h	b	h	b	h
v	v	v	v	v	v	v	v
2 × 2		1.5 × 1.5		8 × 8		7.5 × 7.5	
2 × 3		1.5 × 2.5		8 × 10		7.5 × 9.5	
2 × 4		1.5 × 3.5		8 × 12		7.5 × 11.5	
2 × 6		1.5 × 5.5		8 × 14		7.5 × 13.5	
2 × 8		1.5 × 7.25		8 × 16		7.5 × 15.5	
2 × 10		1.5 × 9.25		8 × 18		7.5 × 17.5	
2 × 12		1.5 × 11.25		8 × 20		7.5 × 19.5	
2 × 14		1.5 × 13.25		8 × 22		7.5 × 21.5	
				8 × 24		7.5 × 23.5	
3 × 3		2.5 × 2.5					
3 × 4		2.5 × 3.5		10 × 10		9.5 × 9.5	
3 × 6		2.5 × 5.5		10 × 12		9.5 × 11.5	
3 × 8		2.5 × 7.25		10 × 14		9.5 × 13.5	
3 × 10		2.5 × 9.25		10 × 16		9.5 × 15.5	
3 × 12		2.5 × 11.25		10 × 18		9.5 × 17.5	
3 × 14		2.5 × 13.25		10 × 20		9.5 × 19.5	
3 × 16		2.5 × 15.25		10 × 22		9.5 × 21.5	
4 × 4		3.5 × 3.5		12 × 12		11.5 × 11.5	
4 × 6		3.5 × 5.5		12 × 14		11.5 × 13.5	
4 × 8		3.5 × 7.25		12 × 16		11.5 × 15.5	
4 × 10		2.5 × 9.25		12 × 18		11.5 × 17.5	
4 × 12		2.4 × 11.25		12 × 20		11.5 × 19.5	
4 × 14		3.5 × 13.25		12 × 22		11.5 × 21.5	
4 × 16		3.5 × 15.25		12 × 24		11.5 × 23.5	
6 × 6		5.5 × 5.5					
6 × 8		5.5 × 7.5					
6 × 10		5.5 × 9.5					
6 × 12		5.5 × 11.5					
6 × 14		5.5 × 13.5					
6 × 16		5.5 × 15.5					
6 × 18		5.5 × 17.5					
6 × 20		5.5 × 19.5					

Table 6.3 **Dressed Abbreviations**	
S1S	Surfaced one side
S2S	Surfaced two sides
S4S	Surfaced four sides
S1S1E	Surfaced one side, one edge
S1S2E	Surfaced one side, two edges
CM	Center matched
D & M	Dressed and matched
T & G	Tongue and grooved
EV1S	Edge vee on one side
S1E	Surfaced one edge

for engineered designs compared to sugar pine. Sugar pine is not commonly used for framing members because of minimal structural capacities and therefore is primarily employed in cabinet work, millwork, and specialty items.

Grade

The function of lumber grading is to set a standard of values between mills that manufacture the same or similar wood and to harmonize the natural differences that may exist between different stocks of lumber. A given grade then represents the same value and can be used for the same purpose regardless of the mill from which it comes. Official grade rules conform to the American Lumber Standards.

The mere fact that a piece of lumber is clear and completely free of knots, shake, wave, and other natural growth characteristics does not necessarily mean that it is better than some other less perfect piece. It is possible that a knotty 2″ × 6″ will support two times as much weight as will a clear piece of the same size and species because strength is based on lumber fiber stress, rather than appearance. Therefore, it saves expense, delay, and misunderstanding

Table 6.4

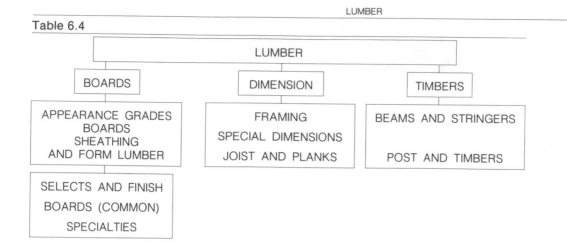

if the right grades of lumber are specified on construction projects.

Generally, grades and sizes are classified into groups, which then identify the uses for the various classifications of grades. Table 6.4 illustrates a grade classification chart.

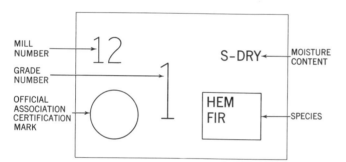

Figure 6.3 Grading stamp example.

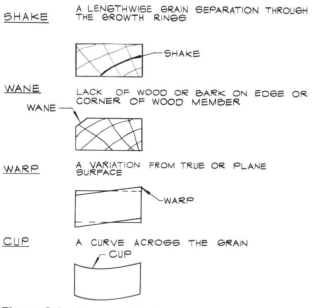

Figure 6.4 Common defects.

All lumber delivered to a construction site has a grade stamp. Official grade stamps may appear in various combinations; however, the necessary information is always shown. A grade stamp contains the following information: the official association certification mark, the assigned mill number, grade mark abbreviation, species mark, and the moisture content mark when the lumber was manufactured. A grading stamp example is illustrated in Figure 6.3.

When inspectors grade lumber, they look for natural and manufacturing defects. These defects affect the strength and appearance of a piece of lumber and influence the grade selection. Some of the most common defects are defined and graphically illustrated in Figure 6.4. Not shown graphically are a knot, which is a limb embedded in the lumber, and mold and stain, which is discoloration caused by fungi.

Treatment

The durability and longevity of wood is improved by preservative treatment techniques. The treatment of wood is usually recommended for two reasons: the location of a member that is subject to an unsafe amount of moisture content and the climate or site conditions in specific regions that are susceptible to decay and termite infestation. Regions of the country vary in their susceptibility to termite infestation. Figure 6.5 illustrates regions that are subject to termites in varying degrees.

When a structure is supported by wood members embedded in the ground, the members should be of an approved pressure-treated wood. Wood is treated by the pressure method when it is impregnated with toxic chemicals at elevated pressures and temperatures. One of the following classes of preservatives is commonly used: (1) creosote and creosote solutions, (2) oil-borne preservatives, (3) water-borne preserva-

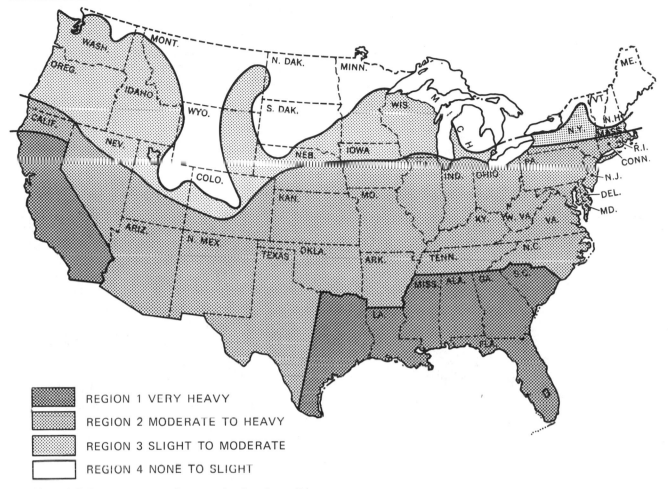

REGION 1 VERY HEAVY

REGION 2 MODERATE TO HEAVY

REGION 3 SLIGHT TO MODERATE

REGION 4 NONE TO SLIGHT

Lines defining areas approximate only. Local conditions may be more or less severe than indicated by the region classification.

Figure 6.5 Regions of termite infestation. (Courtesy of Melville Publishing Co., A.I.A. *Graphic Standards.*)

tives, and (4) water-repellent preservatives. Standards for preservatives and treatments should be in accordance with the American Wood Preservers Association. Water-borne or water-repellent preservatives should be specified when members are to be painted or when finished materials are to be nailed to the members.

Wood members, such as sills, ledgers, or sleepers, that come in contact with concrete or masonry that itself is in direct contact with earth should be of an approved treated wood.

The effectiveness of treated wood depends on the following factors: (1) type of chemical used, (2) amount of penetration, (3) amount of retention, and (4) uniform distribution of the preservative.

In the course of detailing, the architect should be cognizant of the application of treated wood. Examples of details incorporating a treated wood mudsill, ledger, and sleeper are illustrated in Figures 6.6, 6.7, and 6.8.

Creosote and creosote solutions for preservation of wood pile foundations are relatively common and therefore should be called out when detailing this assembly. An example of a detail depicting this condition is illustrated in Figure 6.9.

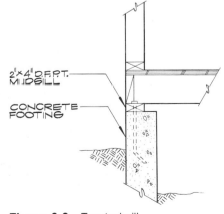

2"x4" DEPT. MUDSILL

CONCRETE FOOTING

Figure 6.6 Treated sill.

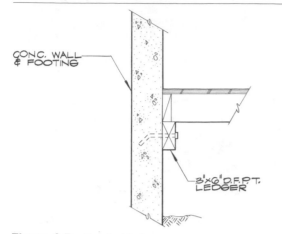

Figure 6.7 Treated ledger.

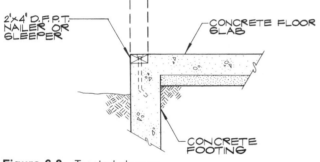

Figure 6.8 Treated sleeper.

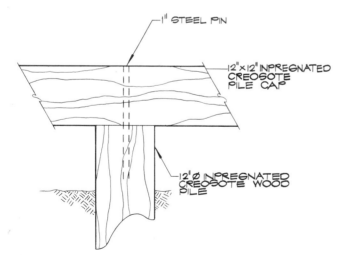

Figure 6.9 Treated pile and cap.

It should be emphasized that damage from decay or termites develops slowly; therefore, inspections should be provided to assure that proper clearances are being maintained and that termite barriers have been implemented correctly.

Lamination

Structural glued laminated lumber is any member comprising an assembly of wood laminations in which the grains of all laminations are generally parallel longitudinally and the laminations are bonded with an approved adhesive. Laminations may vary concerning species, size, number, shape, and thickness. The design and fabrication of structural glue laminated lumber should conform to the standards of the American Institute of Timber Construction (AITC) or other recognized authorities.

Most manufacturers can fabricate structural glued laminated lumber into any practical shape and to any desired size. Close tolerances can be maintained, and since most seasoning action has already taken place, the glued laminated members remain dimensionally stable after placement in the building. An example of the flexibility of glued laminated shapes is shown in Figure 6.10 illustrating an arch.

Glued laminated timbers may be fabricated using more than one species, such as a combination of Douglas fir and larch wood.

The maximum net thickness of individual laminations must not exceed 2 inches. Generally, it is recommended in the industry to use a nominal 1 and 2 inch thickness for laminating. Lumber of a nominal 1″ thickness is generally dressed to $\frac{3}{4}$″ and is primarily employed in curved structural members. Nominal 2″ dressed thick laminations are normally dressed to $1\frac{1}{2}$″ and are generally used for straight structural members. Standard widths, for most fabricators, are $2\frac{1}{4}$″, $3\frac{1}{8}$″, $5\frac{1}{8}$″, $6\frac{3}{4}$″, $8\frac{3}{4}$″, $10\frac{3}{4}$″, $12\frac{1}{4}$″, and $14\frac{1}{4}$″.

Unlike other timber where the call-out size is the nominal size, the call-out size for glued laminated timbers is the dressed or actual size. For example, if the architecture draftsperson selects a glued laminated timber with 10-$1\frac{1}{2}$″ thick laminations, the actual depth is 15 inches. An example of a glued laminated timber with its call-out size is illustrated in Figure 6.11.

Glued laminated members are also fabricated for such other uses as wood columns and tongue and

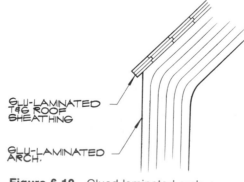

Figure 6.10 Glued laminated arch.

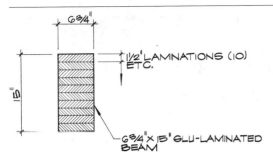

Figure 6.11 Glued laminated beam.

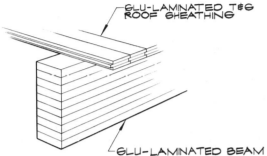

Figure 6.12 Glued laminated wood members.

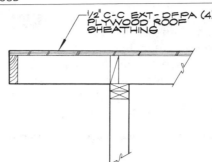

Figure 6.13 Eave detail.

grooved roof sheathing. Laminated roof sheathing affords the flexibility of having the bottom laminations be a species, such as cedar, with the remaining laminations Douglas fir. This gives the designer an option for interior wood finishes. Figure 6.12 illustrates an assembly of glued laminated wood members.

Plywood

The uses of plywood in structures have multiplied in recent years because of advanced adhesives and quality-control processing of plywood laminations and finishes. The American Plywood Association has provided a quality-control program for the manufacturing of plywood.

Plywood is an engineered panel fabricated from a number of thin sheets of wood. These sheets are referred to as veneers. A plywood panel is made by bonding together an odd number of veneers—three, five, seven, and nine, for example. Adjacent veneers are fabricated at right angles to one another to take advantage of the wood's along-the-grain strength. This arrangement results in panel strength in both directions.

Plywood is manufactured in two types: exterior and interior. The type is determined by glue bond capabilities and the grade of veneer to be used.

Exterior type plywood is manufactured with a completely waterproof glue and a veneer grade that is rec-

ommended for exterior use. The glue bond used is stronger and more durable than the wood itself.

The interior-type plywood is made with a highly water-resistant or waterproof glue and the veneer grade is lower than that used in the exterior type. The veneer grade is evaluated on appearance quality and allowable defects.

Plywood is manufactured using a softwood or hardwood species. For construction purposes, a softwood plywood is used, such as the Douglas fir or larch wood species. Hardwood plywood has a face ply of hardwood such as teak, oak, birch, hickory, maple, or walnut. The backing plies must have the equivalent hardness to prevent warping.

Plywood panel sizes are usually 4' wide with lengths of 8', 10', or 12'. The thickness of panels ranges from $\frac{1}{16}$" to $1\frac{1}{4}$".

When architectural details incorporate the use of plywood, the size and grade of the plywood recommended for a specific detail should be called out. Figure 6.13 illustrates an eave detail incorporating plywood roof sheathing. The plywood call out for this detail indicates $\frac{1}{2}$" thick, C.C. EXT-DFPA (4). The letters C.C. represent the veneer quality; EXT. is the abbreviation for exterior type, DFPA (Douglas Fir Plywood Association) is the sign of a quality tested and

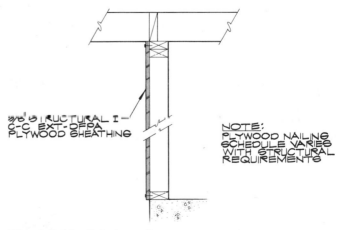

Figure 6.14 Exterior wall.

inspected product; and numeral (4) represents the face veneer quality and inner plies.

Plywood sheathing for exterior walls is excellent for resisting lateral forces, such as wind loads and earthquake forces. Engineered plywood sheathed wall details provide the call-out size and grade as specified by the engineer or architect. Figure 6.14 illustrates an exterior wall with plywood sheathing call-out size and grade.

Information on plywood, such as grades, description, structural capability, and suggested uses is available from wood associations such as the American Plywood Association. Publications by wood associations are highly recommended.

Regional Differences

When dealing with lumber, the species and lengths available will vary from region to region. When it is feasible, a species of lumber native to a region should be used. This not only provides better availability, but its use will reduce shipping costs.

In some regions species with higher stress values will be needed to satisfy special structural requirements. Also, regions that have an infestation problem will require a specific species of pretreated lumber to combat this problem.

Summary

This chapter introduced the process and definitions used in the lumber industry. This chapter conveyed the actual lumber sizes that are used when providing architectural details. It is important to be aware of various types of wood species and their application in construction as well as grading techniques used in the lumber industry.

This chapter explained and illustrated the processes of treated lumber and furnished examples of where it is incorporated in specific structures. Information has been provided concerning the fabrication of wood timbers and plywood panels along with an evaluation of the uses for these manufactured products.

7
METALS

Preview   Chapter 7 introduces various metals and their applications found in light-frame structures. The first part of the chapter deals with the reasons for the need of reinforcing bars, placement, and shapes and sizes. The reasons for and applications of metal flashing are discussed and illustrated and related to framing intersections and moisture control. Examples of metal door frames and various types of metal thresholds are illustrated and discussed and related to wood frame construction. The final sections of this chapter deal with the connection of wood members through the use of metal framing connectors, nails, lag bolts, and machine bolts. Illustrations, both pictorial and in detail form, describe assemblies for light- and heavy-loaded wood frame connections.

An understanding of the availability and applications of metals in light frame construction will help architectural draftpersons in their approach to detailing wood framing connections.

Upon completion of this chapter, the architectural draftsperson will:

1. Understand the reason for the use of reinforcing bars, their shapes and sizes, and how reinforcing bars are delineated in detail form.
2. Be aware of the importance of metal flashing, as well as the various gauges, treatment, and types of flashing that are utilized in light-frame construction and where flashing applications may occur.
3. Understand in detail form the application of metal door frames and metal thresholds in wood frame construction; learn the availability of many shapes and sizes that may satisfy specific conditions.
4. Be able to realize the need for various metal connectors and their application in framing connection details.
5. Understand the various sizes and finishes of nails and code requirements for the nailing of specific wood members.
6. Be able to differentiate among lag bolts, anchor bolts, and machine bolts, their sizes, shapes and where they are normally found.

Reinforcing Bars

The purpose of reinforcing bars embedded in concrete is to provide resistance to tensile stresses. Concrete in its hardened state is capable of resisting compressive forces, but it is relatively weak in tension.

The forces of tension and compression can be simulated by holding a piece of string between two hands. The string held in a taut position depicts a tension force. The opposite reaction of this force is compression, demonstrated by a loosely held string. See Figures 7.1 and 7.2. Therefore, to satisfy the weakness of concrete in tension, reinforcing bars are re-

quired. This is illustrated in Figures 7.3 and 7.4. It also should be noted that the combination of concrete and reinforcing steel primarily provides a marriage of two materials acting as one unit.

Sizes, spacing, and placement of reinforcing bars are normally accounted for from engineering calculations done by the engineer or architect. Therefore, the designer should be aware of these design requirements prior to commencing a specific detail.

Reinforcing bars — or as often referred to, "rebars" — are made from billet steel and old-rail steel. Billet steel comes in three grades: structural, intermediate, and hard. Of the three grades, the intermediate grade of billet steel is probably the most commonly used.

Reinforcing bars are manufactured in plain and deformed shapes. See Figure 7.5. The plain bar is used more infrequently because stresses depend on the adhesive factor between concrete and steel; the deformed bar, more commonly used, provides a much greater bonding capacity than does the plain bar. This bonding capacity is accomplished with the use of lugs that give a mechanical bond that is not dependent on an adhesive factor. The shapes of bars are round or square, with round bars more commonly used because they are easier to bend.

Reinforcing bars are primarily sized from $\frac{1}{4}''$ to $1''$ and greater. The symbol ϕ means round in call outs on details. The call-out size of a reinforcing bar might be stated: #3 bars @ 24" on center. The actual size of this bar would be $\frac{3}{8}''$. Bar number call outs are interpreted in $\frac{1}{8}''$ intervals, as shown in Figure 7.6. It should be noted that a $\frac{1}{4}''$ round bar is called out as $\frac{1}{4}''$ reinforcing bar.

The architect or designer delineates reinforcing bars with a heavy dot when the detail is in a section,

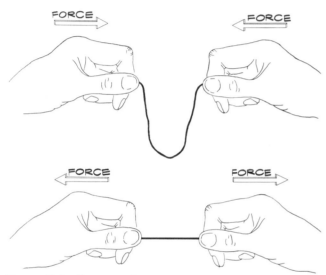

Figure 7.1 Compression and tension analogy.

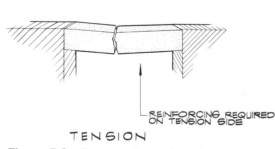

Figure 7.2 Compression and tension forces.

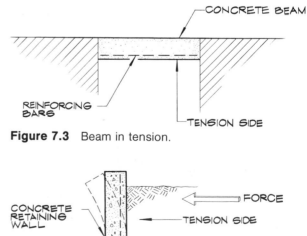

Figure 7.3 Beam in tension.

Figure 7.4 Wall in tension.

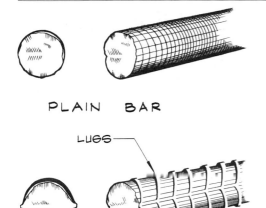

PLAIN BAR

LUGS

DEFORMED BAR

Figure 7.5 Reinforcing bar shapes.

#3 bar = $\frac{3}{8}''$
#4 bar = $\frac{1}{2}''$
#5 bar = $\frac{5}{8}''$
#6 bar = $\frac{3}{4}''$
#7 bar = $\frac{7}{8}''$
#8 bar = $1''$

Figure 7.6 Reinforcing bar sizes.

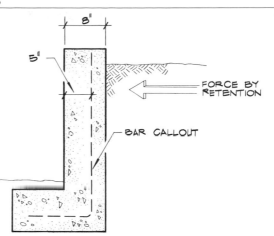

Figure 7.8 Retaining wall section.

Figure 7.9 Footing section.

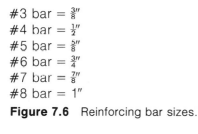

NORMALLY 3" MIN. CLEARANCE FROM EARTH

SECTION   ELEVATION

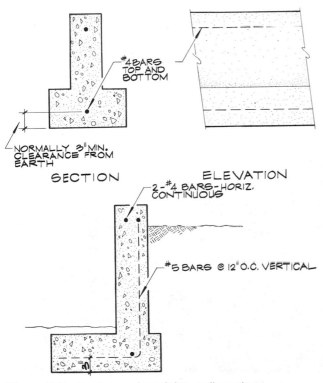

Figure 7.7 Footing and retaining wall sections.

or a heavy broken line when a detail is in an elevation or plan view. See Figure 7.7.

The placement of reinforcing bars in a concrete or masonry wall may vary depending on the type of wall and its function. Placement dimensions of rebars are derived from the engineer's computations or minimum code requirements, whichever may govern. An example of this is seen in Figures 7.8 and 7.9.

The type of reinforcing bar and its properties are normally given in the specifications of a set of working drawings under the title "steel reinforcing bars." It is therefore not necessary to call out these facts on the specific detail. The main concern is size, placement, and spacing.

Dowels

Primarily, the function of dowels is to unite two concrete elements together to resist separation. Dowel sizes and shapes are the same as those of reinforcing bars. Deformed shapes are primarily used because of their bonding capabilities and obviously would be more suitable for holding two elements together.

The delineation of a dowel in a section is a heavy dash, and a heavy broken line in a plan or elevation view. Dowels are placed in the building footing form

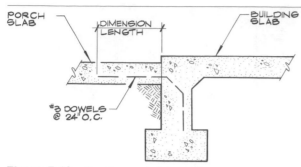

Figure 7.10 Footing and slab section.

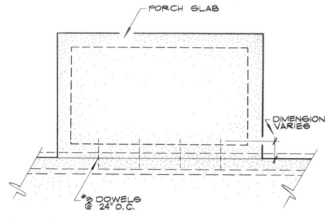

Figure 7.11 Foundation plan view.

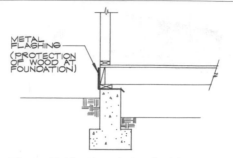

Figure 7.12 Foundation flashing.

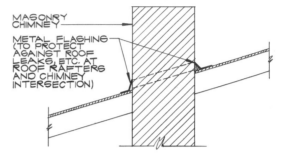

Figure 7.13 Chimney flashing.

prior to the pouring of concrete and are made ready for a later stage of pouring of concrete porch slab. An application and call out of the use of dowels can be seen in Figure 7.10. Figure 7.11 shows dowel placement in plan view.

Flashing

The term "flashing" refers to a material such as sheet metal, a combination of sheet metal and building paper, or just building paper that surrounds or covers the intersection of two or more building members. In this chapter only the use of sheet metal flashing is discussed. The designer, when involved in architectural details, should rely on his or her judgment to determine the need for metal flashing on a specific detail.

The purpose of flashing material is to produce a protective covering for a wood member or to seal a joint of two intersecting members, such as a masonry chimney and the roof framing. Two examples showing where metal flashing would be required are seen in Figures 7.12 and 7.13.

As indicated in Figure 7.12 metal flashing is installed to protect the wood floor system at the foundation wall from moisture, dry rot, and other deterio-

rating sources. See Figure 7.14 for an example of foundation flashing. Figure 7.13 depicts the use of metal flashing around a chimney at its intersection with the roof framing. The purpose here is to protect against leaks from rain, water, snow, and so forth. It should be noted, as shown in Figure 7.13, that the metal flashing is set in a mortar joint or saw cut into the masonry chimney to provide a good seal.

Metal flashing, most commonly used in wood structures, is derived from flat galvanized iron sheets ranging from gauges of No. 7 to No. 30, in which the No. 7 gauge has an approximate thickness of $\frac{3}{16}$" down to No. 30 gauge, which is approximately $\frac{1}{80}$" in thickness. For the remaining intermediate gauges, see Table 7.1.

For most installations, No. 26 gauge galvanize sheet metal is used. Because of its thickness, it af-

Figure 7.14 Photograph of foundation flashing.

Table 7.1

Number of Gauge	Thickness	Weight
	Approximate Thickness in Fractions of an Inch	Weight per Square Foot in Pounds
7	$\frac{3}{16}''$	7.50
8	$\frac{11}{64}''$	6.87
9	$\frac{5}{32}''$	6.25
10	$\frac{9}{64}''$	5.62
11	$\frac{1}{8}''$	5.0
12	$\frac{7}{64}''$	4.37
13	$\frac{1}{11}''$	3.75
14	$\frac{5}{64}''$	3.12
15	$\frac{9}{128}''$	2.81
16	$\frac{1}{16}''$	2.50
17	$\frac{9}{160}''$	2.25
18	$\frac{1}{20}''$	2.0
19	$\frac{7}{160}''$	1.75
20	$\frac{3}{80}''$	1.50
21	$\frac{11}{320}''$	1.37
22	$\frac{1}{32}''$	1.25
23	$\frac{9}{320}''$	1.12
24	$\frac{1}{40}''$	1.0
25	$\frac{7}{320}''$	0.87
26	$\frac{3}{160}''$	0.75
27	$\frac{11}{640}''$	0.68
28	$\frac{1}{64}''$	0.62
29	$\frac{9}{640}''$	0.56
30	$\frac{1}{80}''$	0.5

fords the sheet metal installer more flexibility to form, bend, and cut the material on the job site. A heavier gauge, such as No. 18, would necessitate bending, forming, and cutting to be done with shop machinery.

Where flashing members are joined together, they are bonded by a soldering process or overlap one another with the use of an approved sealing compound.

An acceptable abbreviated call out for a flashing element on a detail might be stated as #26 ga. G.I. flashing. Twenty-six (26 ga.) refers to the gauge of the metal and G.I. is the abbreviation for galvanized iron. See Figure 7.15.

Metal Door Frames

Metal door frames are used in wood structures for durability and fire door assemblies and in specific types of building where their use requires metal door frames because of building code regulations.

Manufacturers' designs vary in sizes and shapes with different installation techniques; however, most manufacturers use steel extrusions with gauges ranging from No. 14 to No. 18. For wood doors, No. 18 gauge is recommended. Frames are available in a complete one-piece welded assembly with mitered corners and can be delivered to the job site primed or prepainted.

A typical frame installation provides an anchoring clip that is nailed to the door frame stud in the framing stages and is used to provide a secure interlocking connection with the finished door frame.

An example of an installation is seen in Figure 7.16. It should be noted that the finishing of the walls has been completed prior to the installation of the steel door frame.

Thresholds

The member that is secured to the floor just below the bottom of a door is termed a threshold. A threshold

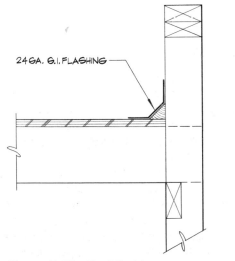

Figure 7.15 Roof flashing.

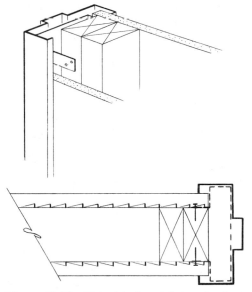

Figure 7.16 Pictorial of metal door jamb; section of metal door jamb.

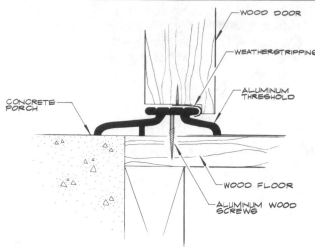

Figure 7.17 Metal threshold.

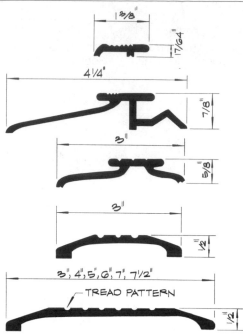

Figure 7.19 Metal threshold shapes.

can be made from hardwood, such as oak, or a metal alloy, such as aluminum or brass. In dealing specifically with metal thresholds, you will find that manufacturers of metal thresholds vary in their designs, sizes, and finishes.

Extruded aluminum thresholds are more economical in cost and are low in maintenance. These thresholds are designed for interior and exterior doors. Types that are designed for exterior doors have provisions for weatherstripping, which restricts the admission of water or cold air into a building. An aluminum threshold for a weatherstripping door is seen in Figure 7.17.

The slots that are located at the top of the threshold are linear and provide an abrasive surface to minimize slip hazards. These extruded slots are referred to as tread patterns. The design of tread patterns also varies considerably among manufacturers.

Thresholds are fastened in place by means of aluminum screws, attached directly to the subfloor,

when used on wood floor construction. When thresholds are to be fastened to a concrete floor, a pressure treated sleeper or expansion plugs can be installed to secure the threshold. See Figure 7.18.

When reviewing literature for the selection of a threshold to satisfy a specific detail, the designer has the following alternatives to select from: size, tread pattern design, interior or exterior door conditions to facilitate weatherstripping of a door, and, finally, the finish of the metal. The finish might be of natural aluminum, bronze, or whatever specific color a specific manufacturer might offer. Some examples of standard aluminum thresholds are shown in Figures 7.19 and 7.20.

Metal Connectors

Various types of metal connectors are used in today's wood construction. Metal connectors are manufactured in various gauges of galvinized iron and flat steel. The primary purpose of metal connectors is to join wood framing members securely together in buildings of wood construction.

An application of a use of a metal connector is provided in Figure 7.21. This type of connector may be referred to as a framing anchor, and is manufactured from 18 gauge heavily coated galvanized steel. With the use of metal connections, framing anchors, or metal fasteners, the following attributes are recognized: ease and speed in construction, increased

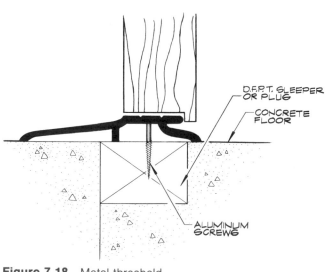

Figure 7.18 Metal threshold.

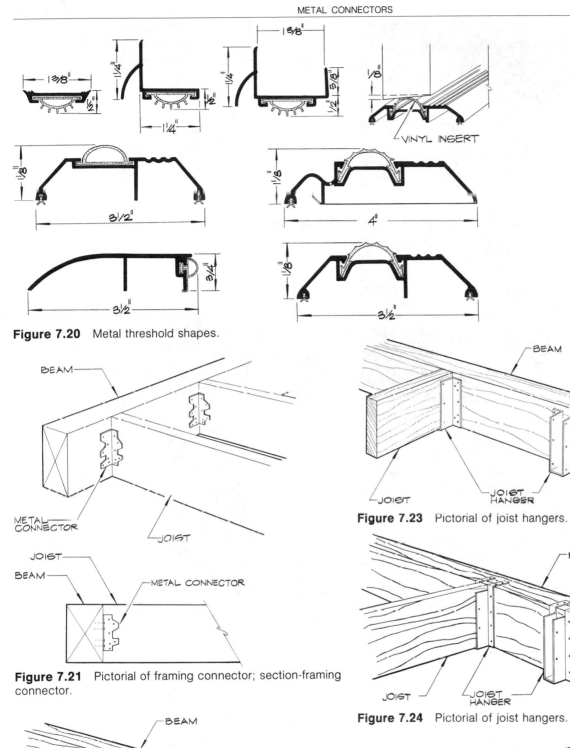

Figure 7.20 Metal threshold shapes.

Figure 7.21 Pictorial of framing connector; section-framing connector.

Figure 7.22 Pictorial of joist hangers.

Figure 7.23 Pictorial of joist hangers.

Figure 7.24 Pictorial of joist hangers.

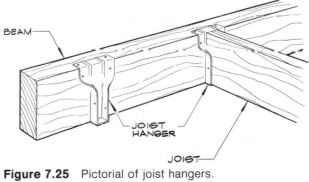

Figure 7.25 Pictorial of joist hangers.

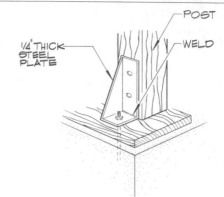

POST HOLDDOWN
Figure 7.28 Pictorial of post holddown.

Figure 7.26 Photograph of joist hangers.

Figure 7.29 Photograph of post holddown.

structural capability, and the opportunity for connections for a variety of special framing conditions. Figures 7.22, 7.23, 7.24, and 7.25 are examples of manufactured joist hangers and their applications. It should be noted that connectors have predrilled holes for nailing and bolting purposes. Figure 7.26 illustrates an example of framing connectors.

Wherever heavy loads are concentrated on wood members, connectors made of flat steel are necessary. Steel plate $\frac{3}{16}''$ and $\frac{1}{4}''$ thick is most commonly used. Plates are joined together by a fillet weld.

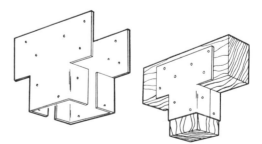

Figure 7.30 Pictorial of post-to-beam connectors.

An example of connectors assembled with flat steel plates is shown in Figures 7.27 and 7.28. Figure 7.29 shows an example of a post holddown.

The use of metal connectors for post to beam conditions as well as a post to base connection is highly recommended. Connectors at these specific points

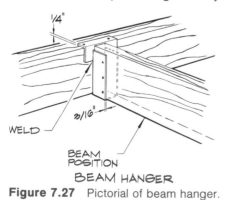

BEAM HANGER
Figure 7.27 Pictorial of beam hanger.

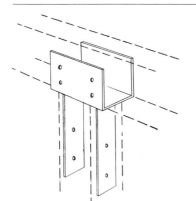

Figure 7.31 Pictorial of post-to-beam connector.

Figure 7.34 Photograph of post-to-beam connector.

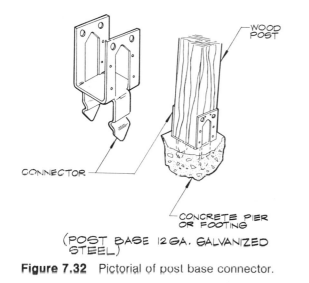

(POST BASE 12 GA. GALVANIZED STEEL)

Figure 7.32 Pictorial of post base connector.

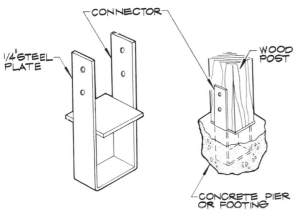

Figure 7.33 Pictorial of post base connector.

Figure 7.35 Photograph of post base connector.

afford a positive structural link. Manufactured connectors for these applications are illustrated in Figures 7.30, 7.31, 7.32, and 7.33. Figure 7.34 shows a steel saddle similar to Figure 7.31 and a post connector embedded in concrete is depicted in Figure 7.35.

When draftspersons are involved with a detail that necessitates a metal connector, they should have access to manufacturers' literature on metal connectors to enable them to satisfy a specific condition. The use of standard metal connectors is more economical to a project than that of custom-made connectors fabricated in a shop.

Nails

Nails that are used for framing in wood structures are generally employed for fastening 1″ and 2″ framing

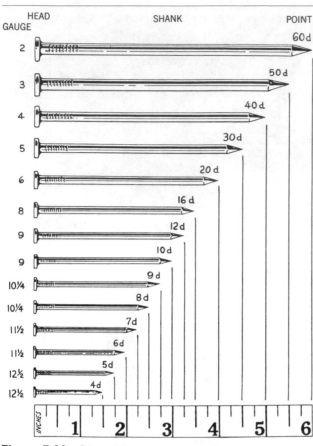

Figure 7.36 Sizes of common wire nails.

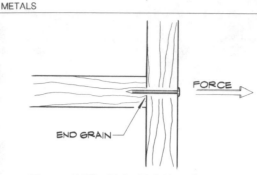

Figure 7.38 Nailed joint section.

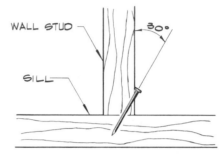

Figure 7.39 Toe nailed joint section.

members. These nails are referred to as common wire nails. Common nails vary from #2 ga. to #12½ ga., and range in lengths of 1½" to 6". For exterior use, cement-coated nails are employed to provide a resistance to corrosion. Others have a finish termed "bright flat."

When specifying nails for a particular detail, the architecture draftsperson refers to a nail size such as 4d, 8d, or 16d. Figure 7.36 illustrates the gauge, size, and call-out size for common wire nails.

Structural capabilities of nailed joints are strongest when a force is acting at right angles to the nails. An example of this is depicted in Figure 7.37.

The weakest nailing condition occurs where the nail is fastened into the end grain of the wood member with an applied force parallel to the nail in such a way

Table 7.2 **Recommended Nailing Schedule Using Common Nails**

Joist to sill or girder, toe nail	3-8d
Bridging to joist, toe nail each end	2-8d
Ledger strip	3-16d at each joist
1" × 6" subfloor or less to each joist, face nail	2-8d
Over 1" × 6" subfloor to each joist, face nail	3-8d
2" subfloor to joist or girder, blind and face nail	2-16d
Sole plate to joist or blocking, face nail	16d @ 16" o.c.
Top plate to stud, end nail	2-16d
Stud to sole plate, toe nail	4-8d
Doubled studs, face nail	16d @ 24" o.c.
Doubled top plates, face nail	16d @ 16" o.c.
Top plates, laps and intersections, face nail	2-16d
Continuous header, two pieces	16d @ 16" o.c. along each edge
Ceiling joists to plate, toe nail	3-8d
Continuous header to stud, toe nail	4-8d
Ceiling joists, laps over partitions, face nail	3-16d
Ceiling joists to parallel rafters, face nail	3-16d
Rafter to plate, toe nail	3-8d
1-inch brace to each stud and plate, face nail	2-8d
1" × 8" sheathing or less to each bearing, face nail	2-8d
Over 1" × 8" sheathing to each bearing, face nail	3-8d
Built-up corner studs	16d @ 24" o.c.
Built-up girders and beams	20d @ 32" o.c. along each edge

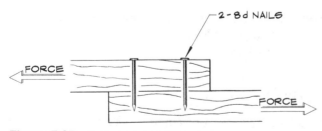

Figure 7.37 Nailed joint section.

so as to cause withdrawal. An application of this is seen in Figure 7.38.

A common nailing method for fastening wall studs to a sill is termed toe nailing; it is where the nail is driven at an approximate angle of 30°. This provides a more positive connection than that of nailing into end grain. See Figure 7.39.

Most building codes and wood construction data literature still provide a table for a recommended nailing schedule for various wood members to be fastened together. See Table 7.2 for an example.

Lag Bolts

Lag bolts provide better structural capabilities for fastening two wood members together than nails.

Lag bolts may be used to secure two wood beams together when nails are not structurally adequate or when it is not feasible to drill completely through two members and provide a machine-bolted connection.

Table 7.3 **Lag Bolt Table**

Lag Bolt (in inches)

Diameter (in inches)	Decimal Equivalent	Length
$\frac{1}{4}$	.250	1–6
$\frac{5}{16}$	.313	1–10
$\frac{3}{8}$	.375	1–12
$\frac{7}{16}$	.438	1–12
$\frac{1}{2}$	.500	1–12
$\frac{5}{8}$	.625	$1\frac{1}{2}$–16
$\frac{3}{4}$	.750	$1\frac{1}{2}$–16
$\frac{7}{8}$	.875	2–10
1	1.00	2–16

An application of a lag bolt connection is seen in Figures 7.40 and 7.41.

Lag bolts may be obtained in bright plate finish or galvanized for exterior use.

Table 7.3 illustrates diameters and lengths of the most commonly used lag bolts.

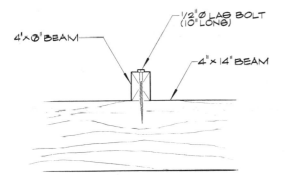

Figure 7.40 Lag bolt connection.

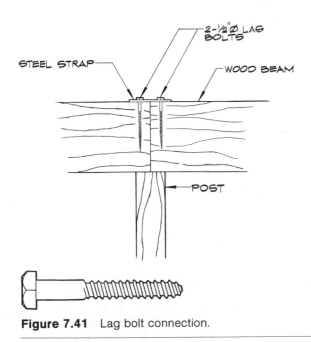

Figure 7.41 Lag bolt connection.

Bolts

Two types of bolts that are most commonly used in today's light wood structures are foundation anchor bolts and machine bolts. Foundation anchor bolts, embedded in concrete, are galvanized and sized from $\frac{1}{2}''$ to 1″ in diameter.

Standard anchor bolts have a length of 10″ and bend to form a hook at the bottom to provide resistance against withdrawal from the concrete. Types of anchor bolts are shown in Figure 7.42.

Generally, foundation anchor bolts will be $\frac{1}{2}''$ ϕ in diameter, 10″ long, and spaced not more than 6′-0″ on centers with a maximum distance of 12″ from the corners. Minimum embedment into the concrete is approximately 7″ deep. Figure 7.43 is an example of anchor bolt placement.

Machine Bolts

Machine bolts are primarily used for the fastening of wood members when metal connectors are involved,

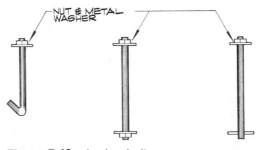

Figure 7.42 Anchor bolts.

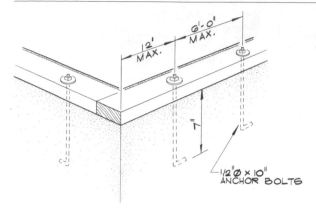

Figure 7.43 Pictorial of anchor bolts.

and when structural requirements are not satisfied by the use of nails or lag bolts.

Diameters of machine bolts range from $\frac{1}{2}''$ ϕ to $1\frac{1}{2}''$ ϕ and standard lengths are $3\frac{1}{2}''$ to 30″ long. Heads of bolts come in hexagonal or square shapes.

Machine bolts are available in galvanized or bright plate finishes. A typical application of machine bolts in wood structures is shown in Figure 7.44.

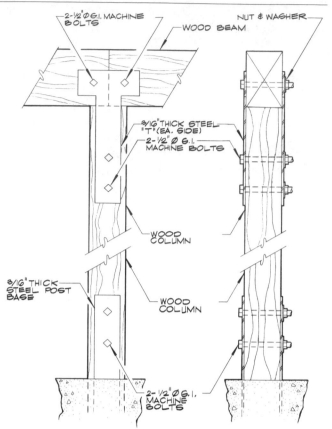

Figure 7.44 Elevation of machine bolt connections; section of machine bolt connections.

Regional Differences

In areas in which lateral forces are considered in the structural design of concrete and masonry buildings, the use of reinforcing bars will be required. Some metal connections, such as holddowns, are not required in regions in which lateral forces are not a factor in the structural design of a building.

Summary

This chapter has illustrated the various types of metals that are used in light wood frame construction and describes their application in detail form. The architectural draftsperson should now understand the reason for reinforcing bars and shapes, and the placement of these bars relative to design criteria.

The draftsperson must be informed about the availability of the types of metals that can be selected for the solution of a framing detail, or for a finished threshold.

8
MASONRY

Preview Chapter 8 introduces the subject of masonry and its implications for light-frame construction. This chapter is, however, limited to brick and concrete block and a discussion of the material used to bond them together. Background information for both brick and concrete block is provided to give architectural draftspersons a firm base on which they can develop and draft details. Each of these building materials is dealt with in terms of available size, stacking methods, nomenclature, types of joints used, symbols needed to represent them on a detail, and so on.

A set of working drawings of a masonry building appears at the end of this chapter showing a finished plot plan, foundation plan, floor plan, and elevations and the source of the details with which the architect will be dealing.

Additional knowledge in masonry makes architectural draftspersons more valuable to their employers since they are not limited just to wood construction.

After reading this chapter, the architectural draftsperson will:

1. Understand the specific nomenclature applying to masonry construction.
2. Be able to relate information to subsequent chapters where specific applications are available.
3. Comprehend the materials used in masonry construction.
4. Become familiar with the typical units that are manufactured.
5. Realize the advantages of strength and weakness of moisture absorption in masonry construction.
6. Be able to select the correct method of designating brick and concrete block.
7. Be able to designate how to stack masonry units, using different patterns.
8. Be able to produce various visual effects by stacking methods and arranging the way in which the joints are finished.

Types of Masonry Units

Masonry can be divided into two categories. The first is clay masonry, which includes (1) solid masonry units, such as brick, (2) hollow masonry units, such as structural clay tile, and (3) architectural terra cotta. The second is concrete masonry, which includes (1) concrete block, both hollow and solid, and (2) special units, such as decorative, split faced, and faced block.

To simplify the description of clay and concrete masonry, one from each category is discussed here and in subsequent chapters. Brick and concrete block are selected because they are of different materials (one is solid, the other is hollow) and because of their extensive use throughout the country.

Justification for using masonry units rather than wood involves its special characteristics. Masonry units are fireproof, durable, and long lasting; they have a high degree of compressive strength that is important when using load-bearing walls of masonry with substantial roof loads. There is very little need for painting, the units are immune to termites and rotting, and there is no corrosion. In fact, masonry used in conjunction with poured concrete and wood provides a very flexible and desirable combination for light construction.

In describing the size of a masonry unit, the width is expressed first, the height second, and the length third. Therefore, a $6 \times 8 \times 16$ concrete block means that the block is 6 inches wide, 8 inches tall, and 16 inches long. See Figure 8.1.

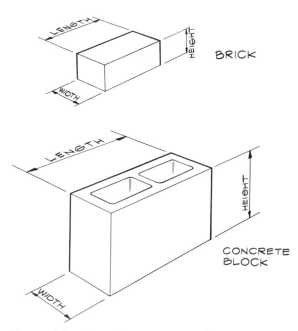

Figure 8.1 Describing masonry units.

Brick Background

Brick is made of burned clay, shale, fire clay, or a combination of these materials. It is shaped, while in a plastic state, and burned (fired) in a kiln at a high temperature, which tends to fuse or bond the ingredients. Surface clays that are commonly used to make brick are of a sedimentary character and are found most often on the earth's surface. Shale, however, is a harder form and comes in the form of slate. This material is ground, crushed, and pulverized prior to being formed into brick. The purest and hardest form of clay is fire clay found extremely deep and used as firebrick.

Since brick is synthetic, there is a great deal of control over its final appearance. Brick comes in a variety of colors—greys, creams, buffs, reds, purples, maroons, and even black. The surface textures can also be controlled by the forms used. The architectural draftsperson should become familiar with such brick textures as smooth, matt-vertical or horizontal markings, rugs, barks, stipple, sandmold, waterstruck, and sandstruck. Each of the names is indicative of final appearance. A vertical matt, for example, has vertical markings on the face of the brick, the stipple appears to have a series of dots on the surface, and so on.

Brick has a greater compressive strength compared to concrete block. Compressive strength is measured in pounds per square inch (psi) and ranges from 1500 psi to 20,000 psi. Strength of the brick is based on the ingredients and, mostly, on the burning of the brick itself. Deterioration, however, does occur. This happens when the brick freezes, then thaws in the presence of water. If the area in which the structure is to be built has an annual precipitation of 20 inches or more and freezing does occur during this time, the architectural draftsperson should be aware that a brick with a high compressive strength, or low absorption, or both should be used.

Solid masonry refers to brick. This does not mean that holes cannot be introduced to reduce weight. Such holes are called cores, and they are often the diameter of a pencil. When the core area begins to exceed 25 percent of the total area, the brick units are no longer classified as solid masonry units, but rather as hollow units.

The absorption rate of the brick has much to do with the quality of construction and the strength of the system. If the brick absorbs too much water, it will extract it from the mortar when it is being installed and thus weaken the joint. This causes poor bonding and, consequently, poor joints. The penetration of water through a masonry wall also causes a moisture problem.

Absorption is usually calculated in a C/B ratio. "C" is the cold water exposure the first 24 hours and is measured in a percentage of the total weight of a dry unit. "B" refers to a 5-hour boiling test and the amount absorbed as a percentage of total weight. The suggested ratio in Southern California is 100. The architectural draftsperson should check the local region for the suggested ratio there.

There is also a rate of absorption that is the amount of water absorbed in 1 minute. The ideal unit absorbs 10 to 20 grams per minute.

Brick Sizes

Architectural draftspersons should be aware of the available sizes in their areas. Sizes are listed as either net or nominal. "Net" means the actual size of the brick and "nominal" size includes the thickness of the mortar in between the brick. For example, a $2\frac{1}{2}'' \times 3\frac{7}{8}'' \times 8\frac{1}{4}''$ standard brick is the actual or net size, while a $4 \times 4 \times 8$ economy brick is the nominal size and includes a $\frac{3}{8}''$ mortar thickness. Thus, the $4 \times 4 \times 8$ brick is actually $3\frac{5}{8}'' \times 3\frac{5}{8}'' \times 7\frac{5}{8}''$ net. Sizes of brick may also vary slightly according to manufacturers and regions of the country. In most instances, bricks manufactured today are modular, for ease of construction and planning.

Position of Brick in a Wall

The positions of brick in a wall are indicated by certain terms that the architectural draftsperson should be aware of. When, for example, the height and length are exposed, the unit is called a "stretcher." See Figure 8.2A. When the height and width are ex-

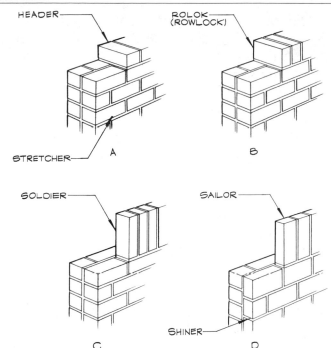

Figure 8.2 Terms applied to brick positions.

posed on the face of the wall, the unit is called a "header." Using the same situation, with the width and the height exposed and the unit resting on the smaller of the two dimensions, the same unit is called a "rolok" (or rowlock) as shown in Figure 8.2B. When the units are sitting on their ends and the height is showing, this is called a "soldier." When the width is showing, the position is termed "sailor." If the sailor unit sits on its side rather than its end, it is called a "shiner." See Figures 8.2C and 8.2D.

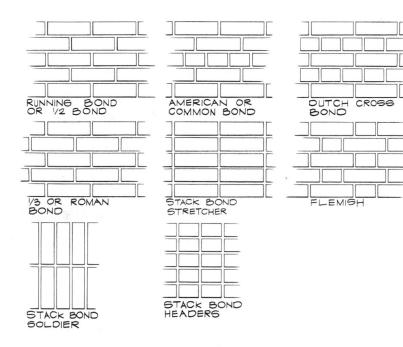

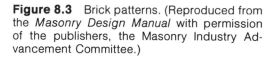

Figure 8.3 Brick patterns. (Reproduced from the *Masonry Design Manual* with permission of the publishers, the Masonry Industry Advancement Committee.)

Methods of Stacking Brick

The method of stacking the brick one on another can form a series of patterns. For ease of description, names have been given to the patterns formed — see Figure 8.3 on the previous page. When, for example, you stack a brick on top of another so that each layer overlaps the previous layer in the middle, this is called running or $\frac{1}{2}$ bond. If each brick had overlapped the brick below by $\frac{1}{3}$ or $\frac{1}{4}$ rather than $\frac{1}{2}$, the stacking method would have been called $\frac{1}{3}$ or $\frac{1}{4}$ bond.

The American, or Common Bond as it is often referred to, is very similar to the Dutch Cross Bond, except that headers appear every other row on the Dutch Cross Bond and every third row on the Common Bond.

Joint Terminology

Each row of brick is called a wythe as shown in Figure 8.4. When there are two rows of brick, as shown in Figure 8.4, this is termed two wythe of brick. The space between may be an airspace, called a cavity, or a large space filled with grout and steel for structural purposes. The space may also be a joint between the two wythe of brick and is called a collar joint. Vertical joints, on the other hand, are called head joints and horizontal joints are called bed joints. Sizes of joints can vary, but a $\frac{3}{8}''$ joint is typical.

Joint Finishes

There are a variety of ways of finishing joints and a majority of them are shown in Figure 8.5. These finishes are used for many reasons, such as appearance, shadow patterns, and drainage of water away from the building. As you will notice in the figure, some require the use of a special tool, while others can be produced by a simple trowel.

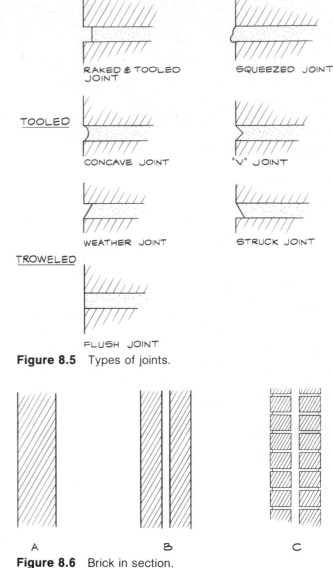

Figure 8.5 Types of joints.

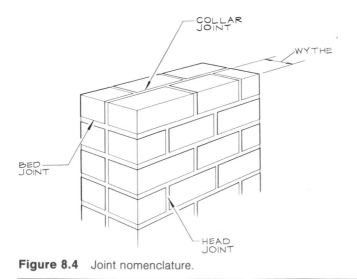

Figure 8.4 Joint nomenclature.

Figure 8.6 Brick in section.

Symbols Used to Represent Brick

In drawing a brick wall in section, one of three methods can be employed. Figure 8.6A illustrates the simplest. Figure 8.6B is used when it becomes necessary to show the cavity or to call out the solid grouting and/or steel between the two wythe of brick. The third, Figure 8.6C, is the most sophisticated method, but is often not used by architectural offices because of the time needed to draw each brick.

A typical view of a brick wall is shown in Figure 8.7; Figure 8.8 indicates the nomenclature applied to it.

Concrete Block Background

Concrete blocks, also called molded concrete units, are made from relatively dry portland cement, aggre-

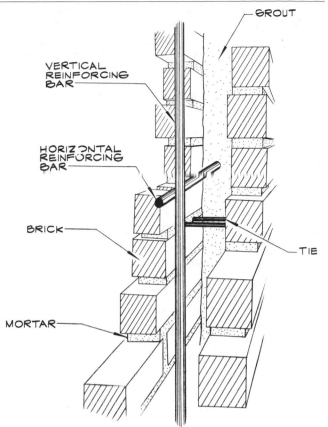

Figure 8.8 Typical brick wall.

Figure 8.7 Vertical and horizontal reinforcing bars between two Wythe of brick.

gates, and water. They are compacted in forms by means of vibrating, and usually cured under controlled temperature and moisture conditions. A precise period of aging is necessary for maximum strength.

Aggregate, which constitutes 90 percent of the block by weight, should be selected in size so that the largest piece does not exceed one-third of the smallest section of the block shell.

Strength of Concrete Block Units

The type of aggregate also determines the strength of the unit and the water absorption that is measured in pounds per cubic feet of concrete. Normal-weight blocks use sand and gravel or limestone or air-cooled slag. Lightweight blocks might use such materials as expanded shale or slag, cinders, pumice, and scoria. Therefore, the compressive strength might range from as little as 700 to 1800 psi depending on the material and 7 to 16 pounds of water per cubic foot of concrete. There are, however, blocks that exceed

3000 psi in some concrete block units when the ingredients and the method of production are controlled to a very high degree.

The compressive strength range of 700 to 1800 is based on a gross-bearing area that includes the core areas. To compute the actual strength of the net area, the figures provided by the manufacturer should be multiplied by 1.8. That is, of course, if the figures provided are gross area figures. For water absorption, a figure of 4 to 5 to a maximum of 20 should be used.

It should be noted here that a two-core design of a concrete block unit is good for a running bond or common bond (see Figure 8.16) because the design of the concrete blocks is such that the face of the block is slightly thicker at the center where the strength is most needed. There is also less cracking because less shrinkage occurs when using this unit in a running bond.

Many figures have been calculated to compare the relative cost of a concrete block building to a stud wall construction. Some literature indicates that the cost will vary as much as 10 percent in favor of concrete block. The variation may be due to the need for reinforcing and grouting, waterproofing, sound insulation, insulation against heat loss, and so on, depending on the region. For example, where hurricanes and earthquakes are a problem, the local codes require reinforcing. This alone raises the cost. Some of the sound can be absorbed by the concrete block itself by using a block with a great deal of surface texture.

Airspaces in Concrete Block Units

The airspaces in the concrete block (cores) can be used for many purposes. As previously mentioned, reinforcing is required in earthquake and hurricane areas, and this reinforcing can be placed in the cores. Insulation can also be put in these voids as well as some type of barrier to moisture. Therefore, it is important that these spaces be free of mortar droppings when the joints are being worked on. Such droppings may create a bridge between the hollow areas, allowing water to pass to the interior side of the wall.

Another way of insulating a concrete block wall is to apply some form of rigid insulation to the face of the wall. Batt or blanket insulation can be applied to the inside face of the masonry wall by attaching wood or metal furring strips, placing the insulation in between them, and covering the system with paneling or lath and plastic or conventional interior wall finishing material. See Figure 8.9.

Flashing should be used at the base, around windows and doors, and at roof intersections, when there is severe or moderate wind and precipitation. The following list explains the three classifications.

Severe — annual precipitation of 30″ or over and 30 lb per square foot of wind.
Moderate — annual precipitation of 30″ or over and winds 20 to 25 lb per square foot.
Slight — precipitation of less than 30″ and wind 20 to 25 lb per square foot or precipitation of less than 20″.

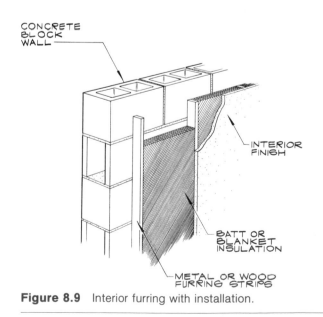

Figure 8.9 Interior furring with installation.

With very few exceptions nationally, building codes allow 6″ wide concrete blocks to be used as a load bearing wall for a one-story building (9′-0″ maximum wall height), assuming the peak of the roof does not exceed 15 feet.

Sizes of Concrete Block Units

Figures 8.10 through 8.12 show the variety of typical concrete block sizes that are available and their respective dimensions. Of special interest to the architectural draftsperson are their uses. The unit labeled standard is the basic unit used to construct a concrete masonry wall. The sash is a unit with a slot formed in one side to allow special metal or wood pieces to be attached by means of grout. See Figure 13.31 for practical application of this unit. A lintel is a U-shaped unit for use over openings such as windows and doors. The sash lintel is the unit employed in Figure 13.31. The bond beam is a unit used to allow horizontal reinforcing to penetrate. A practical application of the bond beam can be seen in Figure 11.28 and pictorially in Figure 8.15.

The open-ended units are used for setting attachment pieces into the concrete block. See Figures 12.42 and 12.44 for examples. The $\frac{1}{2}$ and $\frac{3}{4}$ units are used when a running bond (Figure 8.17) requires a small block to end a sequence.

Figure 8.13 shows a typical pilaster unit and is the same unit described in Chapter 20 and illustrated in Figure 20.53. The units below the pilasters are, as the name indicates, accessory blocks. Finally, Figure 8.14 shows a variety of units used in conjunction with the typical units. The cap or paving unit is just what its name indicates — a unit to cap off the open unit at the top of the wall, or to use for paving purposes. Slumped units are the same as regular units; however, when taken out of the form, they settle and get a slight bulge at the sides. The split units are mechanically split for textural purposes. The center scored unit is used to produce a variety of face patterns when stacked in a variety of ways, as is the offset face. The screen block is used most often as a decorative fence or wall. Figure 8.15 shows the typical assembly of a reinforced concrete block wall. Note that the joints are mortar and the cavity filled with grout. The main difference in this case is that the grout is of a slightly more soupy consistency to make it easier to pour into the cavity, and the mortar somewhat stiff to maintain the joint thickness. A further description follows later in this chapter.

Figure 8.16 illustrates the visual appearance of concrete block when stacked. These examples show only the most typical patterns. A designer may find other combinations that are more pleasing for a particular structure.

8″ WIDE WALL

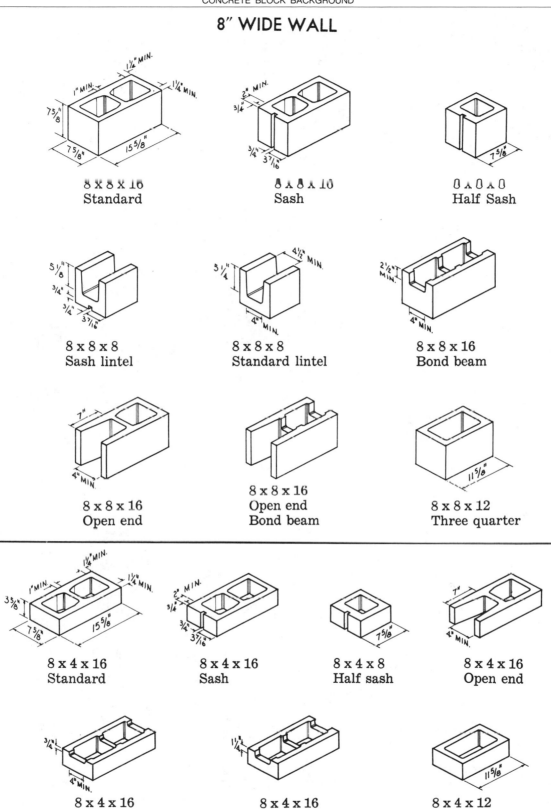

8″ HIGH UNITS

8 X 8 X 16
Standard

8 X 8 X 16
Sash

8 X 8 X 8
Half Sash

8 x 8 x 8
Sash lintel

8 x 8 x 8
Standard lintel

8 x 8 x 16
Bond beam

8 x 8 x 16
Open end

8 x 8 x 16
Open end
Bond beam

8 x 8 x 12
Three quarter

4″ HIGH UNITS

8 x 4 x 16
Standard

8 x 4 x 16
Sash

8 x 4 x 8
Half sash

8 x 4 x 16
Open end

8 x 4 x 16
Channel

8 x 4 x 16
Bond beam

8 x 4 x 12
Three quarter

Figure 8.10 8″ wide—4″ and 8″ high units. (Reproduced from the *Masonry Design Manual* with permission of the publishers, the Masonry Industry Advancement Committee.)

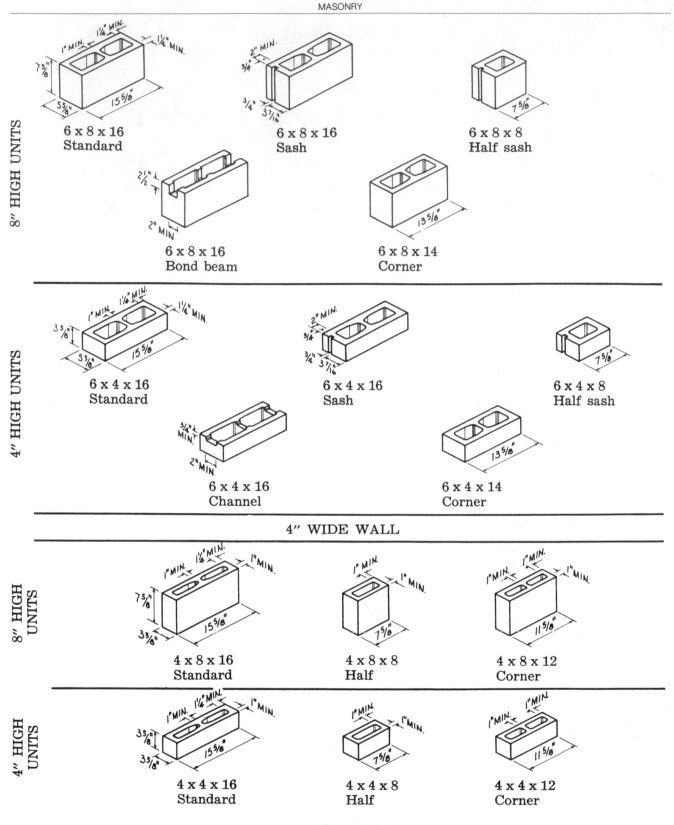

Figure 8.11 6″ wide — 4″ and 8″ high units; 4″ wide — 4″ and 8″ high units. (Reproduced from the *Masonry Design Manual* with permission of the publishers, the Masonry Industry Advancement Committee.)

12" WIDE WALL

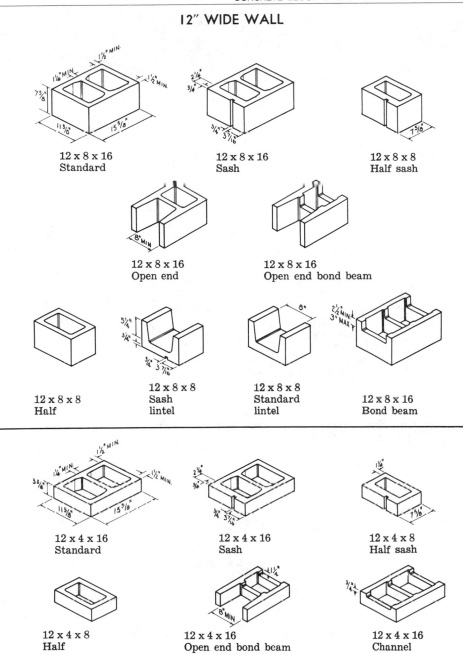

8" HIGH UNITS

12 x 8 x 16
Standard

12 x 8 x 16
Sash

12 x 8 x 8
Half sash

12 x 8 x 16
Open end

12 x 8 x 16
Open end bond beam

12 x 8 x 8
Half

12 x 8 x 8
Sash
lintel

12 x 8 x 8
Standard
lintel

12 x 8 x 16
Bond beam

4" HIGH UNITS

12 x 4 x 16
Standard

12 x 4 x 16
Sash

12 x 4 x 8
Half sash

12 x 4 x 8
Half

12 x 4 x 16
Open end bond beam

12 x 4 x 16
Channel

Figure 8.12 12″ wide wall—4″ and 8″ high units. (Reproduced from the *Masonry Design Manual* with permission of the publishers, the Masonry Industry Advancement Committee.)

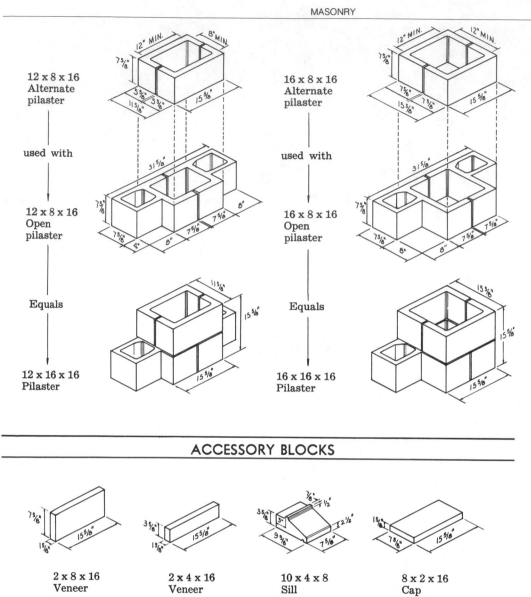

ACCESSORY BLOCKS

2 x 8 x 16
Veneer

2 x 4 x 16
Veneer

10 x 4 x 8
Sill

8 x 2 x 16
Cap

Figure 8.13 Pilaster and special blocks. (Reproduced from the *Masonry Design Manual* with permission of the publishers, the Masonry Industry Advancement Committee.)

ARCHITECTURAL FEATURE UNITS

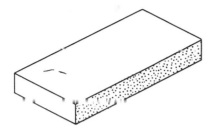

Cap or paving unit

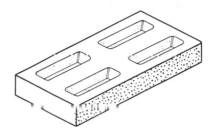

Cap or paving unit (reversed)
some units are manufactured
with indentations on underside
which acts as a mortar key.

CAP OR PAVING UNIT SIZES															
MODULAR								STANDARD							
UNIT NO.	A	B	C	UNIT NO.	A	B	C	UNIT NO.	A	B	C	UNIT NO.	A	B	C
1 M	3 5/8"	2 1/4"	7 5/8"	8 M	7 5/8"	2 1/4"	15 5/8"	1 S	3 3/4"	2 1/4"	8"	8 S	8"	2 1/4"	16 1/2"
2 M	3 5/8"	2 1/4"	15 5/8"	9 M	9 1/4"	2 1/4"	15 5/8"	2 S	3 3/4"	2 1/4"	16 1/2"	9 S	10"	2 1/4"	16 1/2"
3 M	5 5/8"	2 1/4"	7 5/8"	10 M	11 5/8"	2 1/4"	15 5/8"	3 S	5 7/8"	2 1/4"	8"	10 S	12 1/4"	2 1/4"	16 1/2"
4 M	5 5/8"	2 1/4"	15 5/8"	11 M	15 5/8"	2 1/4"	15 5/8"	4 S	5 7/8"	2 1/4"	16 1/2"	11 S	3 3/4"	1 5/8"	16 1/2"
5 M	7 5/8"	2 1/4"	7 5/8"	12 M	3 5/8"	1 5/8"	15 5/8"	5 S	8"	2 1/4"	8"	12 S	5 5/8"	1 5/8"	16 1/2"
6 M	7 5/8"	2 1/4"	9 1/4"	13 M	5 5/8"	1 5/8"	15 5/8"	6 S	8"	2 1/4"	10"	13 S	8"	1 5/8"	16 1/2"
7 M	7 5/8"	2 1/4"	11 5/8"	14 M	7 5/8"	1 5/8"	15 5/8"	7 S	8"	2 1/4"	12 1/4"	14 S	12 1/4"	1 5/8"	16 1/2"

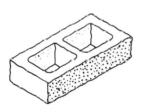

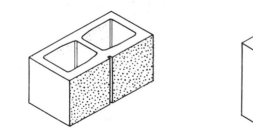

Slumped

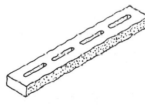

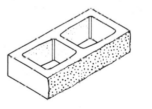

Split faced

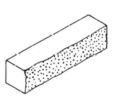

Center scored   Screen block   Offset face

Figure 8.14 Architectural feature units. (Reproduced from the *Masonry Design Manual* with permission of the publishers, the Masonry Industry Advancement Committee.)

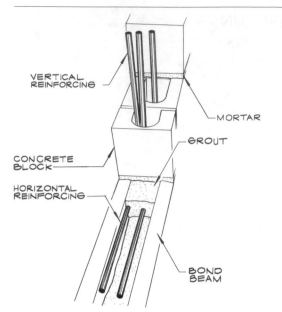

VERTICAL
REINFORCING

MORTAR

GROUT

CONCRETE
BLOCK

HORIZONTAL
REINFORCING

BOND
BEAM

Figure 8.15 Typical masonry (concrete block) wall with reinforcing.

Modular System

Figure 8.17 is included to emphasize the need for concern for the units worked with. In almost all cases, these units are modular, and to break the modular system is very costly at the construction stage. A block layout plan, Figure 8.18, shows how this modular system looks in plan format.

Figures 8.19 and 8.20 show the various units in place pictorially for a residence and a commercial structure. Remember that reinforcing is used over openings in hurricane or earthquake zones. Also, see if you can identify the various units described in Figures 8.10 through 8.14 in these pictorial assembly drawings.

When these components are presented in a drafted version they take on a slightly different appearance. Figure 8.21A shows how various offices have chosen to represent concrete block in a small scale such as $\frac{1}{4}'' = 1'\text{-}0''$. In a larger scale, the actual block is drawn and shown in Figure 8.21B.

Methods of Representing Concrete Block Units

Figure 8.22 illustrates the various methods employed to show concrete block in section. Figure 8.22A is very commonly used but can be mistaken for brick. This symbol should be used only if one building material is used. Figure 8.22B is a variation of the first, suggested by the military. Figure 8.22C is recommended by the Task Force #1, Committee on Office Practice as published in the *A.I.A. Journal.* Figure 8.22D is approved by a local chapter of the A.I.A. Fig-

ure 8.22E is suggested by the Masonry Institute, and Figure 8.22F is used by the A.I.A. Standards.

Whatever system is employed, the architect should always consider the office standard he or she is expected to follow, speed of execution, and clarity of detail as a guide for selection.

Mortar and Grout

Mortar is found between the joints of concrete block and brick, while grout is used to fill the cavity when the local code requires it. Because of their location, they are composed of basically the same material but with differing consistencies.

Mortar is made of sand and cement and is relatively stiff. High-strength mortar may achieve strength up to 2000 to 3000 pounds per square inch and more. Strength of mortar bonds is classified usually by letter—such letters as M, S, N, O, and K, with "M" being high strength and "K" being very low.

Typical mortar joints measure $\frac{3}{8}''$, but this can vary depending on the unit being used, the desired visual appearance, and the modularity of the units in conjunction with the dimension of the joints.

Grout, on the other hand, has a "soupier" consistency so that it can be poured into place. Its purpose is to bond required steel found in the cavity to the brick or concrete block, thus producing a stronger unit. Grout is found mostly in earthquake or hurricane areas where the walls require reinforcing.

Efflorescence

In dealing with both concrete block and grout, large amounts of portland cement and water are used. This often produces an undesirable condition called efflorescence, illustrated in Figure 8.23. There are two types of efflorescence. The first is produced by water-soluble salts, which are sulfates of sodium and potassium contained in the cement. The second type of efflorescence is produced by insoluble carbonates and results over a long period of time from some form of continuous water penetration, such as water pouring out of a downspout onto the brick surface.

Efflorescence, as shown in Figure 8.23, occurs mostly during high-humidity and low-temperature conditions. Warm, dry conditions also produce efflorescence but it does not show up in the face of the brick because the evaporation takes place behind the face of the masonry. Because efflorescence happens as a result of water-soluble salts in the cement, grouted brick masonry walls are apt to have this condition the most.

WALL PATTERNS

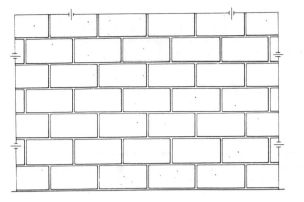

Common bond
8″ high and 16″ long units

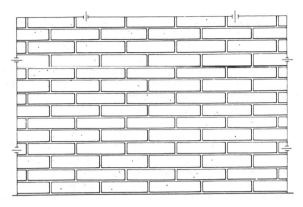

Common bond
4″ high and 16″ long units

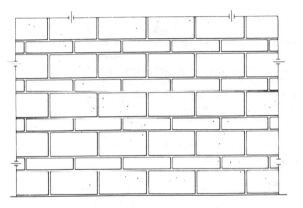

Coursed ashlar
8″ x 16″ and 4″ x 16″ units

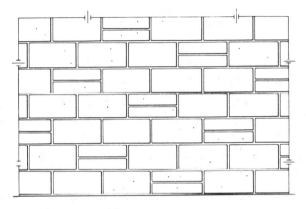

Coursed ashlar
8″ x 16″ and 4″ x 16″ units

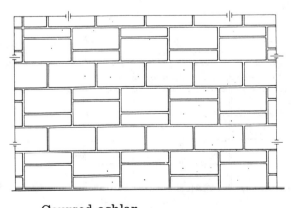

Coursed ashlar
8″ x 16″ and 4″ x 16″ units

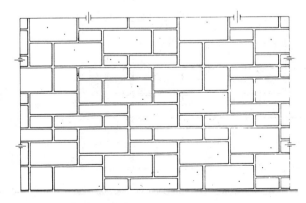

Random ashlar
8″ x 16″, 8″ x 8″, 4″ x 16″ and 4″ x 8″ units

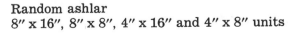

Figure 8.16 Wall patterns in concrete block. (Reproduced from the *Masonry Design Manual* with permission of the publishers, the Masonry Industry Advancement Committee.)

WALL PATTERNS

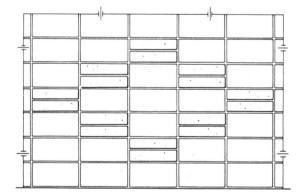

Stack bond
8″ high and 16″ long units

Stack bond
4″ high and 16″ long units

Stack bond
8″ x 16″ and 4″ x 16″ units

Stack bond
8″ x 16″ and 4″ x 16″ units

Stack bond
8″ x 8″ units

Stack bond
8″ x 16″ and 4″ x 16″ units

Figure 8.16 (continued)

8″ MODULAR LAYOUT DETAILS

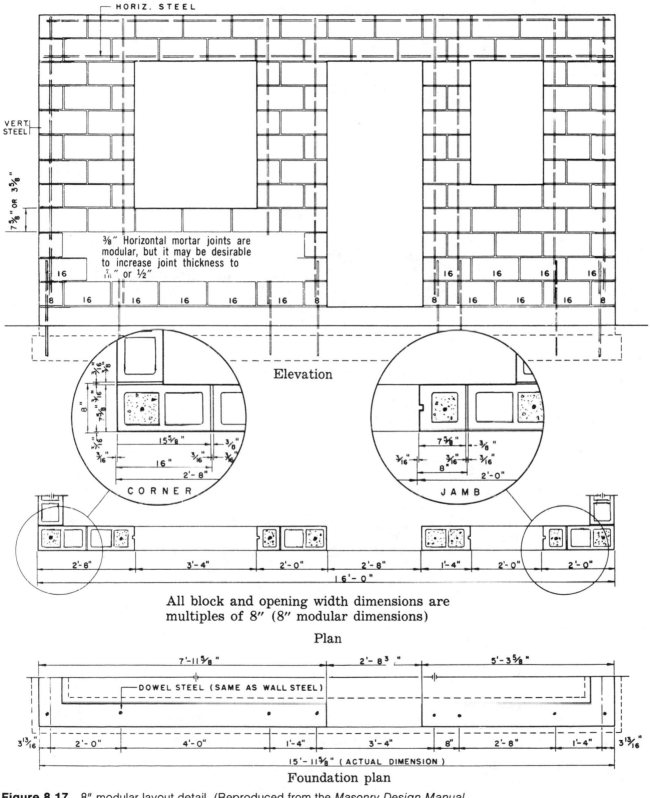

Figure 8.17 8″ modular layout detail. (Reproduced from the *Masonry Design Manual* with permission of the publishers, the Masonry Industry Advancement Committee.)

RESIDENCE — BLOCK LAYOUT PLAN

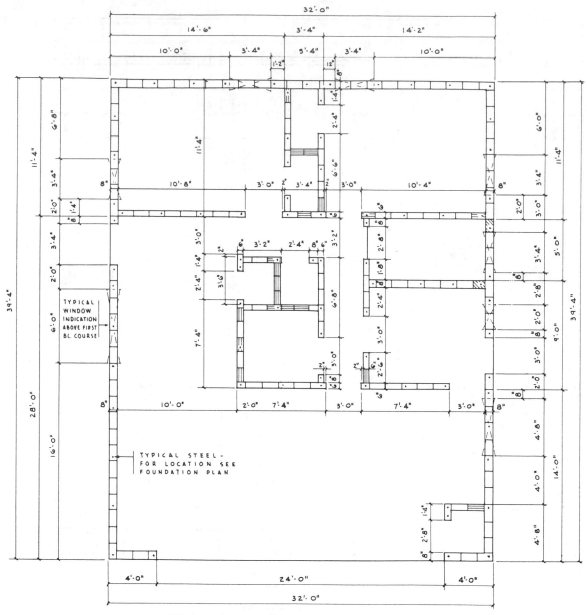

PLAN AT FIRST BLOCK COURSE

scale ⅛″ = 1′-0″

☐ 16″ long block
☐ 8″ long block
▤ 14″ long block
▨ 12″ long block

Figure 8.18 Concrete block layout plan. (Reproduced from the *Masonry Design Manual* with permission of the publishers, the Masonry Industry Advancement Committee.)

TYPICAL RESIDENTIAL CONSTRUCTION

Detail number

Page number

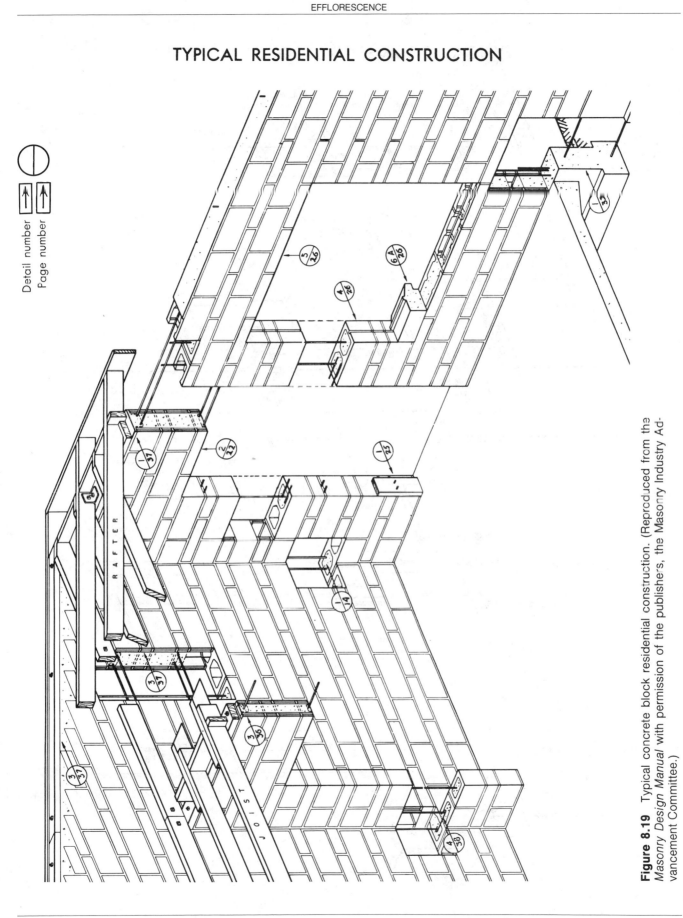

Figure 8.19 Typical concrete block residential construction. (Reproduced from the *Masonry Design Manual* with permission of the publishers, the Masonry Industry Advancement Committee.)

TYPICAL COMMERCIAL CONSTRUCTION

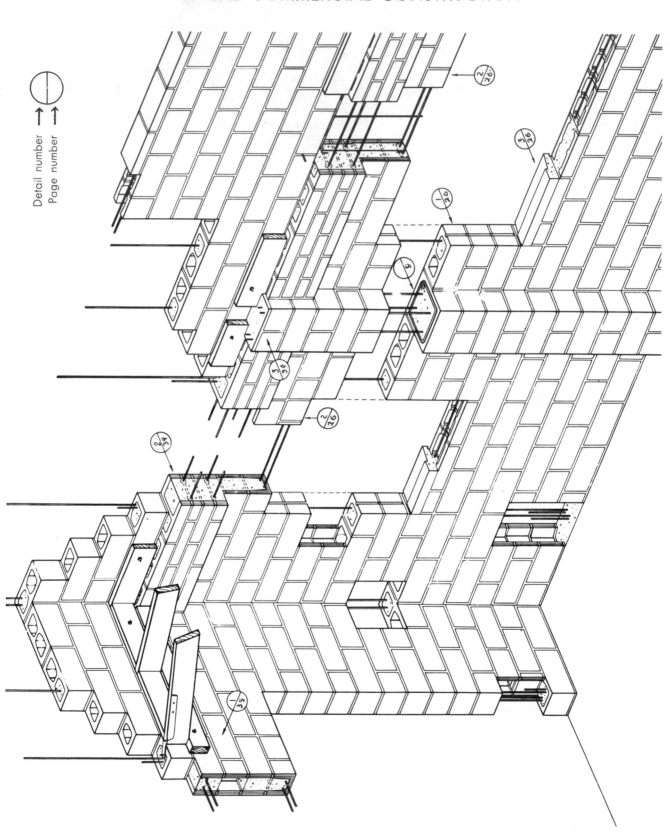

Figure 8.20 Typical concrete block commercial construction. (Reproduced from the *Masonry Design Manual* with permission of the publishers, the Masonry Industry Ad-

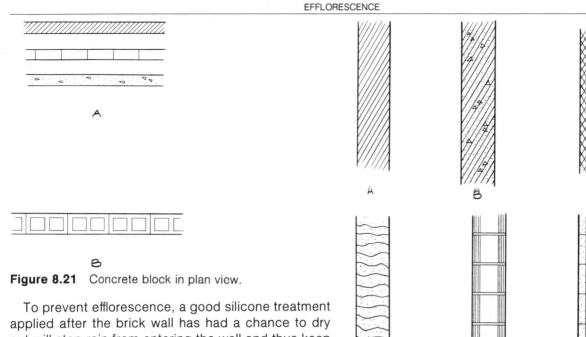

Figure 8.21 Concrete block in plan view.

To prevent efflorescence, a good silicone treatment applied after the brick wall has had a chance to dry out will stop rain from entering the wall and thus keep the salts from reaching the surface. No paint or water repellent should be applied to a grouted masonry wall until several months after the completion of the structure or following the rainy season. In the meantime, efflorescence can be cleaned off this wall by a zinc-sulfate wash or a dilute (1:20) solution of muriatic acid and water.

For specific solutions to different conditions in brick or concrete block, refer to the following chapters.

Figure 8.22 Concrete block in section.

Chapter
9 — Footing details
10 — Exterior walls

11 — Roof to wall
12 — Doors
13 — Windows
18 — Fireplaces
20 — Beam connections
21 — Miscellaneous details

Figure 8.23 Efflorescence in brick walls.

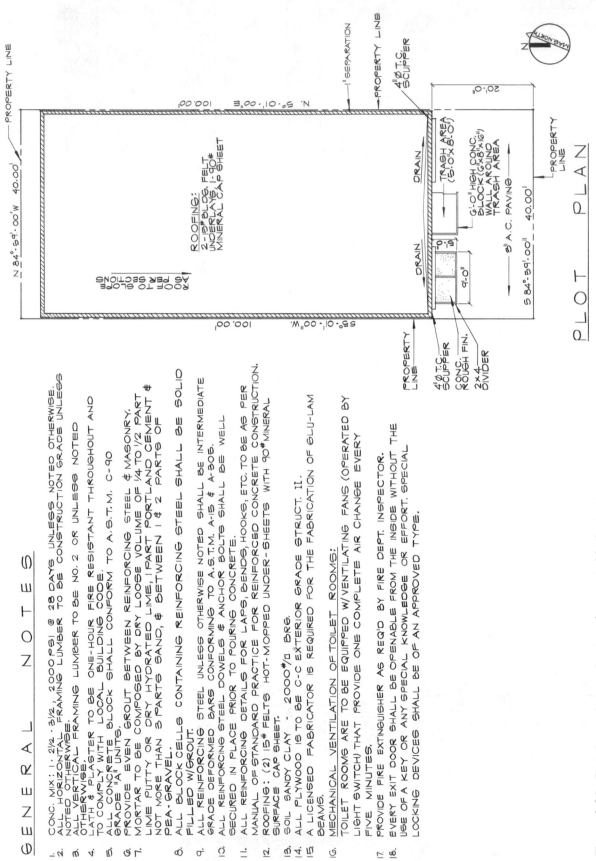

G E N E R A L   N O T E S

1. CONC. MIX: 1:2½:3½, 2000 PSI @ 28 DAYS UNLESS NOTED OTHERWISE.
2. ALL HORIZONTAL FRAMING LUMBER TO BE CONSTRUCTION GRADE UNLESS NOTED OTHERWISE.
3. ALL VERTICAL FRAMING LUMBER TO BE NO. 2 OR UNLESS NOTED OTHERWISE.
4. LATH & PLASTER TO BE ONE-HOUR FIRE RESISTANT THROUGHOUT AND TO COMPLY WITH LOCAL BUILDING CODE.
5. ALL CONCRETE BLOCK SHALL CONFORM TO A.S.T.M. C-90 GRADE "A" UNITS.
6. PROVIDE EVEN GROUT BETWEEN REINFORCING STEEL & MASONRY.
7. MORTAR TO BE COMPOSED BY DRY LOOSE VOLUME OF ¼ TO ½ PART LIME PUTTY OR DRY HYDRATED LIME, 1 PART PORTLAND CEMENT & NOT MORE THAN 3 PARTS SAND, & BETWEEN 1 & 2 PARTS OF PEA-GRAVEL.
8. ALL BLOCK CELLS CONTAINING REINFORCING STEEL SHALL BE SOLID FILLED W/GROUT.
9. ALL REINFORCING STEEL UNLESS OTHERWISE NOTED SHALL BE INTERMEDIATE GRADE DEFORMED BARS CONFORMING TO A.S.T.M. A-15 & A-305.
10. ALL REINFORCING STEEL DOWELS & ANCHOR BOLTS SHALL BE WELL SECURED IN PLACE PRIOR TO POURING CONCRETE.
11. ALL REINFORCING DETAILS FOR LAPS, BENDS, HOOKS, ETC. TO BE AS PER MANUAL OF STANDARD PRACTICE FOR REINFORCED CONCRETE CONSTRUCTION.
12. ROOFING: (2) 15# FELTS HOT-MOPPED UNDER-SHEETS WITH 90# MINERAL SURFACE CAP SHEET.
13. SOIL SANDY CLAY - 2000#/□ BRG.
14. ALL PLYWOOD IS TO BE C-C EXTERIOR GRADE STRUCT. II.
15. A LICENSED FABRICATOR IS REQUIRED FOR THE FABRICATION OF GLU-LAM BEAMS.
16. MECHANICAL VENTILATION OF TOILET ROOMS:
    TOILET ROOMS ARE TO BE EQUIPPED W/VENTILATING FANS (OPERATED BY LIGHT SWITCH) THAT PROVIDE ONE COMPLETE AIR CHANGE EVERY FIVE MINUTES.
17. PROVIDE FIRE EXTINGUISHER AS REQ'D BY FIRE DEPT. INSPECTOR.
18. EVERY EXIT DOOR SHALL BE OPENABLE FROM THE INSIDE WITHOUT THE USE OF A KEY OR ANY SPECIAL KNOWLEDGE OR EFFORT. SPECIAL LOCKING DEVICES SHALL BE OF AN APPROVED TYPE.

Figure 8.24 Plot plan and general notes of concrete block structure.

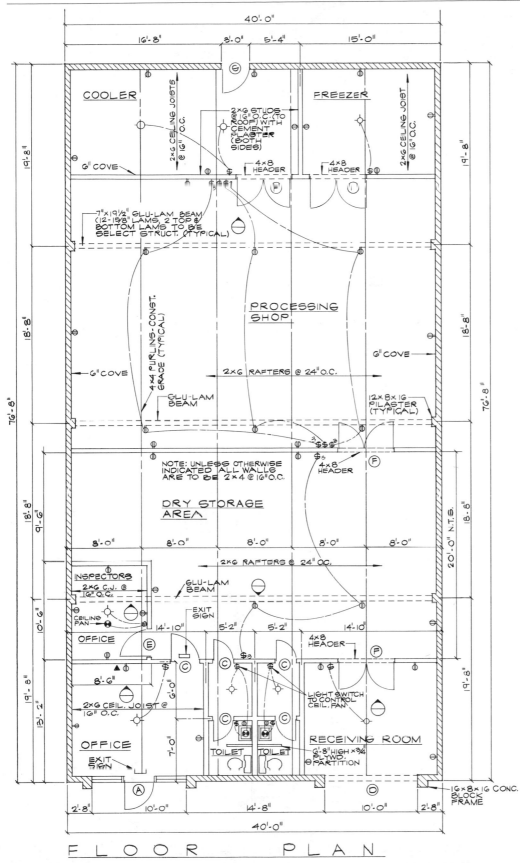

FLOOR PLAN

Figure 8.25 Floor plan of concrete block structure.

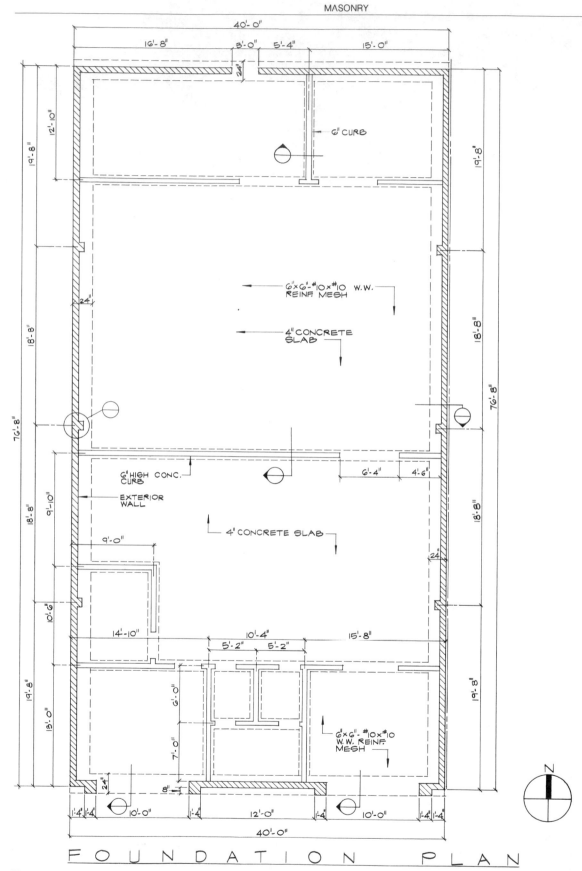

Figure 8.26 Foundation plan in concrete block structure.

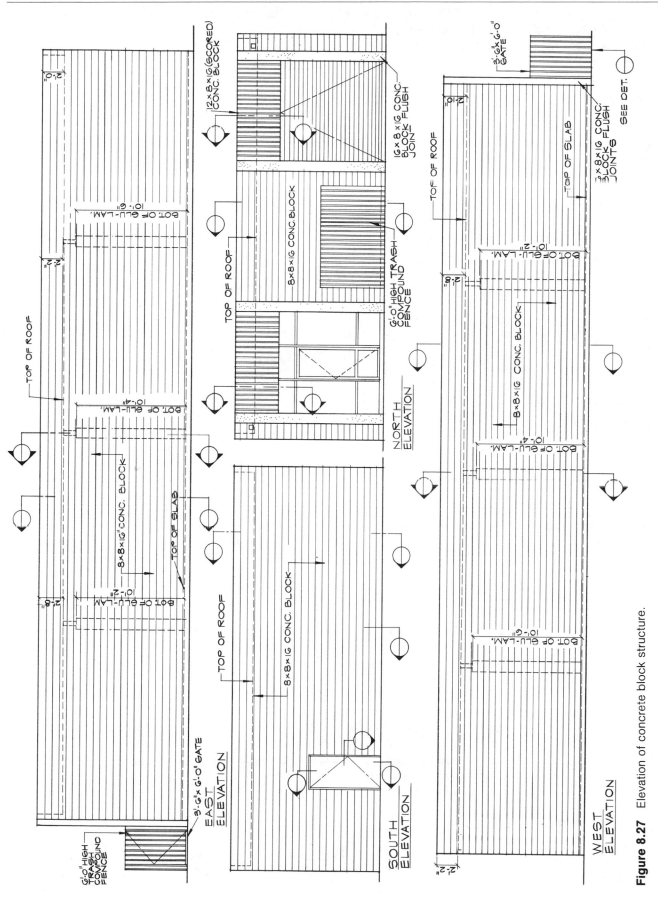

Figure 8.27 Elevation of concrete block structure.

Each of these chapters deals with a specific application of masonry and includes a detailed explanation of that respective condition.

Working Drawings in Masonry Construction

To help the architectural draftsperson understand the source of many of the details encountered in the chapters cited, an abbreviated set of working drawings has been included. They are bound in Figures 8.24 through 8.27. (See preceding four pages.) Figure 8.24 shows general notes and a plot plan. The purpose of the plot plan here is to locate the structure on the site and explain the material surrounding the building. Figure 8.25 is a floor plan; this is a horizontal section taken at eye level and is used to locate walls, windows, doors, special architectural features, often electrical outlets, and so forth. Figure 8.26 illustrates a foundation plan, also a horizontal section. Its main purpose is to explain all the concrete features of the structure at the base level. Figure 8.27 demonstrates the elevation, which is comparable to the front or side view in mechanical drafting. It shows the various conditions and materials used on the exterior face of the building.

Specific details for this working drawing set are left out because they are repeated in corresponding chapters.

In the general notes, much information omitted from the detail is covered by notes elsewhere. For example, a footing detail very seldom gives the mixture ratio or strength of the concrete since this information is covered in the general notes.

The plot plan usually does not have a direct detail reference. Only special conditions, such as fences, planters, parking bumpers, benches, and so on, would be referred to a detail from the plot plan.

The floor plan can refer to a detail indirectly or directly. It does this indirectly by locating specific windows or doors by use of symbols, such as designating a masonry wall by diagonal lines, and by providing the location of beams and headers. If there is a detail of any of these, the reader is referred to another principle drawing for detail reference. For example, from the floor plan, we can arrive at the location of a window or door. The reader can then look at the elevation to locate windows and see the detail reference bubble that in turn refers to a detail.

A direct reference method is one in which a note or reference bubble directs the reader to a specific detail.

From the floor plan you may get structural references, such as one that directs the reader to a pilaster detail; an architectural feature such as a cabinet reference; or even a means of allowing the reader to anticipate a condition, such as the note in the cooler room. In this room there is a cement plaster note, and the reader can immediately anticipate this material's appearance on the details of this wall.

The foundation plan usually refers to details directly. Reference can be made to footing details, structural conditions that involve concrete, or decorative problems that also involve concrete. A footing detail or pilaster reference is a good example of this principle.

The elevations explain parapets, doors, windows, pilasters, fences, and so on. If not directly explained on the elevation, there should be a detail drawn or a reference made.

The information contained on this set of working drawings was used for two reasons: first, to illustrate the differences and similarities found between wood frame construction and masonry construction, and, second, to show the potential sources of details and the need for them.

Regional Differences and Building Codes

When dealing with masonry, regional differences and building codes can be discussed concurrently, because one usually reflects the other. For example, earthquake and winds produce a need to consider the lateral force acting on a masonry wall. The resistance to this lateral force is accomplished by the introduction of grout and reinforcing steel into the cavity of the masonry wall. Building codes of areas dealing with wind and earthquake problems reflect this as a specific requirement.

Since the weather varies so drastically from one region to another, it also plays a major role in the design and treatment of a masonry wall. Where temperatures vary drastically, heat loss and heat gain, through masonry walls, become a significant consideration in the design. Building departments have established minimum "R" and "U" values (refer to Chapter 2) to which masonry structures must adhere.

Masonry is basically an absorbent material, so rain and snow also produce problems for the detailer, depending upon the region. This situation is compounded by a combination of various temperatures and water, because moisture freezes in the masonry units and its joints, thereby causing rapid deterioration of the system. As discussed in the chapter, this also causes efflorescence.

Therefore, before proceeding to detail, the architectural draftsperson should first check with a structural engineer, the local building department, suppliers of masonry units, or masonry institutes to discover the unique implications to the region. These would be in the form of structural problems, caused by such things as wind, earthquake, and moisture, and insulation problems, caused by weather, and even soundproofing problems, caused by the use of the structure and its setting.

Summary

The two basic types of masonry are concrete and clay, and each has its own characteristics—such as strength, absorption of water, shape, and size. The popularity of masonry is primarily due to its strength, fireproof quality, and durability. Other advantages are that it is termiteproof and certainly is not subject to corrosion. But masonry does have its weaknesses. Brick and concrete block are not good insulating materials, and additional insulation must frequently be introduced. They also are not initially waterproof. Therefore, moisture protection does become a problem.

Since both brick and concrete block are synthetic, there is a great deal of control over their color, texture, and even their strength. This allows flexibility in the final appearance of the structure.

Both come in modular sizes so the architectural draftsperson must become familiar with their modular limits and detail to them. Odd or nonmodular dimensions can be costly since they require custom (nonstock) units or cutting of the units on the job.

Another major concern for the detailer involves the various shapes available, their proper use and position, and the names assigned to each. Such knowledge is essential for the architectural draftsperson to converse fluently about masonry construction. Review very carefully the name of the position of each unit, the various stacking methods, and how the joints are to be finished.

9

FOOTING DETAILS

Preview   Chapter 9 introduces the subject of concrete footings and the importance that they have in architecture.

This chapter is basically divided into four sections. The first deals with the component parts of a footing and their implications. The second describes wood floors and their relationship to concrete footings. The third deals with slab (concrete) floors. The last section discusses masonry walls and their relationship to wood and concrete slab footings.

Each section strives to explain the parts and how they will look in detail form. A variety of conditions are explained to provide an opportunity to solve a variety of problems.

After reading this chapter, the architectural draftsperson will:

1. Understand how concrete is poured and what its limitations are.
2. Be familiar with the vocabulary as it relates to footings.
3. Be able to perform simple arithmetical tasks in relationship to the footing bearing surface.
4. Comprehend the relationship that exists between the grade (the soil) and the footing.
5. Be aware of the various components, such as membranes, anchor bolts, reinforcing, and so forth, and their interrelationship.
6. Be able to draft various types of footing details.
7. Understand how to strengthen concrete by the introduction of reinforcing.
8. Be able to deal with hillside lots and changes of level.
9. Be prepared to handle footings of various types in conjunction with masonry walls.

A footing is that part of a structure that distributes the weight of the structure to the ground or soil. Its configuration or shape resembles a man's foot, wider where it comes in contact with the ground so that the weight can be more equitably distributed. A footing functions in much the same manner as a surfboard that spreads a person's weight over a larger area or like wide tires on a car that allow one to drive over soft soil by distributing the weight over a larger area.

The footing is a vital base in establishing a stable structure. Therefore, certain considerations must be provided for in the construction of a stable footing: type of soil on which the footing is placed, amount of weight the soil can support (bearing capacity), weight of structure to be placed upon the footing (dead load), and alterative characteristics of the ground by nature (weather, earthquakes, or termites).

After analyzing the foregoing considerations, the footing is then made to certain specifications and detailed by the architectural draftsperson. The design and sizing of the footing are critical, because if the house settles at a different rate from one side to the other or moves too drastically due to temperature change, it causes cracks in the plaster or on the inside of the structure.

Soil

The type of soil has much to do with the final size and possibly the shape of the footing. While certain soils cannot resist greater amounts of weight, others can, and this is usually calculated in pounds per square foot (indicated #/□′). For example, hard clay can accept more weight (referred to as the bearing capacity of soil) than can sandy clay. Compact coarse sand can accept greater weight than can adobe but less weight than can sandy clay. See Figure 9.1 for sample ratings.

When determining the particular type of soil on a piece of property, it is best to have a soil engineer investigate and supply you with geological data. For example, if the soil in question was soft clay with a bearing capacity of 1000 lb per square foot (see Figure 9.1) and the weight of the structure was 800 lb per lineal foot excluding the footing along the exterior foundation wall of a building (see Figure 9.2), then the task becomes that of distributing the weight of the building over the soil so as not to exceed 1000 lb per square foot.

If we used a concrete configuration similar to Figure 9.2 with a 12 inch wide and 6 inch high footing and with a 6 inch wide foundation wall approximately 12 inches high, this would equal approximately 1 cubic foot of concrete per lineal foot of foundation. Con-

ROCK	5000 or 20 percent of ultimate crushing value
SAND	
Coarse compact	1500
Fine compact	1000
Fine loose	500
CLAY	
Hard	3000
Sandy	2000
Soft	1000
ADOBE	1000
SILT	
Dry	500

ᵃ Per square foot.

Figure 9.1 Bearing pressure of soil. (Reproduced from *Architectural Drrawing and Planning* with permission of the publisher, the McGraw-Hill Book Company.)

crete weighs 150 lb per cubic foot. This weight must be added to the 800 lb per lineal foot of building (design load). The total of this design load and the concrete footing weight gives us the total load. The total load is 800 lb plus 150 lb, which equals 950 lb per lineal foot.

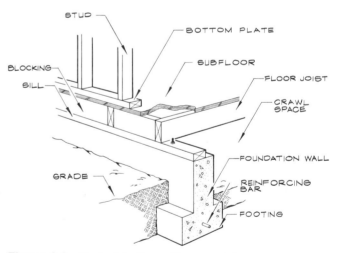

Figure 9.2 Typical footing with a wood floor.

Thus, if we take a square foot section of the footing as shown in Figure 9.3, we find that the ground is capable of holding up 1000 #/□′ while the weight is 950 #/□′, thus producing a safe situation. If the total load was greater than the 1000 #/□′, the width of the footing would have to be increased to accommodate it.

Another factor to consider about soil is its characteristic of expansion; this is caused by a variety of factors. Earthquakes shift the earth in different directions, as do moisture and any drastic temperature change.

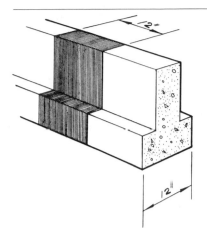

Figure 9.3 One-foot section of a footing.

In those areas of our country where the temperature falls below freezing, a level called the frost line or frost depth must be considered. See Figure 9.4. The figures given on the map are in inches and are for general use only. Frost lines should be checked because they are established by local codes.

The National Code requires that a footing be placed at a minimum of 1'-0" below the frost line. The ground does not freeze below the level that causes expansion.

Where swelling of the soil (called expansive soil by soil engineers) is a problem, reinforcing bars or a bed of sand are introduced to the footing. (For size of the reinforcing bar, see Chapter 7.)

The sand under the footing also works as a cushion against expanding soil. See Figure 9.5. Since this load is a uniform load — as opposed to a concentrated or point load — the objective of the footing is also to distribute this load as uniformly as possible to the grade.

Grade

The term "grade" indicates the level of the soil around the structure. In discussing grade, the following terms are encountered: (1) natural grade, (2) existing grade, (3) finished grade, (4) fill, (5) compacted fill, (6) uncompacted fill, (7) cut, and (8) backfill. See Figure 9.6 for the typical location of each of these terms.

Natural grade refers to undisturbed soil. It assumes that no soil has been added. Most building departments use this as a point of reference below which you take your footing.

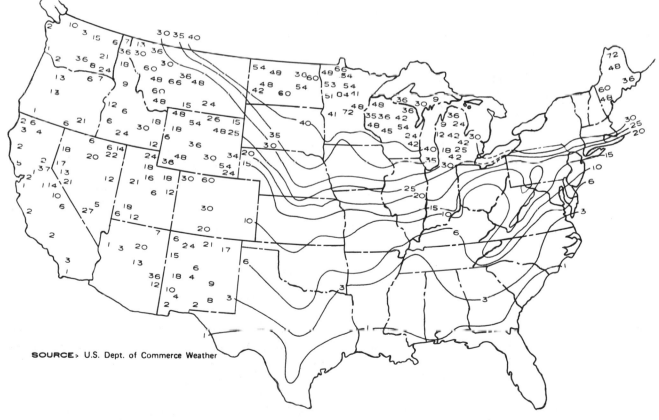

SOURCE: U.S. Dept. of Commerce Weather

AVERAGE DEPTH OF FROST PENETRATION – H INCHES

Figure 9.4 Frost depths. (Reproduced from *Architectural Graphic Standards* with permission from John Wiley & Sons, Inc.)

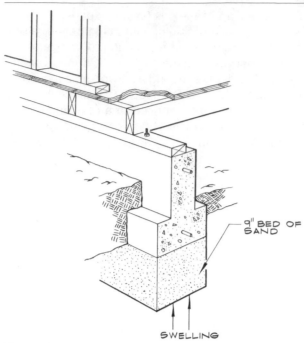

Figure 9.5 Sand bed for expansive soil.

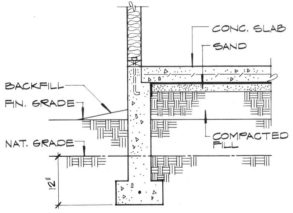

Figure 9.6 Grade terms.

it has been added. Compacted fill, which is the only type of fill allowed in many parts of the country, is soil that is brought to the site and added very systematically to ensure proper weight-bearing capacity. It is usually wet down and mechanically compacted. This process normally achieves 90 percent compaction when tested.

Cut refers to the removal of soil from a particular level; backfill refers to the return of soil above and beyond the original soil. It is often found around foundations to keep water from undermining the footing. (See Figure 9.12, Step #4, for an example.)

Again, a reminder that when a soils expert is called in to determine the bearing capacity of the soil, the terms such as natural grade can just be called grade.

Expansion of Concrete

If large amounts of concrete are used, such as the long concrete slab of a concrete driveway, its reaction to changes in temperature must be considered. Concrete will expand and contract with great variations in temperature. Thus expansion joints are introduced to prevent the slab of concrete from buckling. See Figure 9.7.

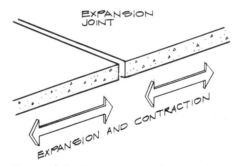

Figure 9.7 Expansion and contraction.

Reinforcing

Reinforcing refers to the process of including additional material to strengthen the concrete. In footings, reinforcing is the addition of steel rods to the poured concrete. These rods are called reinforcing rods or rebars and their values, sizes, and descriptions are covered in Chapter 7.

The reinforcing bars at the top of the footing combat breakage at that point and the rebar at the bottom fights against breakage there. Both breakage situations may be caused by expansive soil as shown in Figure 9.8.

Existing grade refers to the grade as it is at the time construction begins or when the property was purchased. It may be natural grade in that no soil was added to it, or the natural grade may be below it.

Finished grade refers to the level of the soil when the structure is finished. As cited in the example, it may be the same as the natural grade and/or may be higher or lower than the existing grade depending on the grading required for the structure.

The term ''fill'' must be broken down into compacted and uncompacted fill. Uncompacted fill refers to soil being brought upon the site and used to raise the level of the grade with no consideration as to how

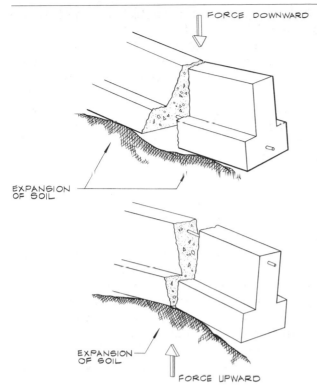

FORCE DOWNWARD

EXPANSION OF SOIL

EXPANSION OF SOIL

FORCE UPWARD

Figure 9.8 Location of reinforcing.

Slab Reinforcing

In much the same manner that the footing needs reinforcing, the concrete slab floor also needs some type of reinforcing to prevent it from cracking.

One method is to run a series of reinforcing bars each way. This is called matting. Size and spacing are determined by an engineer based on the soil report.

Another way of reinforcing, when the stability of the soil is not so much in question, is to use what is called mesh. See Figure 9.9 and Chapter 7. Mesh is usually made of No. 10 wire and is spaced 6 inches apart

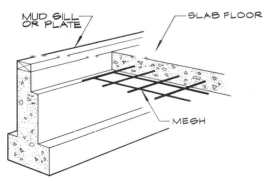

MUD SILL OR PLATE

SLAB FLOOR

MESH

Figure 9.9 Use of mesh in slab.

each way. The intersections of these wires are electrically welded and the mesh comes in rolls already spaced and welded.

It is laid on the ground and concrete is poured over it. The workers then grab the mesh and pull it upward until it is sitting on the top of the poured concrete. A second layer of concrete is immediately poured, thus bringing the concrete to its desired thickness with the mesh in the center. A photograph of mesh installation is shown in Figure 9.10.

Figure 9.10 Mesh installation.

Another method is to lay the mesh on top of the large pieces of gravel and pour the concrete over it. This ensures that the mesh is not at the very bottom of the concrete.

Forms

Poured concrete is the most popular material used in foundations because of its ability to be shaped into almost any configuration. However, it should be noted

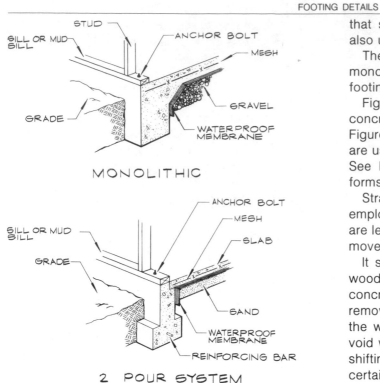

MONOLITHIC

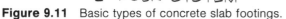

2 POUR SYSTEM

Figure 9.11 Basic types of concrete slab footings.

that stone, brick, and concrete block (precast) are also used.

There are basically two types of slab footings: monolithic, which is the one-pour system or one solid footing, and the multipour system. See Figure 9.11.

Figure 9.12 shows the basic steps of pouring a concrete footing. When a trench is dug, as shown in Figure 9.13, and the concrete poured, wood forms are usually used to control and contain the concrete. See Figure 9.14 for the actual appearance of the forms.

Straps, as shown in Figure 9.12, Step #2, are often employed to keep the form boards equally apart and are left in the concrete footing after the forms are removed.

It should be remembered by the detailer that the wood used for form boards cannot be left under the concrete. All wood in contact with the soil must be removed because of subterranean termites. Leaving the wood might result in its rotting, thus causing a void where the wood originally was and possibly the shifting of the concrete. See Figure 9.15. Therefore, certain shapes cannot be made because the form boards cannot be removed.

Figure 9.12 Basic steps in pouring a concrete footing.

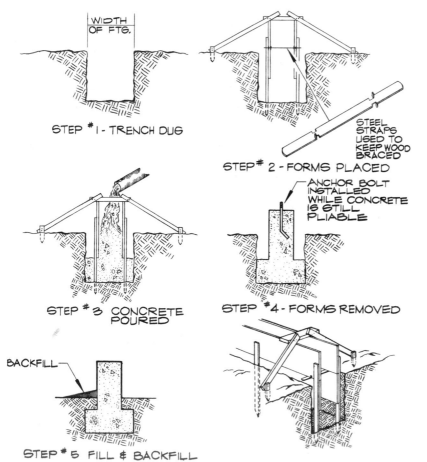

Figure 9.13 Digging the trench.

Figure 9.14 Forms.

Note the buildup of soil on the outside, called back-fill (Figure 9.12, Step #5). This is to ensure that rain washes away from the perimeter of the house and does not undermine the footing.

Still another way of keeping water away from the bearing surface (bottom of the footing) is the use of drain tiles on the footing or beside it. See Figure 9.16. The drain tiles sit on a gravel bed (about 2 inches) and are placed about $\frac{1}{4}$ inch apart with 4"–6" of gravel above it. The $\frac{1}{4}$ inch space between one drain tile and another is covered with building felt that is a building paper impregnated with an oil. The water

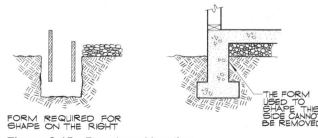

FORM REQUIRED FOR SHAPE ON THE RIGHT

THE FORM USED TO SHAPE THIS SIDE CANNOT BE REMOVED

Figure 9.15 Form board location.

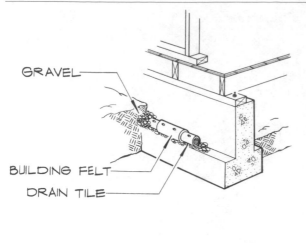

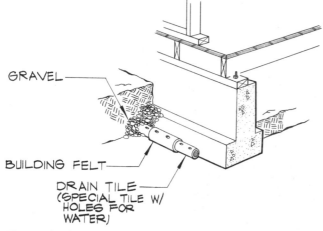

Figure 9.16 Use of drain tiles.

trapped by this drain tile is carried to a storm drain (storm sewer) or to a dry well. If there is a location on the building site where water accumulates, a french drain similar to that shown in Figure 9.17 can be used. Strategically located, this type of drain will keep the rainwater from accumulating around the structure and will prevent the water from undermining the foundation.

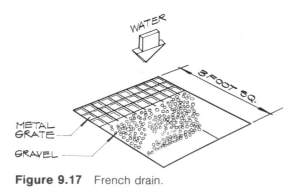

Figure 9.17 French drain.

Waterproofing Foundation

It is often desirable to waterproof the foundation wall. This applies to basements, planters on the sides of homes, or anywhere the floor level of the room inside is lower than the grade on the outside. Bituminous material applied to the foundation wall waterproofs it as well as building felt or polyethylene film. See Figure 9.18.

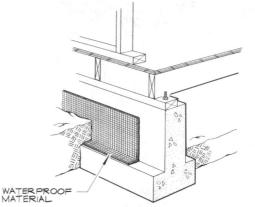

Figure 9.18 Waterproofing foundation wall.

Slab Treatment

Where a slab of concrete is used for a floor, a variety of combinations are employed to combat moisture or to strengthen the concrete. When it comes to combating moisture, the architect should remember that concrete is much like a sponge and absorbs moisture rapidly (try spilling a cup of water on a concrete surface and watch it become absorbed by the concrete). If concrete absorbs any moisture from the soil, it will work its way between the concrete slab and the finished floor.

Material such as vinyl tile or a hardwood floor either warps, as in the case of wood, or breaks the adhesive bond, as in the case of vinyl tile. To prevent this, a moisture barrier can be introduced directly under the slab. A barrier such as polyethylene film has gained in popularity in recent years because of its strength, cost, and water-resistant quality.

When the membrane is used in conjunction with sand or crushed gravel, it is placed between the gravel or sand and the slab. See Figure 9.11 for such a slab.

If strength of the slab is the major consideration, and moisture on the top surface of the slab is not a problem, sand or gravel is placed under the slab without the membrane.

Sand or fine, well-compacted gravel is used rather than large gravel, because the intent is initially to remove the moisture but not the cement. If large gravel was used, the paste (cement) is drawn into the cavity between the gravel, and the concrete loses its strength. In either case — sand or crushed gravel — a 2 to 4 inch amount is considered a minimum.

Second, the intent is to hold some of the water, so sand is a better material than crushed gravel. As the concrete is poured over the sand bed, the moisture is absorbed by the sand slowly and allows the concrete to cure (harden). As the concrete dries, it pulls the moisture from the sand back into the slab and slows the curing process. This slower curing process strengthens the concrete. Had a membrane been used, this stronger concrete would not have been possible.

Dowels

Dowels resemble reinforcing bars in appearance; their main difference is in function. The dowel has as its primary function the holding together of two different pours of concrete: separate pours such as a house and a porch, the house and the garage, or two slabs that must be tied together.

Doweling is a process whereby short rods are put into the first slab when it is poured and still pliable at the point where the connection is to be made and half of these rods are left exposed. See Figure 9.19. The second portion is poured right over these rods, thus bonding the two together.

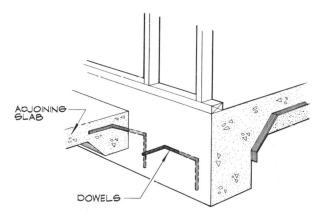

ADJOINING SLAB

DOWELS

Figure 9.19 Use of dowel to hold slab to structure.

Termite Protection

There are basically three ways to protect a structure from termites. While none of these procedures is 100 percent termiteproof, each has certain features that discourage subterranean termites.

The first is a method of using wood treated with a termite-resistant chemical; this process is called pressure treated and is especially needed where wood comes in contact with concrete. It is called out on the detail as 2×4 D.F.P.T. (Douglas Fir pressure treated).

The second method of prevention is to treat the soil around the structure with a termite-repellent chemical. This is especially important under concrete slabs where the slightest crack or space entices subterranean termites to create a tunnel and consume the finished wood floor from the underside. While it is possible to fumigate the ground under a wood floor, this is not feasible with a slab floor. If termites are found under the slab, holes must be drilled into the slab in close intervals and gas forced through them to kill the termites.

Finally, a termite shield made of metal must be placed between the wood and concrete. Termites build mud tunnels up the side of the foundation wall to the wood unless a shield can prevent them. See Figure 9.20. All foundations built of hollow concrete blocks should be filled to discourage mud tunnels from appearing, hidden from view, on the inside.

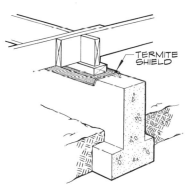

TERMITE SHIELD

Figure 9.20 Placement of termite shield.

Subterranean termites thrive on the combination of wood and moisture, so any preventative measure to negate moisture aids in avoiding termites. Hence, all states require that wood does not come in contact with soil even if it is treated. A recommended dimension is 6 or more inches from wood to the nearest soil. For a detailed description of treatment of wood, see Chapter 6.

Anchor Bolt

The transition of one material to another always causes a problem of bonding, as with the transition from footing (concrete) to the frame of the structure (wood). A simple introduction of a third material solves this problem. The item used is a bolt and nut system.

This special bolt is called an anchor bolt. It is a long steel rod threaded on one end and bent on the other. While the footing concrete is still soft, these bolts are placed into the concrete bent side down. Because of the bend in the anchor bolt, it cannot be withdrawn after the concrete has hardened.

The first piece of wood to come in contact with the concrete has a series of holes drilled into it, spaced the same as the anchor bolt and placed over it. A washer and a nut are used to attach the wood firmly to the footing. See Figure 9.21. On the detail, the anchor bolt is represented by a center line or the actual shape of the bolt itself is drawn. See Figure 9.22 for examples of an anchor bolt in drafted form.

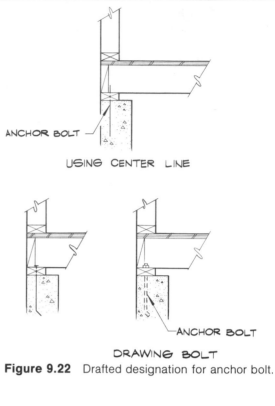

USING CENTER LINE

ANCHOR BOLT

DRAWING BOLT

Figure 9.22 Drafted designation for anchor bolt.

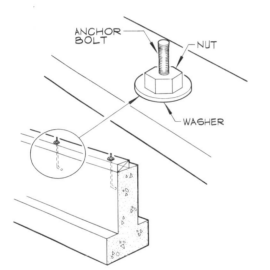

Figure 9.21 Anchor bolt.

In some cases, the bolts are shot through the wood into the concrete by means of a low-caliber gun. These are called shot-ins (powder actuated) and are usually limited to interior walls. The anchor bolt resembles a nail, and the washer (with no hole in it) is used to prevent the nail type anchoring device from totally going through the wood. See Figure 9.23. Both standard anchor bolt and shot-in are shown in Figure 9.24 for a visual comparison.

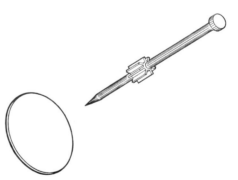

Figure 9.23 Powder-actuated bolt.

Insulation

Because of the great range in temperature in some regions of our country, it may become highly desirable to insulate the footing. Figure 9.25 shows an example of a footing with 1 inch of rigid insulation between the slab and footing to prevent excess cold

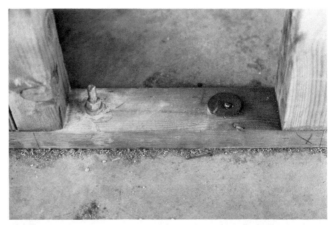

Figure 9.24 Regular anchor bolt and powder-actuated bolt.

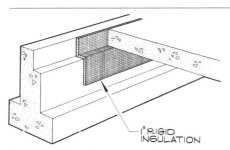

Figure 9.25 Footing insulation.

from reaching the slab and ultimately the inside of the house. Because of our concern for preserving energy and fuel, the rigid insulation is a good investment for those areas with extremely cold weather. See Figure 9.4.

Stepped Footing

If all buildings were built on flat lots, the study of foundations would be easy. The configuration or the shape of the footing would remain the same throughout the perimeter of the structure if such were the case. However, this is usually not the situation.

If, for example, the site you were dealing with had a severe slope to it, you could not use the same shape footing throughout the structure because of the excessive increase in the usage of concrete due to the fluctuation of the foundation wall height. To combat this, we use what is called a stepped footing. See Figure 9.26.

This system allows the base of the footing to rise or fall as the terrain requires yet maintains a constant

depth below the grade. One should not drastically change directions, however. See the suggested minimum and maximum on Figure 9.26 for heights and lengths of stepped footings.

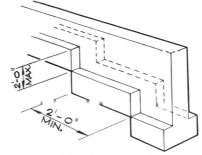

Figure 9.26 Stepped footing.

Cripples

Even with a stepped footing, it is impossible to accommodate a hillside lot, especially with concrete. The shaded area shown in Figure 9.27 illustrates the difficulty encountered. This area can be built with wood.

Figure 9.27 Use of cripples on stepped footing.

Figure 9.28 Stepped footing with cripples above.

This situation is treated much like a two-story structure with the shaded area being the wall of the first story. This area is built of vertical wood members similar to studs in a wall and called cripples. See Figures 9.28 on the previous page, and 9.29 for an example of this situation. They are usually 2 × 4 members and are spaced at 16″ o.c. (on center).

It should also be noted that minimum heights for cripple walls are established by local codes. If the cripples are too short, it becomes impossible to brace to prevent lateral movement of the structure.

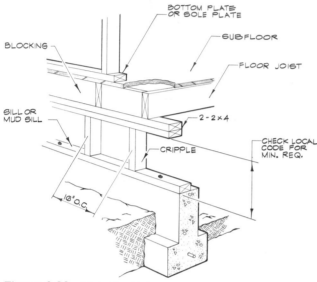

Figure 9.29 Use of cripple.

Footing with Wood Floor

Exterior Bearing Footing

Exterior bearing footing refers to any footing found on the outside of the structure that carries a load other than itself. The load may be from the roof structure or the ceiling. The most typical shape found is an upside down T-shaped footing, as shown in Figures 9.2 and 9.30.

The critical items to remember, other than calling out the sizes of the various members, include giving the minimum depth to which the footing goes below the grade (level of the earth), the width of the bearing surface (bottom of the footing), the distance between grade and any wood, and the crawl space under the floor joist.

Since everything is in relationship to the grade, this should be drawn first as shown in Figure 9.31 and the footing arranged around it. The distance that the foundation wall extends above grade line is determined by how close the local building code allows

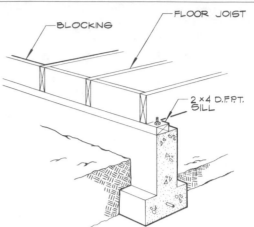

Figure 9.30 Typical exterior bearing footing with a wood floor.

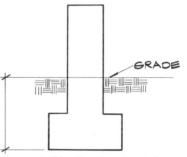

Figure 9.31 Footing depth into earth.

wood to be to the grade. The dimension is usually 6 to 8 inches on the outside.

An example of how soil can be removed from the interior side of the foundation and give the illusion of a lower building is illustrated in Figure 9.32. The crawl area under the house is maintained by using this method, but the removal of soil allows the floor joist to be at a lower level to the outside grade. It is for this

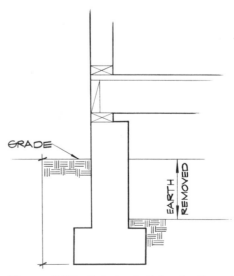

Figure 9.32 Exterior bearing footing with earth removed on inside of footing.

reason that the major dimension of grade to bottom of footing is placed on the outside since the inside can vary.

The next step in drawing a footing detail is to place the related material in position. The first member to come into contact with the concrete is called a sill, often also called mud sill and in some cases a plate. (Sill seems to be the most acceptable term.) The sill is attached to the foundation wall by means of an anchor bolt. Because the sill is the first piece of wood to come in contact with concrete, it is the most vulnerable to termites, and, as such, it should be pressure treated.

The size of the sill depends upon the member directly above it called the floor joist. If the floor joist extends to the edge of the sill, a 2 × 4 is sufficient as in Figure 9.30. However, if it does not, as in Figure 9.33, the sill should be larger, say, 2 × 6. The smaller the floor joist, the weaker it is, but at the same time it acts to reduce the height of the structure. To keep the floor joist from overturning, blocking or header joists are used. See Figures 9.30 and 9.33.

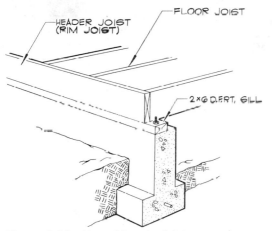

Figure 9.33 Use of header joist.

Directly above the floor joist is the subfloor. The subfloor can be made of 1 × 6 wood, preferably diagonally laid at a 45° angle to the floor joist or plywood for structural stability. The spacing of the floor joist not only depends on the span and the size of the floor joist but also on the type of subfloor used.

The first horizontal member of the wall is called a bottom plate or sole plate and is usually the same size as that used in the wall itself. Directly above the bottom plate (in some instances called sill), you will find the vertical members called studs or studding. These are normally 2 × 4 for one- and two-story structures and are spaced 16″ o.c. to accommodate finished material that is applied to them.

If it is desirable to keep the exterior finishing material or structural material, such as plywood, flush with the face of the concrete foundation wall, the sill, floor joist, and wall can be moved back slightly. See Figure 9.34. A typical detail drafted by an architect is illustrated in Figure 9.35.

Footing details are normally drawn at $\frac{3}{4}″ = 1′\text{-}0″$ or $1″ = 1′\text{-}0″$.

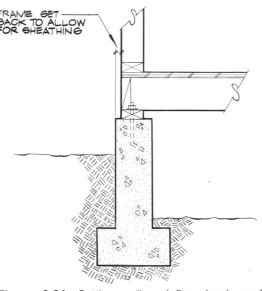

Figure 9.34 Setting wall and floor back on footing for sheathing.

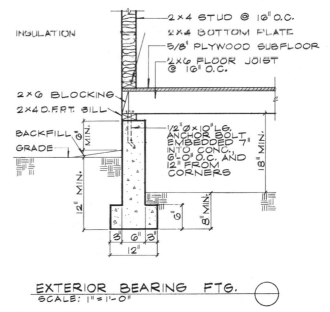

Figure 9.35 Drafted detail of typical exterior bearing footing.

Pier and Girder

In small wood structures, it is not economical to attempt to span great distances with floor joists. Large spans just increase the size of the floor joist, which in turn increases the height of the structure.

To reduce the span of a floor joist, an intermediate support is introduced. This member, called a girder, runs perpendicular to the floor joists. It is, in turn, supported by a series of wood posts that rest on a pad of concrete called piers. Since most local codes require an 18″ crawl space between the floor joist and the grade on the inside of the structure and 12″ between the grade and any member supporting the floor joist, a 4 × 6 is a very popular size for girders. A 4 × 4 piece of wood can be used, but since it is square, it does not make absolute use of the strength of horizontal members. Rectangles are much stronger. See Figure 9.36.

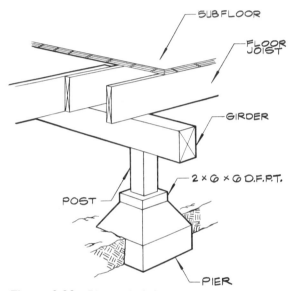

Figure 9.36 Pier and girder.

The top truncated portion of a pier is usually precast in advance. Prior to the concrete hardening, a piece of 2 × 6 × 6 wood, with nails driven in it at an angle from the underside, is placed on the truncated pyramid. At the building site a square hole of 12 × 12 or 16 × 16 is dug 6 to 8 inches deep. Concrete is poured into this square hole and the truncated form placed on top of it to form the pier. See Figure 9.37.

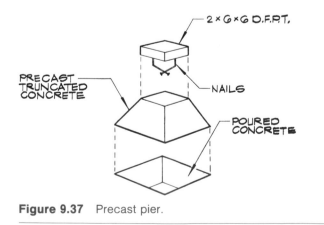

Figure 9.37 Precast pier.

The 2 × 6 × 6 allows for the 4 × 4 post usually placed above it to be toe nailed (nailed at an angle) into the pier.

Above the post is the girder and above that the normal sequence for a wood floor: floor joist, subfloor, bottom plate, and studs. Figure 9.38 shows this area from the underside of the floor. Note that on Figure 9.39, the pier and girder is drawn with the floor joist coming toward you and that on Figure 9.40, it is drawn with the girder coming toward you. Both are acceptable, but Figure 9.40 is more often drawn.

An additional lateral brace in Figure 9.39 that is not in Figure 9.40 should be noted. This brace is introduced when the post begins to exceed 2½ to 3 feet in height and is used to stabilize the total system.

Figure 9.38 Pier and girder.

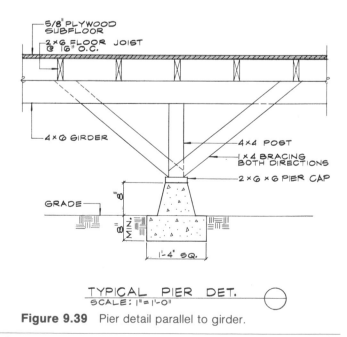

Figure 9.39 Pier detail parallel to girder.

130

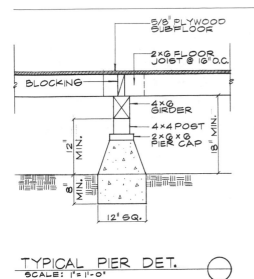

TYPICAL PIER DET.
SCALE: 1" = 1'-0"

Figure 9.40 Pier detail perpendicular to girder.

Interior Bearing Footing

The function of an interior bearing footing is the same as the exterior bearing footing, except that it is found on the interior of a structure. Its purpose is twofold: first, to bring cohesion to a total foundation system of an irregular shape (see Figure 9.41); second, to be used under walls that are interior load bearing walls.

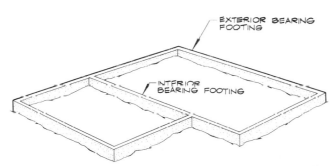

Figure 9.41 Interior and exterior foundation.

Whichever the case may be, it is possible to have a structure with exterior bearing footings and piers and girders only, void of any interior bearing footings. As far as appearance is concerned, the interior bearing footing looks the same as an exterior bearing footing, except that the sill is in the center of the foundation wall. See Figure 9.42.

When used with an exterior bearing footing, as shown on Figure 9.34 the footing should go the full depth of the exterior bearing footing. When used with one similar to Figure 9.32, where the soil on the inside has been removed, the interior bearing footing need

go only as deep as the exterior footing is on the inside. This creates absolute cohesion in the foundation system as one intersects another.

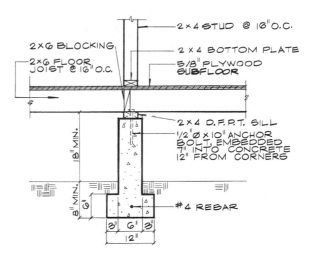

INTERIOR BEARING FOOTING
SCALE: 1" = 1'-0"

Figure 9.42 Drafted detail of interior bearing footing with wood floor.

Planking

It is possible to void the floor joist completely and go to a system where the girders are placed closer together, say, 5 or 6 feet apart, and use a heavier subfloor material that is capable of spanning the 5 or 6 feet. The suggested subfloor material used is a 2 × 6 tongue and groove material that is illustrated in Figure 9.43.

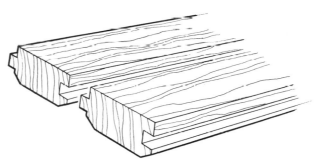

Figure 9.43 Tongue and groove planks.

Since we have no floor joist, the minimum crawl area is measured 18 inches from the grade to the underside of the subfloor and 12 inches from grade to the bottom of the girder. See Figure 9.44. Notice on this detail that the minimum is 12 inches between the grade and the bottom of the girder. While this is a minimum code requirement, it is not practical or good practice because it is almost impossible to crawl between a 12-inch space for maintenance or repair.

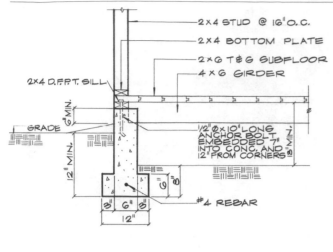

EXTERIOR BEARING FTG.
SCALE: 1"=1'-0"

Figure 9.44 Drafted detail of a wood floor system without floor joist.

Change in Level

It is often desirable to change the floor level in a structure — to accommodate a sloping site or for aesthetic reasons such as producing a sunken living room. For whatever reason, it is also common to use two different floor materials. For example, the transition from a house floor to a garage floor automatically indicates a change from wood to concrete. The concrete floor is called a slab. Figure 9.45 shows such a relationship.

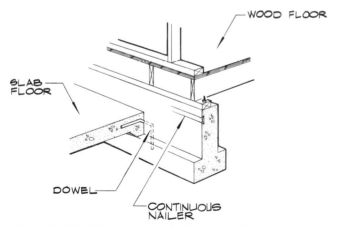

Figure 9.45 Change in level of a wood floor to concrete slab.

Notice the introduction of steel to hold the two floors together. This steel member is called a dowel and is placed in the footing while the concrete is still soft. After the concrete has hardened, the dowels are bent into position. The slab floor is then poured over the dowels to create a maximum bond between con-

crete and concrete. For information about the treatment of the slab as shown in Figure 9.46 and the underside of it, read the section in this chapter "Footings with Slab Floors."

Note the nailer at the intersection of the slab and foundation. This nailer is made of pressure-treated wood and is placed into the concrete as it is being poured. When finish material is applied to this surface, it becomes a member into which you can nail.

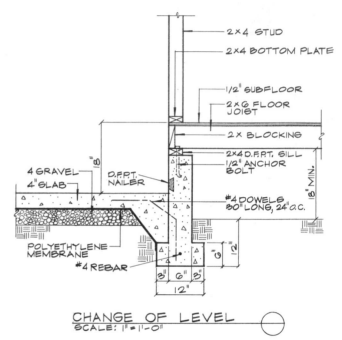

CHANGE OF LEVEL
SCALE: 1"=1'-0"

Figure 9.46 Drafted detail of change of level of a wood floor to a concrete slab.

Because the intent of the detail is to show the difference between one level and another and how this is accomplished, the dimension between floors is a very important item.

It is also very common to find a change of level incorporating the same floor material. This becomes more of a framing problem except where the foundation has to be preformed.

Three simple solutions are presented here involving a change of level using the same floor material. The first involves the use of a cripple system. The second incoprorates a structural piece called a ledger. The third method employs preforming the footing to accommodate both levels. See Figure 9.47, 9.48, and 9.49 for these examples.

Figure 9.50 shows the drafted version of the cripple. Notice the size and spacing of the cripple. It is the same as a standard framed wall.

Figure 9.51 illustrates the use of the ledger in drafted form. Since most codes require that the floor joist bear 1½ inches minimum, a 3″ × member was

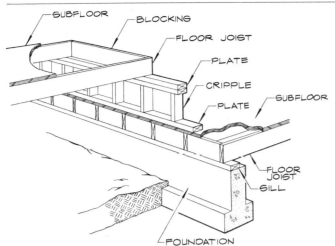

Figure 9.47 Change of level from a wood floor to a wood floor using cripples.

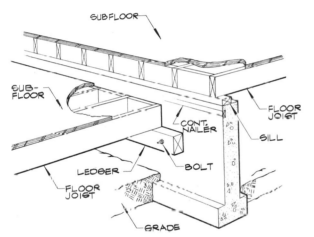

Figure 9.48 Change of level from a wood floor to a wood floor using a ledger.

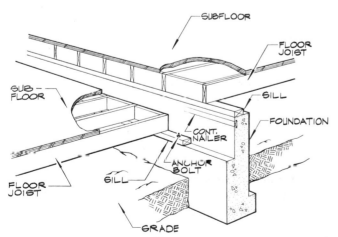

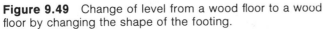

Figure 9.49 Change of level from a wood floor to a wood floor by changing the shape of the footing.

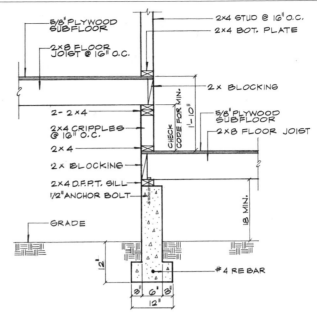

CHANGE OF LEVEL
SCALE: 1"=1'-0"

Figure 9.50 Drafted detail of a wood floor to wood floor using a cripple.

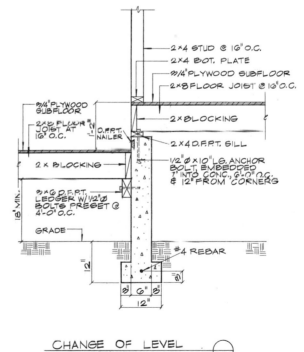

CHANGE OF LEVEL
SCALE: 1"=1'-0"

Figure 9.51 Drafted detail of a wood floor to a wood floor using a ledger.

used. The only difficulty here is the presetting of the bolts because of location.

The final drafted example, Figure 9.52, shows a preformed ledge on which the floor joist sits. The ledge has a 2″ × 3″ anchored with bolt. The 2″ × 3″ allows for the floor joist to be nailed down.

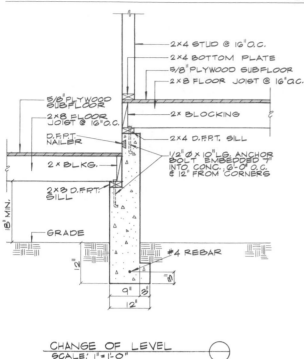

CHANGE OF LEVEL
SCALE: 1"=1'-0"

Figure 9.52 Drafted detail of a wood floor to a wood floor changing the shape of the footing.

Areaway

The purpose of the areaway is to keep earth away from openings in a wall below grade. This applies to windows, as found in a basement, called window wells or those found around stairs.

Two materials are most often used here: metal and concrete. The metal areaway or window well is preformed and put into position. Its appearance is not as desirable or as durable as one made of concrete. A concrete areaway is shown in Figure 9.53. The distance away from the opening should be equal to or larger than the height of the opening, and in all cases the top of the opening must be higher than the grade.

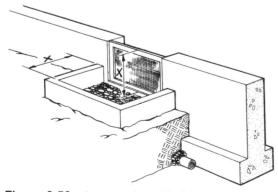

Figure 9.53 Areaway (crawl hole).

To prevent an accumulation of water, some type of drain is often provided where the rainfall is great. In all cases, the base of the areaway is filled with gravel. If the areaway becomes excessively deep, a railing should be provided to prevent people, especially children, from falling into this area. Figure 9.54 shows the typical areaway, often referred to as a crawl hole.

Note how the U-shaped concrete areaway is tied to the structure by means of a continuous piece of reinforcing bar at the top and bottom. The reinforcing bar also acts like a dowel here in tying the U-shaped piece to the structure.

Since there is an opening, the weight of the building that would have normally been placed at this point must be redistributed around the opening. This is especially critical when the floor joists run perpendicular to the wall that has the opening in it because the floor load is usually the heaviest. When a header joist system is used, either a ledger strip or joist hangers can be used effectively. See Figures 9.55 and 9.56.

If the floor joists extend all the way out to the end of the sill and blocking is used, the blocking over the opening is replaced with two 2 × members, and again joist hangers are used. See Figure 9.56.

Porch Connection

Assuming that there is a detail of an exterior bearing footing, the porch connection detail need concern itself mainly with what has not been previously covered. Time is money in an office, and a draftsperson must be aware of what information is the most necessary to get the job done. With that in mind, we can pursue the problem of connecting a concrete porch to a footing with a wood floor.

Look at Figure 9.57 and note that for the first time, we have concrete coming into contact with more than one wood piece—that is, the sill and the floor joist. If the porch is hosed off with water, this adds moisture to the wood, causing it to expand and contract and also making it more conducive to termite invasion. A moisture barrier called flashing is introduced. Flashing is a galvanized metal sheet of 26 gauge material.

The second problem to consider is the distance between the floor level of the structure and the grade. Assuming the distance between the grade and the underside of the floor joist is 18 inches, the floor joist of a 2 × 6 (net $5\frac{1}{2}$ inches) and $\frac{1}{2}$ inch of plywood subfloor, the total will be 24 inches. It is desirable to slope the porch away from the structure. If we sloped the porch 1 inch, and had 2 inches between the floor of the structure and the concrete porch, this leaves 21 inches for steps. Using 7 inches as a dimension for the riser, we have three risers.

Third, the detailer should note that the porch is above grade level. The fill should be wetted down and

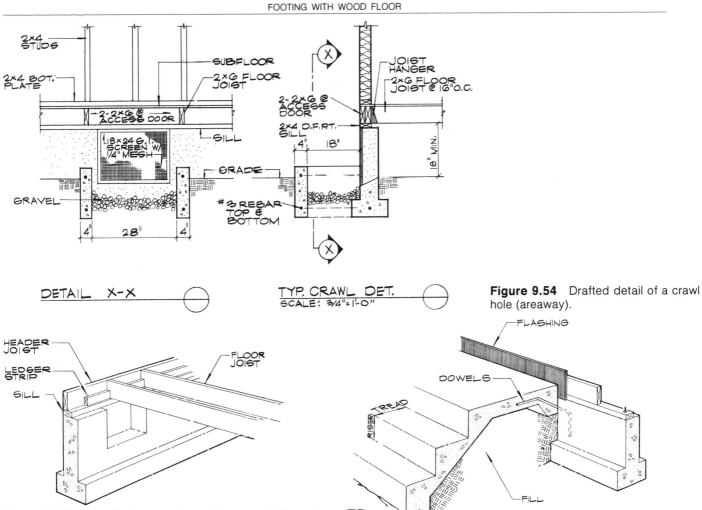

DETAIL X-X

TYP. CRAWL DET.
SCALE: 3/4"=1'-0"

Figure 9.54 Drafted detail of a crawl hole (areaway).

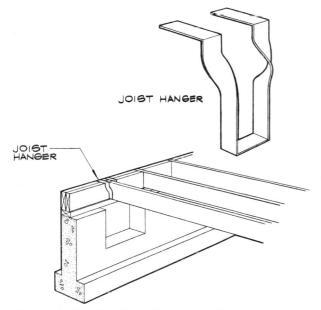

Figure 9.55 Use of ledger for floor joist support. (From *Architectural Drafting and Design*, 2nd ed., by Ernest R. Weidhaas, copyright © 1972 by Allyn & Bacon, Inc. Reprinted by permission of the publisher.)

Figure 9.57 Use of galvanized flashing to protect the wood from moisture.

Figure 9.56 Use of joist hanger for floor joist support.

tamped (compressed) firmly so it will not fall away from the underside of the porch.

Fourth, the porch must also be firmly attached to the foundation of the house to prevent a gap at its intersection. The solution for this is a series of dowels.

Finally, the portion of the step and porch that comes into contact with the grade does not have to be the full width of a standard footing since it carries very little weight. Also, it needs to go into the grade far enough so that it does not become exposed by a slight shifting of the earth. See Figure 9.58 for a sample of a drafted detail of this connection.

Grade Beam

In many instances, the earth at the surface is not stable enough to carry the weight of a structure. However, let us assume that many feet below the surface, the earth is stable. If it were recommended to try to

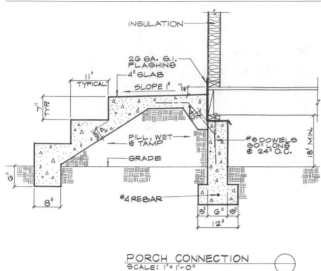

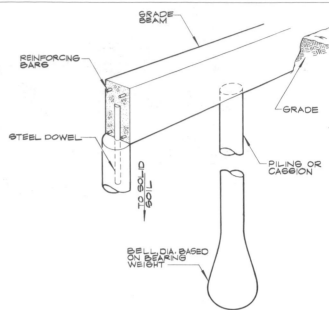

Figure 9.58 Drafted detail of a porch connection.

Figure 9.60 Piling and grade beam.

reach this stable level with the complete foundation, a beam called a grade beam is employed.

The first step of this system is the construction of piling. Piling is made of concrete and poured into a hole dug into the earth until it reaches a stable soil level. The frequency, depth, and size of the piling are determined by soil condition and the weight of the structure. These factors are in turn usually determined by the structural engineer for the architectural draftsperson.

Let's assume that the decision is to use 10 inch diameter piling and 7'-0" o.c. A beam is placed across the 7'-0" span. Since the beam is into the grade, concrete is used rather than wood. (If the beam were above the grade, wood may be used.) This concrete beam is called a grade beam. Figure 9.59 gives an example of a trench and reinforcing prior to pouring a grade beam. See Figure 9.60. The framing above the grade beam follows the normal procedure as previously discussed. See Figure 9.61.

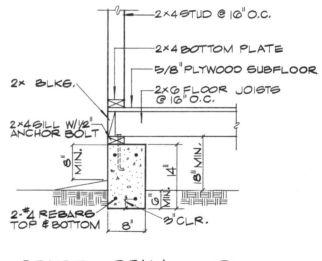

GRADE BEAM
SCALE: 1" = 1'-0"

Figure 9.61 Drafted detail of a grade beam. (Reproduced from *Standard Structural Details for Building Construction* with permission of the publisher, the McGraw-Hill Book Company.)

Footing with Slab Floors

Monolithic — Exterior Bearing

A monolithic system, as the prefix mono indicates, is a one-pour system. The footing and the slab (the floor) are poured together, and hence the architect is

Figure 9.59 Preparation for grade beam.

reminded that forms on the inside of the footing under the slab are never used because they cannot be removed. The trenches themselves become the forms for the poured concrete on the inside. The most typical shape is shown in Figure 9.62. As shown in Figure 9.63, the bulk of the load is placed on the extreme outside; this produces a rotation and cracks the concrete at its weakest point.

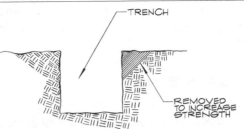

Figure 9.64 Trench preparation to strengthen footing at critical points.

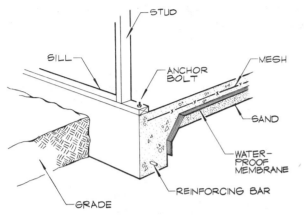

Figure 9.62 Monolithic footing.

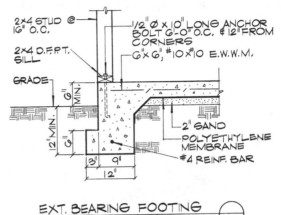

Figure 9.65 Drafted detail of a typical exterior bearing footing.

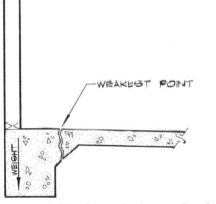

Figure 9.63 Strengthening weak points.

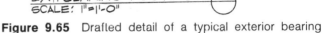
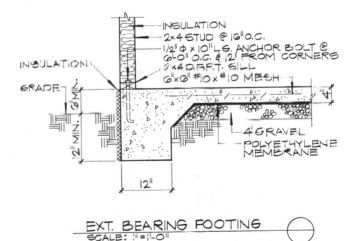

Figure 9.66 Drafted detail of a monolithic footing.

For this reason this area is "beefed up" and strengthened. The procedure is simple. The hard edge of the trenches is removed as shown in Figure 9.64. To redistribute the weight toward the center, one form board is used on the outside and later removed, thus producing a shape shown in Figure 9.65. Exterior bearing, as before, means that this footing is found on the exterior of the structure and acts as a load-bearing footing. The load may be from the ceiling or the roof but not from the floor as it rests on the ground.

The bearing surface, as drawn in Figure 9.66 is 12 inches—a minimum in many states for a single-story structure and 12 inches into the grade. As previously mentioned, there must be 6 to 8 inches between the grade and the first piece of wood for termite protection.

Since there is only one horizontal wood member, as compared with the wood floor system, the member may be called a sill or a bottom plate. Sill seems to be the more common term here. Special attention must be paid the mesh, which is unique to slabs and the gravel and sand used. A very popular combination involves 2 or more inches of sand, which acts as a cushion against expansive soil, and a polyethylene membrane located above the sand to act as a barrier against moisture.

T-Shaped — Exterior Bearing

The principles, dimensions, and limitations are the same in a T-shaped system as in the monolithic slab system. However, as seen in Figure 9.67, the system is a two-pour system with the foundation poured first and the slab afterward. Gravel and insulation has been used in the detail in Figure 9.68 to show variety.

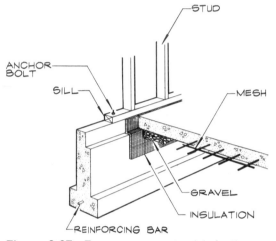

Figure 9.67 Two-pour concrete slab footing.

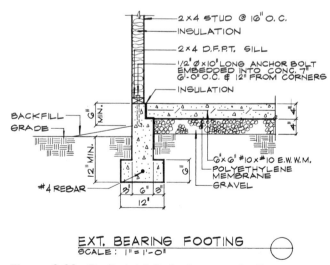

EXT. BEARING FOOTING
SCALE: 1" = 1'-0"

Figure 9.68 Drafted detail of a two-pour footing.

Since a slight separation may occur at the joint, it is best to locate the joint at the intersection between the floor and wall plane. This means that the width of the concrete at the sill should be the same size as the sill itself.

Interior Bearing

Interior bearing footing, like exterior bearing footing, carries additional weight besides the wall above it. Weight from the ceiling and the roof are typical loads. The detailer should remember that when using monolithic exterior footing, the interior must also be monolithic as shown in Figure 9.69. If the two-pour system is used, a two-pour interior bearing footing should be used that is similar to Figure 9.70. The depth of the interior bearing footing should coincide with that of the exterior so that when they join at the outside perimeter a sound unit results.

The original grade line is often drawn in all details to remind the people in the field, as well as the draftsperson, that they should be aware of the relationship existing between exterior and interior footings.

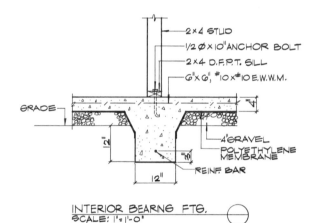

INTERIOR BEARING FTG.
SCALE: 1" = 1'-0"

Figure 9.69 Drafted detail of interior bearing monolithic footing.

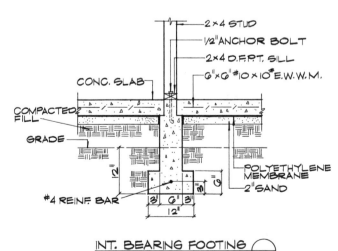

INT. BEARING FOOTING
SCALE: 1" = 1'-0"

Figure 9.70 Drafted detail of a two-pour interior bearing footing.

Interior Nonbearing

Interior nonbearing footing carries only the load of the wall above it, not any ceiling or roof load. As can be seen in Figure 9.71, its thickness is sufficient only to accommodate the anchor bolt. The monolithic sample shown can be used with any type of system.

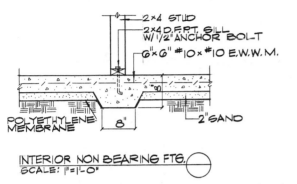

Figure 9.71 Drafted detail of an interior nonbearing footing.

Since the cost of form work can constitute up to 75 percent of the cost of constructing the foundations, any time there is an opportunity to redesign a detail to decrease the use of forms, it should be encouraged. Figures 9.72 and 9.73 show a slight adjustment to the configuration used in Figures 9.68 and 9.70. Figures 9.72 and 9.73 are also different because they are for a two-story structure.

The area where the sill attaches to the footing is notched out to accept the slab of the floor on Figures 9.68 and 9.70. In the new examples, there is no need to use wood forms on the interior bearing footing to develop this notch, thus saving a great deal of money.

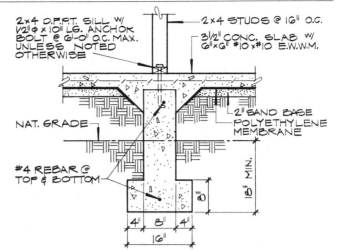

Figure 9.73 Two-story interior bearing footing.

Footing at Property Line

When dealing with most sites, there is a required setback. A city building department may require that you set the structure away from the property line; however, many commercial and industrial buildings are allowed to go right up to it.

In such a situation, if a T-shaped footing is used, the flange of the T shape extends into the neighboring site, provided the exterior wall is right on the property line. For this reason, a detail such as the one shown in Figure 9.74 was developed. Admittedly, the load is not squarely distributed in the center, but considering the prevailing conditions, it is the best that can be done.

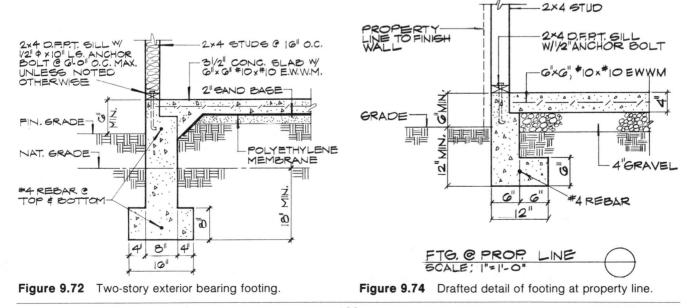

Figure 9.72 Two-story exterior bearing footing.

Figure 9.74 Drafted detail of footing at property line.

Because finished material is applied to this surface and the setback is measured to the finished wall, a hidden line should be added to the detail showing the property line and finished wall material.

Change of Level

As in the wood floor footing, a change of level within a structure may be highly desirable for aesthetic reasons or could be forced on you to accommodate the site.

For whatever reason, the connection is an easy one to make. See Figure 9.75. Note that in the example, the new level is resting on one leg of the T shape. If the change of level had been less, this base could have been raised to accommodate the intersection and give the new slab a firm base to sit on. See Figure 9.76.

When this is drawn in detail form (Figure 9.77), the original outline is drawn in hidden line form and called out as ''trace of footing beyond.'' This means that after the change of level ends, there is no need for the raised platform and the footing returns to its original form. If the footing does not return to its original form

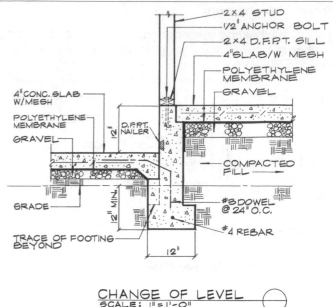

CHANGE OF LEVEL
SCALE: 1" = 1'-0"

Figure 9.77 Drafted detail of change of level of a concrete slab floor to a concrete slab floor.

within that foundation wall, the hidden line and note are eliminated from the detail.

If fill is required on the underside of the new floor level, the earth should be compacted, As can be seen on the sample, dowels are used here to ensure a good connection. Since this is a change of level from one floor to another, the dimension between them becomes an important item to remember. Notice also on the detail that the point of contact on the edge of the slab has been increased in both vertical and horizontal dimensions. Minimum construction may not increase the contact area but can carry the 4 inch slab dimension right up to the footing with which it is coming in contact.

If the change of level is rather small or needs to adapt itself for a particular floor material, the change is called a depressed slab. For example, if ceramic floor tiles are used in an area, the slab must be depressed to allow the use of mortar. The combination of mortar and ceramic tile requires more thickness than most finished floor materials.

If the floor is to be kept even throughout the structure, certain slabs may have to be depressed. See Figure 9.78. Notice how one layer of concrete overlaps the other by 12 inches to ensure a good structural connection. The depression in the concrete need be only as deep as required to accommodate the finish material.

Porch Connection

The problems we face with a porch connection to a slab footing are not nearly as severe as those en-

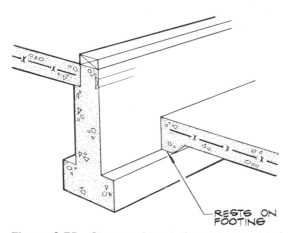

Figure 9.75 Change of level of a concrete slab footing to a concrete slab footing.

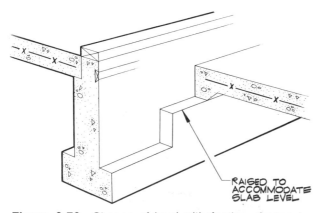

Figure 9.76 Change of level with footing change to accommodate concrete slab floor.

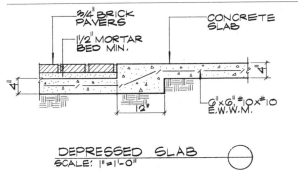

DEPRESSED SLAB
SCALE: 1"=1'-0"

Figure 9.78 Drafted detail of a depressed slab to accommodate a change of floor material.

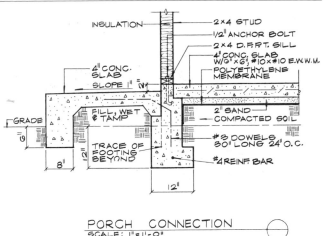

PORCH CONNECTION
SCALE: 1"=1'-0"

Figure 9.80 Drafted detail of a porch connection.

countered with a porch connection to a wood floor footing. The first major difference is that here there is no need for flashing since the contact is concrete to concrete. See Figure 9.79.

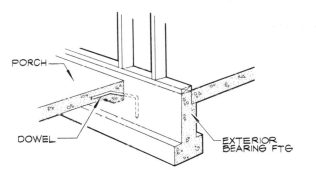

Figure 9.79 Porch connections.

Second, the floor to grade level is usually 6 to 8 inches, thus voiding the need for many steps. On a hillside lot, this may not apply because of the irregularity of the site.

Third, there is very little fill required on the underside of the porch. What is required, however, must be wet and firmly tamped down.

Finally, dowels must still be used to keep the objects from separating. See Figure 9.80 for a drafted sample.

Garage

Garage footing creates a unique situation because the floor of the garage must be kept rather close to the existing grade on the outside to allow a smooth transition for the vehicle being driven in or out. If we kept the garage at the same level as the house, the 6 to 8 inch drop would be too much for the car to negotiate.

If the floor of the garage is lower than the existing grade on the outside, we introduce the problem of water during rain or when the driveway is washed. The compromise is 1 to 3 inches in height difference

—just enough to keep the water out while allowing a comfortable exit.

The difference between the two levels is taken care of by a sloping portion in front of the garage door called an apron. The requirement to keep all wood 6 to 8 inches above the grade still remains. Because of it, we are forced to come up with an odd and very unique shape. See Figure 9.81. Notice how the portion closest to the grade is raised to fulfill the 6 to 8 inch requirement while the slab floor remains within a few inches of the grade.

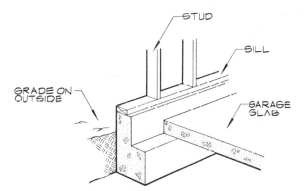

Figure 9.81 Exterior bearing footing of a garage.

Dimensions and structural pieces remain the same as those for the exterior bearing footing except that the surface on which the sill rests (bearing surface of sill) should be 6 inches. See Figures 9.82 and 9.83 for a two-pour and a monolithic system.

The driveway detail (see Figure 9.84) should be traced directly off the garage footing. See Figure 9.85. Notice how the footing portion is also shown in sections; this is because it continues under the driveway. Note also the outside edge of the garage and how the apron ties into it. The projection at the top

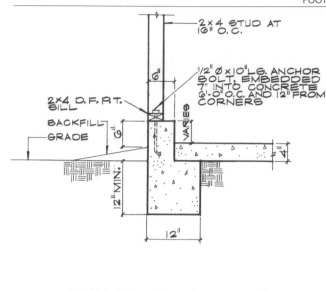

GARAGE FOOTING
SCALE: 1" = 1'-0"

Figure 9.82 Drafted detail of a garage exterior bearing footing with a two-pour system.

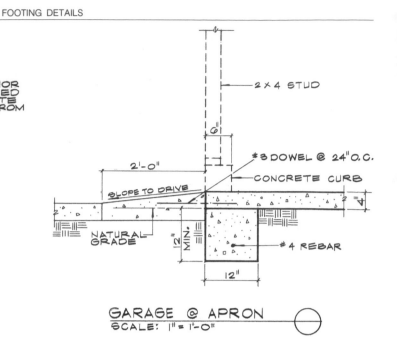

GARAGE @ APRON
SCALE: 1" = 1'-0"

Figure 9.85 Drafted detail of a garage apron.

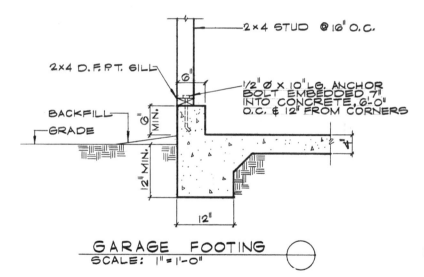

GARAGE FOOTING
SCALE: 1" = 1'-0"

Figure 9.83 Drafted detail of an exterior bearing monolithic footing for a garage.

Figure 9.84 Garage apron.

that the sill sits on is not in sections. It stops at each end of the door to allow cars to drive in and out and should be represented as an elevation.

Also, there are times when an architect encounters a situation in which a garage is required but the terrain is not level. One solution is to build a concrete wall (called a retaining wall) and fill the area with earth to produce a terrain level enough to accept a slab. See Figure 9.86.

Another solution is to pour concrete over a wood base. (The wood is used to accommodate the terrain.) Figure 9.87 shows a drafted detail of this situation. It is unusual because concrete is poured right over the wood floor.

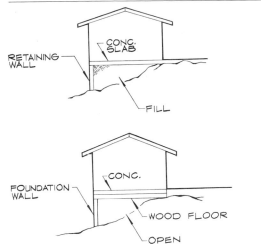

Figure 9.86 Comparison of floor systems.

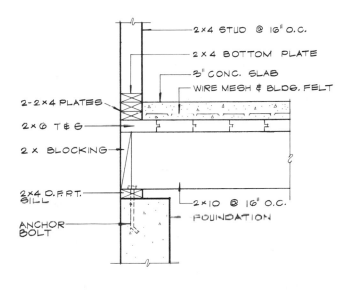

Figure 9.87 Drafted detail of concrete poured on a wood floor system.

Notice the use of a heavy subfloor (2″ × 6″ tongue and groove), a combination of mesh and building felt (tar paper), and the 3 inch concrete that is the thickness of two 2 × 4 members surrounding the perimeter.

Footings with Masonry Walls

Prior to reading this section, which deals with masonry walls and their relationship to footings, the reader should review Chapter 8 and also consult the masonry portion of Chapter 10.

The main features the architectural draftsperson must be aware of in developing a footing for a masonry wall are the weight being supported and the soil condition capable of resisting that weight.

Brick as a Wall

As the title indicates, this is a system where the complete brick wall comes down to the concrete footing. See Figure 9.88. There are two withe (vertical rows) of brick with a solid grout in between. The grout can be eliminated in parts of the country that do not have

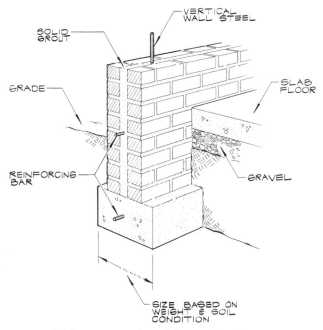

Figure 9.88 Masonry foundation wall at footing in brick.

strong earthquakes or high winds. Figure 9.89 shows what a detail of the pictorial drawing looks like. Note the diagonal lines used to represent the brick. The type of joint, size of brick, and method of stacking are usually written in the specifications or indicated on the elevation where the brick patterns and joints show best. Some offices do, however, insist on putting this information on the details as well.

Brick Wall above the Floor

Figure 9.90 depicts a condition similar to Figure 9.88, except that in this particular situation the brick begins at the intersection of the slab floor and the wall. The slab floor might intersect the foundation wall as shown or be poured on top of it, extending the floor to the outside. In either case, the joint between the foun-

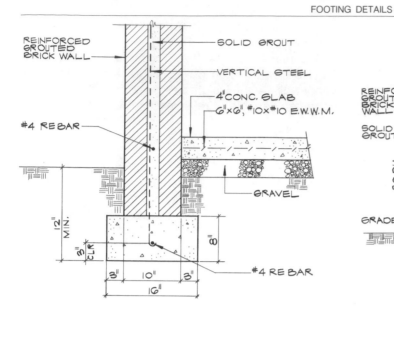

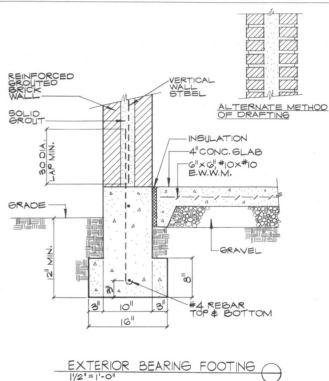

Figure 9.89 Drafted detail of masonry (brick) foundation wall.

Figure 9.91 Drafted detail of footing for masonry brick wall and alternate method of representing brick.

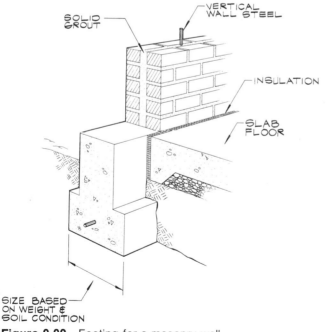

Figure 9.90 Footing for a masonry wall.

shows an alternate method of representing brick used by some offices, but one that is somewhat time consuming to draft. Notice that dowels are not used to connect the slab to the foundation wall. Since the floor is on the interior of the structure, there is nowhere for the floor slab to go. Also, any time the vertical steel reinforcing is not continuous but is in separate pieces, these must be lapped. Local codes dictate the amount to be lapped. In some instances, these pieces are even welded together. The main purpose of lapping is to make it easier to build; it becomes very cumbersome if steel runs the full height from footing to the top of the wall.

Concrete Block as a Wall

There is very little difference between the way an architect deals with brick and concrete block as shown in Figure 9.92. A key is used here to keep the wall located correctly in relationship to the footing. A key is also often used with brick. (Figure 9.93 presents this situation detailed.) Note how the concrete block is represented. It can also be shown with two vertical lines to indicate the outside of the concrete block and cross-section lines as done with the original brick. Another item to note in Figure 9.93 is the very superior two-pour concrete slab system.

dation wall and the brick or the floor slab and the brick is seen on the exterior. A drafted detail of this condition is illustrated in Figure 9.91. This detail

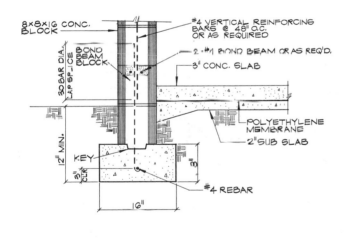

Figure 9.92 Masonry (concrete block) foundation wall at footing.

MASONRY FOUNDATION WALL ◯
1½" = 1'-0"

Figure 9.93 Drafted detail of masonry (concrete block) foundation wall.

Brick Veneer

The different methods of attaching a brick veneer to a stud wall are described in Chapter 10. Figure 9.94 shows the intersection of the brick veneer and footing. A noteworthy feature is the incorporation of flashing to protect the wood from moisture. A detail of a brick veneer on a footing with a concrete slab floor is drafted in Figure 9.95.

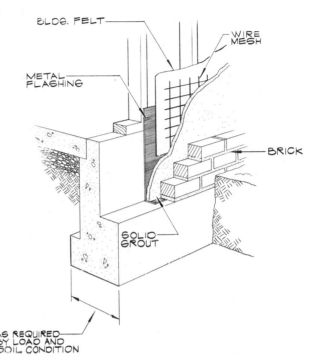

Figure 9.94 Footing variation for brick veneer.

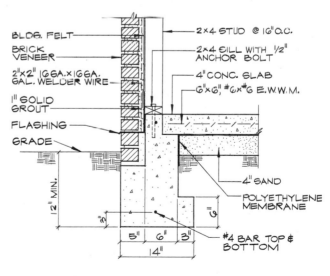

FOOTING @ VENEER ◯
1½" = 1'-0"

Figure 9.95 Drafted detail of footing for brick veneer on a conventional wood frame wall.

Masonry and a Wood Floor

The method of dealing with a wood floor in conjunction with a masonry wall varies very little between brick and concrete block. Therefore, only concrete block is shown here. Figure 9.96 illustrates a wood floor attached to a masonry wall by means of a ledger. The system is very similar to that encountered earlier in Figure 9.51 except that the foundation wall is masonry. A joist hanger can be used in conjunction with the ledger (see Figure 9.97) when the underside of the floor is required to be kept visually or structurally clear. This might occur in a basement or a multi-story building. Figure 9.98 shows how the wood floor can be accommodated by changing the width of the concrete block. In this instance, a sill is installed by means of anchor bolts and the floor joist nailed to it. Figure 9.99 shows the formally drafted version of the use of the ledger at the floor joist. The reader should also consult Chapter 11 because many of the connections used in that chapter also apply here.

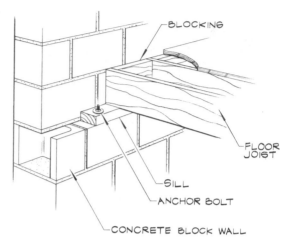

Figure 9.98 Use of a sill at the intersection of the floor joist and masonry foundation wall.

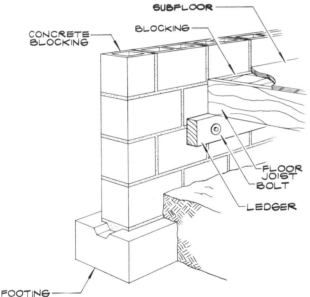

Figure 9.96 Intersection of a masonry foundation wall and a wood floor.

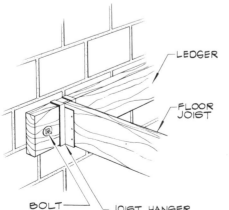

Figure 9.97 Use of a ledger and joist hanger at the intersection of the floor joist and masonry foundation wall.

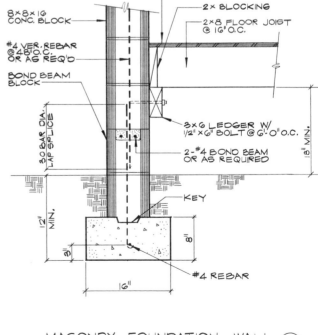

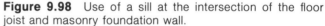

Figure 9.99 Drafted detail of masonry foundation wall.

Brick Veneer at the Wood Floor

A footing supporting a brick veneer with a slab floor, Figure 9.95, is not too different from that of a wood floor. See Figure 9.100. In this instance, however, note how the sill was set back on the foundation wall to accept wood sheathing, which is more commonly used in the East. Note also in this illustration that the Bower wire veneer tie method was employed where the wire is spaced 16″ o.c. horizontally and not more than 18″ o.c. vertically or as the local code requires. Figure 9.101 gives a sample of a drafted version of this condition. Notice how the detail shows a hidden line at the base of the footing and noted "trace of footing beyond." This is a situation where the veneer does not extend the full face of the elevation; in other words, the brick veneer is only on a portion of the building face and the footing size varies. Finally, weep holes, usually spaced at 2'-0″ o.c., can be noted directly above the flashing at the joint. The function of the weep holes is to void any water that may get behind the brick.

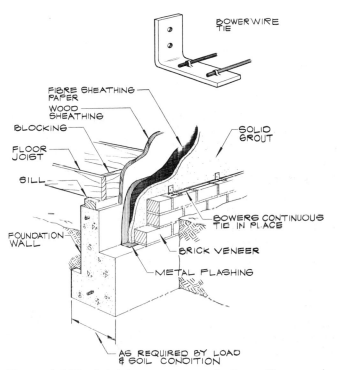

Figure 9.100 A brick veneer on a footing with a wood floor.

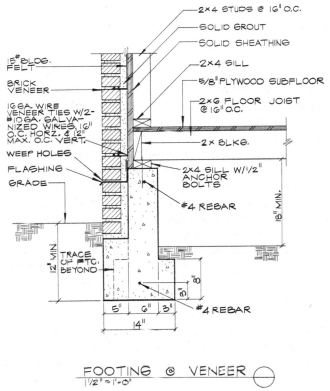

FOOTING @ VENEER

Figure 9.101 Drafted detail of a footing for a brick veneer with a wood floor.

Regional Differences

Regional differences tend to be rather great in dealing with foundations due to the varying surrounding conditions. An architectural draftsperson must be aware of local conditions and develop foundations to accommodate the particular area. In developing foundations for wood frame construction, the architectural technician should be aware of the following conditions:

Wind, including hurricanes and cyclones
Moisture, including humidity and rain
Various soil conditions
Various temperature ranges, including frost lines and snow loads
Termites
Seismic conditions
Availability of material

In dealing with wind, the connection between the wall and floor, whether concrete or wood, is a major design factor.

If rain or humidity is a problem in the local area, the designer must raise the floor off of the ground (if it is wood) or introduce some type of moisture barrier between a concrete floor and the soil itself.

Soil condition can be obtained from a soils engineer and dictates the amount of weight the soil is capable of resisting. Difference in soil conditions is more than just regional. It can vary drastically, depending on location, within a relatively short distance.

Varying temperatures, especially cold, produce additional implications for foundations in the form of snow loads and frost lines. See Figure 9.102. Additional snow load means a wider footing to accommodate the extra load and placing footing far below the frost line. Colder climates also suggest the use of some type of insulation attached to the underside of a wood floor or under a slab and around the exterior perimeter of the foundation.

Termites are also a problem in many parts of the country. To prevent them, wood is treated and a termite shield introduced on wood floor systems.

Earthquake possibilities create additional problems for the foundation and vary in intensity in different parts of the country. Seismic risk maps can be obtained from your local building and safety department or are usually included in building codes. Parts of Washington, South Carolina, and all of California are in what is called major damage areas, while the lower parts of Texas and Florida are in no damage areas.

Architectural draftspersons must become familiar with the materials available in their particular regions and the type of construction typically used. For example, in California a light-frame construction usually calls for a T-shaped footing to be poured all at once as explained in this chapter. Other areas of the country may use two pours to accomplish the same shape, with the footing poured separately from the foundation wall. When this is done, a key is often used. See Figure 9.103.

Finally, masonry construction methods do differ regionally because of weather, soil, and earthquake problems. While reinforcing steel and solid grouting are used in California because of the earthquake problem, many other parts of the country use what is called a cavity wall construction. In fact, a lateral force produced by wind or earthquake changes the design of masonry wall construction.

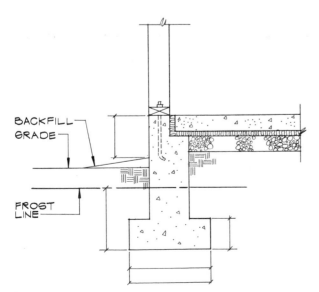

Figure 9.102 Measuring the footing below the frost line.

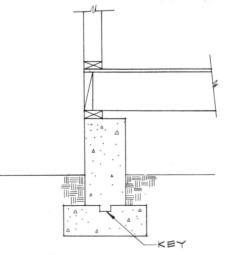

Figure 9.103 Use of a key on a two-pour system.

Building Code

Codes differ so much from one area of the country to the next that it would be impossible to cite minimum and maximum sizes that can be used nationally for footings. In lieu of this, the architectural draftsperson should check the local code requirements for the following factors when drawing a footing detail:

1. Minimum width of footing allowed.
2. Grade or frost line to bottom of footing, measured on the exterior side of the footing.
3. Minimum distance between grade and the nearest piece of wood.
4. Minimum requirements for crawl space if any; minimums include distance between grade and girder or between grade and floor joist.
5. Minimum insulation required by energy board.
6. Size and spacing of anchor bolts.

Summary

One can readily see from reading this chapter, concrete is a highly desirable material to use for foundations because of its strength and adaptability to varying conditions. It is also compatible with a variety of different building materials: wood, steel, polyethylene, brick, and so on. However, it should be remembered that concrete does absorb water and is a very brittle media.

Critical consideration must be given wherever and whenever different materials, such as earth, wood, steel, come into contact with concrete. The earth expands and is often in motion. Wood must be protected from termites in some regions and not only from excessive moisture. Although steel strengthens the concrete when its placement is well thought out, it does rust.

The architectural draftsperson should formulate carefully the intent of the detail and determine why it is being detailed and dimension accordingly. Selection of notes must be based on what information is needed to describe the important parts and how they are located.

10
EXTERIOR WALLS

Preview   Chapter 10 describes in narrative and detail form the types of framing techniques found in light-wood-frame construction. The first three sections of this chapter deal with the three basic framing techniques: platform framing, balloon framing, and post and beam construction. Each one of these techniques is discussed in detail along with pictorial and detailed illustrations. These illustrations provide the basics required for framing sections and their related connections. The fourth section deals with one-story exterior masonry wall construction. The walls discussed are reinforced and unreinforced brick and concrete block assemblies. The fifth section examines the reasons for shear walls and shows, in detailed form, an example of the makeup of a wood shear wall and its key connections. Final sections deal with various types of exterior and interior finish materials and their application in light-wood-frame construction. A complete understanding of these framing techniques and their related details will help architectural draftspersons in analyzing various types of framing conditions.

After reading this chapter, the architectural draftsperson will:

1. Understand the nomenclature and differences in detailing for different types of wood framing techniques.
2. Be familiar with the problems faced by the framing carpenter when erecting wood walls.
3. Be able to detail an exterior wood frame wall relative to its framing technique.
4. Understand the vocabulary and terms for light-frame construction and the basic structural members found in these assemblies.
5. Be able to detail reinforced and unreinforced masonry exterior walls and understand the primary differences among walls that are built in different regions of the country.
6. Understand wood shear walls and their detailed key connections.
7. Have a knowledge of the availability of exterior finishes in wood and masonry veneer and their application to a wood frame wall.
8. Be familiar with basic interior wall finishes and their applications to a wood framed wall.

Exterior wall framing should be structured so that it can support vertical loads from the roof, ceiling, and floors. Walls should also be able to resist lateral forces resulting from wind and earthquakes.

Exterior walls for one- and two-story buildings are comprised of 2″ × 4″ studs with the 4″ dimension perpendicular to the direction of the wall. For three-story buildings, studs at the first floor level have a minimum dimension of 2″ × 6″. Spacing of studs is normally dimensioned at 16″ on center.

Primarily, there are two conventional methods for framing wood stud walls: platform frame construction and balloon frame construction.

Platform Frame Construction

Platform frame construction, also termed western frame construction, is best used for one-story residences; however, many two- and three-story structures are framed by this method. For platform framing, 2″ × 4″ wood studs are nailed to a continuous 2″ × 4″ member at the base of the wall, which is commonly referred to as the bottom plate or sole plate. Eventually, when the wall is raised and aligned, the bottom plate is nailed to the floor system.

At the top of the wall, two 2″ × 4″ plates are nailed to the studs. The doubled 2″ × 4″ plates are overlapped and spliced rather than butted together. The overlapped splice is normally a minimum of 4′-0″ and provides continuity to tie the walls of the structure together. Wall framing and its members is shown in Figure 10.1.

Openings

Where openings—such as windows and doors—occur in a wall, a horizontal member is built into the wall. This member is referred to as a header or lintel. The header must be sized to support vertical loads adequately across the opening that are contributed from the roof, ceiling, floor, and wall loads. Where small openings occur, such as a 3′-0″ wide window, headers may be supported at the ends by a 2″ × 4″ or by metal framing fasteners.

Where large openings in a wall occur, such as 6′-0″ and greater, it is good practice to provide two 2″ × 4″ to support the ends of the header. Examples of header construction are illustrated in Figures 10.2, 10.3, and 10.4. Figure 10.5 shows window openings in a framed wall.

The use of platform or western frame construction affords more ease in the erection of walls since a flat

Figure 10.1 Wall framing.

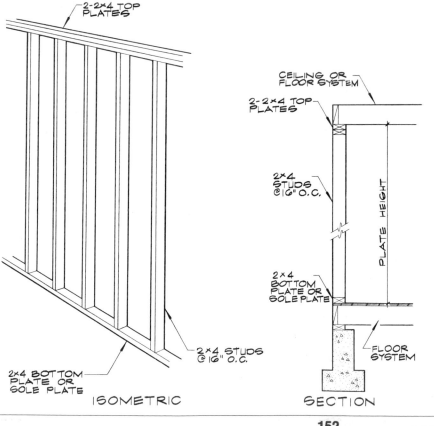

ISOMETRIC   SECTION

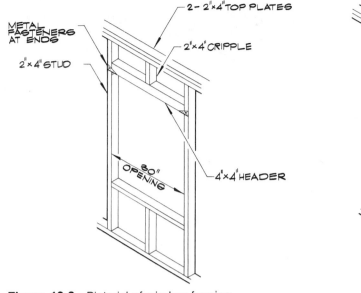

Figure 10.2 Pictorial of window framing.

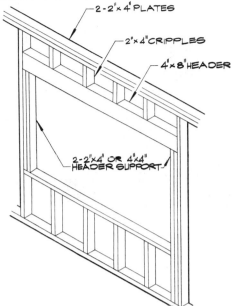

Figure 10.4 Pictorial of window framing.

surface is provided at each floor level. This in turn, allows the wall framing to be assembled on the floor and then to be raised in place by tilting the entire unit up to a vertical position. A photograph of this is shown in Figure 10.6.

Balloon Frame Construction

Balloon frame construction, also referred to as braced framing, is primarily used for two-story construction and is recommended when the exterior finish is of brick or stone veneer or exterior plaster.

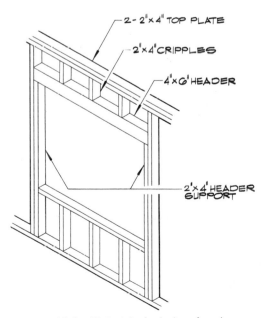

Figure 10.3 Pictorial of window framing.

The advantage of using balloon framing when masonry veneer is used on exterior walls is that there is less chance of shrinkage or movement between the wood framing and the masonry veneer. Shrinkage or movement in most cases is the direct cause of cracks on stucco walls or separation of masonry units at the joints. Exterior wall studs for balloon frame construction span from the mud sill, which in this method is a 4″ × 6″ treated member, to the two top plates of the second floor. Floor joists at the first floor are supported at the mud sill. On the second floor, floor joists are supported at the exterior walls by a continuous 1″ × 4″ that is perpendicular to the direction of the wall, and the 4 inch dimension stud. This member is referred to as a ribbon strip, which is "let in" to the inside edges of the studs. In this case, the term "let in" refers to the notching of the studs to accommodate the ribbon strip. Fire blocking is provided between the studs and flush with the top of the 1″ × 4″ ribbon. Figure 10.7 illustrates a section of a two-story balloon framed exterior wall.

As shown in Figure 10.7, solid blocking is installed between floor joists at each floor, which enables the carpenter to nail down the subfloor between the floor joist at the edges. The blocking also affords a nailing strip for finish ceiling material beneath the second floor. Figure 10.8 illustrates blocking at the first floor level, and Figure 10.9 depicts it at the second floor level.

Because this chapter deals specifically with exterior walls, the architect or designer should be aware that interior bearing partitions, in conjunction with balloon framing, do not span from the mud sill to the second

Figure 10.5 Photograph of window framing.

floor top plates. These partitions terminate at the first floor ceiling level and are tied together with a single top plate. Since a single plate is used at the top of the wall, floor joists at the second floor level are installed directly over the wood stud below. Figure 10.10 illustrates second floor framing over an interior bearing partition.

Openings in exterior walls, in conjunction with balloon framing, are framed in a fashion similar to platform framing. For platform frame construction or balloon frame construction, various arrangements of exterior corner studs are utilized. These arrangements are designed to satisfy the attachment of exterior and interior materials selected. Figure 10.11 illustrates three varying arrangements.

Exterior walls should be braced regardless of the method of construction. Bracing for exterior walls may be achieved with the use of solid diagonal

Figure 10.6 Photograph of wall framing.

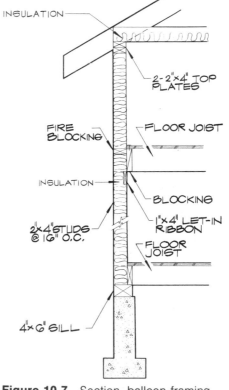

Figure 10.7 Section, balloon framing.

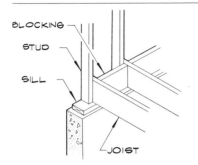

Figure 10.8 Pictorial of floor blocking.

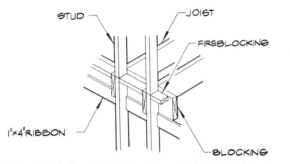

Figure 10.9 Pictorial of floor blocking. (Courtesy of National Forest Products Association.)

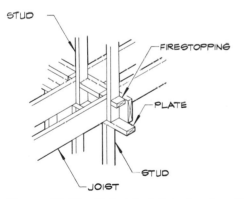

Figure 10.10 Pictorial of floor framing. (Courtesy of National Forest Products Association.)

sheathing or the use of 1" × 4" members that are let in to the outside face of the studs at an angle of 45° and are nailed to the top, bottom plates, and studs. Bracing is installed to provide lateral stability to the walls. See Figure 10.12 to compare these two basic methods of frame construction. It can be said that balloon framing is less expensive than platform framing; however, balloon framing does not provide the rigidity and fire resistance that platform frame construction does. Primarily, this is because in platform framing only exterior studs span from floor to floor and are separated at each level by two 2" × 4" continuous top plates, thus providing an excellent fire stop. Examples of platform and balloon frame construction and their specific members are illustrated in Figures 10.12 and 10.13.

Post and Beam Construction

Post and beam construction is relatively new and less commonly used than is platform and balloon frame construction in residential framing. However, post and beam framing has been used in heavy timber buildings for many years.

The principal difference between post and beam construction and conventional exterior wall framing is the use of a beam-to-post module that facilitates the use of 2 inch roof or floor planking. A visual comparison of a post and beam system and that of conventional framing is illustrated in Figure 10.14.

For maximum utilization of this system for residential construction, the designer should provide for a specific module or post and beam spacing that is used for planning criteria. Depending on the building code or location, 2 inch roof planking may be supported on roof beams spaced up to 8'-0" center to center. In this case a module of beams and posts is spaced 8'-0" center to center. Exterior walls between posts are provided with supplementary framing for required attachment of exterior and interior finishes.

The term "planking," when used with this framing system, refers to members that have a minimum depth of 2 inches and a width of from 6 to 8 inches. Edges of this member are normally tongued and

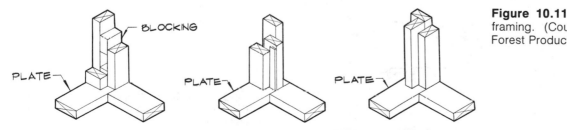

Figure 10.11 Pictorial of floor framing. (Courtesy of National Forest Products Association.)

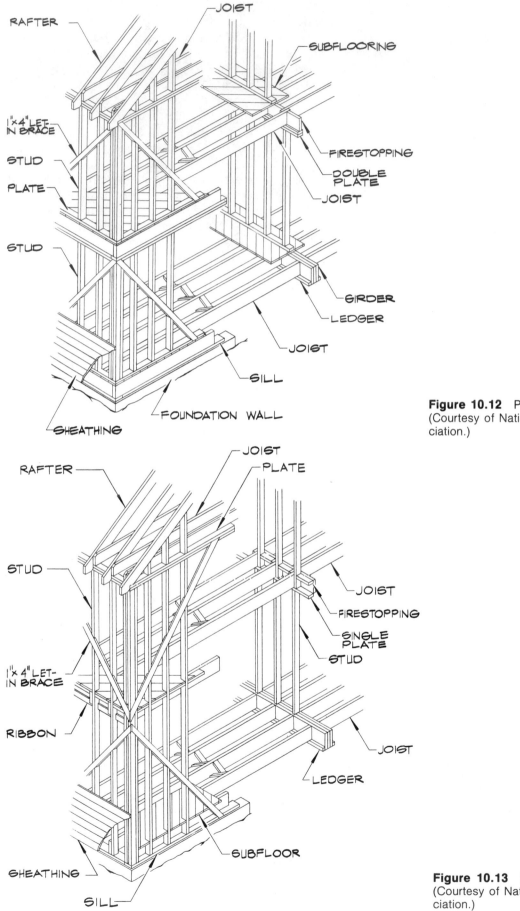

RAFTER

JOIST

SUBFLOORING

1"×4" LET-IN BRACE

STUD

PLATE

STUD

FIRESTOPPING

DOUBLE PLATE

JOIST

GIRDER

LEDGER

JOIST

SILL

FOUNDATION WALL

SHEATHING

Figure 10.12 Pictorial of platform framing. (Courtesy of National Forest Products Association.)

RAFTER

JOIST

PLATE

STUD

JOIST

FIRESTOPPING

SINGLE PLATE

STUD

1"×4" LET-IN BRACE

RIBBON

JOIST

LEDGER

SUBFLOOR

SHEATHING

SILL

Figure 10.13 Pictorial of balloon framing. (Courtesy of National Forest Products Association.)

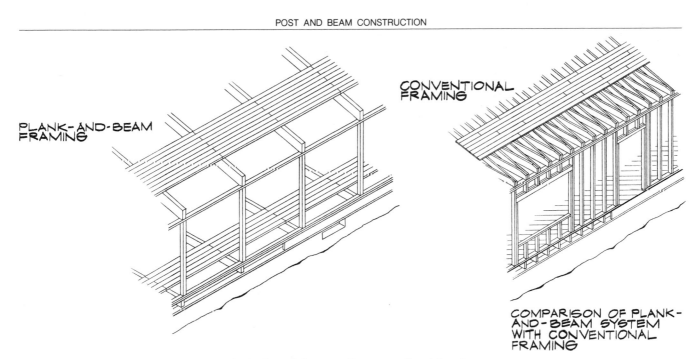

Figure 10.14 Pictorial comparison of plank and beam with conventional framing. (Courtesy of National Forest Products Association.)

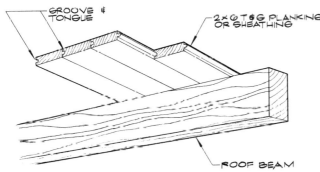

Figure 10.15 Pictorial of roof planking.

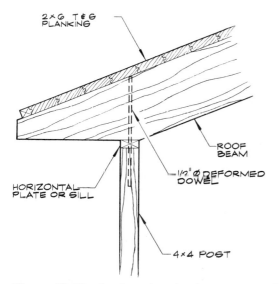

Figure 10.16 Section of post-to-beam connection.

grooved. The use of such edges enables a continuous joining of members so that a specific concentrated load is distributed into adjacent members. This would help to resist deflection in the one member affected. An acceptable abbreviation for tongued and grooved planking or sheathing in architectural detailing is "T & G." Figure 10.15 illustrates a commonly used planking with tongued and grooved edges.

When designers are involved with the wall detailing of a post and beam system, they should pay careful attention to the connection of the beam to post and the post to floor.

When the beam is not stayed laterally by blocking or by a framed filler wall, the use of dowel or pin is acceptable. The dowel may be a $\frac{1}{2}''$ ϕ deformed reinforcing bar that is driven down from the top and

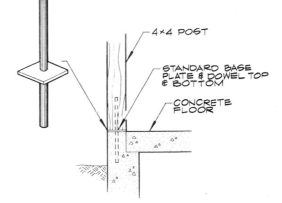

Figure 10.17 Section of post base dowel.

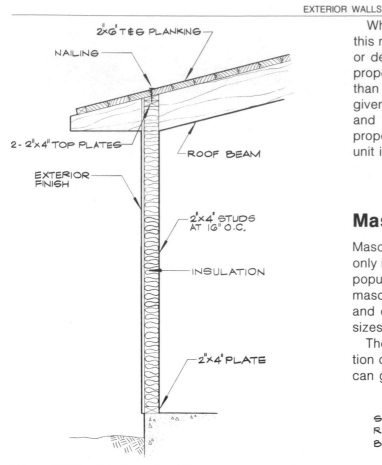

Figure 10.18 Exterior wall section.

through the beam and into the column. This method is preferred when glass is to be installed between the beams, whereas the use of metal fasteners or straps would pose an undesirable visual and installation problem. The use of post caps, saddles, and so forth, as discussed in Chapter 7, provide a more rigid connection and is recommended when visual and installation criteria have been satisfied. Figure 10.16, on the preceding page, illustrates a doweled beam-to-post connection.

Posts that are supporting roof beams are secured to the floor by metal post base connectors or dowels. (Information about and examples of metal post connectors are given in Chapter 7.) The use of dowels for a post base connection is acceptable when, like the beam to post connection, metal connectors are not desirable or when glass is to be installed and metal connectors cannot be concealed. An example of a doweled post base is shown in Figure 10.17 on the preceding page.

Where wood studs occur between the posts on an exterior wall, it is advantageous to frame the studs from the bottom plate to top plates directly under the planking. This allows nailing along the planking to the top plates, which aids to stiffen the structure laterally. Figure 10.18 illustrates this condition.

When assigned to provide architectural details for this method of framing, the architectural draftsperson or designer should strive to detail members that are properly fastened together. With fewer pieces used than in conventional framing, particular care must be given to connections where beams abut each other and where beams join posts. Connections that are properly fastened together allow the house to act as a unit in resisting external forces.

Masonry Construction

Masonry for exterior structural walls is utilized not only in commercial and industrial buildings but is very popular for residential construction. The two leading masonry units found in today's construction are brick and concrete block, and they are available in many sizes, shapes, textures, and colors.

The principal advantages for exterior wall construction of masonry are its fire-resistance qualities, which can give excellent fire ratings ranging from 2 to 4 or

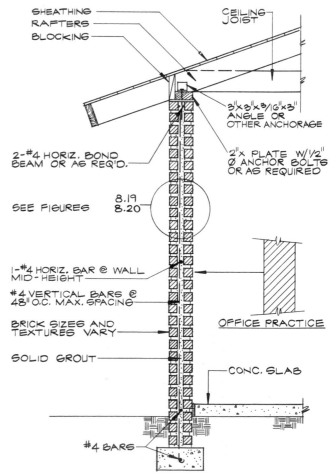

Figure 10.19 Section of reinforced grouted brick masonry wall.

more hours, and its ability to act as an excellent barrier to sound transmission.

When using solid brick units for an exterior structural wall, the assembly is determined by the region of the country in which the wall is to be constructed. If the region is subjected to earthquakes or very high winds, the use of steel reinforcing bars and solid grout is necessary to resist these forces.

An example of a reinforced grouted brick masonry wall is illustrated in Figure 10.19. Note the two horizontal bars located at the top of the wall. These bars form a bond beam that is designed to take the longitudinal flexure and tensile forces. This condition usually occurs at roof and floor levels. Sizes and placement of the remaining horizontal and vertical reinforcing steel are determined by local codes and regional requirements. For clarity, individual bricks are delineated in this section. However, when drawing details for a set of construction documents, Figure 10.20 is also an acceptable method for delineating a reinforced grouted brick wall because less drawing time is required.

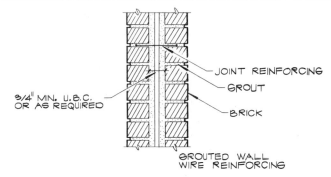

Figure 10.21 Grouted wall wire reinforcing.

There are two basic methods for reinforcing a grouted masonry wall: wire reinforcing and bar reinforcing. Wire reinforcing is placed between the joints to provide joint reinforcement. This is done in conjunction with the required vertical steel. Figure 10.21 illustrates an example of this method.

The second method, bar reinforcing, provides for horizontal reinforcing bars in the grouted wall space of the wall. The spacing of horizontal and vertical reinforcing bars depends on code and regional requirements. An example of a grouted wall with bar reinforcing is illustrated in Figure 10.22.

In areas where there is no concern for earthquakes or high winds, the use of the brick cavity wall is considered excellent for exterior wall construction. Two 3" or 4" walls of brick are separated with a 2" airspace or cavity. The cavity provides a suitable space for insulating materials and the two masonry walls are bonded together with metal ties set in mortar joints. A wall section illustrating the cavity wall is shown in Figure 10.23.

Concrete Block Wall

Hollow masonry units for exterior structural concrete block walls generally are 6 to 8 inches thick, depending on the height of the wall. The hollow sections of

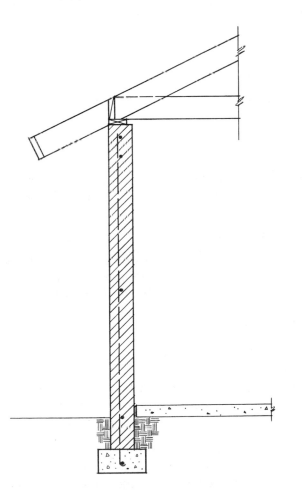

REINFORCED GROUTED BRICK MASONRY WALL

Figure 10.20 Reinforced grouted brick wall section.

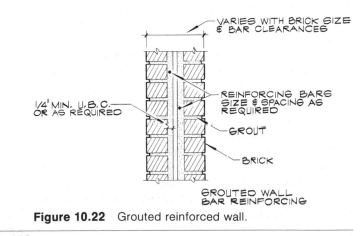

Figure 10.22 Grouted reinforced wall.

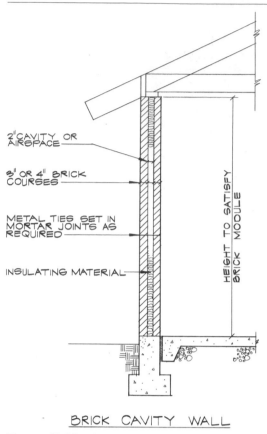

Figure 10.23 Brick cavity wall section.

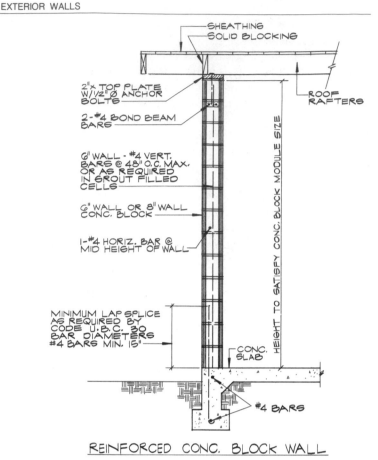

Figure 10.24 Reinforced concrete block wall section.

these units are called cells. These vertical cells may be left clear or filled solid with grout and reinforcing steel. This depends on the region and its code requirements. To enhance the insulating qualities of concrete block construction, open cells may be filled with a suitable insulating material.

When detailing an exterior concrete block wall, the architectural draftsperson should dimension the height of the wall or plate height to satisfy the modular heights of the masonry units selected. When wood partitions abut to a masonry wall, they have double studs bolted to the masonry wall with $\frac{1}{2}''$ bolts spaced not farther than 24" apart. When the wall is to be reinforced, horizontal steel is placed not more than $2\frac{1}{2}''$ from the outer face of the wall. When supporting a roof structure, the bearing wood plates are not to be less than 2 inches by 4 inches and bolted to the top of the wall with $\frac{1}{2}''$ bolts having not less than 6 inches of embedment and spaced no farther apart than four feet. A reinforced, grouted exterior concrete block wall is illustrated in Figure 10.24.

In many cases, concrete block may be used as a structural wall for economic reasons and then faced with a masonry veneer for architectural design requirements. Primarily, the attachment of a veneer depends on the following: the type of veneer to be used,

the region of the country, and local code requirements. Figure 10.25 illustrates a detail for 5 inch maximum brick veneer bonded to a concrete block structural wall for a region that is subject to seismic forces.

Wood Shear Walls

In areas where structures must be designed to resist lateral forces resulting from earthquakes or winds, exterior wood stud walls may be so designed to resist these forces. These walls are commonly referred to as "shear walls."

Wood shear walls, which are subjected to heavy forces, are normally stiffened by using plywood sheathing. The plywood sheathing is nailed to the studs with a specific nailing schedule that has been established by local building codes. These nailing schedules are based on the magnitude of the lateral forces, and they deal primarily with edge nailing and field nailing. Edge nailing considers the boundary or perimeter of the shear wall and field nailing refers to nailing within the boundary of the shear wall. In the course of detailing a wood shear wall, the designer should be aware of the following key connections: (1) floor or roof sheathing connections to the joist or

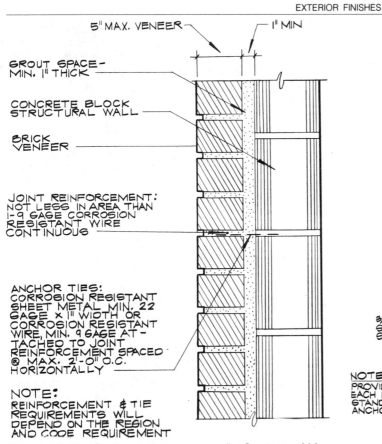

5" MAX. VENEER

1" MIN

GROUT SPACE—MIN. 1" THICK

CONCRETE BLOCK STRUCTURAL WALL

BRICK VENEER

JOINT REINFORCEMENT: NOT LESS IN AREA THAN 1-9 GAGE CORROSION RESISTANT WIRE CONTINUOUS

ANCHOR TIES: CORROSION RESISTANT SHEET METAL MIN. 22 GAGE × 1" WIDTH OR CORROSION RESISTANT WIRE, MIN. 9 GAGE ATTACHED TO JOINT REINFORCEMENT SPACED @ MAX. 2'-0" O.C. HORIZONTALLY

NOTE: REINFORCEMENT & TIE REQUIREMENTS WILL DEPEND ON THE REGION AND CODE REQUIREMENT

Figure 10.25 Section, brick veneer wall. (Courtesy of Masonry Institute of America.)

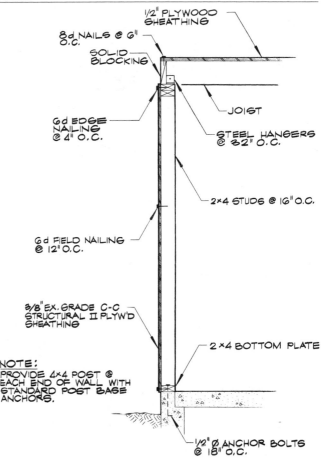

1/2" PLYWOOD SHEATHING

8d NAILS @ 6" O.C.

SOLID BLOCKING

6d EDGE NAILING @ 4" O.C.

JOIST

STEEL HANGERS @ 32" O.C.

2×4 STUDS @ 16" O.C.

6d FIELD NAILING @ 12" O.C.

3/8" EX. GRADE C-C STRUCTURAL II PLYW'D SHEATHING

2×4 BOTTOM PLATE

NOTE: PROVIDE 4×4 POST @ EACH END OF WALL WITH STANDARD POST BASE ANCHORS.

1/2" ∅ ANCHOR BOLTS @ 18" O.C.

Figure 10.27 Section, wood shear wall.

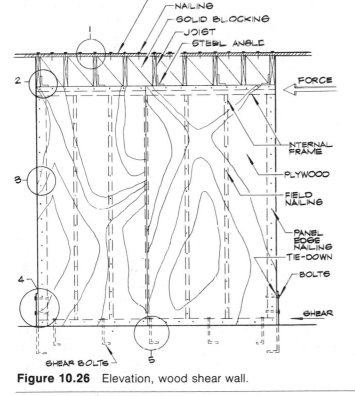

PLYWOOD DIAPHRAGM

NAILING

SOLID BLOCKING

JOIST

STEEL ANGLE

FORCE

INTERNAL FRAME

PLYWOOD

FIELD NAILING

PANEL EDGE NAILING

TIE-DOWN

BOLTS

SHEAR

SHEAR BOLTS

Figure 10.26 Elevation, wood shear wall.

rafters, (2) joist or rafter connection to top of wall, (3) 4" × 4" posts at each end of wall and edge nailing, (4) metal tie-down straps and bolts, if required by magnitude of force, and (5) number of anchor or shear bolts that are required to keep the wall from sliding off the foundation. An elevation of a wood stud shear wall and its key connections is illustrated in Figure 10.26.

The makeup of wood shear walls varies, depending on the forces they are designed to resist. An example of a section of a shear wall and the call out of the connections required is illustrated in Figure 10.27

Exterior Finishes

A variety of exterior finishes that may be attached to exterior wood stud walls are available. Of these materials, the most generally used are masonry veneer, wood siding, and cement stucco.

Masonry Veneer

Masonry veneer includes the use of brick, concrete block units, or stone. The maximum thickness of ma-

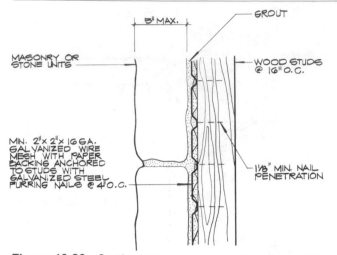

Figure 10.28 Section, masonry veneer. (Courtesy of Masonry Institute of America.)

sonry veneer is regulated by most building codes and is generally recognized as 5 inches. The term ''masonry veneer'' may be defined as strictly a masonry finish that is nonstructural and generally used for appearances.

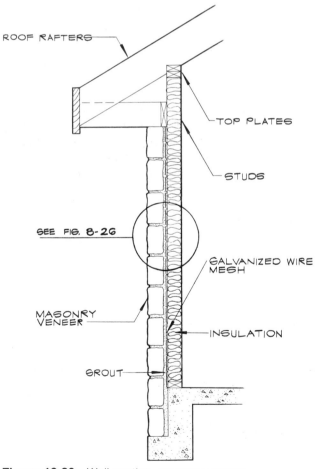

Figure 10.29 Wall section, masonry veneer.

Code requirements for the attachment of masonry or stone veneer units may vary depending on whether or not the locale is subject to earthquakes. In areas where this is a possibility, a positive bond between the veneer and stud wall is necessary. An example of a detail that provides an acceptable bond for this condition is illustrated in Figure 10.28.

After detailing an exterior wall section, using masonry veneer as an exterior finish material, it is good practice to provide a larger-scale detail showing the exact bonding technique to be used. See Figure 10.29. Figure 10.30 shows a masonry veneer on wood stud wall framing.

Wood Siding

Wood siding for exterior use on wood walls is available in various sizes and shapes and the method of attachment may vary with the locale.

Some of the more commonly used sidings and their recommended nailing techniques are illustrated in Figure 10.31.

Plywood is also widely used for exterior siding and is available in many grades and surface textures. Sheet sizes range from 8'-0" to 10'-0" in length and from $\frac{5}{16}$" to 1" in thickness.

For all types of exterior siding, proper nails should be specified. Aluminum or hot-dipped galvanized nails are recommended for exteriors because they will eliminate nail stains.

It is recommended that building paper be placed directly behind the siding. This blocks out water seepage and allows any vapor trapped within the stud spaces to escape.

Two acceptable methods for attaching wood siding to exterior walls are illustrated in Figure 10.32.

In cases where vertical siding has been selected, such as 1" × 6" tongue and groove, horizontal blocking between the studs should be provided to allow nailing of siding members that occur between studs.

Cement Stucco

Exterior lath and plaster over wood stud walls is one of the least expensive finishes used in today's construction. Its recommended sequence of application, when dealing with open wood stud construction, is as follows: No. 18 gauge wire is attached to the wood studs horizontally at 6" on center and stretched taut; over the wire a water-resistant building paper is applied to the vertical surfaces with the long dimension at right angles to the supports and the upper courses of the paper lapped over the lower not less than 6 inches; over the paper, woven wire fabric lath is applied to vertical surfaces with the long dimension at

Figure 10.30 Photograph of brick veneer construction.

right angles to the supports. Wire fabric lath joints should be lapped a minimum of 1 inch. The final step is the plaster. This is applied in three separate coats: scratch, brown, and finish coat. To finish the bottom of the wall, a drip screed is nailed to the mudsill. The total minimum thickness is $\frac{7}{8}$ inch.

Figure 10.33 illustrates the application sequence of exterior lath and plaster for open and sheathed frame construction. For sheathed wood frame construction, these steps are followed except for the use of the No. 18 gauge wire attached to the studs. See Figure 10.34.

Interior Finishes

Interior finishes on wood stud walls vary depending on what the architect specifies. In residential design, interior lath and plaster, drywall, and wood paneling or siding are most commonly used.

Interior lath and plaster are generally comprised of $\frac{3}{8}''$ or $\frac{1}{2}''$ thick solid or perforated gypsum lath nailed

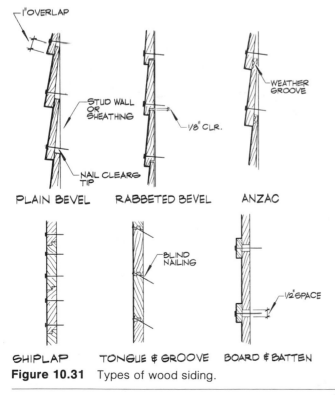

Figure 10.31 Types of wood siding.

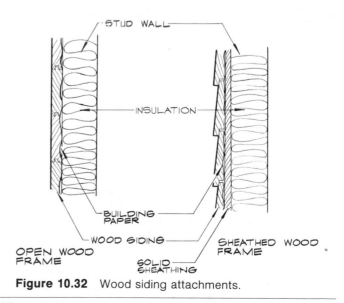

Figure 10.32 Wood siding attachments.

163

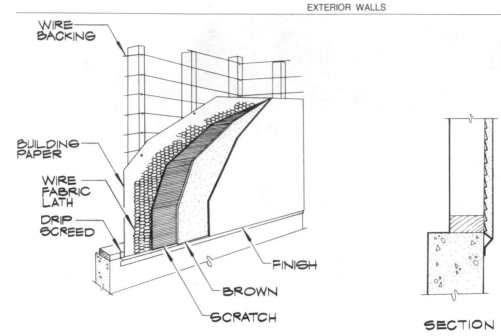

WIRE BACKING

BUILDING PAPER

WIRE FABRIC LATH

DRIP SCREED

FINISH

BROWN

SCRATCH

SECTION

Figure 10.33 Pictorial, exterior wall open frame construction.

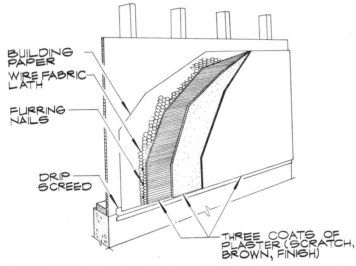

BUILDING PAPER

WIRE FABRIC LATH

FURRING NAILS

DRIP SCREED

THREE COATS OF PLASTER (SCRATCH, BROWN, FINISH)

1" SOLID SHEATHING

SECTION

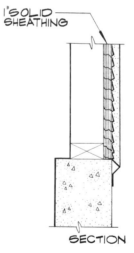

Figure 10.34 Pictorial, exterior wall sheathed frame construction.

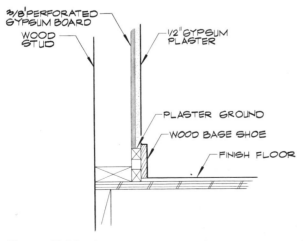

3/8" PERFORATED GYPSUM BOARD

WOOD STUD

1/2" GYPSUM PLASTER

PLASTER GROUND

WOOD BASE SHOE

FINISH FLOOR

Figure 10.35 Section, interior wall finish.

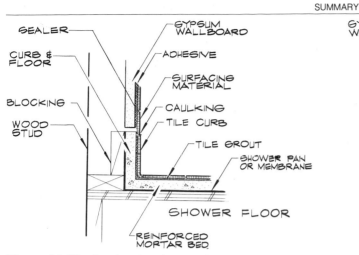

Figure 10.36 Section, interior wall finish.

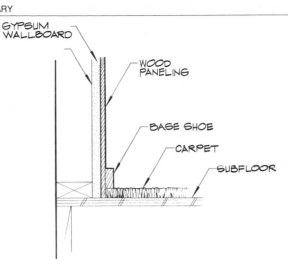

Figure 10.37 Section, interior wall finish.

directly to the wood studs. The perforated gypsum has $\frac{3}{4}$" diameter holes through the lath and is spaced at 16" on centers. These holes are provided to bond a finish coat of $\frac{1}{2}$" minimum thickness gypsum plaster to the lath.

Gypsum drywall ranges in thickness from $\frac{1}{4}$ inch to 1 inch, and is available in sheet sizes from 24" to 48" wide, and from 7' to 16' long. Gypsum wallboard is factory guaranteed and not dependent on job site workers. Drywall is nailed directly to the studs with the nails slightly indented so the nailhead may be concealed by a nail-spotting compound. Taping compounds are used to conceal the joints as the sheets are abutted together. Drywall also provides an excellent backing for wood paneling that is attached to the wall with an adhesive compound. Suggested interior wall sections using these materials are illustrated in Figures 10.35, 10.36, and 10.37.

Regional Differences

Some regions will require little or no reinforcing steel in the construction of masonry walls. Other regions, such as those subject to excessive wind pressure or seismic activity, will require extensive reinforcing steel in the walls.

Different regions will also vary in their exterior wall insulation requirements. For example, regions that experience cold temperatures will require more insulation than will regions with milder temperatures.

There will be variations among regions using exterior veneer wall construction and the attachment technique. Those regions subject to earthquakes will require a positive bonding method that must satisfy the building code requirements for that area.

The construction techniques for wood stud and cement stucco walls will vary according to regions. For example, open frame construction is primarily used in the western United States, whereas the solid sheathed frame construction is mainly used in the eastern United States.

Summary

Often, the architectural draftsperson is confronted with different exterior wall framing conditions for a specific structure. This chapter discussed and illustrated various framing techniques and their related details that are required to structure an exterior wall.

It is important to understand and evaluate the most logical framing technique for a specific structure before proceeding with architectural details. The designer must determine why one technique is more applicable than another.

11
ROOF TO WALL

Preview Chapter 11 deals with various types of roofs and their assemblies as they are structured to exterior walls. Types of roof materials discussed are wood, tile, and hotmopped tar and gravel. Examples of wood roof framing and how they are structured to wood, concrete, and masonry exterior walls are discussed and illustrated.

Upon completion of this chapter, the architectural draftsperson will:

1. Know about wood shingled roof with variations of eave and rake design to exterior wood stud wall.
2. Understand pitched clay tile roof with boxed-in eave and exposed ratters.
3. Know about built-up composition and gravel roofing with level and sloping rafters, including detailing at parapet walls.
4. Understand roofing conditions that necessitate the use of flashing, coping, gravel guards, reglets, and aluminum fascias.

Eave Detail

The architectural detail that incorporates the roof to the wall assembly is commonly referred to as an eave detail. Members that may be incorporated into a roof to wall eave detail are defined as follows.

Fascia—A finished horizontal member varying in size; it is normally secured to the ends of the rafters.
Rake—The roof-to-wall assembly that occurs on the sloping or pitched edge of the roof.
Soffit—An enclosed or boxed-in assembly directly below or under the roof rafters and perpendicular to the exterior wall.
Parapet—A low wall that projects above the finished roof and may be a continuation of a wall below or erected independently upon the roof structure.

Wood Shingles

Prior to beginning an eave detail, the architect should have information on the following:

Roof material
Rafter size and spacing
Roof or eave overhang
Architectural design of eave
Roof pitch
Roof sheathing
Exterior wall material

The architectural scale used for an eave detail may vary from $\frac{3}{4}'' = 1'\text{-}0''$ to $1\frac{1}{2}'' = 1'\text{-}0''$, depending on the complexity of the assembly.

An eave detail for a wood shingle roof with the following criteria is illustrated in Figure 11.1. A pictorial view is given in Figure 11.2.

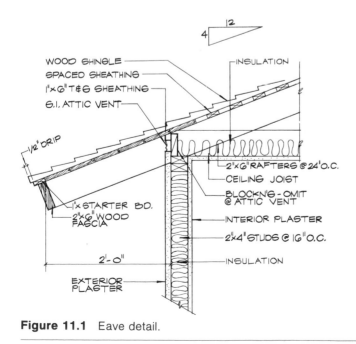

Figure 11.1 Eave detail.

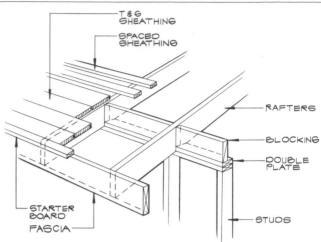

Figure 11.2 Pictorial, eave detail.

Roof material: Wood shingles
Roof pitch: 4 in 12
Roof overhang: 2'-0"
Rafter size and spacing: 2" × 6" @ 24" o.c.
Roof sheathing: 1" × 4" spaced, 1" × 6" T & G (exposed)
Fascia board: 2" × 6"
Exterior wall: 2" × 4" woods with exterior plaster finish

Tail Rafters

The design of the eave detail has a major influence on the overall design of a structure, and the use of tail rafters helps to establish its character. The tail rafter is an exposed wood member that is spliced to the common roof rafters or nailed to intermediate blocking between the roof rafters. Normally, tail rafters are spaced farther apart than are the roof rafters, ranging anywhere from 32" o.c. (on center) to 48" o.c., depending on the design selection.

Generally, tail rafters have a minimum thickness of 3", with the end of the tail rafter cut to a design that is harmonious with the architectural character of the building. An eave detail incorporating tail rafters is shown in Figure 11.3; a pictorial view is found in Figure 11.4.

Boxed Eave or Soffit

A boxed-in or soffited eave detail results when additional framing is used completely to enclose the rafters that extend beyond the wall line. It is most important that provisions are made in the detail for ventilating the attic space when designing a boxed-in eave—assuming that no other ventilating method is used.

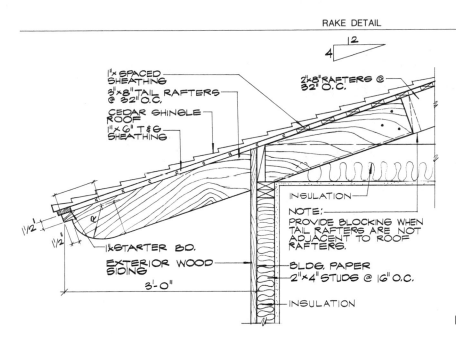

Figure 11.3 Eave detail.

The finish of the boxed-in eave may be of any acceptable exterior material. Figure 11.5 illustrates a soffited eave detail.

Rake Detail

Prior to detailing the rake section, it is recommended that the eave detail be completed since its design dictates the members to be incorporated into the rake assembly. As defined previously, the rake is the assembly that occurs along the sloping edge of a roof. This is shown pictorially in Figure 11.6.

Rake

In many cases, the overhang for the rake is different from that of the eave. An example of a rake detail, which would be compatible with the eave-detail illustrated in Figure 11.1, is shown in Figure 11.7. It should be noted that the roof rafters at the rake assembly are not notched at the top plate, whereas the rafters are at the eave assembly, as illustrated in Figures 11.1, 11.3, and 11.5.

Built-up Composition and Gravel

The components of a roof-to-wall assembly vary with the type of finish roof specified. In the case of the

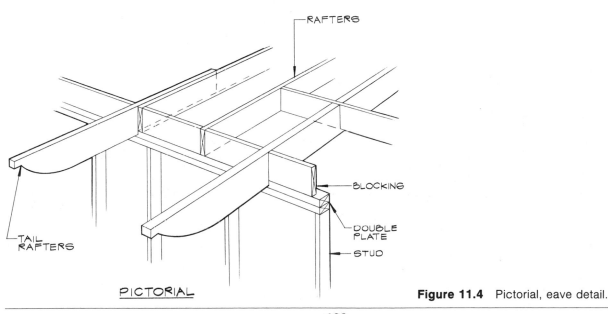

Figure 11.4 Pictorial, eave detail.

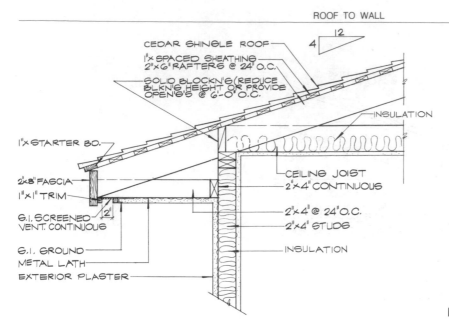

Figure 11.5 Eave detail.

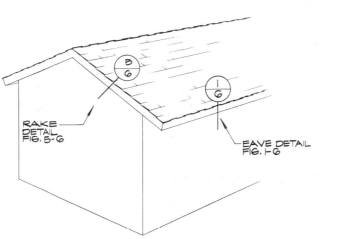

Figure 11.6 Pictorial, eave and rake location.

built-up composition and gravel roof, the pitch may vary from 0″ in 12″ to 3″ in 12″ and—obviously—the roof sheathing is solid rather than spaced. The procedure for detailing an eave detail with a built-up composition and gravel roof, $2\frac{1}{2}$: 12 roof pitch, $\frac{1}{2}$″ plywood roof sheathing, 2″ × 8″ roof rafters @ 24″ o.c., 2″ × 8″ redwood fascia and 2′-0″ overhang is illustrated in Figures 11.8 and 11.9.

The designer should first select the scale that is most suitable to illustrate clearly the members in the assembly. The roof pitch and main members should then be drawn lightly and to scale. This procedure is illustrated in Figure 11.8. The same scale that is to be used for the detail may be used to establish the roof pitch by scaling 12″ along the horizontal at the top plate and scaling $2\frac{1}{2}$″ vertically. Upon completion of laying out the detail, the designer may finalize the detail and call out the members that comprise the assembly. This procedure is illustrated in Figure 11.9.

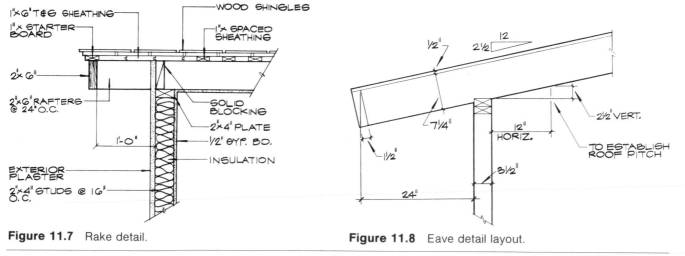

Figure 11.7 Rake detail.

Figure 11.8 Eave detail layout.

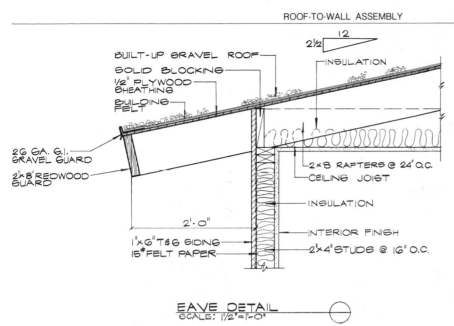

Figure 11.9 Eave detail.

Roof-to-Wall Assembly

The roof-to-wall assembly, for plank and beam construction, varies according to the beam and plank direction; that is, whether the planking is parallel or perpendicular to the exterior wall. It is important that the top plates are nailed directly to the planking whenever possible because this helps to stiffen a structure laterally when framed by this method. A roof-to-wall assembly is illustrated in Figure 11.10. Note that the 2″ × 6″ T & G planking is parallel to the exterior wall.

Parapets

The roof-to-wall assembly for parapet walls in wood construction generally incorporates balloon framing for walls that extend above the roof to facilitate a parapet. The use of balloon framing supports the parapet wall structurally since it is subject to wind and seismic forces. An example of the framing of a parapet wall with the use of balloon framing is illustrated in Figure 11.11.

Prior to adding the finished wall and roofing materials, it is most important that steps are taken to alleviate the possibilities of water leaks into walls and ceiling. Starting at the top of the parapet wall, a metal

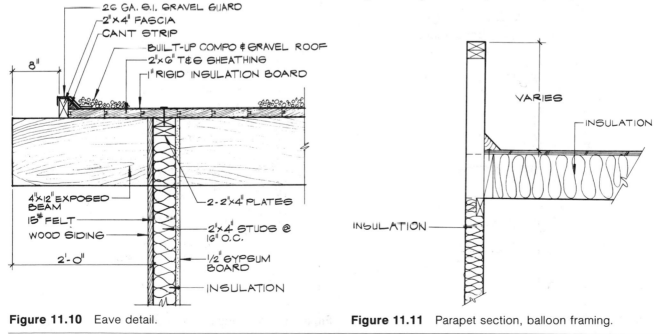

Figure 11.10 Eave detail.

Figure 11.11 Parapet section, balloon framing.

cap may be used. This member is referred to as a "coping cap" and may be made of galvanized sheet metal or aluminum with sections up to 10'-0" in length. To join the sections, a soldered connection is recommended.

The attachment of the metal coping to the top of the wall may be accomplished with the use of an approved construction adhesive. As you move down the wall to the roof intersection, you find a vunerable condition exists for the possibility of water leaks, and it is therefore necessary to provide a well-flashed assembly. One method for water control is to attach a metal flashing member to the wall just above the roof plane. This member is referred to as a "reglet" and may be made from galvanized iron or aluminum sheet metal of varying shapes and sizes. The reglet should be level and nailed securely to the stud wall; it may act as a plaster ground for the exterior finish of the wall above. After the roofing is applied, a metal flashing member is snapped into the reglet without the use of nails or screws and lapped a minimum of 3" at all joints. This member provides a cover over the finish roofing and wall intersection. Figures 11.12 and 11.13 illustrate these techniques for a wood stud and plaster parapet wall, in section and pictorial views.

Masonry and concrete parapet walls are primarily found in commercial and industrial structures. The detailing of the roof-to-wall intersection is the most

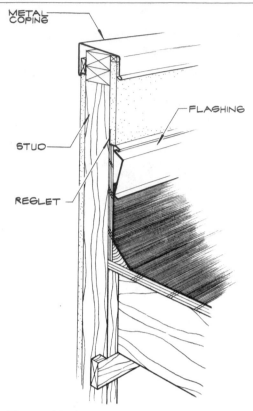

Figure 11.13 Pictorial, parapet wall.

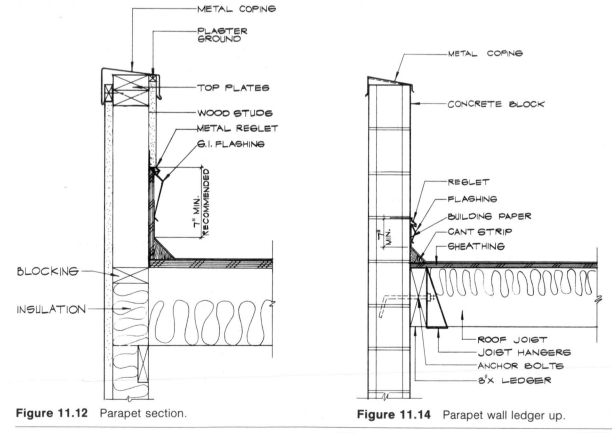

Figure 11.12 Parapet section.

Figure 11.14 Parapet wall ledger up.

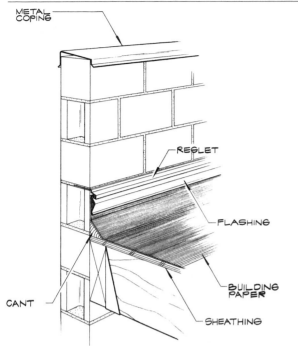

Figure 11.15 Pictorial, parapet wall ledger up.

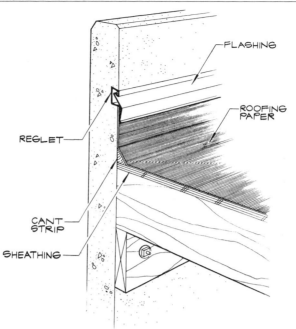

Figure 11.17 Pictorial, concrete parapet wall.

critical factor since this joint is the most vulnerable to roof leaks. The structuring of a wood roof to a masonry or concrete parapet wall may vary, depending upon the selection of the architect or engineer. One method of attachment involves hanging the roof rafters from a ledger bolted to a masonry wall using joist hangers or framing anchors. This method allows the ledger to be in the same plane as the roof rafters. Figures 11.14 and 11.15 illustrate this condition. Fig-

ure 11.16 depicts a ledger bolted to a concrete parapet wall at the bottom of the roof rafters, thus eliminating the need for framing anchors or joist hangers. Figure 11.17 shows the situation pictorially.

Metal Fascias

Metal fascias for an eave assembly are primarily used in commercial or industrial designed buildings. Most metal fascias are manufactured from .050 gauge aluminum and come in various sizes and shapes.

Many metal fascia designs may be an integral part of a roof flashing system since they may be incorporated as a gravel guard, coping, and fascia design in one complete unit. An example of a aluminum fascia acting as one complete unit is illustrated in Figures 11.18 and 11.19. Figures 11.20 and 11.21 show the use of aluminum as a fascia only.

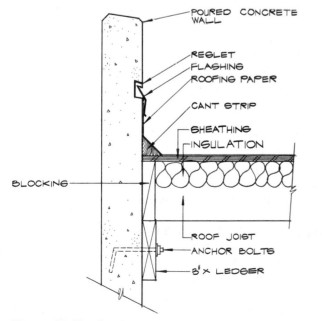

Figure 11.16 Section, concrete parapet wall.

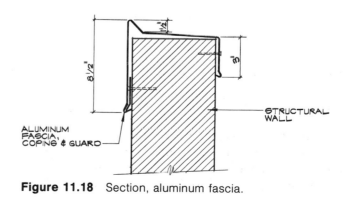

Figure 11.18 Section, aluminum fascia.

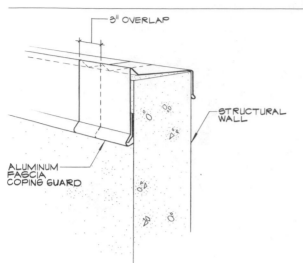

Figure 11.19 Pictorial, aluminum fascia.

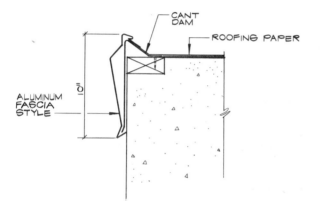

Figure 11.20 Section, aluminum fascia.

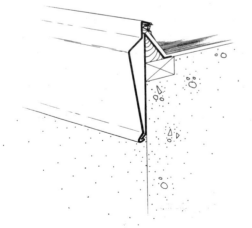

Figure 11.21 Pictorial, aluminum fascia.

Tile Roof

The roof-to-wall assembly that employs the use of clay tile as a finish roofing material is similar to a built-up composition and gravel roof in that it requires solid roof sheathing and felt roofing paper hotmopped. The

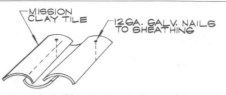

Figure 11.22 Pictorial, tile roof fastening.

Figure 11.23 Pictorial, tile roof fastening.

roofing paper and hotmopping application are the primary deterrents against roof leaks, whereas clay tile is for beauty and architectural style.

When selecting clay tile as a finish roofing material, the architectural draftsperson must realize that tile is one of the heaviest finish roofing materials used and requires larger framing members such as rafters and supporting beams to hold the additional weight. Three acceptable methods for securing the tiles to the roof are the use of 12 gauge galvanized wire, 10 gauge copper wire, or .084 diameter stainless steel wire. Figures 11.22 and 11.23 illustrate these two methods of fastening tile to a wood roof structure. A complete eave assembly using clay tile as a finish roof material is illustrated in Figure 11.24.

Masonry Construction

The roof-to-wall assembly for wood roof construction and masonry walls depends primarily on bolted connections for the main structural attachment. The roof structure bears upon wood plates bolted to the top of a masonry wall with the bolt size and spacing governed by the code requirements of the region in which the structure is to be built. When wood rafters are used, as in residential construction, rafters are attached to the top plate with steel clip angles that are bolted to the rafter and top plate. However, other approved attachment methods may be employed.

At the top of a masonry wall, or at the roof or ceiling line, a continuous bond beam assembly is comprised of horizontal reinforcing steel bars a minimum of 15 inches deep and filled solid with grout. The bond beam design serves to absorb the longitudinal flexural and tensile forces that may be induced in a masonry wall. Wood roof construction to a reinforced brick masonry wall is illustrated in Figure 11.25.

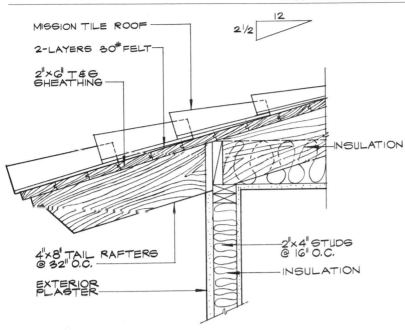

MISSION TILE ROOF

2-LAYERS 30# FELT

2"x6" T&G SHEATHING

2 1/2 | 12

INSULATION

4"x8" TAIL RAFTERS @ 32" O.C.

EXTERIOR PLASTER

2"x4" STUDS @ 16" O.C.

INSULATION

Figure 11.24 Eave detail.

Parapet Walls

Parapet walls, of masonry construction, are primarily used in commercial and industrial buildings. Basically, the reason for a parapet wall is to deter the spreading of fire from one building to another. The minimum height of parapet walls and reinforcing depends on local code requirements. The method of structuring wood roof construction to a brick masonry parapet wall depends on the selection of the architect or engineer. Figure 11.26 illustrates an assembly method

where a 4 inch ledger is bolted to a reinforced brick wall with the use of approved joist hangers supporting intersecting roof members. The size and spacing of the anchor bolts depends upon engineering design requirements. Directly below this assembly is the bond beam with its required reinforcing and depth. As previously indicated, the roof-to-wall intersection assembly is very critical since it is susceptible to roof leaks. As shown in Figure 11.26, the use of a cant strip, building paper, flashing, and a reglet are recommended for proper sealment to prevent roof leaks.

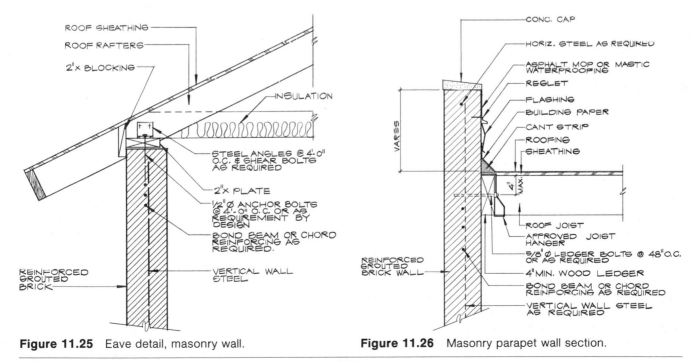

ROOF SHEATHING

ROOF RAFTERS

2"x BLOCKING

INSULATION

STEEL ANGLES @ 4'-0" O.C. & SHEAR BOLTS AS REQUIRED

2"x PLATE

1/2" Ø ANCHOR BOLTS @ 4'-0" O.C. OR AS REQUIREMENT BY DESIGN

BOND BEAM OR CHORD REINFORCING AS REQUIRED.

REINFORCED GROUTED BRICK

VERTICAL WALL STEEL

Figure 11.25 Eave detail, masonry wall.

CONC. CAP

HORIZ. STEEL AS REQUIRED

ASPHALT MOP OR MASTIC WATERPROOFING

REGLET

FLASHING

BUILDING PAPER

CANT STRIP

ROOFING

SHEATHING

VARES

4" MAX.

ROOF JOIST

APPROVED JOIST HANGER

5/8" Ø LEDGER BOLTS @ 48" O.C. OR AS REQUIRED

4" MIN. WOOD LEDGER

BOND BEAM OR CHORD REINFORCING AS REQUIRED

VERTICAL WALL STEEL AS REQUIRED

REINFORCED GROUTED BRICK WALL

Figure 11.26 Masonry parapet wall section.

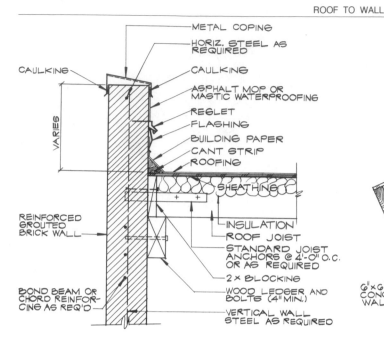

(LEDGER DOWN)

Figure 11.27 Masonry parapet wall section.

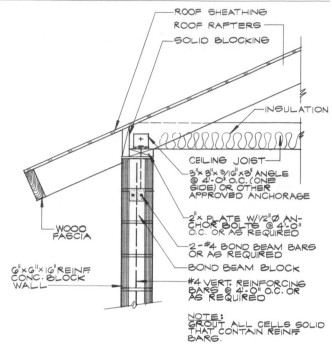

Figure 11.28 Eave detail, masonry wall construction.

The top of the parapet wall may be finished with a concrete cap and mastic waterproofing as indicated. In regions subject to earthquakes, masonry parapet wall reinforcement is designed for lateral loads prescribed by governing codes.

Figure 11.27 illustrates an alternate method for a roof-to-wall assembly where the wood ledger is located below the intersecting roof members and joist anchor straps are utilized to provide a positive bond between the roof system and the masonry bearing wall. Recommended sealment techniques are illustrated in this figure, as in Figure 11.26. However, metal coping is used at the top of the parapet wall in lieu of a concrete cap. A metal coping at the top of a parapet wall is highly recommended to prevent moisture from entering the wall.

Concrete Block

The attachment of wood roof construction assemblies to concrete block exterior walls is connected in the same manner as that for brick masonry wall. The primary difference is the placement of the bond beam bars. Concrete block manufacturers have provided a special bond beam block that allows bond beam bars to be placed adjacent to one another rather than vertically as in brick masonry construction. In concrete block construction, only the cells containing reinforcing bars are filled and grouted solid. A concrete block wall with wood roof construction is illustrated in Figure 11.28.

A reinforced concrete block wall and parapet with an intersecting wood roof structure are illustrated in Figure 11.29. The use of bond beam block and the placement of horizontal and vertical steel reinforcing

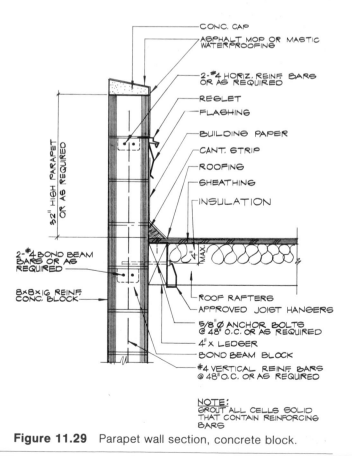

Figure 11.29 Parapet wall section, concrete block.

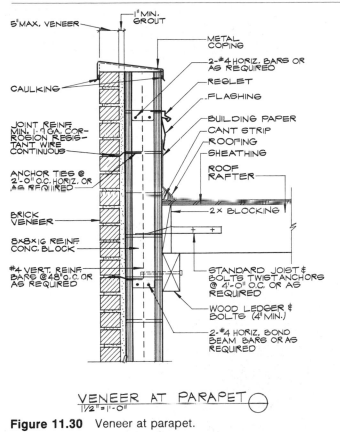

5" MAX. VENEER

1" MIN. GROUT

CAULKING

JOINT REINF. MIN. I-9 GA. COR-ROSION RESIS-TANT WIRE CONTINUOUS

ANCHOR TIES @ 2'-0" O.C. HORIZ. OR AS REQUIRED

BRICK VENEER

8×8×16 REINF. CONC. BLOCK

#4 VERT. REINF. BARS @ 48" O.C. OR AS REQUIRED

METAL COPING

2-#4 HORIZ. BARS OR AS REQUIRED

REGLET

FLASHING

BUILDING PAPER

CANT STRIP

ROOFING

SHEATHING

ROOF RAFTER

2× BLOCKING

STANDARD JOIST & BOLTS TWIST ANCHORS @ 4'-0" O.C. OR AS REQUIRED

WOOD LEDGER & BOLTS (4" MIN.)

2-#4 HORIZ. BOND BEAM BARS OR AS REQUIRED

VENEER AT PARAPET
1/2" = 1'-0"

Figure 11.30 Veneer at parapet.

bars are only applicable in areas where structural design criteria and building codes require this assembly.

In many cases, the architect chooses to use concrete block mainly as a structural wall and selects a veneer for an exterior appearance. In so doing, the attachment or bonding of the veneer is dependent on the region in which the structure is to be built.

In Figure 11.30, an illustration of this condition is shown in detail form. The following assemblies should be observed: a metal coping and caulking that completely covers and seals possible leaks through the veneer, grout space and concrete block wall, joint reinforcement, and anchor ties as specified by region and code requirements.

Regional Differences

In considering roof-to-wall assemblies, one of the most significant differences found between regions is the bonding of the roof-to-wall elements to satisfy lateral design requirements. Roof and wall insulation requirements will vary according to the climatic conditions of a region. The roof pitch and roof materials may also be selected for climatic conditions particular to a region, such as having a steeper roof pitch in areas with heavy snow conditions.

Summary

Architectural draftspersons should be cognizant of the various roof-to-wall assemblies that may be influenced by a specific architectural design. However, they should understand that there are basic connections that must be satisfied regardless of the architectural design.

An important factor to be stressed is the necessity for acceptable flashing methods for parapet walls and the intersection of roof framing members to deter the possibilities of roof leaks.

This chapter also intended to illustrate various bolted connection assemblies that are required when joining wood roof members to exterior masonry walls.

12
DOORS

Preview Chapter 12 introduces the subject of doors and their detailing implications. The chapter is divided into five sections. The first deals with the framing around the door and the structural complications that arise when an opening is created in a wall for a door. The second covers the finished framing found around and immediately adjacent to the door. The third examines a variety of doors that an architectural draftsperson might encounter when dealing with exterior doors, such as hinged or sliding doors, and even varying conditions around the exterior doors, such as wood frame or concrete slab floors. The fourth describes the various interior doors and shows them in pictorial and detail form: hinged, sliding, wardrobe, accordian, and folding doors. The final section concerns doors in masonry walls.

A complete understanding of doors not only helps an architectural draftsperson to understand their component parts and how they work but also enables the drawing of accurate and precise elevations as well.

After reading this chapter, the architectural draftsperson will:

1. Understand the structural implications of locating doors in a wall.
2. Become familiar with the vocabulary relating to doors.
3. Become familiar with the problems faced by the finish carpenter when installing doors.
4. Understand fire rating of doors and its implication to the architectural industry.
5. Be able to differentiate between various types of doors.
6. Know how to weatherproof the door against wind, rain, and noise.
7. Be able to draw elevations with a greater degree of accuracy.
8. Be equipped to solve the problems presented by a variety of conditions and the use of a variety of materials.
9. Understand the various sizes of the different parts of a door.
10. Comprehend how wood and metal jambs are installed into a masonry wall.
11. Appreciate the need for modular units and their effects on door details.
12. Understand how to detail a door in a brick veneer.

The study of door detailing must start with a complete understanding of the framing that exists around a door.

Openings for a door, in a wood framed wall, involve breaking the normal pattern of studs placed at 16″ o.c. If and when the stud pattern is broken, the weight of the wall itself must be distributed around the opening. This is done by placing a beam called a lintel (sometimes referred to as a header) over the opening. This lintel is supported by a double stud system as shown in Figure 12.1.

Since the lintel is housed in a stud wall, its width cannot increase. For additional strength (needed for larger openings), the vertical dimension or height is increased. The opening that is created is considered the rough opening and is made by a rough carpenter—the finish carpenter then puts in the finishing touches.

Door Nomenclature

The top of the door is called the head; the sides are referred to as the jamb. The bottom or base of the door is called the sill.

An interior door usually has no sill since the floor continues, unless there is a change of level. In detailing, these terms become the titles to the details themselves.

Door Frame

The door frame fits around the door itself and the rough framing. The terms used to describe it may vary somewhat. One source calls the total frame a jamb, the top frame a head jamb, and the sides a finished jamb. This book reserves the term jamb to describe the side portion of a window or door and consequently calls the top of the door frame a finished head, and the sides a finished jamb.

These frames can be made on the job or purchased preassembled at the plant and suppliers. Since there are only three sides to an interior door frame, the frame may come precut but usually not assembled. An exterior door frame, in contrast, usually comes precut and assembled.

The rough opening is measured much larger than the door frame requires. This allows for ease of installation and, if there is any deflection of the lintel or twisting of the studs, the door frame remains unaffected. The space between the frame and the rough opening is called a shim space. If the lintel is not absolutely perpendicular with the studs, the shim space still allows for a good square door frame to fit. See Figure 12.2.

When the door is closed, there is a wood strip on the frame that prevents the door from going any farther. This piece is called the doorstop, and it can be nailed to the frame after the door is installed, or the frame can be purchased with the doorstop already planted or milled in the frame.

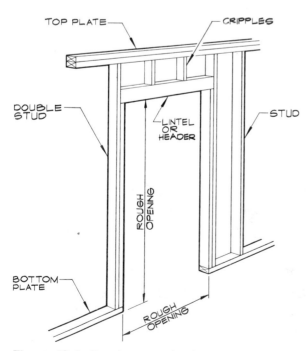

Figure 12.1 Framing around a door.

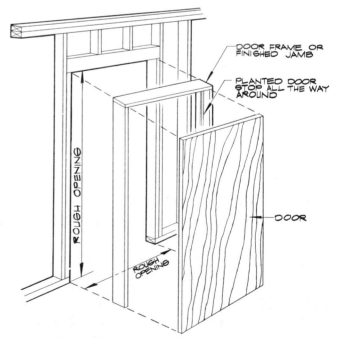

Figure 12.2 Rough and finished carpentry. (From *Architectural Drafting and Design,* 2nd ed., by Ernest R. Weidhaas, copyright © 1972, by Allyn & Bacon, Inc. Reprinted by permission of the publisher.)

Fire Rating

It would be well to note here that other than considerations of strength and durability, fire rating (rate of consumption by fire) becomes a factor in selecting a type of door. In residences, one need not be too concerned about fire rating of doors, except if there is a door between the house and garage where the required rating is 1 hour.

In areas dealing with many people, such as industrial or commercial buildings, the building codes require certain fire-rated doors. The physical appearance of a 1 and 2 hour door may be the same but one may be rated higher because of the special chemical treatment it received or the material with which it is made.

Fire rating is established by the American Society of Testing and Measurement (ASTM).

Exterior Hinged Door

A hinged door fits snugly into the door frame and is hinged on one side. The opening left by the door frame is about $\frac{1}{4}$ inches larger than the door itself. The door's thickness usually depends on the location: $1\frac{3}{4}$ inches for exterior doors and $1\frac{3}{8}$ inches for interior doors. The door is very seldom made of one solid material but rather is a series of laminations or of pieces.

Basically, doors can be categorized as (1) flush, often called slab doors, and (2) panel doors. A flush door can be subdivided into the solid slab, or solid core, and the hollow core.

The solid slab is the better of the two doors and is made of a core of lumber, particle board (wood chips glued together), or chemically treated gypsum (which looks like chalk) with a veneer covering of mahogany, birch, ash, or other finishes. See Figure 12.3. Because it is solid, it weathers better and is not subject to warping as the hollow core is during extreme temperature changes.

The hollow core has the advantage of being lightweight, easier to install, and easier to open and close. It is made of a frame consisting of vertical stiles, a top rail, and a bottom rail of Douglas fir or ponderosa pine.

In between the stiles and rails exists a network either of cardboard, much like an egg crate, or cross bands of wood. In fact, one manufacturer uses small wooden spirals packed together to form a honeycomb structure. See Figure 12.3.

Panel doors are made of solid stiles and rails with recessed portions called panels. These panels can be left plain or can be handcarved—manufacturers' literature should be consulted to see the various patterns

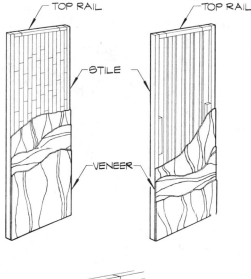

Figure 12.3 Interiors of hollow and solid core doors. (Courtesy of Edward J. Muller, *Architectural Drawing and Light Construction,* copyright © 1967. By permission of Prentice-Hall, Inc., Englewood Cliffs, N.J.; also courtesy of the Strait Door & Plywood Corporation.)

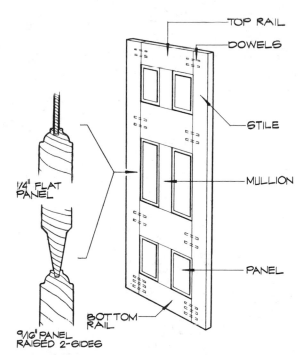

Figure 12.4 Panel door construction. (Courtesy of Fir & Hemlock Door Association/Western Wood Products Association.)

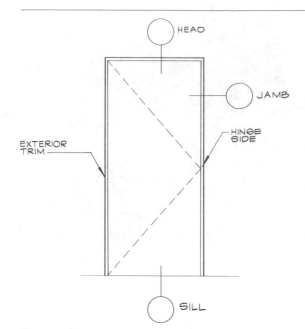

Figure 12.5 Elevation of exterior door.

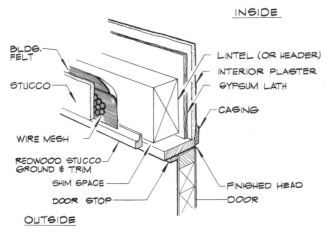

Figure 12.6 Head section of a door.

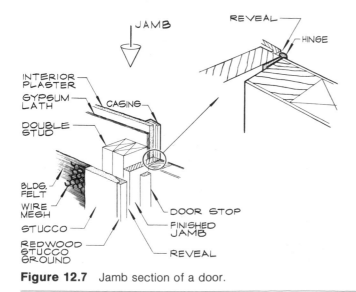

Figure 12.7 Jamb section of a door.

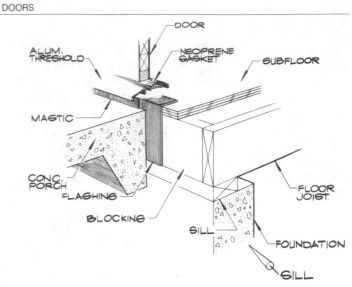

Figure 12.8 Sill section of a door.

available. Some of the panels may be replaced with glass to produce further flexibility of design. Depending upon the method of construction and thickness, panels can be used on the exterior of a structure as well as the interior. See Figure 12.4 on the preceding page.

A slight variation of the slab and the panel is the plant-on, which is usually a solid slab door with a decorative raised molding glued directly on the door. This might be done on one side or both sides, depending upon the need and desire of the client.

When drafting a hinged door, remember that you are cutting through a head, jamb, and sill.

A view, as found in Figure 12.5, may help to explain the detailing process. In the figure, a door similar to one found on an exterior elevation is shown. Notice how the reference bubbles cut through the head (top), the jamb (side), and the sill (bottom). These reference bubbles are saying: "There are details of these areas."

A pictorial representation of the head, jamb, and sill

Figure 12.9 Exterior view of the head and jamb.

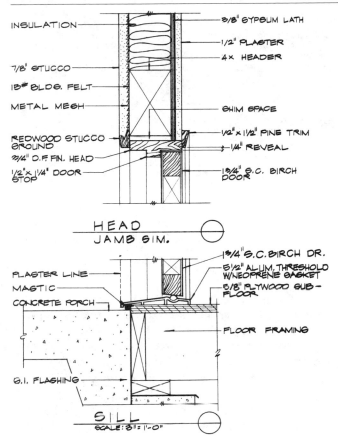

Figure 12.10 Drafted detail of an exterior door.

is shown in Figures 12.6, 12.7, and 12.8. Also note the photograph of the almost complete door head in Figure 12.9.

Note how much the head and jamb are alike. Except for the difference between the lintel and the studs, they are exactly alike. In a situation when objects will look alike in the final detail, one is eliminated. In window and door details, it is sufficient to draw the head only and indicate "JAMB SIMILAR" in the title as done in Figure 12.10, above.

Notice the use of the casing to cover the joint between the finished jamb and the plaster, Figure 12.7. Note also on the drafted detail, Figure 12.10, that there is a little space left below the pine trim (casing) and the redwood stucco ground. This area is called a reveal. If the casing and the Douglas fir finished jamb are left flush, this appears as a crack between the wood rather than a planned event. Also, the reveal is needed to allow space for the hinge. Look at doors around your home and notice this reveal.

The header is called out as a 4 × rather than a 4 × 6 or 6 × 8 in Figure 12.10. This indicates that the draftsperson is not sure of the size and, rather than hazard a guess, is forcing the contractor to look elsewhere for this measurement — which should be found on the roof framing plan. Another reason is that this one detail may be used for a variety of widths of doors and each may have a different header size.

The shim space indicates the amount of the space left between the rough opening and the door frame. The thin lines running down to the break line represent the members on the jamb. For example, the two lines running down the redwood stucco ground on Figure 12.10 represent the same piece on the jamb. It is shown in this manner because it is a true section with the portions not being cut represented as an elevation. Refer to Figure 12.7.

Always be sure to keep this head and the sill lined up. The outer edge of the header should *always* line up with the outer edge of the blocking on the sill.

Exterior Hinged Door with Sill

As an alternate solution to the previous detail, a metal casing and the use of a sill are discussed. See Figure 12.11. Note the use of the metal casing (often called casing beads). This is a bent piece of galvanized material shaped so as to allow the interior plaster to end abruptly.

Unlike the wood casing that sticks out beyond the plaster, the metal casing allows everything to be flush with the plane of the wall. See the sketch accompanying Figure 12.11. A reveal is still used so that a hinge can be installed in the jamb portion. The trim is reduced in size; notice how the door location has been changed compared with the previous detail — it is now closer to the outside.

The addition of a sill requires a knowledge of what happens to the frame around it. To accommodate the sill, the floor joists are beveled at an angle. See Figure 12.12. Blocking is put in its normal position, but a sec-

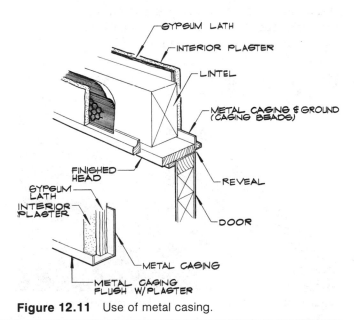

Figure 12.11 Use of metal casing.

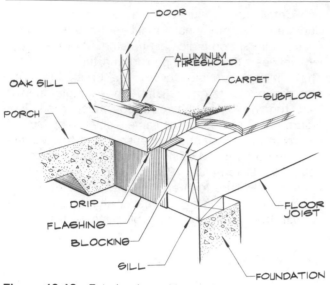

Figure 12.12 Exterior door with wood sill.

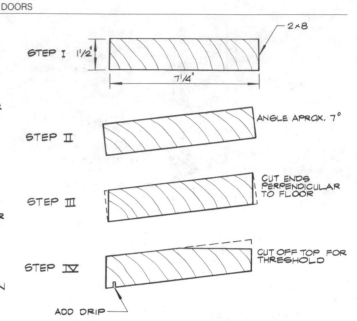

Figure 12.14 Sequence showing development of a sill.

ond blocking is located between floor joists to give a sound base for the sill.

The sill comes already preformed and attached to the rest of the door frame. It is usually 2 inches in thickness (1½ inches net) and 6 or 8 inches in width as the need requires. The material composing the sill should be hardwood such as oak, since it must withstand much wear. The angle the sill makes with the floor joist is approximately 7°. Figure 12.13 shows the finished appearance of the sill.

For drawing purposes, the detailer should take a sheet of paper, follow the steps outlined in Figure 12.14, and prepare a sill that can be slipped under the detail for location and size.

On the underside of the sill, you will notice a drip. The purpose of the drip is to prevent any water that might reach this point from going any farther up the underside. The sill should be placed slightly higher than the subfloor to allow for the finished floor of hardwood, carpet, and so on.

To keep the area waterproof, note the use of flashing and a sealant called mastic. Mastic is somewhat flexible and moves with the structure around it. See Figure 12.15. Notice also on the detail that the doorstop and the trim are one and the same piece. You can purchase the frame made in this way.

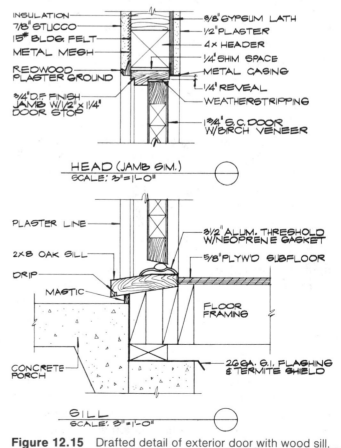

Figure 12.15 Drafted detail of exterior door with wood sill.

Figure 12.13 Photograph of exterior door with wood sill.

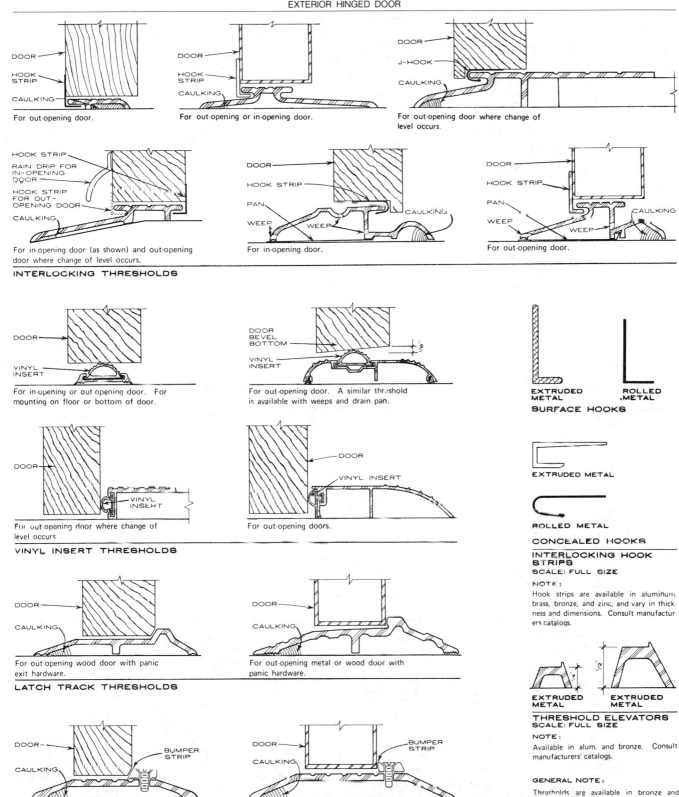

Figure 12.16 Exterior saddle and weatherstrip. (Reproduced from *Architectural Graphic Standards* with permission from John Wiley & Sons, Inc.)

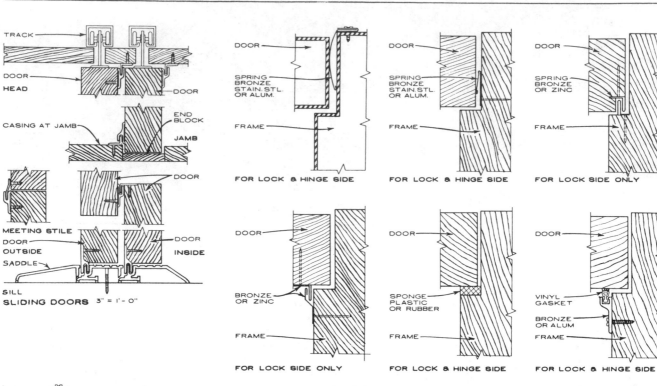

SLIDING DOORS 3" = 1'-0"

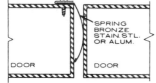

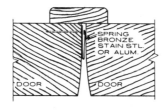

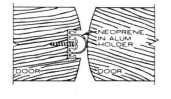

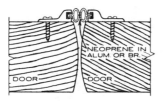

MEETING STILES

DOOR JAMBS
SCALE: HALF SIZE
NOTE: Door heads are similar except where noted otherwise.

DOOR SILLS
SCALE: HALF SIZE

Dan Cowling and Associates, Inc.; Little Rock, Arkansas

Figure 12.17 Weatherstrip for doors. (Reproduced from *Architectural Graphic Standards* with permission from John Wiley & Sons, Inc.)

Finally, the door can be weatherstripped. Weatherstripping is a process of adding material around the perimeter of a door to prevent dirt, draft, light, or sound from entering. This material can be thin sheets of bronze nailed to either the door or frame that is compressed when the door is closed. Aluminum, neoprene (a pliable rubberlike substance), felt, and even sponge rubber have been used. See Figure 12.16. An interlocking type is one in which a preformed metal piece fits into another. See interlock samples in Figure 12.17.

Exterior Door with Slab Floor

The head and jamb are usually not affected by a change of floor material, and, therefore, the section confines itself to the sill portion. For head and jamb treatment, refer to the previous section. In fact, as seen in Figure 12.18, the treatment is the same as in Figure 12.8 except for the floor material.

Figure 12.19 illustrates a drafted sample of the door sill. When a wood sill is introduced to this area, the problems are compounded somewhat because of the necessity of preforming the concrete. When the original concrete footing is poured, a piece of lumber (2 × 6 or larger) is put into place. When the concrete dries, the lumber is removed and replaced with a wood sill of the same length. An example of this is illustrated by the oak sill in Figure 12.20.

To attach the oak sill to the concrete, a variety of procedures can be used. One of the more popular methods is to employ a device called a tamp-in. It consists of a cylindrical lead outside, threaded on the inside, with a plug on the end. See Figure 12.21. A hole is drilled into the concrete the same size as the lead shield.

On striking this lead shield, the plug at the bottom that is a tampered shape forces the lead shield to ex-

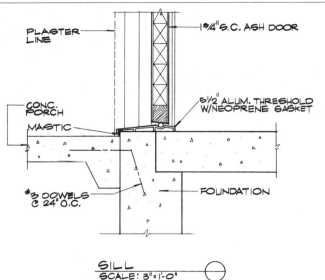

Figure 12.19 Drafted detail of exterior door with slab footing.

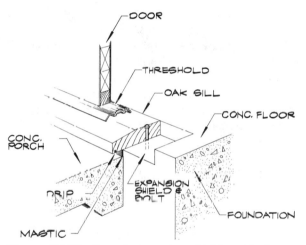

Figure 12.20 Use of expansion shield and bolt.

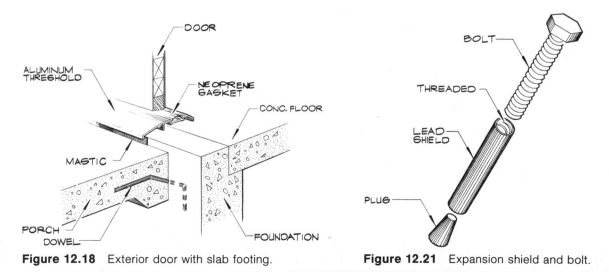

Figure 12.18 Exterior door with slab footing.

Figure 12.21 Expansion shield and bolt.

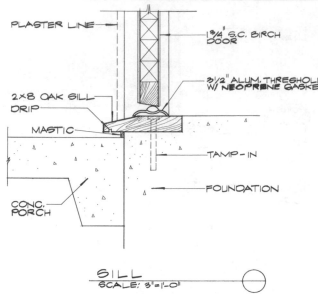

Figure 12.22 Drafted detail of sill using tamp-in.

pand against the concrete. The harder one hits the shield, the better the grip the shield has on the concrete. A bolt can now be installed through the oak sill into the shield, thus producing a good connection. See Figure 12.22, above.

Another method is to use a wood sleeper that is placed into the footing when the concrete is poured into the form. Galvanized anchors are located on the underside of the sleeper prior to placement to ensure a good bond. The wood sill is then nailed or screwed to this sleeper. See Figure 12.23.

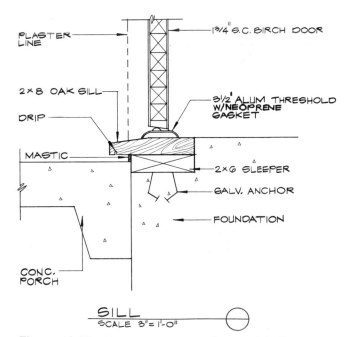

Figure 12.23 Use of a sleeper under a wood sill.

To keep the water away from the underside of the sill, mastic and a drip are incorporated once again. See Figures 12.22 and 12.23 for drafted samples of the detail.

Exterior Sliding Door

Aluminum and steel, as well as wood, are widely used in this country for sliding doors. They are manufactured and brought on the job for installation. Since they are premade, there is very little a draftsperson can do to alter their size or shape.

Some firms prefer to have detailers show all aspects of the sliding door—the stationary parts as well as the moving ones. By doing this, it is felt that the people looking at the detail can draw elevations of the door more accurately and understand better how the mechanical parts function. Without drawing them, many things, such as whether the screen is on the inside or outside, cannot be easily recognized.

However, with very little control over the moving parts, other offices prefer their time to be best spent showing how the door frame fits into the wall, how the surrounding area is affected, and what pieces are needed to control the problem of good joints, water

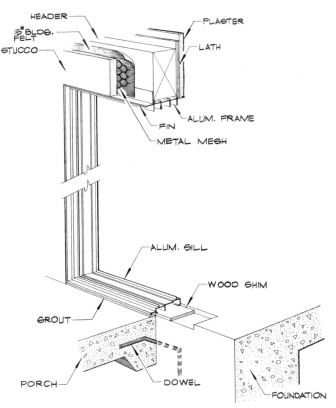

Figure 12.24 Aluminum sliding door. (Series 750 Arcadia Sliding Window, manufactured by Northrop Architectural Systems.)

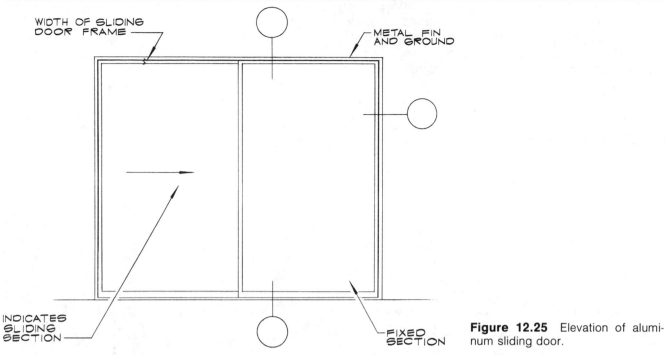

WIDTH OF SLIDING DOOR FRAME

METAL FIN AND GROUND

INDICATES SLIDING SECTION

FIXED SECTION

Figure 12.25 Elevation of aluminum sliding door.

coming into the structure, the airtightness of the unit, and so on. Figure 12.24 is a pictorial drawing of an aluminum sliding door without the moving parts; Figure 12.25 shows the source of the detail in elevation form; and Figure 12.26 depicts how this would appear with the moving parts and is drafted as you would see it on a set of working drawings.

Figure 12.27 illustrates a wood sliding door in detail form without the moving parts illustrated. All parts in this detail are made of specially treated wood except the sill, which is made of aluminum. However, as the detail shows, the aluminum can only be seen on the outside. From the inside, the door appears to be made totally of wood.

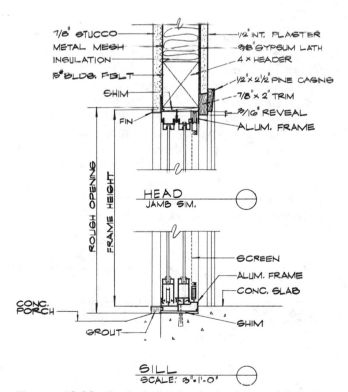

7/8" STUCCO
METAL MESH
INSULATION
15# BLDG. FELT
SHIM
FIN

1/2" INT. PLASTER
3/8" GYPSUM LATH
4 × HEADER
1/2" × 2 1/2" PINE CASING
7/8" × 2" TRIM
3/16" REVEAL
ALUM. FRAME

HEAD
JAMB SIM.

SCREEN
ALUM. FRAME
CONC. SLAB
SHIM

CONC. PORCH
GROUT

ROUGH OPENING
FRAME HEIGHT

SILL
SCALE: 3"=1'-0"

Figure 12.26 Drafted detail of aluminum sliding door showing moving parts. (Series 750 Arcadia Sliding Window, manufactured by Northrop Architectural Systems.)

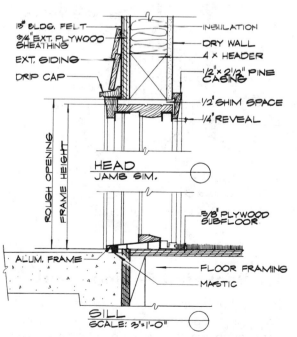

15# BLDG. FELT
3/4" EXT. PLYWOOD SHEATHING
EXT. SIDING
DRIP CAP

INSULATION
DRY WALL
4 × HEADER
1/2" × 2 1/2" PINE CASING
1/2" SHIM SPACE
1/4" REVEAL

HEAD
JAMB SIM.

3/8" PLYWOOD SUBFLOOR

ALUM. FRAME
FLOOR FRAMING
MASTIC

ROUGH OPENING
FRAME HEIGHT

SILL
SCALE: 3"=1'-0"

Figure 12.27 Drafted detail of sliding door excluding moving parts. (Courtesy of Rolscreen Company, Pella Division.)

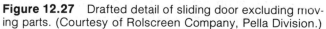

A closer look at the manufacturer's literature shows how much of the wood has been reinforced by some type of metal, such as aluminum, but not exposed visually. This is to keep the wood from twisting or warping and from binding into the moving parts.

Interior Hinged Doors

The discussion of interior hinged doors is a very easy one in that usually the head and jamb are alike and there is very seldom a need to draw a sill. Also, you must treat the interior hinged door like the inside portion of the exterior door for visual continuity. Two solutions have been drafted and are found in Figure 12.28.

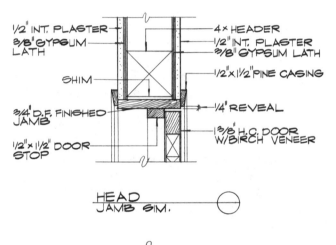

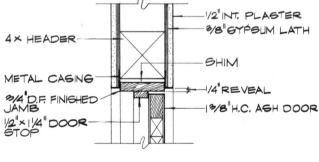

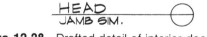

Figure 12.28 Drafted detail of interior door.

Interior Pocketed Sliding Door

The frame, as well as the door and hardware, of a pocketed sliding door is premanufactured and available at most suppliers. It consists of a frame similar to the one pictorially described in Figure 12.29.

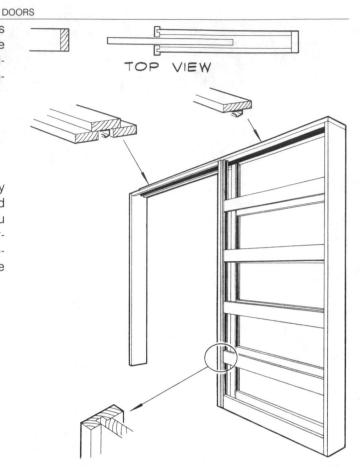

Figure 12.29 Pocketed sliding door. (Courtesy of the Nordahl Mfg. Co., Inc.)

Also note the top view. The head section is made up of three pieces of wood over the opening, and the very top pieces continue into the pocket portion.

The jamb of the opening is normally as wide as the studs plus the thickness of the interior finish material. The jamb of the opening on the pocket side is also as wide as the studs plus the finish material but is made so that a $\frac{3}{4}$ inch to $1\frac{3}{8}$ inch thick door can slide into the pocket. The width of the pocket is only as wide as the studs.

The track on which the door will slide is built right into the head section. See Figure 12.30 for an exam-

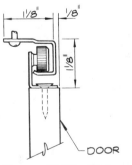

Figure 12.30 Sliding door hardware: Rocket® Grant®.

ple of the type of hardware that might be used and its dimensions. For a 2'-6" wide door, a 5'-0" wide space is needed for the frame, which thus causes the use of a larger header over the opening.

For a drafted detail, three drawings are necessary to describe the complete unit. See Figure 12.31. First, the head showing how the frame fits into the opening, what the track and door look like in relation to the head, and how the surrounding area is finished.

Notice the use of additional doorstops on all three details; they are necessary to keep the door in place after it is installed. Also, if there is any need to repair the hardware or remove the door, one simply removes the doorstops.

The second detail shows how the door slides into the pocket and its framing. Finally, the bottom detail shows the jamb opposite the pocket. The two doorstops on this detail are not necessary. If used, the door is easier to hang since any irregularity is hidden. Without them, the door must be hung properly and great care must be taken to see that there is no space between the door and the jamb.

Wardrobe or Closet Doors

Wardrobe and closet doors come in a variety of different types as well as thicknesses. The smaller hinged doors can use the details previously described; but larger doors, like a 8'-0" wide wardrobe door, should use solid materials to keep them from warping. Plywood with a good veneer finish is often used for sliding wardrobe doors, but lumber core doors seem to resist warpage the best.

Thickness of sliding wardrobe doors ranges from $\frac{3}{4}$ to $1\frac{3}{8}$ inches, 6'-8" in height, and whatever width that is required. If excessive weight is encountered, such as a mirror on the face of the door, it is best to run the track on the bottom. Otherwise, most doors are suspended from a track above with hardware similar to that described in Figure 12.32 and with nylon floor guides at the bottom. This type of hardware is for doors up to 50 pounds.

For doors weighing up to 100 pounds, hardware as shown in Figure 12.33 is used. While the number of rollers appears to have doubled, they have in fact quadrupled. Each bracket looks like an upside down roller skate with four rollers. Notice in the drafted version, Figure 12.34, how the lower portion is kept in place by means of nylon guides, with the extra large casing used to hide the hardware, and the lack of casing on the interior of this wardrobe, an area one will never visually see. Figure 12.35 illustrates how a metal casing bead is used to reduce the excessive

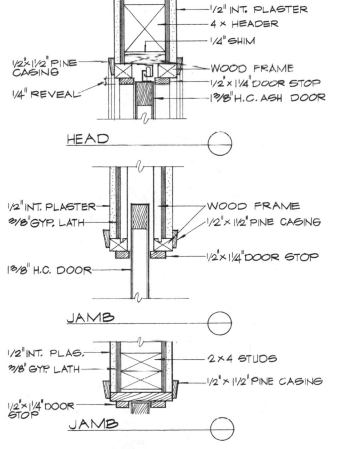

Figure 12.31 Drafted detail of interior sliding door.

Figure 12.32 Wardrobe door hardware: Rocket® Grant®.

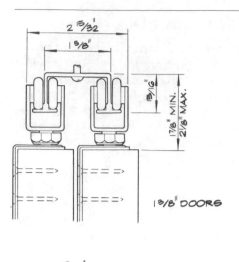

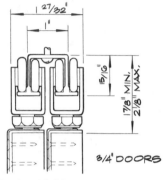

Figure 12.33 Heavyweight sliding door hardware: Rocket® Grant®.

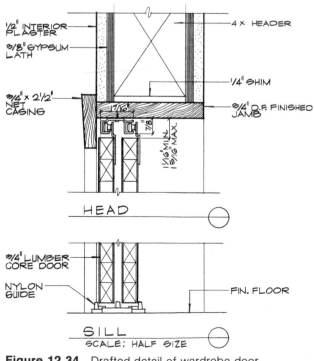

HEAD

SILL
SCALE: HALF SIZE

Figure 12.34 Drafted detail of wardrobe door.

HEAD
HALF SIZE

JAMB
HALF SIZE

Figure 12.35 Drafted detail using metal casing bead at wardrobe door.

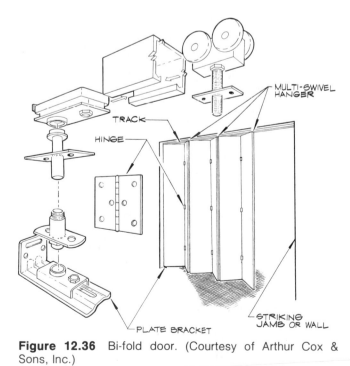

Figure 12.36 Bi-fold door. (Courtesy of Arthur Cox & Sons, Inc.)

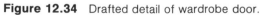

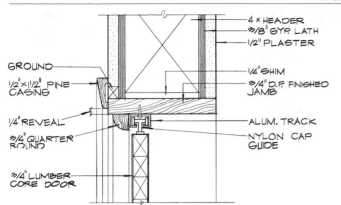

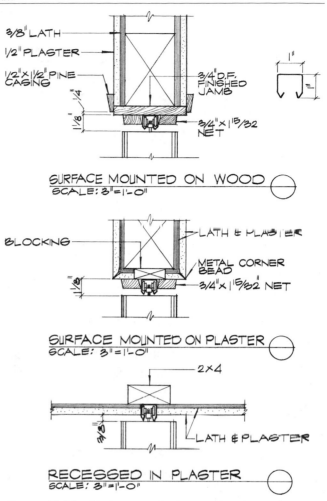

Figure 12.37 Drafted detail of bi-fold door.

lines created by the pine trim and increase simplicity of the finish.

There are two types of folding doors that are popular for wardrobe or closet doors: the bi-fold doors that fold open from the center toward the jamb and the folding doors that fold open only to one side.

The more popular bi-fold door has four panels—two folds to the right and two folds to the left. If there are many panels hinged together as shown in Figure 12.36, the door is not only pivoted on one jamb but requires a track and rollers. Each pair is pivoted on its respective jamb.

If the weight of these doors is not too great (for example, using a $\frac{3}{4}$ inch door), a track and roller at the top are not used. This does, however, require a track and guide as shown in the drafted version of this detail on Figure 12.37, above.

Visually, the second type of folding door looks like an accordion. Better quality folding doors are made of wood, but they can be obtained in plastic, fabric, and synthetic leather, such as vinyl. They can be mounted on wood, surface mounted on plaster, or recessed in plaster. See Figure 12.38 for jamb drawings; see Figure 12.39 for drafted samples.

Figure 12.39 Drafted detail of accordian door. (Courtesy of Rolscreen Company, Pella Division.)

Masonry

Before reading this section, the architectural draftsperson should review Chapter 8 and become familiar with the nomenclature, method of assembly, and drafted representation used.

Prior to this section, we have dealt primarily with wood construction. While there are many implications in dealing with wood, such as weatherproofing, correctness of representation, source of detail, variation of construction, and sequence of construction, there was never a problem with the size of the door being detailed. The rough opening was mentioned briefly because the height of the header or the location of double st...   could be placed ...   the location of studs and the location of the door could significantly raise the cost of construction when it is too often off the normal 16″ o.c. spacing, yet in masonry

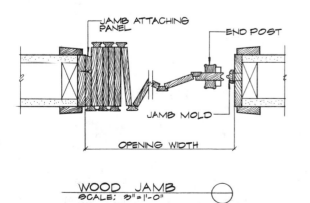

Figure 12.38 Drafted detail of accordion door at jamb. (Courtesy of Rolscreen Company, Pella Division.)

construction, it becomes almost mandatory to understand not only how a door is installed but what space is available for the detailer to work with. This space, called the masonry opening, is based on the size of the masonry units used and the size of the joints in between. Consequently, this section first discusses

1. How the door size dictates the detail.
2. How the masonry unit size dictates the detail.
3. How the size of the joint dictates the final detail configuration.

To illustrate best the implication for the architect, the authors used a publication called *Masonry Design Manual,* published by the Masonry Industry Advancement Committee. A great deal of research went into the study of the most efficient and practical door system used in a concrete block structure. Notice the basic construction used around doors and windows in Figure 12.40.

Doors come in a variety of sizes from 2'-0" to 3'-0" or more. It was discovered that a 4 inch system worked the best. Since doors differ in width normally by 2 inches, the following categories were established.

Group 1—includes doors 2'-0", 2'-4", 2'-8", and 3'-0" wide.

Group 2—includes doors 2'-2", 2'-6", 2'-10", 3'-2", and 3'-6" wide.

The width of either group can be increased by multiples of 4".

Group 1 doors have, by design, a $2\frac{3}{16}$" head and a $2\frac{3}{16}$" jamb width when using a 4" or 8" concrete block. Look at Figure 12.41 and locate a chart called Scheme A. On this chart, you will note this system employs a $\frac{3}{8}$" mortar joint. Note, also, that for a 6"-8" door, the first concrete block, in the wall, must be either $2\frac{3}{16}$" or $6\frac{3}{16}$" below the floor line and $2\frac{3}{16}$" below the floor line for a 7'-0" door. This information has a direct bearing on the foundation details.

The details on Figure 12.41 are designed for this system of $\frac{3}{8}$" mortar joints with a 4" or 8" concrete block, a 6'-8" or 7'-0" door with a specified distance below the floor line, and a $2\frac{3}{16}$" head. Details 1, 2, 3, and 4 are designs for exterior doors, while details 5 and 6 are for interior doors. In either case, the first piece coming into contact with the concrete block is called a buck and should be $1\frac{1}{2}$" thick. A $1\frac{1}{2}$" piece is $1\frac{3}{16}$" net. The finished jamb below it should be a 1" piece that will be $\frac{3}{4}$" net. The space between is the shim space and is approximately $\frac{1}{4}$". The total of these measurements gives us the desired $2\frac{3}{16}$" needed for a 6"-8" or 7'-0" door.

The corresponding jamb details for these head details on Figure 12.41 can be found in Figure 12.42. On Figures 12.41, 12.42, and the pictorial drawing on Fig-

ure 12.46, there is an extra piece of wood between the finished jamb and the concrete block. This is called a buck. It is nothing more than a spacer, subjamb, or shim piece to accommodate the required space between the masonry opening and the door opening. The buck is not a structural member in the sense that it does not hold up the masonry units.

Because the finished jambs are $2\frac{3}{16}$", a 2'-0" door requires a $2'-4\frac{3}{8}$" masonry opening, a 2'-4" door requires a $2'-8\frac{3}{8}$" masonry opening, a 2'-6" requires a $3'-0\frac{3}{8}$" opening, 3'-0" door a $3'-4\frac{3}{8}$" opening, and so on. The $2'-4\frac{3}{8}$" and $3'-0\frac{3}{8}$" openings require a 12" long concrete block, while the $2'-8\frac{3}{8}$" + $3'-0\frac{3}{8}$" necessitate concrete blocks that are 8" long or multiples of 8" such as 16" long blocks. Thus it can readily be seen that selection of the correct size concrete block affects the door details.

If it is desired to use other than $\frac{3}{8}$" joints, Scheme B in Figure 12.41 should be used. In Scheme B, three joint sizes are recommended. They are $\frac{3}{8}$", $\frac{7}{16}$", and $\frac{1}{2}$". All start with the first row of blocks, even with the floor level, and require the doors to be cut to a smaller size. Using the $\frac{1}{2}$" joint, with 4" concrete blocks, the door opening ends up greater than the standard 6'-8" or 7'-0" door and requires a space of almost 1" at the bottom of the door. This space can be accounted for by the use of a correctly sized threshold.

Group 2 is for doors that are 2'-2", 2'-6", 2'-10", 3'-2", and 3'-6", or 4" multiples of them. They require no buck since the finished $1\frac{1}{2}$" jamb ($1\frac{3}{16}$" net) is applied directly to the concrete block. See Figure 12.43 for their schemes.

As with the Group 1 doors, the Group 2 doors require a

$2'-4\frac{3}{8}$" masonry opening for a 2'-2" door.
$2'-8\frac{3}{8}$" masonry opening for a 2'-6" door.
$3'-0\frac{3}{8}$" masonry opening for a 2'-10" door.
$3'-4\frac{3}{8}$" masonry opening for a 3'-2" door.
$3'-8\frac{3}{8}$" masonry opening for a 3'-6" door.

Also note that masonry openings of $2'-4\frac{3}{8}$", $3'-0\frac{3}{8}$", and $3'-8\frac{3}{8}$" require 12" long blocks and $2'-8\frac{3}{8}$" and $3'-4\frac{3}{8}$" require a 8" module block. See Figure 12.44 for jamb details and dimensions.

Under no circumstances should Group 1 doors be mixed with Group 2 doors. If this happens, the total modular system is useless; not only are there different door heights, but chaos occurs in the placement of concrete blocks in the wall to accommodate the doors.

The way the door is attached to the concrete block wall is illustrated in Figure 12.45. A pictorial view of one of the typical methods is illustrated in Figure 12.46. A pictorial illustration of the corresponding head section can be found in Figure 12.47.

TYPICAL RESIDENTIAL CONSTRUCTION

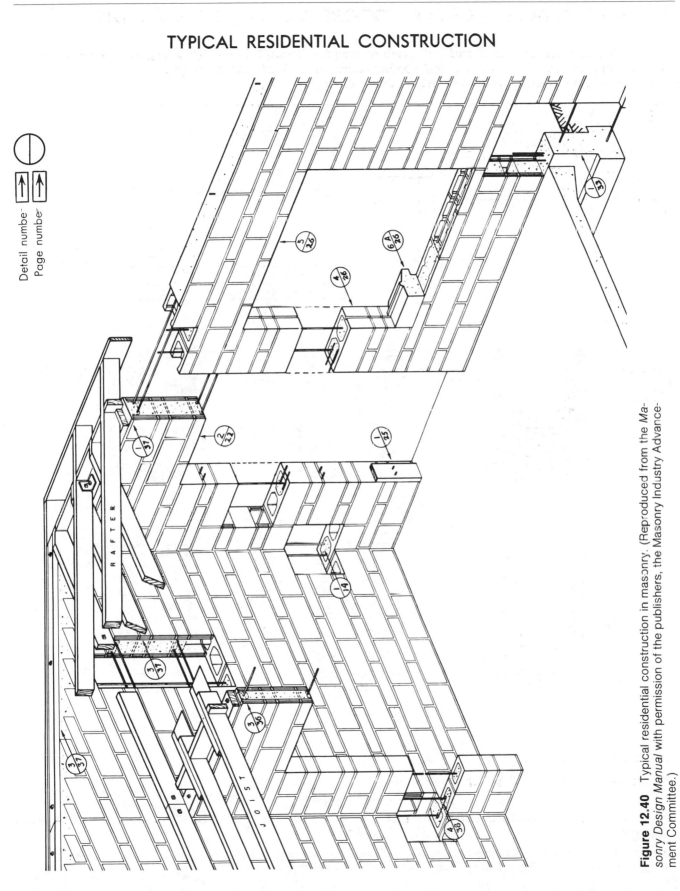

Detail number
Page number

Figure 12.40 Typical residential construction in masonry. (Reproduced from the *Masonry Design Manual* with permission of the publishers, the Masonry Industry Advancement Committee.)

HEAD DETAILS — GROUP 1 DOORS (2'-0", 2'-4", 2'-8" & 3'-0" WIDE)

In order to have 2⅞" head and 2⅞" jamb widths for Group 1 doors either scheme A or B shown below should be used — (when using combinations of 8" high and 4" high units a detailed wall section should be made to establish height dimensions)

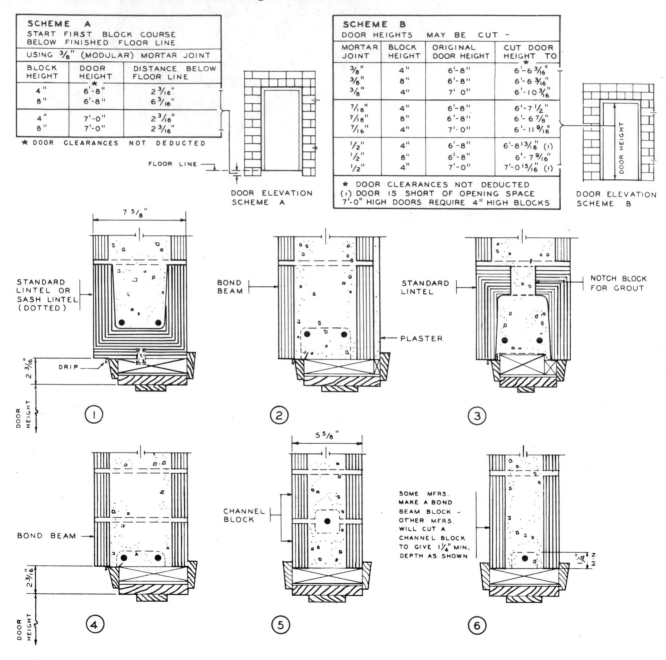

SCHEME A

START FIRST BLOCK COURSE BELOW FINISHED FLOOR LINE

USING ⅜" (MODULAR) MORTAR JOINT

BLOCK HEIGHT	DOOR HEIGHT ★	DISTANCE BELOW FLOOR LINE
4"	6'-8"	2 3/16"
8"	6'-8"	6 3/16"
4"	7'-0"	2 3/16"
8"	7'-0"	2 3/16"

★ DOOR CLEARANCES NOT DEDUCTED

SCHEME B

DOOR HEIGHTS MAY BE CUT —

MORTAR JOINT	BLOCK HEIGHT	ORIGINAL DOOR HEIGHT	CUT DOOR HEIGHT TO ★
⅜"	4"	6'-8"	6'-6 3/16"
⅜"	8"	6'-8"	6'-6 3/16"
⅜"	4"	7'-0"	6'-10 3/16"
7/16"	4"	6'-8"	6'-7 1/2"
7/16"	8"	6'-8"	6'-6 7/8"
7/16"	4"	7'-0"	6'-11 9/16"
1/2"	4"	6'-8"	6'-8 13/16" (1)
1/2"	8"	6'-8"	6'-7 9/16"
1/2"	4"	7'-0"	7'-0 15/16" (1)

★ DOOR CLEARANCES NOT DEDUCTED
(1) DOOR IS SHORT OF OPENING SPACE
7'-0" HIGH DOORS REQUIRE 4" HIGH BLOCKS

Details 1, 2, 3 and 4 are for exterior doors

Details 5 and 6 are for interior doors

Note—Do not mix Group 1 doors with Group 2 doors because head heights and jamb widths will vary—   scale 1½" = 1'-0"

Figure 12.41 Head details of Group 1 doors. (Reproduced from the *Masonry Design Manual* with permission of the publishers, the Masonry Industry Advancement Committee.)

JAMB DETAILS — GROUP I DOORS (2'-0", 2'-4", 2'-8" & 3'-0" WIDE)

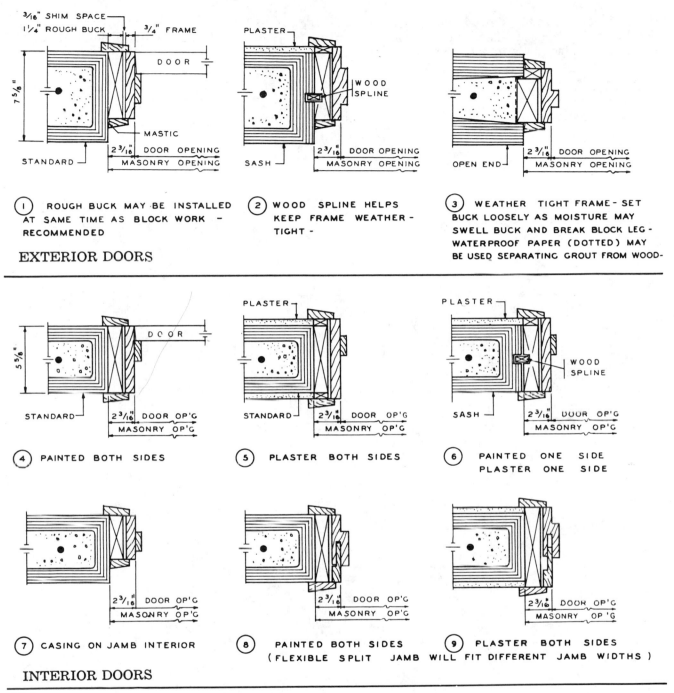

EXTERIOR DOORS

① ROUGH BUCK MAY BE INSTALLED AT SAME TIME AS BLOCK WORK — RECOMMENDED

② WOOD SPLINE HELPS KEEP FRAME WEATHER - TIGHT -

③ WEATHER TIGHT FRAME - SET BUCK LOOSELY AS MOISTURE MAY SWELL BUCK AND BREAK BLOCK LEG - WATERPROOF PAPER (DOTTED) MAY BE USED SEPARATING GROUT FROM WOOD-

④ PAINTED BOTH SIDES

⑤ PLASTER BOTH SIDES

⑥ PAINTED ONE SIDE PLASTER ONE SIDE

⑦ CASING ON JAMB INTERIOR

⑧ PAINTED BOTH SIDES (FLEXIBLE SPLIT JAMB WILL FIT DIFFERENT JAMB WIDTHS)

⑨ PLASTER BOTH SIDES

INTERIOR DOORS

Notes—
Above jamb details are designed for Group 1 doors (2'-0", 2'-4", 2'-6" and 3'-0" door widths) with corresponding masonry opening widths of 2'-4⅜", 2'-8⅜", 3'-0⅜" and 3'-4⅜"—
2'-4⅜" and 3'-0⅜" masonry opening widths require 12" long blocks (4" module)
2'-8⅜" and 3'-4⅜" masonry opening widths are based on 8" module—

Note—Do not mix Group 1 doors with Group 2 doors because jamb widths and head heights will vary—

Figure 12.42 Jamb details of Group 1 doors. (Reproduced from the *Masonry Design Manual* with permission of the publishers, the Masonry Industry Advancement Committee.)

HEAD DETAILS — GROUP 2 DOORS (2'-2", 2'-6", 2'-10", 3'-2" & 3'-6" WIDE)

In order to have $1\frac{3}{16}$" head and $1\frac{1}{16}$" jamb widths for Group 2 doors either scheme A or B shown below should be used—(when using combinations of 8" high and 4" high units a detailed wall section should be made to establish height dimensions)

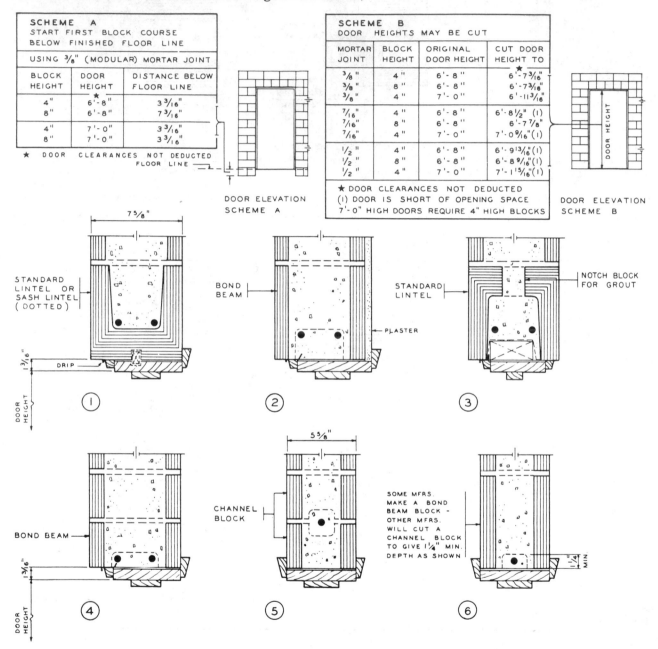

SCHEME A
START FIRST BLOCK COURSE BELOW FINISHED FLOOR LINE
USING ⅜" (MODULAR) MORTAR JOINT

BLOCK HEIGHT	DOOR HEIGHT	DISTANCE BELOW FLOOR LINE
4"	6'-8"★	3 3/16"
8"	6'-8"	7 3/16"
4"	7'-0"	3 3/16"
8"	7'-0"	3 3/16"

★ DOOR CLEARANCES NOT DEDUCTED

SCHEME B
DOOR HEIGHTS MAY BE CUT

MORTAR JOINT	BLOCK HEIGHT	ORIGINAL DOOR HEIGHT	CUT DOOR HEIGHT TO
⅜"	4"	6'-8"	6'-7 3/16"★
⅜"	8"	6'-8"	6'-7 3/16"
⅜"	4"	7'-0"	6'-11 3/16"
7/16"	4"	6'-8"	6'-8 1/2"(1)
7/16"	8"	6'-8"	6'-7 7/8"
7/16"	4"	7'-0"	7'-0 9/16"(1)
1/2"	4"	6'-8"	6'-9 13/16"(1)
1/2"	8"	6'-8"	6'-8 9/16"(1)
1/2"	4"	7'-0"	7'-1 5/16"(1)

★ DOOR CLEARANCES NOT DEDUCTED
(1) DOOR IS SHORT OF OPENING SPACE
7'-0" HIGH DOORS REQUIRE 4" HIGH BLOCKS

DOOR ELEVATION SCHEME A

DOOR ELEVATION SCHEME B

Details 1, 2, 3 and 4 are for exterior doors
Details 5 and 6 are for interior doors

Note—Do not mix Group 2 doors with Group 1 doors because head heights and jamb widths will vary—   scale 1½" = 1'-0"

Figure 12.43 Head details of Group 2 doors. (Reproduced from the *Masonry Design Manual* with permission of the publishers, the Masonry Industry Advancement Committee.)

JAMB DETAILS — GROUP 2 DOORS (2'-2", 2'-6", 2'-10", 3'-2" & 3'-6" WIDE)

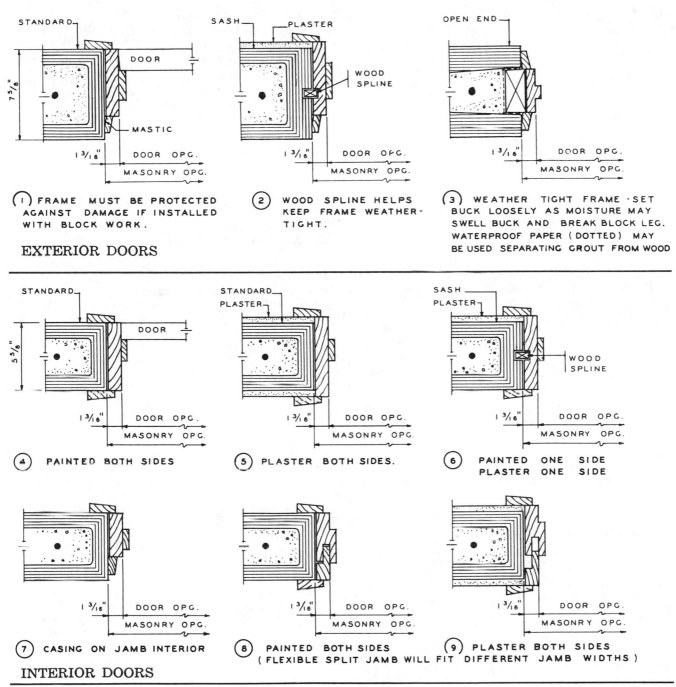

EXTERIOR DOORS

(1) FRAME MUST BE PROTECTED AGAINST DAMAGE IF INSTALLED WITH BLOCK WORK.

(2) WOOD SPLINE HELPS KEEP FRAME WEATHER-TIGHT.

(3) WEATHER TIGHT FRAME · SET BUCK LOOSELY AS MOISTURE MAY SWELL BUCK AND BREAK BLOCK LEG. WATERPROOF PAPER (DOTTED) MAY BE USED SEPARATING GROUT FROM WOOD

(4) PAINTED BOTH SIDES

(5) PLASTER BOTH SIDES.

(6) PAINTED ONE SIDE PLASTER ONE SIDE

(7) CASING ON JAMB INTERIOR

(8) PAINTED BOTH SIDES (FLEXIBLE SPLIT JAMB WILL FIT DIFFERENT JAMB WIDTHS)

(9) PLASTER BOTH SIDES DIFFERENT JAMB WIDTHS

INTERIOR DOORS

Notes—
Above jamb details are designed for Group 2 doors (2'-2", 2'-6", 2'-10", 3'-2", and 3'-6" door widths) with corresponding masonry opening widths of 2'-4⅜", 2'-8⅜", 3'-0⅜", 3'-4⅜" and 3'-8⅜"
2'-4⅜", 3'-0⅜" and 3'-8⅜" masonry opening widths require 12" long blocks (4" module).
2'-8⅜" and 3'-4⅜" masonry opening widths are based on 8" module.

Note—Do not mix Group 2 doors with Group 1 doors because jamb widths and head heights will vary—

Figure 12.44 Jamb details of Group 2 doors. (Reproduced from the *Masonry Design Manual* with permission of the publishers, the Masonry Industry Advancement Committee.)

JAMB ANCHORAGE

(1) Stagger bolts or place side by side. Buck may be installed with or after block work—

scale 1½″ = 1′-0″

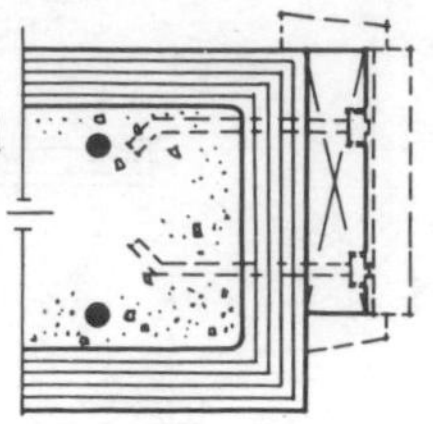

(2) Drive nails ¾″ thru buck bend over then drive flush. Nail heads and hooked ends embedded in grout will provide tight anchorage. Buck must be installed with block work. Frame can not be tightened after installation—

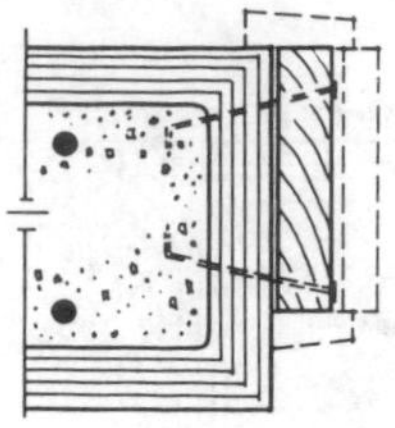

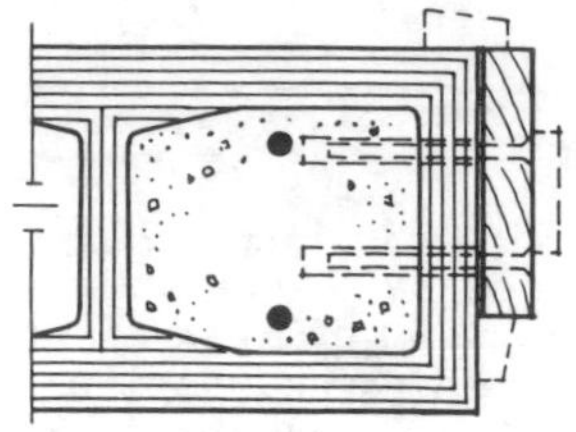

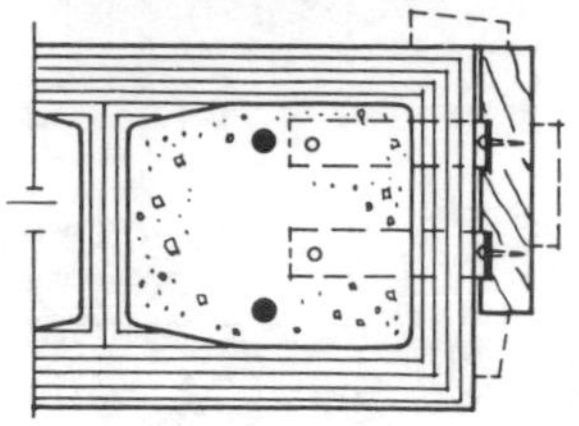

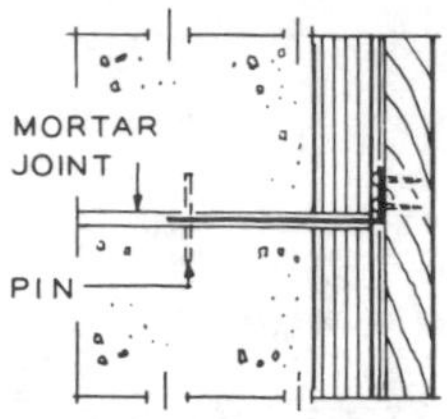
MORTAR
JOINT
PIN

Vertical section

(3) Flat head bolts used with conc. anchors or threaded (closed bottom) shield so that frame may be tightened after installation.

(4) Metal anchors embedded in grout. Bend ends and screw to frame. Frame must be installed with block work. Frame can not be tightened after installation.

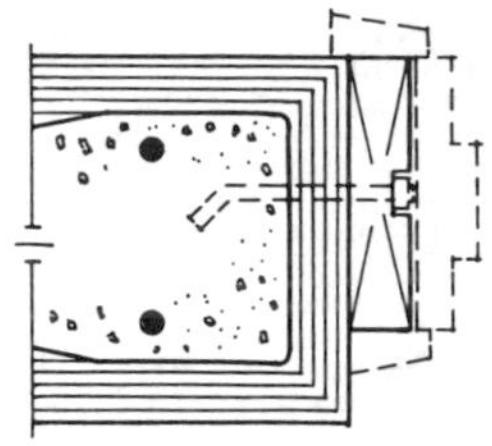

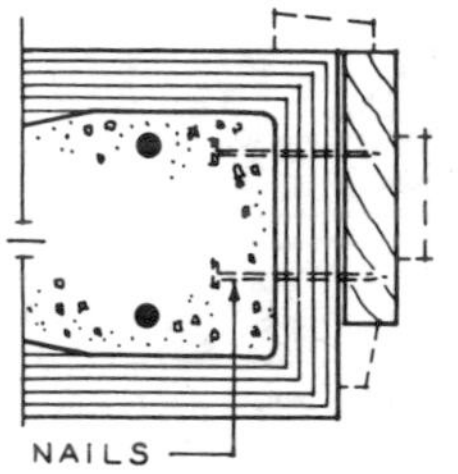
NAILS

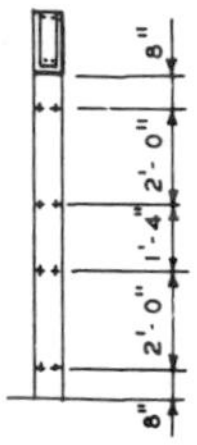
8"
2'-0"
1'-4"
2'-0"
2'-0"
8"

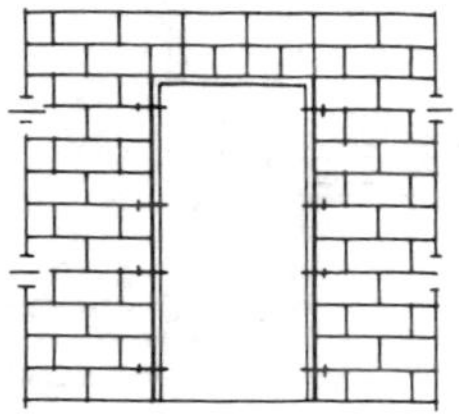

(5) Single bolt will tend to wrap or split buck. **Not recommended.**

(6) Jambs will work loose. **Not recommended.**

Section Elevation

(7) Anchorage spacing scale ⅛″ = 1′-0″

METAL DOOR FRAMES — MODULAR

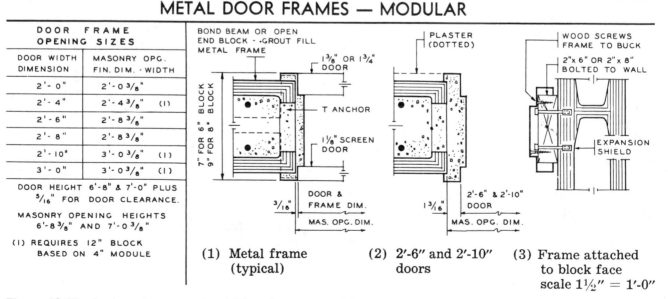

DOOR FRAME OPENING SIZES

DOOR WIDTH DIMENSION	MASONRY OPG. FIN. DIM. - WIDTH
2'-0"	2'-0 3/8"
2'-4"	2'-4 3/8" (1)
2'-6"	2'-8 3/8"
2'-8"	2'-8 3/8"
2'-10"	3'-0 3/8" (1)
3'-0"	3'-0 3/8" (1)

DOOR HEIGHT 6'-8" & 7'-0" PLUS 5/16" FOR DOOR CLEARANCE.

MASONRY OPENING HEIGHTS 6'-8 3/8" AND 7'-0 3/8"

(1) REQUIRES 12" BLOCK BASED ON 4" MODULE

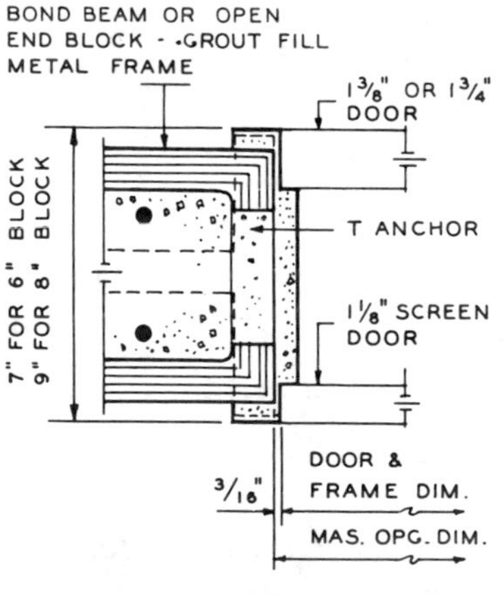
BOND BEAM OR OPEN
END BLOCK - -GROUT FILL
METAL FRAME
1 3/8" OR 1 3/4"
DOOR
T ANCHOR
1 1/8" SCREEN
DOOR
7" FOR 6" BLOCK
9" FOR 8" BLOCK
3/16"
DOOR &
FRAME DIM.
MAS. OPG. DIM.

(1) Metal frame (typical)

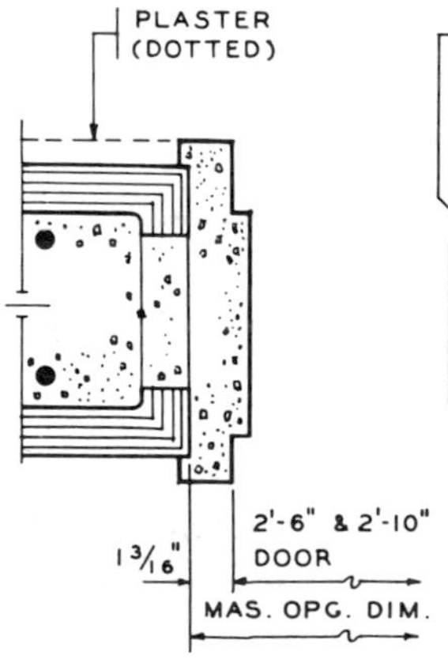
PLASTER
(DOTTED)
1 3/16"
2'-6" & 2'-10"
DOOR
MAS. OPG. DIM.

(2) 2′-6″ and 2′-10″ doors

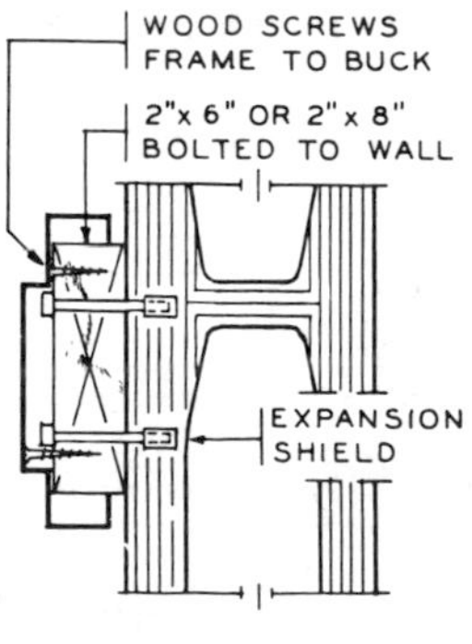
WOOD SCREWS
FRAME TO BUCK
2"x 6" OR 2"x 8"
BOLTED TO WALL
EXPANSION
SHIELD

(3) Frame attached to block face scale 1½″ = 1′-0″

Figure 12.45 Jamb anchorage and metal door frames—modular. (Reproduced from the *Masonry Design Manual* with permission of the publishers, the Masonry Industry Advancement Committee.)

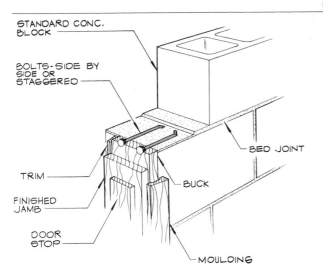

Figure 12.46 Jamb anchorage by bolts.

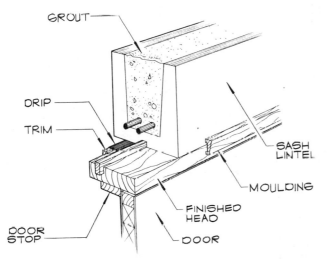

Figure 12.47 Head detail of wood frame—masonry construction.

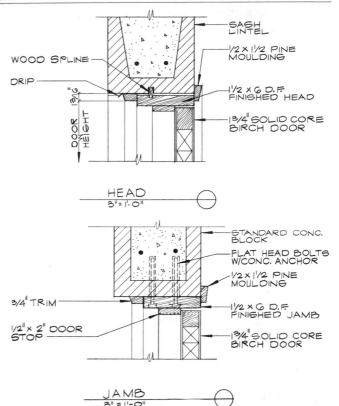

HEAD
3" = 1'-0"

JAMB
3" = 1'-0"

Figure 12.48 Drafted detail of wood framed door at head and jamb.

A drafted detail of Figures 12.46 and 12.47 is detailed in Figure 12.48.

This same modular analysis should be employed when detailing a door in a brick wall. Brick also comes in modular sizes, and the joints can be the standard $\frac{3}{8}''$, $\frac{7}{16}''$, and $\frac{1}{2}''$. In fact, the configuration for a wood door with a wood jamb is similar to the previously discussed doors for concrete block.

There are instances in light-frame construction where the building code requires a metal door and metal jamb. The primary reason is fire and smoke.

Architects should refer to literature from a manufacturer for available door dimensions and methods of attachment to the masonry wall. A sample of a typical unit is drawn in Figure 12.49. While $4\frac{3}{4}$, $5\frac{3}{4}$, $6\frac{3}{4}$, and $8\frac{3}{4}$ inch widths are the most typically found nationally, there are manufacturers that make widths available in increments of $\frac{1}{8}$ of an inch. Therefore, sizes such as $4\frac{5}{8}$, $4\frac{3}{4}$, $4\frac{7}{8}$, 5, $5\frac{1}{8}$, $5\frac{1}{4}$, $5\frac{3}{8}$, $5\frac{1}{2}$, $5\frac{5}{8}$, $5\frac{3}{4}$, and so on are not

uncommon. It should be noted that, while we are dealing primarily with masonry in this section, metal door jambs can also be used with wood stud construction.

The metal door jamb can be attached to the masonry wall in a variety of ways. The different anchoring devices are shown in Figure 12.50. Figure 12.51 shows a pictorial illustration of how one of these anchoring methods (the loose T anchor) is employed with a metal door jamb and masonry wall. Notice that the T anchor is located in the joints and must be installed with the door during the construction of the masonry wall. Note also the use of caulking to prevent air, moisture, sound, and even smoke penetration. Figure 12.52 depicts a metal door being installed

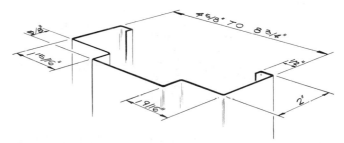

Figure 12.49 Typical metal door jamb.

JAMB ANCHORS

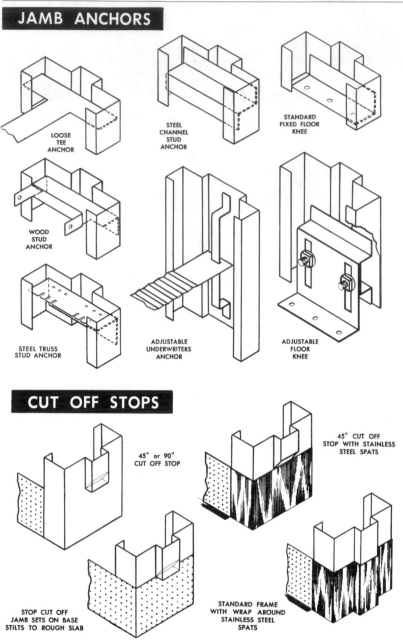

LOOSE TEE ANCHOR

STEEL CHANNEL STUD ANCHOR

STANDARD FIXED FLOOR KNEE

WOOD STUD ANCHOR

STEEL TRUSS STUD ANCHOR

ADJUSTABLE UNDERWRITERS ANCHOR

ADJUSTABLE FLOOR KNEE

CUT OFF STOPS

45° or 90° CUT OFF STOP

45° CUT OFF STOP WITH STAINLESS STEEL SPATS

STOP CUT OFF JAMB SETS ON BASE STILTS TO ROUGH SLAB

STANDARD FRAME WITH WRAP AROUND STAINLESS STEEL SPATS

Figure 12.50 Metal jamb anchors and cut-off stops. (Courtesy of Allied Steel Products, Inc. A subsidiary of Richford Industries, Inc.)

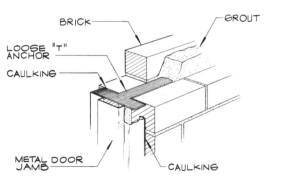

BRICK

GROUT

LOOSE "T" ANCHOR

CAULKING

METAL DOOR JAMB

CAULKING

Figure 12.51 Metal door jamb installation in grouted masonry wall.

along with the erection of the masonry wall. Figure 12.53 shows a drafted detail of this condition.

The example shown in Figure 12.54 involves a condition where the metal door jamb is located in the center of the wall. In some cases it may be desirable to have it flush with the interior wall for appearance. See Figure 12.55 for an example. Figure 12.56 shows what is referred to as a wraparound unit. In this unit, the door jamb is larger than the masonry wall.

Veneer

A final condition that the architect might encounter is that of a combination of brick and concrete or brick

Figure 12.52 Metal door jamb is installed as masonry wall is being built.

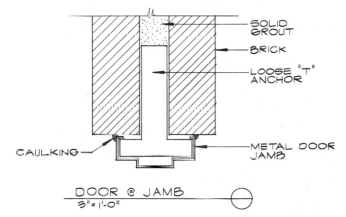

DOOR @ JAMB
3" = 1'-0"

Figure 12.53 Drafted detail of metal door jamb in masonry wall.

and wood frame. Both these conditions were discussed in Chapter 10.

In the case of a brick veneer on a wood frame construction, codes usually require that the weight of the veneer *not* be placed on the wood frame but rather is self-supporting. This requires a second lintel over a door — one for the wood frame that has been interrupted by the door and one under the brick at the opening. The lintel over the door that supports the brick at this point is usually steel and is called a steel lintel angle. See Figure 12.56. The example shown here has a solid wood sheathing usually not found on the West Coast.

A drafted detail of a door at a veneer wall is shown in Figure 12.57.

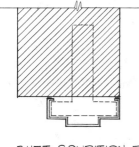

BUTT CONDITION-FRAME
FLUSH WITH INTERIOR FACE
OF WALL

Figure 12.54 Butt condition — frame flush with interior face of wall.

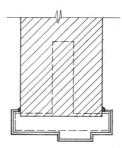

WRAP AROUND CONDITION

Figure 12.55 Metal door in wraparound condition.

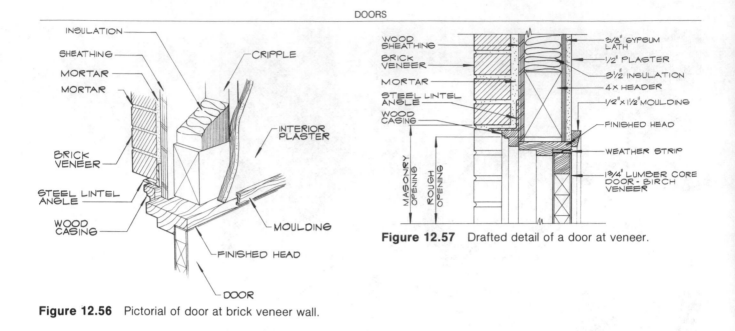

Figure 12.56 Pictorial of door at brick veneer wall.

Figure 12.57 Drafted detail of a door at veneer.

Regional Differences

When drawing a door detail, the two main differences from one geographical location to another in our country are construction differences due to weather and the weather itself. In very mild climates, sheathing is very seldom used under siding. This may not be the case in areas with colder weather. These differences must be reflected in the detail. The architectural draftsperson must first find out the material used around the door for the specific location and then ascertain the procedure used to apply the covering on the exterior. Due to the concern for energy conservation, almost all walls—mild climate included—have some type of insulation.

The second concern is for the weather. This may involve high wind, driving rain, or great ranges of temperature difference between the exterior and the interior. Weatherstripping around the door is the answer here, and the typical and best type used for a given area depends highly on the problems encountered. In a problem area, an interlock type might be employed, while in milder climate a neoprene cushion may be all that is needed.

Since there is a regional difference in how a masonry wall is built, plus the required horizontal and vertical reinforcing, the need for insulation, the waterproofing of the surface, and so on, the method of door installation may vary slightly, but the basic theory remains the same. The distribution of weight from the ceiling, the roof, or another floor above an opening, along with the weatherproofing of the door against the rain, wind, and even sound must be a primary concern for the architectural draftsperson.

Building Codes

Building codes dealing with doors differ very little from one part of the country to the next in wood frame construction. Residential door heights are normally 6'-8", while industrial and commercial structures may use 7'-0". Widths of doors depend pretty much on function. In a public building, doors normally open out and are a minimum of 3'-0". Specialized structures may require larger doors, for example, hospitals where equipment used usually dictates the size. Sizes can be verified by calling the local Department of Building and Safety, or they may be published in a local code book or pamphlet.

Building codes do vary when dealing with doors in masonry construction. Some regions require a solid grouted wall while others allow a hollow cavity. In either case, the door detail appears different because of this structural requirement.

Summary

Often, two different craftspeople are involved with the installation of a door: first, the rough carpenter and, second, the finish carpenter or window manufacturer. In either case, the architect should be constantly aware of the limitations and abilities of each. The rough carpenter is working with tolerances of about $\frac{1}{2}$", with a main concern about the weight from the roof and ceiling and any wall load above the door and how to redistribute it around the door. To this end, the lintel or header becomes a critical item in the detail.

Rain, wind, noise, and even safety in the form of fire-rated doors are also major concerns for the architectural draftsperson. If you can trace a drop of rainwater down the side of a building and prevent it from reaching the interior side or the structural pieces around the door, you have reached a degree of rain security.

The detail of the head, jamb (if used), and sill should be drawn one above another with the sill on the bottom, the jamb next, and the head at the top. Be sure to see that the outside surface of the header lines up with the studs in the jamb section and with the end of the foundation.

Doors in masonry construction should take joint thickness, unit size, and the modular system used to determine the configuration of the door detail. These required details often affect the footing details because they necessitate placing the first row of masonry units below the floor line for a 6'-8" or 7'-0" door.

Metal door jambs require a special anchorage. There are many manufacturers of masonry anchors. An architectural draftsperson need only consult *Sweet's Catalog* or the A.I.A. Standards (formally called *Graphic Standards*) for specific installation data and for size.

13
WINDOWS

Preview   Chapter 13 deals with window assemblies detailed in constructions of wood frame, concrete block, solid brick, and brick veneer exterior walls.

The first section defines window nomenclature in narrative and pictorial form, thus providing the designer with the basic knowledge of the members that constitute a window assembly. The second section illustrates in detail and pictorial form examples of metal casement and sliding windows, wood sash and fixed glass sections as they are assembled in wood frame construction.

The third section deals with metal, wood, and fixed glass window assemblies with examples of detailed sections in concrete block construction, solid brick construction, and brick veneer.

In general, the window details illustrate a degree of flexibility of interior and exterior trim and frame design.

After reading this chapter, the architectural draftsperson will:

1.   Understand the nomenclature used for window construction.
2.   Be able to detail window frames in wood and masonry construction.

The components that make up a finished window assembly primarily depend on the following elements: the architectural design of the structure, the region of the country and its weather conditions, the material of the structure in which the window is to be installed, and the type of window and material that has been selected.

Window manufacturers provide brochures and literature describing their products in narrative and detail form; it is recommended that the designer become familiar with the various manufacturers and their suggested installation details. This helps the detailer in selecting a window that will satisfy the various requirements for a particular project.

In general, it should be emphasized that window assemblies are detailed in many different ways depending on their design requirements. However, the architectural draftsperson should strive to accomplish competent detailing based on the following: proper weatherproofing, the sequence of installation, and simplicity of assembly.

Window Nomenclature

There are three basic terms that refer to a window assembly: head, jamb, and sill.

The head section is found at the top of the window. Directly above the head of the window opening is a structural member called a "lintel" or "header." This member distributes roof and ceiling loads to the sides of the window opening and alleviates stresses on the window and glass.

The sides of a window are referred to as the jamb. Adjacent to the jamb, at each side of the window opening, is a structural column. These columns support the lintel or header that occurs above the window opening.

The bottom of the window is called the sill. This member is designed to expell moisture to the outside of the structure.

A pictorial example of the members that constitute a window assembly in a wood frame construction is illustrated in Figure 13.1.

Window Assemblies in Wood Construction

Requirements for detailing window assemblies in wood frame construction may vary for the following reasons: the type of window, the architectural design, the region of the country, and the cost of installation.

Many types of windows are utilized in today's buildings. However, the most prevalent are casement windows, horizontal sliding windows, awning windows, louvre windows, double-hung windows, and fixed sash.

Casement windows are available in wood, steel, and aluminum. They are hinged at the jamb sections and may be inswinging or outswinging. A prime factor for utilizing casement windows is that they provide maximum ventilation and light. When drawing the elevation of a casement window, the architect should provide the following information: the width of the window frame, the hinged point for the operable section, the exterior trim and millwork as the window has been detailed, and the detail reference symbols for the head, jamb, and sill sections.

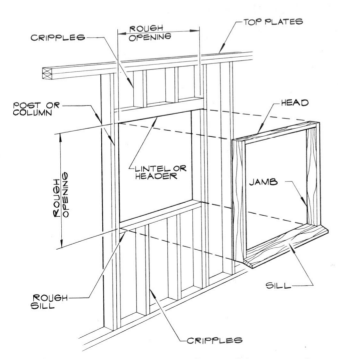

Figure 13.1 Window assembly in wood frame construction.

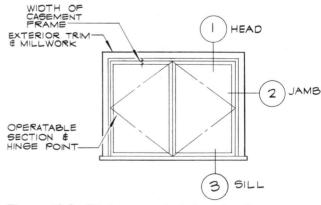

Figure 13.2 Steel casement window elevation.

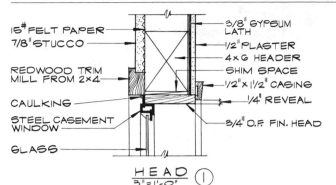

Figure 13.3 Head section.

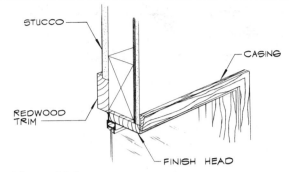

Figure 13.6 Pictorial, head section.

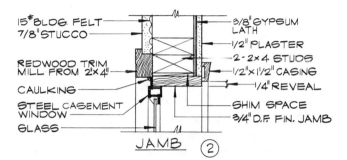

Figure 13.4 Jamb section.

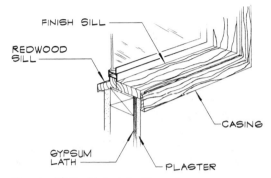

Figure 13.7 Pictorial, sill section.

An elevation of a steel casement window, its related information, and how it will be shown on exterior elevations are depicted in Figure 13.2.

Window details for the head, jamb, and sill sections are generally detailed at a scale of 3" = 1'-0" to half size depending on the complexity of the assembly.

Figures 13.3, 13.4, and 13.5 are examples of the head, jamb, and sill sections for a steel casement window assembly in wood frame construction. Figures 13.6 and 13.7 depict, in pictorial form, the head and sill section.

Horizontal aluminum sliding windows are predominantly used in residential construction. The shape and complexity of the section for aluminum sliding windows vary, depending on the quality of the window and the manufacturers' specifications. Because of the diversity of these window sections, the designer will find that the components of the window assembly also vary according to the shape and size of the aluminum window section.

An elevation of an aluminum sliding window, its related information, and how it is depicted on exterior elevations are shown in Figure 13.8.

Generally, aluminum sliding window sections are constructed from 6063-T5 aluminum alloy and are available in colors as well as an aluminum finish. Glazing channels are available for $\frac{3}{16}$", $\frac{7}{32}$", or $\frac{1}{4}$" thick single glazing and $\frac{1}{2}$" or $\frac{5}{8}$" double-glazed insulating glass. Screens are installed at the sliding vent section. Examples of a head, jamb, and sill section for an aluminum sliding window with single glazing in open

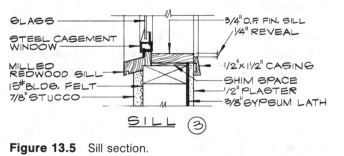

Figure 13.5 Sill section.

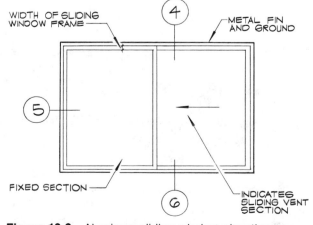

Figure 13.8 Aluminum sliding window elevation.

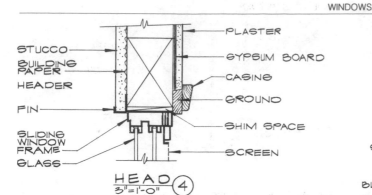

Figure 13.9 Head section.

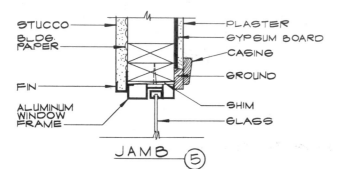

Figure 13.10 Jamb section.

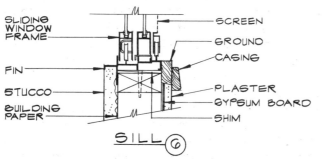

Figure 13.11 Sill section.

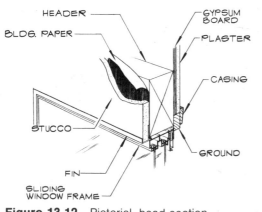

Figure 13.12 Pictorial, head section.

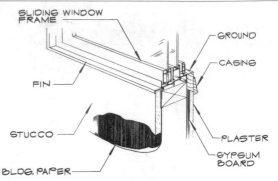

Figure 13.13 Pictorial, sill section.

wood frame construction are shown in Figures 13.9, 13.10, and 13.11. Pictorial representation is depicted in Figures 13.12 and 13.13. Figure 13.14 shows jamb and sill sections attached to framing.

Note on this particular window assembly that the exterior trim is a metal fin (finish) and ground. Therefore, this would be depicted on the exterior window elevation. (See Figure 13.8).

Windows with frames and sash constructed of wood are available in such types as casement windows, projecting windows, sliding windows, and double-hung windows. These windows accommodate single and double glazing as well as screens for the openable sections.

The architectural draftsperson should know that the selection of wood windows and their assemblies is dependent on the requirements of a specific region of the country. For example, when asked to select and detail a wood casement window for a region that is subjected to extreme cold temperatures, the following information should be considered: a wood frame and sash window that provide an assembly designed to deter the passage of air and moisture to the inside, plus proper flashing and weatherstripping and wood sash to accommodate double glazing.

An exterior elevation of a wood casement window and sash with a structural mullion or column is illustrated in Figure 13.15. This elevation depicts the exterior trim and wood sash as it is detailed in the window sections.

Window section reference symbols, as indicated in Figure 13.15, are keyed to the head, jamb, sill, and structural mullion detailed sections. Figures 13.16 through 13.19 show these sections, for closed wood frame construction, in detail and pictorial form. Note that the head and jamb sections are identical except for the framing of the lintel at the head section and the two 2″ × 4″ column at the jamb for lintel support. The architect must provide window sections for every condition that occurs on a specific project.

The use of fixed glass sections and their assemblies in wood frame construction varies according to

Figure 13.14 Photograph of window installation.

what the architect is striving for in his or her design. In many cases, the head, jamb, mullions, and sill sections are not manufactured but are milled in accordance with window sections furnished in the architect's drawings. It is therefore pertinent that these sections satisfy the following requirements: simplicity of millwork, proper sealment from the outside, and continuity of the assembly components relative to other types of windows used on the project.

The delineation of an exterior elevation for fixed glass windows and related information is drawn as indicated in previous exterior window elevations. Figure 13.20 illustrates an example of an exterior elevation of fixed glass sections in a milled wood frame with related sectional symbols.

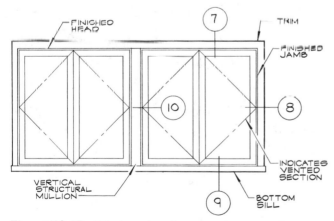

Figure 13.15 Window elevation, wood casement.

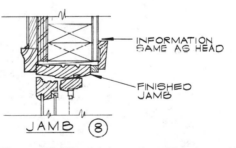

Figure 13.17 Jamb section. (Courtesy of Rolscreen Company, Pella Division.)

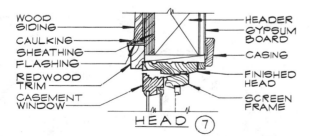

Figure 13.16 Head section. (Courtesy of Rolscreen Company, Pella Division.)

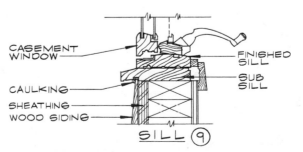

Figure 13.18 Sill section. (Courtesy of Rolscreen Company, Pella Division.)

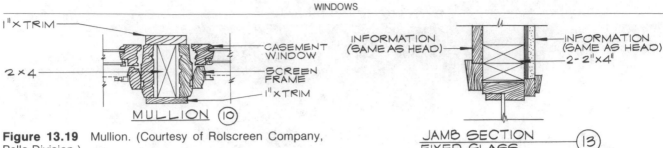

Figure 13.19 Mullion. (Courtesy of Rolscreen Company, Pella Division.)

JAMB SECTION
FIXED GLASS ⑬

Figure 13.23 Jamb section.

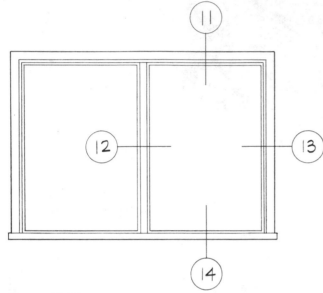

Figure 13.20 Fixed glass, exterior window elevation.

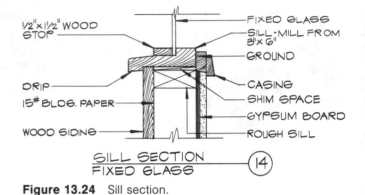

SILL SECTION
FIXED GLASS ⑭

Figure 13.24 Sill section.

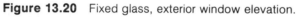

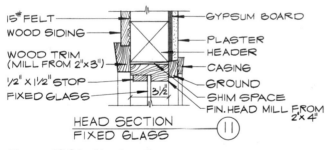

HEAD SECTION
FIXED GLASS ⑪

Figure 13.21 Head section.

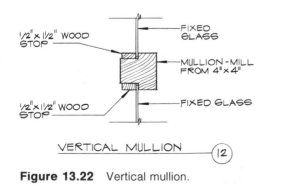

VERTICAL MULLION ⑫

Figure 13.22 Vertical mullion.

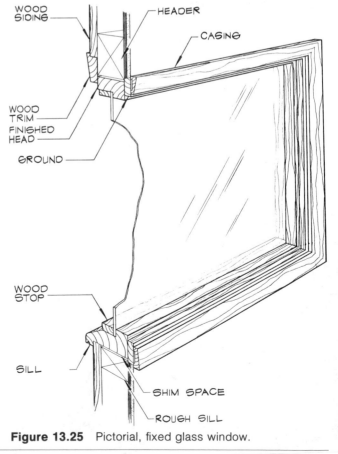

Figure 13.25 Pictorial, fixed glass window.

As indicated previously, window elevations are drawn to depict how the window will look relative to the head, jamb, mullion, and sill sections.

For the head, jamb, mullion, and sill sections for the fixed glass window assembly, the detailer should strive to utilize standard lumber sizes wherever possible. This will alleviate waste and help to reduce the cost of construction. Figures 13.21 through 13.25 illustrate window sections in detail and pictorial view for fixed glass windows using milled head, jamb, mullion, and sill assemblies. Note that structure is open wood frame construction.

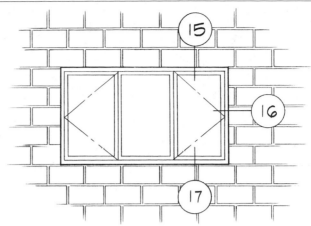

Figure 13.26 Steel casement window elevation.

Window Assemblies in Masonry Construction

Concrete Block

Design of window assemblies in concrete block construction has a degree of inflexibility because of the mechanics of concrete block construction.

In general, building code regulations for industrial buildings require that window assemblies be constructed of incombustible materials. The following figures illustrate a steel casement incombustible window assembly for a light industrial building using concrete block units for the exterior walls. Whenever possible, the horizontal and vertical dimensions of the window should relate to the dimensions of the concrete block units. Figure 13.26 illustrates the exterior elevation of this casement window drawn relative to the window sections.

Since the requirements for this window assembly do not allow combustible materials to be used, the window frame may be attached to the concrete block by a snap-in metal clip or an attached metal fin solid grouted to the concrete block. An example of the use of an attached fin grouted in place is illustrated in Figures 13.27, 13.28, and 13.29. Note that the sill section in Figure 13.29 is a standard 16″ long concrete sill block used to satisfy the requirement for combustible materials. Figure 13.30 illustrates, in pictorial view, a steel casement window in concrete block wall construction.

For concrete block residential construction, the use of wood sash may be incorporated, provided that the window dimensions are compatible with the concrete block modular dimension.

An example of an exterior elevation of a wood sliding window with concrete block exterior walls is illustrated in Figure 13.31. Details for the head, jamb, and sill sections are shown in Figures 13.32, 13.33, and

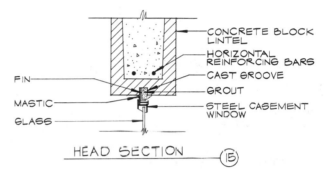

Figure 13.27 Head section.

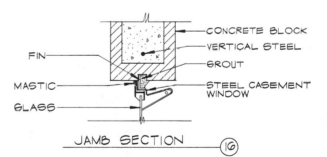

Figure 13.28 Jamb section.

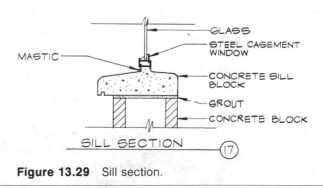

Figure 13.29 Sill section.

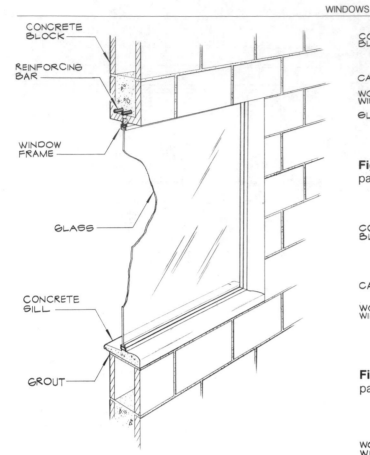

Figure 13.30 Pictorial, casement window in concrete block construction.

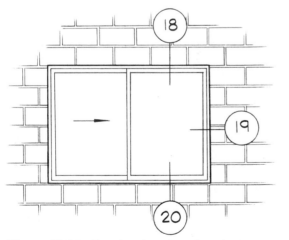

Figure 13.31 Exterior elevation of wood sliding window.

13.34. A pictorial illustration of this window assembly is shown in Figure 13.35.

Brick

Window assemblies in solid brick construction provide a higher degree of flexibility for the detailer than do those of concrete block construction. This is be-

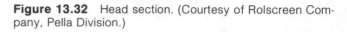

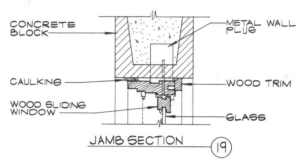

Figure 13.32 Head section. (Courtesy of Rolscreen Company, Pella Division.)

Figure 13.33 Jamb section. (Courtesy of Rolscreen Company, Pella Division.)

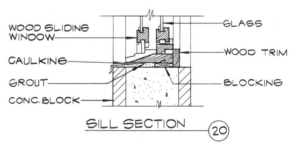

Figure 13.34 Sill section. (Courtesy of Rolscreen Company, Pella Division.)

cause solid brick units are smaller in size and may be cut to satisfy various window sizes and design conditions. Solid brick construction is generally erected with two courses of brick, which allows for additional design flexibility at the head, jamb, and sill sections.

The principal structural difference between solid brick and concrete block construction generally occurs at the head section of the window assembly. Concrete block construction relies on a reinforced grouted concrete block lintel, whereas solid brick construction utilizes steel angles to provide a structural lintel.

Figure 13.36 illustrates an exterior elevation of a wood casement window, and its section symbols, assembled in solid brick wall construction. Observe the following in the window sections: head section 21 provides steel angles for a structural lintel in lieu of a steel reinforced grouted lintel (see Figure 13.37)

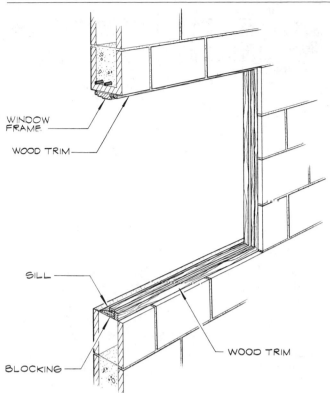

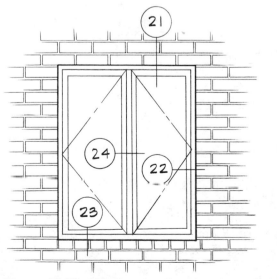

Figure 13.35 Pictorial, wood sliding window in concrete block construction.

and all sections are detailed to receive interior drywall finish. Figure 13.38 depicts the jamb section. Figure 13.39 depicts the sill section, and Figure 13.40 illustrates the section through the vertical mullion. A pictorial view of this window assembly is shown in Figure 13.41.

An exterior window elevation of fixed glass with masonry veneer construction is illustrated in Figure

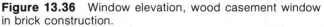

Figure 13.36 Window elevation, wood casement window in brick construction.

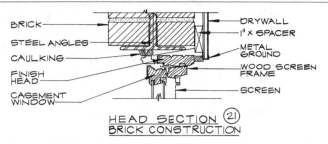

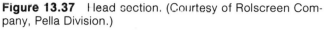

HEAD SECTION ㉑
BRICK CONSTRUCTION

Figure 13.37 Head section. (Courtesy of Rolscreen Company, Pella Division.)

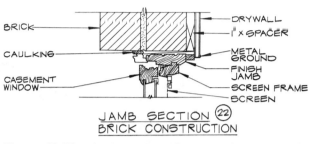

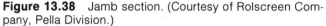

JAMB SECTION ㉒
BRICK CONSTRUCTION

Figure 13.38 Jamb section. (Courtesy of Rolscreen Company, Pella Division.)

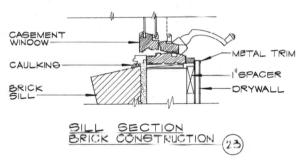

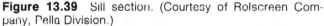

SILL SECTION
BRICK CONSTRUCTION ㉓

Figure 13.39 Sill section. (Courtesy of Rolscreen Company, Pella Division.)

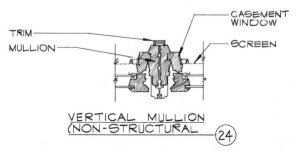

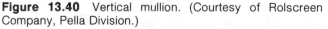

VERTICAL MULLION
(NON-STRUCTURAL ㉔

Figure 13.40 Vertical mullion. (Courtesy of Rolscreen Company, Pella Division.)

13.42. Note that the window frame is delineated relative to the window section assembly.

Since this window assembly is incorporated in wood frame construction with a brick veneer exterior finish, the brick veneer at the head section is supported independently by a steel angle. See head section detail ㉕, Figure 13.43. In this case, solid sheathing is applied on the outside of the wood studs

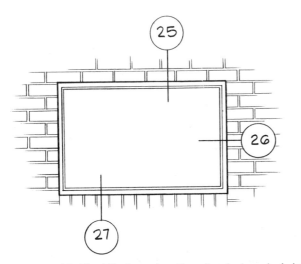

Figure 13.41 Pictorial, wood casement window in brick construction.

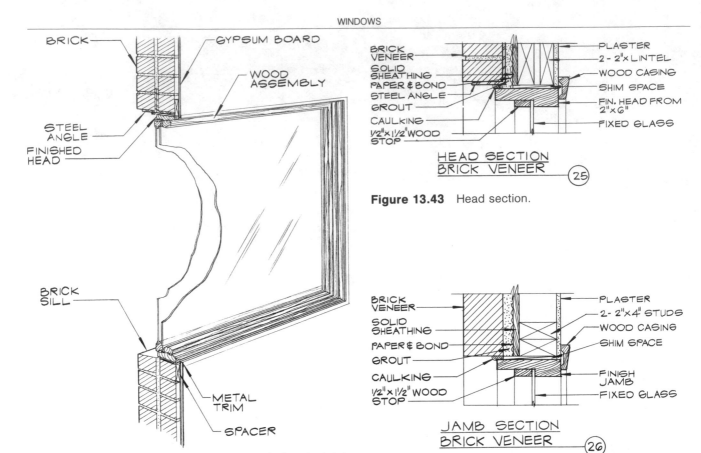

Figure 13.43 Head section.

Figure 13.44 Jamb section.

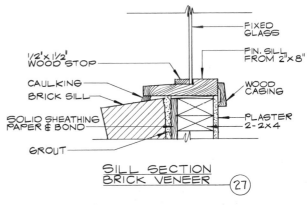

Figure 13.45 Sill section.

Figure 13.42 Window elevation, fixed glass in brick construction.

with an acceptable bonding method for the brick veneer. Figure 13.44 shows jamb detail ㉖ . (See Chapter 10 on exterior walls.) Note that in window section ㉗, Figure 13.45, a brick sill is incorporated below a wood sill. This architectural detail is left to the

discretion of the designer and is an example of the flexibility of brick units in window assemblies. Figure 13.46 illustrates, in pictorial view, this window assembly.

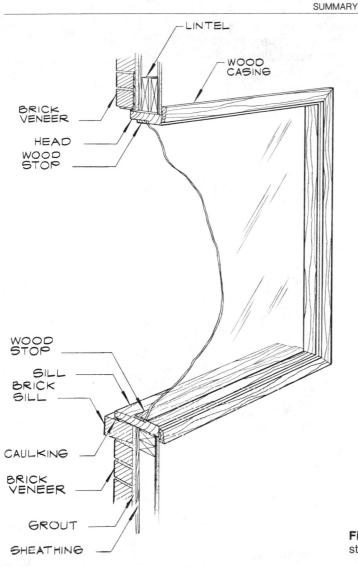

Figure 13.46 Pictorial, fixed glass in brick veneer construction.

Regional Differences

The severe differences in weather conditions among various regions require that the following be considered in window assemblies:

The type of window
Weatherproofing
Single/double glazing
Window material
Codes and governing energy conservation requirements

Summary

This chapter defined the various components that make up a window assembly and provided examples of how different types of windows are assembled in wood frame and masonry construction.

Various types of manufactured windows and custom shop-milled frames found in today's residential and light commercial structures were illustrated.

By illustrating various types of windows and their assemblies, we hope to provide an awareness of how a selected type of window may dictate the various components required to complete the window assembly. We also emphasized proper weather sealment around the perimeter of the window assembly.

14
STAIRS

Preview   Chapter 14 introduces the subject of stairs in general. Specific details and material applications are dealt with in later chapters.

The chapter starts with establishing a need and purpose for stairs and laying a foundation toward an understanding of stairs by delving into nomenclature unique to stair construction and the necessary framing around stairs.

A few varieties of stairs are discussed, such as winder, reverse, and straight. This chapter then deals with the various ways to approach a stair design and its layout by the use of formulas and charts.

Finally, the structural aspects and design limitations of handrails and guardrails are discussed, using simple examples and arithmetical computations.

General information of this type is necessary before dealing with wood or steel applications to stairs.

After reading this chapter, the architectural draftsperson will:

1. Develop an appreciation for stairs by understanding their component parts.
2. Be familiar with the vocabulary applied to stairs.
3. Be able to design riser-tread ratios by simple arithmetical calculations.
4. Understand the relationship that exists between the rough framing and the stairs itself.
5. Be able to lay out a stair system step-by-step between floors.
6. Differentiate between guardrails and handrails. Also understand the connections necessary.

Figure 14.1 Interior wood stairs.

The main purpose of stairs is to allow the flow of traffic to be accommodated when there is a change of floor level within a structure. This should be done with the least amount of physical strain on one's body. The change of level could be as simple as a sunken living room or as complex as a flight of stairs between two floors. Stairs may exist on the interior, as shown in Figure 14.1, above, which is the case with most residences, and on the outside, as in many apartment structures.

Stairs can be categorized into three groups: wood stairs, steel stairs, and concrete stairs. Since there is a preponderance of the first two groups in wood frame structures, these are dealt with in great detail following this introductory section.

Terms

When applied to stairs certain terms gain a particular significance. An architectural draftsperson must learn these terms and make them a part of everyday vocabulary. Once mastered, these terms can be discussed intelligently.

The following are definitions as well as pictorial descriptions of those terms most often encountered.

Tread—the horizontal portion of a stair on which you step when ascending or descending. See Figure 14.2.
Riser—the vertical portion between the treads. See Figure 14.2.
Nosing—located at the intersection of the riser and the tread. It is usually a $1\frac{1}{8}''$ projection of the tread over the riser. See Figure 14.2.

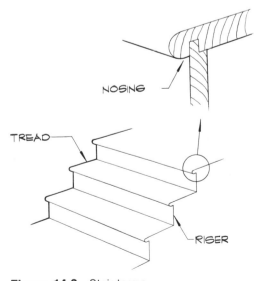

Figure 14.2 Stair terms.

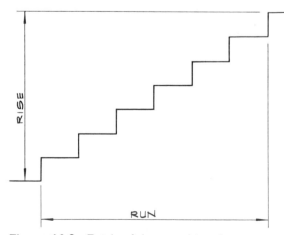

Figure 14.3 Totals of risers and treads.

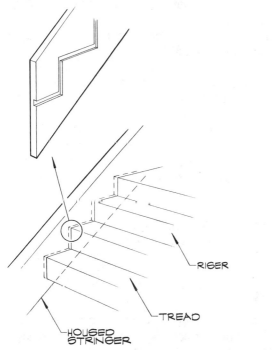

Figure 14.4 Pictorial of a closed stringer.

Run—the total of all the treads or the total horizontal distance traveled when ascending or descending a flight of stairs. See Figure 14.3.

Rise—the total of all the risers or the total vertical distance traveled. Rise is the distance between floors and is measured perpendicularly to, not diagonally with, the floor. See Figure 14.3.

Landing—the floor at the beginning or end of a flight (run) of stairs. This term also describes an intermediate platform between the two floors.

Carriage or stringer—these terms are often used interchangeably, with stringer being more familiar to those in the field. They form the structural support for the riser and tread, which is positioned diagonally as shown in Figures 14.4 and 14.5.

Closed stringer—that area covering the ends of the tread and riser. The closed stringer, when seen from the side, does not expose the stairs. When this stringer is grooved to receive the treads and risers, it is called a housed stringer. See Figure 14.4.

Platform—an intermediate landing between floors.

Handrail—as the name indicates, the handrail is a member that parallels the angle of the stairs and allows a person to grasp it by the hand to aid in going up or down stairs. See Figure 14.6.

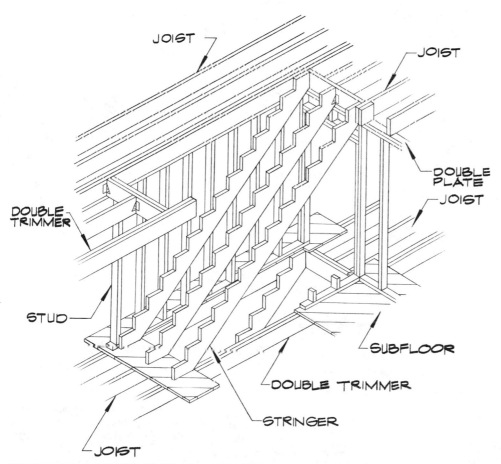

Figure 14.5 Typical stair framing—wood frame. (Courtesy of National Forest Products Association.)

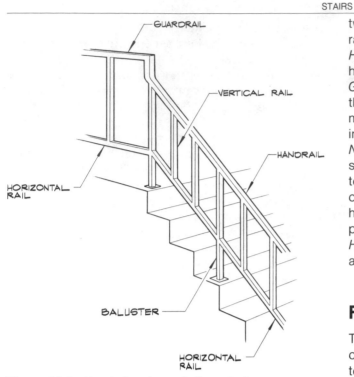

Figure 14.6 Handrail and guardrail terminology.

Baluster — the member that holds up the handrail and any other rails attached to the handrail. It is the structural component of this system.

Vertical rails — those members found between the balusters to prevent people from falling through be-tween the handrail and the stairs. They may be decorative in pattern.

Horizontal rail — any member, besides the handrail, horizontal to the handrail.

Guardrail — found on a balcony, deck, or platform, the topmost rail similar to the handrail except that its main function is containment of people rather than aid in climbing.

Newel — the large terminating post at the bottom of a stair or a landing often found on very fancy stair systems. If you can imagine a large mansion with a large circular descending staircase, with a highly decorated handrail, the very last baluster is a large ornamental piece — the newel.

Head room — the clearance between the nosing and any part of the structure above.

Framing

The framing around an interior stair is a standard procedure. Since the normal sequence of floor joist is interrupted by the stairs, the floor joist on either side of the opening is normally doubled. The floor joists are called double trimmer. The members perpendicular to the double trimmer, called *headers,* transfer the weight of the floor joists that have been interrupted to the double trimmer. If there is no wall below the headers, they should be doubled and called double header. See Figure 14.7.

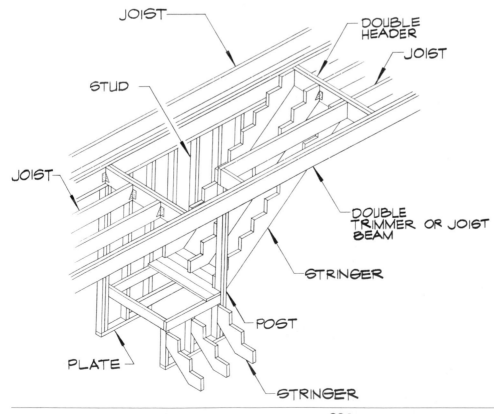

Figure 14.7 Typical stair framing around a right-angle stair. (Courtesy of National Forest Products Association.)

In either case, framing anchors similar to the one shown in Figure 18.4 should be used. See Figures 14.5 and 14.7 for samples of this framing procedure.

If there is support below the joist, such as the one between the two sets of double trimmers, as shown in Figure 14.7, it need not be doubled.

Types of Stair Systems

There are three basic types of stair systems, and many combinations and variations of each. Fundamentally, the three types are the straight run, the right angle, and the reverse.

The straight run is a system in which one does not change direction. See Figure 14.8.

A right angle run, often called "L"-shaped system, is one in which a 90° directional change is negotiated by the person ascending or descending the stairs. This system incorporates a landing to initiate the 90° turn that is normally in the center.

If the platform is located toward the top or bottom, this is called a long L stair. A double L has two platforms.

If the step continued in place of the landing, it would be called a winder. Winders are not desirable because the steps become wedge shaped as they

make the 90° turn. The tread size is reduced and can be very dangerous.

Finally, a reverse or U-shaped stair is one in which a person ascends a set of stairs, reaches a platform, and makes a 180° turn before continuing to ascend. If the two sets of stairs are close together, this is called a narrow U. If the two sets of stairs are set apart so as to produce a stairwell, this is termed a wide U.

Stair Design

Because of the proportions of the human body, certain ratios of riser to tread have been researched and developed. If risers are too great, climbing stairs becomes tiring and one tends to fatigue easily. If the treads are too long or too short, the normal walking gate is broken, and one must stretch to reach the next step or trip because of the inability of the stair to accommodate the size of the feet.

Before you draw your first stair detail, watch someone walk. This may sound like an absurd thing to do, but if you observe, you will realize that the person's trailing leg will go backward slightly as it is raised. When the knee is bent and the leg raised, the foot moves back. The leg is then raised and thrust forward.

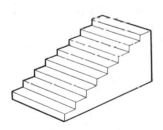

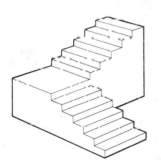

STRAIGHT RUN   RIGHT ANGLE OR "L"

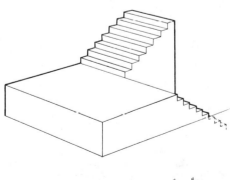

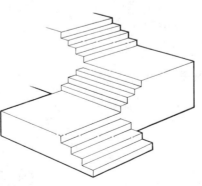

REVERSE OR "U"   DOUBLE "L"

Figure 14.8 Types of stair systems.

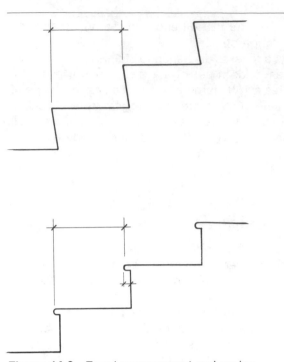

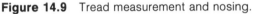

Figure 14.9 Tread measurement and nosing.

At maximum velocity, the foot travels at about 30 miles per hour — which is why it hurts so much to stub your toe prior to slowing down and putting your foot down. The backward movement of your foot also prevents tripping over the nosing of the tread. These concepts of motion and speed are important for designing stairs.

There is also a fatigue factor when negotiating a large amount of stairs. For this reason, it is suggested that landings be used anytime there are more than 16 steps. A stair angle of 30 to 35° has been found to be the optimum for preventing fatigue.

Every step must also be the same size and proportion; otherwise, an accident is likely. Most local codes do not allow even the slightest difference in step size.

The optimum ratio of tread to riser has been developed after many years of experimentation. This ratio is a 7″ to 7½″ riser and 9½″ to 10½″ tread. This tread measurement does not include the 1⅛″ nosing. This is somewhat misleading because on the details you are asked to draw the tread is usually measured from nosing to nosing. See Figure 14.9, above.

When you measure from nosing to nosing, the total depth of the tread is not measured. There are, of course, suggested maximum and minimum ratios. A 5″ riser to a 16″ tread is the absolute minimum ratio while a 9″ riser to an 8″ tread becomes the maximum.

When you look at these figures carefully, you will notice that the increase in riser size decreases the tread size. This is an attempt to maintain the 30 to 35° angle of the stair. In fact, people who design stairs use a very simple series of rules to govern their ratio. Simply stated it reads

Riser + tread = 17 or 17½ inches
and/or
2 × riser + tread = 24 or 25 inches
and/or
Riser × tread = 70 to 75 inches*

Apply the optimum suggested sizes to these rules of thumb and you find the following, using a 7″ riser and a 10″ tread.

$$7r + 10t = 17″$$
$$2 \times 7r + 10t = 24″$$
$$7r \times 10t = 70″$$

Let's check the minimum and see how it compares with the optimum.

$$5r + 16t = 21″$$
$$2 \times 5r + 16t = 26″$$
$$5r \times 16t = 80″$$

As you can see, all exceed the rule of thumb. In this case, the tread size should be reduced to 14 inches. Thus,

$$5r + 14t = 19″$$
$$2 \times 5r + 14t = 24″$$
$$5r \times 14t = 70″$$

Although all the rules were not satisfied, at least two out of three were making a more comfortable minimum riser stair.

The final aspect of stair design is determining the number of risers, treads, size of rise, and length of run. This can be done by charts or arithmetically. In either case, the floor-to-floor measurement must be known.

Let us set up a hypothetical situation and solve it.

Given	Floor to ceiling height	=	8′-0″
	Ceiling thickness	=	1″
	2nd floor floor joist size	=	10½″
	2nd floor subflooring material thickness	=	½″
	Total	=	9′-0″
			or 108″

Desired riser size = 7″
Desired tread size = 10″

Solve for riser size.

Solution

Step 1.   Take the 108 inches (floor-to-floor measurement) and divide by the desired riser

---

* Courtesy of Edward J. Muller, *Architectural Drawing and Light Construction,* copyright © 1967. By permission of Prentice-Hall, Inc., Englewood Cliffs, N.J.

size to find the number of risers:

$$\frac{108}{7} = 15.43 \text{ risers}$$

Step 2. Decide, based on the answer, whether you wish 15 or 16 risers. You cannot have a fraction at this stage since all steps must be alike. If you select 15, the height of the risers will be slightly larger than the desired 7" riser. If you select 16, the risers will be slightly smaller than the desired 7" riser.

Step 3. Assuming that you choose 15, the total floor to floor dimension is now divided by 15 to get the actual size of the riser.

$$\frac{108}{15} = 7.2 \text{ inches per riser}$$

Step 4. To find the total run, multiple the number of treads times 10". Always remember the number of treads is one less than the number of risers because we do not count the floors at each end as treads; therefore, your stairs will begin and end with a riser.

$$14t \times 10'' = 140'' \text{ or } 11'8''$$

Solution by chart of Figure 14.10.

Step 1 Locate floor-to-floor dimension on the left side of the chart.

Step 2 Follow the curved lines downward until it intersects a vertical and a horizontal line simultaneously. Only the intersection of these three lines can be used. Use the vertical lines nearest 7 inches since this was the riser size.

Step 3 All three lines intersect at $6\frac{3}{4}$ inches or $7\frac{1}{4}$ inches. You must now decide which of these you will use.

Step 4 Assuming that $7\frac{1}{4}$ inches was used, follow the intersection horizontally until you reach the first number (15). This number represents the number of risers you have in this system.

Step 5 Still traveling horizontally, the next number represents the number of treads (14). From here follow the angular line upward until it intersects the vertical line representing the size of tread. As before, three lines should intersect to read this chart accurately.

Step 6 The sample shows the intersection of three lines above the $10\frac{3}{4}$ inch mark. From this intersection, travel horizontally to the right to find the total length of run. Each line represents 2 inches, so the total length of run equals 12'-6".

Step 7 The lines at the bottom connecting height of risers and length of treads represent the original "tread times riser = 75 inch" rule. According to these lines, it would have been better to select a tread closer to 10 inches.

Scale

The scale of the drawing depends on the use and intent of the drawing. A $\frac{1}{2}'' = 1'-0''$ is a popular scale for section drawings of stairs. If many details at a larger scale are to be drawn, you may draw the section at a scale as small as $\frac{1}{4}'' = 1'-0''$. This $\frac{1}{4}''$ scale will, however, make the various connections very difficult to read. If and when details of the various components are made, they should be drawn at $1\frac{1}{2}'' = 1'-0''$ or $3'' = 1'-0''$.

A scale of $\frac{3}{4}'' = 1'-0''$ or $1'' = 1'-0''$ is also used if the parts you are detailing are large enough, or if the space requirement dictates this.

Stair Layout

To develop a good stair detail, there are certain steps a draftsperson or architect must follow to ensure an accurate representation of the design. The steps are simple and are based on previous calculations, whose results are

A. Floor to floor = 9'-0" or 108"
B. 7.2 inch per riser
C. 15 risers
D. 140" or 11'-8" run
E. 14 treads
F. 10" treads
G. 6'-8" headroom (or as required by code)

Step 1 Select the appropriate scale for the drawing. See Figure 14.11. The floor-to-floor measurement of 9'-0" is first measured and two parallel guidelines drawn.

Step 2 Since it is difficult to measure 7.2 inches individually and draw them accurately, the floor-to-floor distance is geometrically divided into the total number of risers. Select a measurement that is slightly larger than the distance between the lines divisible by 15. Any scale will do. Start with the 0 (zero) placed at any location on the top line and the selected measurement at the bottom. This angle that the scale makes with the horizontal lines will vary depending upon

STAIR DATA

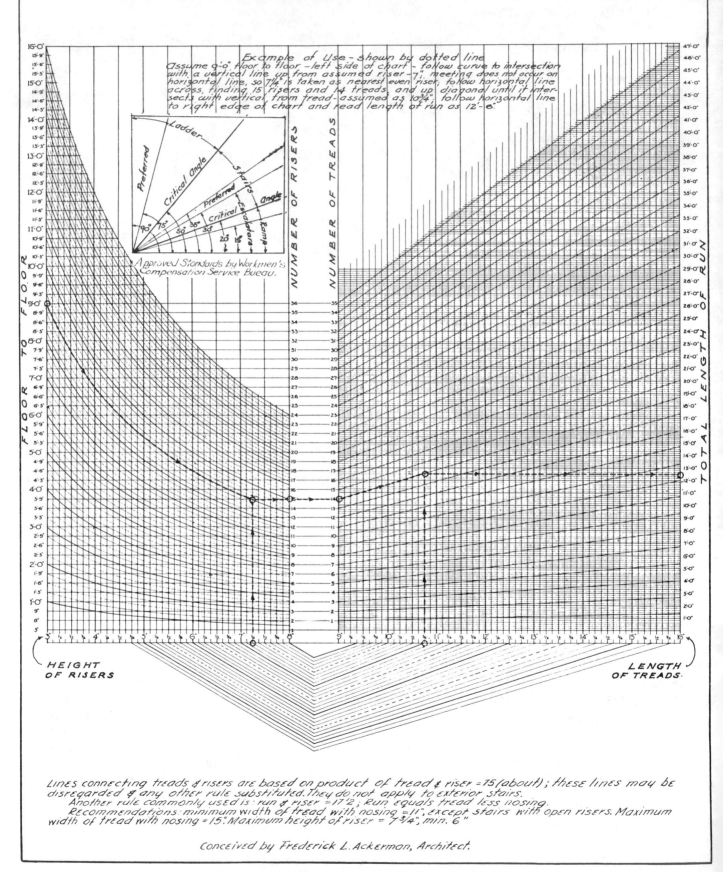

Figure 14.10 Stair data chart for finding out heights of risers, length of tread, and numbers of treads and risers. (Reproduction from *Architectural Graphic Standards* with permission from John Wiley & Sons, Inc.)

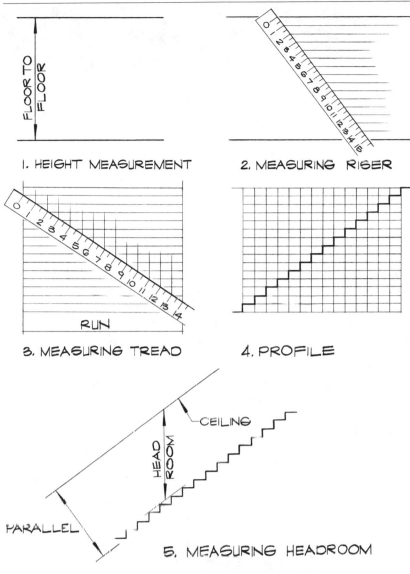

1. HEIGHT MEASUREMENT

2. MEASURING RISER

3. MEASURING TREAD

4. PROFILE

5. MEASURING HEADROOM

Figure 14.11   Steps for laying out stairs.

the size of the scale selected. Place a tick mark at each division, remove the scale, and draw light horizontal lines at each tick mark. Each space should measure 7.2 inches in scale.

Step 3   The next step deals with the treads. As with the risers, it is hard to measure 10 inch treads accurately so the total run ends up 11'-8". It is better that the reverse take place. Measure 11'-8" with two guidelines. Lay a scale across it and repeat step 2, but divide the space into 14 equal divisions. Make tick marks and a series of light vertical lines with your triangle. Each horizontal dimension should be 10 inches.

Step 4   Starting at the top right corner or bottom left corner, begin to profile each horizontal and vertical line of the steps as they intersect each other.

Step 5   Measure 6'-8" (headroom) above any nosing (intersection of tread and riser) and construct a light line parallel to the stairs. The space between the stair and this diagonal line is called the headroom, and no structure may enter this area.

Structural Aspects of Handrails and Guardrails

Many times a stair is designed in such a way that it is exposed on one or two sides. The handrails now become guardrails to prevent people from falling off the edge of the stair. Balconies and decks must also have some type of guardrailing to prevent people from falling off.

Since the stair handrail serves two purposes—aiding a person ascending a stair and serving as protection—the height remains the same: 30 inches to a maximum of 34 inches.

The height of the guardrail for the balcony may vary depending on the type of activity taking place in the structure and whether it is a private residence or public building. Heights vary from 36 to 42 inches. Some codes require the stringent 42 inches for all balcony handrails regardless of whether the building is a residence or an office.

Some codes require the vertical rails on a stair or balcony to be constructed so that a person does not fall through. A 9 inch minimum is often recommended for this measurement.

The most complex of the guardrail requirements is structural stability. Here it would be safe to say that if we could accommodate a thrust on the guard rail of 20 pounds per linear feet (indicated #/lin.'), it would satisfy most codes. This 20 pounds of thrust must be transferred down through the balusters and again to the bolts holding the baluster to the deck.

If the balusters were spaced at 5'-0" o.c. as shown in Figure 14.12, each baluster must withstand a thrust of 20 pounds times 5'-0" or 100 pounds. However, this thrust is at the top of the baluster, and the bolt is 3 feet below it. Similar to using a long wood stick to move a boulder, we have developed what is called a lever arm.

The calculation of this lever arm system is simple. We multiply the thrust at the top times the length (or height, in this case) of the arm. One hundred pounds times 3'-0" gives a product of 300 foot pounds.

If the bolts holding the baluster down were on opposite sides (one on the outside of the guardrail and one on the inside), the inside bolt would usually be the first to give way when you pushed against the guardrail. When pulling the guardrail, the situation is just the opposite. The outside bolt is primarily responsible for the strength. If both were bolted in a line parallel to the guardrail, each would share the thrust in either direction.

For the holding power of bolts and screws, an engineer should be consulted or the local building department official may have the necessary information for the minimum required safety standard.

Remember, however, that this analysis assumes that you have selected a sufficiently strong material to resist bending or the collapse of the system prior to the transference of force. A $1\frac{1}{4}$" square times 15 ga. (.072 wall) tube welded to a $\frac{1}{4}$" plate at the bottom is sufficient.

Since the handrail is 30" to 34" and the guardrail on the balcony is 36" to 42" in height, a transition must take place at the top of the stairs. This transition is called a *gooseneck*. See Figure 14.13.

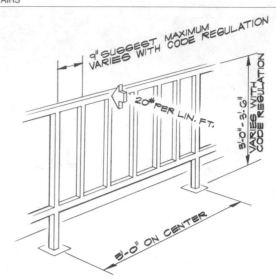

Figure 14.12 Forces acting on guardrail.

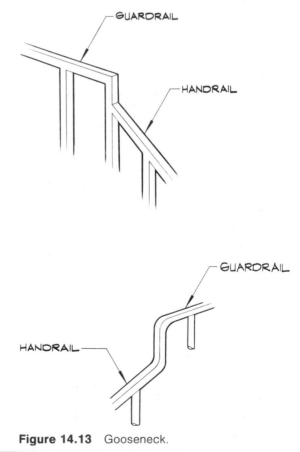

Figure 14.13 Gooseneck.

Regional Differences

Since we are primarily dealing with health and safety of the human body, there is very little regional difference in the design of a stair except for the structure around it and the regional differences that affect it.

Building Codes

Code differences on stairs usually revolve around the following requirements:

1. Head clearance
2. Maximum and minimum treads
3. Maximum and minimum riser
4. Difference in maximum and minimum of types of stairs   private or public
5. Handrail heights
6. Guardrail heights
7. Vertical rail or horizontal rail spaces
8. Stair requirements for handicapped

Summary

This chapter showed the relationship that exists between stairs and the needs of the human body where safety and minimal physical exertion become the primary concern.

Designs of stairs are based on well-established and acceptable standards devised by stair specialists. These standards have been developed over a long period of time and should be precisely followed.

The ultimate goal of this chapter has been to introduce the general information pertaining to stairs so that the architectural draftsperson can approach the design and layout of wood or steel stairs with some degree of uniformity. Wood and steel stairs are dealt with in greater detail in the next chapter.

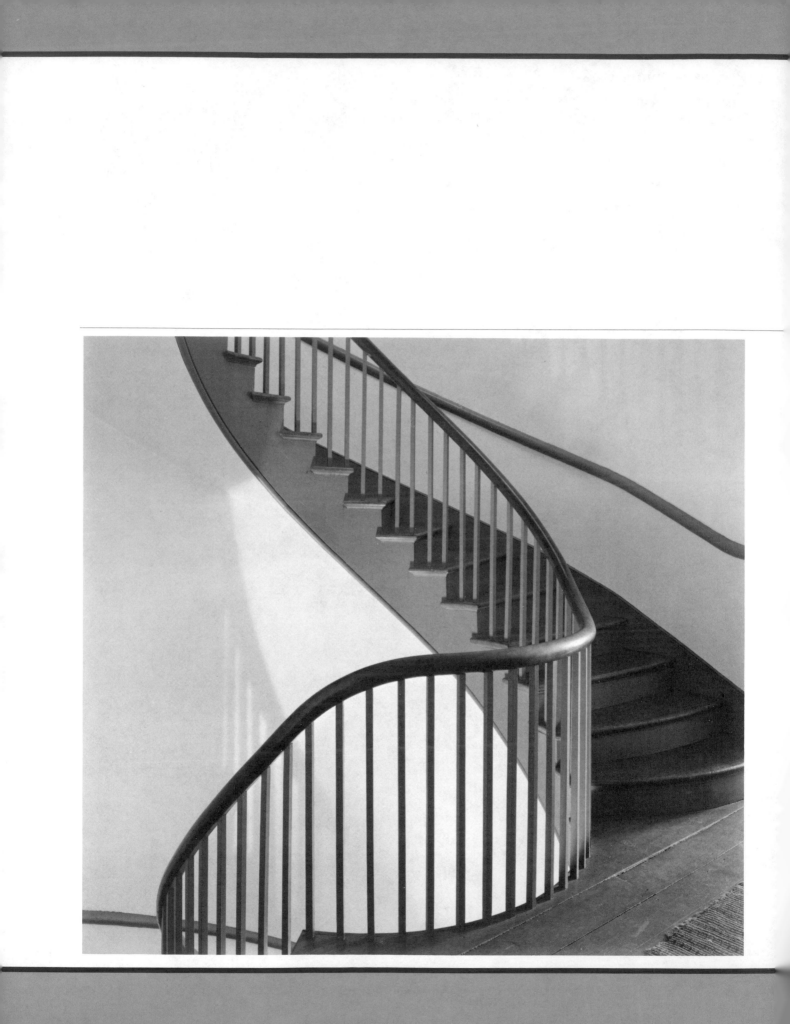

15
WOOD STAIRS

Preview   Chapter 15 describes in narrative and detail form two types of wood stair design. Design criteria for each stair are given so that the necessary drawings and details can be implemented. The first section deals with a given straight-run stair design with explanations and details of the handrail assembly, stringer connections, and tread assembly. The second section provides drawings and details for a reverse or U-shaped wood stair design. It shows the stair section and specific details necessary to build a given stair design.

Each stair design is analyzed in drawing form to show the necessary details required to complete a set of stair details.

After reading this chapter, the architectural draftsperson will:

1. Be cognizant of stair connections that should be clearly detailed.
2. Realize the various methods in which wood stairs are assembled.

The design and assembly for stairs in residential construction generally demand the use of wood for rough and finished members. For other types of structures, building codes require that stair supporting members are constructed of incombustible materials, such as steel and concrete. As in residential construction and other types of buildings, the design of the stairs is a major design element and normally is compatible with the architectural design of the building, whether traditional or contemporary in style.

When the project designer has completed studies for the design of a specific stair, the detailer then incorporates this information into a composite set of stair details for construction purposes. Regardless of the stair design, the detailer should employ the basic principles for stair design and construction. Chapter 13 illustrated the basic physical requirements, code requirements, and nomenclature necessary for the detailing of a specific stair design.

Before starting to detail a stair assembly, the architect should verify the dimensions on the floor plan that pertain to the width and run of the stair to see if they satisfy physical and code requirements. The architect should also compute the exact dimensional height from one floor to the other.

Straight-Run Stairs

Let us assume that we have been given a stair design to detail. The stair is a straight-run rise with a wood handrail, black iron balusters, open wood treads, and exposed wood stringers.

The first task is to draw the stair elevations in accordance with the design criteria, dimensional height from floor to floor, and the selected rise and run. (It should be noted that the detailer must take the responsibility for accurately computing the rise and run prior to commencing the finish details.)

Figure 15.1 illustrates our stair elevation and the referenced sections that we will be detailing. A recommended architectural scale for stair sections and elevations is $\frac{1}{2}'' = 1'-0''$.

When the drawing of the stair elevation is complete, it allows us to analyze the critical connections that should be detailed accurately. The first important connection occurs at the top of the stair run where we must detail the exposed stringer and second floor connection.

Since the stair structure is exposed, we provide an exposed bolted connection for each stringer. The detailer is furnished with the number and bolt sizes necessary to support the stair structure. This may be done by the engineer or the architect. Figures 15.2 and 15.3 illustrate the stringer connection at the top of the stall run in detail and pictorial views.

The remaining structural connection occurs at the bottom of the stair run; it is designed principally to secure the stair horizontally. Figures 15.4 and 15.5 illustrate this connection in detail and pictorial view.

This specific stair design enables the architectural draftsperson to incorporate in one section the handrail, baluster, and tread assemblies.

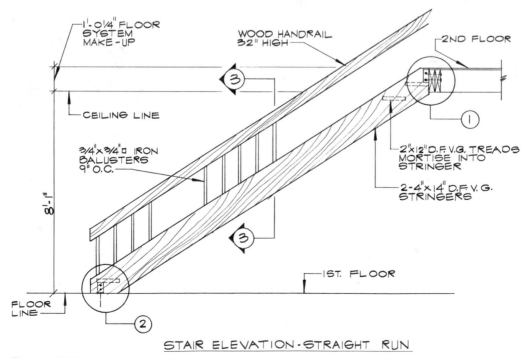

STAIR ELEVATION - STRAIGHT RUN

Figure 15.1 Straight-run stair elevation.

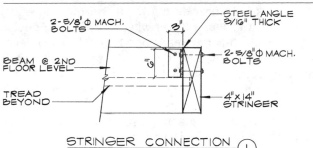

STRINGER CONNECTION ①

Figure 15.2 Stringer connection.

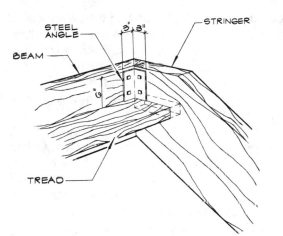

Figure 15.3 Pictorial, stringer connection.

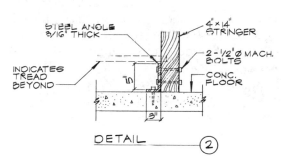

DETAIL ②

Figure 15.4 Stringer connection.

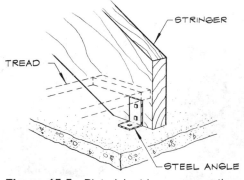

Figure 15.5 Pictorial, stringer connection.

Since the designer has asked for exposed stringers and treads, there are some options for the tread to stringer connection. The tread can be supported below with a steel angle or block, or the tread can be mortised into the stringer. In this case, a mortise connection is shown on the detail. Figure 15.6 shows the stringer with mortise for tread connection. Figures 15.7 and 15.8 illustrate handrail, baluster, and tread connections in detail and pictorial view.

Figure 15.6 Photograph of wood stringer.

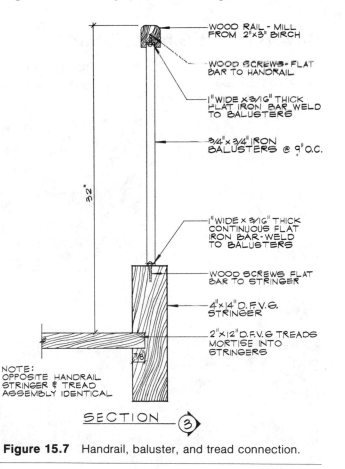

SECTION ③

Figure 15.7 Handrail, baluster, and tread connection.

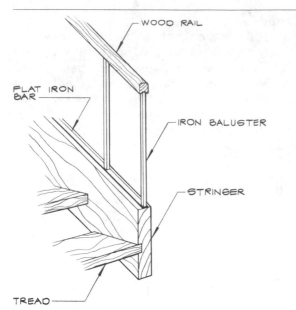

Figure 15.8 Pictorial, stringer tread, and handrail assembly.

It should be noted that this stair was designed for exposed wood treads. However, other finishes, such as carpeting, may be incorporated. Figure 15.9 shows exposed wood treads and stringers in framing stage.

Reverse or U-Shaped Stair

As explained and illustrated in Chapter 14, the reverse or U-shaped stair generally provides a landing at midheight between floors.

The task is to provide drawings and the necessary details for a U-shaped stair with the following design criteria: floor-to-floor dimensions of 9'-2", wood handrail and iron balusters, enclosed risers, and treads with carpet as a finished floor material.

As indicated previously, it is most important for the detailer to verify the dimensional space allotted for the stair on the floor plans to ascertain that it satisfies the rise and run dimensions required.

With the design criteria given, a section is drawn through the stair using an architectural scale of $\frac{1}{2}'' = 1'\text{-}0''$. On completion of the section, the critical structural connections are keyed and analyzed. Figure 15.10 illustrates the stair section and the keyed structural connections for the stringer to the second floor level, stringer to the landing, and stringer to first floor level. Figure 15.11 depicts in pictorial form the framing assembly for the run from the landing to the upper floor level. Figure 15.12 shows stair framing from landing to upper floor.

Detail ④, at the top of the stair run in Figure 15.13, shows a stringer-to-floor connection using a standard joist hanger or framing connector. This type of framing connection is required where a bearing wall is not located directly below the top of the stair run. Note that a beam is provided at the top of the stair run to support the stair's live and dead loads.

Detail ⑤ shows the stringer connections at the landing and the members that are required to support the stair's live and dead loads. Since a bearing wood stud wall is located directly under the front of the landing, the use of framing connectors is not necessary. In this case, the stringers are supported by 2" × 4" or 2" × 6" ledgers nailed continuously along

Figure 15.9 Photograph of stair assembly.

236

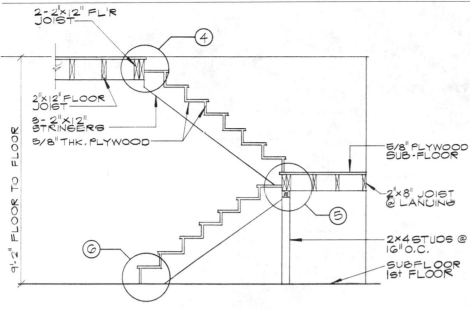

STAIR SECTION - REVERSE RUN

Figure 15.10 Stair section, reverse run.

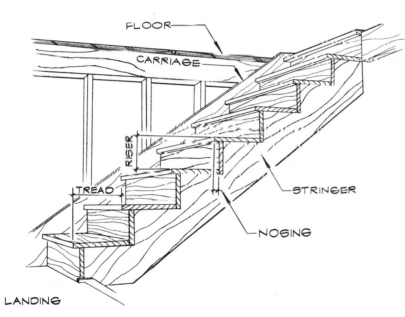

Figure 15.11 Pictorial of stair framing.

the wood stud framing. Figure 15.14 illustrates this framing condition. Figure 15.15 shows this detail in pictorial form.

Detail 6 depicts the framing condition at the bottom of the stair run. The principal structural members, for this connection, are the 2″ × 4″ plate nailed to the subfloor to resist horizontal shear and the two 2″ × floor joist located directly below the stringers to support the stair's live and dead loads. This detail is illustrated in Figure 15.16.

For this specific stair design, the remaining details deal with the handrail assembly. The first task is to draw a large scale elevation of the handrail and the supporting members. For detail and clarity, an architectural scale of $1\frac{1}{2}″ = 1′-0″$ is recommended. The elevation should show the following elements: material and height of handrail, material, size, and spacing of vertical rails, the material and size of the supporting baluster, and the material and size of the bottom rail. This elevation should also provide locations for keyed

Figure 15.12 Photograph of stair assembly.

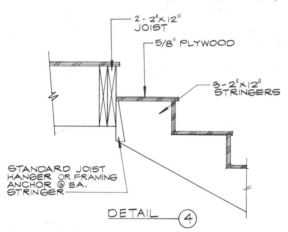

2 - 2"x12" JOIST

5/8" PLYWOOD

3 - 2"x12" STRINGERS

STANDARD JOIST HANGER OR FRAMING ANCHOR @ EA. STRINGER

DETAIL ④

Figure 15.13 Stringer-to-floor connection.

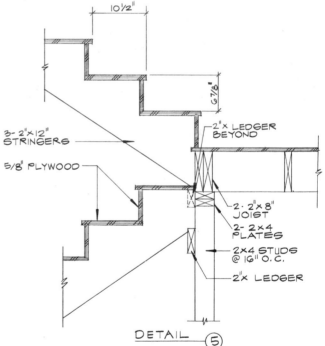

10½"

6⅞"

3- 2"x12" STRINGERS

5/8" PLYWOOD

2"x LEDGER BEYOND

2- 2"x 8" JOIST

2- 2x4 PLATES

2x4 STUDS @ 16" O.C.

2"x LEDGER

DETAIL ⑤

Figure 15.14 Stringer-to-landing connection.

section symbols for additional details. Figure 15.17 shows an elevation of the handrail assembly.

Since the designer has asked for a wood handrail, a full-size detail of this connection should be provided. Detail ⑦ in Figure 15.18 shows the selection of a handrail milled from birch wood with dimensions as noted and the attachment to the flat bar and vertical rails.

The final detail, ⑧, shows the baluster's structural connection to the stringer. The size and penetration of lag screws should be designed to resist the lateral forces, governed by the local building code. Figure 15.19 illustrates the baluster connection at the base support and Figure 15.20 shows this detail pictorially.

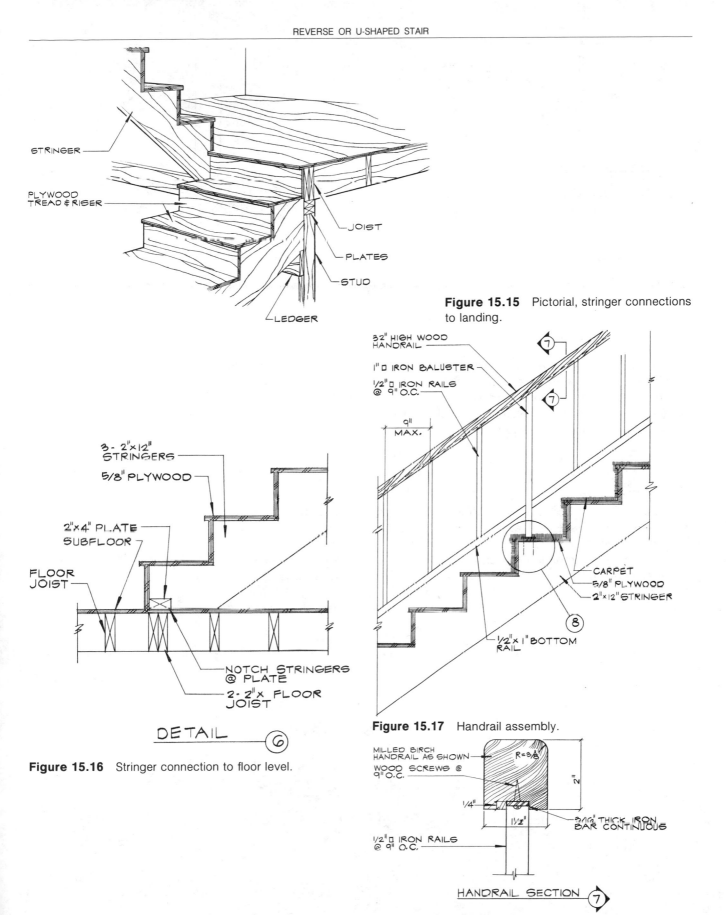

STRINGER

PLYWOOD
TREAD & RISER

JOIST

PLATES

STUD

LEDGER

Figure 15.15 Pictorial, stringer connections to landing.

32" HIGH WOOD HANDRAIL

1"□ IRON BALUSTER

1/2"□ IRON RAILS @ 9" O.C.

9" MAX.

CARPET

5/8" PLYWOOD

2"×12" STRINGER

1/2"×1" BOTTOM RAIL

Figure 15.17 Handrail assembly.

3 - 2"×12" STRINGERS

5/8" PLYWOOD

2"×4" PLATE
SUBFLOOR

FLOOR JOIST

NOTCH STRINGERS @ PLATE

2 - 2"× FLOOR JOIST

DETAIL 6

Figure 15.16 Stringer connection to floor level.

MILLED BIRCH HANDRAIL AS SHOWN

WOOD SCREWS @ 9" O.C.

R=3/8"

2"

1/4"

1/2"

1/2"□ IRON RAILS @ 9" O.C.

3/16" THICK IRON BAR CONTINUOUS

HANDRAIL SECTION 7

Figure 15.18 Handrail section.

239

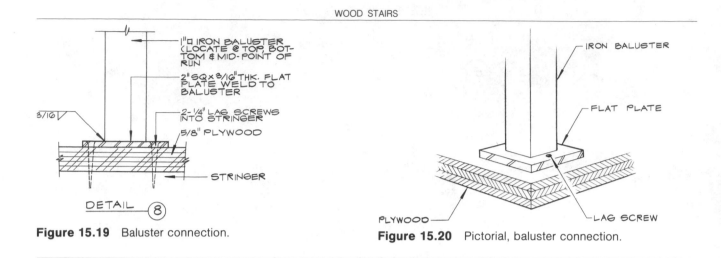

Figure 15.19 Baluster connection.

Figure 15.20 Pictorial, baluster connection.

Regional Differences

Many states have adopted various standards to facilitate handicap access to buildings. It is recommended that the governing standards for stair design within the region be reviewed. In some cases, it was found that building codes will vary in their space requirements for stair design as well as in their dimensional limitations for risers and treads.

Summary

This chapter presented an approach to the detailing of two different types of wood stair designs. It illustrated in narrative and detail form the design and structural connections that are detailed for a specific stair assembly.

Recommended architectural scales for specific details have been shown to provide more information and clarity for detailed connections. This chapter also emphasized the need for the detailer to verify all floor plan dimensions relative to the stair design prior to commencing with finished stair drawings and details.

16
STEEL STAIRS

Preview This chapter discusses the reasons why steel stairs are utilized in today's building and provides examples of stair designs and an approach to detailing these assemblies.

The first section deals with a straight-run stair design and explains in narrative and detail form an approach to the drawings that is necessary to complete a set of stair details. Illustrations of these details are shown along with recommended scales to provide clarity for a specific detail.

In the second section a right angle or L-shaped stair design is illustrated and discussed in detail with the approach to the drawings required for this stair assembly.

After reading this chapter, the architectural draftsperson will:

1. Understand the reasons for the use of steel in stair construction.
2. Be able to detail steel stringers to wood floor construction and precast concrete treads to steel assemblies.

The use of steel as a material for stair assemblies and designs may be recommended for the following reasons: building code requirements for specific structural types, structural stability, and designs that are more compatible with today's contemporary buildings.

In most cases, building codes require that specific types of buildings, such as office buildings, have stair assemblies constructed of incombustible materials, such as steel or concrete. Structural considerations may also influence the use of steel stringers when there are long spans designed to carry excessive live and dead loads. And the aesthetics of today's contemporary buildings are often enhanced by the use of various types of steel stair designs. The designs of steel stairs vary considerably because steel sections are available in many sizes and shapes and steel fabrication affords great flexibility.

As in any stair design—whether constructed in wood, concrete, or steel—the detailer should adhere to basic principles. These principles have been explained and illustrated in Chapter 14 and should be reviewed before beginning stair details.

As previously stated in Chapter 15 the detailer should verify the dimensions of the floor plan concerning the width and run of the stair and be sure they satisfy physical and code requirements. The dimensional height from floor to floor should be computed accurately, so that the riser and tread dimensions may also be computed.

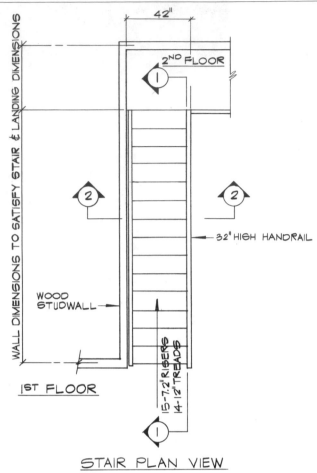

Figure 16.1 Stair plan view.

Straight-Run Stairs

As illustrated in Figure 16.1, the detailer has been given a plan view of a straight-run stair that is constructed of steel members. The first step is to verify the wall and landing dimensions and determine if they satisfy the number and width of the treads selected. Section symbols should be on the plan view as a reference to detailed stair sections.

For this specific stair design, a cross section should be drawn showing the following information: the exact dimensional height from the first floor to the second floor and the selected steel stringers and stringer connections that occur at the first and second floors. These connections should be given section symbols for enlarged details, for clarity. A recommended architectural scale for this section is $\frac{1}{2}'' = 1'-0''$. Figure 16.2 illustrates stair section ①, from Figure 16.1.

Detail ③, which occurs at the top of the stair run, is drawn to an architectural scale of $1\frac{1}{2}'' = 1'-0''$. The larger-scale drawing enables the detailer to show clearly the members required to structure this connection. As indicated on this detail, machine bolts and a flat plate are used to connect the stringer to the floor beam at the landing. For further clarity, a front view of the steel plate and bolts is shown. When detailing, it is good practice to provide as much clarity as possible. Figure 16.3 illustrates the stringer to second floor connection. Figure 16.4 shows an alternate stringer connection. Figure 16.5 illustrates a pictorial view of this connection. The call out for the steel stringer, C10 × 15.3, translates "C" for channel, 10 for 10", and 15.3 for a beam weight of 15.3# (pounds per linear foot).

The remaining structural connection occurs at the first floor level. The enlarged detail ④, which is referenced on the stair section, clearly shows the members necessary to satisfy this connection. See Figure 16.6; Figure 16.7 shows this detail in pictorial form.

Cross section ② is drawn to show the dimension from stringer to stringer as well as their relationship to the stud wall. Also included in this section are the type of treads to be used and their connection to the stringer, as well as the handrail location and detail ref-

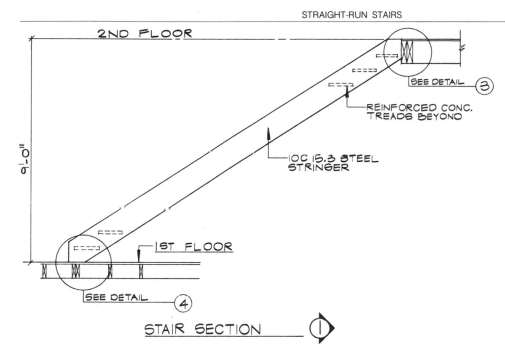

Figure 16.2 Stair section.

erence and the height of the handrail and connection to the stringer. Figure 16.8 illustrates this section.

Figure 16.9 shows the handrail elevation and the members that make up this assembly. For this particular elevation, a scale of 1″ = 1′-0″ was selected. It Is recommended that you provide large-scale drawings when detailing steel members that are small in dimension, such as the vertical and horizontal rails and the continuous flat bars. This elevation shows, graphi-

cally, the design and connections of the members selected for this assembly as well as further detail references that are used for more clarity, such as the

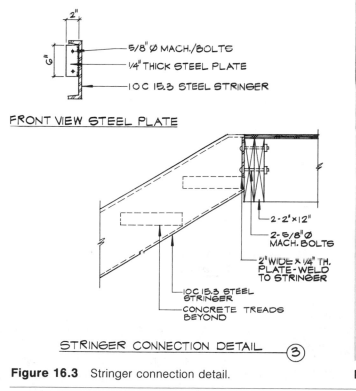

Figure 16.3 Stringer connection detail.

Figure 16.4 Photograph of stringer connection.

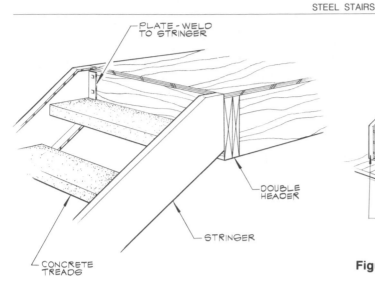

Figure 16.5 Pictorial, stringer-to-floor connection.

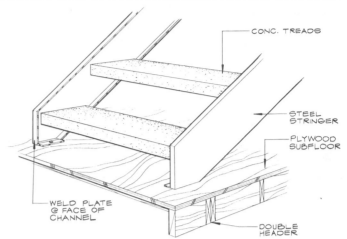

Figure 16.7 Pictorial, stringer-to-landing connection.

wood handrail size, shape, and connection to the iron vertical rails.

As referenced on the handrail elevation, detail ⑤ is provided to show a large-scale drawing of the wood handrail in section and the connection of the vertical rails. It is recommended that a scale of half size or full size be used to depict this type of handrail assembly. A specific type of wood and its milled dimensions may be clearly shown as well as the connection of the handrail to a $\frac{1}{4}''$ thick continuous flat bar that is welded to the iron vertical members.

Figure 16.10 illustrates these members and their connections.

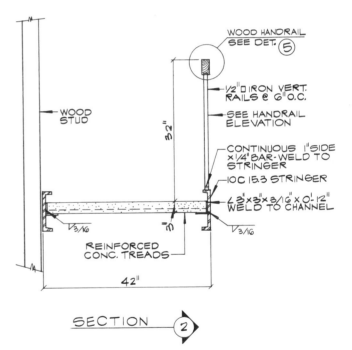

Figure 16.8 Handrail and tread section.

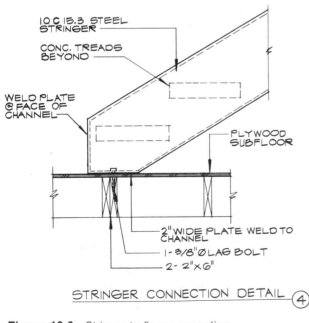

Figure 16.6 Stringer-to-floor connection.

Right Angle Run or L-Shaped Design

The right angle or L-shaped stair run, as explained and illustrated in Chapter 14, changes direction at the midheight between floors as do most reverse or U-shaped stair designs.

The first procedure in preparing stair details and drawings for a right angle stair design is to draw a

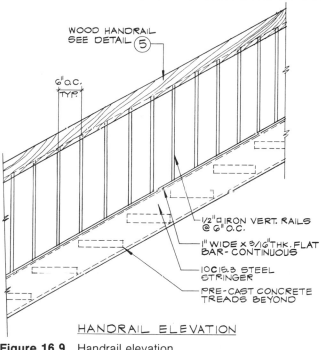

Figure 16.9 Handrail elevation.

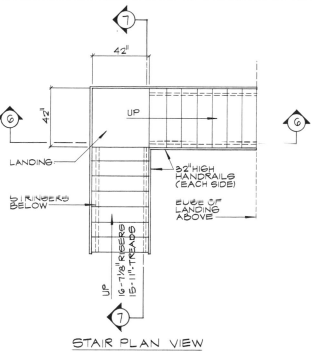

Figure 16.11 Stair plan view.

floor plan of the stair design using a scale of $\frac{3}{8}$ = 1'-0". This scale of the plan affords more accuracy than what is normally shown on a floor plan. The plan view should indicate the following: dimensional width of each stair run, the direction of each run, locations and heights of handrails, number and sizes of risers and treads, location of stringers and cross sectional reference symbols. Figure 16.11 illustrates the plan view of a right angle stair design and related information.

The stair plan indicates handrails on both sides of the stair run. This is done because the walls are not located adjacent to the stair runs.

The next step in detailing this particular stair design is to draw the stair sections as referenced on the stair plan view.

Stair run section 6 is taken from the second floor level to the landing. From this section, we can analyze which connections should be detailed in a larger scale to provide more detail and clarity. Also indicated on this section are the dimensional height from first floor to the second floor and that of the landing

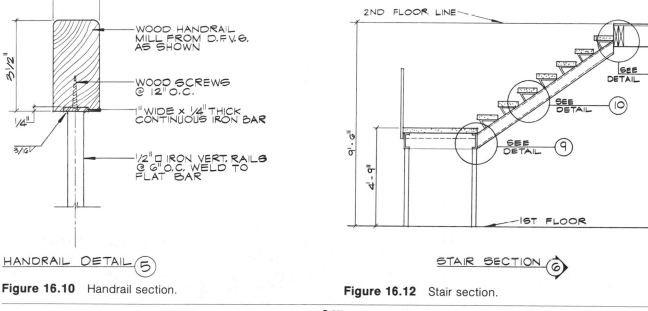

Figure 16.10 Handrail section.

Figure 16.12 Stair section.

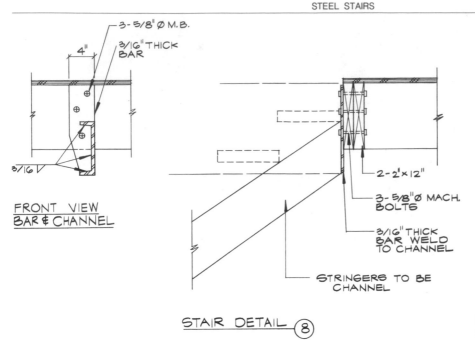

FRONT VIEW
BAR & CHANNEL

STAIR DETAIL (8)

Figure 16.13 Stringer-to-floor connection.

above the first floor. Figure 16.12 on the preceding page illustrates this stair section and includes keyed detail symbols that are drawn at a larger scale to provide more information and clarity for these specific connections. A recommended scale for stair sections is $\frac{1}{2}'' = 1'-0''$.

Stair detail (8) is drawn using an architectural scale of $1\frac{1}{2}'' = 1'-0''$. This detail shows the connection of a stringer to the second floor level. Note that the section shows a flat bar welded to the channel and bolted to the second floor beam. For further clarity, it is good practice to provide a front view of the shape and size of the flat bar, bolt positions, and definite weld locations. Figure 16.13 illustrates this detail and its related information.

The connection of the upper stringers to the landing is drawn at the same scale as detail (8) and is re-

ferred to as detail (9). This detail provides the following information: the structural member around the landing, the type of connection specified for the stringer and landing assembly, and whether it is a bolted or welded connection. Figure 16.14 illustrates detail (9) and the information required to fabricate this assembly. Figure 16.15 shows this detail in pictorial form.

An enlarged drawing should be provided to show clearly the tread design and connection to the steel stringers. Detail (10) depicts the material, size, and shape of the treads that have been selected, as well as the attachment of steel brackets to the supporting steel channel. This detail also shows the riser and tread dimensions and the overlap dimension. Figure 16.16 illustrates detail (10). Figure 16.17 shows the view below tread, bracket, and stringer. Precast concrete treads were selected for this design; however, other options are available, such as a bucket tread filled with concrete or a steel channel filled with concrete.

The remaining stair section (7), which extends from the landing to the first floor, also defines the two critical connections that occur at the landing and first floor levels. These connections are keyed with detail numbers as in section 6. This section and its related information are illustrated in Figure 16.18.

As indicated on section (7), detail (11) shows the connection of the stringer to the landing. This detail is drawn using a scale of $1\frac{1}{2}'' = 1'-0''$. This larger-scale drawing shows clearly the welded connection of the reinforced concrete landing to the supporting landing member. The connection is achieved by a weld plate embedded in the concrete landing and welded to the

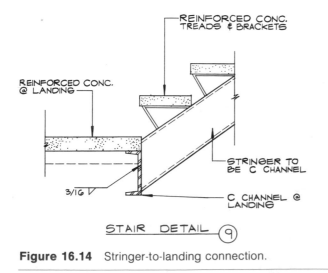

STAIR DETAIL (9)

Figure 16.14 Stringer-to-landing connection.

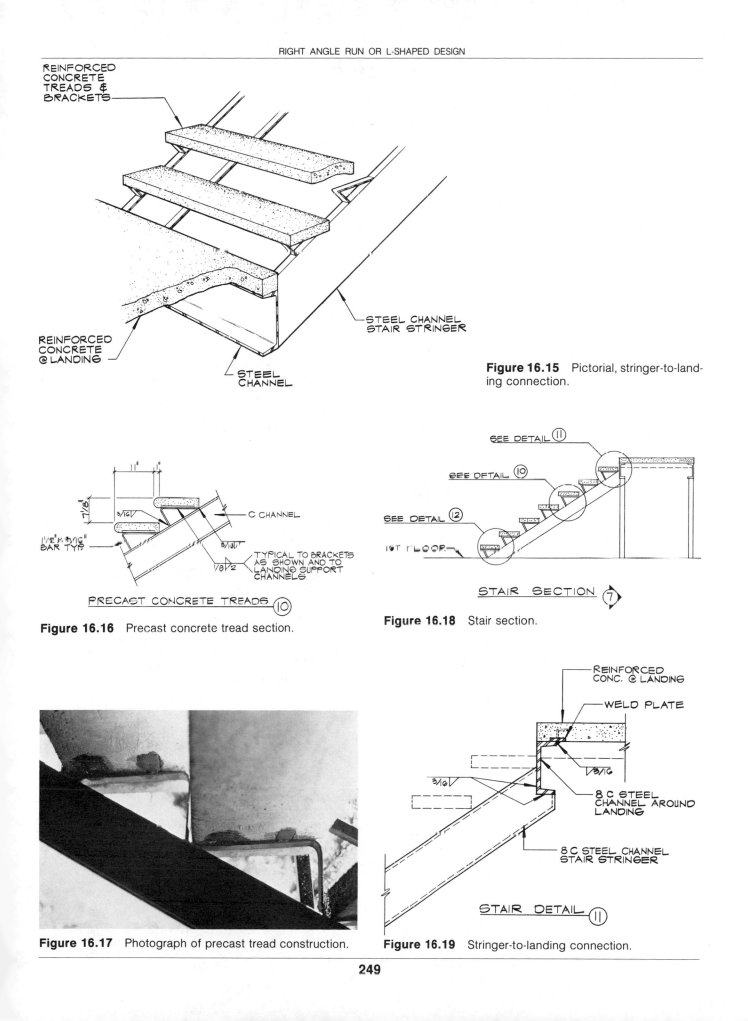

REINFORCED
CONCRETE
TREADS &
BRACKETS

REINFORCED
CONCRETE
@ LANDING

STEEL
CHANNEL

STEEL CHANNEL
STAIR STRINGER

Figure 16.15 Pictorial, stringer-to-landing connection.

C CHANNEL

TYPICAL TO BRACKETS
AS SHOWN AND TO
LANDING SUPPORT
CHANNELS

PRECAST CONCRETE TREADS ⑩

Figure 16.16 Precast concrete tread section.

SEE DETAIL ⑪

SEE DETAIL ⑩

SEE DETAIL ⑫

1ST FLOOR

STAIR SECTION ⑦

Figure 16.18 Stair section.

Figure 16.17 Photograph of precast tread construction.

REINFORCED
CONC. @ LANDING

WELD PLATE

8 C STEEL
CHANNEL AROUND
LANDING

8 C STEEL CHANNEL
STAIR STRINGER

STAIR DETAIL ⑪

Figure 16.19 Stringer-to-landing connection.

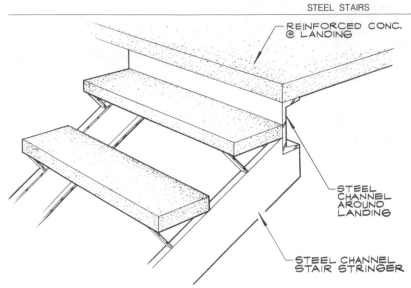

REINFORCED CONC. @ LANDING

STEEL CHANNEL AROUND LANDING

STEEL CHANNEL STAIR STRINGER

Figure 16.20   Pictorial, stringer-to-landing connection.

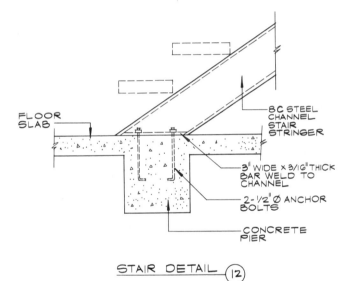

FLOOR SLAB

8C STEEL CHANNEL STAIR STRINGER

3" WIDE × 3/16" THICK BAR WELD TO CHANNEL

2-1/2" Ø ANCHOR BOLTS

CONCRETE PIER

STAIR DETAIL ⑫

Figure 16.21   Stringer-to-concrete slab connection.

steel channel supporting the landing. Note that the stair stringer has been notched and welded to the landing supporting member to provide a cleaner connection. Figure 16.19 on the preceding page illustrates this assembly graphically plus the call out of the various members. Figure 16.20 depicts this detail in pictorial form.

The remaining structural connection is shown in detail ⑫, which occurs at the first floor level, in Figure 16.21. This detail shows graphically the bolted connection of the steel stringer to the concrete floor slab and foundation. A pictorial view is shown in Figure 16.22.

A large-scale drawing of the handrail elevation and the desired members that comprise this assembly is given in Figure 16.23. In this drawing, it is good practice to include a main supporting member, such as the $1\frac{1}{2}'' \times 1''$ iron baluster shown. This allows the detailer to reference a section of the baluster to provide clarity for the attachment to the stair stringer. Section

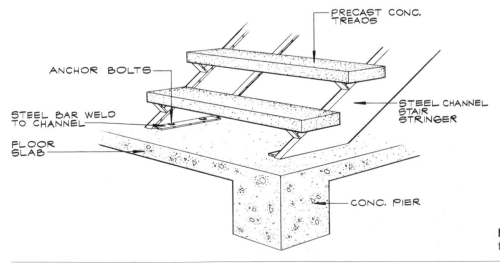

PRECAST CONC. TREADS

ANCHOR BOLTS

STEEL BAR WELD TO CHANNEL

FLOOR SLAB

STEEL CHANNEL STAIR STRINGER

CONC. PIER

Figure 16.22   Pictorial, stringer-to-concrete slab connection.

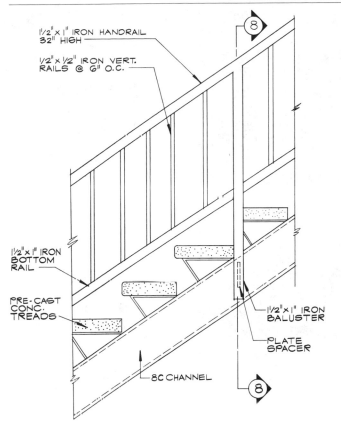

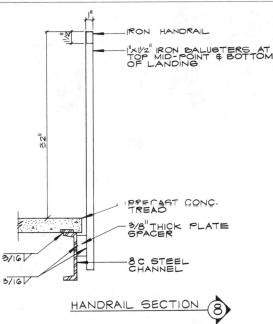

Figure 16.24 Handrail section.

Figure 16.23 Handrail elevation.

reference symbol ⑧ illustrates this condition. The handrail elevation is shown in Figure 16.23.

As discussed previously, a section of a supporting baluster member is detailed to provide more clarity for this structural connection. Figure 16.24 illustrates this

section, drawn with an architectural scale of $1\frac{1}{2} = 1'\text{-}0''$. Note that all members are designated and dimensioned.

Figure 16.25 shows a pictorial view of the handrail, concrete treads and bar supports, and steel stringer. This type of drawing is usually not shown in a set of stair details, but it has been included here as a visual aid. Figure 16.26 illustrates baluster, precast treads, brackets, and stringer.

Building codes require a guardrail dimension at stair landings from 36″ to 42″ in height. Conse-

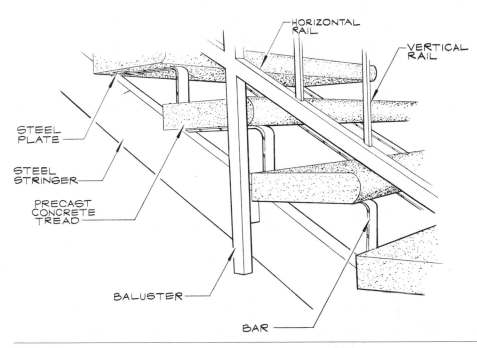

Figure 16.25 Pictorial, handrail, stringer, and tread connection.

Figure 16.26 Photograph of precast tread and baluster assembly.

quently, the stair handrail, which generally is 32″ in height, intersects the landing handrail somewhat below the top rail. This connection is illustrated in pictorial form in Figure 16.27.

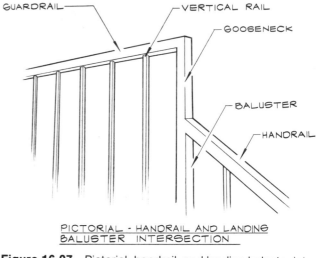

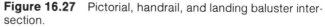

PICTORIAL - HANDRAIL AND LANDING BALUSTER INTERSECTION

Figure 16.27 Pictorial, handrail, and landing baluster intersection.

Regional Differences

Many states have adopted various standards to facilitate handicap access to buildings. It is recommended that the governing standards for stair design within the region be reviewed. In some cases, it was found that building codes will vary in their space requirements for stair design as well as in their dimensional limitations for risers and treads.

Summary

This chapter related the importance of clarity in detailing stair assemblies and described the recommended scales to achieve this task.

We also discussed reasons for the use of steel in stair assemblies and methods for connecting various members. Many illustrations of different types of detailed connections were presented to illustrate the various methods that may be employed to satisfy the assembly of stair members.

17
CABINETS

Preview Chapter 17 introduces the subject of cabinets. A variety of different types of cabinets are compared to show the construction techniques used to improve and produce varying qualities. Terms unique to cabinets are defined and shown pictorially to familiarize the draftsperson with the component parts, their relationship, and their function.

A section of this chapter is also devoted to the variety of materials used in cabinets and their implications. The materials are not limited to various woods. Ceramic tile, cultured marble, and plastic laminate are discussed in terms of construction methods, durability, and so on. Drawers and sinks and their installation, depending on the surrounding material, are also discussed.

Three types of cabinets — flush, flush overlay, and lip — are described. These examples are explained with reference to upper and lower cabinets and the various grades of cabinets predominantly found in the field.

After reading this chapter on cabinets, the architectural draftsperson will:

1. Be familiar with the various parts of a cabinet.
2. Be familiar with the term exclusively used in cabinetmaking.
3. Know the major difference between shop- and job-built cabinets.
4. Know the various grades of cabinets.
5. Become aware of the various material employed in cabinetmaking and their construction implications.
6. Be able to detail upper and lower cabinets of varying materials, grades, and conditions.
7. Increase his or her value to an office by the ability to draft better interior elevations.

Cabinets, or case work as it is sometimes called, deal with storage units. They are most frequently found in kitchens or bathrooms in residences. However, cabinets are not limited to residences. Hospitals, medical and dental offices, department stores, and other commercial structures of various sorts use cabinets.

The bulk of information contained in this chapter is derived from the standards of the industry as compiled and adapted by the Woodwork Institute of California. These standards are also used in Arizona and Oregon. While their information is not the final word in cabinets and case work, much research has been incorporated into this area, and it should be studied carefully and with regard to regional differences, if any.

Types of Cabinets

Cabinets can be categorized into three general areas. The first deals with housing and tract homes. This type is the most inexpensive and does not have the longevity of other types.

Architectural mill is a second type, and we will focus most of our attention on it in this chapter. It uses good sound building procedures as well as good materials and precise equipment to maintain high standards.

The final classification is showcase. Showcase cabinets are made like fine furniture, custom-made for each job. You will find these cabinets in exclusive offices, high-fashion stores, and even banks.

Terms

Most of the terms in cabinet or case work are self-explanatory, such as drawer, shelf, and so on. Others are not and they are explained here:

Concealed portions—those parts of a cabinet that are never exposed to view.

Coped—to cut out a member to fit the form of another.

Eased edge—slightly rounding off a corner.

Edge band—to cover the edge of a piece of plywood, particle board, and so forth with a thin strip of wood.

Ends and divisions—The vertical sheets that are used at the sides of a cabinet are called ends; the vertical sheets used on the inside to divide portions of the cabinet are called divisions.

Exposed portion—any part of a cabinet that is left exposed when the drawers and doors are left in a closed position.

Face frame—the framework around the front or sides of the cabinet that is not sheet material and is usually found around doors and drawers.

Opaque finish—any finish that conceals the grain of the wood.

Plough (plow)—rectangular groove or slot cut in a piece of wood parallel to the grain in contrast to dado, which is cut perpendicular to the grain.

Scribe—the process of marking and cutting a piece of wood that abuts a wall in such a way to void any gaps.

Self-edge—to apply to the edges of a piece of plywood or particle board the same material that covers the surface.

Semi-exposed—portions of the cabinet that become exposed when doors or drawers are opened.

Spacer—often called cleat; see Figure 17.8 for pictorial view. Its main function is to structurally hold up the cabinet. The ends, top, and back, if any, are usually attached to it.

Trim—any nonstructural or nonoperating member used to decorate or hide a joint. In cabinets the trim is usually used to cover bad joints or intersections of two materials.

Web frame—a structural frame system to which finished material is applied. A sample web frame is shown on Figure 17.19.

Materials

Cabinets incorporate a variety of different types of materials. The quality, the location, and the innate strength of the materials dictate its use.

Hardboard—a generic term of materials such as masonite, often called tempered hardboard. It is manufactured and consolidated under heat and pressure in a hot press.

Hardwoods with closed grain—red alder, red birch, white birch, birch, cherry, gum, and maple.

Hardwood with open grain—ash, butternut, chestnut, African and Honduras mahogany, Philippine mahogany, red oak, white oak, and walnut.

Laminated plastic—layers of fibrous sheet materials impregnated with a thermosetting condensation resin and consolidated under heat and pressure. It is waterproof and somewhat heat- and acidproof.

Particleboard—small consistent particles of wood bonded together with a synthetic resin. It is cured (hardened) under high pressure and heat.

Plastic backing sheet—a thin sheet, usually phenolic, applied to the opposite side of a piece of plywood that has laminated plastic on it. It prevents undue moisture to be absorbed by the opposite side.

Plywood—a series of thin layers of wood veneer combined and glued at right angles to each other. See Chapter 4 for further description.

Job versus Shop Construction

Some cabinets are made directly on the job. For this, the cabinet must not only be simple in design but require very little intricate cutting—which is not the case with most cabinets. They do require special tools to form the plastic laminate on the countertop, or superior equipment to ensure precise joints.

However, even the best shop-made cabinets leave some of the work to be done on the job because of the condition of the walls, ceiling, or other objects with which they may come in contact. The perpendicularity with the floor or other walls may not be right, and some adaptation must be made. Or, as in the case with ceramic tile countertops, it is better to do it on the job to ensure a perfect fit or to keep it from cracking upon delivery.

Classification of Cabinets

Within architectural mill, cabinets can be easily divided into three classifications: *economy,* the lowest grade; *custom,* the average grade; and *premium,* the top of the line. To the untrained eye, it is sometimes difficult to tell the difference.

There are some telltale signs that one might look for when recommending cabinets to a client. For example, an economy-grade cabinet has no back and usually has a lipped door (covered later in this chapter). The underside of the counters is not specially treated and thus may produce some warpage.

The custom cabinet, in contrast, does have a back in all its construction. The edges of all the exposed plywood are covered, the ends and division between one area and another are solid as opposed to just a frame, and the drawers have hardwood guides for better wear.

The premium cabinet is made with the best construction procedures and materials. The corners are mitered (see the section on joints), and there are solid panels between drawers to prevent dust from going from one area to another. Drawers are made completely of hardwood and constructed with a device to prevent them from falling out and down. The tops are attached with hidden clips or screws, not nailed, and all joints are screwed or glued with blocks.

Size of Cabinets

The Woodwork Institute of California has recommended minimum thicknesses for various parts of a cabinet. For specific thickness see Figure 17.1.

The upper cabinets generally range between 11″ and 13″ in depth; the height depends upon the space above the counter, the ceiling height of the room, and whether a soffit exists or not.

A soffit is an enclosed area above the cabinet used for mechanical or electrical items, such as air-conditioning ducts, or it may be an unused area enclosed for aesthetic purposes.

Since it is impossible to reach this high, many designers close this area off. Figure 17.2, an extract from Federal Housing Administration's "Minimum Property Standards for One and Two Living Units" describes suggested horizontal and vertical dimensions. Average dimensions are as follows.

Upper cabinet depth	12″
Lower cabinet depth	24″
Height of lower cabinet (kitchen)	36″
Height of lower cabinet (bathroom)	30″

It is suggested that the kick space (the area allotted for your shoe when standing close to the counter) is around $3\frac{1}{2}$ inches high and a minimum of 3 inches deep. It is recommended that drawers are not more than 12 inches high or more than 16 inches wide. This is to ensure their good operating and efficiency.

Width of material also becomes a problem. This is especially true of doors that are not braced around the perimeter as in the cabinet itself. If you begin to exceed 20 to 24 inches in width, this may result in warpage and doors that do not close properly.

Sizes of Hardwood and Softwood

Figures 17.3 and 17.4 show the nominal rough size (the call-out size) and the net thickness and width (actual size) of hardwoods and softwoods. For the actual classification of hardwoods and softwoods, refer to Chapter 6.

Size Notation

In cabinet drawings (often called shop drawings), the normal procedure is to draw and call out everything in its net size. Unlike a wall section or a detail of a footing, cabinets call out the exact size required. The architectural draftsperson must, therefore, understand what sizes are available for maximum usage of material. It would be foolish to call out for a $1\frac{3}{4}$″ thick hardwood when $1\frac{5}{8}$″ is available and this size will do while

	Thickness
Face frame	$\frac{3}{4}''$
Ends and divisions	
Flush overlay	$\frac{3}{4}''$
Economy	$\frac{1}{2}''$
Custom premium	$\frac{5}{8}''$
Shelves	
economy	
Solid stock or particleboard	$\frac{3}{4}''$
Plywood	$\frac{5}{8}''$
Custom and premium	$\frac{3}{4}''$
Length	
Over 3'-6" in length and adjustable	$1''$
Over 4'-0" in length and adjustable	$1''$
Tops and bottom	
Economy	Same as shelves
Custom and premium	$\frac{3}{4}''$
Length over 4'-0"	$1''$
Web members or stretcher	$\frac{3}{4}'' \times 2''$
Backs	
Economy untempered hardboard	$\frac{1}{8}''$
Custome and premium—Plywood or	
tempered hardboard	$\frac{1}{4}''$
Exposed backs	$\frac{3}{4}''$
Breadboards	$\frac{3}{4}''$
Drawers	
Side, sub fronts and backs	
Economy	$\frac{7}{16}''$
Custom and premium	$\frac{1}{2}''$
Bottoms	
Economy (18" maximum width)	$\frac{1}{8}''$
Economy (over 18")	$\frac{1}{4}''$
Custom and premium	$\frac{1}{4}''$
Cabinet door faces	
All grades	$\frac{3}{4}''$

Figure 17.1 Suggested minimum sizes for parts of a cabinet.

a $1\frac{3}{4}''$ would have to be cut from a $2\frac{1}{2}''$ piece. See Figure 17.4 for available sizes.

Some offices do, however, insist on using nominal and net sizes. In this case, nominal sizes are called out in the normal fashion while net sizes would be called out as follows.

$$\frac{3}{4}'' \times 1\frac{1}{2}'' \text{ (net) trim}$$

If some doubt still exists, it would be a simple matter to note ''All sizes net'' under the title or as a note on the side of the drawing.

The sizes indicate the final appearance and do not include such things as scribe. If, for example, you wished a $\frac{3}{4}'' \times 1\frac{1}{2}''$ face frame and this piece was to be scribed into the wall, it is merely enough to call for a $\frac{3}{4}'' \times 1\frac{1}{2}''$ piece, show the scribe with a hidden line, and call it as being scribed.

Joints

To appreciate good cabinet work, an architectural draftsperson must be able to identify the various types of joints used. The pictorial drawings in Figure 17.5 are self-explanatory. Familiarize yourself with them to be able to recognize them in a detail by name.

Types of Cabinet Doors

There are basically three types of doors. Variations of them do exist, but fundamentally they are *lip, flush,* and *flush overlay.* See Figure 17.6.

The lip is the most inexpensive because of its ease of installation. Slight variations in opening or door size can be absorbed by the lip on the door.

The flush door must be cut precisely to the opening. Any irregularity must be reflected in the door. If, for example, the opening was not true 90° at each corner and somewhat of a parallelogram, the door must also be the same shape.

The flush overlay has gained popularity with contemporary homes because of the simple lines it pro-

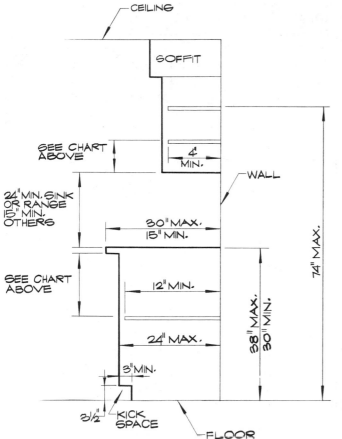

DEPTH OF SHELF (INCHES)	MINIMUM SPACING (INCHES)
4 TO 6	5
6 TO 10	6
10 TO 15	7
15 TO 24	10

Figure 17.2 Suggested minimum dimensions for cabinets.

Nominal Rough	Douglas Fir Hemlock Western Red Cedar		Redwood		Ponderosa Pine Sugar Pine	
	Thickness	Width	Thickness	Width	Thickness	Width
1″	$\frac{11}{16}″$		$\frac{11}{16}″$		$\frac{3}{4}″$	
1$\frac{1}{4}$″	$\frac{15}{16}″$		1″		1″	
1$\frac{1}{2}$″	1$\frac{3}{16}″$				1$\frac{1}{4}″$	
2″	1$\frac{7}{16}″$	1$\frac{1}{2}″$	1$\frac{1}{2}″$	1$\frac{1}{2}″$	1$\frac{1}{2}″$	1$\frac{1}{2}″$
3″	2$\frac{7}{16}″$	2$\frac{1}{2}″$	2$\frac{1}{2}″$	2$\frac{1}{2}″$	2$\frac{1}{2}″$	2$\frac{1}{2}″$
4″	3$\frac{7}{16}″$	3$\frac{1}{4}″$	3$\frac{1}{2}″$	3$\frac{1}{2}″$	3$\frac{1}{2}″$	3$\frac{1}{2}″$
5″		4$\frac{1}{4}″$		4$\frac{1}{2}″$		4$\frac{1}{2}″$
6″		5$\frac{1}{4}″$		5$\frac{1}{2}″$		5$\frac{1}{2}″$
8″		7″		7$\frac{1}{4}″$		7$\frac{1}{4}″$
10″		9″		9$\frac{1}{4}″$		9$\frac{1}{4}″$
12″		11″		11$\frac{1}{4}″$		11$\frac{1}{4}″$
Over 12″		1″ Off		$\frac{3}{4}″$ Off		$\frac{3}{4}″$ Off

Figure 17.3 Size of finished lumber — softwoods. (Reproduced from the *Manual of Millwork,* with permission of the publishers, the Woodwork Institute of California.)

Nominal Rough	Thickness	Width
1″	$\frac{3}{4}″$	
1$\frac{1}{4}$″	1″	
1$\frac{1}{2}$″	1$\frac{1}{4}″$	
2″	1$\frac{1}{2}″$	1$\frac{1}{2}″$
3″	2$\frac{1}{2}″$	2$\frac{1}{2}″$
4″	3$\frac{1}{2}″$	3$\frac{1}{2}″$
5″		4$\frac{1}{4}″$
6″		5$\frac{1}{4}″$
8″		7″
10″		9″
12″		11″
Over 12″		1″ Off

Figure 17.4 Size of finished lumber — hardwoods. (Reproduced from the *Manual of Millwork,* with permission of the publishers, the Woodwork Institute of California.)

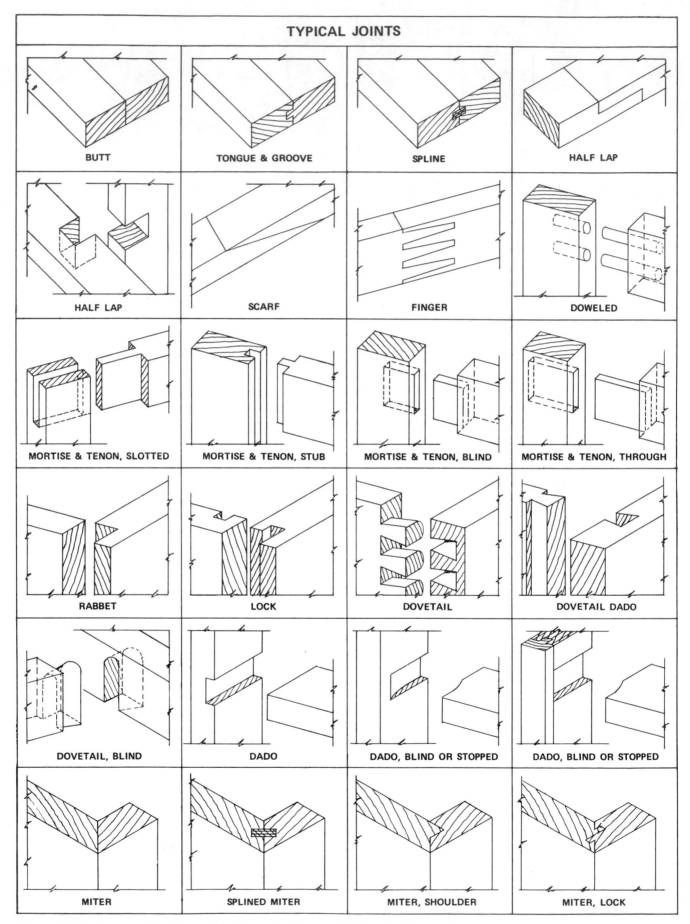

Figure 17.5 Typical joints. (Reproduced from the *Manual of Millwork,* with permission of the publishers, the Woodwork Institute of California.)

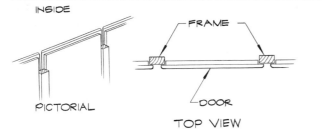

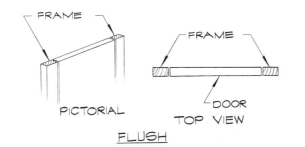

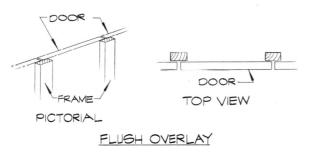

Figure 17.6 Types of cabinet doors.

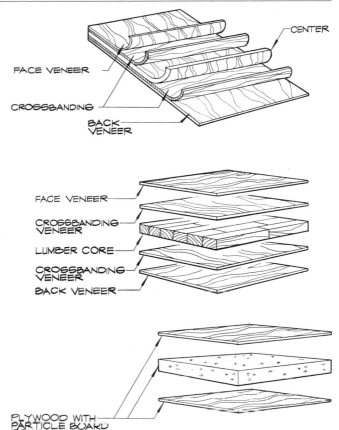

Figure 17.7 Hardwood plywood. (Reproduced from the *Manual of Millwork,* with permission of the publishers, the Woodwork Institute of California.)

duces. The cabinet frames are completely covered, with only the doors showing.

Cabinet doors are made in a variety of different ways. The three most used material combinations are shown in Figure 17.7. The top illustration is called a veneer core with no veneer greater than $\frac{1}{4}$ inch. Lumber core, as the name indicates, is filled with solid lumber of a lesser quality in the center. The particleboard, or shaving board, shown at the bottom, is composed of wood chips bonded together and sandwiched between two pieces of plywood.

Lumber core seems to be the most highly regarded material from the standpoint of durability and freedom from warpage.

Upper Cabinets

The drawings of economy, custom and premium cabinets as shown in Figures 17.8, 17.9, and 17.10 illustrate generally how upper cabinets are assembled.

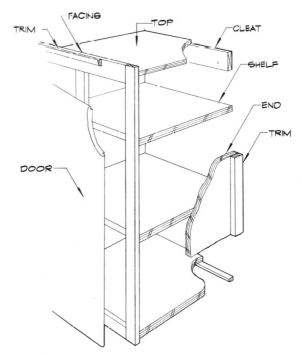

Figure 17.8 Pictorial of economy cabinet.

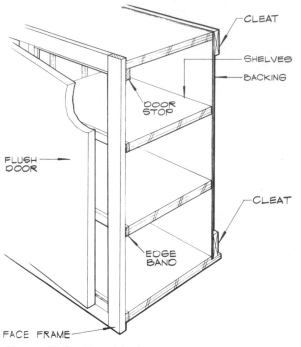

Figure 17.9 Pictorial of custom cabinet.

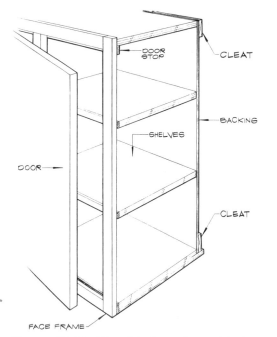

Figure 17.10 Pictorial of premium cabinet.

Inexpensive houses and apartments use economy-type cabinet construction, while the bulk of cabinets made follow the custom method of construction. Premium is used when striving for excellence.

Figure 17.11 shows the precise construction detail at each joint using economy, custom, and premium assembly. A specific explanation of each of these joints and the recommended sizes are indicated at the end of this chapter in the section "Explanation of Case Work Construction Details—Upper Cabinet at the Ceiling" (Appendix 17a).

Adjustable Shelves

Most shelves in kitchens of residences are fixed—the shelves cannot be moved. In offices, stores, and other parts of a residence, it may be highly desirable to be able to adjust shelves to any height. This is accomplished by some type of adjustable bracket. The adjustable shelf standard, as shown in Figure 17.12, is shaped like a channel and usually runs the total vertical height of the division. It has horizontal slots cut in approximately $\frac{1}{4}''$ spacing so that a bracket can be placed and the shelf located at any height. Good construction calls for this standard to be placed slightly beyond the surface of the division; in other words, *not* flush with it, so any adjustable shelf will not rub against the finished or painted surface of the division.

A pin shelf rest is also often employed. This type of construction is used in exposed bookcases to avoid the often unsightly vertical channels. These pin shelf rests are mounted into bored holes. See Figure 17.12. Again, the thickness of the pin keeps the adjustable shelves from touching the divisions.

Shelf Limits

Shelves should be made of solid stock, plywood, or particleboard. Less than $\frac{3}{4}''$ is acceptable for economy grade, but $\frac{3}{4}''$ minimum is suggested for all grades.

The shelves should not exceed 3'-6" in length. Beyond this, it becomes necessary to increase the vertical support members for the possible added weight they will have to support.

Cabinet Details

Figures 17.13, 17.14, and 17.15 show samples of formally drafted details. Remember that all members are drawn net size, not nominal, and that the size indicated is the final actual size and does not include extra need to scribe. Also, any variations or combinations are possible as the need and desire of the client

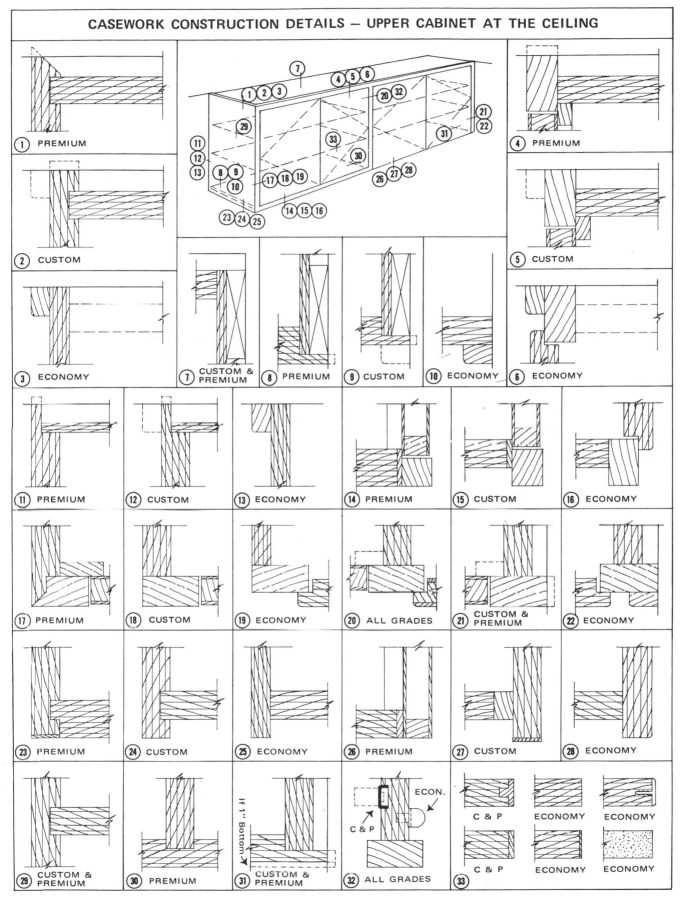

Figure 17.11 Case work construction details—upper cabinets at the ceiling. (Reproduced from the *Manual of Millwork,* with permission of the publishers, the Woodwork Institute of California.)

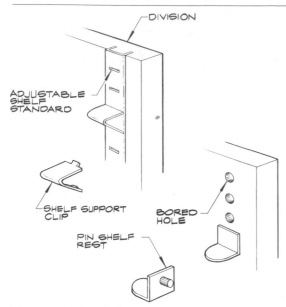

Figure 17.12 Shelf supports.

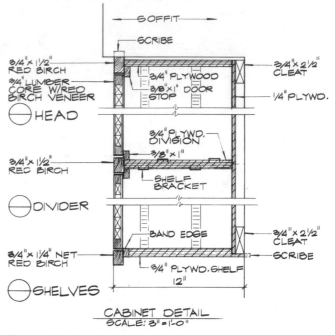

CABINET DETAIL
SCALE: 3" = 1'-0"

Figure 17.14 Drafted detail of custom cabinet.

dictate. The architectural draftsperson should be aware when drawing a cabinet detail with the division being shown at the center of the detail that each section should be labeled and possibly even a reference number given as the examples show. If the center section had been a shelf rather than a division, each section would not need to be labeled.

Drawers

A drawer is simply a wood box, with a front, back, sides, and a bottom. Like any other box, we must consider strength, capacity, and method of construction. A drawer 20″ wide and 20″ high gives great capacity but will produce weakness in the joints. A 3″

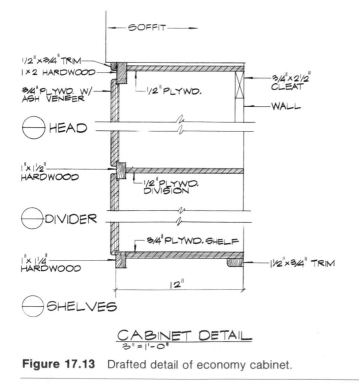

CABINET DETAIL
3" = 1'-0"

Figure 17.13 Drafted detail of economy cabinet.

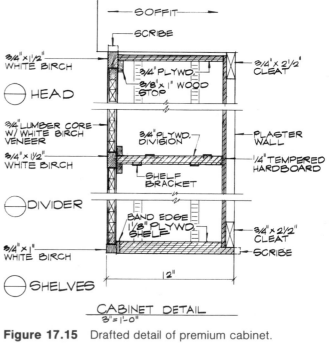

CABINET DETAIL
3" = 1'-0"

Figure 17.15 Drafted detail of premium cabinet.

high by 20″ wide drawer gives great strength but very little capacity and utility. A maximum suggested size is 12″ high and 16″ wide; the minimum should be based upon its function.

The design of the face (whether a lip, flush, or flush overlay door is used) should be compatible with the rest of the cabinets surrounding it. However, there are times when a flush drawer is used above a lip door. The method of construction of a drawer is shown in Figure 17.16. A specific explanation of these joints and sizes is included at the end of this chapter in the section "Explanation of Drawers" (Appendix 17b).

Stretchers

The better made cabinets use what is referred to as stretchers (often called sleepers). A stretcher is a 1″ × 4″ or 2″ × 4″ that becomes the base of a cabinet in a shop-made cabinet or is positioned right on the floor on a job-made cabinet. See Figure 17.17. These pieces rest on the 1 or 2 inch side and elevate the base some 4 inches (3½″ net).

Not all floors are perfectly flat, so these stretchers are notched on the underside as shown by the pictorial drawing. This ensures good contact at the front and back whether the floor may bow upward or downward.

A 1″ × 4″ piece of wood is nailed to the rear and front to prevent these stretchers from toppling over. Maximum spacing for these stretchers is 3′-0″ o.c., which is determined by the fact that normally a ¾″ piece (called the base) will go directly above it. Had the base of the cabinet been thicker, the spacing could have been greater, but it would be more expensive and serve no purpose.

The 3½ inch height of these stretchers automatically produces the height for the kick space for a person's toe. Any division (solid vertical partition) will, therefore, come down to the base of the cabinet but not the floor. This acts to keep bugs out of lower cabinet areas and drawers. It also makes it easier to remove objects from cabinets since items need not be lifted over the kick area.

The total depth of the stretchers plus the 1 × 4 piece of wood at the front and back totals 19¾″. The ¾″ base material is 22½″. With the face frame and the overhang of the countertop, the total depth of the base cabinet should be 2′-0″.

When stretchers are not used, the area behind the kick is often left open. The vertical divisions then come directly to the floor, as in Figure 17.18. The front bottoms of the division are notched to receive the kick. The floor is not seen when you have drawers in this area but is seen when hinged doors are opened.

Base Cabinets

The study of base cabinets is divided into three sections. The first deals with how the base cabinet comes into contact with the floor. The second, and most extensive, describes the actual cabinet itself with the exception of drawers, covered in a previous section.

The final segment deals with how the top is finished with such items as ceramic tile, sink installation, and the use of laminated plastic tops and cultured marble.

Construction of Base Cabinets

Figures 17.18 and 17.19 show two typical methods of constructing cabinets. Figure 17.18 illustrates one that is a more economical and cheaper one to build. Notice the exposed floor and how the area of the kick is handled.

The drawer guide can be suspended from the spacer or from the division as shown on the pictorial drawing. Also worth noting is the lack of stretchers and how the divisions go all the way down to the floor. These divisions actually carry the weight of the countertop or any additional weight on the countertop.

The tilt strip above the drawer is located to prevent the drawer from tilting or tipping downward when open, a problem usually caused by pulling the drawer out more than half way. It is the back of the drawer that hits the tilt strip.

Figure 17.19 shows a much better quality cabinet and derives its shape from the custom-grade cabinets. Of the cabinets built by the Woodwork Institute of California or according to their standards, 95 percent of these are built in this manner.

Notice the use of stretchers, the inclusion of a back, a dust panel between the drawer and the area below, and especially the use of a web frame to which the countertop will be attached.

If a solid dust panel is not desired, the center (solid sheet stock) is omitted, and you have basically a web frame. Tilt strips are used when center, side, or corner runners are used on the drawer. If the side runner is inserted into the dado in the division and the drawer, it may be voided. (See the section on drawers in this chapter.)

For specific illustrations of the connections and intersections of various parts of a cabinet and the contrast between construction methods, see Figure 17.20. A specific explanation of these joints, the intent of the cabinetmaker, and the recommended sizes are indicated in a section at the end of this chapter titled "Explanation of Case Work Construction Details — Base Cabinet" (Appendix 17c).

All base cabinets described in this section are with-

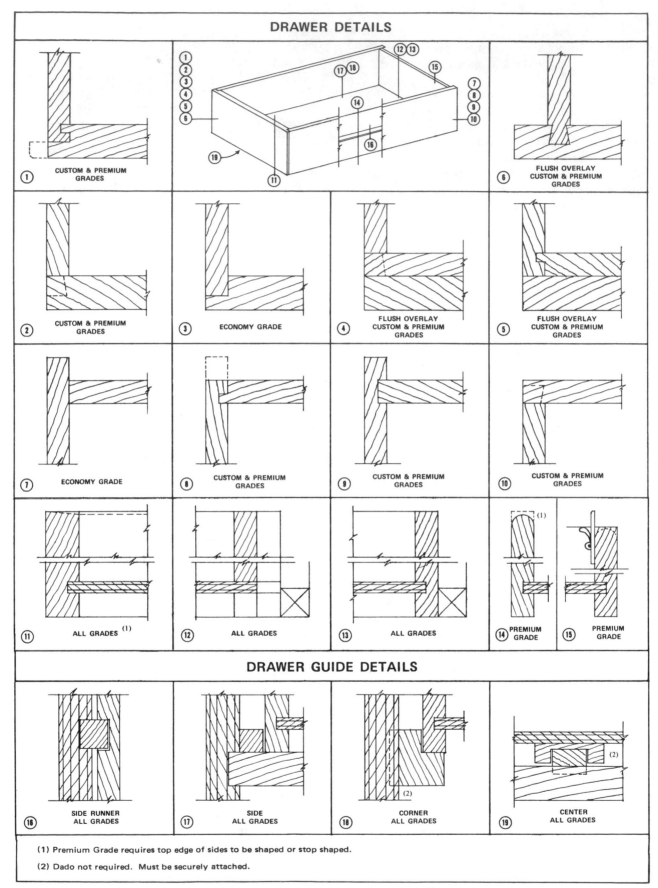

Figure 17.16 Drawer details. (Reproduced from the *Manual of Millwork,* with permission of the publishers, the Woodwork Institute of California.)

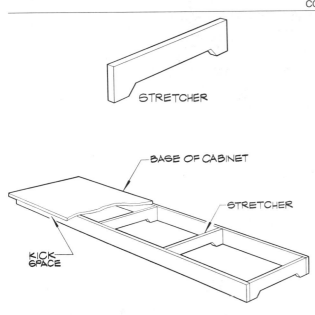

Figure 17.17 Stretcher.

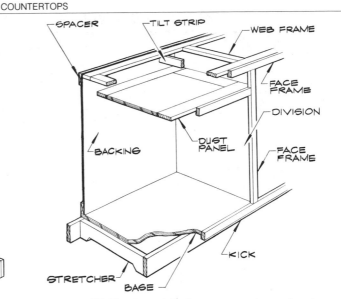

Figure 17.19 Pictorial of custom and premium base cabinet.

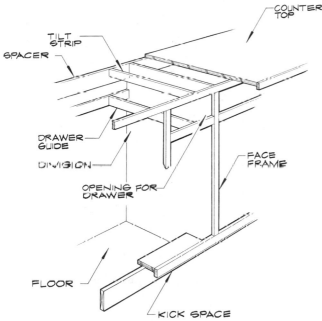

Figure 17.18 Pictorial of economy base cabinet.

out countertops attached. Countertops are discussed in a later part of this chapter.

Kick Space

The intersection of the base cabinet and the floor is called the kick space or toe space. See Figure 17.18. Three of the more popular methods of dealing with this area are illustrated in Figure 17.21. The first illustration uses a $\frac{1}{4}''$ plywood with a veneer similar to the material used on the exposed surface of the cabinet. The irregularity that might appear between the floor

and this piece of plywood is hidden by a wood piece called a shoe. If two pieces are used, the first and larger is called a base and the second the shoe.

A second method is to use a flexible rubber strip called a topset. Since this rubber topset is pliable, it will cover any irregularities that might result. The final method is used when the finished floor material is applied to the floor in sheet form, such as vinyl, instead of in individual forms, such as tile squares. In this method, the floor material is rolled under the base cabinet. A piece of wood, with the desired arc, is used behind the floor material to prevent it from cracking.

Some very exclusive case work might eliminate the problem altogether by mounting the cabinet on the wall and leaving a large space below the cabinet. The floor material would still be dealt with by using a topset, a shoe or base and shoe, or coving. The main difference is that the intersection takes place at the wall and the floor rather than the floor and the bottom front face of the cabinet.

Countertops

A countertop, located above and on the base cabinets, is the surface to which sinks, cooking tops, and so on are attached. Depending upon the need, cost, and appearance desired, a variety of materials can be used: ceramic tiles, plastic laminates, and imitation marbles. Each has its limitations and strengths as well as installation procedures. The architect should be aware of the information required for detailing purposes.

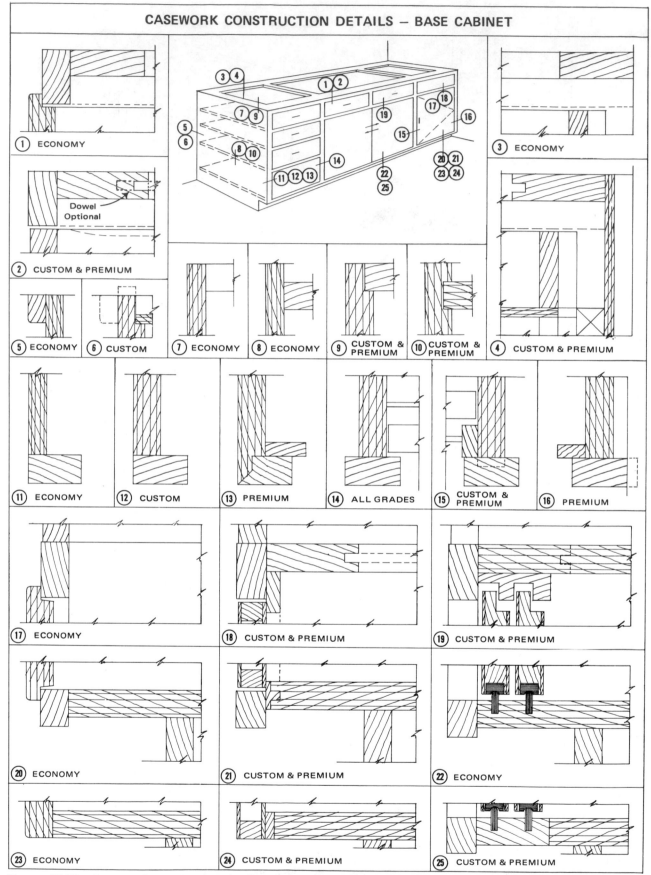

Figure 17.20 Case work construction details—base cabinet. (Reproduced from the *Manual of Millwork,* with permission of the publishers, the Woodwork Institute of California.)

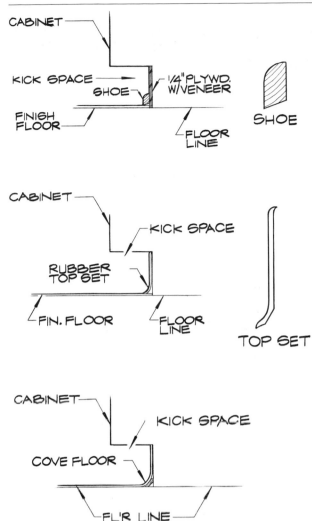

Figure 17.21 Intersection of base cabinet and floor.

Ceramic Tile Countertops

Simply put, ceramic tile is a clay that has been fired (burned under intense heat) to force the clay mixture to fuse together. The mixture that is completely fused together is called vitreous and that partly fused is called semivitreous.

The basic difference is that of color. Vitreous colors are white, silver, grey, cream, green, blue-green, pink, and light and dark blues. The semivitreous colors are buff, salmon, various shades of grey, red, brown, and black.

Semivitreous color ceramic tile is called unglazed tile. It does stain somewhat with such items as beets, wine, coffee, or tea, and is not recommended for countertops but rather for floors.

The tile that should be used for countertops is glazed tile. Glazed tile is made by applying a paste (composed of feldspar, silica, and metallic oxides for glaze coloring) on the unglued tile and firing this tile twice. The glazed tile can result with one firing by applying the paste on the initial firing.

The glazed tile comes in a variety of different finishes. Tiles can be purchased with a high gloss or a dull matte finish; they are available in a variety of different colors and even different textures. Some are even sculptured with a three-dimensional pattern embossed upon them, which is called low relief or high relief. Tiles can be obtained in a variety of different sizes. The most popular size is $4\frac{1}{4}'' \times 4\frac{1}{4}''$. Other typical sizes and shapes are shown in Figure 17.22.

This ceramic tile can be applied to a counter in two different ways. Both require a good sound base to work from and a $\frac{3}{4}''$ exterior plywood (exterior to resist moisture) seems to be a popular media.

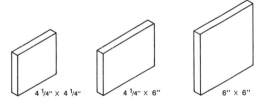

Types of Ceramic Tile

GLAZED WALL TILE

Nominal thickness = $\frac{5}{16}''$, Actual = $\frac{1}{16}''$ to $\frac{3}{8}''$.

Normally used on interior walls or where freezing temperature will not be encountered. For exposure to freezing use frost proof glazed tile. For light or moderate traffic on floors use an extra duty crystalline glaze.

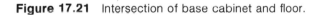

STANDARD SIZES (NOMINAL) OF FLAT TILE

Actual tile size is $\frac{1}{16}''$ less (joint size):

Special sizes available from some manufacturers: $4\frac{1}{4}'' \times 8\frac{1}{4}''$, $6'' \times 9''$, $6'' \times 12''$, $3'' \times 3''$, $3'' \times 6''$, $4''$ octagon, $1\frac{3}{8}'' \times 1\frac{3}{8}'' \times 1\frac{3}{8}''$

Shapes shown to the right are standard trimmers. Special trimmer shapes are available from some manufacturers.

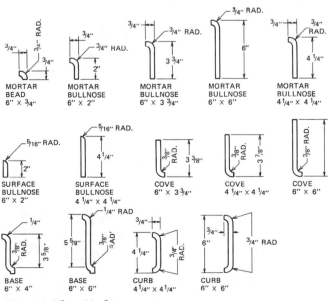

Figure 17.22 Types of ceramic tile. (Reproduced from *Architectural Graphic Standards* with permission from Melville Publishing Company.)

The first application involves a system where the ceramic tile is literally applied to a $\frac{3}{4}''$ plywood. The $\frac{1}{2}''$ epoxy mortar is applied to the plywood and the ceramic tile applied directly above it. See Figure 17.23. An epoxy grout is used in between the joints. This is a very inexpensive method, and its main drawback is that is does not last very long.

The second, and much better method, is to establish a mortar bed on top of which the ceramic tile is set. A photograph of this is shown in Figures 17.24 and 17.25. The layers are as follows:

1. $\frac{3}{4}''$ exterior plywood.
2. A 15-pound building felt that is paper impregnated with weatherproof material.
3. A metal lath to hold the mortar to the wood.
4. A punched metal strip to reinforce the front edge of the counter.
5. The mortar bed itself that is made of cement, a lime-base material.
6. A thin coat called neat cement coat.
7. The ceramic tile itself.

The spaces between the ceramic tiles are filled with portland cement grout. The mortar is $\frac{3}{4}''$ to $1\frac{1}{4}''$ in thickness.

The front edge has a punched metal strip to allow the piece at the edge, called the sink trim, to extend out farther. Without the punched metal strip, you would not be able to bring the sink trim out this far because of the need to keep the mortar contained. A reinforcing bar, which has the diameter of a pencil, called a pencil rod, is often installed at this point.

If a sink were to be installed in this countertop, it is located first and held up with some type of wood framing and tiled later. This is different from the method used for laminated plastic, that is covered later in this chapter. Figures 17.26 and 17.27 show a sink installed in a ceramic tile counter.

Plastic Laminate Countertops

As the name indicates, laminated plastic is a veneering material applied to another material such as plywood. These high-pressure plastic laminates have become popular for a number of reasons, with cost being a major contributor to their popularity. Unlike ceramic tile, laminated plastic has no grout lines that

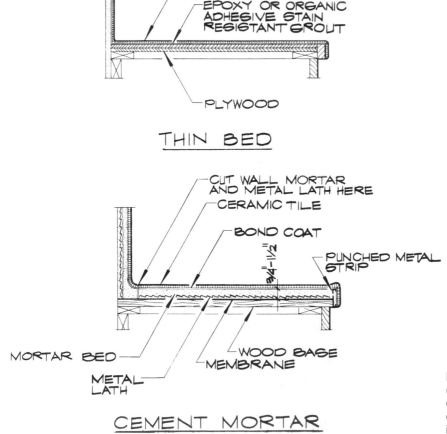

THIN BED

CEMENT MORTAR

Figure 17.23 Ceramic tile countertops. (Reproduced from the *1975 Handbook for Ceramic Tile Installation* with permission of the publisher, the Tile Council of America, Inc.)

Figure 17.24 Ceramic tile with mortar bed.

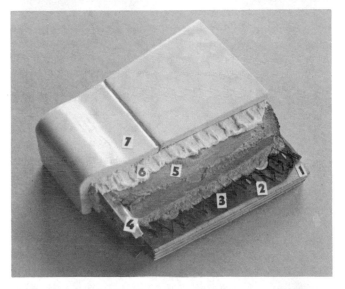

Figure 17.25 Parts of a cement mortar bed.

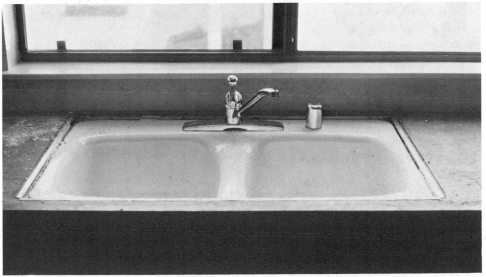

Figure 17.26 Preparation for ceramic tile around sink.

Figure 17.27 Ceramic tile counter top with sink.

can get stained; it also is relatively free from scratching, chipping, and burn marks under low heat.

Laminated plastic comes in four finishes: gloss, satin, furniture, and textured. Figure 17.28 shows a variety of conditions that might be encountered and possible solutions.

The illustration on the top left corner shows a countertop with splash around it. The splash is a vertical portion behind the counter that protects the wall; it is mounted to the countertop at the back or on top. The drawing to the right shows the same condition with the intersection coved (made of one continuous material).

It is, however, impossible to cove the end splash. A 90° bend is not possible with this material since a 1 inch radius is about as small as a craftsperson can make. When a 90° edge is desired, it will require two pieces and the dark edge of the plastic laminate will show unless the edges are painted or laminated plastic, whose color is the same throughout, is used. See Figures 17.29 and 17.30 for such a sample. This type of material is called Colorcore® surfacing material and is made by Formica Corporation.

Another way of avoiding the edge of the laminated plastic from being seen is to use a beveled edge. See Figures 17.31 and 17.32. Figure 17.31 shows an example of using different shades of the laminated plastic material and the clean edge that is possibly by using this method. Figure 17.32 shows the appearance as if one laminated color and pattern has been used. Figure 17.33 shows a mockup counter above a drawer using this system. The space between the base cabinet and countertop was painted black to make the counter look as if it were floating and to give the illusion that the countertop was 1½ inches thick.

Figure 17.34 shows a detail of the countertop on a conventional base cabinet. This beveled edge can also be used for the splash area or partition between, say, teller windows in a bank.

Toward the right center of Figure 17.28, a fully formed top is shown. It comes with top, coved intersection, splash, a bullnose, and enough material extended beyond the splash to allow for scribing.

Two methods of attaching a sink are also illustrated here. The hole for the sink is cut after the plastic laminate is bonded to the plywood. A special metal sink rim called a Hudee ring is used. See Figure 17.35 for a full-scale drawing of the sink rim.

Cultured Marble Countertops

Often called imitation marble, cultured marble countertop material resembles marble with its subtle lines. It is not as porous as marble and, therefore, does not stain.

The countertop comes with a splash, bullnose, and an integral sink with the advantage of being all one piece. This complete unit is made of limestone and a gel coat of polyester resin to give it the marble illusion. Hard abrasives cannot be used and it will not stand up to an extreme impact. Once the polyester resin is worn, the appearance is very poor.

Corian* Countertops

This is a product made of filled methyl methacrylate with marble veins. It is not like cultured marble in that

* Du Pont's registered trademark for its methyl methacrylate material.

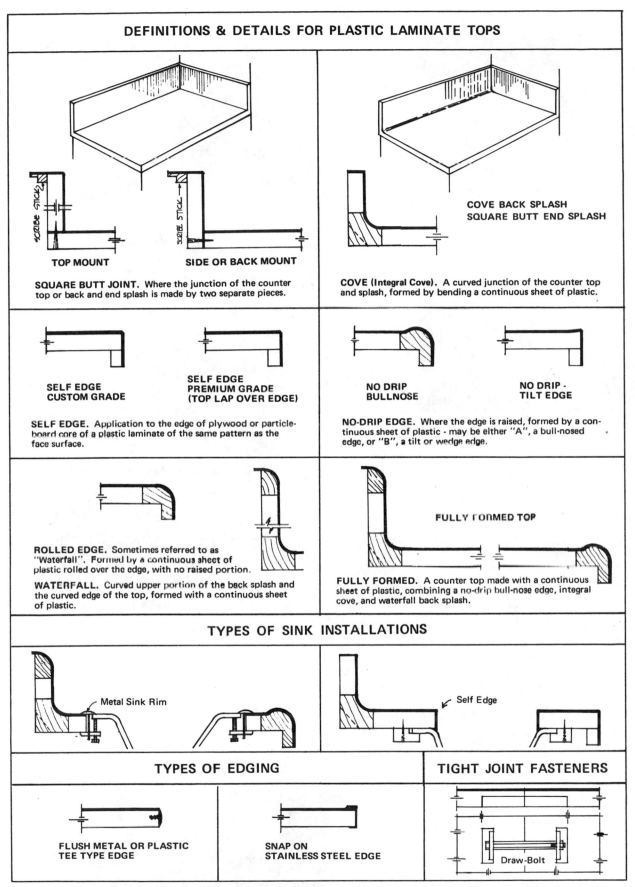

Figure 17.28 Definitions and details for plastic laminate tops. (Reproduced from the *Manual of Millwork,* with permission of the publishers, the Woodwork Institute of California.)

Figure 17.29 Colorcore® surfacing material. (Courtesy of Formica Corporation.)

Figure 17.31 Bevel-edge laminated plastic. (Courtesy of Suncraft Bevel-Edge Moulding, Inc.)

Figure 17.32 Bevel-edge laminated plastic (Courtesy of Suncraft Bevel-Edge Moulding, Inc.)

Figure 17.30 Colorcore® sample. (Courtesy of Formica Corporation.)

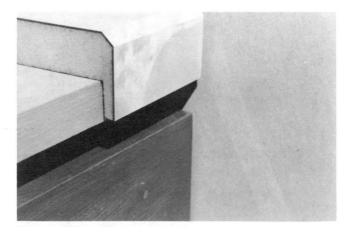

Figure 17.33 Simulated installation of bevel-edge counter-top above a drawer. (Courtesy of Suncraft Bevel-Edge Moulding, Inc.)

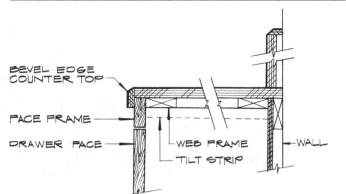

Figure 17.34 Bevel-edge counter.

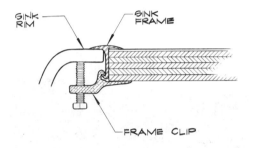

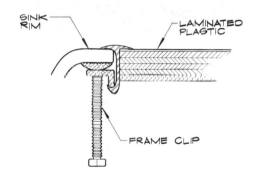

Figure 17.35 Sink installation into plastic laminate countertop. (Courtesy of Ronald C. Smith, *Principles and Practices of Light Construction,* copyright © 1963. By permission of Prentice-Hall, Inc., Englewood Cliffs, N.J.)

If the Corian is allowed to extend beyond the edge of a counter (cantilever), a $\frac{1}{2}''$ sheet can extend 6″ and $\frac{3}{4}''$ sheets can extend as much as 12″.

Figure 17.36 shows two of the more conventional methods used. The apron (front face) of the illustration can use almost any thickness starting from $\frac{1}{4}''$ sheet to $\frac{3}{4}''$ sheet. The front corner is usually slightly eased with about $\frac{1}{16}''$ radius. The lower illustration shows a $\frac{1}{2}''$ setback. This setback is painted black, giving the illusion of a floating slab.

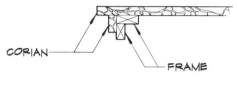

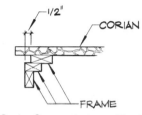

Figure 17.36 Corian® countertop. (Du Pont's registered trademark for its methyl methacrylate material.)

With the introduction of a special joint adhesive for the Corian countertop, many countertop edge treatments are now possible. When a piece of Corian is glued to another piece of Corian, the seam is inconspicuous. Figure 17.37 shows two pieces of Corian joined together with a Roman ogee carved into the top with a $\frac{1}{16}''$ radius. Both pieces are $\frac{3}{4}''$ thick. Many variations are possible from the joining of two pieces of $\frac{3}{4}''$ Corian. For example, the edge can be rounded

it is made totally of one material. Although similar in appearance to marble, it is better than marble because the pattern is consistent throughout with a nonporous surface; scratch marks can be removed with fine-grained sandpaper.

Corian can be purchased in $\frac{1}{4}''$ to $\frac{3}{4}''$ thick sheets, and, although the material cost is higher than other products, shop fabrication costs are much reduced. The in-place costs are consistent with the long-term performance of Corian.

The expansion is about $\frac{1}{32}''$ in an 8′-0″ length when the temperature increases 20°F. A 25″ wide $\frac{3}{4}''$ thick piece weighs about $14\frac{1}{2}$ pounds running foot.

Figure 17.37 Corian®-edge treatment.

with a ½″ radius, top and bottom, to give the illusion of a rounded 1½″ thick Corian counter. In reality, only the edge is 1½″ thick. The top and bottom can be routed with a Roman ogee to produce a classic look about the edges.

Acrylic strips can be used between two pieces of Corian, thus allowing the designer to add color to the edge of the counter. See Figure 17.38 for a photograph of such a combination. This example shows the edge with a ½″ radius top and bottom. Other possibilities are as follows:

1. Recess the acrylic to produce a shadow pattern.
2. Inlay a strip on the top side to match the front or on the splash at the back of the counter.
3. Laminate a series of the same color by alternating between Corian and acrylic.

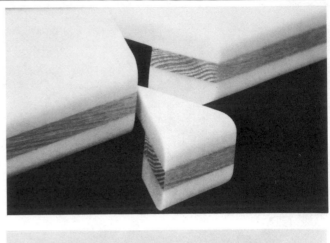

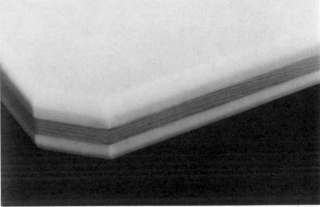

Figure 17.39 Corian® edge with wood insert.

Figure 17.38 Corian® with acrylic insert.

Wood can now be used in conjunction with Corian as shown in Figure 17.39. Different materials do not always need to be sandwiched between pieces of Corian. Figure 17.40 shows a detail of a piece of finished wood joined with Corian and chamfered together to form a neat edge treatment.

By joining the smaller piece in front of the countertop and slightly above the top surface, a no-drip edge can be designed. The seam between the two pieces will barely be seen. See Figure 17.41 for a detail of such a combination.

Figures 17.42 and 17.43 show a simulated installation of the foregoing units over a drawer in a base cabinet. Note how they incorporate the conventional recess, which is painted black.

For bathroom application, Corian countertops can be purchased with an integral sink.

AVONITE*

AVONITE is a new patented man-made material that simulates marble or stonelike products such as granite, parchment stone, and onyx. (See Figure 17.44.) It is used in countertops, bath surrounds, bar tops, and anything that requires marble or stone such as bank teller stations.

AVONITE comes in $\frac{3}{8}$″, $\frac{1}{2}$″, and $\frac{3}{4}$″ thicknesses ($\frac{1}{2}$″ being the preferred size used) and in 3′ by 10′ sheets. It can be cut easily, and patching kits are available for large chips.

This product cuts like wood (cutting powders), can be parqueted to form grain patterns, and comes in a variety of colors. AVONITE was 10 years in its development.

* AVONITE © 1985.

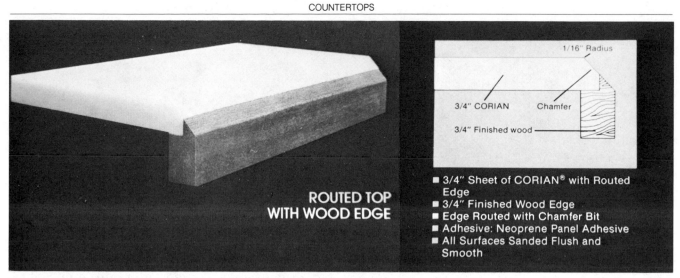

1/16" Radius

3/4" CORIAN   **Chamfer**

3/4" Finished wood

**ROUTED TOP
WITH WOOD EDGE**

- 3/4" Sheet of CORIAN® with Routed Edge
- 3/4" Finished Wood Edge
- Edge Routed with Chamfer Bit
- Adhesive: Neoprene Panel Adhesive
- All Surfaces Sanded Flush and Smooth

Figure 17.40 Routed top with wood edge. (Courtesy of Formica Corporation.)

CORIAN joint adhesive   1/8" Radius

3/4" CORIAN sheet

Height optional

ANGLED NO-DRIP EDGE

- 3/4" Sheet of CORIAN® with 3/4" No-Drip Facing
- Facing Sanded for Exact Fit
- Adhesive: CORIAN® Joint Adhesive

Figure 17.41 Angled no-drip edge. (Courtesy of Formica Corporation.)

Figure 17.42 Wood-laminated Corian® base cabinet.

Figure 17.43 Acrylic-laminated Corian® base cabinet.

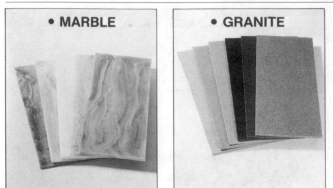

• MARBLE • GRANITE • PARCHMENT STONE • BLACK ONYX

Figure 17.44 Avonite® countertop. (Courtesy of Avonite®).

Suggestions for Detailing

Figure 17.45 shows an inexpensive base cabinet with a plastic laminate countertop. If you wish to include a sink (see Figures 17.28 and 17.35), eliminate the complete drawer except the front of the drawer. This front will be a false drawer front to match the other drawers for the face frame.

Note the use of hardwood for the face frame. Many break-lines are used to reduce the size of the detail when drawing at 3″ = 1′-0″ but remember not to destroy the proportion of the original cabinet.

Figure 17.46 shows a finished detail of a base cabinet of a better quality using flush doors and a ceramic countertop. Because of the great amount of lettering and lines, the architectural draftsperson must take

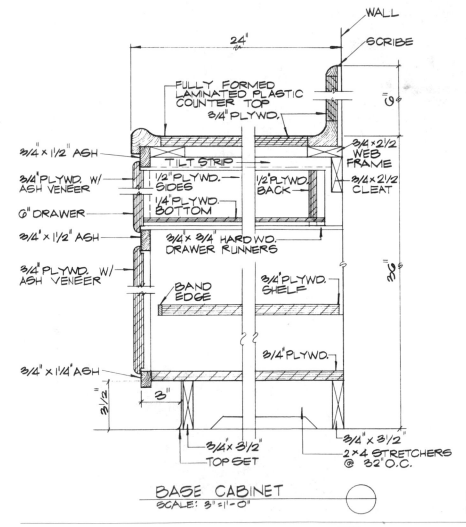

Figure 17.45 Drafted detail of economy base cabinet.

great care in planning every move—organize everything before you darken in.

Figure 17.47 is included in this chapter to show how flush overlay details would look. A complete section is shown in illustration #1 and #5 (base cabinet) and a combination of #2 and #3 gives you a complete detail of the upper cabinets. The rest of the detail shows various conditions you might encounter.

Figure 17.48 provides some additional details on case work. These are laminated plastic covered case work for ease of maintaining; use might be in an office, medical office, or restaurant where the surface of the case work needs to be constantly wiped clean.

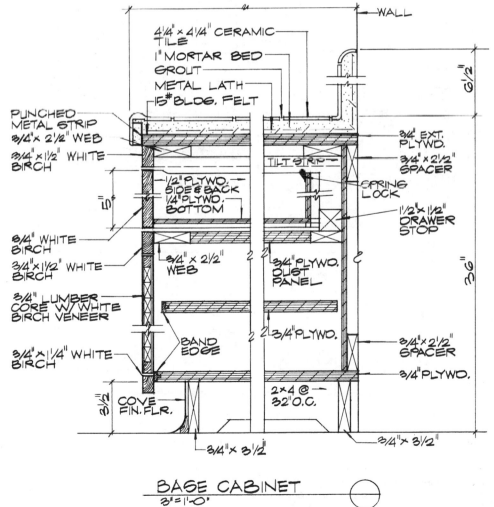

BASE CABINET
3"=1'-0"

Figure 17.46 Drafted detail of custom and premium base cabinet.

FLUSH OVERLAY TYPE CASEWORK CONSTRUCTION DETAILS

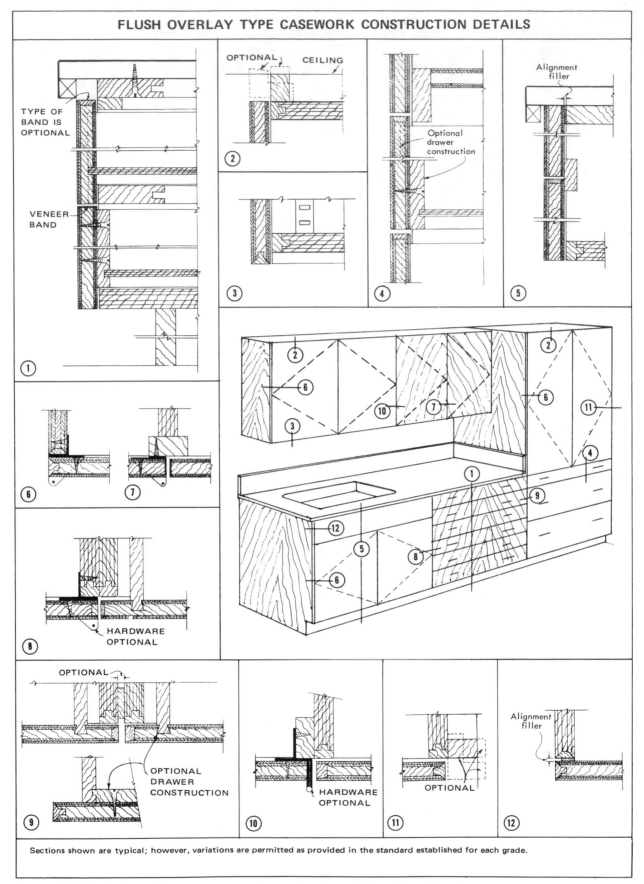

Sections shown are typical; however, variations are permitted as provided in the standard established for each grade.

Figure 17.47 Flush overlay type case work construction details. (Reproduced from the *Manual of Millwork,* with permission of the publishers, the Woodwork Institute of California.)

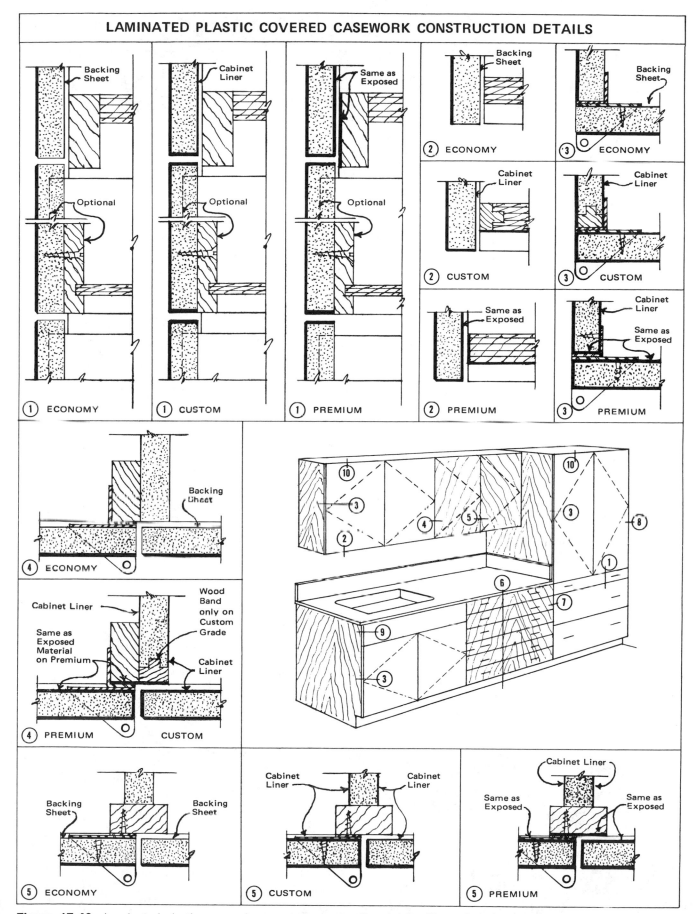

Figure 17.48 Laminated plastic covered case work construction details. (Reproduced from the *Manual of Millwork,* with permission of the publishers, the Woodwork Institute of California.)

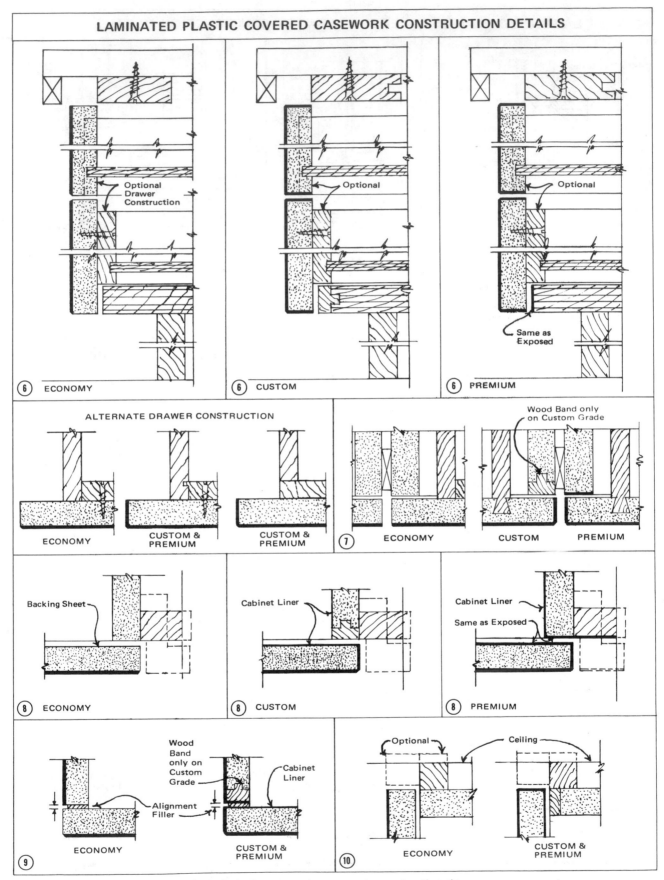

Figure 17.48 (*Continued*) Laminated plastic covered case work construction details.

Regional Differences

Since cabinets are found in the interior of a structure and are not affected by the immediate environment (such as wind, rain, extreme temperature change), there is very little difference in the physical makeup of cabinets from one area to the next. The major difference may be the availability of materials in a certain region and/or cost.

Building Codes

Very few code requirements affect cabinet construction. Most specify maximum and minimum heights of cabinets, their depth and clearance when cook tops and sinks are installed. Many loan companies do, however, establish minimums for drawers, number of shelves, quantity of counter space, and so forth. This has more to do with the resale value of the structure rather than with the health and safety of the individuals using it.

Summary

Although only a few architectural draftspersons will be asked to draw cabinet details (unless employed by cabinet shop or a firm that deals with cabinets as a speciality), the knowledge of cabinets becomes extremely important when developing interior elevations accurately. This is also one way of ensuring that an architect comprehend the total scope of any project, whether store or residence. It allows the draftsperson to make critical decisions concerning appearance and cost of cabinets and the inherent qualities of a variety of materials.

EXPLANATION OF CASE WORK CONSTRUCTION DETAILS— UPPER CABINET AT THE CEILING

The following numbers correspond to the numbers that appear in Figure 17.11.

1. **Premium** An intersection of a top to end of cabinet. The ends and tops are of $\frac{3}{4}''$ plywood. The angular cut at the very top of the end allows this piece of wood to be scribed easily to fit the ceiling.

2. **Custom** An intersection of a top to end of cabinet where the end is exposed. The ends and top are $\frac{3}{4}''$ plywood. The hidden line at the top shows an excessive amount of end that can be scribed to the ceiling. The hidden lines to the left illustrate another method of covering what might be a bad joint if it were not scribed. If the end is not scribed, a trim is used. The trim is $\frac{1}{2}'' \times 1\frac{1}{4}''$ hardwood to match the exposed surface of the cabinet.

3. **Economy** An intersection of the end with ceiling. A top may or may not be used here in this type of cabinet. The hidden line represents some type of frame to which the sides and front might be attached or can designate a $\frac{3}{4}''$ plywood top. See Figure 17.8. The end is $\frac{1}{2}''$ plywood, and the trim to hide the contact area is $\frac{1}{2}'' \times 1\frac{1}{4}''$ and of hardwood, the same finish as the exposed material.

4. **Premium** An intersection of front face, top, and ceiling are shown. Facing material is $\frac{3}{4}'' \times 1\frac{1}{2}''$, and hidden lines show how it is scribed into the ceiling. Directly below the facing is a lumber core door self-edged in a flush position. Door is also $\frac{3}{4}''$ wide. The member to the right of the door represents a door stop. The door stop is $\frac{3}{8}'' \times \frac{1}{2}''$ or larger, as desired.

5. **Custom** An intersection of the front face frame of $\frac{3}{4}'' \times 1\frac{1}{2}''$ of the cabinet, the top, and ceiling. The face frame is not scribed and if any gap is developed, a trim (shown by hidden lines) can be used. The trim is $\frac{1}{2}'' \times 1\frac{1}{4}''$ hardwood. Directly below the face frame is the lumber core door (self-edged) and the door stop ($\frac{3}{8}'' \times \frac{1}{2}''$ or larger) behind it.

6. **Economy** An intersection of the front face frame and the ceiling with a $\frac{3}{4}''$ lip door below it. The face frame is $\frac{3}{4}'' \times 1\frac{1}{2}''$ hardwood and is not scribed to the ceiling. As such, it requires a trim to cover the gaps that may be produced. The trim is $\frac{1}{2}'' \times 1\frac{1}{4}''$. The hidden lines represent a web frame (similar to that shown in Figure 17.19) to which the face frame is attached or an optional $\frac{3}{4}''$ top with its location within the hidden lines.

7. **Custom and premium** The intersection of the top to the back wall is revealed here. A cleat (see Figures 17.9 and 17.10) is shown with a $\frac{1}{4}''$ tempered hard board or $\frac{1}{4}''$ plywood backing. The cleat is used structurally to suspend the cabinet to the wall. It is a $\frac{3}{4}'' \times 2\frac{1}{2}''$ piece.

8. **Premium** The intersection of the rear of the 1'' thick plywood base to the wall is shown. Note the use of a rabbet joint here. The 1'' piece is extended beyond what is needed for scribing purposes. The vertical plywood piece represents the $\frac{1}{4}''$ back and behind it is found the $\frac{3}{4}'' \times 2\frac{1}{2}''$ cleat (often called spacer).

9. **Custom** The intersection of the $\frac{3}{4}''$ plywood base and the wall is illustrated here. Notice how the base is rabbetted and extended for scribing. A trim below may be used. The vertical members are the $\frac{1}{4}''$ plywood backing and the $\frac{3}{4}'' \times 2\frac{1}{2}''$ cleat. The cleat carries much of the weight of the cabinet.

10. **Economy** The intersection of the $\frac{3}{4}''$ base against the back wall is illustrated here. Notice the $\frac{1}{2}'' \times 1\frac{1}{4}''$ trim below it. The base is held up by its attachment to the division pieces and the ends. The division pieces and the ends are in turn attached to the top or the web members. All transfer their weight to the cleat at the top and any cleat that abuts an adjacent wall.

11. **Premium** A view looking down at the intersection of the end and the back as it joins the wall is shown here. The end is rabbetted to accept the back and scribed to the wall. As you

compare the premium with the custom or economy, you will become aware of the lack of a trim to cover the intersection of the cabinet and the walls. The lack of a trim forces the finish carpenter to scribe this intersection perfectly; it also produces a clean-looking cabinet, void of excessive trim lines.

12. **Custom** A view looking down at the intersection of the end and the back as it joins the wall is illustrated here. The end is rabbetted and could be scribed, or this joint can be covered with a trim as shown by the hidden lines to the left of the end piece.

13. **Economy** This is a view looking down at the intersection of the end and the wall. The end is $\frac{1}{2}$" plywood and is not scribed. Lack of scribing requires the use of a $\frac{1}{2}$" × $1\frac{1}{4}$" trim.

14. **Premium** This view shows how the door intersects the base and the face frame. The face frame at this location is a $\frac{3}{4}$" × $\frac{3}{4}$" and made of solid hardwood stock. The base is 1" plywood that has been banded. The bottom is left flush for appearance and the difference between the 1" base and the $\frac{3}{4}$" × $\frac{3}{4}$" face frame creates a ledge that functions like a door stop. The line directly behind the door represents the door stop on the vertical face frame, along the sides of the door. The premium requires a door stop all the way around it, while the others require stops only at the top and bottom.

15. **Custom** This view shows how the door intersects the base and the face frame at the bottom front of the cabinet. The face frame is an 1" × $1\frac{1}{2}$" and is attached to the $\frac{3}{4}$" plywood base which has had the edge banded. Notice how the plywood at the base has been offset to produce a ledge to stop this door.

16. **Economy** How the door intersects the base and the face frame at the bottom front of the cabinet is illustrated here. The face frame is a $\frac{3}{4}$" × $1\frac{1}{2}$" solid hardwood and is attached flush with the $\frac{3}{4}$" plywood base. A ledge is not needed because the door is of a lip variety and will stop itself. Note how the edge of the door is slightly rounded (eased edge).

17. **Premium** A sectional view looking down at the face frame and the exposed end is shown here. Quality shows very much here with the use of a shoulder miter much like that used in making furniture. The face frame that is metered is a $\frac{3}{4}$" × $1\frac{1}{2}$" solid hardwood of the same species as veneered on the end plywood. A larger door stop is employed because of the size face frame ($\frac{3}{4}$" × $1\frac{1}{2}$").

18. **Custom** A sectional view looking down at the front face frame and the exposed end is shown. The face frame ($\frac{3}{4}$" × $1\frac{1}{2}$") of solid hardwood is placed against the plywood end. No door stop is employed here, only at the top and bottom.

19. **Economy** This is a sectional view looking down at the front face frame and the exposed end. Exposed end is $\frac{1}{2}$" plywood and the face frame is $\frac{3}{4}$" × $1\frac{1}{2}$" solid hardwood. The door is a $\frac{3}{4}$" door.

20. **All grades** This view shows a horizontal section of the face frame, which is $\frac{3}{4}$" × $1\frac{1}{2}$" solid hardwood, and a division (a vertical partition). Also shown are the various ramifications such as how a lip door would look with this face frame, how a flush door would look, and how a door stop on a flush door for the premium grade would appear.

21. **Custom and premium** This view shows what the end would look like had it come in contact with an adjacent wall. The space between the end wall and the wall is absorbed by a cleat above and below. See illustrations #7, #8, and #9 on Figure 17.11. The face frame is a $\frac{3}{4}$" × $1\frac{1}{2}$" solid hardwood and the hidden line indicates that it is scribed. The hidden line indicates the door stop for the premium grade.

22. **Economy** This view, which is a horizontal section, shows the end as it abuts an adjacent wall. The end is $\frac{3}{4}$" plywood, the face frame $\frac{3}{4}$" × $1\frac{1}{2}$" solid hardwood, not scribed and, therefore, requires a $\frac{1}{2}$" × $1\frac{1}{4}$" trim. The door is lip.

23. **Premium** The connection between the end and the base is illustrated here. The end is $\frac{3}{4}$" plywood, and the base is 1" plywood. The end piece is banded with the same material that is veneered over the surface of the plywood. The joint is a rabbet and dado. Notice the bottom is flush.

24. **Custom** The connection between the end and the base is shown here. The joint is a dado. Both pieces are $\frac{3}{4}$" plywood.

25. **Economy** The connection between the end and the base is shown here. The joint is a butt joint and is nailed. The end is $\frac{1}{2}$" plywood and the base $\frac{3}{4}$" plywood.

26–28. **All grades** In many cases, it is desirable to use a face frame on the three sides and let the door extend beyond the base. In other words, there is no face frame at the bottom as in illustrations #14, #15, and #16 in Figure 17.11. Such is the case here.

26. **Premium** This illustrates the intersection of the door and base. The 1" plywood base is banded. When you compare this banded edge with that shown in illustration #27, you will note that it is thinner. In fact, some banded edges are as little as $\frac{1}{16}$" due to a thermobonding process now being employed. The thinner banding looks better but employs another step in construction that raises the cost; thermobonding.

27. **Custom** This illustrates the intersection of the door and the base. The $\frac{3}{4}$" plywood base is banded as in the bottom of the door if it is plywood. Read the description for illustration #26 about banding.

28. **Economy** This illustrates the intersection of the door and base. Both members are $\frac{3}{4}$" plywood and neither is banded. The door has an eased edge.

29. **Custom and premium** Dado connection of shelf and end is shown here. Adjustable shelf standards can also be used.

30. **Premium** Dado connection of division and the base is illustrated here.

31. **Custom and premium** Horizontal sectional view shows how the end that runs against a wall is joined with the base. Both premium and custom are scribed and the hidden line at the bottom represents the thicker 1" base for the premium.

32. **All grades** This view shows the face framing coming into contact with the face frame. The dark outline on the left side denotes an adjustable shelf standard. See Figure 17.12. The opposite side of the division shows what is called a pin shelf rest. Figure 17.12 also shows a pin shelf rest.

33. **All grades** This illustration shows how the edge of the shelves are handled.

APPENDIX

EXPLANATION OF DRAWERS

The numbers listed on the following pages correspond to the numbers that appear on Figure 17.16.

1-6. These show the intersection of the front face of the drawer and one of its sides.

1. The sides are made of $\frac{1}{2}''$ solid stock and the front, $\frac{3}{4}''$ stock. This type of joint is a combination called dado tongue and rabbet or simply lock. The hidden line shows the optional lip construction that might be used.

2. The use of a dovetail joint is illustrated here. Sizes are the same as illustration #1.

3. Sides here could be as narrow as $\frac{7}{16}''$, but the front remains $\frac{3}{4}''$ in thickness. The joint is called a rabbet.

4-5. An example of a drawer with the facing attached is illustrated here. They are separated pieces of wood. The inside is called an "inner drawer." The purpose is to keep the face of the drawer flush with the doors on the cabinet that are flush overlay. Thickness of the inner drawer is the same as the sides, while the exposed face will be $\frac{3}{4}''$ in thickness. The joint is #4 is a dovetail and #5 is a dado and rabbet.

6. This sample shows the drawer face extending beyond the sides. This allows the face of the drawer to extend beyond the face frame and be flush with the doors around it.

7-10. These examples show the sides as they intersect the back. Except for the sides and back of an economy that can be as thin as $\frac{7}{16}''$, all others are $\frac{1}{2}''$ minimum.

7. This is an intersection with butt joint.

8. This is an intersection with dado and rabbet joint.

9. This intersection shows a dado joint. Note how the side extends beyond the back.

10. This intersection shows a dovetail.

11. This illustration shows how the front face intersects the bottom. The thickness of the bottom can be as thin as $\frac{1}{8}''$ for economy but a minimum of $\frac{1}{4}''$ for all other grades. The bottom is not attached to the bottom of the side but rather fits in a plough (a slot cut in the sides). The dashed line at the top indicates a slight shaping (rounding) for premium grades. For appearance, see #14.

12. This illustration shows the rear as it is attached to the base. Notice how the dado and the plough extend the total length and width of the sides and are represented by two continuous lines beyond the bottom and rear. The block at the rear of the drawers keeps the drawer from going in any farther. This is no problem with a lip construction, as the lip will stop the drawer at the face frame, but this may not be the case with a flush or flush overlay. A piece of wood is placed at the rear of the drawer. This piece can be any size. A $\frac{3}{4}'' \times \frac{3}{4}''$ square is shown here.

13. This illustration shows the same principle as #12 except the side does not extend beyond the back.

14. The picture shows how the side and the bottom intersect. Notice how the top of the side is rounded for premium construction.

15. This illustration shows connection of the bottom and the back. The unusual looking mechanical device is a spring catch that prevents the drawer from being pulled out too far, thus causing it to fall out of the drawer slot. The bottoms are set about $\frac{1}{2}''$ from the lowest point of the drawer.

16-19. These illustrations show the variety of methods used to slide the drawer in and out smoothly. They are called runners or drawer guides. They should be made of hardwood to ensure longevity.

16. A $\frac{3}{4}'' \times \frac{3}{4}''$ runner is inserted into a dado that is cut into a division and a slightly larger dado is cut into the side of the drawer.

17. This illustration shows a solid dust panel between the drawer and a drawer space below. The drawer slides on the dust panel and the guide shown next to the drawer keeps it in line. The size of the guide is $\frac{1}{2}'' \times \frac{1}{2}''$ or larger, depending upon the need.

18. This illustration shows a corner guide, and the dashed line indicates a stopped or blind dado (see Figure 17.5). These corner guides are about $1\frac{3}{4}''$ in height and $1\frac{5}{16}''$ to $1\frac{3}{4}''$ in width depending upon where they are used. The larger guides are used at the ends. The slot is around $\frac{1}{2}''$ square.

19. A center guide is illustrated here installed with a stop or blind dado to the horizontal piece or solid dust panel.

EXPLANATION OF CASE WORK CONSTRUCTION DETAILS — BASE CABINET

The description and their numbers correspond to the numbers listed in Figure 17.20.

1. **Economy** The intersection of the lip drawer and the top of the cabinet are illustrated here. The drawer is $\frac{3}{4}''$ plywood stock with some type of finished lumber veneered onto it. The perimeter of the drawer faced is eased. The solid line behind the face indicates the side of the drawer, and the dashed line above it (see Figure 17.20) indicates the tilt strip. The face frame above the door is of solid hardwood stock and is $\frac{3}{4}'' \times 1\frac{1}{2}''$ in size. The member behind is a web frame and is optional. It can be eliminated for cost purposes.

2. **Custom and premium** The intersection of a flush drawer and the top of the cabinet is illustrated here. The drawer face could be plywood with a veneer or solid stock. Solid stock is mandatory on premium grade. The drawer face is $\frac{3}{4}''$ thick. The solid line behind the drawer face indicates the side of the drawer and the slightly arced line below it represents the rounded sides on premium. See the section on drawers. The dashed line above the drawer represents the tilt strip. Above the door is the face frame that is made of solid stock and is $\frac{3}{4}'' \times 1\frac{1}{2}''$ in size. The piece behind the face frame is the web frame. Notice the tongue and groove construction and the optional dowel for added quality construction.

3. **Economy** This illustration is the continuation of illustration #1 as it hits the back wall. The two top lines show the web member (had it been used). It, in turn, sits on a spacer (not shown here). The dashed line is the back portion of the tilt strip and the lines at the bottom represent the top back of a drawer.

4. **Custom and premium** This illustration is the continua-tion of illustration #2. The top piece represents the web frame. The vertical member behind it is the backing of $\frac{1}{4}''$ in thickness made of tempered hardboard or plywood. The area behind the backing and the wall is the area absorbed by a spacer (not shown). These spacers are not as urgent as they were in the upper cabinets, since they are not depended upon to carry all the weight. The dashed line below the web frame is the back half of the tilt strip. The drawing below that represents the back half of the drawer. The block at the bottom right of the illustra-tion is installed to prevent the drawer from going farther back than necessary.

5. **Economy** The intersection of the end and the wall is shown here. The $\frac{1}{2}''$ plywood end is *not* scribed into the wall and irregularities are covered by a $\frac{1}{2}'' \times \frac{3}{4}''$ or $\frac{1}{2}'' \times 1\frac{1}{4}''$ trim.

6. **Custom** The intersection of the end and the wall is shown here. End is $\frac{3}{4}''$ and rabbetted to ac-cept the back. It can be scribed or a trim can be used.

6. **Premium (not shown)** The description is the same as in custom except that it must be scribed and no trim is used.

7. & 9. **All grades** The connection between the end and a web frame is shown here. Illustration #7 shows a butt joint where custom and premium illustration #9 shows a rabbet. Sizes remain the same as previously described.

8. & 10. **All grades** This shows how dust panels intersect the ends. Again the economy (illustration #8) shows a butt joint while custom and premium (illustration #10) show a dado. The dust panels are made of $\frac{3}{4}''$ stock.

11–13. **All grades** All these illustrations show the intersection of the ends with the face frame of $\frac{3}{4}'' \times 1\frac{1}{2}''$ solid hardwood. The economy $\frac{1}{2}''$ end and the $\frac{3}{4}''$ custom end both use a butt joint while the premium uses a shoulder miter. The economy uses a lip door so stops are not required as they are in the other grades. The custom has these stops at the top and the bottom, while the premium has them all the way around the door opening.

14. **All grades** This illustration is a sectional view looking down on the intersection of the division and the face frame. Divisions for all grades are $\frac{3}{4}''$ in thickness and the face frame is $\frac{3}{4}'' \times 1\frac{1}{2}''$ solid hardwood. Since the right half is an illustration of a sliding door, only one door will be seen at one time. The two lines drawn close together represent the fiber, aluminum, or nylon guides that the doors slide upon, while the two widely spaced lines below it represent the sliding door itself.

15. **Custom and premium** This is the opposite side of illustration #14 and, again, the wide lines represent the door while the narrow lines represent the guide. The hidden lines indicate that a dado may be used here where the division comes in contact with the face frame. If the sliding doors bang against the divisions constantly, the dado might be a good idea. The small solid hardwood piece adjacent to the division and the face frame is located so that when both sliding doors are in a closed position, one will not see the division. The division at this point becomes an exposed surface and must be covered.

16. **Premium** This view shows how a cabinet may fit against a wall. The face frame is $\frac{3}{4}'' \times 1\frac{1}{2}''$ solid hardwood and is scribed to the wall. Had this been custom, the face frame would also look like this but may not be scribed and a trim used. The economy would be handled with no scribe used and a trim. Also note the use of a door stop on the premium detail. The amount of the door stop exposed and touching the door should be $\frac{1}{4}''$ minimum and $\frac{3}{4}''$ maximum.

17, 20, 23. **Economy** Illustration #17 shows an unusual combination of a flush drawer at the top, a lip door below, and a $\frac{3}{4}'' \times 1\frac{1}{2}''$ face frame in between. It is unusual because most cabinets with lip doors will have lip drawers as well. Notice on the lip portion of the door that this slot has a angle greater than 90°. It is cut this way on better lip doors to ensure clearance of this area when opening or closing. If it were cut at 90°, the inside edge may hit the face frame.

Illustration #20 shows how this lip door intersects the base. In this situation, a the stretcher may be $\frac{3}{4}''$ hardwood or $\frac{3}{4}''$ softwood with a $\frac{1}{4}''$ veneer of the same finish as the cabinets attached to it. In fact, the floor material can also be coved to cover the area. Coving is the process of taking the floor material and tucking it under the kick space. Three samples are illustrated in Figure 17.21.

Illustration #23 is also an example of how a lip door might intersect the base. The main difference between #20 and #23 is the elimination of the face frame. The door is allowed to come down to the very bottom of the cabinet. The bottom of the door need not have a lip since a lip would serve no purpose. The base material must be extended farther than that with a face frame.

18, 21, 24. **Custom and premium** Illustration #18 shows the intersection of a flush drawer and a flush door below. In between is a horizontal face frame of $\frac{3}{4}'' \times 1\frac{1}{2}''$ size and a solid dust panel between or a web frame. The web frame is made of $\frac{3}{4}'' \times 2\frac{1}{2}''$ tongue and groove stock. The door below is a $\frac{3}{4}''$ lumber core self-edged door with a hardwood veneer. A door stop large enough to stop the door is installed. At least $\frac{1}{2}''$ of contact is suggested here between the door and the door stop. The dashed line below it represents the door stops along the side (jamb) of the door that are optional on custom.

Illustration #21 shows how the flush door will intersect the base. Notice how the $\frac{3}{4}'' \times 1\frac{1}{4}''$ solid hardwood face frame is lowered slightly to function as a door stop. Since this procedure exposes the ugly edge of the plywood, it is banded. The dashed line above this represents the door stop along the side.

Illustration #24 illustrates the same location as #21 except that the face frame is removed and the door allowed to extend to the base. Since the total edge of the plywood is exposed and unsightly, it is banded. The base is usually $\frac{3}{4}''$ plywood.

19, 22, 25. **All grades** This set of illustrations shows how to treat the top and bottom of a sliding door in a cabinet. Illustration #19 shows a $\frac{3}{4}'' \times 1\frac{1}{2}''$ face frame with a $\frac{3}{4}''$ dust panel behind it. Below the dust panel is a hardwood track with sliding doors below it. The doors are rabbetted to fit into the track. The rabbet is cut large and a space is left in the track to allow for easy removal by lifting the doors up and out.

Illustrations #22 and #25 show how the sliding doors intersect the base. Note the use of fiber tracks at the base. Also note that the $\frac{3}{4}''$ plywood base will be exposed partly even with the $\frac{3}{4}'' \times 1\frac{1}{2}''$ hardwood face frame. It is exposed because when the doors are closed, the area in front of the rear door is left exposed visually. This is why a $\frac{3}{4}'' \times 2\frac{1}{2}''$ solid hardwood band is used in front of the plywood in the custom and the premium.

18
FIREPLACES

Preview Chapter 18 introduces the fireplace as a decorative item as well as a primary source of heat. The fireplace is described according to the five basic implications it has for the architectural draftsperson: first, the framing around the fireplace; second, the size of the openings; third, the relationship between the opening and the size of the chimney required; fourth, the relationship between chimney and roof structure; and, finally, the shape or configuration based on good practice and codes.

Various types of fireplaces are described, and the most typical are dissected for study. The interior workings of the throat, connection with the house, and methods of representation are discussed. After reading this chapter on fireplaces, the architectural draftsperson will:

1. Understand what design aspects dictate the detailing process.
2. Be aware of the various shapes possible in the design of a fireplace.
3. Understand the necessary framing that is required around the fireplace.
4. Comprehend the relationship between the structure and the fireplace and chimney.
5. Be able to calculate the size of flue based on the fireplace opening.
6. Be aware of how a fireplace actually works, along with the function of such items as the damper, spark arrester, ash dump, and bond beam.
7. Be aware of the minimum construction details necessary.
8. Be able to draw a more accurate set of exterior and interior elevations based on knowledge of fireplaces.
9. Be able to detail any part of a fireplace.
10. Be able to interpret local code requirements as they relate to various parts of a fireplace.

The concept of a fireplace is almost as old as civilization, as people have always used open fire for heat. The control of smoke has led to what we know as the present-day fireplace. Today, the fireplace is more a luxury and decorative item than a primary source of heat. For whatever reason the fireplace is needed, certain facts must be observed to develop a well-functioning fireplace.

There are five main areas of concern when designing a fireplace: first, the structural framing around the fireplace; second, the size and type of opening; third, the relationship of the opening to size of the chimney and the opening within it; fourth, the amount the chimney extends above the roof; and finally, the limitation of the configuration as established by good practice, engineering, codes, or safety.

The fireplace, in many respects, is like a house; to understand all its implications and ramifications fully, the architectural draftsperson must be familiar with the total scope of what is involved.

To understand a home, one must study the elevation, the floor plans, the sections, the foundation, the framing, and the details. All this must transpire simultaneously. One cannot just look at the floor plan and understand the rest of the drawings.

So it is with fireplaces. To understand fireplaces, the architectural draftsperson must use pictorial drawings to get an idea visually of the basic shape that will be encountered. Then comes a study of the terminology involved so as to be able to understand the design and code limitation that are employed in respect to fireplaces.

A true understanding of a section drawing must be at a draftsperson's command, because the fireplace is cut in a full vertical section. The architect must also be able to comprehend the relationship between the plan and the framing around it, as well as the chimney and the framing around it. Simply put, you must be able to look at different drawings simultaneously and understand different views of the same principle.

Types of Fireplaces

Figure 18.1 shows a few of the more popular fireplaces that are now available. Of these, the single-faced is by far the most popular. As seen in the first two illustrations, this type may protrude into the room or be flush with the wall. In either case, the exterior

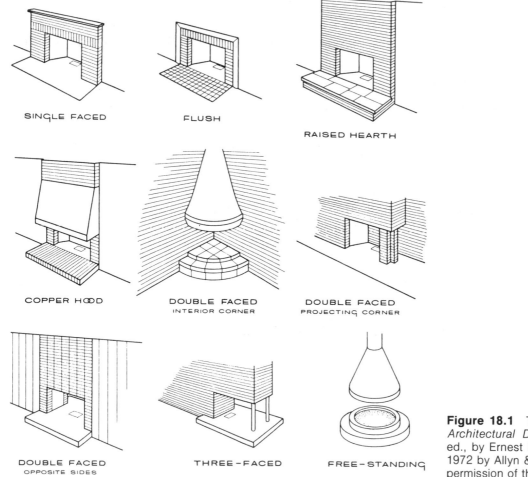

SINGLE FACED

FLUSH

RAISED HEARTH

COPPER HOOD

DOUBLE FACED
INTERIOR CORNER

DOUBLE FACED
PROJECTING CORNER

DOUBLE FACED
OPPOSITE SIDES

THREE-FACED

FREE-STANDING

Figure 18.1 Types of fireplaces. (From *Architectural Drafting and Design,* 2nd ed., by Ernest R. Weidhaas, copyright © 1972 by Allyn & Bacon, Inc. Reprinted by permission of the publisher.)

Figure 18.2 Wood framing around fireplace.

elevation is affected by its thickness protruding on the outside.

The third illustration shows how the raised hearth can have a platform under it or be cantilevered out to give the illusion of a floating hearth.

Other materials can be incorporated, such as a copper hood or wood panel instead of brick. Wood, however, must be kept away from the fire. Some are double-faced and some are three-faced. In fact, the last example is one that is found at mountain resorts and is called the freestanding.

Wood Framing

One of the fundamental principles of framing around a fireplace is that no wood or combustible material is allowed to touch any part of the fireplace, its founda-

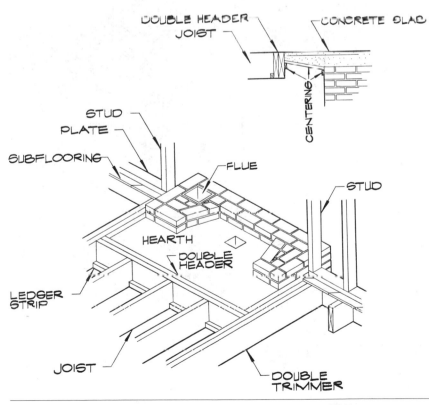

Figure 18.3 Floor framing around a fireplace. (Courtesy of National Forest Products Association.)

tion, or chimney. Most codes require a 2″ clearance all the way around. You are also not allowed to rest any structural piece on the fireplace and use it as support. See Figure 18.2 on the preceding page for an example of a beam over a fireplace.

Figure 18.3 on the preceding page shows the basic framing (wood floor) at the floor joist. The example shows floor joists that would normally rest on a foundation on the exterior of a building being interrupted by a fireplace. The floor joists that are immediately to each side of the fireplace, called trimmers, are doubled. They are doubled because these trimmers carry the extra weight of the floor joists that cut short because of the fireplace. The transfer of weight is made possible by way of the double header.

Two members, the same size as the floor joists, are placed perpendicular to the trimmers. These are called double headers. These headers should not exceed 10′-0″, or the trimmers will not be able to support all the weight.

Joist hangers or framing anchors, shown in Figure 18.4, can be used at this intersection or a ledger, illustrated in Figure 18.3. In this case, the ledger is nailed to the double header. The notched joists rest on this ledger. The nails in the ledger, as well as the framing anchors, are in "shear" as opposed to being pulled out. This is the strongest aspect of a nail.

Figure 18.5 shows what the chimney would look like going through the roof of a structure. The illustration depicts a sloping roof, but the procedure is the same for a flat roof or ceiling joists. The framing is the

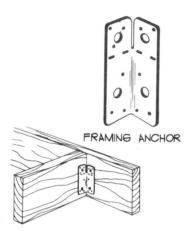

FRAMING ANCHOR

Figure 18.4 Framing anchor. (Courtesy of Easy-Arch Rib division of Easy on Manufacturing Co.)

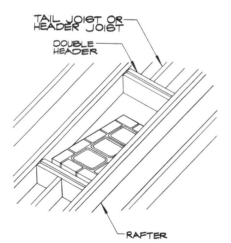

TAIL JOIST OR HEADER JOIST

DOUBLE HEADER

RAFTER

Figure 18.5 Framing around chimney at the rafters. (Courtesy of National Forest Products Association.)

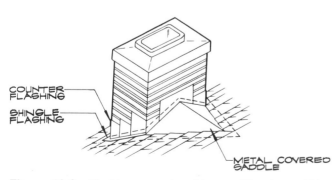

COUNTER FLASHING

SHINGLE FLASHING

METAL COVERED SADDLE

Figure 18.6 Flashing around a chimney. (Courtesy of National Forest Products Association.)

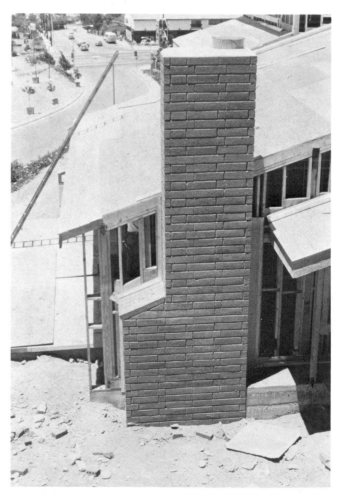

Figure 18.7 Flashing on exterior intersection.

same as that at the floor with double trimmers and double headers used.

The joists that are cut short and run into the double header are called tail joists. If the tail joists are over 6'-0" long, framing anchors should be employed. The header can also be single when the distance between the trimmers is only a few feet (4'-0" maximum).

Finally, if the roof is sloped and the chimney interrupts the normal flow of rain, a saddle (often called a cricket) is used. See Figure 18.6. This diverts the water around the chimney. Also note the inclusion of flashing around the chimney to seal this joint and make it waterproof. See Chapter 7 for a more detailed description of flashing.

See Figure 18.7 on the previous page for an example of a chimney outside the structure. Note the flashing at the joint of the wood and masonry.

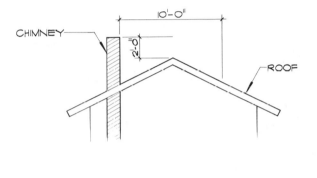

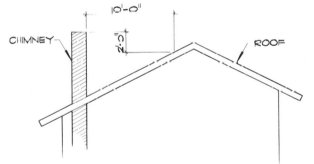

Figure 18.8 Height of chimney above a roof.

Chimney Heights

We shall now examine the heights of chimneys in their relationship to the roof itself. Most areas of the country stipulate that the chimney be raised 2' to 2'-6" above the roof. The main reason is to prevent a downdraft into the chimney, which forces smoke downward and into the room. Some codes suggest a height of 2'-0" above any part of the roof, while a more popular approach is to require the chimney to be 2'-0" above any part of the roof within 10'-0" horizontally measured to the nearest roof plane of the chimney. See Figure 18.8.

Where downdraft is a problem because of the landscape or tall structures, a chimney cover as illustrated in Figure 18.9 is used. This cover is also an effective way of dealing with areas that have heavy snow and rain. The higher the chimney, the greater the velocity of the air current inside the chimney and, therefore, the greater the ability to remove smoke.

Lined and Unlined Flues

In the chimney, there exists an area called the flue through which combustion gases and smoke travel. This flue may be lined or unlined. Flue liners are used because mortar joints can deteriorate due to excessive heat.

When lined, fire clay is usually used. Because of its smooth and uniform characteristics, it produces a better downdraft and thus requires a smaller flue.

An unlined flue must be thicker, and there is a chance that the gases and smoke may leak through the unlined flue area.

Each area that burns material must have a separate flue. If, for example, you had a fireplace in the livingroom on the first floor and a fireplace in the recreational room directly above, with each room using a common chimney, their flues must be different and separated by at least 4 inches of material.

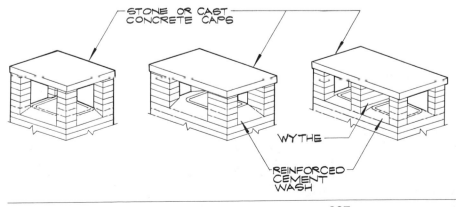

Figure 18.9 Chimney caps. (Reproduced from *Architectural Graphic Standards* with permission from Melville Publishing Company.)

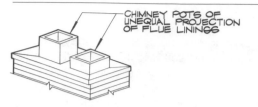

Figure 18.10 Unequal projection of flue lining. (Reproduced from *Architectural Graphic Standards* with permission from Melville Publishing Company.)

At the very top of the chimney where the flues terminate, the flue lining must, at all cost, be kept at unequal levels. This is to prevent the smoke of one chimney from entering another. See Figure 18.10, above. If multiple flues are incorporated into one chimney, each must be separated by at least 4 inches. See Figure 18.11.

There are times, however, when it is desirable to increase the width of the chimney for aesthetic reasons and not because of the presence of more than one flue. Rather than make the complete chimney solid, with a flue in it, a void is left. The flue is either centered or located to the side. The vertical reinforcing runs the complete height of the flue and around it, but the horizontal ties run completely around the exterior perimeter of the chimney. See Figure 18.12.

Firebox and Fireplace Opening

As indicated by the term, the firebox (often called combustion chamber) is the actual area in which the fire is burned. The bottom or base of this firebox is called the inner hearth and is the surface upon which the fire is burned. See Figure 18.13.

If the space below it allows, as in a wood floor system, a small door called an ash dump is installed. It becomes a simple matter, after burning a fire, to drop the ashes through this door and remove the ashes (after they accumulate) through another door called the clean out (not shown in Figure 18.13) that exists on the outside behind the ash pit.

The side walls of the firebox are angled inward at approximately 70° to radiate heat into the room while the rear wall is made with a slight curve to it to produce a good updraft needed to remove the smoke from the firebox.

The firebox is made of firebrick. Unlike common brick that has been fired (process of burning in a kiln) at a lower temperature, firebrick has been fired at a sufficient temperature so that it will not be affected by any normal burning in the firebox.

Common brick or any hard substances like it, such as concrete, cannot be used because it expands in heat. If and when it expands and is surrounded by additional material, it moves in the direction of the least resistance — into the firebox. This is why we never use a blow torch on concrete. The concrete will expand and explode toward you because that is the direction of the least resistance for expansion.

In front of the firebox is the outer hearth. It must be made of noncombustible material, and its main purpose is to keep the fire and heat from reaching the floor materials as well as prevent sparks from landing on wood or carpeted floors.

WIDE CHIMNEY — 2 FLUES

WIDE CHIMNEY — 3 FLUES

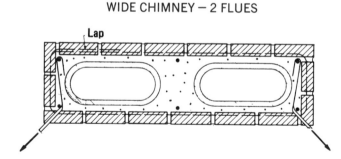

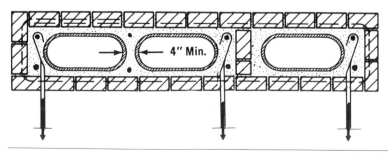

Figure 18.11 Wide chimneys of two and three flues. (Reproduced from *Residential Fireplace and Chimney Details* with permission of the publishers, the Masonry Institute of America.)

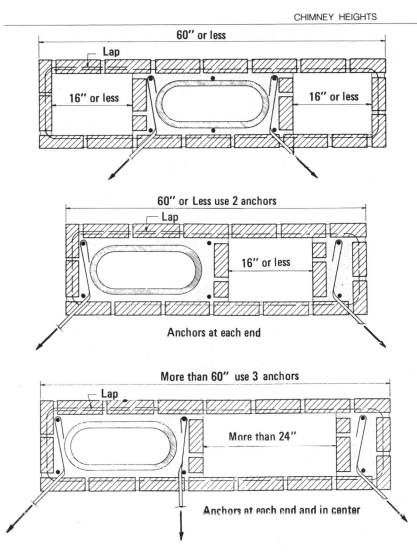

Figure 18.12 Wide chimneys with a single flue. (Reproduced from *Residential Fireplace and Chimney Details* with permission of the publishers, the Masonry Institute of America.)

The fireplace opening is the height and width of the opening in front of the firebox. The width of the fireplace opening should always be equal to or, better yet, greater than the height. There is a close correlation between this opening and the flue. (See the ratio of flue to firebox later in this chapter.)

The area above and to each side of the fireplace opening is called the face. This face protects any combustible material that may surround the fireplace opening from the fire being burned.

The top face is held up by a steel angle (called a lintel) located on the inside in order to hide it from view. See Figure 18.13. Another way is to reinforce the masonry to create a beam that spans this distance. Of the two, using the steel angle is the cheaper and more common procedure.

The area above the face is called the chimney breast. The area above that is called a mantel shelf; more contemporary homes usually eliminate the mantel shelf.

Smoke Chamber

The transition from the firebox to the flue is called the smoke chamber. It consists of a throat, smoke shelf, and a damper. It is that area directly below the flue lining responsible for controlling and regulating burning and eliminating smoke and combustion gases. If it is incorrectly designed, a poor fireplace will result.

The throat, similar to a human throat, channels the smoke into the smoke chamber so it can be dissipated. This throat is usually fitted with a mechanical device, made of metal, called a damper.

The damper runs the full width of the throat, and its function is twofold. It controls and regulates the quantity of air that passes through the throat, and it is used to close off the opening when the fireplace is not in use. If left open, much of the heat can be lost through this area. The lack of damper resembles a window left open at all times—there is a constant cold draft and loss of heat.

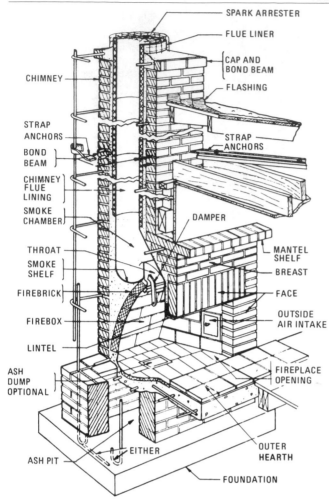

Figure 18.13
Parts of a fireplace and chimney. (Reproduced from *Residential Fireplace and Chimney Details* with permission of the publishers, the Masonry Institute of America.)

The smoke shelf is found at the base of the smoke chamber. Its primary function is to keep any air current from coming down into the firebox and forcing smoke into the room. It also prevents soot and debris from entering the firebox.

Cap and Spark Arrester

The very top of the chimney has a cap on it, with the flue lining generally extending a few inches beyond it. The cap serves many functions. It keeps water away from the lining, and because of its sloping shape it forces wind currents upward. This helps the draft inside of the flue. If the slope had been the other way, it would force wind into the flue as well as moisture.

There should be a spark arrester at the very top of the flue. This is a screen device that prevents sparks from leaving this area and passing on to the roof.

Bond Beam

A support level is established at various levels of the chimney, such as at the top of the chimney, the intersection of the roof and the chimney or ceiling and the chimney. This supplemental support comes in the form of a member poured right on the masonry itself.

Ratio of Flue to Firebox

It is crucial that the ratio of the fireplace opening be in proportion to the flue. These proportions are called effective flue areas based on fireplace opening and are expressed in a fraction, such as $\frac{1}{8}$, $\frac{1}{10}$, or $\frac{1}{12}$. The most typical ratio found seems to be $\frac{1}{10}$, but other factors, such as height of chimney, whether this flue is lined or unlined, or local codes, may change the ratio.

When calculating the ratio, we must first find the affected firebox area. This is based on the type of fireplace used. For example, if a single-face fireplace is to be calculated (see Figure 18.14), it is sufficient to multiply the height times the width. Each illustration is accompanied with its respective formula.

After the area is calculated, this area should be multiplied by $\frac{1}{10}$ or whatever ratio that would apply to find the effective flue area.

EXAMPLE

A single-face fireplace 30 inches wide and 26 inches high. Since

$$A = h \times w$$

then

$$A = 26 \times 30$$

and

$$A = 780 \text{ inches}$$
$$\text{Effective flue area} = 780 \times \tfrac{1}{10}$$
$$= 78 \text{ square inches}$$

Looking at the bottom chart in Figure 18.15 in the center, select the measurement that is equal to or next largest to the one required. You will find an effective flue area of 87 square inches. (The one above it, the 69 square inches is too small.) Reading horizontally, you will find that it is a $8\frac{1}{2}'' \times 17''$ oval with an actual measurable dimension on the outside of $8\frac{1}{2}'' \times 16\frac{3}{4}''$.

The graph above it allows you to determine this information directly. For example, if you had a 32 inch high by 42 inch wide opening, you would find the 32 inch figure on the bottom, the 42 inch figure on the left vertical column, and then follow the two lines until they intersect. The first curved line to the right gives you the suggested flue size: 13×17 with 134 square inches of effective area.

AREA = h × W

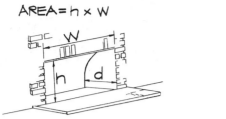

SINGLE-FACED FIREPLACE

AREA = h (d + W)

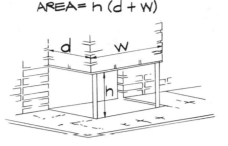

THREE-FACED FIREPLACE

AREA = 2(W × h)

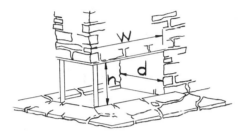

THREE-FACED FIREPLACE

AREA = h $\sqrt{d^2 \times W^2}$

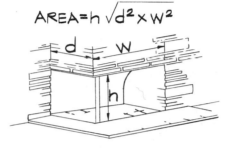

L-SHAPED OR SWEDISH FIREPLACE

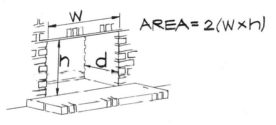

AREA = 2(W × h)

LOOK-THRU FIREPLACE

Figure 18.14 Fireplace openings and required flue size formulas. (Reproduced from the *Residential Fireplace and Chimney Handbook* with permission of the publishers, the Masonry Institute of America.)

It should be pointed out, however, that this chart is calculated for single-faced fireplaces using a $\frac{1}{10}$ ratio. Selection of flue linings is more a matter of getting what is available in a particular region of the United States rather than obtaining the precise size that is indicated by size on a chart.

You will notice letter call outs rather than actual sizes. These are discussed in the next section and the actual appearance of a finished detail is shown at the end of this chapter.

Minimum Construction Details

The main drawings are the section (as shown on Figure 18.16), the plan, and the bond beam anchorage when necessary for earthquake purposes. An enlarged detail of the vertical flashing is also desirable. (This is an enlargement of the plan where the studs meet the masonry.)

Suggested Sizes and Limits

The figures that are listed here are typical sizes found throughout the country. For specific areas, the local department of building and safety should be contacted for precise limitations. These letters correspond to Figures 18.16, 18.17, and 18.28.

A. *Hearth slab thickness*—Most codes require 4" minimum thickness. Some will allow the slab to

FLUE SIZES

The area of the fireplace opening is multiplied by the flue area ratio to obtain the minimum required effective flue area.

The size of the modular flue lining selected should be equal to or larger than the required computed area.

PROBLEM:

Find proper flue size at 1/10 fireplace area for a fireplace 48" wide by 30" high.

SOLUTION:

1. Find 48" fireplace width at bottom of chart
2. Find 30" fireplace height at left side of chart
3. Follow height line across and width line up until they intersect.
4. Proper flue size will be nearest curve above intersection. Use 17" x 17" or 13" x 21" nominal flue lining size.

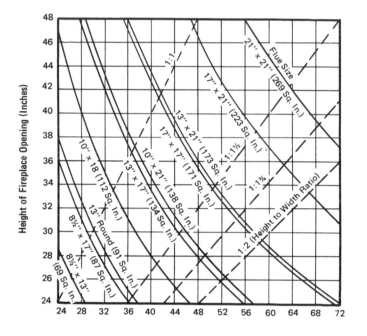

GRAPH TO DETERMINE PROPER FLUE SIZE FOR SINGLE FACE FIREPLACE

FLUE AND CHIMNEY SIZES

Nominal Dimension of Flue Lining	Actual Outside Dimensions of Flue Lining	Effective Flue Area	Max. Area of Fireplace Opening	Minimum Outside Dimension of Chimney
8½" Round	8½" Round	39 sq. in.	390 sq. in.	17" x 17"
8½" x 13" oval	8½" x 12¾"	69 sq. in.	690 sq. in.	17" x 21"
8½" x 17" oval	8½" x 16¾"	87 sq. in.	870 sq. in.	17" x 25"
13" Round	12¾" Round	91 sq. in.	1092 sq. in.	21" x 21"
10" x 18" oval	10" x 17¾"	112 sq. in.	1120 sq. in.	19" x 26"
10" x 21" oval	10" x 21"	138 sq. in.	1380 sq. in.	19" x 30 '
13" x 17" oval	12¾" x 16¾"	134 sq. in.	1340 sq. in.	21" x 25"
13" x 21" oval	12¾" x 21"	173 sq. in.	1730 sq. in.	21" x 30"
17" x 17" oval	16¾" x 16¾"	171 sq. in.	1710 sq. in.	25" x 25"
17" x 21" oval	16¾" x 21"	223 sq. in.	2230 sq. in.	25" x 30"
21" x 21" oval	21" x 21"	269 sq. in.	2690 sq. in.	30" x 30"

Figure 18.15 Flue sizes for single-faced fireplace. (Reproduced from *Residential Fireplace and Chimney Details* with permission of the publishers, the Masonry Institute of America.)

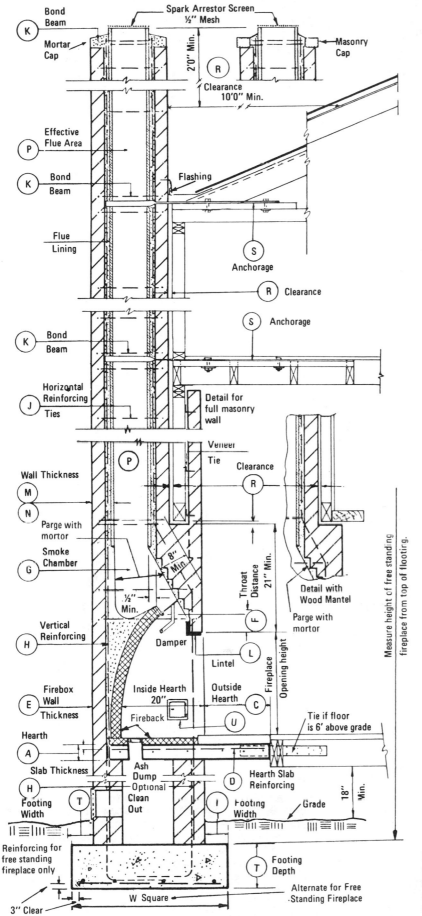

Spark Arrestor Screen ½" Mesh

(K) Bond Beam
Mortar Cap

Masonry Cap

2'0" Min.

(R) Clearance 10'0" Min.

(P) Effective Flue Area

(K) Bond Beam
Flashing

Flue Lining

(S) Anchorage

(R) Clearance

(S) Anchorage

(K) Bond Beam

(J) Horizontal Reinforcing Ties

Detail for full masonry wall

Veneer Tie

(P) Clearance (R)

Wall Thickness
(M)
(N)
Parge with mortor

Smoke Chamber
(G)

8" Min.

½" Min.

Throat Distance

Damper

Detail with Wood Mantel

Parge with mortor

Vertical Reinforcing
(H)

(F)

(L) Lintel

Fireplace Opening height

Measure height of free standing fireplace from top of flooring.

Firebox Wall Thickness
(E)

Inside Hearth 20"

Fireback

Outside Hearth
(C)

(U)

Hearth
(A)

Tie if floor is 6' above grade

Slab Thickness

Ash Dump
Optional Clean Out

(D) Hearth Slab Reinforcing

18" Min.

Footing Width
(H)
(T)

(I) Footing Width

Grade

Reinforcing for free standing fireplace only

Footing Depth
(T)

3" Clear

W Square

Alternate for Free Standing Fireplace

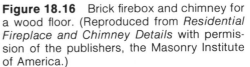

Figure 18.16 Brick firebox and chimney for a wood floor. (Reproduced from *Residential Fireplace and Chimney Details* with permission of the publishers, the Masonry Institute of America.)

303

SMALL CHIMNEY ONE FLUE

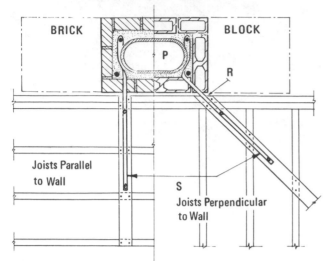

BRICK

BLOCK

P

R

Joists Parallel
to Wall

S

Joists Perpendicular
to Wall

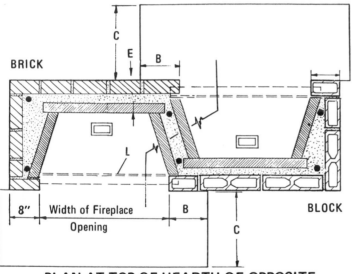

C

E

B

BRICK

L

BLOCK

8"

Width of Fireplace
Opening

B

C

PLAN AT TOP OF HEARTH OF OPPOSITE
FACING DOUBLE FIREPLACE

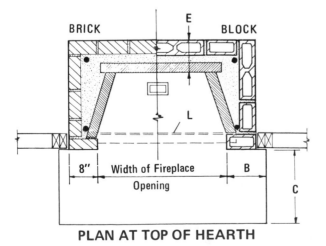

E

BRICK

BLOCK

L

8"

Width of Fireplace
Opening

B

C

PLAN AT TOP OF HEARTH

Figure 18.17 Small chimney showing connection of joist with material variation, plan at top of hearth of opposite facing double fireplace, and a plan at top of hearth. (Reproduced from *Residential Fireplace and Chimney Details* with permission of the publishers, the Masonry Institute of America.)

be tapered, 5″ at the beginning and 3″ at the outer edge.

B. *Hearth slab width* — This is measured on each side of the opening. Eight inches is suggested for an opening of less than 6 square feet and 12″ for an opening of more than 6 square feet.

C. *Hearth length* — This measurement refers to the distance in front of the fireplace. Use 16″ for openings less than 6 square feet and 20″ for opening greater than 6 square feet.

D. *Hearth slab reinforcing* — Number 3 rebars at 6″ o.c. when perpendicular and #3 rebars at 12″ o.c. parallel to the front face seem to satisfy most requirements.

E. *Thickness of walls of firebox* — Most codes require at least 8 inches thickness, of which 4 inches must be firebrick. When firebrick is not used, the thickness increases to between 10 and 12″.

F. *Distance from top of opening to throat* — Some areas allow you to go as small as 6″ but an 8″ minimum is recommended.

G. *Smoke chamber* — As shown by the drawing, the edge of the shelf to the inside front edge of the flue is measured to be ½″. The rear wall thickness is 6″, and the front and side wall thickness should be 8″ or more.

H. *Bond beam* — If required by local codes, this requirement can be satisfied by two ¼″ bars at the top bond beam 4″ high and two ¼″ bars at the anchorage bond beams 5″ high.

J. *Horizontal reinforcing* — Again a concern only for earthquake zones. The most severe areas are satisfied by a ¼″ bar at between 18″ and 24″ o.c. minimum. Notice that it is called out as ¼″ rather than #2 bar — see Chapter 7.

K. *Bond beams* — As the above, this requirement is for high earthquake zones. The need is satisfied by the use of two #¼ bars (called ties at this location) in the cap of the chimney and two #¼ tie bars at the roof anchorage.

L. *Fireplace lintel* — The lintel should be made of some incombustible material such as steel. The size varies depending upon the opening and the weight to be carried. A steel angle is the most popular. Sizes range from 2½″ × 3″ × 3/16″ minimum to 4″ = 4″ × 3/8″. Whatever the size, the lintel should bear at least 3″ on the ends.

M. *Walls with flue lining* — This dimension includes the brick, the grout (approximately 1″) around the flue lining, and the flue lining itself, which is a minimum of 4″ to the outside face of the chimney.

N. *Walls with unlined flue* — In the majority of cases, this dimension is a minimum of 8″. When the chimney is unlined, there is a possibility that

some heat will be lost, thus reducing the uplift capability of the chimney. The chimney depends on the principle of heat rising.

O. *Distance between adjacent flues* — When two or more flues exist in one chimney, the distance between the flues should be at least 4″. This 4″ dimension may include the flue lining.

P. *Effective flue area* — As indicated previously, the effective flue area is based on the fireplace opening area. Generally speaking, 1/10 seems to be a widely acceptable figure. If round linings are used, as opposed to rectangular lining, some codes call for a 1/12″ or 1/8″ requirement for unlined chimneys or those less than 15 feet high. In fact, some codes also indicate a minimum square inch, such as round lining — 1/12″ or 50 square inches minimum.

R. *Clearances* — This requirement must be divided into three categories:

   1. *Wood frame* — Many codes require 2″, but some call for less in specific areas, for example, 3/4″ from subfloor or floor and roof sheathing or if the fireplace is entirely inside a structure.

   2. *Combustible material* — In most cases, it is 6″ to the fireplace opening.

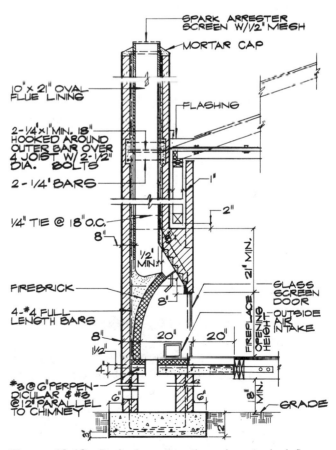

Figure 18.18 Drafted section through a typical fireplace and chimney.

3. *Above roof*—In most cases, it is 2'-0" above the ridge or the highest point within 10'-0".

S. *Anchorage*—Again, this is a problem for earthquake zones. Two $\frac{3}{16}$" or $\frac{1}{4}$" × 1" straps are used. These straps are embedded at least 18" into the chimney and are to be fastened to at least three to four joists with two $\frac{1}{2}$" diameter bolts. If lag bolts (see Chapter 7) are used, a $\frac{3}{8}$" × 3" will meet the requirement or six 16d (d indicates penny, a measurement of nail size—see Chapter 7). If the anchorage is made to the ceiling joist, a 2" × 4" is nailed across four joists at 45° angle. The strap is bolted, screwed, or nailed to this 2" × 4" which is called a runner. See Figure 18.17.

T. *Footing*—The footing should be a minimum of 12" in thickness and extend 6" to 12" beyond the base of the fireplace or as soil conditions indicate.

U. *Outside air intake*—Six square inches is usually sufficient.

See Figure 18.18 on the preceding page for a sample of a drafted section through a fireplace and lined chimney.

Drafting a Vertical Section of a Fireplace

(All drawings in this section courtesy of Mr. Fred Hassouna, FIAL, AIA, AICP.)

Preliminary Procedure

A. Calculate fireplace area (see Figure 18.19)

$$Area = width \times height$$

B. Calculate the effective flue area based on local code requirements.

C. Select flue liner size from manufacturers' literature.

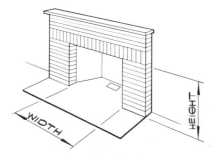

Figure 18.19 Calculating the effective flue area based on fireplace opening.

Steps in Drafting a Vertical Section—See Figures 18.20 to 18.27

Step 1. Draw the flue. If there are two different dimensions (e.g., 8" × 17"), use the smaller.

STEP I

Figure 18.20 Step 1 in drafting a fireplace section.

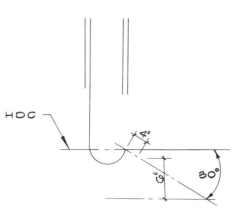

STEP II

Figure 18.21 Step 2 in drafting a fireplace section.

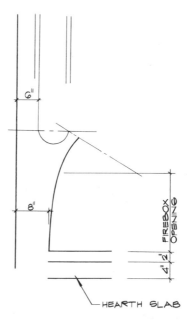

STEP III

Figure 18.22 Step 3 in drafting a fireplace section.

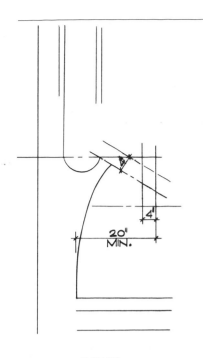

STEP IV

Figure 18.23 Step 4 in drafting a fireplace section.

Then construct a circle with a diameter $\frac{1}{2}''$ (or more) larger than the inside diameter of the flue starting with the inside face of the flue lining.

Step 2. At the horizontal diameter of the circle (HDC), draw a line 30° from the horizontal. On this 30° line measure 4 inches to find

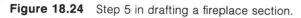

STEP V

Figure 18.24 Step 5 in drafting a fireplace section.

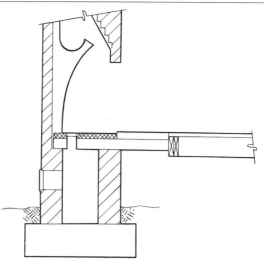

STEP VI

Figure 18.25 Step 6 in drafting a fireplace section.

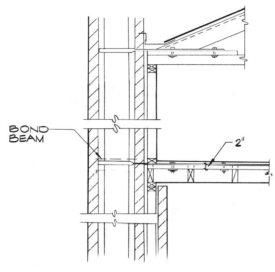

STEP VII

Figure 18.26 Step 7 in drafting a fireplace section.

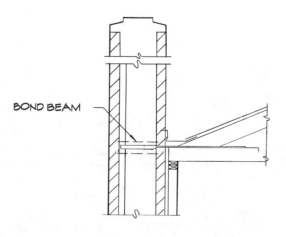

STEP VIII

Figure 18.27 Step 8 in drafting a fireplace section.

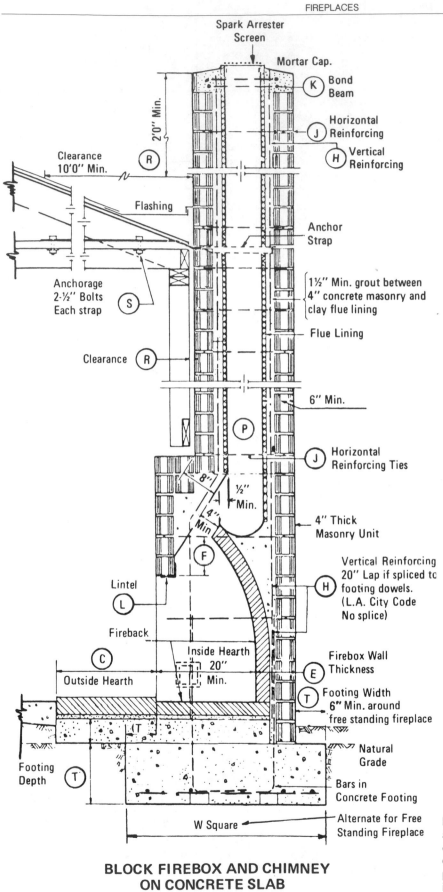

Spark Arrester Screen

Mortar Cap.

(K) Bond Beam

2'0" Min.

(R)

Horizontal Reinforcing (J)

(H) Vertical Reinforcing

Clearance 10'0" Min.

Flashing

Anchor Strap

Anchorage 2-½" Bolts Each strap

(S)

1½" Min. grout between 4" concrete masonry and clay flue lining

Flue Lining

Clearance (R)

6" Min.

(P)

Horizontal Reinforcing Ties (J)

8"

½" Min.

4" Min.

(F)

4" Thick Masonry Unit

Lintel (L)

Vertical Reinforcing 20" Lap if spliced to footing dowels. (L.A. City Code No splice) (H)

Fireback

(C)

Inside Hearth 20" Min.

Firebox Wall Thickness (E)

Outside Hearth

Footing Width 6" Min. around free standing fireplace (T)

(T)

Natural Grade

Footing Depth

(T)

Bars in Concrete Footing

W Square

Alternate for Free Standing Fireplace

BLOCK FIREBOX AND CHIMNEY ON CONCRETE SLAB

Figure 18.28 Concrete block firebox and chimney on concrete slab. (Reproduced from *Residential Fireplace and Chimney Details* with permission of the publishers, the Masonry Institute of America.)

the throat starting at the intersection of the circle and the 30° line. From the lower point of the 4 inch measurement, measure 6 inches (8 inches is recommended) to establish the top of the firebox opening.

Step 3. Establish the outside face of the chimney by measuring 6 inches from the interior face of the flue and the height of the firebox opening. Measure 8 inches and construct the rear of the firebox with an arc. (Use a french curve.) Establish the hearth below the firebox opening by constructing a line 2 inches below the firebox opening. Measure and establish the hearth slab thickness.

Step 4. From the interior face of the firebox measure 20 inches (or more) to establish the exterior face of the firebox. Measure in 4 inches from the exterior face of the firebox at the top of the firebox opening and establish a vertical line. Measure a minimum 4 inch throat opening.

Step 5. Draw a line at 60° minimum, intersecting the interior face of flue and the line established in step 4 to find the top of the throat opening.

Step 6. Draw in desired type of foundation as per local code.

Step 7. Establish wall and plate line and superimpose on fireplace in section. Draw ceiling joist (floor joist is more than one story) and allow for 2 inch airspace between joists and brick. Draw a 1″ × 6″ flat over ceiling joist (for floors, notch floor joist) to support $\frac{3}{16}$″ × 1″ straps. Check local codes since some states do not require this bond beam. Locate the center of bond beam 2 inches below top of strap and draw bond beam.

Step 8. Locate rafters. Place saddle and complete motor cap and spark arrester. Be sure chimney extends far enough above roof to meet local codes.

Concrete Masonry Fireplace and Chimney

Fireplaces can also be made of concrete masonry as well as brick. They are usually made of 4, 6, or 8 inch solid grouted masonry units. Figure 18.28 shows a recommended configuration for such a fireplace published by the Concrete Masonry Association of California. Again, as in previous chapters, the requirement for steel is based on local circumstances such as wind, earthquake, and soil conditions.

Energy Conservation Requirements

Because of the great concern for the preservation of energy in this country, many municipalities have included various ways to make a fireplace more effective and energy efficient. Constantly burning gas pilot lights like the ones that are used in older gas stoves are no longer permitted. An outside air intake with its own flue damper is required; it can be seen in Figure 18.13. A tight-fitting closable glass or metal door is often required if it does not interfere with any special energy-saving device, tool, or instrument used in the fireplace.

While many of the building codes leave such things as glass screen doors optional, other agencies such as the Federal Housing Administration and many local ordinances require them.

Regional Differences

One of the main regional differences is a concern about earthquakes. Regions not affected by earthquakes need not worry about reinforcing to a high degree about tying the chimney to the structure with strap anchors.

In contrast, earthquake regions must put their major efforts into this area. See the section "Suggested Sizes and Limits," in this chapter.

Building Codes

There are small differences from one area of the country to another when it comes to fireplace codes, but the main difference is in the requirement for steel. Listed here are the majority of items an architectural draftsperson must check before starting to detail.

1. Minimum thickness for the hearth slab
2. The amount the hearth slab must extend on either side of the opening
3. The amount of hearth slab required in front of the fireplace opening
4. Minimum thickness of the walls of the firebox.
5. Distance between the top of the opening and the beginning of the throat
6. Requirements around the throat and base of the chimney
7. Minimum vertical reinforcing
8. Minimum horizontal reinforcing
9. Bond beams, if required
10. Allowed material for fireplace lintel
11. Requirements around flue lining
12. Minimum thickness for unlined flues
13. Horizontal distance between flues if more than one
14. Effective flue area ratio
15. Clearance of wood, horizontally and vertically
16. Chimney height to roof slope
17. Size of anchorage and fastening sizes
18. Allowable footing sizes
19. Outside air intake
20. Glass screen door

Summary

The fireplace is a product of centuries of evolution to its present configuration. Its shape, proportions, and fundamental design must be carefully protected to ensure proper air flow and maximum efficiency. Most critical are the area around the throat, the smoke chamber, and smoke shelf; also important is the ratio of the fireplace opening to the size of the flue.

Since there are so many small bits and pieces of information, maximums, and minimums, the architectural draftsperson must follow some systematic approach to detail an accurate and functional fireplace. The step-by-step approach used in this chapter is a good method and will aid in the successful completion of a fireplace detail.

Because this is primarily a detailing book, we have been referring to the detailing of a fireplace, but the final drawing is more of a section than a detail.

19
PREFABRICATED FIREPLACES

Preview Chapter 19 discusses the various reasons for the widespread use of prefabricated fireplaces in today's buildings. These reasons are explained in detail to enable the architectural draftsperson to understand the advantages of these units and the influences on their use.

The first section provides illustrations of framing details that are necessary to accommodate a specific prefabricated fireplace.

The second section deals with a circulating fireplace and the advantages of this type of unit for heating purposes.

Then chimney designs are discussed and illustrated and a description is included of the framing and minimum clearances necessary for a chimney chase.

After reading this chapter, the architectural draftsperson will:

1. Understand the framing techniques necessary to satisfy the installation of prefabricated fireplaces.
2. Know about the various options for interior finishes.

Prefabricated metal fireplaces are being extensively used in modern buildings. Their popularity has been influenced by the development of the flexibility of planning them, their design, and their economic advantages.

Planning advantages are such that these fireplaces may be located on any floor level without concern for a supporting foundation. The only planning restrictions that may arise involve the flue locations for multistory buildings. However, many manufacturers provide elbows and bends to allow for flue offsets. Most manufacturers have various sizes and shapes that allow the designer additional flexibility for the location of fireplaces. Prefabricated fireplaces are available in wood burning and gas burning units.

The wood burning units require a flue, while gas burning units demand only a vent similar to that of a water heater.

The interior design or facing of prefabricated fireplaces affords a great latitude for the use of various materials. These materials may include brick or stone veneer, wood paneling, marble, or interior plaster.

The economic advantages for using prefabricated fireplaces results from their not requiring a foundation, the minimum amount of time and labor involved for installation, and the normal framing assemblies that accommodate the firebox and flue.

Types of wood burning prefabricated fireplaces are also manufactured to provide the ability to circulate warm air into a room with the use of front and side supply registers that may distribute the air with a mechanical fan. Such an installation becomes more significant with the growing need for fuel conservation.

Wood Burning Fireplaces

When detailers are confronted with a project that involves the use of a wood burning metal prefabricated fireplace, they should first verify that the selected prefabricated fireplace meets building code requirements. Then, they should research the clearances re-

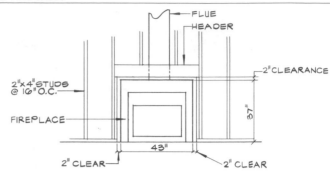

Figure 19.2 Fireplace framing elevation. (Courtesy of The Majestic Company — An American Standard Company, Huntington, Ind.)

quired by the code or the manufacturer's recommendations. (These clearances relate to combustible materials.)

The first step in providing drawings and details for a specific type of fireplace is to draw a plan view showing the rough opening size and the required clearances from the wood framing. Figure 19.1 illustrates a plan view depicting the wall framing, clearances, and the position of a prefabricated fireplace.

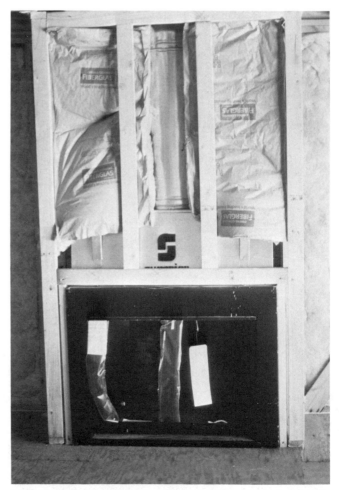

Figure 19.3 Photograph of framing for fireplace installation.

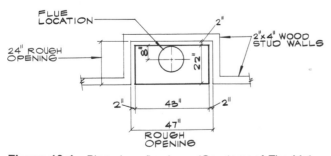

Figure 19.1 Plan view, fireplace. (Courtesy of The Majestic Company — An American Standard Company, Huntington, Ind.)

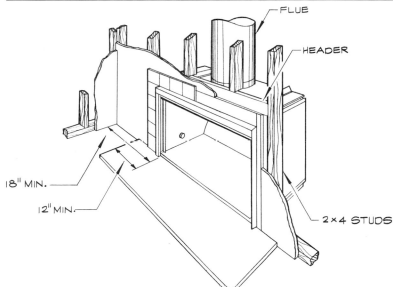

Figure 19.4 Pictorial, fireplace facing material. (Courtesy of The Majestic Company — An American Standard Company, Huntington, Ind.)

Framing Elevation

The next step is to provide a framing elevation showing the height of the specified fireplace and the vertical clearances required by code and manufacturers recommendations. This drawing should also give the size and location of the header designed to carry the wall, ceiling, and roof loads that may be distributed to this area. An example of a framing elevation is illustrated in Figure 19.2. Figure 19.3 shows framing, insulation, metal fireplace, and flue.

Fireplace Facing

As discussed previously, the interior finish of the fireplace facing may be a combination of various mate-

rials applied to wood stud construction. Figure 19.4 illustrates a pictorial view of the wood framing, prefabricated fireplace, and fired clay tile facing applied in conjunction with a gypsum board finished wall material. Figure 19.5 is a view of a metal fireplace with gypsum board wall finish.

Fireplace Elevation

After completing the necessary framing drawings, the detailer should draw an elevation of the selected fireplace and all the required sections that complete this assembly from the floor level through the ceiling and roof framing and the required chimney or cap height above the finished roof level. This drawing enables

Figure 19.5 Photograph of fireplace and wall finish.

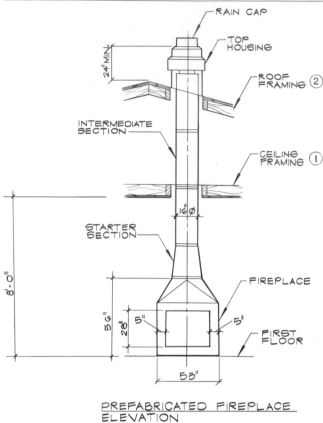

PREFABRICATED FIREPLACE ELEVATION

Figure 19.6 Prefabricated fireplace elevation. (Courtesy of The Majestic Company—An American Standard Company, Huntington, Ind.)

the detailer to key and symbol enlarged details for the ceiling and roof framing as well as the flashing connections that occur above the roof level. Figure 19.6 illustrates this elevation and the keyed details.

Ceiling and Roof Framing

In the fireplace elevation illustrated in Figure 19.6 details ① and ② are keyed to other figures. Detail ① illustrates the framing members that occur at the ceiling level and the rough opening dimensions

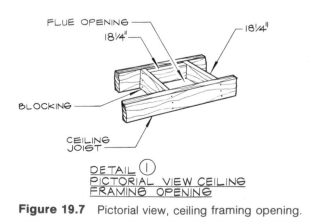

DETAIL ①
PICTORIAL VIEW CEILING
FRAMING OPENING

Figure 19.7 Pictorial view, ceiling framing opening.

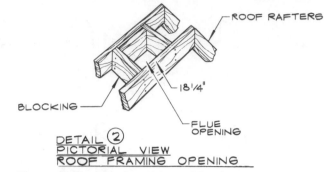

DETAIL ②
PICTORIAL VIEW
ROOF FRAMING OPENING

Figure 19.8 Pictorial view, roof framing opening.

required to satisfy the opening and clearance needed for a selected flue size. Figure 19.7 illustrates this detail in pictorial form. Detail ② depicts the framing at the roof level and the required dimensional opening. This is shown in pictorial form in Figure 19.8. These details have been drawn in pictorial form to provide more clarity than a cross section would show.

Chimney Flashing

Where chimneys penetrate the roof framing—whether it is metal or masonry—flashing details should be shown. Most prefabricated fireplace manufacturers provide chimney flashing collars for various chimney section sizes. The detailer may specify the manufacturer's flashing collar item or designate the collar to be fabricated locally. Figure 19.9 illustrates the chimney flashing section utilizing a manufacturer's collar item.

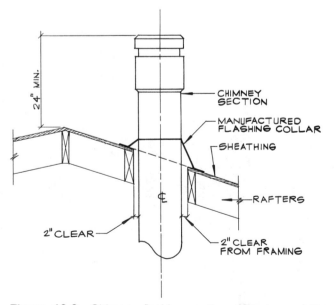

Figure 19.9 Chimney flashing section. (Courtesy of The Majestic Company—An American Standard Company, Huntington, Ind.)

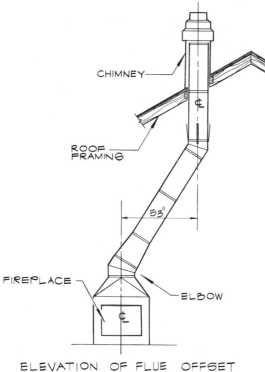

CHIMNEY

ROOF FRAMING

53"

FIREPLACE

ELBOW

℄

ELEVATION OF FLUE OFFSET

Figure 19.10 Elevation of flue offset. (Courtesy of The Majestic Company — An American Standard Company, Huntington, Ind.)

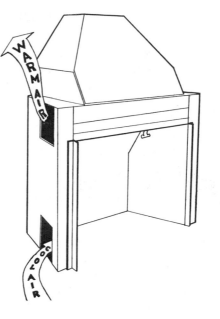

WARM AIR

COOL AIR

PICTORIAL VIEW CIRCULATING FIREPLACE

Figure 19.11 Pictorial view of circulating fireplace. (Courtesy of The Majestic Company — An American Standard Company, Huntington, Ind.)

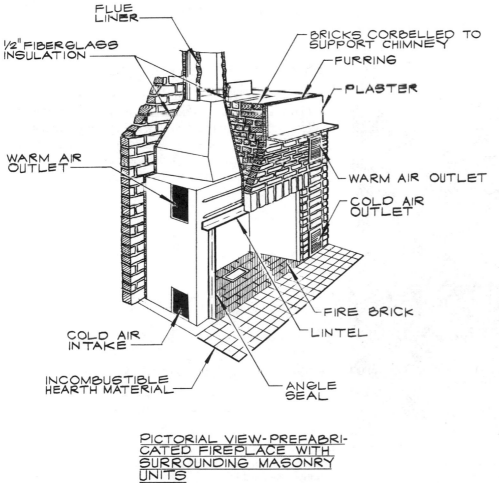

FLUE LINER

½" FIBERGLASS INSULATION

BRICKS CORBELLED TO SUPPORT CHIMNEY

FURRING

PLASTER

WARM AIR OUTLET

WARM AIR OUTLET

COLD AIR OUTLET

FIRE BRICK

LINTEL

COLD AIR INTAKE

INCOMBUSTIBLE HEARTH MATERIAL

ANGLE SEAL

PICTORIAL VIEW-PREFABRICATED FIREPLACE WITH SURROUNDING MASONRY UNITS

Figure 19.12 Pictorial view, prefabricated fireplace with surrounding masonry units. (Courtesy of The Majestic Company — An American Standard Company, Huntington, Ind.)

Flue Offsets

As discussed earlier, prefabricated fireplace flues provide the flexibility to offset from the fireplace to the roof. This is accomplished by the use of elbows, which are generally a manufacturer's item. An example of a fireplace elevation incorporating a flue offset is illustrated in Figure 19.10.

Heat Circulating Fireplaces

As mentioned briefly in the beginning of this chapter, there are prefabricated fireplaces designed to utilize the heat from the fireplace and circulate this warm air into a room with the use of a mechanical fan. These fireplaces are built of a heavy-gauge steel and have supply registers to discharge warm air. In view of the need to conserve fuel, this type of fireplace provides an excellent tool for supplying or supplementing the need for heating residences. An example of a circulating fireplace, shown in pictorial view, is illustrated in Figure 19.11.

Figure 19.13 Photograph of fireplace with interior finished materials.

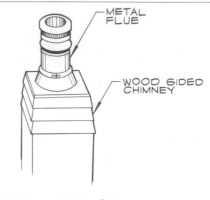

PICTORIAL VIEW OF CHIMNEY DESIGN

Figure 19.14 Pictorial view of chimney design. (Courtesy of The Majestic Company—An American Standard Company, Huntington, Ind.)

A circulation fireplace unit, which is generally constructed of heavy-gauge steel, may be completely housed with a masonry material. Figure 19.12 on the preceding page shows a pictorial view of masonry units surrounding the steel firebox and flue. Note that a steel angle lintel is provided to support the masonry units. Figure 19.13 illustrates masonry veneer around a fireplace. The hearth requirements for prefabricated fireplaces are the same as those for masonry fireplaces.

Exterior Chimney Design

When the architect or designer desires a special or unusual architectural design motif for a chimney, the detailer should then provide drawings and details that show minimum clearances and required ventilation for proper draft. Figure 19.14 depicts, in pictorial form, a chimney design with ship-lap siding as an exterior material.

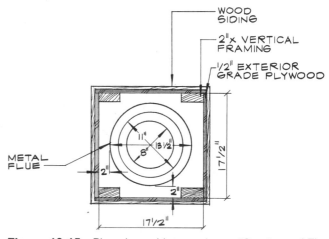

Figure 19.15 Plan view, chimney chase. (Courtesy of The Majestic Company—An American Standard Company, Huntington, Ind.)

The assembly of materials that house the metal flue is referred to as a chase. A good practice is to draw a plan view of the chase showing the metal flue, minimum clearances to combustible materials, and the framing members that support the chase. An example of this plan view is illustrated in Figure 19.15.

Regional Differences

The types of manufactured fireplaces that are acceptable in a region should be verified with the governing municipality and building codes. The minimum clearances from the metal to combustible materials will also vary in some regions. Check local codes for minimum clearances.

Summary

This chapter explained the types of prefabricated fireplaces available and the advantages in using these units.

This chapter also illustrated the drawings and details that are required when a detailer is confronted with a project that includes this type of fireplace.

20
BEAM CONNECTIONS

Preview Chapter 20 introduces the subject of beam connection. This is the process of holding up a building, or part of a building, by means of a horizontal beam supported by a series of vertical columns. The columns studied in this chapter are made of wood, steel, and masonry. The beam studied is made of wood.

The chapter starts by building an understanding of the various implications for this type of structure, such as the forces acting on it, where and how to determine the weight on the beam and column, allowances for wind, and characteristics of the material.

The second portion discusses the connection between the beam and the column and the footing. Post caps and post bases of a variety of shapes and sizes are introduced.

The final portion deals with what the architectural draftsperson must know to develop a detail. The chapter systematically describes a typical computation and design of such a problem.

After reading this chapter, the architectural draftsperson will:

1. Be able to understand the various forces acting upon beams and columns.
2. Be able to determine by arithmetical calculation the maximum and minimum requirements for drilling holes in wood.
3. Solve simple problems of loads on columns, beams, and footings.
4. Be able to design and detail simple connections of wood and pipe columns.
5. Be able to design and detail simple masonry columns.

Study of Beams and Columns

As you look about, you will find many examples of beams supported by some type of column. These beams are made of steel, wood, or reinforced concrete masonry. Their support can be made of similar materials or combinations of these materials.

Since this book deals primarily with wood, this chapter addresses itself to wood beams and wood, steel, and masonry columns that will transfer the weight from the beam to the pad of concrete below.

The need to study and understand the various features of a column to beam and column to footing becomes paramount when one considers the variety of applications, such as any projected overhang of a structure. Factors such as cost, aesthetics, structural stability, or even code restrictions are also important.

For whatever reason, beam connections involve a condition where a uniformly distributed load, such as that from a roof on a beam, is concentrated through a column (type of vertical post) and through a pad of concrete that is subsequently distributed to the ground. See Figures 20.1 and 20.2 for examples.

Influencing Factors

Of the many factors involved in this study, the most important is weight. While it is not usually the detailer's responsibility to compute the weight of the structure, you should be aware of where such calculations originate. To solve the weight problem, the architect, structural engineer, or whoever is responsible for such decisions must compute the weight of the part of the structure that will have a direct bearing on the strength and durability of the whole structure.

The shaded area, called the tributary area, in Figure 20.3 shows the area on the structure that is calculated to put weight on the beam. This weight plus an additional weight of the beam is placed on the center

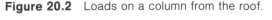

Figure 20.2 Loads on a column from the roof.

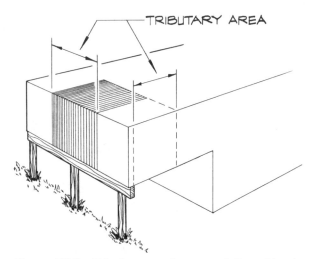

Figure 20.3 Tributary area for computation of loads.

column. The computation includes such weight as rafters, floor joists, studs, and all material applied to them such as flooring material, plaster, siding, and so on.

Wind pressure and seismic loads also play an important part in determining the size of lumber used, bolt sizes, and other factors.

The type of material used must also be considered, since each type has certain inherent qualities that will work against as well as for the designer. In small structures, wood beams are commonly used in conjunction with wood, steel, and masonry columns.

If, for example, wood posts are used, a 4 × 4 post 2 feet tall can withstand a great deal of weight before the fibers of the wood begin to fail. The wood post, because of its height, will hardly bend. See Figure 20.4. The same 4 × 4 post 15 feet tall now begins to bend under excessive weight before the fibers begin to deteriorate. See Figure 20.5.

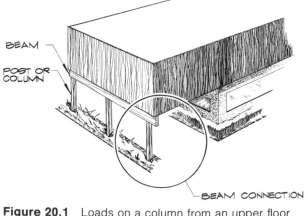

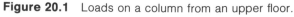

Figure 20.1 Loads on a column from an upper floor.

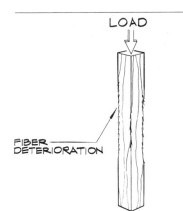

Figure 20.4 Limits on wood columns.

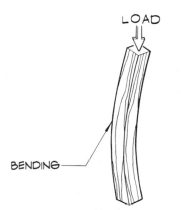

Figure 20.5 Bonding with applied loads.

Drilling Holes in Column or Beam

As we deal with wood, it often becomes necessary to drill holes in the column or beam for bolts. A good rule of thumb when drilling is *not* to drill closer than *seven* times the diameter of the bolt being used from the ends of the lumber and *four* times the diameter of the bolts between holes and away from the edges. See Figures 20.6 and 20.7.

Example of $\frac{1}{2}$ inch bolt:

7 × dia. = required distance from end of lumber
7 × $\frac{1}{2}$" = $3\frac{1}{2}$" from end of wood

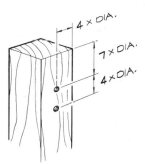

Figure 20.6 Drilling limits to edge of wood and between holes.

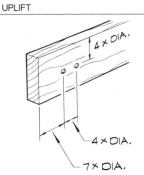

Figure 20.7 Drilling limits to end of wood and between holes.

4 × dia. = required distance from edge or between holes
4 × $\frac{1}{2}$" = 2" between holes and from edge

Example of $\frac{3}{4}$ inch bolt:
7 × dia. = required distance from end of lumber
7 × $\frac{3}{4}$ or .75 = 5.25 or $5\frac{1}{4}$" from end
4 × dia. = required distance between holes and from edge
4 × $\frac{3}{4}$ or .75 = 3.00 or 3" between holes and from edge

It is hoped the reader realizes that one cannot drill a 2" hole in a 3" member. A large percentage of the wood must remain. Again, a good rule of thumb is not to drill a hole larger than one-fifth the width of the member. See Figure 20.8.

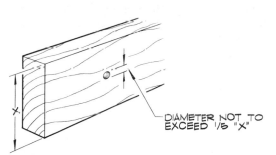

Figure 20.8 Maximum size of holes in a wood member.

Uplift

Bolts and metal post caps are used to tie the beam to the column but do more than hold the unit together; they also prevent what is known in the profession as uplift.

An overhanging projection of any kind is subject to the downward force due to the weight and also has the potential of being literally uplifted by the wind. See Figure 20.9.

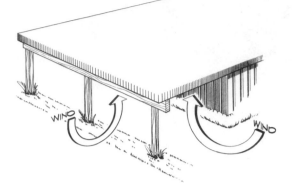

Figure 20.9 Problems of uplift.

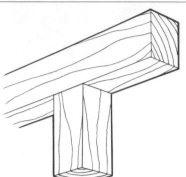

Figure 20.11 Intersection of wood post and continuous beam.

Post Caps

The intersection of the wood post and the wood beam enables a variety of possible conditions. Figure 20.10 shows a beam terminating at the post, while Figure 20.11 shows the beam extending beyond the post or continuing far beyond the post. Figure 20.12 illustrates one beam terminating and another continuing at the post. Figure 20.13 shows a continuous beam sitting atop a post intersected with one or two additional beams that may be required in certain conditions.

The transition between these wood columns and wood beams can be accomplished by means of a preformed member called post cap. Since lumber comes from the mill in specific sizes, the manufacturers have prepared their post caps to fit these sizes. These caps are engineered in advance for uplift and any lateral forces that might be applied.

Caps generally are categorized into three structural divisions: heavy weight, medium, and lightweight. Each category depends on the forces applied to

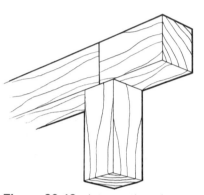

Figure 20.12 Intersection of wood post and spliced beam.

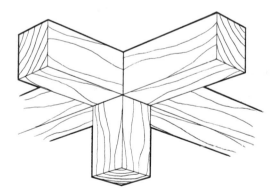

Figure 20.13 Four-way intersection.

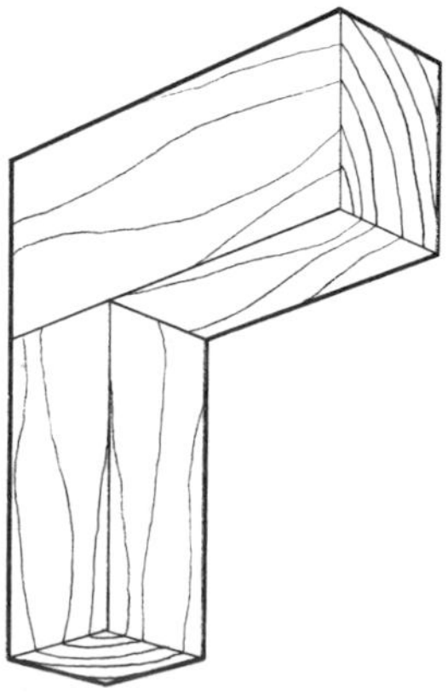

Figure 20.10 Intersection of wood post and end of a beam.

them. For example, Simpson makes a post cap of 16 gauge galvanized material (see Figure 20.14). It can be made to accept an end of a beam or a continuous beam. The 16d nails ($3\frac{1}{2}''$ long) are used with these units and they have the capability of withstanding 1600 pounds of uplift and 1200 pounds of lateral force. Unlike most post caps, the unit wraps around the post for appearance as well as for structural stability.

A very popular metal post cap used for beams that end as shown in Figure 20.10 continuous beams, or

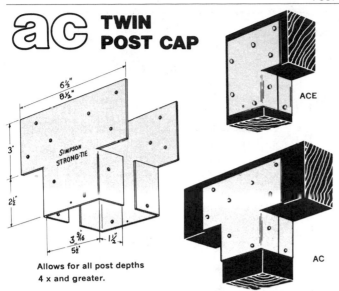

... enhances appearance ... adds structural value

Twin design permits easy installation before, during, or after post and beam erection. Two models for a variety of timber sizes. All corners are enclosed for trim appearance and functional strength. Centerline hole provided for easy alignment of post base.

DESIGN DATA: (a) Nail hole pattern provides UBC safe load **uplift** resistance of 1070 lbs. (b) Nail hole pattern provides UBC rating of 805 lbs. **horizontally** as a beam splice plate.

SPECIFICATIONS

1. Specify as SIMPSON STRONG-TIE AC4 (for 4X dimension post), or AC6 (for 6X dimension post).
2. Specify as ACE4, or ACE6, for post caps to be used at end of beam runs.
3. Material and finish. 16 gauge, galvanized steel.
4. Hole locations are staggered and sized for 16d nails. Use 8 ga. x 2½" nails.
5. Design conforms to criteria of UBC #2506 and #2507 ("Columns & Posts").

APPROVED—See Research Recommendation No. 1211 of the International Conference of Building Officials (Uniform Building Code) for the AC approval.

Figure 20.14 Twin post cap. (Courtesy of Simpson Company, "Strong-Tie Products.")

spliced beams as in Figures 20.11 and 20.12 is a "U" shape with straps attached. See Figure 20.15.

Figure 20.16 illustrates a commercially produced item that fulfills the requirements for end or corner, splicing, and continuous beams.

If the item is to be custom made, it should be engineered to fit the need, and the detailer must indicate the bolt size, size of the "U", and size of the strap and call out the welds, and so on. In fact, a complete description must be given to allow some shop to make it.

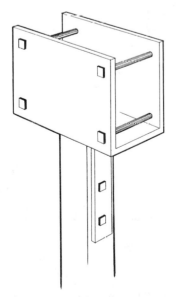

Figure 20.15 Typical post cap. (Courtesy of Easy-Arch Rib division of Easy On Manufacturing Co.)

If, however, a readymade unit is to be used, the detailer need only indicate the brand name and the company's model number. Be sure when indicating brand names that they are readily available. An acceptable substitute should be considered too so that if you insist on the particular brand name and they are not in stock, the job may not be held up for lack of parts.

Post caps are designated by number, based on type and bolt size. For example, a ⅝" machine bolt on a splicing post cap has the number C25 assigned to it.

Figure 20.17 gives the load-bearing capacity of the C25 post cap. The left column on the chart is used for the manufacturing number; the second column, the thickness of the material; and the third column (called BW), the width of the beam itself. This BW column is subdivided again into solid timber and glu-lam. (For further description of glu-lam or glue-laminated timber, see Chapter 6, Lamination.)

Solid lumber is further divided into the various beam sizes. For example, C25 with a 4 × 12 beam (3½" net size) uses column "a" (3⅝"). The bearing load is calculated in kips, which means in 1000 pounds. Thus, 12.9 equals 12,900 pounds.

Notice that a 3⅝" width is used for the 3½" piece of wood. The extra ⅛" allows for any irregularity in the wood. Figure 20.18 gives the "U" channel size number of bolts, strap size, and allowable loads.

Connections called tees and ells are also manufactured by Easy-Arch Rib, as shown in Figure 20.19. Figures 20.20 through 20.23 show a variety of configurations available and produced by Simpson.

POST CAPS
I.C.B.O. Approval 2318.1

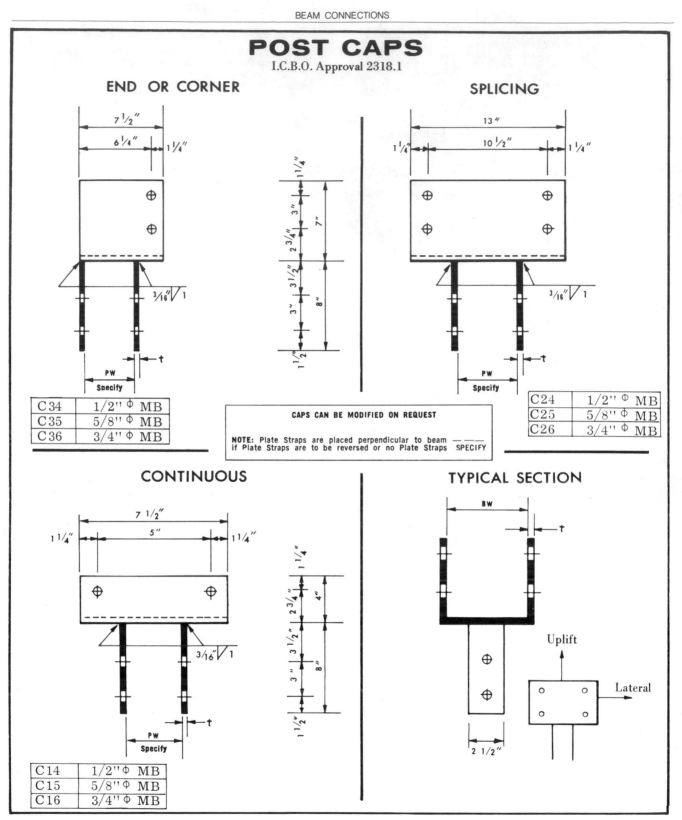

END OR CORNER

C 34	1/2" Φ MB
C 35	5/8" Φ MB
C 36	3/4" Φ MB

SPLICING

C 24	1/2" Φ MB
C 25	5/8" Φ MB
C 26	3/4" Φ MB

CAPS CAN BE MODIFIED ON REQUEST

NOTE: Plate Straps are placed perpendicular to beam ——— if Plate Straps are to be reversed or no Plate Straps SPECIFY

CONTINUOUS

C 14	1/2" Φ MB
C 15	5/8" Φ MB
C 16	3/4" Φ MB

TYPICAL SECTION

Uplift

Lateral

Figure 20.16 Post caps for differing conditions. (Courtesy of Easy-Arch Rib division of Easy On Manufacturing Co.)

POST CAPS

I.C.B.O. Approval 2318.1

WOOD BEARING (LOAD IN KIPS)

CATALOG NUMBER	MAT. THICK-NESS	SOLID TIMBERS DIMENSIONS INCHES				GLULAMS DIMENSIONS INCHES			
		3-5/8" a	5-1/2" b	7-1/2" c	9-1/2" d	3-1/8" e	5-1/8" f	6-3/4" g	8-3/4" h
C— 14	3/16"	12.9	19.9	27.1	34.3	11.3	18.5	24.4	31.6
15	3/16"	12.9	19.9	27.1	34.3	11.3	18.5	24.4	31.6
16	1/4"	12.9	19.9	27.1	34.3	11.3	18.5	24.4	31.6
C— 24	3/16"	22.3	34.4	46.9	59.4	19.6	32.1	42.2	54.7
25	3/16"	22.3	34.4	46.9	59.4	19.6	32.1	42.2	54.7
26	1/4"	22.3	34.4	46.9	59.4	19.6	32.1	42.2	54.7
C— 34	3/16"	12.9	19.9	27.1	34.3	11.3	18.5	24.4	31.6
35	3/16"	12.9	19.9	27.1	34.3	11.3	18.5	24.4	31.6
36	1/4"	12.9	19.9	27.1	34.3	11.3	18.5	24.4	31.6

Figure 20.17 Wood bearing (load in KIPS). (Courtesy of Easy-Arch Rib division of Easy On Manufacturing Co.)

TABLE NO. II
TYPE C—POST CAPS[1]

POST CAP TYPE	CATALOG NUMBER	U-CHANNEL DIMENSIONS (Inches)				PLATE STRAP		ALLOWABLE LOADS (Kips)[2]				
								Uplift Connections			Lateral Connections	
		Length	Over-all Height of Sides	Metal Thick-ness	Number and Size of Through Bolts	Thick-ness	Number and Size of Through Bolts	Post (Bolts)	Beam (Bolts)	Post (Weld-ing)	Post (Bolts)	Beam Axial (Bolts)
For Continuous Beams	C-14 C-15 C-16	7½	4	3/16 7/32 ¼	Two 1/2" " 5/8" " 3/4"	3/16 7/32 ¼	Two 1/2" " 5/8" " 3/4"	4.29 5.35 6.40	2.72 3.22 3.30	1.00	2.58 2.77 2.87	4.29 6.70 9.60
For Splicing Beams	C-24 C-25 C-26	13	7	3/16 7/32 ¼	Four 1/2" " 5/8" " 3/4"	3/16 7/32 ¼	" 1/2" " 5/8" " 3/4"	4.29 5.35 6.40	2.72 3.22 3.30	1.00	2.58 2.77 2.87	4.29 6.70 9.60
For Beam End or Corner	C-34 C-35 C-36	7½	7	3/16 7/32 ¼	Two 1/2" " 5/8" " 3/4"	3/16 7/32 ¼	" 1/2" " 5/8" " 3/4"	4.29 5.35 6.40	2.72 3.22 3.30	1.00	2.58 2.77 2.87	4.29 6.70 9.60

[1]Allowable bolt values, where controlling, are based upon Douglas fir (Coast Region), Douglas fir, larch, or Southern pine, and are to be adjusted for other species of wood in accordance with relative group classification in U.B.C. Standard No. 25-17. Where post caps are exposed to the weather use 75 per cent of tabulated bolt loads. Tabulated allowable loads have been increased for metal sideplates, wind or seismic loads, no other increases are permissible. All dimensions are in inches.
[2]Posts and beams are to be investigated for compression perpendicular to the grain for actual bearing areas involved. Posts and beams are to be investigated for allowable vertical live loads where such loads are critical. The most critical connection tabulated for each type of load is to control that allowable load.

Figure 20.18 Post cap sizes and limits. (Courtesy of Easy-Arch Rib division of Easy On Manufacturing Co.)

TEE'S & ELL'S

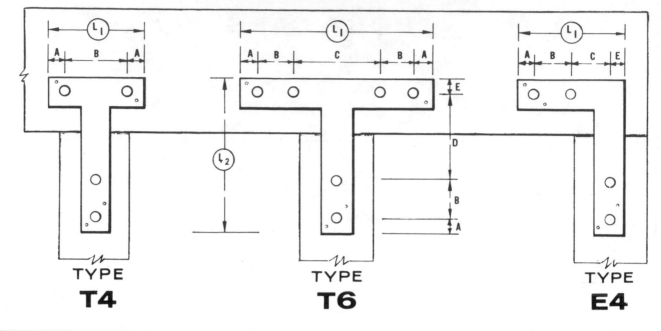

Mfg. Code	Material	Bolt Size	L_1	L_2	A	B	C	D	E	Wt. Per 100
T 4-4	1/8 x 2	1/2	6	12	1 1/2	3	–	6 1/2	1	113#
T 4-5	3/16 x 2 1/2	5/8	6	13	1 1/2	3	–	7 1/4	1 1/4	219#
T 4-6	1/4 x 3	3/4	6	14	1 1/2	3	–	8	1 1/2	361#
T 6-4	1/8 x 2	1/2	16	12	1 1/2	3	7	6 1/2	1	184#
T 6-5	3/16 x 2 1/2	5/8	18	13	1 1/2	3	9	7 1/4	1 1/4	379#
T 6-6	1/4 x 3	3/4	20	14	1 1/2	3	11	8	1 1/2	659#
E 4-4	1/8 x 2	1/2	8	12	1 1/2	3	2 1/2	6 1/2	1	128#
E 4-5	3/16 x 2 1/2	5/8	9	13	1 1/2	3	3 1/4	7 1/4	1 1/4	259#
E 4-6	1/4 x 3	3/4	10	14	1 1/2	3	4	8	1 1/2	446#

NOTE

1. Bolt holes shall be 1/16" larger than nominal diameter of bolt, unless specified otherwise.
2. Tee's & Ell's fabricated from 1/8 x 2" material are stocked and available with 3/16" nail holes (min. 4 per leg).

Figure 20.19 Tee's and ell's. (Courtesy of Easy-Arch Rib division of Easy On Manufacturing Co.)

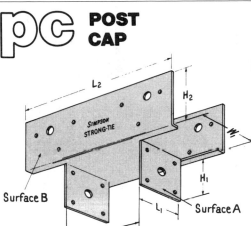

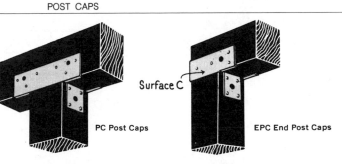

pc POST CAP

Surface C

PC Post Caps   EPC End Post Caps

NEW! HEAVY-SECTION GALVANIZED STEEL

PC and EPC Post Caps provide a custom connection for post-beam combinations in the medium design-load category. The extension beam side plates also function as tie straps where splices occur.

SPECIFICATIONS

MATERIAL: Manufactured of 12 gauge galvanized steel.
Note: This design is available in 16 gauge galvanized steel. To obtain 16 gauge galvanized steel, simply add -16 to the model numbers in Table 13. Example: PC44-16.

INSTALLATION: Install with Joist Hanger nails 16d x 2½". 9/16" holes provided for optional bolting.

Table 13

MODEL NO.	DIMENSIONS								NAILS			I.C.B.O. LOAD VALUES†	
	Beam Width W₁	Post Size (Nominal)	W₂	L₁	L₂	L₃	H₁	H₂	Surface A	Surface B	Surface C	Post Uplift or Lateral Shear	Beam Uplift or Long Shear*
PC44	3⁹⁄₁₆″	4 x 4	3⁹⁄₁₆″	2¹¹⁄₁₆″	11″	7⅜″	3¹¹⁄₁₆″	3½″	4-16d	6-16d	4-16d	1070	1610
PC46	3⁹⁄₁₆″	4 x 6	5½″	2¹¹⁄₁₆″	13″	9¼″	3¾″	3½″	4-16d	6-16d	4-16d	1070	1610
PC48	3⁹⁄₁₆″	4 x 8	7½″	2¹¹⁄₁₆″	15″	11¼″	3¾″	3½″	4-16d	8-16d	6-16d	1070	2145
PC64	5½″	4 x 6	3⁹⁄₁₆″	4⁹⁄₁₆″	11″	7⅜″	3¾″	3½″	4-16d	6-16d	4-16d	1070	1610
PC66	5½″	6 x 6	5½″	4⁹⁄₁₆″	13″	9¼″	3¾″	3½″	4-16d	6-16d	6-16d	1070	2145
PC68	5½″	6 x 8	7½″	4⁹⁄₁₆″	15″	11¼″	3¾″	3½″	4-16d	8-16d	6-16d	1070	2145
PC610	5½″	6 x 10	9½″	4⁹⁄₁₆″	17″	13¼″	3¾″	3½″	4-16d	8-16d	6-16d	1070	2145
PC84	7½″	4 x 8	3⁹⁄₁₆″	6½″	11″	7⅜″	3¾″	3¾″	4-16d	6-16d	6-16d	1070	1610
PC86	7½″	6 x 8	5½″	6½″	13″	9¼″	3¾″	3¾″	4-16d	6-16d	6-16d	1070	1610
PC88	7½″	8 x 8	7½″	6½″	15″	11¼″	3¾″	3¾″	4-16d	8-16d	6-16d	1070	2145
PC810	7½″	8 x 10	9½″	6½″	17″	13¼″	3¾″	3¾″	4-16d	8-16d	6-16d	1070	2145
PC106	9½″	6 x 10	5½″	8½″	13″	9¼″	3¾″	3¾″	4-16d	8-16d	6-16d	1070	2145
PC108	9½″	10 x 8	7½″	8½″	15″	11¼″	3¾″	3¾″	4-16d	8-16d	6-16d	1070	2145
PC1010	9½″	8 x 10 / 10 x 10	9½″	8½″	17″	13¼″	3¾″	3¾″	4-16d	8-16d	6-16d	1070	2145
PC1012	9½″	10 x 12	11½″	8½″	19″	15¼″	3¾″	3¾″	4-16d	8-16d	6-16d	1070	2145

*APPROVED—See Research Recommendation No. 1211 of the International Conference of Building Officials (Uniform Building Code).

† See Approval No. 1211 for detailed bolt values.

Figure 20.20 Heavy-section galvanized steel post cap. (Courtesy of Simpson Company, ''Strong-Tie Products.'')

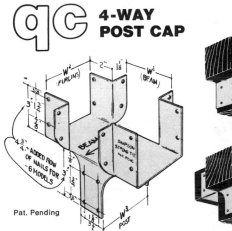

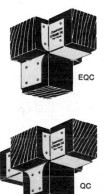

qc 4-WAY POST CAP

Pat. Pending

The first one-piece cap to accommodate a 4-way beam intersection. The first aesthetic connector treatment of this complex intersection. Three basic models fit a variety of beam sizes: QC44 for 4″ x 4″ beams, QC46 for 4″ x 6″, and QC66 for 6″ x 6″.

MATERIAL: 16 gauge galvanized steel

Table 36

MODEL NO.	W¹ Beam	W² Purlin	W³ Post	No. of 16d x 2½″			Uplift		
				Beam	Purlin	Post	Beam	Purlin	Post
QC44	3⁹⁄₁₆″	3⁹⁄₁₆″	3⁹⁄₁₆″	8	8	8	1070	1070	910
EQC44	3⁹⁄₁₆″	3⁹⁄₁₆″	3⁹⁄₁₆″	4	4	8	535	535	910
QC46	3⁹⁄₁₆″	5½″	5½″	12	12	12	1610	1610	910
EQC46	3⁹⁄₁₆″	5½″	5½″	6	6	12	805	805	910
QC66	5½″	5½″	5½″	12	12	12	1610	1610	910
EQC66	5½″	5½″	5½″	6	6	12	805	805	910

APPROVED—See Research Recommendaton No. 1211 of the International Conference of Building Officials (Uniform Building Code).

Figure 20.21 Four-way post cap. (Courtesy of Simpson Company, ''Strong-Tie Products.'')

bc POST CAP/BASE

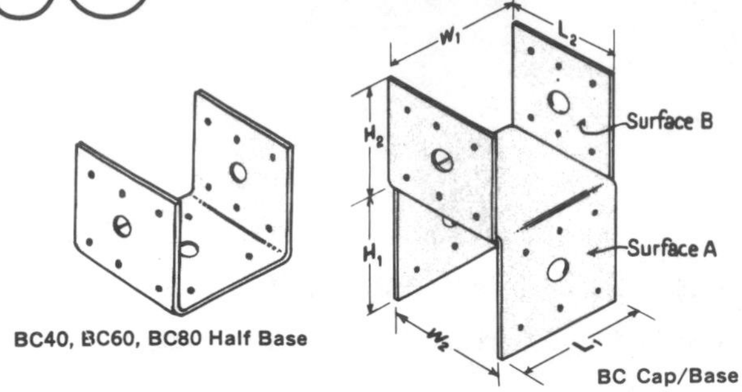

Surface B
Surface A
BC40, BC60, BC80 Half Base
BC Cap/Base

Dual purpose BC Post Cap/Base Combination can be used for post cap or post base connections.

Table 15

MODEL NO.	DIMENSIONS						NAIL SCHEDULE (EACH SIDE)	
	W^1	W^2	L^1	L^2	H^1	H^2	SURFACE A	SURFACE B
BC4	3 9/16"	3 9/16"	3 3/8"	3 3/8"	2 3/4"	2 3/4"	4-16d	4-16d
BC46	3 9/16"	5 1/2"	3 3/8"	3 1/2"	2 3/4"	3"	4-16d	4-16d
BC6	5 1/2"	5 1/2"	5 1/2"	5 1/2"	3"	3"	6-16d	6-16d
BC8	7 1/2"	7 1/2"	7 1/2"	7 1/2"	4"	4"	6-16d	6-16d

APPROVED—See Research Recommendation No. 1211 of the International Conference of Building Officials (Uniform Building Code).

SPECIFICATIONS

MATERIAL: 18 gauge galvanized steel, ASTM Specification A-93. **INSTALLATION:** (1) Install with 16d x 2 1/2" Joist Hanger nails. (2) 9/16" diameter holes may be used for passage of reinforcing steel, when used as a base.

Figure 20.22 Post cap and/or base. (Courtesy of Simpson Company "Strong-Tie Products.")

CC COLUMN CAP

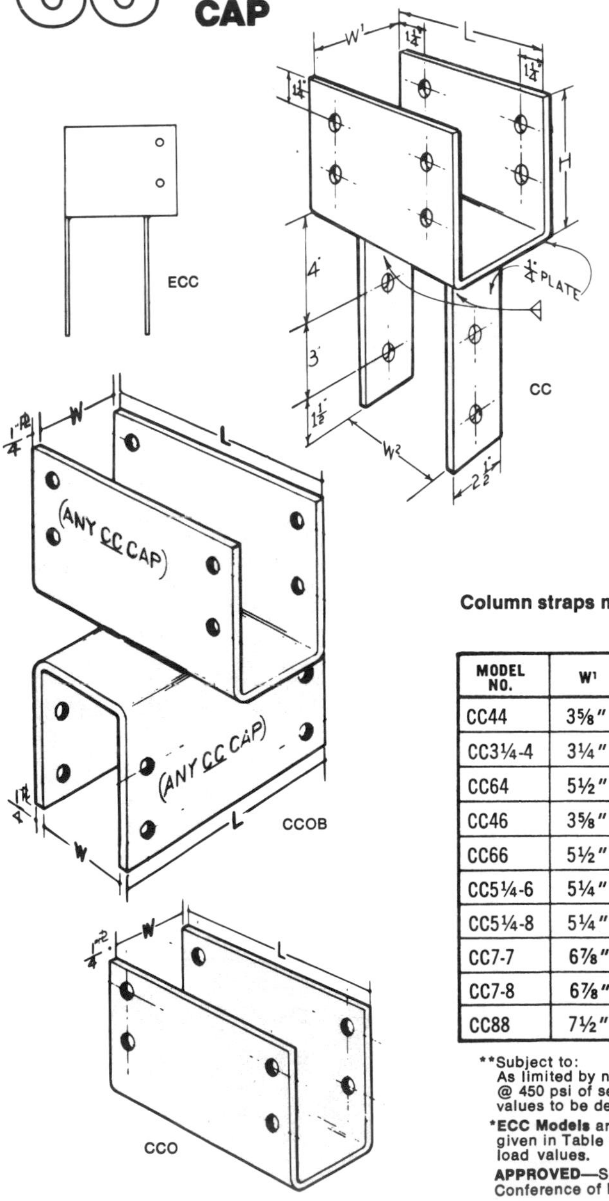

ECC
CC
(ANY CC CAP)
(ANY CC CAP)
CCOB
CCO

FACTORY VALUES!

Precision factory gang-punched holes speed installation and insure full bolt values.

SPECIFICATIONS

1. Special corrosion protection Linear Polymer Formula (Simpson Gray).
2. Straps are fillet-welded both sides to bottom of cap. Welding is by certified welders.
3. Straps are center-positioned both ways upon the cap unless otherwise specified.
4. For complete CC values consult Approval No. 1211.
5. For CCOB beam column cap values, utilize Table 14A or consult Approval No. 1211, applying values no greater than the lesser element employed.

For special or custom sizes, provide dimensions.
*Note: Any W^2 dimension may be specified in combination with any column cap size given. For example, specify as "CC65" for a 5" column and 6" (nominal) beam width requirement. **COLUMN CAP ONLY** may be specified for field-welding to pipe or other column condition by specifying as "CCO—". **SPECIAL COLUMN CAPS** with W^1, "L", "H", and hole schedules different from above may be special ordered. CCOB—Any two CCO's may be specified for back-to-back welding to create the CCOB cross beam connector. For end conditions specify ECC column caps and provide dimensions in accordance with Table 14A.

Column straps may be rotated 90° on special orders where W^1 is greater than W^2.

Table 14A

MODEL NO.	W^1	W^2*	L*	H	MATERIAL	HOLES FOR CAP BOLT	HOLES FOR STRAP BOLT	BOLT VALUES	SEAT LOAD VERTICAL**
CC44	3 5/8"	3 5/8"	7"	4"	1/4" PL	(2) 5/8 MB	(2) 5/8 MB	3024	9430
CC3 1/4-4	3 1/4"	3 5/8"	11"	6 1/2"	1/4" PL	(4) 5/8 MB	(2) 5/8 MB	6050	15470
CC64	5 1/2"	3 5/8"	11"	6 1/2"	1/4" PL	(4) 5/8 MB	(2) 5/8 MB	6050	23290
CC46	3 5/8"	5 1/2"	11"	6 1/2"	1/4" PL	(4) 5/8 MB	(2) 5/8 MB	6050	14820
CC66	5 1/2"	5 1/2"	11"	6 1/2"	1/4" PL	(4) 5/8 MB	(2) 5/8 MB	6050	23290
CC5 1/4-6	5 1/4"	5 1/2"	13"	8"	1/4" PL	(4) 3/4 MB	(2) 3/4 MB	9310	29980
CC5 1/4-8	5 1/4"	7 1/2"	13"	8"	1/4" PL	(4) 3/4 MB	(2) 3/4 MB	9310	29980
CC7-7	6 7/8"	6 7/8"	13"	8"	1/4" PL	(4) 3/4 MB	(2) 3/4 MB	9625	40220
CC7-8	6 7/8"	7 1/2"	13"	8"	1/4" PL	(4) 3/4 MB	(2) 3/4 MB	9625	40220
CC88	7 1/2"	7 1/2"	13"	8"	1/4" PL	(4) 3/4 MB	(2) 3/4 MB	9400	37540

**Subject to:
As limited by nominal beam sizes @ 385 psi or nominal Glulam sizes @ 450 psi of seat area. End bearing value of post, L/R of post, or other values to be deducted.

***ECC Models** are approximately 4" shorter than the "L" dimension given in Table 14A, with consequent decrease in bolt and seat load values.

APPROVED—See Research Recommendation No. 1211 of the International Conference of Building Officials (Uniform Building Code).

Figure 20.23 Column caps. (Courtesy of Simpson Company, "Strong-Tie Products.")

Post Bases

Post bases are also usually made of metal and connect the post to the concrete base below it. Figures 20.24 through 20.26 show a variety of configurations commercially made.

Figure 20.24 illustrates a base made of a series of steel plates welded together to form what is called a bearing plate. This plate is bolted down to the foundation by means of a preset pair of anchor bolts. Note the use of vent holes to allow the water to escape and prevent rot.

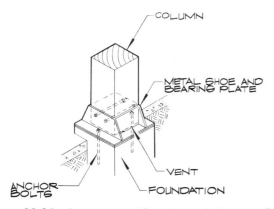

Figure 20.24 Post base. (Courtesy of National Forest Products Association.)

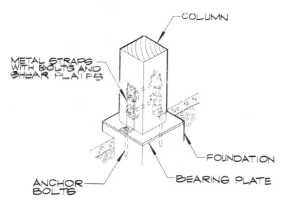

Figure 20.25 Post base with shear plates. (Courtesy of National Forest Products Association.)

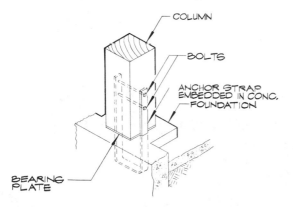

Figure 20.26 Anchor strap. (Courtesy of National Forest Products Association.)

A pair of metal straps is used in Figure 20.25 and held down again by preset anchor bolts. A bearing plate is still used in this system.

If there is enough force to cause the wood to split because of the small bolt diameter, shear plates are used. The shear plates are embedded into the wood, and the bolt must now transfer any force against the shear plates. They in turn can distribute the force over a larger area of wood.

Figure 20.26 shows a popular system that requires the post base to be preset into the concrete. Its main advantage is that it need not concern itself with the top surface of the concrete as do those that are added later using bearing plates.

Actual manufactured dimensions are found in Figure 20.27 and their sizes in Figure 20.28. The chart is very easily read. First, locate the nominal size of the post being used under standard, medium, or heavy, and read horizontally across. The majority of the columns indicate the size of the strap (the "U"-shaped post base) and the thickness of the base upon which the post will sit. The third-to-last column suggests the bolt size, and the last two columns indicate the allowable loads in uplift and lateral that this post cap will resist.

The fourth example of a post base is illustrated in Figure 20.29. Here metal angles called clip angles are used. See Figures 20.30 and 20.31 for proportions, sizes, and bolt sizes. This pair of clip angles is held down to the concrete by a preset anchor bolt. Note the use of a bearing plate to protect the end of the post.

Figure 20.32 illustrates a fifth method using a base that totally covers the base of the post. As shown, the rectangular adjustment plate (the one with the slot in it) allows maximum adjustability for preset anchor bolts.

Another good feature about this unit is that the post sits well above any moisture by means of what is called a stand-off plate. This unit will resist 1200 pounds of uplift. It is made of 12 gauge galvanized material for the rectangular adjustment plate and stand-off plate and 16 gauge for the base cover. Nail holes are for 10d (3" long) nails.

Two additional post bases made by Simpson are illustrated with their specifications in Figures 20.33 and 20.34. The first should be viewed from the standpoint of strength. See uplift and lateral force. The elevated post base is used in areas where moisture and/or sanitation is a problem.

What the Detailer Must Know

While detailers may not be asked to engineer any calculations, there are certain specifics they must know

POST BASES

I.C.B.O. Approval 2318.1

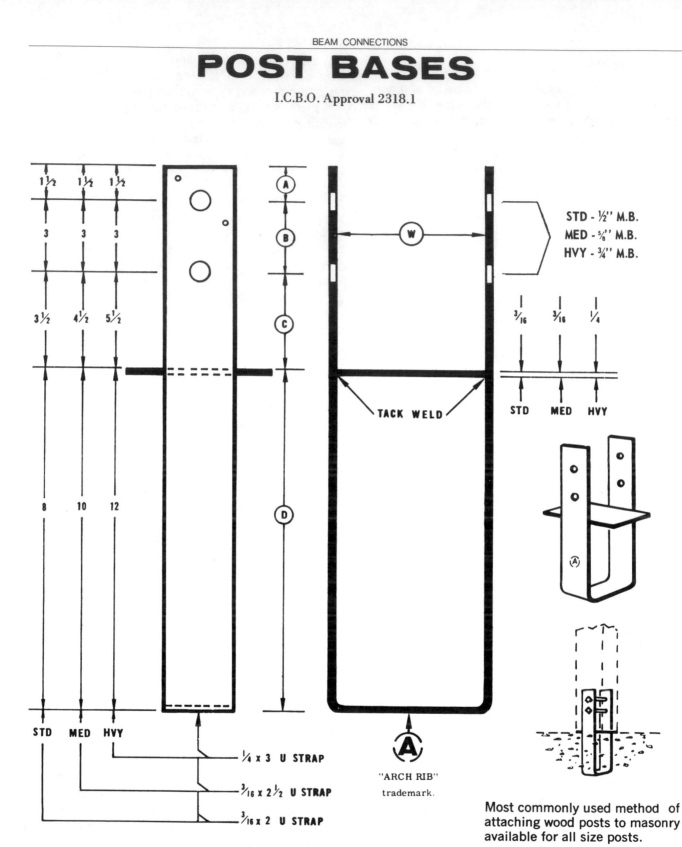

STD - ½" M.B.
MED - ⅝" M.B.
HVY - ¾" M.B.

TACK WELD

ARCH RIB
trademark.

¼ x 3 U STRAP

³⁄₁₆ x 2½ U STRAP

³⁄₁₆ x 2 U STRAP

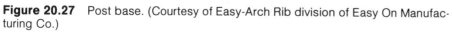

Most commonly used method of attaching wood posts to masonry available for all size posts.

Figure 20.27 Post base. (Courtesy of Easy-Arch Rib division of Easy On Manufacturing Co.)

POST BASES

I.C.B.O. Approval 2318.1

NOMINAL POST SIZE	CATALOG NUMBER	U-STRAP SIZE	DEPTH EMBED-MENT	ⓦ	BASE PLATE SIZE[3]	BOLT SIZE	ALLOWABLE LOAD (Kips) Uplift	ALLOWABLE LOAD (Kips) Lateral[4]
STANDARD — Solid Timbers								
4 x 4 4 x 6 4 x 8 4 x 10 4 x 12	P44-4 P46-4 P48-4 P410-4 P412-4	$\frac{3}{16}$ x 2	8		3⅝ x $\frac{3}{16}$	½	4.29	1.33
6 x 4 6 x 6 6 x 8 6 x 10 6 x 12	P64-4 P66-4 P68-4 P610-4 P612-4	$\frac{3}{16}$ x 2	8		5½ x $\frac{3}{16}$	½	4.29	1.33
8 x 4 8 x 6 8 x 8 8 x 10 8 x 12	P84-4 P86-4 P88-4 P810-4 P812-4	$\frac{3}{16}$ x 2	8		7½ x $\frac{3}{16}$	½	4.29	1.33
MEDIUM — Solid Timbers								
4 x 4 4 x 6 4 x 8 4 x 10 4 x 12	P44-5 P46-5 P48-5 P410-5 P412-5	$\frac{3}{16}$ x 2½	10		3⅝ x $\frac{3}{16}$	⅝	6.70	1.74
6 x 4 6 x 6 6 x 8 6 x 10 6 x 12	P64-5 P66-5 P68-5 P610-5 P612-5	$\frac{3}{16}$ x 2½	10		5½ x $\frac{3}{16}$	⅝	6.70	1.74
8 x 4 8 x 6 8 x 8 8 x 10 8 x 12	P84-5 P86-5 P88-5 P810-5 P812-5	$\frac{3}{16}$ x 2½	10		7½ x $\frac{3}{16}$	⅝	6.70	1.74
10 x 4 10 x 6 10 x 8 10 x 10 10 x 12	P104-5 P106-5 P108-5 P1010-5 P1012-5	$\frac{3}{16}$ x 2½	10		9½ x $\frac{3}{16}$	⅝	6.70	1.74

NOMINAL POST SIZE	CATALOG NUMBER	U-STRAP SIZE	DEPTH EMBED-MENT	ⓦ	BASE PLATE SIZE[3]	BOLT SIZE	ALLOWABLE LOAD (Kips) Uplift	ALLOWABLE LOAD (Kips) Lateral[4]
HEAVY — Solid Timbers								
4 x 4 4 x 6 4 x 8 4 x 10 4 x 12	P44-6 P46-6 P48-6 P410-6 P412-6	¼ x 3	12		3⅝ x ¼	¾	9.52	2.86
6 x 4 6 x 6 6 x 8 6 x 10 6 x 12	P64-6 P66-6 P68-6 P610-6 P612-6	¼ x 3	12		5½ x ¼	¾	9.60	2.86
8 x 4 8 x 6 8 x 8 8 x 10 8 x 12	P84-6 P86-6 P88-6 P810-6 P812-6	¼ x 3	12		7½ x ¼	¾	9.60	2.86
10 x 4 10 x 6 10 x 8 10 x 10 10 x 12	P104-6 P106-6 P108-6 P1010-6 P1012-6	¼ x 3	12		9½ x ¼	¾	9.60	2.86
12 x 6 12 x 8 12 x 10 12 x 12	P126-6 P128-6 P1210-6 P1212-6	¼ x 3	12		11½ x ¼	¾	9.60	2.86

[1]Allowable bolt values, where controlling, are based upon Douglas fir (Coast Region), Douglas fir, larch or Southern pine, and are to be adjusted for other species of wood in accordance with relative group classification in U.B.C. Standard No. 25-17-67. Where post bases are exposed to the weather use 75 per cent of tabulated uplift loads. Tabulated allowable loads have been increased for metal sideplates, wind or seismic loads, no other increases are permissible. All dimensions are in inches. Posts are to be investigated for allowable vertical live loads where such loads are critical.

[2]Post bases are to be embedded in the concrete footings or supporting elements the distance shown, and have the base plate uniformly and fully supported by the concrete. Bolt end distances and spacings in the wood post are as follows:

Bolt Size	End Distance	Spacing	Bolt Hole Size
½″	3½″	3″	$\frac{9}{16}$″
⅝″	4½″	3″	$\frac{11}{16}$″
¾″	5½″	3″	$\frac{13}{16}$″

[3]Base plate size tabulated is actual width of post and base plate between U-strap faces, base plate thickness, with length of base plate to be equal to other actual post dimension.

[4]Lateral allowable loads tabulated are based upon U-strap plate bending stresses.

Figure 20.28 Post base size and limits. (Courtesy of Easy-Arch Rib division of Easy On Manufacturing Co.)

to detail a column to beam and column to a footing successfully.

Size of beam
Size of column or post
Type of post cap
Size and number of bolts (top and bottom)
Material (wood or steel)
Bearing capacity of soil or size of footing and number and size of reinforcing in it
Type of post base

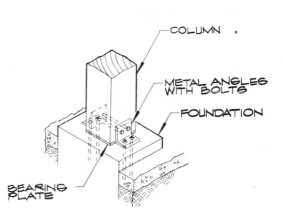

Figure 20.29 Clip angles.

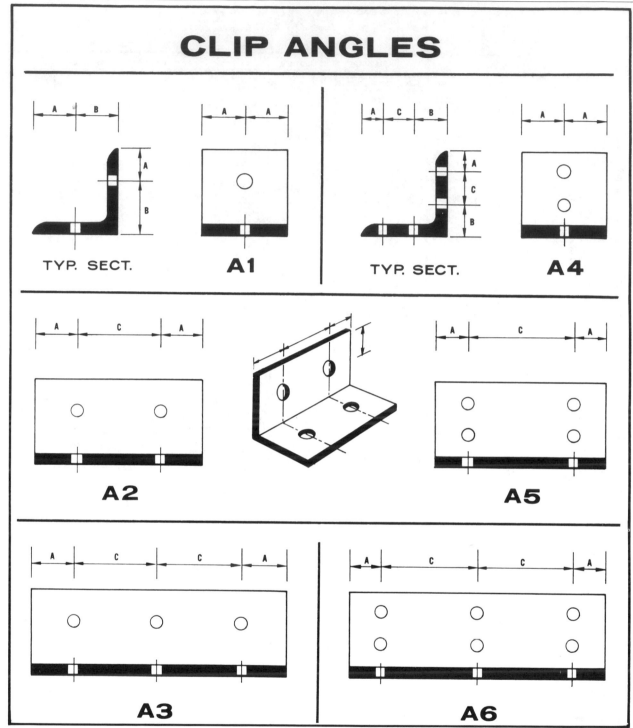

CLIP ANGLES

TYP. SECT.   **A1**

TYP. SECT.   **A4**

A2

A5

A3

A6

Figure 20.30   Types of clip angles. (Courtesy of Easy-Arch Rib division of Easy On Manufacturing Co.)

CLIP ANGLES

Special Sizes or Punching Fabricated on Request

Mfg. Code	Angle Size	Bolt Size	Dimensions			Wt. Per 100
			A	B	C	
A 1-4	3" x 3" x 3/16" ---2 1/2"	1/2	1 1/4"	1 3/4"	- - -	77#
A 1-5	3 1/2"x 3 1/2"x 1/4" - 3"	5/8	1 1/2"	2"	- - -	145#
A 1-6	4" x 4" x 1/4" -----3"	3/4	1 1/2"	2 3/4"	- - -	165#
A 2-4	3" x 3" x 3/16" --- 4 1/2"	1/2	1 1/4"	1 3/4"	2"	139#
A 2-5	3 1/2 x 3 1/2" x 1/4"-5 1/2"	5/8	1 1/2"	2"	2 1/2"	266#
A 2-6	4" x 4" x 1/4" -----6"	3/4	1 1/2"	2 3/4"	3"	330#
A 3-4	3" x 3" x 3/16" ---6 1/2"	1/2	1 1/4"	1 3/4"	2"	201#
A 3-5	3 1/2"x 3 1/2"x 1/4" -8"	5/8	1 1/2"	2"	2 1/2"	387#
A 3-6	4" x 4" x 1/4" -- -9"	3/4	1 1/2"	2 3/4"	3"	495#
A 4-4	5"x 5"x 3/16" - -2 1/2"	1/2	1 1/4"	1 3/4"	2"	128#
A 4-5	6"x 6"x 1/4" --- 3"	5/8	1 1/2"	2"	2 1/2"	245#
A 4-6	7 1/4"x 7 1/4"x 3/8" - 3"	3/4	1 1/2"	2 3/4"	3	466#
A 5-4	5"x 5"x 3/16" - -4 1/2"	1/2	1 1/4"	1 3/4"	2"	231#
A 5-5	6"x 6"x 1/4" --- 5 1/2"	5/8	1 1/2"	2"	2 1/2"	449#
A 5-6	7 1/4"x 7 1/4"x 3/8" -6"	3/4	1 1/2"	2 3/4"	3	877#
A 6-4	5"x 5"x 3/16" - -6 1/2"	1/2	1 1/4"	1 3/4"	2"	333#
A 6-5	6"x 6"x 1/4" --- 8"	5/8	1 1/2"	2"	2 1/2"	653#
A 6-6	7 1/4"x 7 1/4"x 3/8" -9"	3/4	1 1/2"	2 3/4"	3	1315#

NOTE

1. Bolt holes shall be 1/16" larger than nominal diameter of bolt, unless specified otherwise.
2. Where angles not available, bent plates will be used.

Figure 20.31 Clip angles and their limits. (Courtesy of Easy-Arch Rib division of Easy On Manufacturing Co.)

ab ADJUSTABLE POST BASE

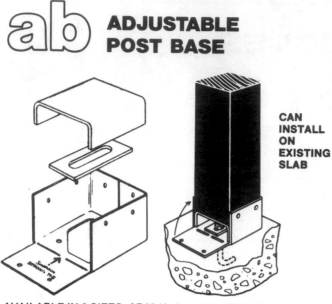

CAN INSTALL ON EXISTING SLAB

AVAILABLE IN 3 SIZES: **AB44** (4x4 posts) • **AB46** (4x6 posts) • **AB66** (6x6 posts) Fully adjustable post base offers moisture protection, structural value, ease of installation, and finish hardware appearance.

Figure 20.32 Adjustable post bases. (Courtesy of Simpson Company, "Strong-Tie Products.")

STAND-OFF PLATE provides **flat-end** bearing area for post; keeps post end 1³⁄₁₆" above surface moisture. **RECTANGULAR ADJUSTMENT PLATE** is secured by base cover to prevent rotation or slippage; provides maximum adjustability to a previously set concrete bolt. **HOLES FOR OPTIONAL NAIL HOLDOWN** in a concrete or timber base, or powder actuated fasteners, are provided in the heavy base cover for non-bolt, adjustable installations.

SPECIFICATIONS

1. Specify as SIMPSON STRONG-TIE AB44 (for 4x4 posts); AB66 (for 6x6 posts) or AB46 (for 4x6 posts).
2. Material and finish: 12 gauge, galvanized steel rectangular adjustment plate and stand-off plate; 16 gauge, galvanized base cover.
3. Nail holes are sized for 10d (9 gauge) galvanized nails. The two optional cement nail tie-down holes are sized for up to ³⁄₁₆" cement nails or "gun" inserts. Rectangular adjustment plate assumes use of ¹⁄₂" bolt (or drilled ¹⁄₂" insert).
4. Supplied as shown: bend up the one base side after positioning and easy-access nut has been secured.

APPROVED—See Research Recommendation No. 1211 of the International Conference of Building Officials (Uniform Building Code).

epb ELEVATED POST BASE

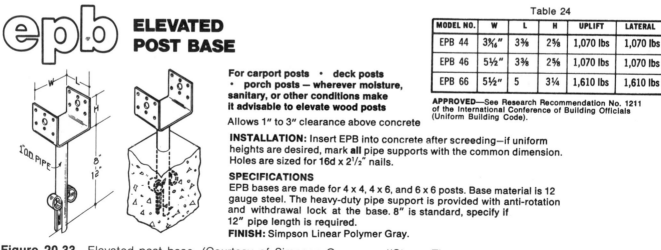

For carport posts • deck posts • porch posts — wherever moisture, sanitary, or other conditions make it advisable to elevate wood posts

Allows 1" to 3" clearance above concrete

INSTALLATION: Insert EPB into concrete after screeding—if uniform heights are desired, mark **all** pipe supports with the common dimension. Holes are sized for 16d x 2½" nails.

SPECIFICATIONS

EPB bases are made for 4 x 4, 4 x 6, and 6 x 6 posts. Base material is 12 gauge steel. The heavy-duty pipe support is provided with anti-rotation and withdrawal lock at the base. 8" is standard, specify if 12" pipe length is required.
FINISH: Simpson Linear Polymer Gray.

Table 24

MODEL NO.	W	L	H	UPLIFT	LATERAL
EPB 44	3⁵⁄₁₆"	3⅜	2⅝	1,070 lbs	1,070 lbs
EPB 46	5½"	3⅜	2⅝	1,070 lbs	1,070 lbs
EPB 66	5½"	5	3¼	1,610 lbs	1,610 lbs

APPROVED—See Research Recommendation No. 1211 of the International Conference of Building Officials (Uniform Building Code).

Figure 20.33 Elevated post base. (Courtesy of Simpson Company, "Strong-Tie Products.")

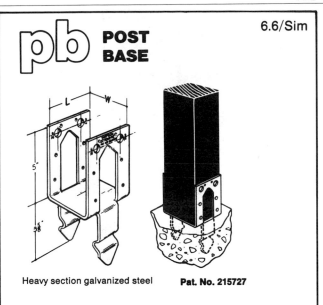

6.6/Sim

pb POST BASE

Heavy section galvanized steel   **Pat. No. 215727**

Provision for optional installation with ½" bolts.

Locking prongs eliminate bolts or inserts in concrete; one-piece design assures maximum strength development.

SPECIFICATIONS

Specify as SIMPSON STRONG-TIE PB44 (for 4x4 posts); PB66 (for 6x6 posts); PB46 (for 4x6 posts); or PB44R (for 4x4 rough posts).

Table 37

MODEL	MATERIAL	W	L	I.C.B.O. LOADS (12-16d NAILS) VERT. UP	I.C.B.O. LOADS (12-16d NAILS) LATERAL	U.B.C. CALC 2-½" MB's VERT. UP
PB44	12 ga. galv.	3⁹⁄₁₆"	3⅜"	1320	1320	—
PB46	12 ga. galv.	5½"	3⅜"	1320	1320	—
PB66	12 ga. galv.	5½"	5⅝"	1610	1610	3225
PB44R (Rough Posts)	12 ga. galv.	4"	3⅜"	1540	1540	—

APPROVED—See Research Recommendaton No. 1211 of the International Conference of Building Officials (Uniform Building Code).

Figure 20.34 Heavy section galvanized steel post base. (Courtesy of Simpson Company, "Strong-Tie Products.")

Sample Problem and Solution

Let us assume:

Size of beam = 4 × 12
Size of Post = 4 × 4
Total weight carried by footing = 4500 pounds
Soil bearing = 1000 pounds per square feet
Cap with strap — Easy-Arch Rib
Post base = Easy-Arch Rib
Height from slab to underside of beam = 9 feet

Before you read on, familiarize yourself with Figures 20.35 and 20.36.

A freehand sketch is always necessary because it affords the detailer the opportunity to view the object and anticipate the drafting problems. The manufacturer's literature furnishes additional information needed about sizes for the post cap and base.

Since the height from slab to the underside fo the beam was 9'-0", find the number 9 on the left side of the chart on Figure 20.35 under the title "Column Height in Feet." Read the chart horizontally to the right from the number 9 until you reach a point below the 4 × 4 column (the size of the post). The intersection of these two columns will tell you how much weight the 4 × 4 column can hold up. In this case, it is 6561 pounds, much greater than the 4500 pounds to be carried. Note that Figure 20.35 is a generalized chart. It is not intended to be used as a definitive solution to structural problems. It is included to help give an approximate idea of the weights that various columns can carry.

Looking next at the chart on Figure 20.36, locate the column marked "Design Load" and find a design load number greater than the needed 4500 pounds. The fifth row down is the closest but greater in number, in this case 5010 pounds. Now reading horizontally to the left, note the footing size to the extreme left, 2'-6" square. Under the "Reinforcing Each Way" column, you will note 2 – #4, which means two number four (½" in diameter) each way.

The pictorial drawing, Figure 20.37, shows what the parts look like assembled, while Figure 20.38 shows how this looks in detail form. For an explanation of the weld symbol, read Chapter 23.

Pipe Column

The pipe column is uniquely different from a wood column in that the pipe column is usually welded directly to the cap (see Figure 20.39, page 361) and the bottom of the pipe column is welded to a bearing plate. This bearing plate in turn is bolted down to a pedestal by means of a prelocated set of anchor bolts. See Figure 20.40.

This plate is a very precise and smooth surface while the top of the concrete may not be. To prevent any irregularity at the joint between the bearing plate and the concrete pedestal, dry pack (cement with very little water) is packed and forced between them thus assuring true perpendicularity of the pipe column with the pedestal as well as firm contact. See Figure 20.41.

For specific sizes of caps, the configuration on Figure 20.16 could be used with the pipe column welded directly to the cap by means of a ¼" fillet weld. See Chapter 23 for suggested weld. However, it is recom-

Column Height in Feet	Wood Column Size					
	3 × 4	4 × 4	4 × 6	6 × 6	6 × 8	8 × 8
4	10500	14700	23100	36300	49500	67500
5	7747	14700	23100	36300	49500	67500
6	5380	14700	23100	36300	49500	67500
7	3953	10846	17044	36300	49500	67500
8	3026	8304	13050	36300	49500	67500
9	2391	6561	10311	36300	49500	67500
10	1937	5315	8352	32409	44193	67500
11	—	4392	6902	26784	36523	67500
12	—	3691	5800	22506	30690	67500
13	—	3145	4942	19177	26150	66305
14	—	2712	4261	16535	22548	57174
15	—	—	—	14404	19642	49805
16	—	—	—	12660	17263	43774
17	—	—	—	11214	15292	38775
18	—	—	—	10003	13640	34587
19	—	—	—	8977	12242	31042
20	—	—	—	8102	11048	28015

Allowable Unit Stress
  Dense No. 1
  $F_c = 1200$
  Modulus of Elasticity = 1.7×10^6
  l/d = 50 Max.

Figure 20.35 Maximum loads on Douglas fir columns (in pounds).

Square Size (L = W)	Reinf. Each Way		Total Load (lbs.)	Ftg. Weight (less pedestal)	Design Load (lbs.)
	16 ksi	20 ksi			
1'-6"	0	0	2210	340	1570
1'-9"	0	0	3060	460	2300
2'-0"	0	0	4000	600	3100
2'-3"	0	0	5060	760	4000
2'-6"	2 – #4	2 – #4	6250	940	5010
2'-9"	2 – #4	2 – #4	7560	1130	6130
3'-0"	2 – #4	2 – #4	9000	1350	7350
3'-3"	2 – #4	2 – #4	10560	1580	8680
3'-6"	2 – #4	2 – #4	12250	1840	10110
3'-9"	3 – #4	3 – #4	14060	2110	11650
4'-0"	3 – #4	3 – #4	16000	2400	13300
4'-3"	3 – #4	3 – #4	18060	2710	15050
4'-6"	3 – #4	3 – #4	20250	3040	16910
4'-9"	4 – #4	4 – #4	22560	3380	18880
5'-0"	5 – #4	4 – #4	25000	3750	20950
5'-3"	6 – #4	5 – #4	27560	4130	23130
5'-6"	7 – #4	5 – #4	30250	4540	25410
5'-9"	8 – #4	6 – #4	33060	4960	27800
6'-0"	9 – #4	7 – #4	36000	5400	30300
6'-3"	10 – #4	8 – #4 or 5 – #5	39060	5860	32900
6'-6"	11 – #4 or 7 – #5	9 – #4	42250	6340	35610
6'-9"	13 – #4 or 8 – #5	10 – #4	45560	6830	38430
7'-0"	14 – #4 or 9 – #5	12 – #4 or 8 – #5	49000	7350	41350
7'-3"	10 – #5	13 – #4 or 8 – #5	52560	7880	44380
7'-6"	12 – #5	14 – #4 or 9 – #5	56250	8440	47510
7'-9"	13 – #5	10 – #5	60060	9010	50750
8'-0"	14 – #5	12 – #5	64000	9600	54100

Soil Pressure = 1000 lb per sq ft
Footing Thickness = 12" typical (T)
Assumed Typ. Pedestal = 300 lb (12" sq × 12" deep)

Figure 20.36 Square footing schedule. (Courtesy of John K. Eardley & Associates.)

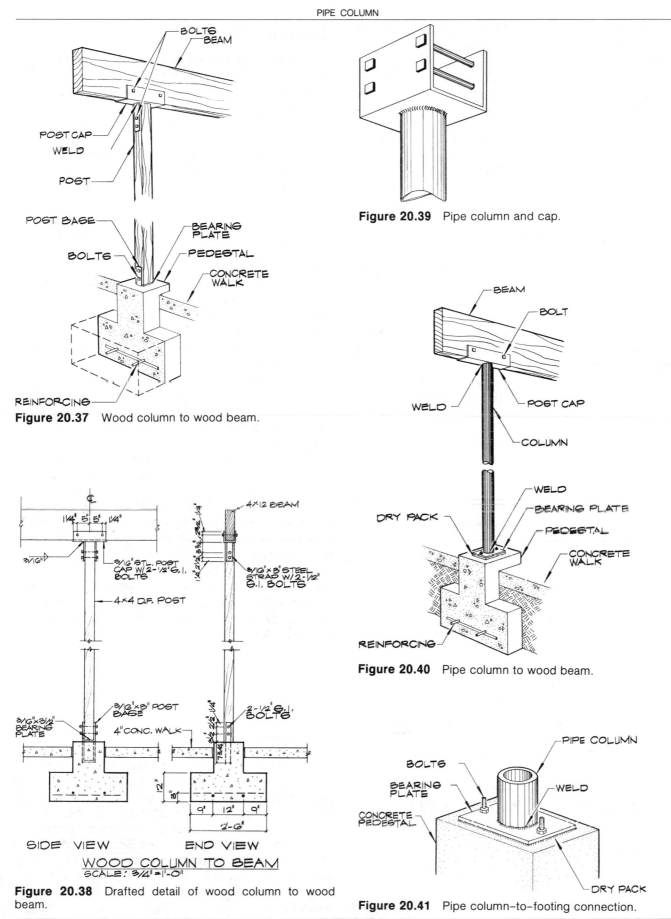

Figure 20.37 Wood column to wood beam.

Figure 20.38 Drafted detail of wood column to wood beam.

Figure 20.39 Pipe column and cap.

Figure 20.40 Pipe column to wood beam.

Figure 20.41 Pipe column–to–footing connection.

SIDE VIEW   END VIEW
WOOD COLUMN TO BEAM
SCALE: 3/4" = 1'-0"

mended that the architectural draftsperson consult a structural engineer or a local manufacturer.

The pipe column is not set directly into the concrete because it is difficult to maintain a true perpendicular condition. Using the method described here, the workers in the field can adjust the pipe column as required.

Note how the pipe column is called out on the detail (Figure 20.42). The 3″ is the diameter of the pipe column and comes first, the name comes next, and finally the weight per foot (7.58 in this case). The weight per foot ensures a particular pipe thickness, which ensures strength.

The drafted detail should also have a detail of the bearing plate with its dimensions.

The chart in Figure 20.43 is much like that Figure 20.35 except that it is calculated for pipe columns. The second horizontal column is the wall thickness of the pipe and directly below it the weight of pipe column per lineal foot. The units are in kips (1000 pounds). Footing for pipe columns can be derived from Figure 20.36.

Figure 20.44 has been included to show extra strong pipe columns. Note the change in wall thickness and weight per lineal foot.

Masonry Columns

Prior to reading this section, the architect should review Chapter 8, to become familiar with the basic terminology. Masonry and its application to the structure is included in Chapters 8, 9, and 10.

In much the same manner that wood and steel columns support concentrated vertical loads, brick and concrete block walls are freestanding masonry columns whose primary function is to support a concentrated vertical load such as a beam or a girder. Figure 20.45 gives an example of a finished masonry column.

Unsupported heights for reinforced masonry columns should not exceed 10 times the smallest cross-sectional dimension. For example, a 16 × 16 masonry column should not be higher than 160 inches (16 × 10) or 15 feet. A good rule of thumb for a hollow unsupported column is four times the smallest cross-sectional dimension. Figure 20.46 illustrates a slump/block with its cavity filled (and including vertical reinforcing).

The footing for a masonry structure is based on the weight to be carried, weight of the column itself, and the soil condition. The procedure for computation is done in the same fashion as previously described in this chapter.

Whether the column is made of brick or concrete block, it must be void of vertical joint. This is accomplished by lapping alternate joints of brick or concrete block. See Figures 20.47 and 20.48. Concrete block can also be obtained in squares voiding vertical joints as shown in Figure 20.49. Note how the wood beam rests in a steel saddle of the same variety used in the wood and pipe columns. The main difference is the use of drypack under the steel saddle to ensure perpendicularity. Figure 20.50 shows a sample of a concrete block column-to-wood beam connection detail in drafted form.

Pilasters

The main difference between pilasters and columns is that pilasters are built into the masonry wall. See the partly finished pilaster in Figure 20.51. Not only are pilasters an integral part of the masonry wall, but they are also for lateral support as well as a support for concentrated vertical loads. See Figure 20.52. Figure 20.53 shows the combination necessary to develop the pilaster, and Figure 20.54 illustrates a drafted version of the connection between the pilaster and a wood beam.

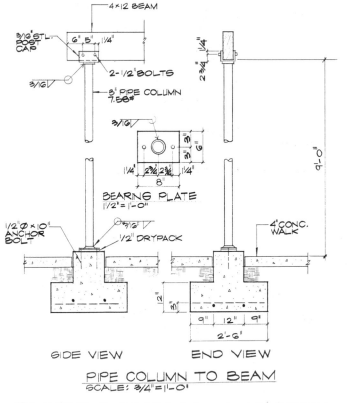

Figure 20.42 Drafted detail of pipe column to wood beam.

$F_y = 36$ ksi

COLUMNS
Standard steel pipe

Allowable concentric loads in kips

Nominal Dia.	12	10	8	6	5	·4	3½	3
Wall Thickness	.375	.365	.322	.280	.258	.237	.226	.216
Weight per Foot	49.56	40.48	28.55	18.97	14.62	10.79	9.11	7.58

Effective length in feet KL with respect to radius of gyration

	12	10	8	6	5	·4	3½	3
6	303	246	171	110	83	59	48	38
7	301	243	168	108	81	57	46	36
8	299	241	166	106	78	54	44	34
9	296	238	163	103	76	52	41	31
10	293	235	161	101	73	49	38	28
11	291	232	158	98	71	46	35	25
12	288	229	155	95	68	43	32	22
13	285	226	152	92	65	40	29	19
14	282	223	149	89	61	36	25	16
15	278	220	145	86	58	33	22	14
16	275	216	142	82	55	29	19	12
17	272	213	138	79	51	26	17	11
18	268	209	135	75	47	23	15	10
19	265	205	131	71	43	21	14	9
20	261	201	127	67	39	19	12	
22	254	193	119	59	32	15	10	
24	246	185	111	51	27	13		
26	238	176	102	43	23			
28	229	167	93	37	20			
30	220	158	83	32	17			
32	211	148	73	29				
34	201	137	65	25				
36	192	127	58	23				
38	181	115	52					
40	171	104	47					

Properties

	12	10	8	6	5	·4	3½	3
Area A (in.²)	14.6	11.9	8.40	5.58	4.30	3.17	2.68	2.23
I (in.⁴)	279.	161.	72.5	28.1	15.2	7.23	4.79	3.02
r (in.)	4.38	3.67	2.94	2.25	1.88	1.51	1.34	1.16
B (Bending factor)	.333	.398	.500	.657	.789	.987	1.12	1.29
a (Multiply values by 10⁶)	41.7	23.9	10.8	4.21	2.26	1.08	.717	.447

Heavy line indicates $Kl/r = 120$.   Values omitted for $Kl/r > 200$.

AMERICAN INSTITUTE OF STEEL CONSTRUCTION

Figure 20.43 Standard steel pipe columns. (Reproduced from the *AISC Manual of Steel Construction* with permission from the American Institute of Steel Construction, Inc.)

3 - 40

$F_y = 36$ ksi	COLUMNS Double-extra strong steel pipe

Allowable concentric loads in kips

Nominal Dia.	8	6	5	4	3
Wall Thickness	.875	.864	.750	.674	.600
Weight per Foot	72.42	53.16	38.55	27.54	18.58
6	431	306	216	147	91
7	424	299	209	140	84
8	417	292	202	133	77
9	410	284	195	126	69
10	403	275	187	118	60
11	395	266	178	109	51
12	387	257	170	100	43
13	378	247	160	91	37
14	369	237	151	81	32
15	360	227	141	70	28
16	351	216	130	62	24
17	341	205	119	55	22
18	331	193	108	49	
19	321	181	97	44	
20	310	168	87	40	
22	288	142	72	33	
24	264	119	61		
26	240	102	52		
28	213	88	44		
30	187	76			
32	164	67			
34	145	60			
36	130				
38	116				
40	105				

Effective length in feet KL with respect to radius of gyration

Properties

Area A (in.²)	21.3	15.6	11.3	8.10	5.47
I (in.⁴)	162.	66.3	33.6	15.3	5.99
r (in.)	2.76	2.06	1.72	1.37	1.05
B (Bending factor)	.567	.781	.938	1.19	1.60
a (Multiply values by 10⁶)	24.2	9.86	4.98	2.27	.899

Heavy line indicates $Kl/r = 120$.   Values omitted for $Kl/r > 200$.

AMERICAN INSTITUTE OF STEEL CONSTRUCTION

Figure 20.44 Double-extra-strong steel pipe columns. (Reproduced from the *AISC Manual of Steel Construction* with permission from the American Institute of Steel Construction, Inc.)

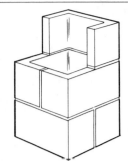

PICTORIAL

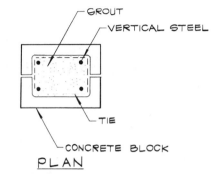

PLAN

Figure 20.47 Concrete block column.

Figure 20.45 Masonry column supporting wood beam.

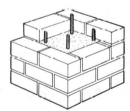

PICTORIAL

Figure 20.46 Slump/block column with reinforcing.

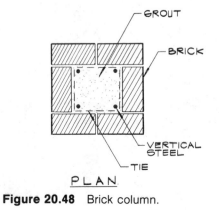

PLAN

Figure 20.48 Brick column.

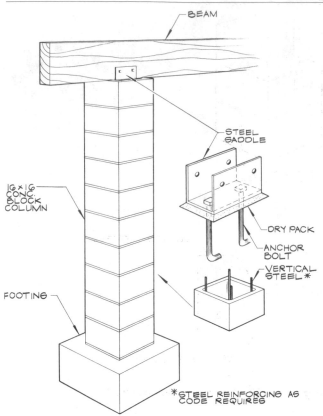

Figure 20.49 Concrete block column to wood beam and concrete pad.

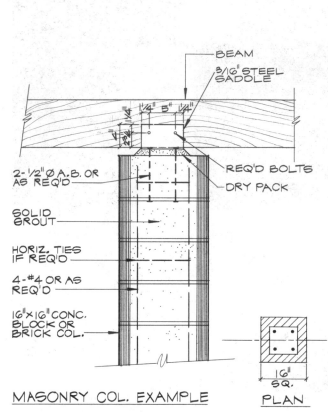

MASONRY COL. EXAMPLE   PLAN

Figure 20.50 Drafted detail of concrete block column with wood beam.

Figure 20.51 Pilaster.

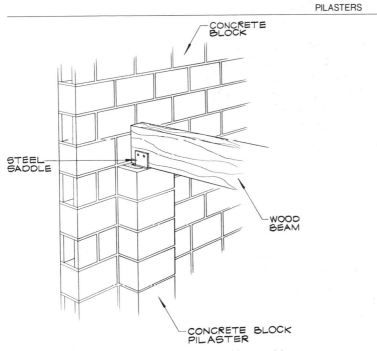

Figure 20.52 Concrete block pilaster with wood beam.

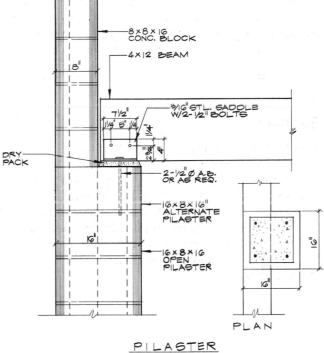

Figure 20.54 Drafted detail of concrete block pilaster.

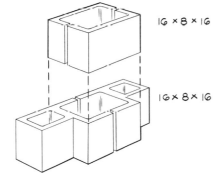

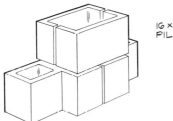

Figure 20.53 Concrete block pilaster. (Reproduced from the *Masonry Design Manual* with permission of the publishers, the Masonry Industry Advancement Committee.)

Regional Differences

The main regional difference for a beam connection involves the weather. Frost lines require a different depth for the footing pad. Earthquake zones demand a more rigid connection and stronger beams and columns. Wind problems also create uplift and produce a greater need for additional stability. And, finally, if wood columns are used, termites must be dealt with if the structure is built in an area of high termite infestation. However, in the majority of cases, this becomes the concern of the engineer responsible for such computations, not the architectural draftsperson.

Building Code

Although the charts included in this chapter are carefully selected and computed by professionals, slight variations may occur from one building department to another; consequently, they may be used for hypothetical cases only and should not be assumed correct for all parts of the country. Most states do require that plans using such beam connections be signed by a licensed architect or engineer. Most building officials also require submission of engineering calculations to confirm the stability of such a structure.

Summary

There are many things to consider when detailing a beam-to-column connection. The concept to be remembered is that an architectural draftsperson, when dealing with a structural design of a building, must always work from the top down. Figure your roof loads, wall load, and floor loads prior to developing a footing or selecting a connection between beam and column or column and footing. Correct selection of the tributary areas as described in this chapter is equally important if you are to calculate the correct weight of the structure.

This chapter brought awareness concerning the various factors that affect the final detail.

21
MISCELLANEOUS DETAILS

Preview Chapter 21 explains and illustrates examples of details that are not always utilized on projects. Ten different conditions are presented, and a brief description of the formulation of the details shown is given.

Various wood framing details are incorporated along with recommended drawings and provisions for the handicapped in the design of a building.

After reading this chapter, the architectural draftsperson will:

1. Be cognizant of miscellaneous details for wood construction and the criteria for their assembly.
2. Understand the recommended design requirements that involve consideration of the handicapped.

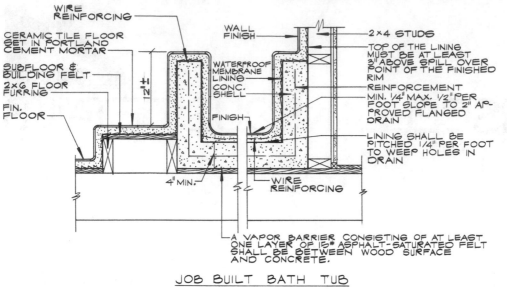

Labels in figure:
WIRE REINFORCING
CERAMIC TILE FLOOR SET IN PORTLAND CEMENT MORTAR
SUBFLOOR & BUILDING FELT
2×6 FLOOR FURRING
FIN. FLOOR
WALL FINISH
WATERPROOF MEMBRANE LINING
CONC. SHELL
FINISH
2×4 STUDS
TOP OF THE LINING MUST BE AT LEAST 3" ABOVE SPILL OVER POINT OF THE FINISHED RIM
REINFORCEMENT
MIN. 1/4" MAX. 1/2" PER FOOT SLOPE TO 2" AP-PROVED FLANGED DRAIN
LINING SHALL BE PITCHED 1/4" PER FOOT TO WEEP HOLES IN DRAIN
4" MIN.
WIRE REINFORCING
A VAPOR BARRIER CONSISTING OF AT LEAST ONE LAYER OF 15# ASPHALT-SATURATED FELT SHALL BE BETWEEN WOOD SURFACE AND CONCRETE.

JOB BUILT BATH TUB

Figure 21.1 Section, job-built bathtub.

The preparation of a set of construction documents for residences and apartment projects may incorporate construction techniques considered standard in detail. Many of these details were explained and illustrated in previous chapters. However, projects often require detailing for unusual or special conditions, and these details may occur for conditions outside the structure as well as within.

In detailing special conditions, the approach is the same as that explained in previous chapters. This approach should include the following information: (1) a preliminary analysis of how a specific detail is assembled, (2) the selection of a scale that provides clarity of the detail, (3) good drafting, and (4) the call out of all the members that constitute a detail.

Roman Tub

The following drawings are examples of special conditions that are required to be detailed for specific projects. The first, drawn in section view, is a detail of a job-built bathtub, also referred to as a roman tub. This detail is designed for wood floor construction with ceramic tile as a finish material; it is illustrated in Figure 21.1. Figure 21.2 shows this detail in pictorial view.

Retaining Walls

The two principal methods used in the construction of retaining walls are poured concrete and concrete ma-

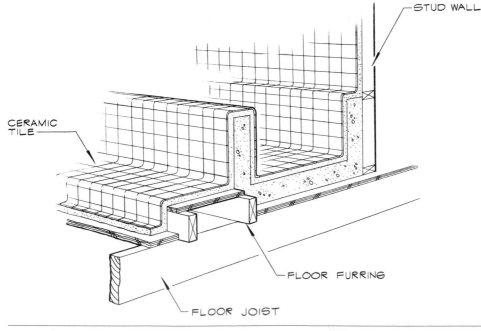

Labels in figure:
STUD WALL
CERAMIC TILE
FLOOR FURRING
FLOOR JOIST

Figure 21.2 Pictorial view, job-built roman tub.

sonry units. The poured-in-place concrete method will necessitate the use of wood forms and the placement of reinforcing steel prior to the pouring of concrete. The size and placement of the reinforcing steel will be decided by the design of the engineer. A 7'-0" high poured concrete retaining wall is illustrated in Figure 21.3. Note the following:

The height of the retention is calculated from the top of the footing to the top of the earth, and on this specific wall design, there is a shear key at the bottom of the footing. This has been incorporated into the design for the purpose of resisting horizontal slide conditions.

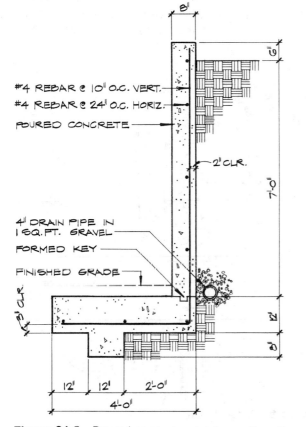

Figure 21.3 Poured concrete retaining wall section.

The use of concrete masonry units, also referred to as concrete blocks, is a method that does not require forming for its construction. The construction sequence for a concrete block retaining wall is as follows:

1. Lay up the units.
2. Install the required reinforcing steel.
3. Fill all the cells solid with grout.

The poured concrete footing, which is installed prior to the erection of the concrete block, will include an inset of key so that when the grout is poured into the block cells, a more positive bond is acquired even

though the reinforcing steel is continuous from the footing to the cells of the wall. Figure 21.4 shows a garden wall retaining 3 feet of earth.

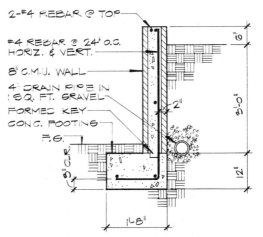

Figure 21.4 Poured concrete retaining wall.

Basement Wall

Basement wall designs vary with the material used and the method of construction the engineer selects.

Two acceptable methods for basement wall designs are a cantilevered wall and a wall that is stayed at the basement and upper floor levels. Since this wall is located below grade, a waterproof membrane, water-repellent admixtures, and drain tile should be incorporated into the wall design. A cantilevered basement wall constructed of concrete block is illustrated in Figure 21.5. It should be mentioned that wall

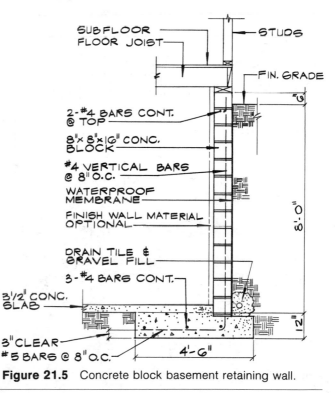

Figure 21.5 Concrete block basement retaining wall.

reinforcing is dependent on the engineer's findings. Figure 21.6 shows this detail in pictorial view.

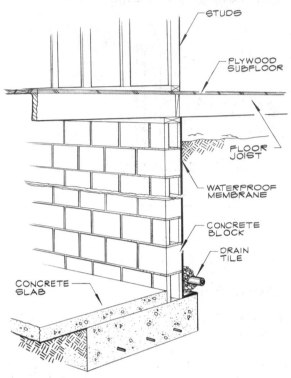

Figure 21.6 Pictorial view, basement wall.

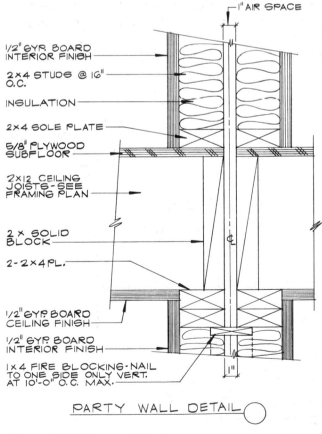

PARTY WALL DETAIL

Figure 21.7 Party wall detail.

Party Wall

In multihousing projects, such as apartment buildings, it is extremely important that the wall assembly, separating one apartment from another, is as soundproof as possible.

Wood construction presents a greater sound transmission problem than does concrete or masonry. In apartments or a row housing project designed for wood frame construction, the separation walls (more commonly referred to as ''party walls'') should be detailed at a large scale. A good method for achieving a low sound transmission coefficient is to detail the party wall utilizing two separate stud walls spaced apart and heavily insulated. This method also allows the floor framing to terminate at the separate walls and thus reduce sound transmission. See Figure 21.7. A pictorial view of this detail is illustrated in Figure 21.8.

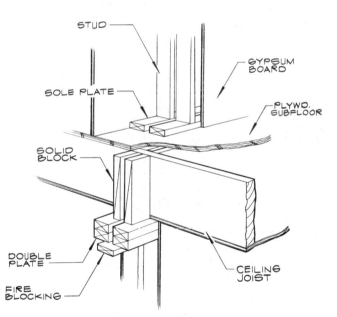

Figure 21.8 Pictorial, party wall detail.

Two-Hour Separation Wall

Another separation wall, which may be required for apartment or office building projects, is a 2-hour area separation wall. This particular wall is required by most building codes or fire department restrictions to separate areas based on a maximum allowable floor area. The 2-hour designation means that under a tested flame condition, the materials used on wood frame construction would resist penetration for 2 hours. A detail of an approved 2-hour wood framed separation wall is illustrated in Figure 21.9. A pictorial view of this detail is shown in Figure 21.10.

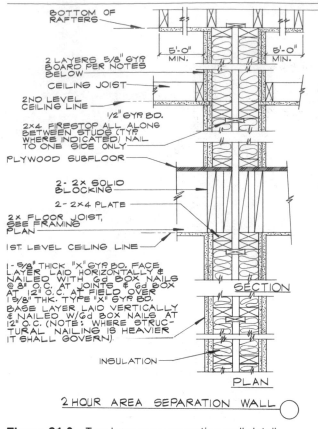

Figure 21.9 Two-hour area separation wall detail.

Fence

A condition that occurs in many building projects regardless of type, is the provision of a fenced-in trash enclosure space. The design of the fence and the details necessary to construct it should be incorporated into the construction documents. An example of a fence detail is shown in Figure 21.11. Figure 21.12 illustrates this detail in pictorial form.

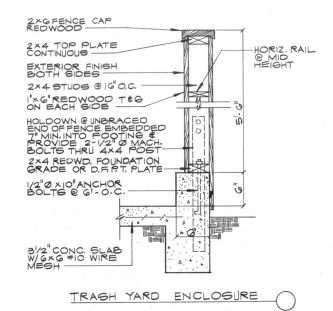

Figure 21.11 Trash yard fence section.

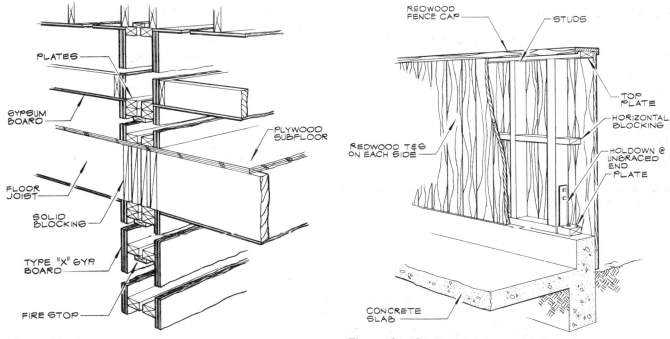

Figure 21.10 Pictorial, 2-hour area separation wall.

Figure 21.12 Pictorial, fence detail.

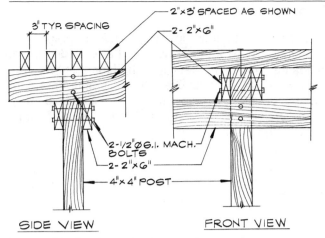

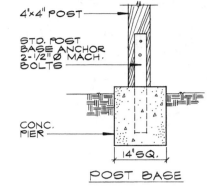

Figure 21.13 Trellis framing sections.

Trellis

In many cases the architect incorporates the use of a trellis in conjunction with a house design. The trellis is detailed along with many details necessary for the house design.

The primary problem involved in a trellis design is that of achieving lateral stability in both directions. The detailer must keep this problem in mind when providing a set of construction details. Figure 21.13 illustrates a trellis design that is freestanding and does not rely on a connection to the structure. Note the two horizontal bolted members that span both directions for lateral stability. Figure 21.14 shows these connections pictorially.

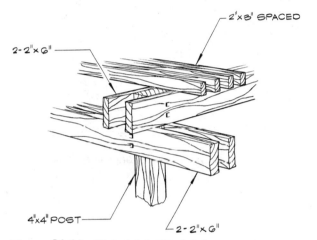

Figure 21.14 Pictorial, trellis detail.

Lighting Soffits

Luminous ceilings and lighting soffit details, when incorporated in the building design, should be detailed according to the architect's design and recommended lighting standards.

The luminous ceiling generally is flush with the ceiling. It is recommended that a minimum of 12″ be provided for the lighting recess and a finish material, such as gypsum board or plaster, be installed to create a reflective surface. See Figure 21.15. Figure 21.16 shows detail in pictorial view.

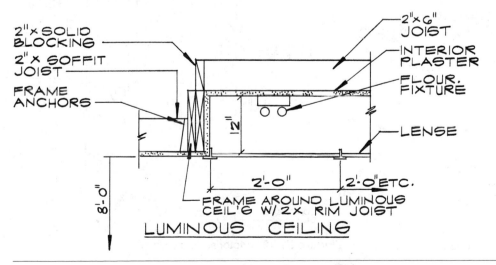

Figure 21.15 Luminous ceiling section.

Lighting soffits are usually located below a ceiling and employ lighting standards similar to the luminous ceiling. Figure 21.17 illustrates a lighting soffit above a bathroom lavatory. Figure 21.18 depicts this detail in pictorial view.

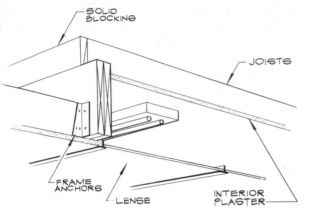
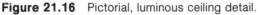

Figure 21.16 Pictorial, luminous ceiling detail.

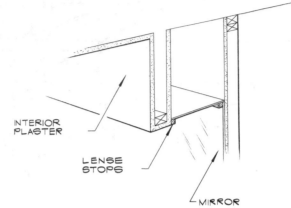

Figure 21.18 Pictorial, lighting soffit detail.

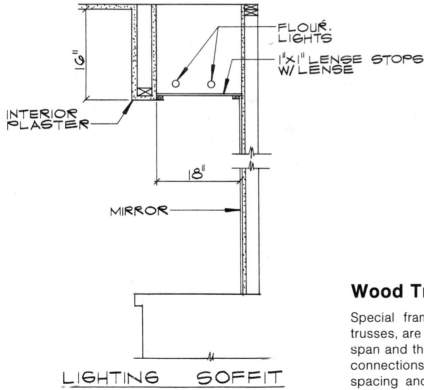

LIGHTING SOFFIT

Figure 21.17 Lighting soffit detail.

Wood Truss

Special framing conditions, such as job-built roof trusses, are engineered and detailed according to the span and the roof's live and dead loads. Wood truss connections require large-scale details since bolt spacing and clearances must be clearly shown. In most cases, trusses are symmetrical and therefore require only one side of the truss to be detailed. Figures 21.19 and 21.20 illustrate details for a specifically designed roof truss. Figure 21.19 depicts the bottom chord connection at the exterior wall and rafter; Figure 21.20 shows the ridge and strut connections. Figure 21.21 depicts the truss in pictorial view.

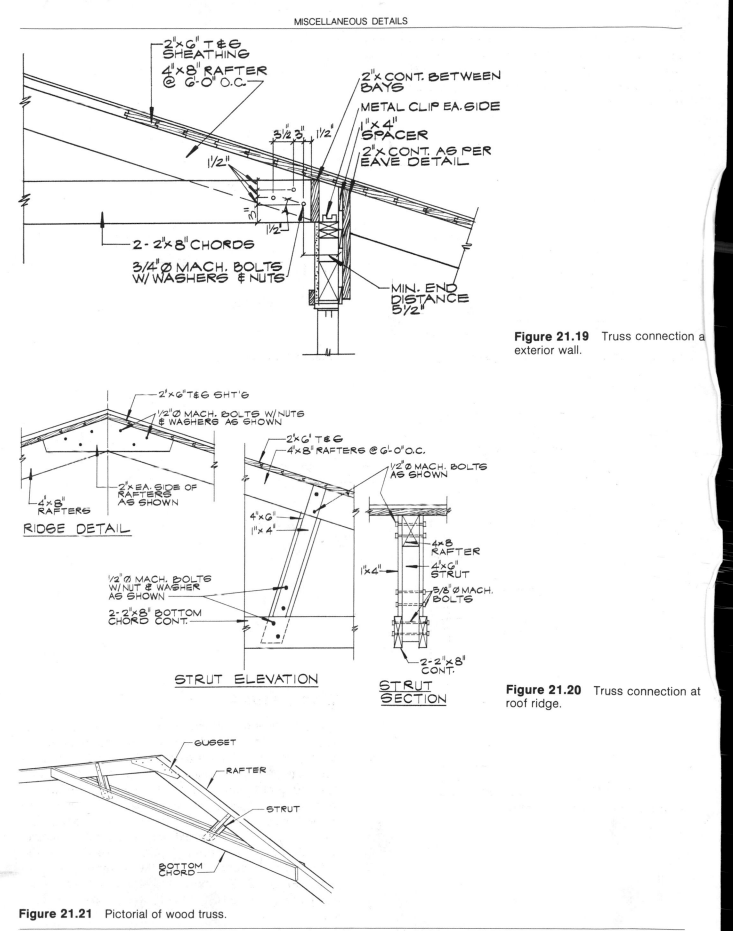

2"×6" T&G
SHEATHING

4"×8" RAFTER
@ 6'-0" O.C.

2"× CONT. BETWEEN
BAYS

METAL CLIP EA. SIDE

1"×4" SPACER

2"× CONT. AS PER
EAVE DETAIL

3½" 3" 1½"

1½"

2 - 2"×8" CHORDS

3/4"Ø MACH. BOLTS
W/ WASHERS & NUTS

1½"

MIN. END
DISTANCE
5½"

Figure 21.19 Truss connection a
exterior wall.

2"×6" T&G SHT'S

½"Ø MACH. BOLTS W/NUTS
& WASHERS AS SHOWN

2"× EA. SIDE OF
RAFTERS
AS SHOWN

4"×8"
RAFTERS

RIDGE DETAIL

2"×6" T&G

4"×8" RAFTERS @ 6'-0"O.C.

½"Ø MACH. BOLTS
AS SHOWN

4"×6"

1"×4"

½"Ø MACH. BOLTS
W/ NUT & WASHER
AS SHOWN

2 - 2"×8" BOTTOM
CHORD CONT.

STRUT ELEVATION

4×8
RAFTER

1"×4"

4"×6"
STRUT

5/8"Ø MACH.
BOLTS

2 - 2"×8"
CONT.

STRUT
SECTION

Figure 21.20 Truss connection at
roof ridge.

GUSSET

RAFTER

STRUT

BOTTOM
CHORD

Figure 21.21 Pictorial of wood truss.

Skylights

The use of skylights or ''skydomes'' is very widespread in many different types of buildings, and they are available in many shapes and sizes. Generally, the detailer selects a specific manufacturer's skylight that is compatible with framing conditions already existing on a project. In addition to the flashing and connection assembly that occurs at the roof level, the detailer should indicate on the drawings the required rough opening dimensions to facilitate the specified skylight. The dimensions are supplied by the manufacturer's information. A skylight assembly is illustrated in Figure 21.22. A pictorial view of this detail is shown in Figure 21.23.

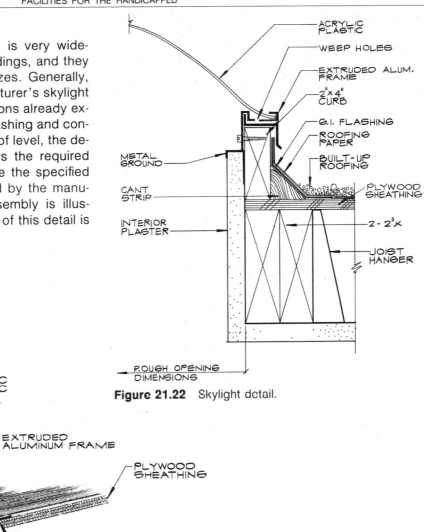

Figure 21.22 Skylight detail.

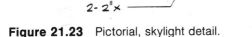

Figure 21.23 Pictorial, skylight detail.

Facilities for the Handicapped

A very important consideration in the design and detailing of many buildings today is provision of facilities for the handicapped. These facilities should consider convenience for people confined to a wheelchair or those who are handicapped.

The following important provisions for the handicapped should be incorporated into the design of a building: (1) door sizes to accommodate wheelchairs, (2) appropriate lavatory facilities, (3) ramp slopes, dropped curb and access walks, (4) handrail designs,

(5) stair treads and nosing design, and (6) openings on floor or ground levels, such as gratings.

To illustrate these provisions graphically, Figures 21.24 through 21.32 have been included. These drawings provide recommended design criteria for the detailer and should be a basis for design solutions.

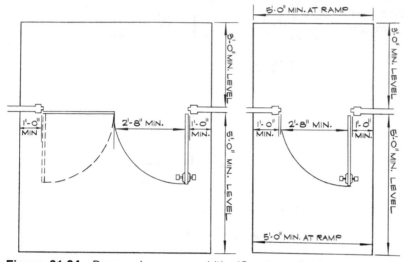

Figure 21.24 Door and passage width. (Courtesy of John C. Worsley, FAIA, State Architect, California Office of Architecture & Construction.)

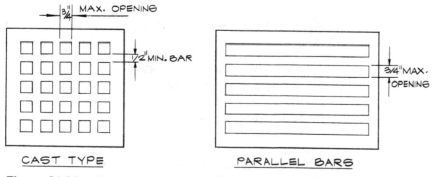

CAST TYPE   PARALLEL BARS

Figure 21.25 Grating openings. (Courtesy of John C. Worsley, FAIA, State Architect, California Office of Architecture & Construction.)

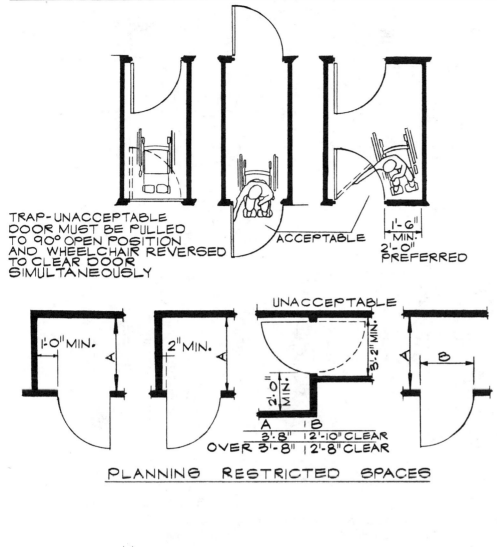

TRAP-UNACCEPTABLE
DOOR MUST BE PULLED
TO 90° OPEN POSITION
AND WHEELCHAIR REVERSED
TO CLEAR DOOR
SIMULTANEOUSLY

ACCEPTABLE

1'-6" MIN.
2'-0" PREFERRED

UNACCEPTABLE

1'-0" MIN. A

2" MIN. A

3'-2" MIN.

2'-0" MIN.

B

	A	B
	3'-8"	2'-10" CLEAR
OVER	3'-8"	2'-8" CLEAR

PLANNING RESTRICTED SPACES

Figure 21.26 Planning spaces. (Courtesy of John C. Worsley, FAIA, State Architect, California Office of Architecture & Construction.)

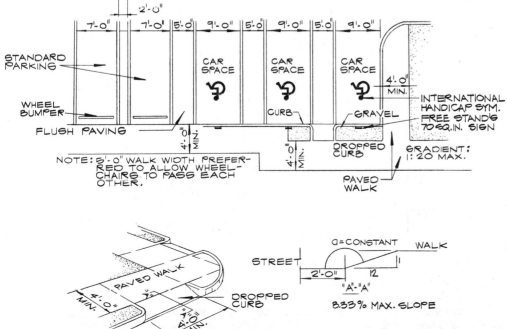

STANDARD PARKING

CAR SPACE

CAR SPACE

CAR SPACE

4'-0" MIN.

WHEEL BUMPER

CURB

GRAVEL

INTERNATIONAL HANDICAP SYM. FREE STAND'G 70 SQ. IN. SIGN

FLUSH PAVING

4'-0" MIN.

4'-0" MIN.

DROPPED CURB

GRADIENT: 1:20 MAX.

NOTE: 5'-0" WALK WIDTH PREFER-RED TO ALLOW WHEEL-CHAIRS TO PASS EACH OTHER.

PAVED WALK

PAVED WALK

4'-0" MIN.

4'-0" MIN.

DROPPED CURB

STREET

a=CONSTANT WALK

2'-0" 12

"A"-"A"

8.33% MAX. SLOPE

Figure 21.27 Drop curb or curb cuts. (Courtesy of John C. Worsley, FAIA, State Architect, California Office of Architecture & Construction.)

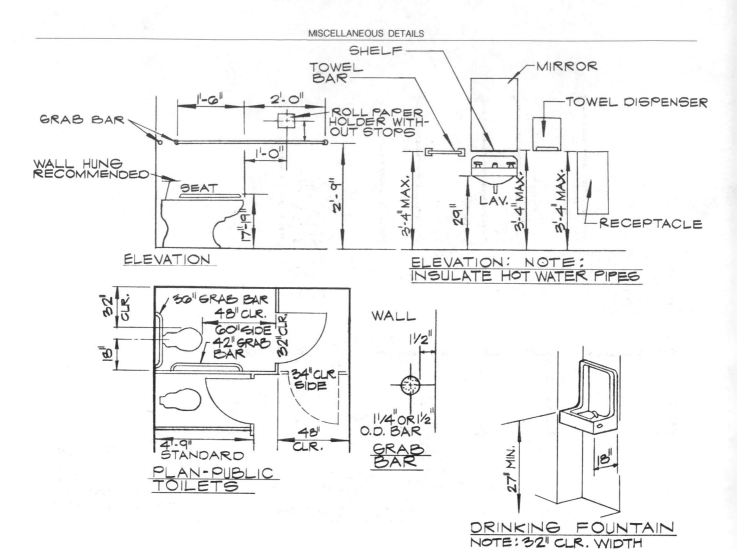

Figure 21.28 Lavatory facilities. (Courtesy of John C. Worsley, FAIA, State Architect, California Office of Architecture & Construction.)

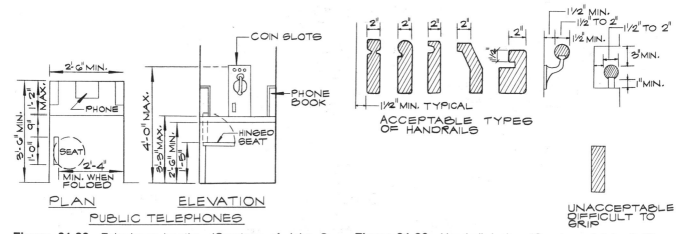

Figure 21.29 Telephone booths. (Courtesy of John C. Worsley, FAIA, State Architect, California Office of Architecture & Construction.)

Figure 21.30 Handrail design. (Courtesy of John C. Worsley, FAIA, State Architect, California Office of Architecture & Construction.)

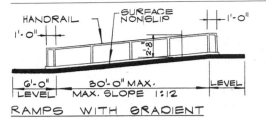

RAMPS WITH GRADIENT

Figure 21.31 Ramp design. (Courtesy of John C. Worsley, FAIA, State Architect, California Office of Architecture & Construction.)

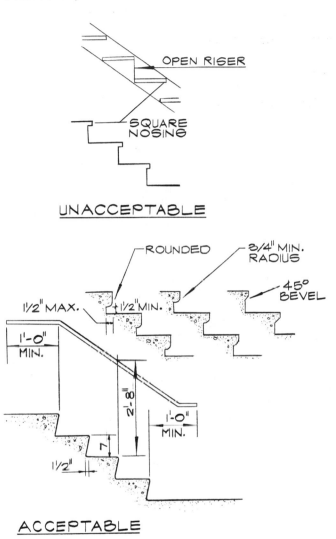

OPEN RISER

SQUARE NOSING

UNACCEPTABLE

ROUNDED — 3/4" MIN. RADIUS — 45° BEVEL

1 1/2" MAX. — 1 1/2" MIN.

1'-0" MIN.

1'-0" MIN.

1 1/2"

ACCEPTABLE

Figure 21.32 Stair design. (Courtesy of John C. Worsley, FAIA, State Architect, California Office of Architecture & Construction.)

Regional Differences

Regional differences may affect the following:

Figure 21.3 — Basement retaining wall — The footing depth and size will vary depending on that region's soil conditions.

Figure 21.19 — Connection of roof truss to exterior wall may be connected with metal clips in earthquake regions, whereas in regions that are not affected by seismic design, the need for such positive connections is not as critical.

Figure 21.22 — Skylight — Because of climatic conditions, many regions will require a dual glazed dome and greater insulation on the roof or between the roof joists to satisfy their temperature requirements.

Figures 21.26, 21.27, and 21.31 — Space planning for the handicapped — These requirements will vary from state to state. Check local codes and recommendations.

Summary

This chapter provided examples of conditions that may require detailing on various projects. The examples selected occur inside or outside the structure. Many conditions that are outside the building boundaries must be detailed and incorporated into the construction documents. The chapter also emphasized that the approach to detailing miscellaneous details should include good graphics, clarity, and complete information.

22
EVOLUTION OF A DETAIL

Preview   The architect must understand and recognize the many facets that influence the development of a detail. Chapter 22 will show the evolution of six different details, each with its own requirements that influence how the detail is made, such as weatherproofing, energy conservation, fire protection, building codes, structural considerations, and architectural design. The details will deal with materials such as wood, masonry, and structural steel.

After reading this chapter, the architectural draftsperson will:

1. Understand the various factors that influence and/or dictate the formulation of a construction detail.
2. Develop a technique of designing a construction assembly with the use of freehand sketches.
3. Be able to develop an architectural detail around established structural members.
4. Have a knowledge of flashing requirements as they apply to various locations in a building.
5. Be familiar with details that incorporate energy conservation requirements.

Creativity, ingenuity, and craftsmanship are just as important in the design of a detail as they are in the overall design of a structure. In addition to these elements, the evolution of an architectural detail is influenced or dictated by some or all of the following: building codes, structural considerations, architectural design, energy conservation, fire protection, weatherproofing, and materials used in the assembly.

Balustrade Detail

In many cases, a detail will evolve around established structural considerations, such as those of the structural members. These members will provide a basis for assembling other members required to formulate the architectural detail. An example is a detail of a balustrade.

Before you begin to develop your detail of a balustrade, make sure you understand the difference between a balustrade and a baluster:

- A baluster is a series of small columns that provide the structural support of a handrail, such as one in a balustrade.

- A balustrade is a combination of a handrail, balusters, and intermediate members.

Structural Members in a Balustrade Detail

The following procedure can be used to develop a successful detail of a balustrade. First, lay out the structural members that are directly related to the handrail assembly. Figure 22.1 illustrates the primary structural members from which the balustrade assembly will evolve. These will be the basic members that support the balustrade and provide a backing for the finished materials. A pictorial view of balustrade assembly is shown in Figure 22.2.

Next, attach the vertical members of the balustrade to the supporting floor members. Figure 22.3 illustrates a method using 2 × 4 vertical members toenailed directly to a 2 × 4 sole plate above the subfloor. Figure 22.4 shows this in a pictorial view. After reviewing the governing building codes, however, we find that this method of attachment is not acceptable for the lateral force design requirements set forth by the building code. Therefore, we must develop a method of attaching the vertical members of a balus-

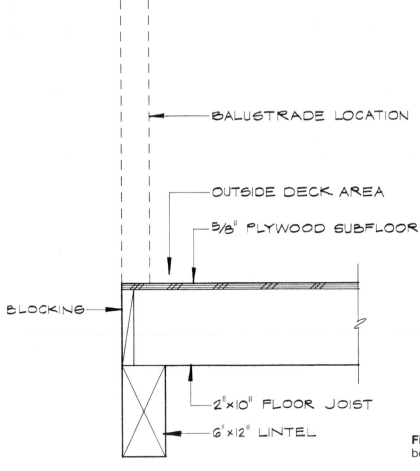

BALUSTRADE LOCATION

OUTSIDE DECK AREA

5/8" PLYWOOD SUBFLOOR

BLOCKING

2"×10" FLOOR JOIST

6"×12" LINTEL

Figure 22.1 Detail showing structural members of a balustrade assembly.

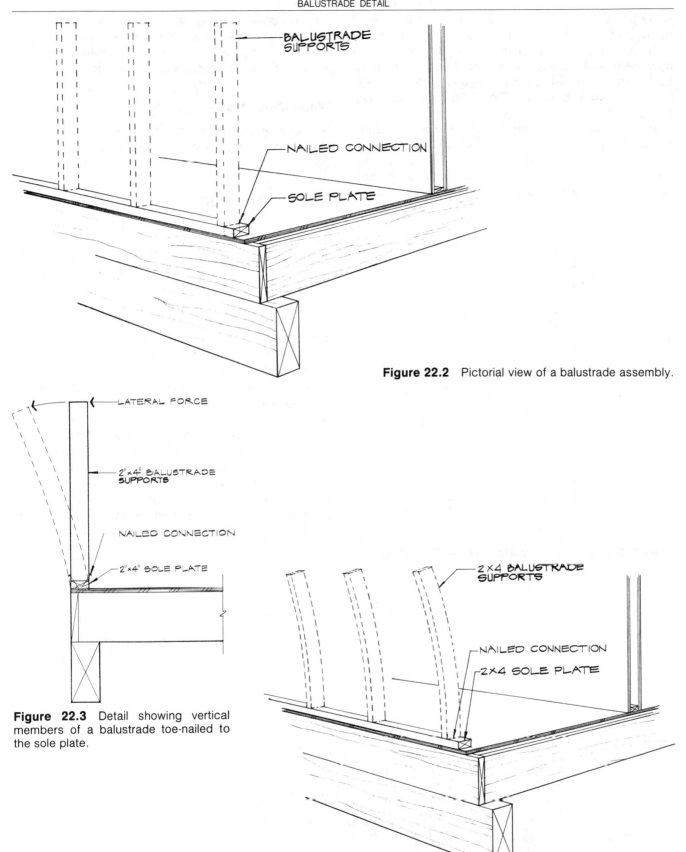

Figure 22.2 Pictorial view of a balustrade assembly.

Figure 22.3 Detail showing vertical members of a balustrade toe-nailed to the sole plate.

Figure 22.4 Pictorial view of vertical supporting members of a balustrade toe-nailed to the sole plate.

trade to the supporting floor members that will satisfy the code requirements for the lateral force factor.

The use of a 3 × 4 baluster attached to two 2 × 10 floor joists with machine bolts has been selected as the method that will satisfy the lateral force factor. This is shown as a detail in Figure 22.5 and pictorially in Figure 22.6.

To complete the balustrade detail, we need additional members and finishes, which are also influenced by building code requirements and architectural design. For example, the balustrade height and the spacing of the vertical rails are governed by the building code (see Figure 22.7). In this case, the balustrade height is 42″ and the vertical rails are spaced not greater than 8″ apart, center to center. A pictorial view of this assembly is shown in Figure 22.8.

Wood Members

Because of the architectural design of the building, stained wood members have been incorporated into our balustrade as the top, bottom, and vertical rails.

Metal Flashing Collar

A $4\frac{1}{2}$″ curb above the deck level was incorporated in the detail to prevent water from the deck spilling over on the face of the finished exterior plaster below. Because of the curb condition, water on the deck will be conducted to the deck drains.

One area of concern relates to the area in which the plaster and the 3 × 4 baluster meet. This is an area of potential water leaks, since the wood baluster will shrink, and the shrinkage leaves a gap between the plaster and wood.

One method of preventing water infiltration at the baluster and plaster intersection is to provide a metal flashing collar that can be recessed into the baluster by making a saw cut around the baluster. (See Figure 22.9.) To provide further assurance of the seal at this point, caulking compound could be injected at the same time the collar is attached. Since the exterior plaster terminates at the collar, the metal can be formed to receive and ground the plaster. (See Figure 22.10 for pictorial view of this assembly.)

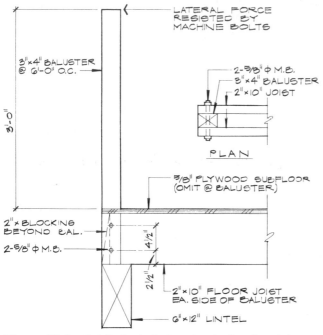

Figure 22.5 Detail of a baluster attached to floor joists.

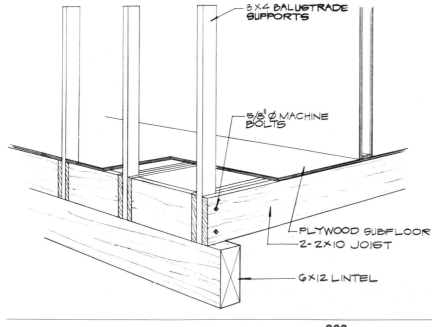

Figure 22.6 Pictorial view of a baluster attached to floor joists.

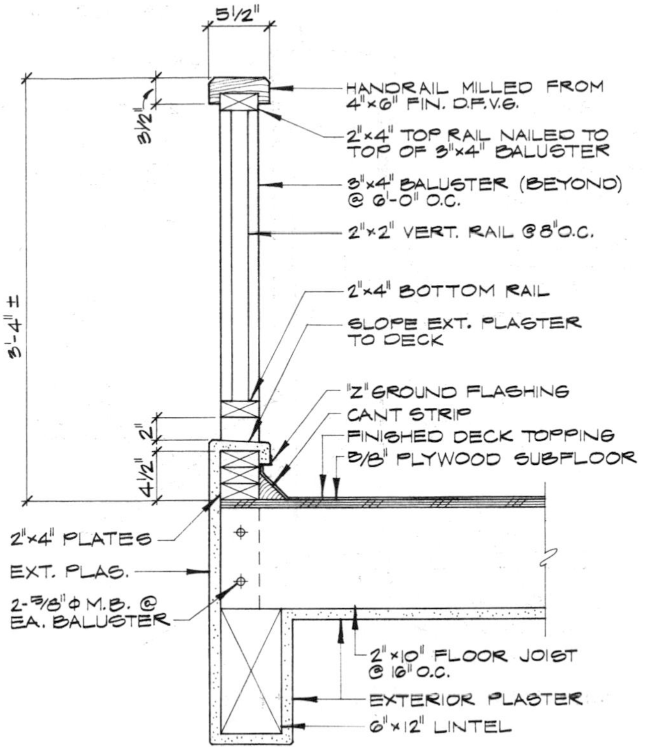
5 1/2"
3 1/2"
3'-4" ±
2"
4 1/2"
HANDRAIL MILLED FROM 4"x6" FIN. D.F.V.G.
2"x4" TOP RAIL NAILED TO TOP OF 3"x4" BALUSTER
3"x4" BALUSTER (BEYOND) @ 6'-0" O.C.
2"x2" VERT. RAIL @ 8" O.C.
2"x4" BOTTOM RAIL
SLOPE EXT. PLASTER TO DECK
"Z" GROUND FLASHING
CANT STRIP
FINISHED DECK TOPPING
5/8" PLYWOOD SUBFLOOR
2"x4" PLATES
EXT. PLAS.
2-5/8" ϕ M.B. @ EA. BALUSTER
2"x10" FLOOR JOIST @ 16" O.C.
EXTERIOR PLASTER
6"x12" LINTEL

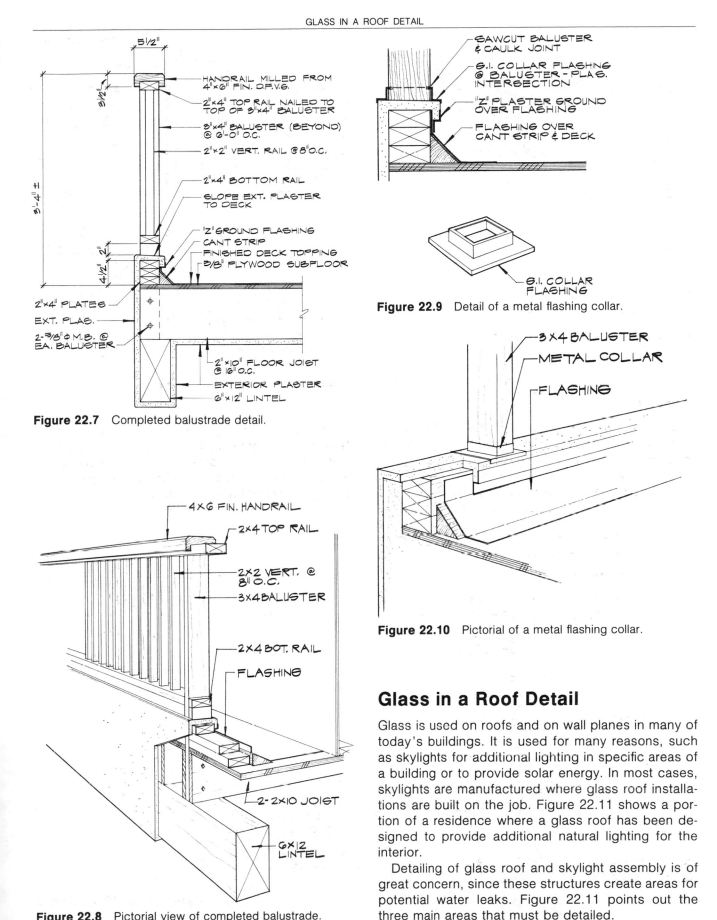

Figure 22.7 Completed balustrade detail.

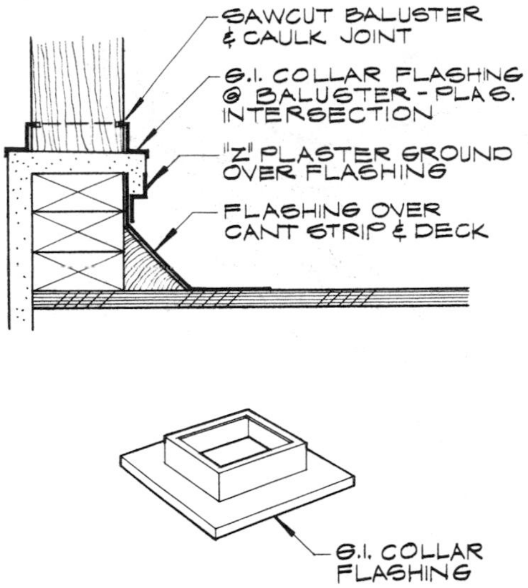
SAWCUT BALUSTER & CAULK JOINT
G.I. COLLAR FLASHING @ BALUSTER - PLAS. INTERSECTION
"Z" PLASTER GROUND OVER FLASHING
FLASHING OVER CANT STRIP & DECK
G.I. COLLAR FLASHING

Figure 22.9 Detail of a metal flashing collar.

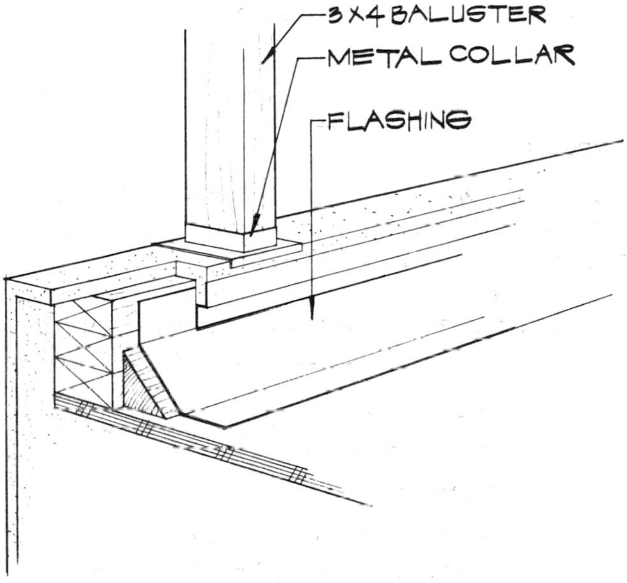
3X4 BALUSTER
METAL COLLAR
FLASHING

Figure 22.10 Pictorial of a metal flashing collar.

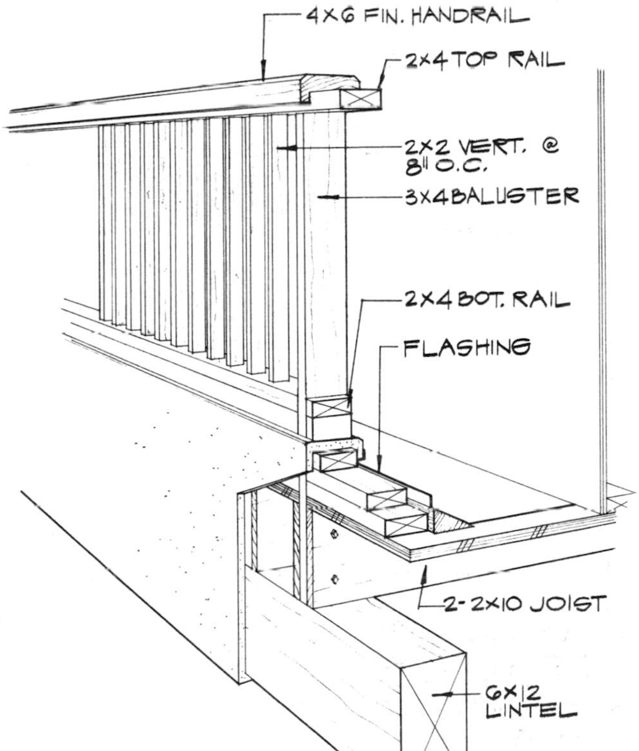
4X6 FIN. HANDRAIL
2X4 TOP RAIL
2X2 VERT. @ 8" O.C.
3X4 BALUSTER
2X4 BOT. RAIL
FLASHING
2-2X10 JOIST
6X12 LINTEL

Figure 22.8 Pictorial view of completed balustrade.

Glass in a Roof Detail

Glass is used on roofs and on wall planes in many of today's buildings. It is used for many reasons, such as skylights for additional lighting in specific areas of a building or to provide solar energy. In most cases, skylights are manufactured where glass roof installations are built on the job. Figure 22.11 shows a portion of a residence where a glass roof has been designed to provide additional natural lighting for the interior.

Detailing of glass roof and skylight assembly is of great concern, since these structures create areas for potential water leaks. Figure 22.11 points out the three main areas that must be detailed.

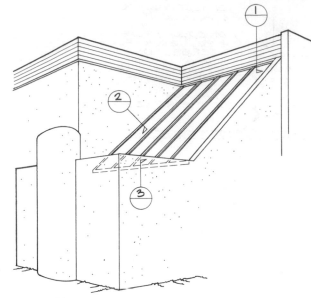

Figure 22.11   Pictorial of a glass roof.

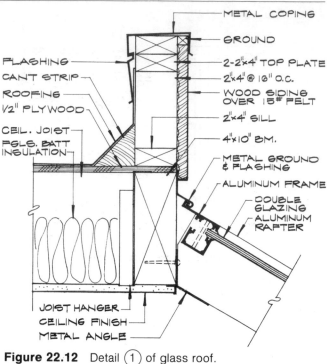

Figure 22.12   Detail ① of glass roof.

Detail ①

In detail ①, which is shown in Figure 22.12, spaced aluminum rafters are attached to a wood beam by metal angles. Figure 22.13 illustrates this condition pictorially. Inside the rafter opening an aluminum frame is attached to the rafter to receive the glass. Most manufacturers provide extrusions that will ac-

commodate a flashing attachment to prevent leaks. Note the metal ground and flashing in Figure 22.12. In most installations, double glazing will be incorporated to satisfy the heat gain and heat loss coefficients of energy conservation design criteria.

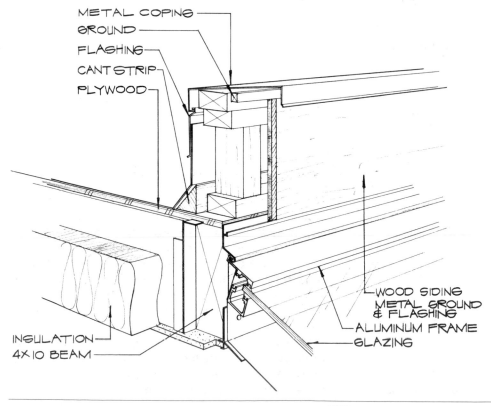

Figure 22.13   Pictorial view of detail ①.

Detail ②

A detail of the exterior wall assembly, area ② in Figure 22.11, is shown in Figure 22.14. Note again that the extrusion above the aluminum rafter has been manufactured to provide an attachment for the wall flashing. For this wall condition, backing or solid blocking will be required behind the flashing so that the flashing can be nailed securely between the 2 × 4 studs. A pictorial drawing for this condition is shown in Figure 22.15.

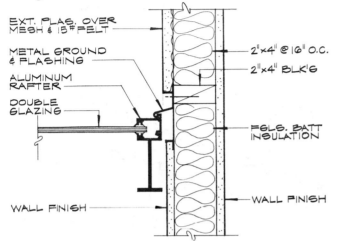

EXT. PLAS. OVER MESH & 15# PELT

METAL GROUND & FLASHING

ALUMINUM RAFTER

DOUBLE GLAZING

2"×4" @ 16" O.C.

2"×4" BLK'G

FGLS. BATT INSULATION

WALL FINISH

WALL FINISH

Figure 22.14 Detail ② of glass roof.

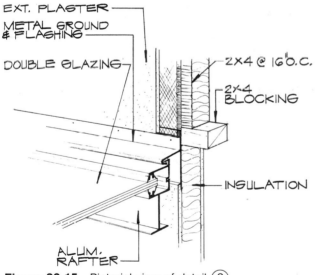

EXT. PLASTER

METAL GROUND & FLASHING

DOUBLE GLAZING

2×4 @ 16" O.C.

2×4 BLOCKING

INSULATION

ALUM. RAFTER

Figure 22.15 Pictorial view of detail ②.

Detail ③

Detail ③ in Figure 22.11 is shown in Figure 22.16. It shows a raised curb at a lower roof and the glass roof attachment to the curb. The recommended flashing for the raised curb can be detailed similar to that of a parapet wall where galvanized metal is cladded over the top of the curb and the metal flashing from the roof below. Above this assembly, the aluminum rafters are attached to the curb, and the manufac-

tured end enclosure is attached to the rafters. Note that openings are provided for moisture that is generated by condensation below the glass. Figure 22.17 shows a pictorial representation of this detail.

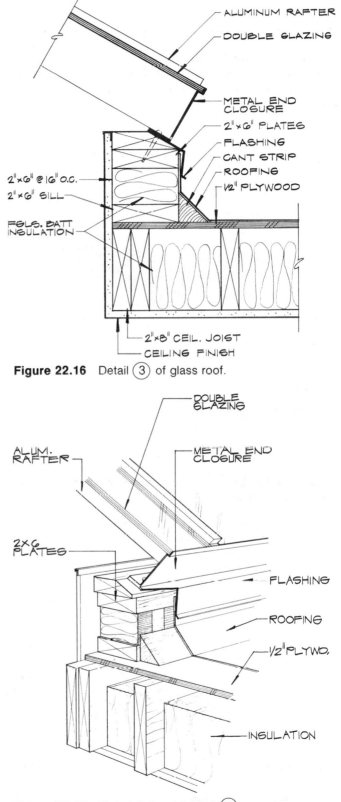

ALUMINUM RAFTER

DOUBLE GLAZING

METAL END CLOSURE

2"×6" PLATES

FLASHING

CANT STRIP

ROOFING

1/2" PLYWOOD

2"×6" @ 16" O.C.

2"×6" SILL

FGLS. BATT INSULATION

2"×8" CEIL. JOIST

CEILING FINISH

Figure 22.16 Detail ③ of glass roof.

DOUBLE GLAZING

ALUM. RAFTER

METAL END CLOSURE

2×6 PLATES

FLASHING

ROOFING

1/2" PLYWD.

INSULATION

Figure 22.17 Pictorial view of detail ③.

Roof Insulation Detail

As discussed in the introduction, the evolution of a detail can be influenced by various factors. One of these factors is energy conservation.

Roof with Planking and Rigid Board Insulation

The method illustrated in Figure 22.18 places a 2" plank directly over the exposed beams. The planking will provide a structural entity for the support of the roof, as well as the exposed sloping wood ceiling. To satisfy the insulation requirements for this method of assembly, rigid insulation board is required. Depending on the specific regional requirements, the thickness of this material may range from $1\frac{1}{2}$" to $3\frac{1}{2}$". Figure 22.19 is a pictorial view of this detail.

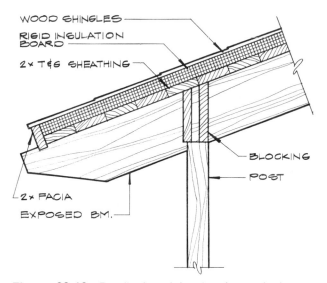

Figure 22.18 Detail of roof framing for a sloping wood ceiling using exposed beams.

Roof with Rafters and Fiberglass Insulation

An alternate method for achieving the desired ceiling design is shown in Figure 22.20. In this method, the roof framing is 2 × rafters that span across the exposed beams to provide structural support for the roof as well as to provide members to attach a sloping wood ceiling. In this case, the 1 × finish wood ceiling would be nonstructural. For this method, insulation such as fiberglass batts can be installed between the plywood roof sheathing and the 1 × T & G finish ceiling. A pictorial of this method is shown in Figure 22.21.

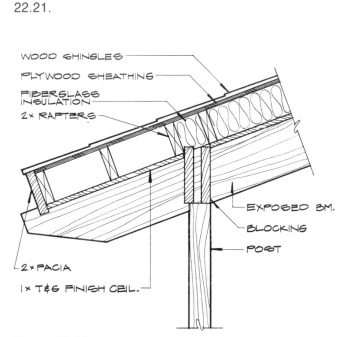

Figure 22.20 Detail of roof framing for a sloping wood ceiling and exposed beams.

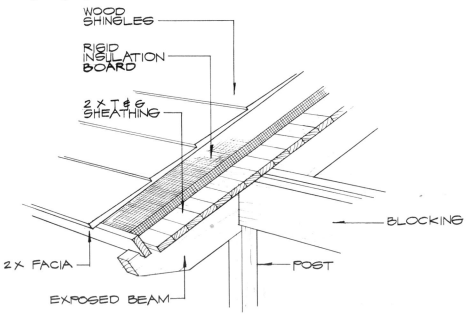

Figure 22.19 Pictorial view of a roof with sloping wood ceiling and exposed beams.

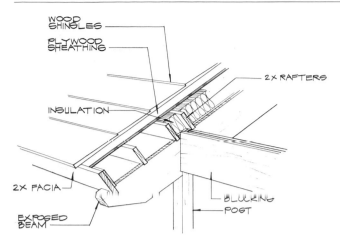

Figure 22.21 Pictorial view of a roof with sloping ceiling and exposed beams.

Masonry Wall Insulation Detail

Insulation requirements for energy conservation coefficients for concrete block walls vary because of regional differences. For example, as shown in Figure 22.22, foam insulation can be used to fill the open cells in a concrete block wall. In some regions of the country, however, the use of insulating foam would be impossible. In such areas, reinforcing steel and solid grouting are required due to seismic and wind forces, and the steel and grout have to go in all or some cells. To satisfy insulation requirements in these areas, we can attach a manufactured panel of styro-

Figure 22.22 Detail of a masonry wall with foam insulation.

Figure 22.23 Detail of a masonry wall with foam and gypsum board insulation.

foam and gypsum board to the concrete block wall, as shown in Figure 22.23. The thickness of these panels depends on the required coefficient. Note that this method of adding thickness to a wall would affect other architectural details, such as door and window details.

Wall Projection Above Roof

Wall projections above a roof, such as those shown in Figure 22.24, require special attention at the areas with potential leakage problems. These walls house glu-lam beams, the main structural members for the support of the roof. A detail of the wall section in Figure 22.25 illustrates the primary framing members required at this assembly. Note that the main areas of

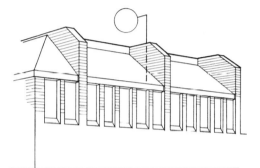

Figure 22.24 Pictorial of major wall projections above a roof.

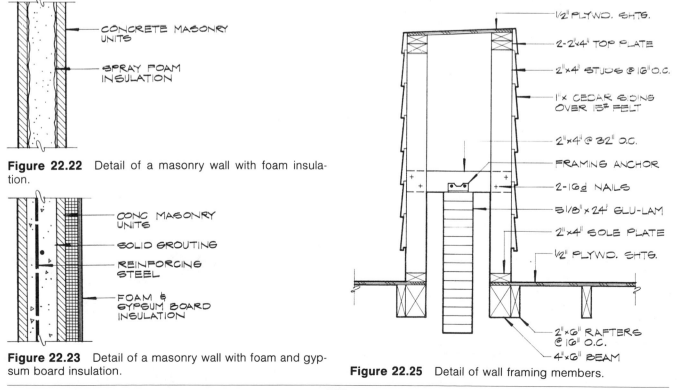

Figure 22.25 Detail of wall framing members.

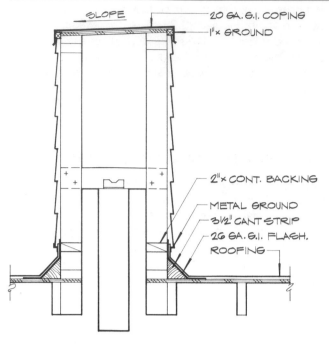

Figure 22.26 Final detail of a roof flashing.

concern for water infiltration are at the top of the wall and at the wall and roof intersections. At the top of the wall, two layers of building paper are applied over and directly above the plywood sheathing. Over the wood siding, there is a 20 gauge galvanized iron coping. This lid should completely seal the various joints at the top of the wall. On each side of the wall, where the wall and roof intersect, a cant is detailed, with 26-gauge galvanized iron flashing going directly above the cant strip and roof sheathing, as well as running vertically up the wall and behind the wood siding and building paper. After the completion of this assembly, the finished built-up roofing application is installed. This final assembly of a roof flashing is shown in Figure 22.26.

Eave Detail

Building code requirements may dictate the major components necessary to complete a detailed assembly. To see how, consider Figure 22.27, which is a preliminary eave detail for a small commercial building. As shown, 3 × 4 wood ledgers bolted to the masonry wall provide the main attachment for the remaining 2 × 4 wood members that formulate the design of this eave. Figure 22.28 illustrates this assembly in a pictorial view. Upon completion of the building plan review, it was found that this specific detail was not allowed to be built of combustible materials such as wood members. Therefore, the detail had to be redesigned using steel members to satisfy

the noncombustible material requirements. Figure 22.29 shows prefabricated steel angles designed to be attached to the masonry wall with anchor bolts. From this point, steel studs are attached to the top angle as well as to a continuous steel stud channel, which is attached to the bottom angle. Expanded metal lath is attached to the steel studs in preparation for the application of cement plaster. This eave detail is shown pictorially in Figure 22.30.

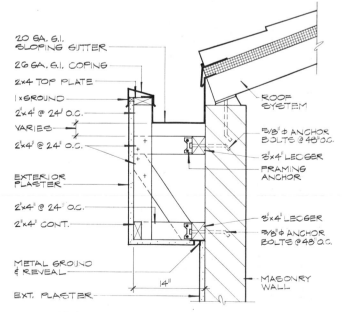

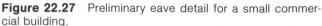

Figure 22.27 Preliminary eave detail for a small commercial building.

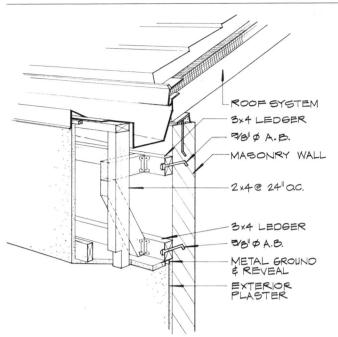

ROOF SYSTEM
3x4 LEDGER
5/8" Ø A.B.
MASONRY WALL
2x4 @ 24" O.C.
3x4 LEDGER
5/8" Ø A.B.
METAL GROUND & REVEAL
EXTERIOR PLASTER

Figure 22.28   Pictorial view of eave assembly.

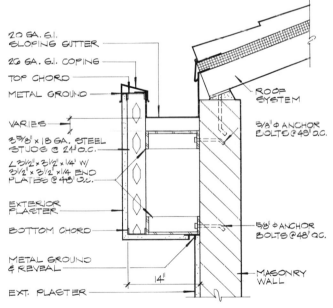

20 GA. G.I. SLOPING GUTTER
20 GA. G.I. COPING
TOP CHORD
METAL GROUND
VARIES
3 5/8" x 18 GA. STEEL STUDS @ 24" O.C.
L 3 1/2" x 3 1/2" x 1/4" W/ 3 1/2" x 3 1/2" x 1/4 END PLATES @ 48" O.C.
EXTERIOR PLASTER
BOTTOM CHORD
METAL GROUND & REVEAL
EXT. PLASTER
ROOF SYSTEM
5/8" Ø ANCHOR BOLTS @ 48" O.C.
5/8" Ø ANCHOR BOLTS @ 48" O.C.
14"
MASONRY WALL

Figure 22.29   Eave detail with prefabricated steel angles.

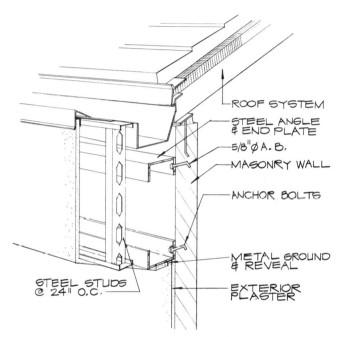

ROOF SYSTEM
STEEL ANGLE & END PLATE
5/8" Ø A.B.
MASONRY WALL
ANCHOR BOLTS
STEEL STUDS @ 24" O.C.
METAL GROUND & REVEAL
EXTERIOR PLASTER

Figure 22.30   Pictorial of eave detail with steel angles.

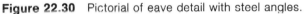

Regional Differences

Architectural details that are formulated as a result of the influences of energy conservation requirements may vary from region to region since many states have adopted their own energy conservation standards.

When detailing a structure using masonry walls, the architect will be highly influenced by the region as to how the walls will be constructed and insulated.

Summary

Architectural draftspersons should be aware of the various factors that influence and dictate the formulation of a detail. This chapter showed how factors such as architectural design, structural design, building code requirements, and energy requirements can influence architectural details.

An important factor is the necessity of creating various methods by which to solve detailing requirements. It is recommended this be done with freehand sketches for review and selection.

23
WELDING

Preview   Chapter 23 introduces welding. Although welding is not a specific detail to be drawn in and of itself in architecture, knowledge of it is absolutely necessary when working with steel.

Like all previous chapters, this one begins by establishing the need and background for welding. Initially discussed are the different methods of welding, the type of joints, and the type of welds commonly used in the architectural industry.

The second part of this chapter deals with the designations used to represent the various welds, the understanding of and need for standard symbols, and suggested minimums established by a national society on welding.

After reading this chapter, the architectural draftsperson will:

1. Understand the different types of welding used in the field.
2. Describe the various types of joints.
3. Differentiate among the types of welds used.
4. Draft, on a detail, the correct welding symbol for the desired weld.
5. Interpret welding symbols drawn by others.

Metals can be bonded together by bolts, rivets, screws, or other fastening devices. Another method, totally different, is welding. Welding plays a large part in the architectural industry, and an architect must be familiar with its implications for detailing.

Weld symbol indicates the type of weld, whereas welding symbol is the shape and form of the symbol being used to communicate the information being conveyed.

Welding uses a combination of symbols, letters, and numbers to denote what is desired and the prescribed method to be employed. The difficult part is that the symbols used may not graphically represent the work to be done. Like chemistry, which uses symbols, welding uses symbols that have a particular significance when drawn in a certain fashion.

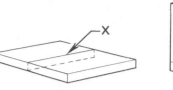
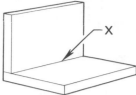

BUTT JOINT   CORNER JOINT

TEE JOINT   LAP JOINT

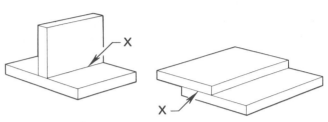

EDGE JOINT
X—AREA TO RECEIVE WELD

Figure 23.1 Types of joints.

Welding Methods

Fundamentally, there are three methods of welding. The first, called the oxyacetylene method, widely known as gas welding, uses a flame of an extremely high temperature that literally melts the metal.

The second is an electric-arc method, commonly called arc-welding. This method uses the heat of an electric arc to fuse or cut metal. The third method is called resistance welding in which metals are held tightly together and electric current is rushed through them. The resistance of the metal to this current eventually causes the metals to fuse (weld) together.

This chapter is primarily concerned with the first two methods, since these are the most widely used in the architectural profession.

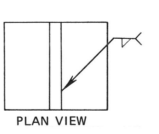

DESIRED WELD

Types of Joints

There are various types of joints that can be achieved with metal: butt joint, corner joint, tee joint, lap joint, and edge joint. These joints are illustrated in Figure 23.1. Each calls for a particular type of weld.

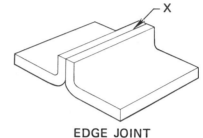

PLAN VIEW

SYMBOL IS   ▽

Types of Welds

We can weld various points by three types of gas and arc welds — the fillet, plug or slot, and spot or seam weld — and seven varieties of the groove weld. These types of welds are shown in Figure 23.2 to 23.13. Each type of weld has a particular symbol assigned to it that is drawn above each pictorial drawing.

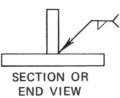

SECTION OR
END VIEW

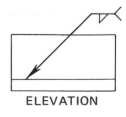

ELEVATION

Figure 23.2 Fillet welds. (Reproduced by permission of the American Welding Society.)

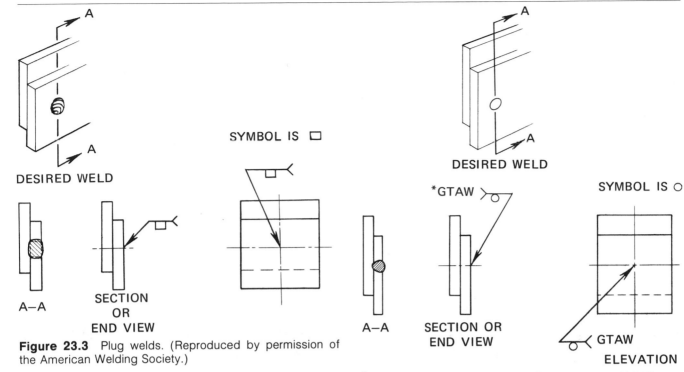

SYMBOL IS □

Figure 23.3 Plug welds. (Reproduced by permission of the American Welding Society.)

SYMBOL IS ○

*TYPE OF WELD (GAS TUNGSTEN—ARC SPOT)

Figure 23.5 Spot weld. (Reproduced by permission of the American Welding Society.)

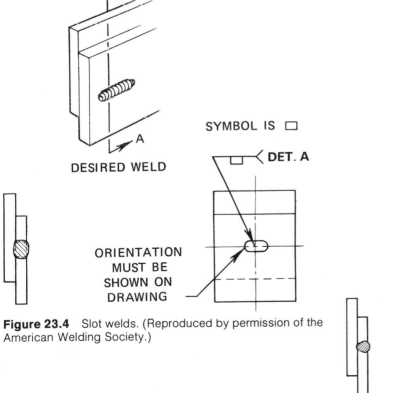

SYMBOL IS □

DET. A

ORIENTATION MUST BE SHOWN ON DRAWING

Figure 23.4 Slot welds. (Reproduced by permission of the American Welding Society.)

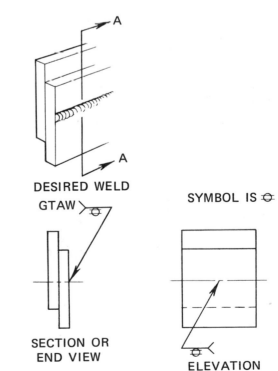

SYMBOL IS ⊖

Figure 23.6 Seam weld. (Reproduced by permission of the American Welding Society.)

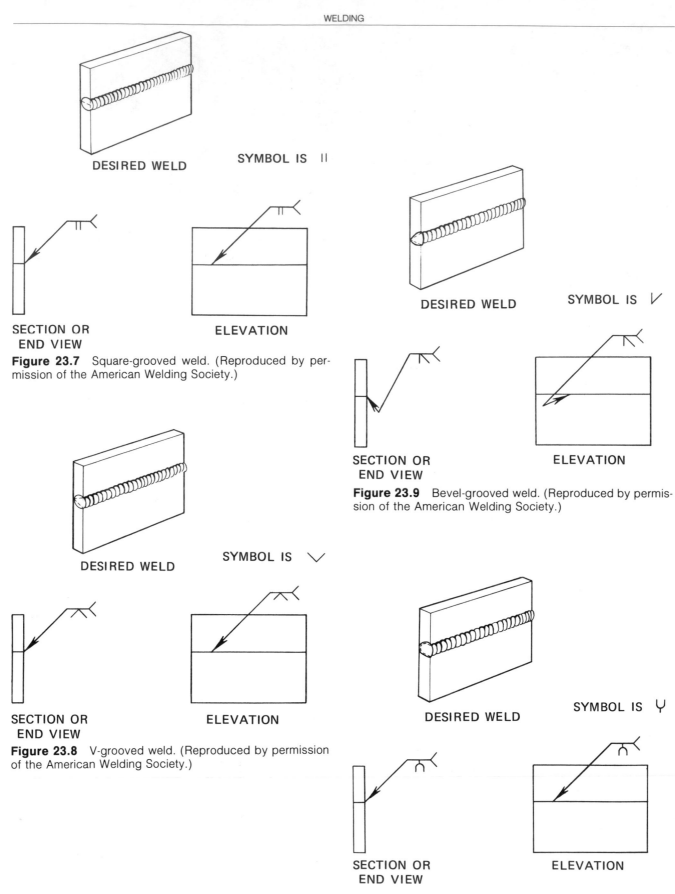

DESIRED WELD   **SYMBOL IS** ‖

SECTION OR END VIEW   **ELEVATION**

Figure 23.7   Square-grooved weld. (Reproduced by permission of the American Welding Society.)

DESIRED WELD   **SYMBOL IS** ∨

SECTION OR END VIEW   **ELEVATION**

Figure 23.9   Bevel-grooved weld. (Reproduced by permission of the American Welding Society.)

DESIRED WELD   **SYMBOL IS** ∨

SECTION OR END VIEW   **ELEVATION**

Figure 23.8   V-grooved weld. (Reproduced by permission of the American Welding Society.)

DESIRED WELD   **SYMBOL IS** ∪

SECTION OR END VIEW   **ELEVATION**

Figure 23.10   U-grooved weld. (Reproduced by permission of the American Welding Society.)

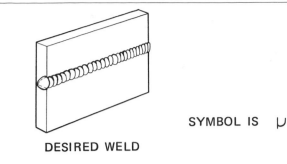

SYMBOL IS ⊔

DESIRED WELD

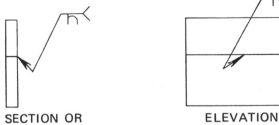

**SECTION OR
END VIEW**

ELEVATION

Figure 23.11 J-grooved weld. (Reproduced by permission of the American Welding Society.)

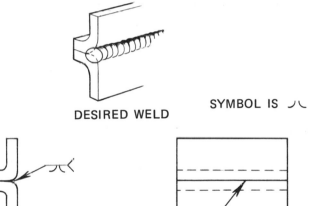

DESIRED WELD

SYMBOL IS ⅃⌣

**SECTION OR
END VIEW**

ELEVATION

Figure 23.12 Flare-V-grooved weld. (Reproduced by permission of the American Welding Society.)

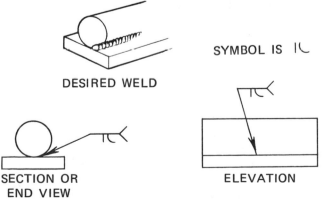

SYMBOL IS I⌣

DESIRED WELD

**SECTION OR
END VIEW**

ELEVATION

Figure 23.13 Flare-bevel-grooved weld. (Reproduced by permission of the American Welding Society.)

Developing Weld Symbols

As shown in Figure 23.14, the basic weld symbols start with an arrow and a leader similar to those used for call outs on a detail. The arrowhead usually points to the location where the weld is to be made, and the horizontal portion of the leader, called the reference line or shank, contains vital information about the weld itself. It is also permissible to use multiple arrowheads on a welding symbol, as in Figure 23.15.

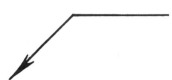

Figure 23.14 Basic welding symbols.

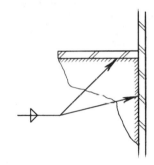
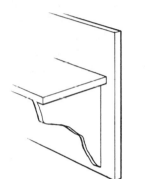

Figure 23.15 Use of multiple arrowheads.

When the symbol is on the underside of the reference line, the weld is to take place where the arrow is pointing. For example, Figure 23.16 shows samples of two fillet welds and a square weld with the weld on the arrow side.

It should be noted that since the fillet weld is not symmetrical, the vertical line of the fillet symbol is always drawn on the left side.

When the symbol is on the top side, the weld takes place opposite to where the arrow is pointing. This affords the detailer greater flexibility because if the detail is crowded on the side of the weld, the symbol can be put on the top of the reference line and can point to the weld from the opposite side.

When the symbol appears on the top and bottom of the reference line, it indicates that the weld is to be done on both sides. Both-side designation is *not* used on plug or slot, spot or projection, and seam welds. If the symbol bisects the reference line, as is the case in Figure 23.33, there is *no* side designation. Three examples of positioning of symbols on the reference line are illustrated in Figure 23.17.

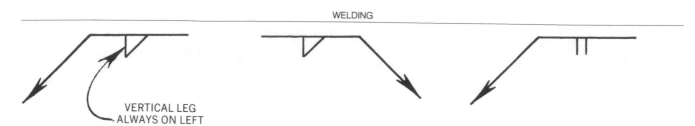

Figure 23.16 Weld on arrow side.

If a round circle is put at the joint of the reference and arrowhead lines, this means "weld all the way around." This is a good symbol to know for such items as pipe columns. See Figure 23.18.

The solid dot shown in Figure 23.18 represents a weld to be done on the job site. This is called a field weld.

A melt-thru symbol, shown in Figure 23.19, is used when the weld is made from one side yet 100 percent joint or member penetration plus reinforcement is required. The only dimension placed on the symbol is that of the reinforcing. The symbol itself is placed on the opposite side of the required welding symbol.

A back or back weld symbol, as shown in Figure 23.20, is still another symbol to show the workers in the field a procedure beyond the normal weld. Its primary purpose is to indicate that a small weld takes place on the opposite side of the weld first, preceding the regular weld.

In developing the symbol, all the leader-type welding symbols point directly to the area to be welded or its opposite side. The one exception is when the area to be welded is not symmetrical. A bevel-groove weld, shown in Figures 23.9 and 23.20, and the J-groove weld, shown in Figure 23.11, are good examples of unsymmetrical welds. Notice the unique shape of the leader. Its arrowhead always points to the side that is perpendicular and the odd leader is used to emphasize that fact.

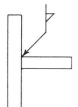

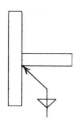

Figure 23.17 Positioning of symbols on the reference line.

Figure 23.18 Weld all-around and field weld.

Figure 23.19 Melt-thru symbol.

DESIRED WELD $\frac{1}{16}$ SYMBOL

Figure 23.20 Back weld symbol. (Reproduced by permission of the American Welding Society.)

Size Designations

The number on the left side of the symbol (usually expressed as a fraction or decimal equivalent with no inch marks) indicates to the welder the size of weld to be made. See Figure 23.21 for an example. If two fractions appear, as shown in Figure 23.22, this indicates a weld having unequal legs: the first fraction indicating the vertical leg distance, the second fraction indicating the horizontal leg distance.

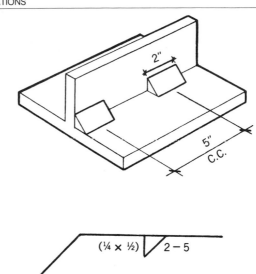

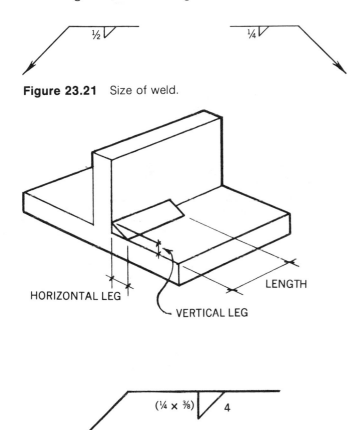

Figure 23.21   Size of weld.

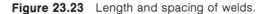

Figure 23.23   Length and spacing of welds.

being welded, because the strength of the metal is not increased by the additional thickness of the weld. For example, it does very little good to call for an $\frac{1}{2}''$ fillet weld for two pieces $\frac{1}{4}''$ in thickness.

If the architect can show the weld graphically, a hatching type of line may be used. See Figure 23.24. The left weld in Figure 23.24 is without definite end lines, while the right weld shows definite end lines.

Figure 23.22   Size and length of weld.

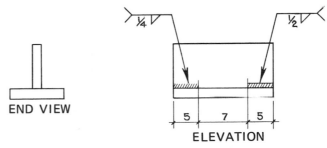

Figure 23.24   Showing a weld graphically.

The length of the weld and its spacing (if any) is on the right side of the symbol, as shown in Figure 23.23. The first number in this example indicates the length of the weld and the second number, the spacing. Thus, Figure 23.23 shows a 2 inch long weld spaced 4 inches center to center (that is 5″ from the center of one 2″ weld to the center of the next 2″ weld).

A second number next to the length of the weld indicates center to center spacing. Figure 23.23 shows a $\frac{1}{4}''$ wide by $\frac{1}{2}''$ high by 2″ long weld 5″ center to center (that is, 5″ from the center of one 2″ weld to the center of the next 2″ weld).

A good rule of thumb is that it is unnecessary to make the weld larger than the thickness of the piece

Welding symbols can be drawn at an angle or vertically if the space requires it. Lettering follows normal noting conventions.

Sizes and their locational descriptions are shown in Figures 23.25 to 23.29.

The reference line is always horizontal and is read from the bottom of the drawing. To this end, vertical or angular reference lines are not used. The line connecting the arrowhead to the reference line can change directions, as shown in Figure 23.11. Only the horizontally drawn reference line should contain sizes, spacing, length of weld, weld symbols, and so on.

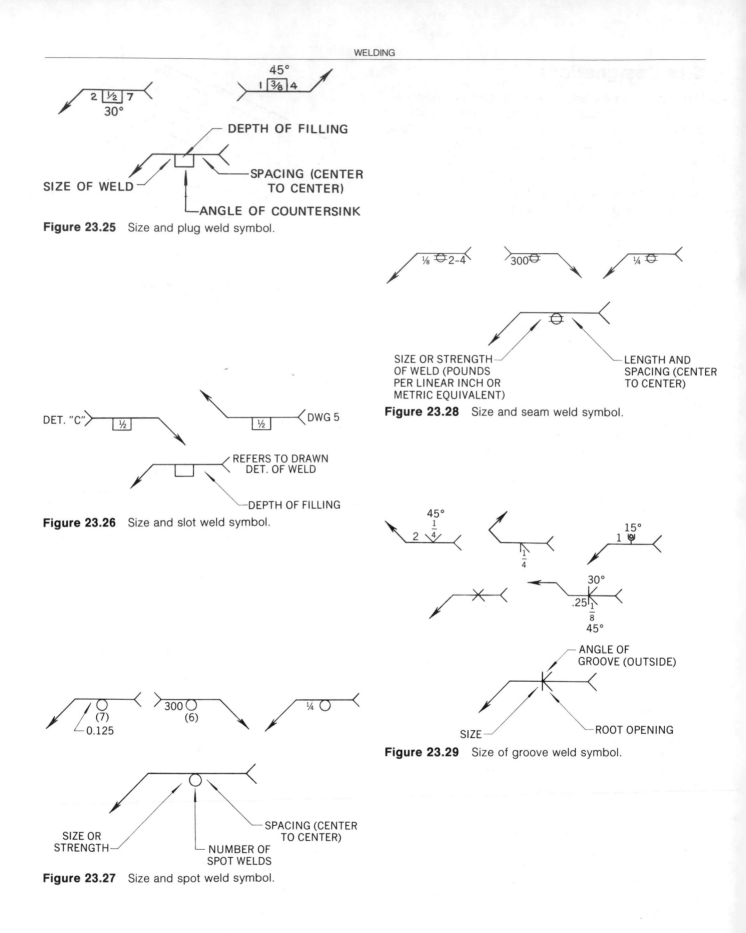

Figure 23.25 Size and plug weld symbol.

Figure 23.26 Size and slot weld symbol.

Figure 23.27 Size and spot weld symbol.

Figure 23.28 Size and seam weld symbol.

Figure 23.29 Size of groove weld symbol.

Weld Finishes

If you wish to have the welded surface finished to a greater degree, a straight line next to the symbol is used. See Figure 23.30. Letters may be used to designate various types of finish. The symbol "G" is used for grinding, "M" for machining, and "C" for chipping. See Figure 23.31 for samples.

Notice that in the final sample in Figure 23.31 the line next to the symbol is drawn with a convex arc. This also represents the acceptable finished shape of the chipped weld.

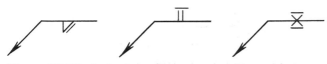

Figure 23.30 Indicating contour on a weld.

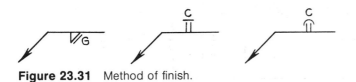

Figure 23.31 Method of finish.

Specifications and References

Additional operational or specification notes on the symbol are put at the end of the shank. References to other locations or other details or notes are also marked in this location. See Figure 23.32. The shank is drawn with two diagonal lines on the end of it, much like the back side of an arrow.

Figure 23.32 References to other details or notes.

Symbol Summary

Figures 23.33 and 23.34 are also included to provide the architectural draftsperson with a reference in summary form of what has been discussed in this chapter. Figure 23.35 gives standard welding symbols used by the American Welding Society.

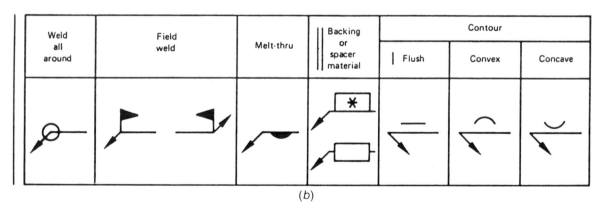

	Groove						
Square	Scarf*	V	Bevel	U	J	Flare-V	Flare-bevel

Fillet	Plug or slot	Spot or projection	Seam	Back or backing	Surfacing	Flange	
						Edge	Corner

(a)

Weld all around	Field weld	Melt-thru	Backing or spacer material	Contour		
				Flush	Convex	Concave

(b)

Figure 23.33 (a) Basic welding symbols, (b) supplementary symbols, and (c) standard location of elements of a welding symbol. (Reproduced by permission of the American Welding Society.)

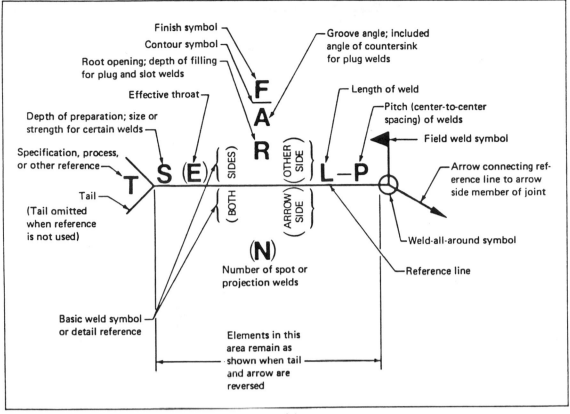

(c)

Figure 23.33 (Continued)

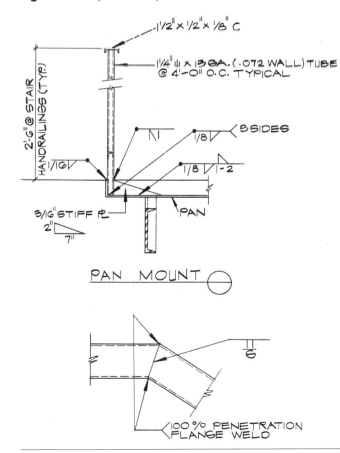

Figure 23.34 Drafted detail with typical welding samples.

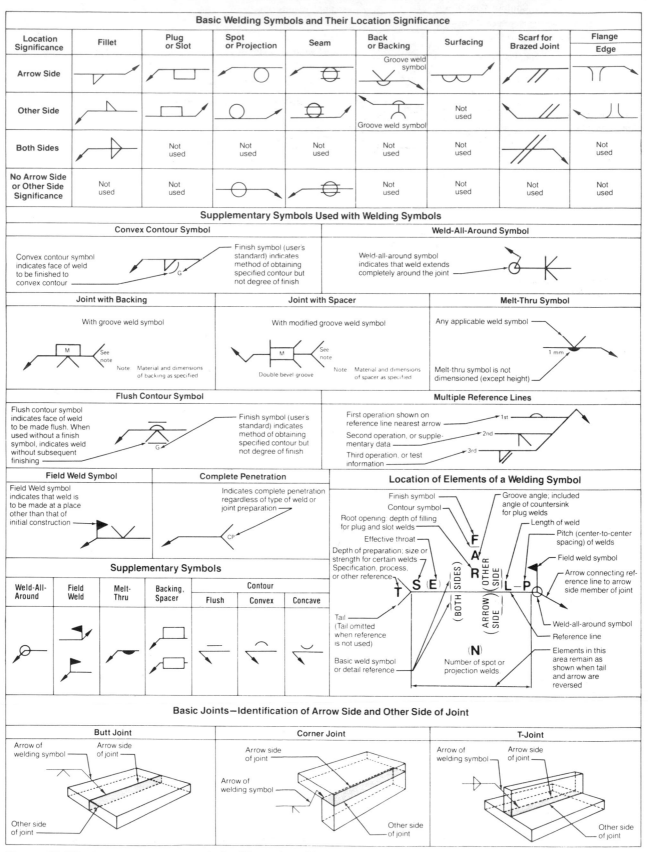

Figure 23.35 Standard welding symbols. (Reproduced by permission of the American Welding Society.)

STANDARD WELDING SYMBOLS

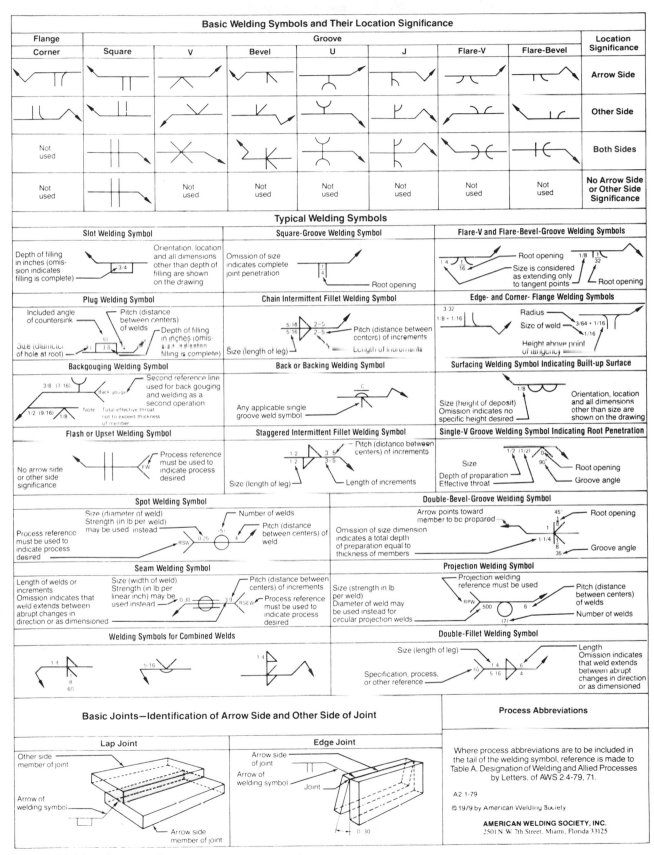

Figure 23.35 *(Continued)*

Regional Differences and Building Codes

As established by the American Welding Society, welding is an acceptable method nationally and the architectural draftsperson need not be concerned with regional or code differences.

Summary

Although welding is not used in every architectural structure, all architectural draftspersons must possess a complete understanding of welding if they are to be of value to an architectural firm. Somewhere in their detailing experiences they will be called on to draft a set of details using steel and, subsequently, welding. It is equally important for the detailer to read and interpret shop drawings that use welding symbols. This understanding allows logical detailing and comprehension of the total scope of the construction. If, for example, parts are to be welded in the field, as designated by detail, the draftsperson must be absolutely sure that the welder has enough space to perform the assigned welding task. One of the functions of the detailer is to avoid unattainable tasks in the field.

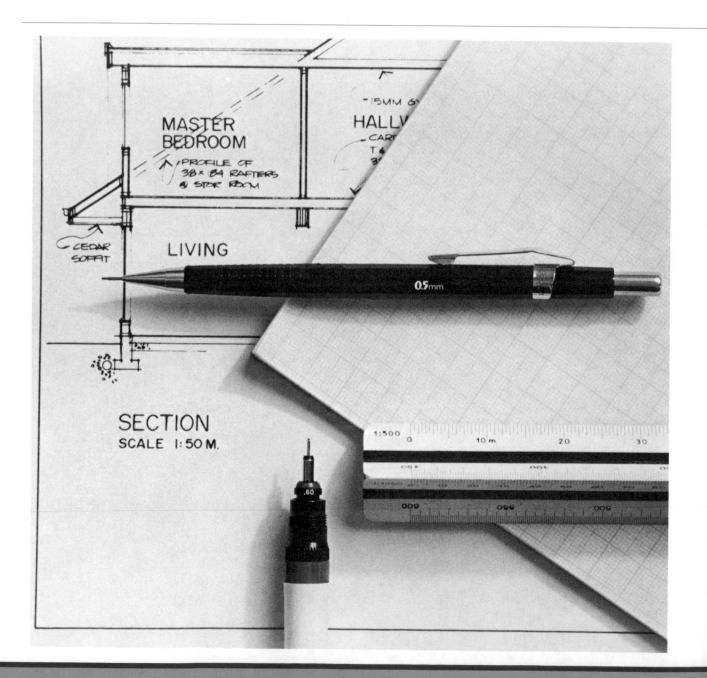

24
METRIC MEASUREMENTS

Preview   Chapter 24 bridges the gap between what is now and what will be —
the conversion from the English system of measurements to the now mandated
metric system. This chapter will use existing trends and previous experience to
develop a method of approach that is sound, with special attention paid to arithmetical conversion.

   After reading this chapter, the architectural draftsperson will:

1. Begin to think metrically rather than think in the English system and convert.
2. Understand the nomenclature unique to the metric system.
3. Translate the values of the English system to the metric system.
4. Convert from one unit of value to another within the metric system.
5. Designate metric values on working drawings and details.
6. Understand how to round off numbers and stay within code limits.

The English system has a basic unit of measurement for everything. Liquid measurement differs from weight, and weight differs from linear measurements. We presently measure in feet, miles, quarts, pounds and so forth, and each unit has a peculiar conversion that is hard to memorize. Four quarts to a gallon, 12 inches to a foot, 16 ounces to a pound are samples of the unusual equivalences.

The metric system is based on tenths and units of tens. In the beginning, you might find this conversion difficult, but it will be much easier in the long run.

Once this total change is made and everything is measured in one system, the problem of converting from one system to another will disappear; however, during the interim we should be able to convert. Until all codes, workers, manufacturers, and others convert, some measurements will be based upon one system or the other. Architectural draftspersons may be able to think metrically and draw using metric scales, but if the code or lumber used is not in metric increments, they must be able to convert.

Nomenclature

An architectural draftsperson deals predominantly with linear measurements as opposed to weights or speed, and so this chapter emphasizes changing from feet and inches to their metric equivalents.

The largest metric unit of measurement for use in the construction industry is the meter. The most recent standard measurement of a meter is the measurement of the swing of a pendulum during a one-second period. This swinging pendulum is made of platinum and is located at 45° latitude in France. Because of the nature of the way the standard meter is measured and the location of this standard, the length of a meter varies slightly throughout the world. It is hoped that attempts at standardization by the International Standards Organization (I.S.O.) will prove successful, because if different lengths are used for the standard meter, building products made in one country might not correspond to the needs of another.*

Since we are working in tenths, the next unit of measurement below a meter is a decimeter or one-tenth of a meter. It should be noted here that the unit decimeter is *not* widely used. One-tenth of a deci-

meter is a centimeter, and one-tenth of a centimeter is a millimeter. The proper sequence is

kilometer	= 1,000 meters	km
*hectometer	= 100 meters	hm
*decameter	= 10 meters	dam
meter		m
*decimeter	= $\frac{1}{10}$ meter	dm
centimeter	= $\frac{1}{100}$ meter	cm
millimeter	= $\frac{1}{1000}$ meter	mm

* Seldom used in modern drawings.

For architectural drafting, the millimeter and the meter are the most desirable units to use.

Notation Method*

Locate the decimal point in the center of the line of numerical value rather than close to the bottom of the line. For example, 304.65 is best written 304·65. However, the original notation is acceptable.

Commas are not used. Rather, spaces are left to denote where commas would have been. For example 10·34674 meters would be written 10·346 74 meters, and 506,473·21 meters would be written as 506 473·21 meters.

Abbreviations of metric units do not have special plural forms. For example, 50 centimenters is written 50 cm, *not* 50 cms. Note, also, the space between the number and the letters. It should read 50, space, centimeters: 50 cm.

Once a standard, such as "all measurements shall be in meters," is established for a set of drawings, it need not be noted on each drawing. A 4 by 8 sheet of plywood shall be called out not as 121 9·2 m × 243 8·4 m plywood but rather as 121 9·2 × 243 8 plywood. However, if a size is in a measure other than meters, this should be noted.

English Equivalents

The closest unit in the English system to a meter is a yard. There is no measurement near a foot. The conversions are as follows.

1 inch	=	2.54 cm
1 foot or 12 inches	=	30.48 cm
39.37 inches	=	1 meter

* Reprinted, by permission, from *The Professional Practice of Architectural Working Drawings,* copyright © 1984 by John Wiley & Sons, Inc.

Unit Change

In the English system, if we have 144 inches and wanted to convert to feet, the procedure would be to take the 144 inches and divide by 12 (12 inches to a foot).

In the metric system, the procedure is much easier — simply move the decimal point to the desired change. For example, to change 30.45 meters to decimeters, you simply move the decimal one digit to the right: 304.5 decimeters. Had you wished to make the measurement in centimeters, you move the decimal still another number to read 3045.0 centimeters.

In reverse, converting 62.54 centimeters into meters would read 0.6254 meters.

Conversion

With the knowledge of English system equivalents and unit changes, we shall now attempt a conversion from the English to the metric system. Let's assume that we wanted to convert 18 inches into centimeters. We can multiply 18 inches by 2.54 (2.54 centimeters per 1 inch) and get 45.72 centimeters, or

$$
\begin{array}{ll}
12'' & = 30.48 \text{ cm} \\
+\ 6'' \left(\dfrac{30.48}{2} \right) & = 15.24 \text{ cm} \\
\hline
18'' & = 45.72 \text{ cm}
\end{array}
$$

For another example, let us convert 27'-9"

$$
\begin{array}{ll}
27' = 30.48 \times 27 = 822.96 \text{ cm} \\
\ \ 9'' = \ \ 2.54 \times \ \ 9 = \underline{\ \ 22.86 \text{ cm}} \\
\ 845.82 \text{ cm}
\end{array}
$$

As shown, the 27 foot measurement is multiplied by 30.48, which is the number of centimeters per foot. Added to this is the product of 9 times 2.54 (the number of centimeters per inch), and the total is 845.82 centimeters. Changing this to meters, it would read 8.4582 meters.

An actual wood member is another problem because it must first be converted to its net size. For example, if we had a 2 × 4 stud that needed to be converted, it would first be reduced to $1\frac{1}{2} \times 3\frac{1}{2}$ — the net size — and then converted metrically. Refer to Chapter 6.

$1\frac{1}{2}$ or $1.5 \times 2.54 = 3.81$ cm or .0381 (meters)
$3\frac{1}{2}$ or $3.5 \times 2.54 = 8.89$ cm or .0889 (meters)

Metric Values

In architectural drafting, most drawings, such as floor plans, exterior elevations, and building sections, are noted and dimensioned in meters because of their sizes. Architectural details can also follow this procedure, and if this system is used, it is not necessary to label meter after each figure used. However, because of the size of the values used to describe the various parts and components in detailing, the drafter may choose to use centimeter or, in some instances, millimeter. To avoid any confusion, the scale of the detail and the unit of measurement should be listed as follows:

Scale 1 : 10   All values in centimeters.

Or each dimension should be noted with the value used.

Actual Versus Nominal*

Presently, lumber uses an odd system of notation. When a piece of lumber is drawn, it is drafted to its actual size (net size). In the notes describing this particular piece of wood, it is called out in its nominal size (call out size). For example, a 2 × 4 piece of wood is drawn at $1\frac{1}{2}'' \times 3\frac{1}{2}''$, but on the note pointing to this piece, it is still called a 2 × 4.

Therefore, when converting to metric, the $1\frac{1}{2}'' \times 3\frac{1}{2}''$ size must be converted and drawn to the actual size. There is no set procedure for the call out. Some drawings convert the 2 × 4 size metrically and note this piece of wood with the $1\frac{1}{2}'' \times 3\frac{1}{2}''$ size converted. A sample note might read as follows:

·0381 × ·0889 (net) STUD

It is hoped that when metric lumber size is established, the net and nominal sizes will be identical.

Limits

Due to the newness of using metrics in the American architectural profession, we are not yet geared to note things metrically. Lumber, reinforcing bars, glass, and other materials are still ordered in the English system. Their sizes, weights, and shapes are also still described in the English system.

There are three approaches that can be employed to cope with this situation. The first is to note only

* Reprinted, by permission, from *The Professional Practice of Architectural Working Drawings,* copyright © 1984 by John Wiley & Sons, Inc.

those things we have control over in metrics, such as the size of a room, the width of a footing, and so on, while noting 2 × 4 studs, #4 reinforcing rods, ½″ anchor bolts and the like, according to the manufacturer until they change to the metric system.

A second method is dual notation. Dimensions, notes, and all call outs are recorded twice. For example, a 35′-6″ dimension has a metric value of 10.8204 written directly below it.

If the bulk of the workers were working under the old system, they would continue to ignore the metric value and depend on the English system. If, however, the majority of the workers used the 10.8204 figure, you have prepared a value that cannot be measured accurately because the decimal is carried out too far. This problem is dealt with later.

The third and final method is to approach everything metrically. This may not be the best way in an office going through a transition, but it is the best method for a student who will eventually be asked to work totally in metrics.

Method of Conversion

If we are to use the method of converting everything to metrics, there are three procedures to consider.

First is that of "holding" certain dimension notes and call outs. If, for example, we were dealing with a #4 rebar (which is ½″ in size) and the manufacturer has not changed to metrics, we must convert the ½″ by multiplying ½″ × 2.54 and note the rebar as

1.27 cm rebar or .0127 rebar

The second procedure requires "rounding off." See Figure 24.1. In this figure, the scale on the top is

an enlarged one that you are accustomed to seeing. The scale directly below is in the same enlarged proportion but in metric units. The numbers in this scale are in centimeters. Notice how 2.54 centimeters equal an inch. Notice also that 1 centimeter is less than ½ inch. Initially, this is a hard proportion to relate to for anyone making the transition. Also note that half a centimeter (.5 cm) is smaller than a quarter of an inch and that 1 millimeter (one-tenth of a centimeter) is less than $\frac{1}{16}$ of an inch.

Now compare this knowledge with an actual number. Assume that you wish to dig a trench 12 inches wide for a footing.

12 inches = (12 × 2.54) = 30.48 cm

Hence, there are 30+ units less than ½ inches in size that we can measure. The .4 is less than $\frac{3}{16}$″, which is very difficult to measure and impossible to maintain on the job for a worker. This is the point when we should begin to round off.

The final number (.08) is even worse. It amounts to just a little more than $\frac{1}{32}$ of an inch — a measurement a draftsperson would have difficulty reading on the scale, let alone the person digging the trench. The final rounded off value should be 31.0 cm or 0.31. This trench is about $\frac{3}{16}$ inches larger than the desired 12 inches but is something the people out in the field can measure with their metric scales.

The third procedure of converting requires the judgment of whether to increase or decrease. Certain measurements must be increased in the rounding off process — the trench discussed previously is a good example. If we round this number off to 30.0 cm or .30, the measurement is less than 12 inches. If the 12 inch requirement were imposed by the local code, you would have thus broken the code. Had it been set at 12 inches for structural reasons, the building could be deemed unsafe. Another example is a planned opening for a piece of equipment. To round off smaller might result in the equipment's not fitting. You must be aware of situations that are dictated by health and safety.

The minimum depth of a step might be 10½ inches or 26.67 cm. Had we rounded this off to 26.0 cm, it would not meet the minimum standards for a stair.

The opposite of this type of converting is the need or process of decreasing the figure. The note for an anchor bolt is a good example for analyzing the feature; it reads

½″ × 10″ φ anchor bolt embedded 7″ into concrete, 6′-0″ o.c. and 12″ from corners.

The spacing of 6′-0″ on center is used to maintain a minimum number of anchor bolts along with their spacing. If we increase this number when converting,

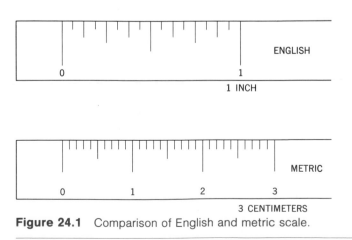

Figure 24.1 Comparison of English and metric scale.

we exceed the minimum spacing and therefore break the requirement as stated in the note.

The 12 inch measurement has the same effect. The intent is to have an anchor bolt at least 12 inches from the corners or less. We must, therefore, decrease the measurement to ensure that there is an anchor bolt closer than 12 inches from every corner.

The $\frac{1}{2}'' \times 10''$ ϕ (ϕ is a symbol for round) becomes a "holding" measurement since it comes from the manufacturer that way.

The final numerical value that reads "embedded 7 inches into concrete" must be thought out wisely. The bolt must be embedded enough for strength, yet left exposed adequately to penetrate a sill and still accommodate enough space for a washer and a nut.

The second and third processes are called *soft* conversion; that is, an English measurement is converted directly into a metric equivalent and then rounded off into a workable metric value. A *hard* conversion is the name given to changing the total approach. It is not just a numerical conversion but a change of media as well. If bricks are the medium for example, the procedure would be to subscribe to a brick that was sized metrically and dimension accordingly.

Listed are some of the recommended rounding off sizes:*

$\frac{1}{8}''$	= 3·2 mm	$1\frac{3}{4}''$	= 44·0 mm
$\frac{1}{4}''$	= 6·4 mm	$2''$	= 50·0 mm
$\frac{3}{8}''$	= 9·5 mm	$2\frac{1}{2}''$	= 63·0 mm
$\frac{1}{2}''$	= 12·7 mm	$3''$	= 75·0 mm
$\frac{5}{8}''$	= 16·0 mm	$4''$	= 100·0 mm
$\frac{3}{4}''$	= 19·0 mm	$6''$	= 150·0 mm
$\frac{7}{8}''$	= 22·0 mm	$8''$	= 200·0 mm
$1''$	= 25·0 mm	$10''$	= 250·0 mm
$1\frac{1}{4}''$	= 32·0 mm	$12''$	= 300·0 mm
$1\frac{1}{2}''$	= 38·0 mm		

Zero is used to avoid error in metrics. For example, .8 is written 0.8 or 0·8.

When other conversions are needed, round off fractions to the nearest 5 mm, inches to the nearest 25 mm, and feet to the nearest 0·1 meter.

Metric Scales

The metric scale is calibrated in much the same manner that the architectural scale is, including a variety

of scales, such as $\frac{1}{2}'' = 1'\text{-}0''$, $\frac{3}{4}'' = 1'\text{-}0''$, $1\frac{1}{2}'' = 1'\text{-}0''$, $3'' = 1'\text{-}0''$. The most common scales found on a metric scale are the following.

1 : 10	1 : 50
1 : 20	1 : 75
1 : 25	1 : 100
1 : 33$\frac{1}{3}$	1 : 125
1 : 40	

While these proportions may not mean anything initially, let us take one example and see what it means. The 1 : 10 scale indicates taking a known measurement (a meter) and making it 10 times smaller. See Figure 24.2. In other words, if you could visualize a meter (39.37 inches) and squeeze it until it was only one-tenth of its original size, you would have a 1 : 10 ratio scale. Everything you draw would be one-tenth of its original size.

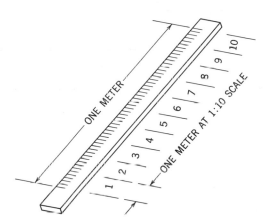

Figure 24.2 Pictorial of reduced scale.

This also applies to any other scale. A 1 : 50 scale means that the original meter has been reduced down 50 times its original value. Figures 24.3 and 24.4 show a full-size scale and its proportions.

If you wished to measure 12 inches or 30.48 cm (.3048 m) on a 1 : 10 scale, see Figure 24.5. If you find it difficult to transfer a $\frac{1}{4}'' = 1'\,0''$ drawing to a metric drawing for example, the chart below should help.

1 : 10 is approximately $1'' = 1'\text{-}0''$
1 : 20 is approximately $\frac{1}{2} = 1'\text{-}0''$
1 : 50 is approximately $\frac{1}{4} = 1'\text{-}0''$
1 : 100 is approximately $\frac{1}{8} = 1'\text{-}0''$

Of the scales mentioned, the 1 : 50 and 1 : 100 come closest to an exact conversion. Also, the conversion charts for feet to meters, and vice versa in Figures 24.6 to 24.10 help reduce arithmatical calculations.

* Reprinted, by permission, from *The Professional Practice of Architectural Working Drawings,* copyright © 1984 by John Wiley & Sons, Inc.

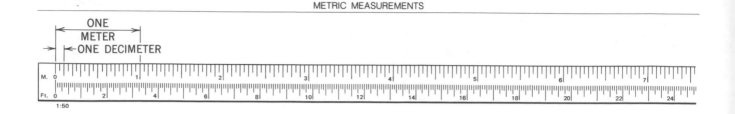

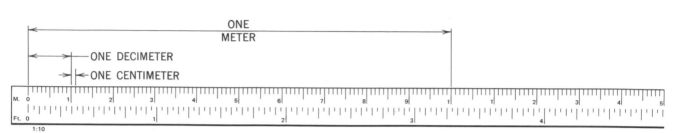

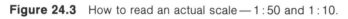

Figure 24.3 How to read an actual scale — 1 : 50 and 1 : 10.

Figure 24.4 How to read an actual scale — 1 : 20 and 1 : 100.

Figure 24.5 One-foot equivalent in metric.

Fractions of inch	64ths of inch	Decimals	Millimeters	Fractions of inch	64ths of inch	Decimals	Millimeters
—	1	.015625	0.397	—	33	.515625	13.097
$\frac{1}{32}$	2	.031250	0.794	$\frac{17}{32}$	34	.531250	13.494
—	3	.046875	1.191	—	35	.546875	13.891
$\frac{1}{16}$	4	.062500	1.588	$\frac{9}{16}$	36	.562500	14.288
—	5	.078125	1.984	—	37	.578125	14.684
$\frac{3}{32}$	6	.093750	2.381	$\frac{19}{32}$	38	.593750	15.081
—	7	.109375	2.778	—	39	.609375	15.478
$\frac{1}{8}$	8	.125000	3.175	$\frac{5}{8}$	40	.625000	15.875
—	9	.140625	3.572	—	41	.640625	16.272
$\frac{5}{32}$	10	.156250	3.969	$\frac{21}{32}$	42	.656250	16.669
—	11	.171875	4.366	—	43	.671875	17.066
$\frac{3}{16}$	12	.187500	4.763	$\frac{11}{16}$	44	.687500	17.463
—	13	.203125	5.159	—	45	.703125	17.859
$\frac{7}{32}$	14	.218750	5.556	$\frac{23}{32}$	46	.718750	18.256
—	15	.234375	5.953	—	47	.734375	18.653
$\frac{1}{4}$	16	.250000	6.350	$\frac{3}{4}$	48	.750000	19.050
—	17	.265625	6.747	—	49	.765625	19.447
$\frac{9}{32}$	18	.281250	7.144	$\frac{25}{32}$	50	.781250	19.844
—	19	.296875	7.541	—	51	.796875	20.241
$\frac{5}{16}$	20	.312500	7.938	$\frac{13}{16}$	52	.812500	20.638
—	21	.328125	8.334	—	53	.828125	21.034
$\frac{11}{32}$	22	.343750	8.731	$\frac{27}{32}$	54	.843750	21.431
—	23	.359375	9.128	—	55	.859375	21.828
$\frac{3}{8}$	24	.375000	9.525	$\frac{7}{8}$	56	.875000	22.225
—	25	.390625	9.922	—	57	.890625	22.622
$\frac{13}{32}$	26	.406250	10.319	$\frac{29}{32}$	58	.906250	23.019
—	27	.421875	10.716	—	59	.921875	23.416
$\frac{7}{16}$	28	.437500	11.113	$\frac{15}{16}$	60	.937500	23.813
—	29	.453125	11.509	—	61	.953125	24.209
$\frac{15}{32}$	30	.468750	11.906	$\frac{31}{32}$	62	.968750	24.606
—	31	.484375	12.303	—	63	.984375	25.003
$\frac{1}{2}$	32	.500000	12.700	1	64	1.000000	25.400

Figure 24.6 Conversion—decimals of an inch to millimeters. (Copyright 1974 Otis Elevator Company.)

Feet	Meters	Feet	Meters	Feet	Meters	Feet	Meters	Feet	Meters
0	0.00000	50	15.24003	100	30.48006	150	45.72009	200	60.96012
1	.30480	1	15.54483	1	30.78486	1	46.02489	1	61.26492
2	.60960	2	15.84963	2	31.08966	2	46.32969	2	61.56972
3	.91440	3	16.15443	3	31.39446	3	46.63449	3	61.87452
4	1.21920	4	16.45923	4	31.69926	4	46.93929	4	62.17932
5	1.52400	5	16.76403	5	32.00406	5	47.24409	5	62.48412
6	1.82880	6	17.06883	6	32.30886	6	47.54890	6	62.78893
7	2.13360	7	17.37363	7	32.61367	7	47.85370	7	63.09373
8	2.43840	8	17.67844	8	32.91847	8	48.15850	8	63.39853
9	2.74321	9	17.98324	9	33.22327	9	48.46330	9	63.70333
10	3.04801	60	18.28804	110	33.52807	160	48.76810	210	64.00813
1	3.35281	1	18.59284	1	33.83287	1	49.07290	1	64.31293
2	3.65761	2	18.89764	2	34.13767	2	49.37770	2	64.61773
3	3.96241	3	19.20244	3	34.44247	3	49.68250	3	64.92253
4	4.26721	4	19.50724	4	34.74727	4	49.98730	4	65.22733
5	4.57201	5	19.81204	5	35.05207	5	50.29210	5	65.53213
6	4.87681	6	20.11684	6	35.35687	6	50.59690	6	65.83693
7	5.18161	7	20.42164	7	35.66167	7	50.90170	7	66.14173
8	5.48641	8	20.72644	8	35.96647	8	51.20650	8	66.44653
9	5.79121	9	21.03124	9	36.27127	9	51.51130	9	66.75133
20	6.09601	70	21.33604	120	36.57607	170	51.81610	220	67.05613
1	6.40081	1	21.64084	1	36.88087	1	52.12090	1	67.36093
2	6.70561	2	21.94564	2	37.18567	2	52.42570	2	67.66574
3	7.01041	3	22.25044	3	37.49047	3	52.73051	3	67.97054
4	7.31521	4	22.55525	4	37.79528	4	53.03531	4	68.27534
5	7.62002	5	22.86005	5	38.10008	5	53.34011	5	68.58014
6	7.92482	6	23.16485	6	38.40488	6	53.64491	6	68.88494
7	8.22962	7	23.46965	7	38.70968	7	53.94971	7	69.18974
8	8.53442	8	23.77445	8	39.01448	8	54.25451	8	69.49454
9	8.83922	9	24.07925	9	39.31928	9	54.55931	9	69.79934
30	9.14402	80	24.38405	130	39.62408	180	54.86411	230	70.10414
1	9.44882	1	24.68885	1	39.92888	1	55.16891	1	70.40894
2	9.75362	2	24.99365	2	40.23368	2	55.47371	2	70.71374
3	10.05842	3	25.29845	3	40.53848	3	55.77851	3	71.01854
4	10.36322	4	25.60325	4	40.84328	4	56.08331	4	71.32334
5	10.66802	5	25.90805	5	41.14808	5	56.38811	5	71.62814
6	10.97282	6	26.21285	6	41.45288	6	56.69291	6	71.93294
7	11.27762	7	26.51765	7	41.75768	7	56.99771	7	72.23774
8	11.58242	8	26.82245	8	42.06248	8	57.30251	8	72.54255
9	11.88722	9	27.12725	9	42.36728	9	57.60732	9	72.84735
40	12.19202	90	27.43205	140	42.67209	190	57.91212	240	73.15215
1	12.49682	1	27.73686	1	42.97689	1	58.21692	1	73.45695
2	12.80163	2	28.04166	2	43.28169	2	58.52172	2	73.76175
3	13.10643	3	28.34646	3	43.58649	3	58.82652	3	74.06655
4	13.41123	4	28.65126	4	43.89129	4	59.13132	4	74.37135
5	13.71603	5	28.95606	5	44.19609	5	59.43612	5	74.67615
6	14.02083	6	29.26086	6	44.50089	6	59.74092	6	74.98095
7	14.32563	7	29.56566	7	44.80569	7	60.04572	7	75.28575
8	14.63043	8	29.87046	8	45.11049	8	60.35052	8	75.59055
9	14.93523	9	30.17526	9	45.41529	9	60.65532	9	75.89534

1 inch = 0.02549 meter	4 inches = 0.10160 meter	7 inches = 0.17780 meter	10 inches = 0.25400 meter
2 inches = .05080 meter	5 inches = .12700 meter	8 inches = .20320 meter	11 inches = .27940 meter
3 inches = .07620 meter	6 inches = .15240 meter	9 inches = .22860 meter	12 inches = .30480 meter

Figure 24.7 Conversion—feet to meters—0′ to 249′.
(Copyright © 1974 Otis Elevator Company.)

Feet	Meters	Feet	Meters	Feet	Meters	Feet	Meters	Feet	Meters
250	76.20015	300	91.44018	350	106.68021	400	121.92024	450	137.16027
1	76.50495	1	91.74498	1	106.98501	1	122.22504	1	137.46507
2	76.80975	2	92.04978	2	107.28981	2	122.52985	2	137.76988
3	77.11455	3	92.35458	3	107.59462	3	122.83465	3	138.07468
4	77.41935	4	92.65939	4	107.89942	4	123.13945	4	138.37948
5	77.72416	5	92.96419	5	108.20422	5	123.44425	5	138.68428
6	78.02896	6	93.26899	6	108.50902	6	123.74905	6	138.98908
7	78.33376	7	93.57379	7	108.81382	7	124.05385	7	139.29388
8	78.63856	8	93.87859	8	109.11862	8	124.35865	8	139.59868
9	78.94336	9	94.18339	9	109.42342	9	124.66345	9	139.90348
260	79.24816	310	94.48819	360	109.72822	410	124.96825	460	140.20828
1	79.55296	1	94.79299	1	110.03302	1	125.27305	1	140.51308
2	79.85776	2	95.09779	2	110.33782	2	125.57785	2	140.81788
3	80.16256	3	95.40259	3	110.64262	3	125.88265	3	141.12268
4	80.46736	4	95.70739	4	110.94742	4	126.18745	4	141.42748
5	80.77216	5	96.01219	5	111.25222	5	126.49225	5	141.73228
6	81.07696	6	96.31699	6	111.55702	6	126.79705	6	142.03708
7	81.38176	7	96.62179	7	111.86182	7	127.10185	7	142.34188
8	81.68656	8	96.92659	8	112.16662	8	127.40665	8	142.64669
9	81.99136	9	97.23139	9	112.47142	9	127.71146	9	142.95149
270	82.29616	320	97.53620	370	112.77623	420	128.01626	470	143.25629
1	82.60097	1	97.84100	1	113.08103	1	128.32106	1	143.56109
2	82.90577	2	98.14580	2	113.38583	2	128.62586	2	143.86589
3	83.21057	3	98.45060	3	113.69063	3	128.93066	3	144.17069
4	83.51537	4	98.75540	4	113.99543	4	129.23546	4	144.47549
5	83.82017	5	99.06020	5	114.30023	5	129.54026	5	144.78029
6	84.12497	6	99.36500	6	114.60503	6	129.84506	6	145.08509
7	84.42977	7	99.66980	7	114.90983	7	130.14986	7	145.38989
8	84.73457	8	99.97460	8	115.21463	8	130.45466	8	145.69469
9	85.03937	9	100.27940	9	115.51943	9	130.75946	9	145.99949
280	85.34417	330	100.58420	380	115.82423	430	131.06426	480	146.30429
1	85.64897	1	100.88900	1	116.12903	1	131.36906	1	146.60909
2	85.95377	2	101.19380	2	116.43383	2	131.67386	2	146.91389
3	86.25857	3	101.49860	3	116.73863	3	131.97866	3	147.21869
4	86.56337	4	101.80340	4	117.04343	4	132.28346	4	147.52350
5	86.86817	5	102.10820	5	117.34823	5	132.50827	5	147.82830
6	87.17297	6	102.41300	6	117.65304	6	132.89307	6	148.13310
7	87.47777	7	102.71781	7	117.95784	7	133.19787	7	148.43790
8	87.78258	8	103.02261	8	118.26264	8	133.50267	8	148.74270
9	88.08738	9	103.32741	9	118.56744	9	133.80747	9	149.04750
290	88.39218	340	103.63221	390	118.87224	440	134.11227	490	149.35230
1	88.69698	1	103.93701	1	119.17704	1	134.41707	1	149.65710
2	89.00178	2	104.24181	2	119.48184	2	134.72187	2	149.96190
3	89.30658	3	104.54661	3	119.78664	3	135.02667	3	150.26670
4	89.61138	4	104.85141	4	120.09144	4	135.33147	4	150.57150
5	89.91618	5	105.15621	5	120.39624	5	135.63627	5	150.87630
6	90.22098	6	105.46101	6	120.70104	6	135.94107	6	151.18110
7	90.52578	7	105.76581	7	121.00584	7	136.24587	7	151.48590
8	90.83058	8	106.07061	8	121.31064	8	136.55067	8	151.79070
9	91.13538	9	106.37541	9	121.61544	9	136.85547	9	152.09550
								500	152.40030

1 inch	= 0.02540 meter	4 inches = 0.10160 meter	7 inches = 0.17780 meter	10 inches = 0.25400 meter
2 inches =	.05080 meter	5 inches = .12700 meter	8 inches = .20320 meter	11 inches = .27940 meter
3 inches =	.07620 meter	6 inches = .15240 meter	9 inches = .22860 meter	12 inches = .30480 meter

Figure 24.8 Conversion—feet to meters—250′ to 500′.
(Copyright © 1974 Otis Elevator Company.)

Meters	Feet	Meters	Feet	Meters	Feet	Meters	Feet	Meters	Feet
0	0.00000	50	164.04167	100	328.08333	150	492.12500	200	656.16667
1	3.28083	1	167.32250	1	331.36417	1	495.40583	1	659.44750
2	6.56167	2	170.60333	2	334.64500	2	498.68667	2	662.72833
3	9.84250	3	173.88417	3	337.92583	3	501.96750	3	666.00917
4	13.12333	4	177.16500	4	341.20667	4	505.24833	4	669.29000
5	16.40417	5	180.44583	5	344.48750	5	508.52917	5	672.57083
6	19.68500	6	183.72667	6	347.76833	6	511.81000	6	675.85167
7	22.96583	7	187.00750	7	351.04917	7	515.09083	7	679.13250
8	26.24667	8	190.28833	8	354.33000	8	518.37167	8	682.41333
9	29.52750	9	193.56917	9	357.61083	9	521.65250	9	685.69417
10	32.80833	60	196.85000	110	360.89167	160	524.93333	210	688.97500
1	36.08917	1	200.13083	1	364.17250	1	528.21417	1	692.25583
2	39.37000	2	203.41167	2	367.45333	2	531.49500	2	695.53667
3	42.65083	3	206.69250	3	370.73417	3	534.77583	3	698.81750
4	45.93167	4	209.97333	4	374.01500	4	538.05667	4	702.09833
5	49.21250	5	213.25417	5	377.29583	5	541.33750	5	705.37917
6	52.49333	6	216.53500	6	380.57667	6	544.61833	6	708.66000
7	55.77417	7	219.81583	7	383.85750	7	547.89917	7	711.94083
8	59.05500	8	223.09667	8	387.13833	8	551.18000	8	715.22167
9	62.33583	9	226.37750	9	390.41917	9	554.46083	9	718.50250
20	65.61667	70	229.65833	120	393.70000	170	557.74167	220	721.78333
1	68.89750	1	232.93917	1	396.90083	1	561.02250	1	725.06417
2	72.17833	2	236.22000	2	400.26167	2	564.30333	2	728.34500
3	75.45917	3	239.50083	3	403.54250	3	567.58417	3	731.62583
4	78.74000	4	242.78167	4	406.82333	4	570.86500	4	734.90667
5	82.02083	5	246.06250	5	410.10417	5	574.14583	5	738.18750
6	85.30167	6	249.34333	6	413.38500	6	577.42667	6	741.46833
7	88.58250	7	252.62417	7	416.66583	7	580.70750	7	744.74917
8	91.86333	8	255.90500	8	419.94667	8	583.98833	8	748.03000
9	95.14417	9	259.18583	9	423.22750	9	587.26917	9	751.31083
30	98.42500	80	262.46667	130	426.50833	180	590.55000	230	754.59167
1	101.70583	1	265.74750	1	429.78917	1	593.83083	1	757.87250
2	104.98667	2	269.02833	2	433.07000	2	597.11167	2	761.15333
3	108.26750	3	272.30917	3	436.35083	3	600.39250	3	764.43417
4	111.54833	4	275.59000	4	439.63167	4	603.67333	4	767.71500
5	114.82917	5	278.87083	5	442.91250	5	606.95417	5	770.99583
6	118.11000	6	282.15167	6	446.19333	6	610.23500	6	774.27667
7	121.39083	7	285.43250	7	449.47417	7	613.51583	7	777.55750
8	124.67167	8	288.71333	8	452.75500	8	616.79667	8	780.83833
9	127.95250	9	291.99417	9	456.03583	9	620.07750	9	784.11917
40	131.23333	90	295.27500	140	459.31667	190	623.35833	240	787.40000
1	134.51417	1	298.55583	1	462.59750	1	626.63917	1	790.68083
2	137.79500	2	301.83667	2	465.87833	2	629.92000	2	793.96167
3	141.07583	3	305.11750	3	469.15917	3	633.20083	3	797.24250
4	144.35667	4	308.39833	4	472.44000	4	636.48167	4	800.52333
5	147.63750	5	311.67917	5	475.72083	5	639.76250	5	803.80417
6	150.91833	6	314.96000	6	479.00167	6	643.04333	6	807.08500
7	154.19917	7	318.24083	7	482.28250	7	646.32417	7	810.36583
8	157.48000	8	321.52167	8	485.56333	8	649.60500	8	813.64667
9	160.76083	9	324.80250	9	488.84417	9	652.88583	9	816.92750

Figure 24.9 Conversion—meters to feet—0 to 249 meters. (Copyright © 1974 Otis Elevator Company.)

Meters	Feet	Meters	Feet	Meters	Feet	Meters	Feet	Meters	Feet
250	820.20833	300	984.25000	350	1,148.29167	400	1,312.33333	450	1,476.37500
1	823.48917	1	987.53083	1	1,151.57250	1	1,315.61417	1	1,479.65583
2	826.77000	2	990.81167	2	1,154.85333	2	1,318.89500	2	1,482.93667
3	830.05083	3	994.09250	3	1,158.13417	3	1,322.17583	3	1,486.21750
4	833.33167	4	997.37333	4	1,161.41500	4	1,325.45667	4	1,489.49833
5	836.61250	5	1,000.65417	5	1,164.69583	5	1,328.73750	5	1,492.77917
6	839.89333	6	1,003.93500	6	1,167.97667	6	1,332.01833	6	1,496.06000
7	843.17417	7	1,007.21583	7	1,171.25750	7	1,335.29917	7	1,499.34083
8	846.45500	8	1,010.49667	8	1,174.53833	8	1,338.58000	8	1,502.62167
9	849.73583	9	1,013.77750	9	1,177.81917	9	1,341.86083	9	1,505.90250
260	853.01667	310	1,017.05833	360	1,181.10000	410	1,345.14167	460	1,509.18333
1	856.29750	1	1,020.33917	1	1,184.38083	1	1,348.42250	1	1,512.46417
2	859.57833	2	1,023.62000	2	1,187.66167	2	1,351.70333	2	1,515.74500
3	862.85917	3	1,026.90083	3	1,190.94250	3	1,354.98417	3	1,519.02583
4	866.14000	4	1,030.18167	4	1,194.22333	4	1,358.26500	4	1,522.30667
5	869.42083	5	1,033.46250	5	1,197.50417	5	1,361.54583	5	1,525.58750
6	872.70167	6	1,036.74333	6	1,200.78500	6	1,364.82667	6	1,528.86833
7	875.98250	7	1,040.02417	7	1,204.06583	7	1,368.10750	7	1,532.14917
8	879.26333	8	1,043.30500	8	1,207.34667	8	1,371.38833	8	1,535.43000
9	882.54417	9	1,046.58583	9	1,210.62750	9	1,374.66917	9	1,538.71083
270	885.82500	320	1,049.86667	370	1,213.90833	420	1,377.95000	470	1,541.99167
1	889.10583	1	1,053.14750	1	1,217.18917	1	1,381.23083	1	1,545.27250
2	892.38667	2	1,056.42833	2	1,220.47000	2	1,384.51167	2	1,548.55333
3	895.66750	3	1,059.70917	3	1,223.75083	3	1,387.79250	3	1,551.83417
4	898.94833	4	1,062.99000	4	1,227.03167	4	1,391.07333	4	1,555.11500
5	902.22917	5	1,066.27083	5	1,230.31250	5	1,394.35417	5	1,558.39583
6	905.51000	6	1,069.55167	6	1,233.59333	6	1,397.63500	6	1,561.67667
7	908.79083	7	1,072.83250	7	1,236.87417	7	1,400.91583	7	1,564.95750
8	912.07167	8	1,076.11333	8	1,240.15500	8	1,404.19667	8	1,568.23833
9	915.35250	9	1,079.39417	9	1,243.43583	9	1,407.47750	9	1,571.51917
280	918.63333	330	1,082.67500	380	1,246.71667	430	1,410.75833	480	1,574.80000
1	921.91417	1	1,085.95583	1	1,249.99750	1	1,414.03917	1	1,578.08083
2	925.19500	2	1,089.23667	2	1,253.27833	2	1,417.32000	2	1,581.36167
3	928.47583	3	1,092.51750	3	1,256.55917	3	1,420.60083	3	1,584.64250
4	931.75667	4	1,095.79833	4	1,259.84000	4	1,423.88167	4	1,587.92333
5	935.03750	5	1,099.07917	5	1,263.12083	5	1,427.16250	5	1,591.20417
6	938.31833	6	1,102.36000	6	1,266.40167	6	1,430.44333	6	1,594.48500
7	941.59917	7	1,105.64083	7	1,269.68250	7	1,433.72417	7	1,597.76583
8	944.88000	8	1,108.92167	8	1,272.96333	8	1,437.00500	8	1,601.04667
9	948.16083	9	1,112.20250	9	1,276.24417	9	1,440.28583	9	1,604.32750
290	951.44167	340	1,115.48333	390	1,279.52500	440	1,443.56667	490	1,607.60833
1	954.72250	1	1,118.76417	1	1,282.80583	1	1,446.84750	1	1,610.88917
2	958.00333	2	1,122.04500	2	1,286.08667	2	1,450.12833	2	1,614.17000
3	961.28417	3	1,125.32583	3	1,289.36750	3	1,453.40917	3	1,617.45083
4	964.56500	4	1,128.60667	4	1,292.64833	4	1,456.69000	4	1,620.73167
5	967.84583	5	1,131.88750	5	1,295.92917	5	1,459.97083	5	1,624.01250
6	971.12667	6	1,135.16833	6	1,299.21000	6	1,463.25167	6	1,627.29333
7	974.40750	7	1,138.44917	7	1,302.49083	7	1,466.53250	7	1,630.57417
8	977.68833	8	1,141.73000	8	1,305.77167	8	1,469.81333	8	1,633.85500
9	980.96917	9	1,145.01083	9	1,309.05250	9	1,473.09417	9	1,637.13583
								500	1,640.41667

Figure 24.10 Conversion—meter to feet—250 to 500 meters. (Copyright © 1974 Otis Elevator Company.)

Metric Detail

To understand the process totally, let us take a typical two-story footing detail, convert its values to metric, and show it using a metric scale. See Figure 24.11.

Step 1. *Convert all sizes to net.*

$$2'' \times 4'' = 1\tfrac{1}{2}'' \times 3\tfrac{1}{2}''$$
$$2'' \times 8'' = 1\tfrac{1}{2}'' \times 7\tfrac{1}{2}''$$
$$\#4 = \tfrac{1}{2}''$$

Step 2. *List required sizes in order.*

$\tfrac{1}{2}''$	$7\tfrac{1}{2}''$
$\tfrac{3}{4}''$	$8''$
$1\tfrac{1}{2}''$	$10''$
$3\tfrac{1}{2}''$	$12''$
$4''$	$16''$
$6''$	$18''$
$7''$	$6'\text{-}0''$

Step 3 *Convert sizes to metric equivalent.*

		Centimeters	Meters
$\tfrac{1}{2} = .5 \times 2.54 =$		1.27 =	.0127
$\tfrac{3}{4} = .75 \times 2.54 =$		1.905 =	.01905
$1\tfrac{1}{2} = 1.5 \times 2.54 =$		3.81 =	.0381
$3\tfrac{1}{2} = 3.5 \times 2.54 =$		8.89 =	.0889
$4 \times 2.54 =$		10.16 =	.1016
$6 \times 2.54 =$		15.24 =	.1524
$7 \times 2.54 =$		17.78 =	.1778
$7\tfrac{1}{2} = 7.5 \times 2.54 =$		19.05 =	.1905
$8 \times 2.54 =$		20.32 =	.2032
$10 \times 2.54 =$		25.4 =	.254
$12 \times 2.54 =$		30.48 =	.3048
$16 \times 2.54 =$		40.64 =	.4064
$18 \times 2.54 =$		45.72 =	.4572
$6'\text{-}0'' \times 30.48 =$		182.88 =	1.8288

Step 4 *Select a scale.*

This is probably the most difficult and crucial step. It involves selecting a scale that would be somewhat equal to what we have been accustomed. The architect must also be able to visualize it, to compound the problem.

A good draftsperson has drawn so many details of footings that without a scale he or she should be able to draw freehand a detail roughly between $\tfrac{3}{4}'' = 1'\text{-}0''$ and $1'' = 1'\text{-}0''$.

After doing many drawings metrically, you will begin to delight in its ease and use it more effectively than the conventional scale now employed.

Step 5 *Draw the detail using appropriate scale.*

In this case, it should be a 1 : 10 scale. The final drawing is slightly larger than the one drawn at $1'' = 1'\text{-}0''$

Step 6 *Verify the hold; increase and decrease the dimension to see that you have progressed correctly.*

Step 7 *Be sure the sums of the parts total.*

A good example of this is shown in the dimensions at the bottom of Figure 24.12. Be sure the three smaller dimensions "total" the overall (.10 + .21 + .10 = .41). In this series of figures, the overall width of the footing is calculated first and enlarged to

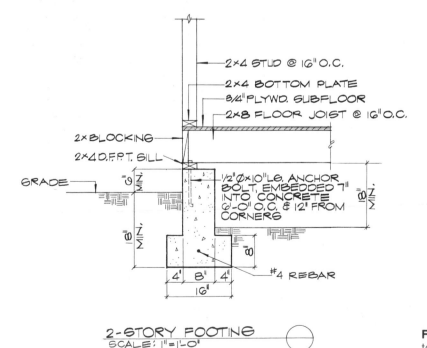

2-STORY FOOTING
SCALE: 1" = 1'-0"

Figure 24.11 Drafted detail to be converted to metric scale.

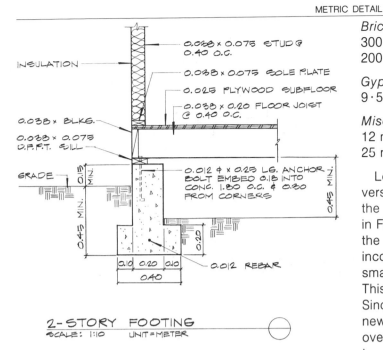

0.038 × 0.075 STUD @ 0.40 O.C.

INSULATION

0.038 × 0.075 SOLE PLATE

0.025 PLYWOOD SUBFLOOR

0.038 × 0.20 FLOOR JOIST @ 0.40 O.C.

0.038 × BLKG.

0.038 × 0.075 D.P.P.T. SILL

GRADE

0.012 ⌀ × 0.25 LG. ANCHOR BOLT EMBED 0.18 INTO CONC. 1.80 O.C. & 0.30 FROM CORNERS

0.012 REBAR

0.10 0.20 0.10
0.40

2-STORY FOOTING
SCALE: 1:10   UNIT = METER

Figure 24.12 Metric detail—hard conversion.

Brick (in mm)

300 × 100 × 100	200 × 100 × 100
200 × 100 × 75	200 × 200 × 100

Gypsum Lath (in mm)
9·5   12·7 or 12·00

Miscellaneous

12 mm diameter for rebar   3 mm for sheet glass
25 mm for sheathing

Look at Figure 24.12 for an example of a hard conversion. This is to be contrasted and compared with the soft conversion and the conventional detail found in Figures 24.11 and 24.12, respectively. Notice how the suggested sizes for wood and rebar have been incorporated. Also note that most of the sizes are smaller than the soft conversion (direct conversion). This will change the strength of the whole structure. Since hard conversion subscribes to a completely new system, the drafter, at this point, must check the overall foundation plan and look for the modular system being used. Also verify sizes for their correct strengths with the structural engineer.

ensure a bearing surface larger than required.

The next value to decide is the foundation wall itself. Again, the approach is to round off larger and subtract this figure from the overall. The remainder is divided equally on either side.

Notice how all lumber, anchor bolt, and rebar sizes are not rounded off. We cannot do anything with these until the manufacturers themselves decide on the new sizes. Also, note that everything is given in net sizes; this may change, but for now it is a calculated guess as to the direction we might go. Until something is certain, we should note under the title that this is the case.

Possible Sizes*

Because the various manufacturers have not converted to a uniform size, it is difficult to predict the final evolution of the various building materials. Suggested sizes and those used by other countries are

Wood (in mm)

38 × 75	44 × 75	50 × 75	63 × 150
38 × 100	44 × 100	50 × 100	63 × 175
38 × 150	44 × 150	50 × 125	63 × 200
38 × 175	44 × 175	50 × 150	63 × 225
38 × 200	44 × 200	50 × 175	
38 × 225	44 × 225	50 × 200	75 × 200
		50 × 300	75 × 300

Exterior Rolling Shutters

An example of a detail that uses metrics is that of the exterior rolling shutter, which has been extensively used in Europe for several decades. It serves many purposes; energy conservation, cutting out sunlight on long daylight hours, and security are its main advantages.

The rolling shutter is made of aluminum or polyvinyl in a double-wall construction that utilizes the space between the double wall by filling it with insulation. It has very good acoustical qualities, provides storm protection, and comes in a variety of colors.

The rolling shutter is opened by a strap (like a drape) or by a hand crank, or an electrical motor can be attached. Because of its unique construction, it allows filtered light or it can be closed to block out nearly 100% of the light. Figures 24.13 and 24.14 show the shutter in a partly open position. Figure 24.15 shows a typical detail drafted metrically, as it might appear on a European detail sheet.

* Reprinted, by permission, from *The Professional Practice of Architectural Working Drawings,* copyright © 1984 by John Wiley & Sons, Inc.

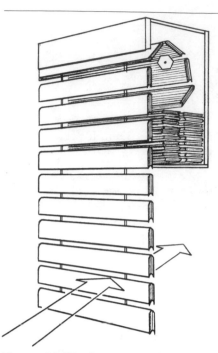

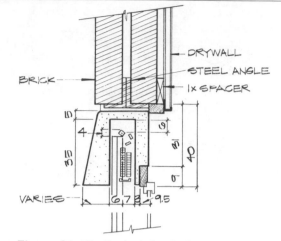

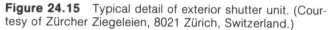

Figure 24.15 Typical detail of exterior shutter unit. (Courtesy of Zürcher Ziegeleien, 8021 Zürich, Switzerland.)

Figure 24.13 Pictorial of exterior shutter unit. (Copyright © by Traber Ltd. CH-9403, Goloach, Switzerland.)

Figure 24.14 Cavity in wall with shutter unit.

Regional Differences

Since this is such a new area, standards have yet to be established.

Summary

The important concept established in this chapter is that there will not be a direct conversion to the metric system but rather a conversion that will follow a transition period. This period will find workers in the field needing help from architects, engineers, and designers to adjust to a complete new way of thinking. Full understanding by the architectural draftsperson is of no value if the people in the field are still confused. This may lead to dual notation for quite some time.

There will also be a period when half the manufacturers have converted and the others have not. Lumber and steel may be the first or last to convert.

Finally, new building codes and charts will have to be established to accommodate this conversion. When the transition comes it will be slow at first and then accelerate rapidly; consequently, architectural draftspersons must prepare now for what is inevitable.

Materials in Section

The following pages have been assembled to show the architectural draftsperson the various methods used throughout the United States to represent different materials in section.

In the first column are material designations assembled by the Committee on Office Practice, American Institute of Architects (National) and published in *Architectural Graphic Standards.** The second column contains material designations published by the Task Force on Production Office Procedures, September 1974, by the Northern California Chapter of the American Institute of Architects.† The final column lists items from other sources such as pamphlets, manufacturers' literature, other textbooks, governmental agencies, and trade and technical organizations or associations.

Our intent is to show where standardization has occurred and where variations exist. For example, all groups agree on the method of representing brick in section, yet there is a great variation in the way concrete block is represented in section.

The final portion shows specialty items from a variety of sources.

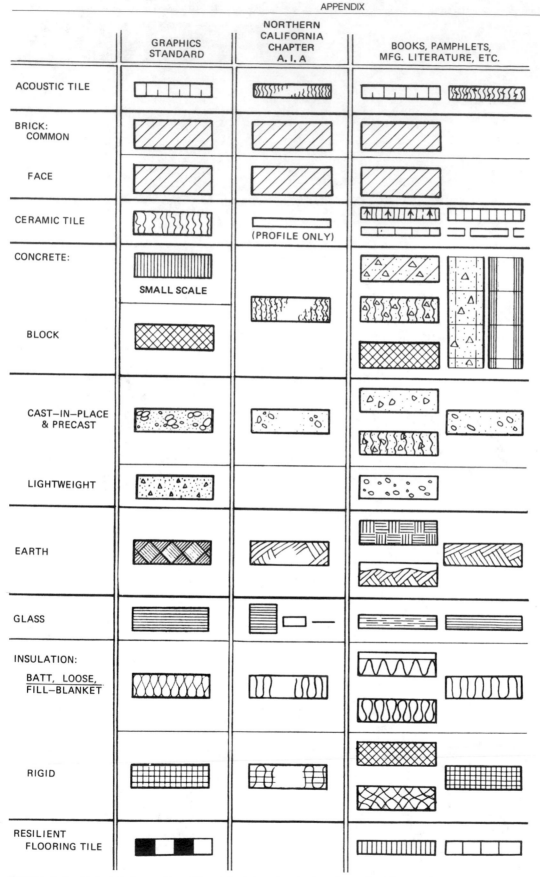

Figure A.1 Materials in section. (Reprinted, by permission, from *Architectural Graphic Standards,* copyright © 1970 by John Wiley & Sons, Inc.)

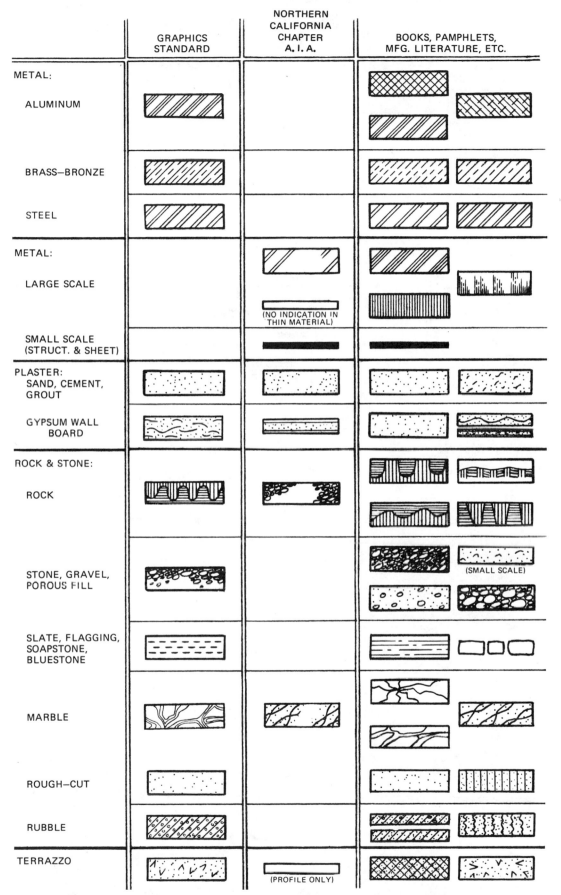

	GRAPHICS STANDARD	NORTHERN CALIFORNIA CHAPTER A. I. A.	BOOKS, PAMPHLETS, MFG. LITERATURE, ETC.
METAL: ALUMINUM			
BRASS—BRONZE			
STEEL			
METAL: LARGE SCALE		(NO INDICATION IN THIN MATERIAL)	
SMALL SCALE (STRUCT. & SHEET)			
PLASTER: SAND, CEMENT, GROUT			
GYPSUM WALL BOARD			
ROCK & STONE: ROCK			
STONE, GRAVEL, POROUS FILL			(SMALL SCALE)
SLATE, FLAGGING, SOAPSTONE, BLUESTONE			
MARBLE			
ROUGH—CUT			
RUBBLE			
TERRAZZO		(PROFILE ONLY)	

Figure A.2 Materials in section. (Reprinted, by permission, from *Architectural Graphic Standards*, copyright © 1970 by John Wiley & Sons, Inc.)

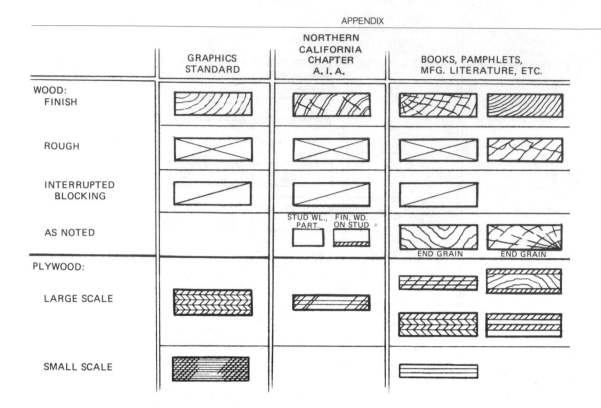

| | GRAPHICS STANDARD | NORTHERN CALIFORNIA CHAPTER A. I. A. | BOOKS, PAMPHLETS, MFG. LITERATURE, ETC. | |

WOOD:
FINISH

ROUGH

INTERRUPTED BLOCKING

AS NOTED

STUD WL., PART.   FIN. WD. ON STUD

END GRAIN   END GRAIN

PLYWOOD:

LARGE SCALE

SMALL SCALE

* TO SAVE VALUABLE DRAFTING TIME, THE NORTHERN CALIFORNIA
CHAPTER RECOMMENDS THAT THE TOTAL DETAIL IN SECTION
NOT BE FILLED IN COMPLETELY BUT JUST ENOUGH TO INDICATE
THE MATERIAL IN QUESTION.

Figure A.3 Materials in section. (Reprinted, by permission, from *Architectural Graphic Standards,* copyright © 1970 by John Wiley & Sons, Inc.)

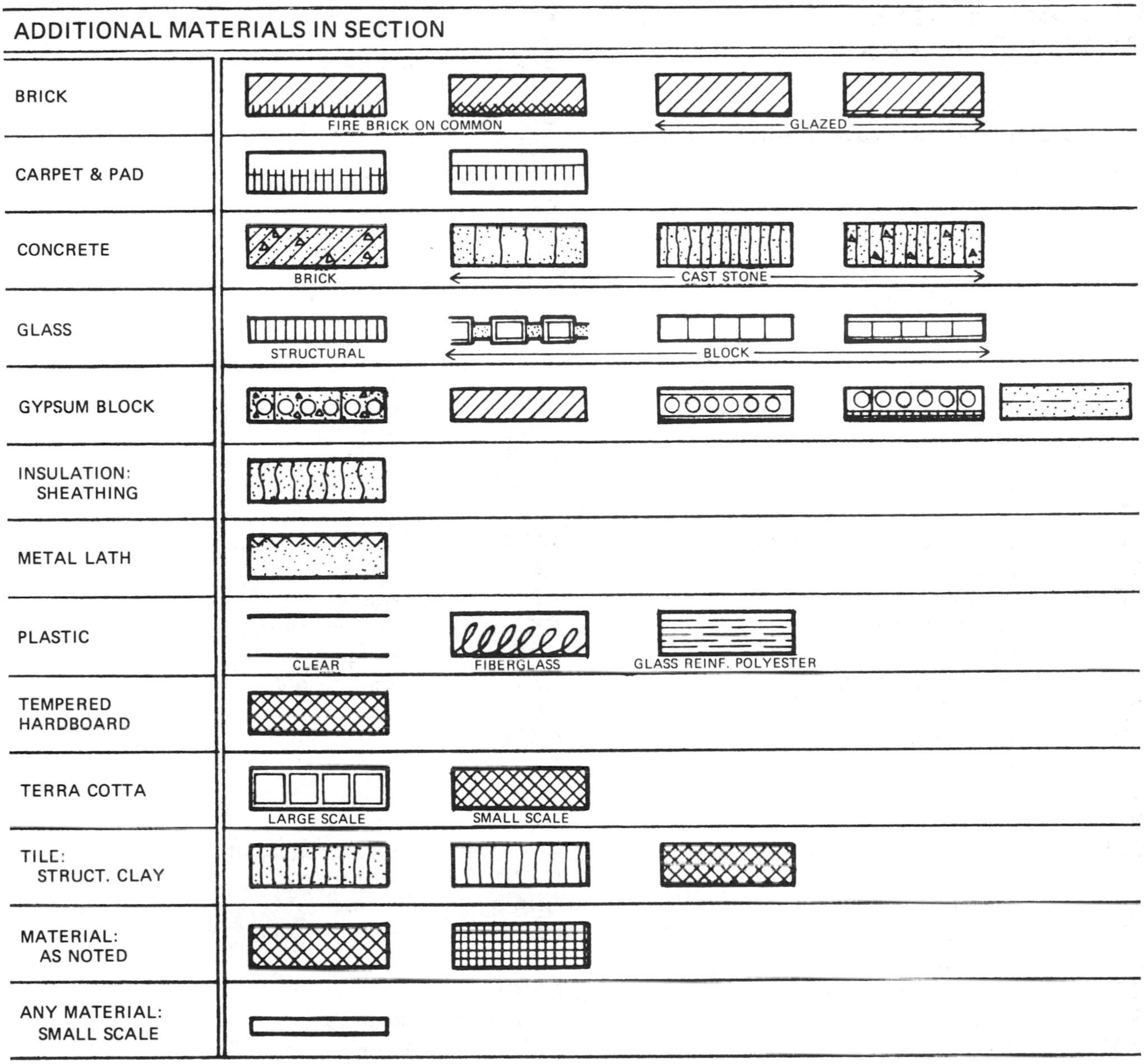

ADDITIONAL MATERIALS IN SECTION

BRICK	FIRE BRICK ON COMMON GLAZED
CARPET & PAD	
CONCRETE	BRICK CAST STONE
GLASS	STRUCTURAL BLOCK
GYPSUM BLOCK	
INSULATION: SHEATHING	
METAL LATH	
PLASTIC	CLEAR FIBERGLASS GLASS REINF. POLYESTER
TEMPERED HARDBOARD	
TERRA COTTA	LARGE SCALE SMALL SCALE
TILE: STRUCT. CLAY	
MATERIAL: AS NOTED	
ANY MATERIAL: SMALL SCALE	

Figure A.4 Additional materials in section. (Reprinted, by permission, from *Architectural Graphic Standards,* copyright © 1970 by John Wiley & Sons, Inc.)

A Uniform System for Working Drawings

Architectural Working Drawing Abbreviations

SYMBOLS USED AS ABBREVIATIONS:

$\angle$ angle
$\not{\mathbb{C}}$ centerline
c channel
d penny
$\perp$ perpendicular
PL plate
ϕ round

ABBREVIATIONS:

ABV	above
AFF	above finished floor
ASC	above suspended ceiling
ACC	access
ACFL	access floor
AP	access panel
AC	acoustical
ACPL	acoustical plaster
ACT	acoustical tile
ACR	acrylic plastic
ADD	addendum
ADH	adhesive
ADJ	adjacent
ADJT	adjustable
AGG	aggregate
A/C	air conditioning
ALT	alternate
AL	aluminum
ANC	anchor, anchorage
AB	anchor bolt
ANOD	anodized
APX	approximate
ARCH	architect (ural)
AD	area drain
ASB	asbestos
ASPH	asphalt
AT	asphalt tile
AUTO	automatic
BP	back plaster (ed)
BSMT	basement
BRG	bearing
BPL	bearing plate
BJT	bed joint
BM	bench mark
BEL	below
BET	between
BVL	beveled

BIT	bituminous
BLK	block
BLKG	blocking
BD	board
BS	both sides
BW	both ways
BOT	bottom
BRK	brick
BRZ	bronze
BLDG	building
BUR	built up roofing
BBD	bulletin board
CAB	cabinet
CAD	cadmium
CPT	carpet (ed)
CSMT	casement
CI	cast iron
CIPC	cast-in-place concrete
CST	cast stone
CB	catch basin
CK	calk (ing) caulk (ing)
CLG	ceiling
CHT	ceiling height
CEM	cement
PCPL	cement plaster (portland)
CM	centimeter(s)
CER	ceramic
CT	ceramic tile
CMT	ceramic mosaic (tile)
CHBD	chalkboard
CHAM	chamfer
CR	chromium (plated)
CIR	circle
CIRC	circumference
CLR	clear (ance)
CLS	closure
COL	column
COMB	combination
COMPT	compartment
COMPO	composition (composite)
COMP	compress (ed), (ion), (ible)
CONC	concrete
CMU	concrete masonry unit
CX	connection
CONST	construction
CONT	continuous or continue
CONTR	contract (or)
CLL	contract limit line
CJT	control joint
CPR	copper
CG	corner guard
CORR	corrugated
CTR	counter
CFL	counterflashing

CS	countersink	**FB**	face brick
CTSK	countersunk screw	**FOC**	face of concrete
CRS	course (s)	**FOF**	face of finish
CRG	cross grain	**FOM**	face of masonry
CFT	cubic foot	**FOS**	face of studs
CYD	cubic yard	**FF**	factory finish
		FAS	fasten, fastener
		FN	fence
DPR	damper	**FBD**	fiberboard
DP	dampproofing	**FGL**	fiberglass
DL	dead load	**FIN**	finish (ed)
DEM	demolish, demolition	**FFE**	finished floor elevation
DMT	demountable	**FFL**	finished floor line
DEP	depressed	**FA**	fire alarm
DTL	detail	**FBRK**	fire brick
DIAG	diagonal	**FE**	fire extinguisher
DIAM	diameter	**FEC**	fire extinguisher cabinet
DIM	dimension	**FHS**	fire hose station
DPR	dispenser	**FPL**	fireplace
DIV	division	**FP**	fireproof
DR	door	**FRC**	fire-resistant coating
DA	doubleacting	**FRT**	fire-retardant
DH	double hung	**FLG**	flashing
DTA	dovetail anchor	**FHMS**	flathead machine screw
DTS	dovetail anchor slot	**FHWS**	flathead wood screw
DS	downspout	**FLX**	flexible
D	drain	**FLR**	floor (ing)
DRB	drainboard	**FLCO**	floor cleanout
DT	drain tile	**FD**	floor drain
DWR	drawer	**FPL**	floor plate
DWG	drawing	**FLUR**	fluorescent
DF	drinking fountain	**FJT**	flush joint
DW	dumbwaiter	**FTG**	footing
		FRG	forged
		FND	foundation
EF	each face	**FR**	frame (d), (ing)
E	east	**FRA**	fresh air
ELEC	electric (al)	**FS**	full size
EP	electrical panelboard	**FBO**	furnished by others
EWC	electric water cooler	**FUR**	furred (ing)
EL	elevation	**FUT**	future
ELEV	elevator		
EMER	emergency		
ENC	enclose (ure)	**GA**	gage, gauge
EQ	equal	**GV**	galvanized
EQP	equipment	**GI**	galvanized iron
ESC	escalator	**GP**	galvanized pipe
EST	estimate	**GSS**	galvanized steel sheet
EXCA	excavate	**GKT**	gasket (ed)
EXH	exhaust	**GC**	general contract (or)
EXG	existing	**GL**	glass, glazing
EXMP	expanded metal plate	**GLB**	glass block
EB	expansion bolt	**GLF**	glass fiber
EXP	exposed	**GCMU**	glazed concrete masonry units
EXT	exterior	**GST**	glazed structural tile
EXS	extra strong	**GB**	grab bar

GD	grade, grading		**LAD**	ladder
GRN	granite		**LB**	lag bolt
GVL	gravel		**LAM**	laminate (d)
GF	ground face		**LAV**	lavatory
GT	grout		**LH**	left hand
GPDW	gypsum dry wall		**L**	length
GPL	gypsum lath		**LT**	light
GPPL	gypsum plaster		**LC**	light control
GPT	gypsum tile		**LP**	lightproof
			LW	lightweight
			LWC	lightweight concrete
HH	handhold		**LMS**	limestone
HBD	hardboard		**LTL**	lintel
HDW	hardware		**LL**	live load
HWD	hardwood		**LVR**	louver
HJT	head joint		**LPT**	low point
HDR	header			
HTG	heating			
HVAC	heating/ventilating/air conditioning		**MB**	machine bolt
HD	heavy duty		**MI**	malleable iron
HT	height		**MH**	manhole
HX	hexagonal		**MFR**	manufacture (er)
HES	high early-strength cement		**MRB**	marble
HC	hollow core		**MAS**	masonry
HM	hollow metal		**MO**	masonry opening
HK	hook (s)		**MTL**	material (s)
HOR	horizontal		**MAX**	maximum
HB	hose bibb		**MECH**	mechanic (al)
HWH	hot water heater		**MC**	medicine cabinet
			MED	medium
			MBR	member
INCIN	incinerator		**MMB**	membrane
INCL	include (d), (ing)		**MET**	metal
ID	inside diameter		**MFD**	metal floor decking
INS	insulate (d), (ion)		**MTFR**	metal furring
INSC	insulating concrete		**MRD**	metal roof decking
INSF	insulating fill		**MTHR**	metal threshold
INT	interior		**M**	meter (s)
ILK	interlock		**MM**	millimeter (s)
INTM	intermediate		**MWK**	millwork
INV	invert		**MIN**	minimum
IPS	iron pipe size		**MIR**	mirror
			MISC	miscellaneous
			MOD	modular
JC	janitor's closet		**MLD**	molding, moulding
JT	joint		**MR**	mop receptor
JF	joint filler		**MT**	mount (ed), (ing)
J	joist		**MOV**	movable
			MULL	mullion
KCPL	Keene's cement plaster			
KPL	kickplate			
KIT	kitchen		**NL**	nailable
KO	knockout		**NAT**	natural
			NI	nickel
LBL	label		**NR**	noise reduction
LAB	laboratory		**NRC**	noise reduction coefficient

NOM	nominal		**QT**	quarry tile
NMT	nonmetallic			
N	north		**RBT**	rabbet, rebate
NIC	not in contract		**RAD**	radius
NTS	not to scale		**RL**	rail (ing)
			RWC	rainwater conductor
			REF	reference
OBS	obscure		**RFL**	reflect (ed), (ive), (or)
OC	on center (s)		**REFR**	refrigerator
OP	opaque		**REG**	register
OPG	opening		**RE**	reinforce (d), (ing)
OJ	open-web joist		**RCP**	reinforced concrete pipe
OPP	opposite		**REM**	remove
OPH	opposite hand		**RES**	resilient
OPS	opposite surface		**RET**	return
OD	outside diameter		**RA**	return air
OHMS	ovalhead machine screw		**RVS**	reverse (side)
OHWS	ovalhead wood screw		**REV**	revision (s), revised
OA	overall		**RH**	right hand
OH	overhead		**ROW**	right of way
			R	riser
			RVT	rivet
PNT	paint (ed)		**RD**	roof drain
PNL	panel		**RFH**	roof hatch
PB	panic bar		**RFG**	roofing
PTD	paper towel dispenser		**RM**	room
PTR	paper towel receptor		**RO**	rough opening
PAR	parallel		**RB**	rubber base
PK	parking		**RBT**	rubber tile
PBD	particle board		**RBL**	rubble stone
PTN	partition			
PV	pave (d), (ing)			
PVMT	pavement		**SFGL**	safety glass
PED	pedestal		**SCH**	schedule
PERF	perforate (d)		**SCN**	screen
PERI	perimeter		**SNT**	sealant
PLAS	plaster		**STG**	seating
PLAM	plastic laminate		**SEC**	section
PL	plate		**SSK**	service sink
PG	plate glass		**SHTH**	sheathing
PWD	plywood		**SHT**	sheet
PT	point		**SG**	sheet glass
PVC	polyvinyl chloride		**SH**	shelf, shelving
PE	porcelain enamel		**SHO**	shore (d), (ing)
PTC	post-tensioned concrete		**SIM**	similar
PCF	pounds per cubic foot		**SKL**	skylight
PFL	pounds per lineal foot		**SL**	sleeve
PSF	pounds per square foot		**SC**	solid core
PSI	pounds per square inch		**SP**	soundproof
PCC	precast concrete		**S**	south
PFB	prefabricate (d)		**SPC**	spacer
PFN	prefinished		**SPK**	speaker
PRF	preformed		**SPL**	special
PSC	prestressed concrete		**SPEC**	specification (s)
PL	property line		**SQ**	square

SST	stainless steel		**VJ**	v-joint (ed)
STD	standard		**VB**	vapor barrier
STA	station		**VAR**	varnish
ST	steel		**VNR**	veneer
STO	storage		**VRM**	vermiculite
SD	storm drain		**VERT**	vertical
STR	structural		**VG**	vertical grain
SCT	structural clay tile		**VIN**	vinyl
SUS	suspended		**VAT**	vinyl asbestos tile
SYM	symmetry (ical)		**VB**	vinyl base
SYN	synthetic		**VF**	vinyl fabric
SYS	system		**VT**	vinyl tile
TKBD	tackboard		**WSCT**	wainscot
TKS	tackstrip		**WTW**	wall to wall
TEL	telephone		**WH**	wall hung
TV	television		**WC**	water closet
TC	terra cotta		**WP**	waterproofing
TZ	terrazzo		**WR**	water repellent
THK	thick (ness)		**WS**	waterstop
THR	threshold		**WWF**	welded wire fabric
TPTN	toilet partition		**W**	west
TPD	toilet paper dispenser		**WHB**	wheel bumper
TOL	tolerance		**W**	width, wide
T&G	tongue and groove		**WIN**	window
TSL	top of slab		**WG**	wired glass
TST	top of steel		**WM**	wire mesh
TW	top of wall		**WO**	without
TB	towel bar		**WD**	wood
TR	transom		**WB**	wood base
T	tread		**WPT**	working point
TYP	typical		**WI**	wrought iron
UC	undercut			
UNF	unfinished			
UR	urinal			

Graphic Symbols

The symbols shown are those that seem to be most common and acceptable, judged by the frequency of use by the architectural offices surveyed. This list can and should be expanded by each office for those symbols generally included in its practice and not indicated here. Again, each professional is urged to accept the task force recommendation by adopting the use of these symbols.

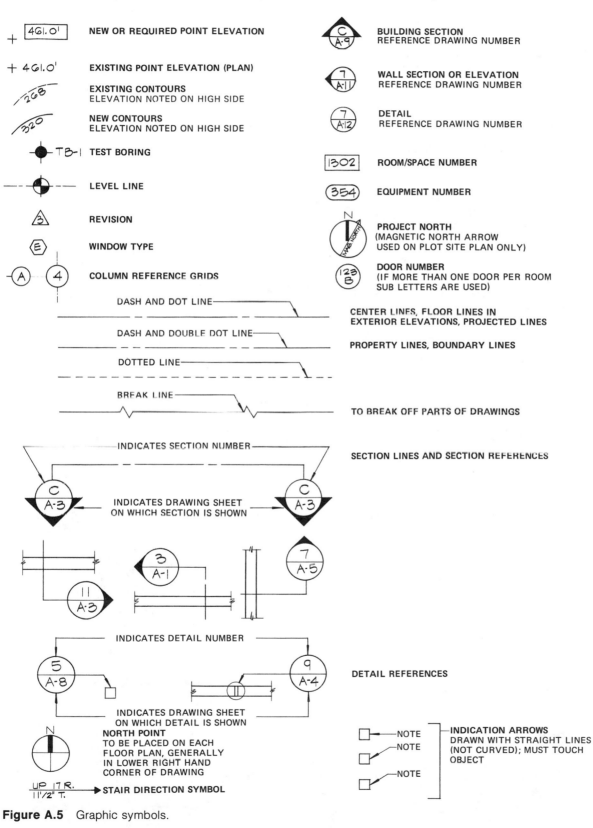

Figure A.5 Graphic symbols.

Photo Credits

INDEX